"Occupy till I Come"

THE ORIGINS OF AURORA UNIVERSITY IN MENDOTA, ILLINOIS

Susan L. Palmer

With a Foreword by
Rebecca Sherrick, President of Aurora University

Printed in the United States of America

First Printing 2020

ISBN 978-1-7352202-0-8

Aurora University
347 South Gladstone Avenue
Aurora, Illinois 60506

www.aurora.edu

Cover Photo: Group portrait of people, standing on the front staircase of the main college building, who were attending the Advent Christian campmeeting held annually on the Mendota College campus.

In Memory of My Wonderful Parents

Donald and Edith Palmer

Who Were Always There for Me with
Love and Support

Contents

Foreword

Over its long history, Aurora University has been home to a number of outstanding historians, excellent teachers who combined their love of the classroom with deep understandings of the institution's distinctive traditions and history. The work of several of these scholars is referenced in the pages that follow. I've known the joy of learning from several of these teachers, including Professor David Arthur who shared generously with a new president and responded with patience to my many questions.

Several others shared Aurora stories with me. Early in my academic career, I worked alongside Dr. Donna Behnke at Carroll College. Donna shared thoughts about her Advent Christian faith and recalled also memories from her time as an Aurora College student and professor. I am thankful to Dorothy Crouse for a long afternoon of conversation in her Dowling Park cottage. And I never will forget a phone call from Chuck Anderson, author of two prior histories of Aurora College. He encouraged me to visit soon, and I was happy to comply.

Shortly after coming to Aurora University in 2000, I began to think about the importance of telling the stories of Aurora College and George Williams College. Both trace their origins to the tumultuous decade of the 1890s and have deep ties to the evangelical movements of the 19th century. Neither was founded as a college, but over time the two matured to make significant educational contributions. Today, Aurora University draws inspiration and meaning from both stories.

In 2005, I turned to Dr. Susan Palmer, longtime Professor of History, with an invitation to write a new history of Aurora College. My request was open-ended. In truth, I don't think either of us appreciated the richness of the sources she would discover—often on the shelves of the university's own Phillips Library. For Susan it was a homecoming of sorts. Her own roots run deep in the Adventist movement. Four generations of her mother's Hartford, Connecticut family were Advent Christians, and her father, Donald, served for almost two decades as a member of the college's Board of Trustees.

Susan and her brother, Scott, both graduated from Aurora College, claiming the institution's most prestigious student award along the way. Susan met her husband and faculty colleague, Richard Westphal, at Aurora College. Over a 37-year career, she made history come alive for generations of students. In the pages that follow, she performs like magic. Settle in for a "good read" as you travel, courtesy of Dr. Palmer, back to a time simpler in some ways ... and quite complicated in others.

You will recognize the story and the broad themes that run through this artful rendering. Here you will learn more about the founding idealism and passion for mission that compelled the tiny institution through its first two decades in Mendota. You will read about sacrifice, courage and leadership. It's an account of dedication, an unwavering commitment to enduring values and timeless virtues. It is our story. Though much has changed, so much remains true yet today.

Rebecca Sherrick, PhD
President of Aurora University
Aurora, Illinois

Acknowledgments and Thanks

President Rebecca Sherrick:
For the year-long sabbatical that launched this project in 2005–6, her continuing support and patience, and her willingness to write the foreword for this book.

John Law (former director of the Aurora University Library) and
Katherine Clark (current director of the university's library):
For John's overall support and helpfulness during this long project, for the time he gave me for our many talks about Mendota College, and for his great enthusiasm for the history of Aurora University in general.

And for Katherine's support of this project over the last two years as my focus shifted from curating the Jenks Collection to finishing this book—especially her patience and helpfulness in covering the Jenks Collection when I could not be there.

Jewel Huggins:
For going through the forty years of *Our Hope's* weekly issues and bookmarking all the articles on Mendota College (and, after 1912, Aurora College). This saved me incalculable hours.

David Arthur (Curator of the Jenks Memorial Collection of Adventual Materials), my dear friend and mentor since my college years:
For introducing me to *Our Hope* and explaining that many of the sources for Mendota College were in the Jenks Collection, not the university archives, as one would expect. His passing, just a month or so after I started this project, was not only terribly sad for those of us who loved him but a real loss to Aurora University. No one had a broader knowledge of Millerism or the school's history.

And last, but by no means least—MY FAMILY:
For their love and support when this project seemed to be never ending and more specifically:

Scott Palmer:

My brother and research assistant—For doing the tedious work of copying the names, hometowns, and areas of coursework of students in the catalogs and then crunching the numbers; taking notes on the Mendota College board minutes so that I could find relevant items in a more streamlined way; looking up random facts for me; and making multiple trips to Mendota's public library to find information on the town itself—in short, for saving me so much time in what was already an incredibly long process. I appreciate your thoroughness and highly recommend your services to anyone who needs a research assistant.

Richard Westphal:

My husband, support system, and editor—For encouraging me; listening to endless stories about Mendota College; spending many hours editing my manuscript (and doing so not only expertly, but with great tact); and preparing many a meal, even when it was my night to cook, because I was working on this book. You are the best husband and editor ever (although we will never agree on commas).

Chapter 1
Mendota College and American Higher Education

"The Bible training school, to help preachers to more successfully spread the truth, and to qualify workers, and help in various ways those whom God has called into this last day gospel service, *is and must be our main object* and our principal department of school work ... All other departments are subordinate to this, tributary to this, and are planned and conducted largely and simply that the Bible training school may be a possibility within the reach of those who need it."

—*Our Hope and Life in Christ*, 1893

The First Class of the Bible Training School, 1893

This is the story of Aurora University's origins—of the institution, named Mendota College, which started it all in 1893 and lasted for nineteen years, until it moved to Aurora and became Aurora College in 1912. It was a small, financially vulnerable, Christian institution that, in all of its nineteen years, produced just 123 graduates (and 20 of them were graduates from the Preparatory Department, which essentially was a high school). Few outside observers would have predicted that the school would not only last nineteen years but would be thriving 125 years after its founding.[1]

The 1800s was a century of college building of all types—small, private schools with religious affiliations (both Catholic and Protestant); large state universities (especially in the Midwest) and large, private universities; the first, all-women colleges, located in the Northeast; and Bible training schools. There were just nine colleges in the colonial period—Harvard, the College of William and Mary, Yale, Princeton, Columbia, the University of Pennsylvania, Brown, Rutgers, and Dartmouth. However, this all changed after the American colonies gained their independence and created a new country.

Higher Education in Antebellum America

In the first half of the nineteenth century, there was an explosion of new colleges. Historians disagree on the exact number, but by the Civil War, there were anywhere from 180 to 250 surviving colleges. (The word "surviving" is used because many more than this had been founded, but they failed fairly quickly. Some had even barely gotten off the drawing boards before they folded.) Historians have described this phenomenon simply as a "college movement," but also as a "frenzy" and a "mania" of college building. The overheated founding of so many colleges reflected what was happening in other areas as well—the constantly moving frontier lines due to Americans' insatiable hunger for land and space; the mania for canal building, which quickly turned into overbuilding; rapid population growth and urbanization; and mining for gold, which quickly became frenzied (as exemplified by the California gold rush). Americans' restlessness and belief in endless progress, even at the expense of rational planning, was very much on display in this era, and the college movement was no exception.[2]

Most of the new four-year private colleges in the antebellum period were founded by various Protestant denominations. Even those that were the most populist sects, ministering to the poorer classes and hostile to the idea that ministers needed an education to be effective (like the Methodists and Baptists, as well as the Millerites and early Advent Christians), eventually changed their minds and joined the college-building movement. It makes sense that college building was largely done by Protestants in the early nineteenth century. The United States was overwhelmingly Protestant at this time—both culturally and in the numbers of people in various Protestant denominations. And in an era when using federal money, even for building national transportation systems, was highly controversial and there were no adequate, dependable federal or state funds for higher education, it was religious groups who had to build and sustain colleges.[3]

This overabundance of colleges was a product of a number of things: the American federal system (with every state having its own institutions); state/regional pride and rivalries; the belief that a college would bring greater social and cultural status as well as economic stimulation to a town; the movement of Americans into new, western lands (and the home missionaries who quickly followed to "tame" the new lands by planting schools); localism and the insularity of many areas in the United States due to poor transportation systems—thus, the inability or unwillingness of potential students to travel far for their education; and religion, especially Protestant denominationalism and sectarianism—each religious group wanting its own schools where it could teach its own distinctive beliefs (but without being so sectarian as to close its doors to everyone outside the denominational fold). Another religious cause was the passionate revivalism of the Second Great Awakening, which swept across the country before the Civil War, creating many new converts and firing up those already in the fold. Some of this enthusiasm went into the founding of small colleges to train Christian workers (especially in the newly settled areas of the West).[4]

However, many of these early colleges were unstable and did not survive. In the pre–Civil War period alone, around 700 colleges failed. (The study from which the number 700 came looked at the failure rate of colleges in the antebellum era. The author of this study found 412 failed colleges, with 104 colleges surviving, in *sixteen* states. In the *remaining eighteen* states, he found 78 surviving colleges. Using the same ratio for failed to surviving colleges as that used for the sixteen states, about 309 additional colleges failed, for a total of around 700.[5]) This much college building was simply not sustainable, especially at a time when just a very small percentage of Americans attended college. One scholar pointed out that, in 1880, all of England, with a population of twenty-three million, had just four universities, whereas Ohio, with a population of only three million, had thirty-seven institutions of higher education. England, of course, had a more concentrated population, which allowed for the consolidation and centralization of educational resources, whereas the United States would have had a more difficult time getting by with so few colleges. American territory was on a grand scale and, for most of the nineteenth century, was thinly settled (especially outside of the Northeast), as Americans were shooting off in various directions to settle new lands. The United States had many more colleges than England in this period because of its vast space, but it was also more difficult to sustain many of them due to the small populations resulting from that large scale. A bit more centralization of educational resources would probably have ensured the survival of more colleges.[6]

The Emergence and Maturation of Universities versus Maturing, Private Colleges in the Late Nineteenth Century

In the last third of the nineteenth century, higher education was redefined and made more widely available as well as more practical (incorporating such new or expanded areas of study as agriculture, science, and technology), both of these changes making it more democratic.

During the Civil War, Congress passed the Morrill Act, which created land-grant colleges. This was the first time that federal power and resources were applied to higher education on such a large scale. Every state was given thirty thousand acres of public land for each of its members of Congress. Those lands would be sold, and then the money would be applied to higher education. These schools were created because of a recognition that, with the rise of industrialization and technology, practical, more scientific studies had become increasingly important. The way that states used these federal education funds varied. For example, some states turned the money over to existing state universities or even private colleges, while others built new schools that competed with existing state universities. In addition to their other programs, they *all* were *supposed* to provide practical, technical studies (mechanics, scientific farming methods, etc.). However, even this basic stipulation was not always met. Sometimes these funds went toward creating institutions that were essentially liberal arts colleges. And southern states created *separate* land-grant colleges for African Americans. In addition to being segregated, they received just the minimal amount of funds that was legally required, most did not provide courses on agriculture and mechanics (the whole point of land-grant funds), and their courses often were taught at a grammar-school level.[7]

Between 1880 and 1910, the modern university was emerging and maturing. A few existed before 1880, but the thirty-year period after 1880 was one in which universities started to appear in substantial numbers. Often they were private institutions funded by wealthy men who had accumulated vast fortunes in industry after the Civil War (like John D. Rockefeller and the University of Chicago). Others emerged out of earlier state and land-grant colleges. The modern university differed from private, four-year colleges in several ways (although there were some differences among the universities as well). Universities were larger (both the student body and the campus facilities); they had a sounder financial foundation, thanks to a new, larger-scale philanthropy; their curricula were broader and included many more practical and professional areas of study, as opposed to just the liberal arts; they gave greater curricular choice to students, especially in the form of electives as well as specialization, in the form of a major; their faculty, trained in research-oriented graduate programs, taught courses in their specialized areas rather than a broad spectrum of subjects; research and publication were emphasized over teaching; they offered graduate programs; and they embraced the idea of providing service to the larger society by helping to find solutions to its problems (i.e., applied scholarship). Because of their size and scope, universities were more impersonal than four-year, liberal arts colleges, and in many ways, took on some of the traits and values of the big, modern corporation. They embraced the idea that schools should be run like a business: corporate values like efficiency, orderliness, quantification, standardization, regimentation, etc.; the rise of specialization and professionalization in teaching, administration, and fundraising; and new, more hierarchical forms of organization (i.e., faculty ranks; departmentalization by specialized disciplines; many, new administrative offices). Universities also enthroned secularism, rationalism, and intellect, unlike the piety and religious beliefs (including those which contradicted science) that dominated in most small colleges at this time. However, even by 1910, the *idea* of the modern university ran ahead of *actual* universities. They tended to be smaller than they are today (while colleges were smaller still), and relatively few faculty members had a PhD.[8]

Many colleges would eventually take on at least some of these characteristics, but years (if not decades) later, and even change their names from "college" to "university." Aurora University certainly followed this path. However, since most small colleges did not have the deep pockets it would take to transform themselves into universities any time soon, they made the most of what they had in the late nineteenth and early twentieth centuries. And they did have some distinctive, highly desirable things to offer. Where universities were weak, colleges could excel. Due to their smaller size, colleges were more intimate and personal. They had much better teacher-student ratios, so students were able to get to know their teachers and receive more individual attention. Related to this, colleges emphasized teaching, whereas many universities were more concerned that their faculty publish and make a name for themselves in their specialized discipline and so neglected teaching. While large universities emphasized their graduate programs, the focus of small colleges was on undergraduates. Whereas the focus of many large universities was divided between their liberal arts program and their growing number of professional, undergraduate programs, colleges generally focused largely on the liberal arts. And colleges such as Mendota College could tout their emphasis on morality and building character because large universities tended to embrace the European model of having no concerns about students outside of the strictly academic realm.[9]

The gulf between universities and colleges of the late nineteenth and early twentieth centuries was not as wide as most descriptions of their characteristics would suggest. Some supporters of the university dismissed colleges as no longer relevant and predicted their imminent extinction, especially if they did not change. Yet for all their dismissive language, universities were dependent on colleges for their very existence. They needed the students of colleges to populate and pay the tuition for their graduate programs. And there continued to be many differences among universities themselves, as they were still trying to define themselves. One scholar described the university of 1910 as "an adolescent—gangly, energetic, and enigmatic."[10] In short, it was still trying to figure out what it wanted to be when it grew up. And the same could also be said of the college. It too had to redefine itself as it saw the university become larger and increasingly more dominant.[11]

Women and Education

Women's educational opportunities expanded after the Civil War as well. Starting in the early 1860s, with the founding of Vassar, several all-women colleges were founded, joining the already-existing Mount Holyoke (and they were known collectively as the "Seven Sisters"—Barnard, Bryn Mawr, Mount Holyoke, Radcliffe, Smith, Vassar, and Wellesley). What made them so important was that, for the first time, women could attend colleges which taught the same kinds of courses, with the same level of difficulty, that men did. The pioneering students who graduated from these colleges went on to become professors and administrators there and elsewhere, as well as to carve out whole new professions for women because they were still mostly kept out of traditional ones. Coeducational schools were developing in much greater numbers as well, especially the land-grant colleges and state universities, and women took advantage of these new educational opportunities. In 1870, only 1 percent of college-age people attended college, and just 21 percent of them were women. This percentage more than doubled by 1910, when out of the 5 percent of college-age people who attended college, 40 percent of them were women. This can be explained, at least in part, by the fact that more women attended and completed high school. In 1900, a mere 7 percent of American teenagers attended high school. A substantial majority of these students were women, and they constituted 60 percent of those who actually graduated. Men were less likely to complete their secondary education because they often left to go to work. And many middle-class men, whether they completed high school or not, were more attracted by the opportunities found in business than in the professions (which required a college degree). This was at a time when the space for students at colleges and universities was growing. The result was that women filled this void.[12]

Women had a long way to go before they were viewed as being capable of higher education. Colonial women were seen as being less rational than and intellectually inferior to men, plain and simple. In an era when few men received much education, women received even less, and it was usually at home. Colonial women also had substantially higher rates of illiteracy than men. After the American Revolution, women were viewed more positively (including society's view of their intellectual capacity), and their education improved somewhat, at least at the lower levels. A republic needed educated citizens if it was to survive, so it became important for women to become better educated and literate. As the mothers of future male citizens and leaders, it was argued, they were their sons' first teachers of republican values. (This is a concept that historians call "Republican Motherhood.") As a result of these new, more positive views of women and the need to give them more education, the antebellum period saw more opportunities for girls' elementary and secondary education (and especially for improving their literacy), but the view remained that the education of women should be different because they were destined for marriage and motherhood. And some people continued to argue that women should not get a college education because they were not up to it, either mentally or physically. In short, women had to prove that they could engage in more and better education without hurting themselves. In 1837, Oberlin College became the first college to admit women, but just six or fewer colleges embraced coeducation before the Civil War. There were also increased numbers of secondary-level academies or seminaries for girls (although of varying quality) and even some colleges for women (although generally unimpressive) in the antebellum era. However, any substantial improvement in higher education for women had to await the Civil War era and beyond.[13]

By the last third of the nineteenth century, women could be found in both coeducational state universities and some coeducational private colleges, but in many ways, the view that women students were different from and even inferior to male students remained. And many people continued to fear that higher education would physically hurt women—the strain of serious intellectual activity would be too much, and so it would lead to a nervous breakdown, their reproductive system would be damaged, and so on. This is one reason why the new all-women colleges after the Civil War were so important. They provided women with an education modeled on that of male students and proved that women could handle serious, varied studies as well as men, both physically and intellectually. Fears also abounded that higher education would make women less feminine and thus less desirable as wives, undermining family stability.[14]

Essentially women—whether students or faculty—remained second-class citizens in coeducational higher education. They were both discriminated against in various ways and largely restricted to specific academic areas that were viewed as the womanly disciplines—in short, domestic science and teaching. The first generation of female students, especially, experienced discrimination and a double standard. For example, at the University of Wisconsin, in the nineteenth century, female students were supposed to remain standing in each classroom until all the male students had seated themselves. And women students, sometimes unwelcome by male students, were kept separate from the men and excluded from most extracurricular activities and organizations (even though they paid the same mandatory activities fee as the men). They also were often ridiculed. University of California male students referred to women students as "pelicans," due to their anatomy, and student publications included humor that was at the expense of the female students.[15]

Faculty women's situation was similar and is nicely summed up by what one scholar calls their confinement to the "academic kitchen."[16] Within most universities, they were isolated within a narrow spectrum of disciplines, marginalized, and, compared to their male peers, undercompensated. They too experienced discrimination and a double standard. For example, at least at some universities, women were excluded from the faculty club and from academic processions. Also, the appointment of women sometimes consisted of a series of special arrangements cobbled together as a job—one without tenure and with low pay. And universities were not eager to hire female professors in the first place. Academic women created strategies to cope with these gender-specific problems, like establishing the Association of American University Women and their own faculty clubs. And when universities would not hire them, they took their expertise to jobs at federal agencies, museums, and laboratories, among others.[17]

African Americans and Education

The post–Civil War era opened up educational opportunities for African Americans as well. A few black colleges were established in the North during the antebellum era, but only a miniscule number of people attended them. The educational situation improved after the war, but many obstacles to educating African Americans remained, so the number of black students in college was still small. In the wake of the South's defeat, most southerners were hostile to the idea of educating African Americans at any level. They viewed people of color as being innately and inalterably racially inferior. By the end of the nineteenth century, many southerners had evolved to the point that they acknowledged the need for public education for African Americans (although publicly subsidized at a minimal level and segregated from whites), but not higher education, which, they feared, could produce leaders who would challenge white supremacy and the place of African Americans in the social order. Not surprisingly, then, in the postwar era, black colleges were established by northern, white, benevolent societies; missionary groups from various denominations; and black charitable societies, followed later by black, Protestant denominations; corporate philanthropic foundations; and wealthy individuals. Since black colleges were founded by so many, different, Protestant denominations or missionary societies and were often established to train ministers and missionaries, they could be considered to be Christian colleges before 1900.[18]

Black colleges faced some serious obstacles. A substantial majority of these schools did not offer college-level work; they were more at the level of an elementary or secondary school. As late as 1916, a Bureau of Education study could name only two black schools that it considered to be real colleges—Fisk and Howard. (Although this was a bigger problem for black colleges, it was also true for many white colleges, including Mendota College. In an era when so few Americans attended high school, most colleges had to have a preparatory department to teach secondary-level courses, and even many college courses were not at the college level.) Like most white colleges founded in the antebellum era, most black colleges founded in the late-nineteenth century did not survive long. It was difficult to bring people into a college who did not have the preparation for higher education provided by public elementary and secondary schools. This was especially a problem for freedmen, who had been denied any kind of formal education as slaves. And funding was always a problem. White southerners were not interested in helping struggling black colleges, black denominations had limited funds, and corporate philanthropists as well as wealthy individuals tended to support schools providing a practical, industrial/agricultural education rather than liberal arts programs.[19]

The late nineteenth to early twentieth century was an era in which white and black Americans alike were divided on the question of what kind of education should be provided to African Americans. Booker T. Washington, founder of Tuskegee Institute, argued that black southerners should be given a practical education focused on developing skills in the mechanical/industrial and agricultural spheres—in short, skilled, manual labor. W. E. B. DuBois denounced Washington's position as giving in to racial bigotry and inequality by training African Americans for lower-level jobs. He wanted at least some African Americans to attend colleges where they would receive a traditional, liberal arts education that would prepare them for professional and leadership positions—a group he called the "the talented tenth."[20]

For the most part, reality differed from DuBois's vision of black Americans getting a liberal arts college education. Very few African Americans received such an education in this period. In 1900, the U.S. commissioner of education reported that just 3,880 people were enrolled in black colleges and professional schools throughout the entire South and Washington, DC. The vast majority of schools that called themselves colleges often did not offer college-level coursework, and many black schools at this time just offered a utilitarian education. This applied to women as well. The small number of

African American women who went on in their education usually attended either teacher training or vocational schools, where they were taught skills, but in women's areas. For example, at Tuskegee Institute, female students did secondary-level academic coursework, while also learning various women's trades—dressmaking, housekeeping, upholstering, millinery, laundry work. Some African American women and men attended black colleges and universities in the South and even integrated universities in the North. However, overall, only a small number attended college. And for those who did, they were frequently reminded that the color of their skin set them apart. If they attended college in the South, they were segregated, having to enroll at an all-black school (which was, more than likely, struggling financially and lacking in resources, status, and support in general). If they attended one of the northern colleges or universities that was racially integrated, they were also set apart and discriminated against. Some schools did not allow African Americans to stay in the dormitories, simply so their white students would not have to live with them. Neither could they join Greek societies, and they were discouraged from even socializing with white students.[21]

Democratizing Effects of Nineteenth-Century Colleges (but within Limits)

The types of educational institutions discussed above had a democratizing and liberating effect on American education—bringing new groups of people into higher education (e.g., people from humbler origins, women, African Americans) and modernizing curricula by supplementing or replacing the old classicism with more practical areas of study. American higher education was not nearly as elitist as it had been in the colonial and antebellum eras, but very few people attended any of these institutions of higher learning in the nineteenth century. Looking at 18- to 21-year-olds in college in the late nineteenth century shows just how miniscule a group college students constituted. In 1870, under 2 percent of this college-age population was enrolled in four-year, post-secondary schools. By the 1890s and 1900, this percentage had risen a bit but was still tiny—just 3 percent and 4 percent, respectively. (Note that these are not percentages of the entire

American population, but of just 18- to 21-year-olds.) Translated into actual numbers, by 1900, there were only about 238,000 undergraduates in the entire United States.[22]

And most of these students attended schools that were academically weak. Like Mendota College, most of the approximately five hundred institutions of higher learning in 1900 hardly qualified as being real colleges or universities. Scholars have estimated that no more than 20 percent of these schools could be considered real colleges or universities—given their low admission standards, poorly prepared students, and low academic standards, among other things. At the turn of the century, Mendota College was not the exception in this regard; it was the norm.[23]

Nevertheless, by the late nineteenth century, colleges were opening up to and being created for groups of people who had been forgotten or given severely limited educational opportunities during the colonial and antebellum periods. Social change generally happens gradually, in fits and starts. The gains made in education by the early twentieth century would be built upon and expanded after World War I, in the 1920s and beyond.

Bible Training Schools

Most private, four-year colleges founded in the nineteenth century were established not just for academic reasons; their denominational founders had religious aims as well—especially, educating Christian workers. This includes all–African American and all-women colleges also. Even an Ivy-League, women's college like Wellesley, one of the prestigious "Seven Sisters," was established for the purpose of educating missionaries and other kinds of Christian workers. And scholars of Christian colleges have argued that even state universities originally were Protestant in nature, citing such things as *mandatory* chapel, Sunday religious services, and religious courses; strict behavioral rules that were hardly different from those at private, Christian colleges; and having presidents who were ministers as well as professing-Christian, faculty members. One of these historians found examples of denominations (especially the Presbyterians) having *more* influence and administrative control over some state universities than the states themselves, noting this about Presbyterian influence: "Though

Miami University was created by the federal congress and established by the State of Ohio, it could not have been more Presbyterian if founded by John Knox."[24] In spite of their religious foundations, however, over time, most of these colleges and certainly all the state universities secularized and took on other goals (as did Aurora College).[25]

The Second Great Awakening of the early nineteenth century reignited evangelism in the United States and produced new colleges, theological seminaries, and especially missionary societies. Some early seminaries were closely related to this new zeal for evangelizing around the world. And the rapid socioeconomic changes taking place in nineteenth-century American society also contributed to the idea that ministers needed more education. Even the leaders of smaller, humbler denominations, like the Methodists and Baptists, who once had rejected the idea that higher education was a necessity for ministers, began acknowledging that clergymen, to be effective in congregations of people who were now better educated, needed more than a call from God; they needed a formal education. Some of these humbler denominations, along with mainline Protestant denominations, founded theological seminaries in the nineteenth century (although the Advent Christians never did). In fact, by the Civil War era, a seminary education to prepare future ministers had become a common expectation for most Protestant denominations. And the denominational seminary, separate from any college (the earliest being Andover, founded in 1808), was probably the first example of an independent graduate school in the United States. As such, it became a prototype for graduate education.[26]

The emergence of seminaries was an important development, but seminaries were not very democratic. They especially posed a problem for women who wanted to devote their lives to Christian service because, at this time, most seminaries would not admit them. Also, in the nineteenth century, they tended not to have programs that would prepare people for Christian work outside of the ministry. Of course, there were some small, Christian schools, like Mendota College, whose overriding purpose was to train Christian workers, including women. But there also was another alternative to all-male seminaries, one that was less academic, but more practical and faster—an institution called a Bible training school (hereafter referred to as BTS).[27]

This type of school was more democratic and inclusive because it admitted many women and others who could not or would not attend seminaries (typically lay people of humble origins). There was always some tension between divinity schools and churches because, early on, seminaries came to be viewed as overly academic—paying more attention to theological scholarship than to preparing people for the practical work of being a church pastor. The mere existence of BTSs was a rebuke to seminaries because they rejected classical, academic learning that took years in favor of practical, mission-focused learning that took a year or two (or even less). Seminaries, in turn, viewed BTSs with disdain, probably because many BTSs did not really offer college-level work (never mind rigorous graduate studies), admitted women, and were not about preparing men for the more prestigious job of minister. Tension often existed between the two, even when they were founded by the same denomination. Religious leaders frequently claimed that the two kinds of schools were complementary rather than competing. The reality was less rosy than this rhetoric suggested because they did represent very different approaches to preparing people for Christian service. Eventually, in the early twentieth century, theological seminaries began incorporating more practical courses for lay training (including for women) into their curriculum while BTSs began offering some "Pastoral Courses." But in the late nineteenth century, when they first appeared, BTSs represented a very different philosophy of religious education from that found in seminaries.[28]

Bible training schools (and their predecessors—missionary training schools) had certain distinctive traits. *First*, their main goal was training people for both home and foreign missions, rather than educating men for the ministry. *Second*, student training was centered on the Bible, which was taken literally because these schools were religiously fundamentalist, and on evangelizing—spreading the Gospel. *Third*, their students were distinctive. Women constituted the majority of students at most schools. Men attended as well, but only those who were not intending to get ordained or were in denominations that did not require many years of education to be ordained. And these students generally came from varied educational backgrounds as well as the middle and lower-middle classes, rather than from the working class (from either farm or factory). *Fourth*,

BTS faculty were distinctive. Almost none of them had earned a graduate degree (and many had not even earned a college degree), and often these teachers received low or no pay. This is probably why many of them worked in some other job, like the ministry or public school teaching. These faculties also had an unusually high percentage of female teachers. *Fifth*, their programs included much coursework on practical topics—like evangelizing strategies—rather than liberal arts or theological courses, as well as hands-on field work (like street revivals or settlement work). *Sixth*, probably the most distinctive trait was the brevity of the programs offered by such schools. Christian workers were needed in the field, but people also feared that if students spent too much time in educational preparation, their enthusiasm for Christian work might fade.[29]

In short, BTSs were religiously fundamentalist and academically weak to mediocre. Yet they were democratic places (given how many women and people of humble background attended). Their aim was to support evangelization by quickly producing workers for home and foreign missions. The word "training" in the name of these schools is significant because it connotes practical studies, rather than academic depth or excellence, as well as efficiency, brevity, and speed. Tensions existed between BTSs and theological seminaries, but this does not mean that BTS leaders thought that theological seminaries should disappear; they looked to them to produce their church leaders. They simply wanted other types of education available so that lay people could quickly acquire training for Christian service. Lay people were needed in churches (pastor's assistants, deacons and deaconesses, church secretaries, Sunday school teachers, Bible teachers, and musicians) as well as in foreign mission fields. There were souls to be saved at home and abroad, and as quickly as possible, so the labor of many people, lay and clerical alike, was needed.[30]

Mendota College and Nineteenth-Century Educational Trends

Where does Mendota fit into this discussion of nineteenth-century colleges and BTSs? The Advent Christian school in Mendota called itself a college, but it also contained a Bible training school. The school was founded to educate ministers and other Christian workers (including women), so this was always considered to be the most important function of the college and the BTS its primary department. However, it also included liberal arts programs as well as studies in business. And the college had many of the same traits as both nineteenth-century colleges and Bible training schools. In short, the college was a hybrid. This is probably why Virginia Lieson Brereton did not include it in her pioneering book, *Training God's Army: The American Bible School, 1880–1940*. She included the Boston Bible School, the other Advent Christian school (founded in 1897), in her study, but not Mendota College. The fact that Mendota College offered liberal arts courses alongside its Bible Training School from the very beginning set it apart from the Bible training schools, even though, in the Mendota years, it shared many characteristics with them.*[31]

The story of Mendota College (and then Aurora College) is not just about how an institution grew and matured academically. It is a very American story about how a religious group founded and shaped a college that would gradually become a much larger, more stable, secularized, four-year college with graduate programs but that in its formative years was thoroughly religious in nature. Religion was its reason for being and was intertwined with virtually every aspect of the school.

*Up through the 1905-06 academic catalog, virtually all the catalogs listed religious studies under the title "Theological Department," and in 1906–7, "Biblical Department," but under those headings appeared another title—"Bible Training School." From 1907–8 on, catalog information about the religious program was listed under just one title—the Biblical Department. The part of the college that taught religion was often referred to as the "Bible Training School," by college people and others, and even informally after 1906–7, when that term disappeared from the catalogs. Perhaps two titles were used for the majority of the Mendota years because the first title had the word "department" in it, which lined up with other areas of study that were called departments.

When I started this project in 2005, my greatest concern was whether there would be enough sources to write a credible history. Mendota College was seldom discussed, other than as the school's founding institution. And given how long ago the Mendota era was and the loss of the school's records in a 1901 fire, I assumed that there would be few sources to work with.

I could not have been more wrong. The university still had most of the Mendota College catalogs (a treasure trove of information about not just the academic program, but also the college's students); its student publications; the minutes of its Board of Directors as well as those for the organization that created the college—the Western Advent Christian Publication Association (hereafter referred to as WACPA)—and that organization's newspaper—*Our Hope and Life in Christ* (hereafter referred to as *Our Hope*)—which was published fifty weeks out of the year.

Since it was WACPA that founded the college, the newspaper contained many articles about it, especially its financial situation and its fundraising, but also its special events, student activities, faculty, and accomplishments. There was even a student column most weeks, which gave some insight into the events, issues, and concerns of students. It literally took years to go through and take notes on nineteen years of *weekly* newspapers with so many relevant articles in each issue, but it was worth it. This source was invaluable, especially in understanding the precarious financial situation of Mendota College throughout its nineteen years. It also was especially valuable at the beginning and end of the Mendota period. *Our Hope* was first published in 1889, so it was able to document the years of argumentation, both for and against starting an Advent Christian school, and decision-making leading up to the founding of the college in 1892 (and its actual opening in 1893). It also documented the process of deciding to move the college, the conflict in deciding where to move it, the fundraising for it, the construction of the Aurora campus, and the actual move to the new campus in April 1912. In short, it is hard to imagine writing this book without *Our Hope*.

As a result of writing this book, I came to understand how important one of Aurora University's special collections—the Jenks Memorial Collection of Adventual Materials—is to the history of Aurora University. I used to think of it as a strictly religious collection, containing materials from the Millerite movement and the Advent Christian denomination. But it is so much more than that because of the parent-child relationship between WACPA and Mendota College. Most of the original sources that I used came from the Jenks Collection. The only major sources that I used from the Colby Archives were the Mendota College catalogs and photographs. This is further evidence of what I stated above—that Mendota College, while offering liberal arts courses (which were usually shunned by Bible training schools) was thoroughly intertwined with religion. As good Advent Christians, Mendota leaders constantly reminded students and Advent Christians in general that time was short because of their belief that Christ's return to earth was imminent. Bible training schools had a similar urgency, thus the brevity of their programs. But the leaders of Mendota College always argued that, however urgent their mission, it would be performed better if their ministers were thoroughly educated, not just in religious studies but in other areas as well. Education was not a luxury; for these early college leaders, it was the key to performing their religious mission effectively. The college's religious mission is why it is important to start Mendota College's story with a discussion of the origins of the Advent Christian denomination in the Millerite movement—the 1830s–40s movement that brought to the world the message that Christ would soon return to earth.

There are several abbreviations used in this book that need explanation:

—BTS – Bible Training School

—ELD. – Elder
This word almost always appears in sources in its abbreviated form. The word "Elder" was used as a title for ministers (instead of "Reverend") by some nineteenth-century Christians (especially Adventists). It was probably used early on because, for Advent Christians, the Bible was at the core of their faith and was to be taken literally. "Elder" is a biblical world—used in both the Old

and New Testaments. In the latter, the term is used interchangeably with the words "pastor" and "bishop." Christ, not a human being, was considered to be the head of every early Christian church, but two or more elders led it and ran it in Christ's name (preaching, teaching, caring for church members like a pastor, etc.). Also, "Elder" was a more humble-sounding title than "Reverend," and the various denominations coming out of the Millerite movement were not high church. Their instinct was *not* to put their leaders on such a high pedestal that they were seen as holier than anyone else. However, by the early twentieth century, more and more Advent Christian ministers were adopting the more conventional title of "Reverend," although Seventh-day Adventists continue to use the title of Elder today (along with "Pastor").[32]

—FIRST ADVENT (of Christ) – Christ's birth

—SECOND ADVENT (of Christ) – Christ's return to earth to raise the dead, punish the wicked, and gather the saved for eternal life

—WACPA – Western Advent Christian Publication Association
This was one of the Advent Christian denomination's publication associations (initially viewed as the publication society for the West [the word "West" being loosely defined]). It founded and nurtured Mendota College.

—*OUR HOPE* – *Our Hope and Life in Christ*
This is the name of the newspaper that was published by WACPA and so closely covered the events and issues of Mendota College (including its founding and, later, move to Aurora).

Chapter 2
Origins of a Denomination: The Millerite Movement

"I was ... brought ... to the solemn conclusion, that in about twenty-five years ... all the affairs of our present state would be wound up."

—William Miller

William Miller

On October 22, 1844, a strange thing happened across the American Northeast. Small numbers of people gathered in public buildings (if authorities had not closed them for fear of mob actions) or in private homes, singing and preaching and praying. Their spiritual bags were packed; they were ready to go to a much better place—a place they had read about and dreamed about and had worked so hard to get to. They were awaiting the arrival of their Lord Jesus Christ, who, they believed, would sweep up the saved, destroy the wicked, and make the earth anew. These people were Millerites, followers of William Miller, who had taught them that the approximate time of the Lord's arrival could be determined through a set of calculations based on Scripture.

Millerism, or the Millerite movement, was just one of a number of new social and religious movements in antebellum America. The three decades leading up to the years of the Civil War (1861–65) were times of tremendous change in the United States. America's industrial revolution, barely visible in the 1790s when the first factory was created, was clearly underway by the 1840s, leaving an especially visible mark on the landscape of the Northeast. This was not simply about economic change. The real revolutionary impact of the industrial revolution was how it was transforming *noneconomic* areas of life—deepening class divisions, encouraging America's first mass immigration, expanding existing cities while also creating new ones, encouraging the westward movement, deepening the differences between the North and the South, and creating the modern middle class with its new value system and new model of family life and gender roles. In short, this was an era of overwhelming change, a situation that generally brings with it great anxiety and conflict.

Accompanying these socioeconomic changes were profound religious changes. Americans were moving away from the more formal, rational, Calvinistic teachings of the colonial era and toward a more personal, emotional, and evangelical approach to religion within a number of Protestant denominations. A large part of this sea change in religion concerned movement away from a belief in predestination (which said that God had determined who would be saved and who would not before each person's birth) and toward a belief in free will (which said that salvation was open to everyone—if they accepted Christ as their savior as part of a rebirth or conversion experience). This belief in free will was reflected in a huge, nondenominational religious revival, in reality consisting of several, successive waves—the Second Great Awakening (the first having been in the eighteenth century of the colonial period). It began in the 1790s, gained steam after 1800, and lasted into the 1840s and 1850s. The movement pioneered such new ways of winning souls as holding a campmeeting. (For those of a more secular nature who were seeking a larger meaning to their lives, there was the transcendentalist movement of Ralph Waldo Emerson, or any number of utopian communities to withdraw to, although some were religious communities as well). In any case, it seems that a fair number of Americans, caught up in dizzying economic, political, and social change, turned to religion.

However, in the antebellum era, religious conversion in the revivals of the Second Great Awakening fed right back into the change. Being converted was not only the end of one kind of life; it was supposed to be the beginning of another—one devoted not just to one's own personal spiritual life but to saving the world. Religious conversion often led to reform activities. It was believed by such converts that a thousand years of love and peace, a veritable godly kingdom on earth, would precede the return of Christ. Given that belief, it made sense to think that whatever Christians could do to reform and purify their society would hasten the coming of this godly, earthly kingdom and, ultimately, the return of Christ. Therefore, many ministers and converts (especially women) marched into battle to fight prostitution, drinking, gambling (and other forms of behavior perceived as immoral), women's educational and legal inequality, and the curse of slavery. They took with them the language and tactics of revivals. They viewed these causes as a fight against sin, not as trying to remedy serious social problems. It is interesting to note that a number of Millerite leaders, most prominently Joshua V. Himes, were participants in one or more of these reform movements, especially the fight to abolish slavery. For them, it seems, Millerism was the ultimate reform, because the return of Christ would end all injustices.[1]

It was during this era of rapid political and socioeconomic change, religious transformation, and widespread reform that a very distinctive religious development—the Millerite movement—arose. Although few people have heard of Millerism today, it was a nationally known movement by at least 1842, its meetings attended not just by the lowly but by ministers and other highly educated people, including members of the United States Congress. It had moved from the countryside of upper-state New York and Vermont to the major cities of the Northeast and made forays into the South and the West. Stories about the movement filled the national press, especially by 1843–44, and William Miller became a household name. Many scholars view it, not as an isolated phenomenon, but as the last wave of the Second Great Awakening. Millerism was taking off just as the earlier revivals were waning.[2]

In short, Millerism, seemingly so irrelevant today, truly mattered in antebellum America. Although the movement disintegrated into various factions after Christ did not come, as predicted, in 1843–44, the movement is not unimportant in American history. A study of the Millerite movement tells us much about the culture and worldview of antebellum America, especially in the North. Millerism also produced six new Protestant denominations, among them the Advent Christian denomination, and, ultimately, a number of Adventist colleges, including Mendota College, the topic of this book. I believe that to fully understand Aurora University in its earliest decades, at Mendota, it is important to understand its Adventist history, because many of the early patterns of the school very much reflected Adventist beliefs and ways of doing things. Understanding Millerism and the Advent Christian denomination that evolved out of it provides insights into the religious culture, worldview, and curriculum of Mendota College.

William Miller's Transformation into a Prophet and Then a Preacher

William Miller (1782–1849), a humble, middle-aged husband, father of ten children, and farmer in Low Hampton, New York, began his life as a preacher in 1831. Who was this uneducated, itinerant preacher, and why did he turn from farming to preaching at a time in his life when most people would be evaluating their life's accomplishments, not venturing into new, life-changing endeavors?

Born in 1782, in Pittsfield, Massachusetts, William Miller lived most of his life in Low Hampton, New York, a small village just a few miles from the Vermont border. Although taught as a child to believe in God by his devout Baptist mother, he became increasingly skeptical about religion in his early adult years and embraced Deism's view of a distant, impersonal God who created the world but then kept his distance from his creation. However, after returning from a stint in the War of 1812 (serving as an officer in the United States Army), he appeared to be disillusioned with his fellow human beings and unhappy with himself.

After wrestling with this disillusionment for several years, he had what appeared to be a conversion experience in 1816. That was not the end of it, however. Miller's rational side said that he needed to study the Bible for himself—to see the Christ presented in the Scriptures—after having experienced Christ through an emotional conversion experience. And so he spent two years in a methodical and thorough study of the Bible. He explained the process that he used like this:

> I determined to lay aside all my prepossessions, to thoroughly compare Scripture with Scripture, and to pursue its study in a regular and methodical manner. I commenced with Genesis, and read verse by verse, proceeding no faster than the meaning of the several passages should be so unfolded, as to leave me free from embarrassment respecting any mysticism or contradictions. Whenever I found anything obscure, my practice was to compare it with all collateral passages; and by the help of Cruden [a concordance], I examined all the texts of Scripture in which were found any of the prominent words contained in any obscure portion. Then by letting every word have its proper bearing on the subject of the text, if my view of it harmonized with every collateral passage in the Bible, it ceased to be a difficulty.[3]

By 1818, this laborious process had not only given him a *rational*, biblical basis for his *feeling* of being saved, it also convinced him, through his study of the prophecies, of the literal, visible, second coming of Christ in the relatively near future: "I was thus brought ... to the solemn conclusion, that in about twenty-five years from that time all the affairs of our present state would be wound up."[4] This was his own conclusion, rooted in his study of the Bible, not a message sent directly via a visible angel or an invisible God, which he never claimed it to be.

One might reasonably expect that such a conviction would cause Miller to go out into the world immediately to start spreading the warning, for time was of the essence. He *did not* do this and *would not* do it for another eleven years. He spent another five years going over and over his assumptions, calculations, and conclusions, raising whatever criticisms he could think of to see if they were valid. Even after a total of eight years of study, he was reluctant to go public. Earlier, he had the excuse of not wanting to mislead people if his ideas should be false, but by 1823, when, in his own mind, he was sure of his beliefs, he still hesitated. His explanation had to do with his own fears about himself:

> I tried to excuse myself to the Lord for not going out and proclaiming it to the world. I told the Lord that I was not used to public speaking, that I had not the necessary qualifications to gain the attention of an audience, that I was very diffident and feared to go before the world, that they would "not believe me nor hearken to my voice," that I was "slow of speech, and of a slow tongue." But I could get no relief.[5]

After he was sure of his beliefs, he did start to mention them privately to some of his neighbors and even a few local ministers, but no one seemed interested. This rejection must have done little to lessen his fears about going public with his beliefs and no doubt gave him little hope that he would find a minister willing to carry his ideas to the world for him. And so he continued to study the Bible for another eight years before finally preaching his first sermon.

Although, by 1831, Miller had successfully put off proclaiming his views to the world, he could not entirely repress the growing conviction within himself that he must begin. According to Miller, to ease his conscience, he struck a bargain with God:

> My distress became so great, I entered into a solemn covenant with God, that if he would open the way, I would go and perform my

duty to the world. "What do you mean by opening the way?" seemed to come to me. Why, said I, if I should have an invitation to speak publicly in any place, I will go and tell them what I find in the Bible about the Lord's coming. Instantly all my burden was gone; and I rejoiced that I should not probably be thus called upon; for I had never had such an invitation: my trials were not known, and I had but little expectation of being invited to any field of labor.[6]

Much to Miller's utter astonishment, an invitation came that very day to preach at a neighboring church. According to Miller, he was "angry with myself for having made the covenant I had; I rebelled at once against the Lord, and determined not to go."[7] After agonizing about it that day, he reached a major turning point in his life, submitting to what he believed was God's mission for him. Miller would delay no more. This cause—of telling the world about the nearness of the Advent—would consume the rest of his days.

The First Stage of Millerism

The first, major phase of the Millerite movement (1831–39) consisted of Miller traveling alone around upper-state New York, parts of New England, and eastern Canada, mostly preaching in small, farming communities—especially in Methodist, Baptist, and Congregational churches. He was so successful at preaching that within a short time, he had many more invitations to speak than he could possibly accept. Especially in the early years of Miller's ministry, many ministers eagerly sought him out (even if they did not accept his Adventist doctrine) because his revivals generally brought an impressive harvest of souls. In December of 1839, Miller complained to Himes, "They like to have me preach, and build up their churches; and there it ends, with most of the ministers, as yet."[8] Although that, no doubt, discouraged him, he kept preaching.

Although Miller downplayed his qualifications before accepting his mission (and even after), he apparently was an effective preacher, given the size of the crowds that flocked to hear him lecture, the great number of conversions that he made, and the endless preaching invitations that he received. His success was not due to his appearance or even his personality. Miller did not cut an impressive figure; he was short, stocky, ruddy-complexioned, and middle-aged, having a slightly shaking head. Nor did he have a charismatic personality. There also was nothing extraordinary about his speaking style. He was not an eloquent preacher and, in fact, had an old-fashioned, provincial way of speaking. The hallmark of his speaking style was simplicity. Scholars have tried to explain why it was that he ultimately attracted huge crowds in some of America's largest cities, kept people enthralled for hours (even while standing), and brought many converts into the Adventist fold.[9]

First, his message was novel and compelling. Although he clearly was not the only person to come up with the idea of the second coming of Christ, even at that time, his Advent message challenged the beliefs and emphases of mainline Protestantism—especially its downplaying or even denial of the *imminent*, visible, personal return of Christ. And what a startling message it was—creating great joy or great distress, depending on the people who heard it. In either case, it made a big impression. Clyde Hewitt, historian of Adventism and longtime history professor at Aurora College, argued that Miller was clearly the most popular and effective of the Millerite preachers. Certainly many people wanted to hear this particular Adventist message from the lips of the man who created it. However, Miller's lieutenants, who supplemented his preaching and stepped in on the many occasions when he was ill, also found receptive audiences, suggesting that the power of the message itself was important.[10]

Second, Miller, although lacking a formal theological education, was impressive in his knowledge of the Bible and history (a knowledge of history being especially important when dealing with prophecy in that, for believers, it shows when and where prophecies are fulfilled). The fifteen years that he had spent in intense biblical study before he took to preaching held him in good stead as he preached, engaged in extensive correspondence, wrote papers and tracts for publication, and responded to the arguments and taunts of critics. His mastery of the Bible even put many ministers to shame. For Miller, every belief he held started and ended with the Bible, which is why it was at the center of his preaching. He had no use for the typical methods and props used by many preachers (like the use of "anxious seats" where people perceived to be ripe for conversion would get special attention from the evangelist) to bring people to a conversion experience. He viewed the sheer power of Scripture as capable of doing that. And he did not expect people to simply take him at his word. He urged people to turn to their own Bibles and test his conclusions.[11]

Third, his carefully reasoned writing and oratorical skills were such that he was able to hold large audiences in rapt attention for up to two hours at a time. Miller did not have anything close to a charismatic personality, and his speech often revealed his frontier origins and lack of formal education, but he seemed to have a talent for painting compelling word pictures. Hewitt argued that "one does not hold an audience 'spellbound,' 'chained to their seats' listening with 'the stillness of death' for up to two hours without employing imaginative, vivid, dramatic, creative language, tinged with an occasional flight into the oratorical or poetic"[12] and that those written sermons that have survived reflect such qualities. However, good oratory is generally enhanced by rational, logical thinking and writing as well. Such vivid imagery may not have been as important as the power of his careful reasoning that was always embedded in Scripture. The editors of one newspaper of the day noted that "allowing his premises to be correct, there is no getting away from his conclusions."[13] Of course many people did not accept his premises and so could not accept his conclusions, but such a comment suggests the logical nature of his reasoning. As historian Francis Nichol pointed out, a number of highly educated clergymen were won over to Miller's views, and they were people who were far more likely to be convinced by carefully reasoned argument backed by Scripture than by fanciful oratory that they were used to employing themselves. Additional evidence for this can be found in the significant numbers of people who embraced Millerism as a result of just *reading* his closely reasoned arguments for Christ's imminent return in published tracts and sermons. Miller's insistence on rationalism over emotionalism to win converts also is reflected in how he wanted people to become convinced of his beliefs. He did not want them to simply take him at his word as a persuasive authority figure but instead urged his listeners to do their own research by reading the Bible themselves.[14]

Fourth, most descriptions of Miller also emphasize his sincerity and passion for his cause and for the people who, in his eyes, remained unsaved and thus in dire straits. One may not have accepted his main message but could still find the man appealing. For example, in the summer of 1844 (after Miller's time period for the return of Christ had elapsed, but before the new date of October 22, 1844), an editor for the *Commercial*, a Cincinnati paper, wrote that "whatever people may think of his belief, which is peculiar, one thing is conceded by all, that he is a Christian at heart."[15] And the Lynn *Record* stated that "no one can hear him five minutes without being convinced of his sincerity."[16] Although he had some severe critics, who made slashing personal attacks, many people took issue with the doctrine rather than with the man. This sincerity and conviction, no doubt, contributed to the conversion rate. It is impossible to know how many of his converts simply came to God and how many also embraced his Adventist beliefs, but the power of his sincerity and convictions probably contributed to the former, thus swelling his conversion rate. Closely related to his sincerity was his passionate concern for those who were yet unsaved. In a letter to Himes, he wrote: "Those souls whom I have addressed in my six months' tour are continually before me, sleeping or waking; I can see them perishing by thousands. ..."[17] Such deep concern for the future well-being of his fellow human beings no doubt came through in his sermons.[18]

Finally, if it is true that hard work brings success, Miller was an excellent example of that truism. When physically able, he worked constantly. Although an old man by the standards of the day and constantly battling various ailments (including palsy), he preached unceasingly, often traveling long distances. In a letter to a friend, Miller wrote that in just one year, between October 1839 and October 1840, he had journeyed 4,560 miles and preached 627 times. And he thought he had brought about five thousand conversions (the majority of them men—ages 30–50). It was in 1839 that Miller began preaching in Massachusetts, which meant that he started preaching in bigger towns—like Lynn, Lowell, and Boston. Such places were much larger than the small villages of northern New England and upper-state New York. By the time that he took on this heavier preaching load, he was older, frailer, and sicker. His precarious health, no doubt, was exacerbated by this new, grueling schedule, which brought him farther from home, required him to use the primitive modes of transportation of the day, and put him in the limelight for the first time, opening him up to much more criticism. Only absolute belief in a cause could have driven a person to undergo such an ordeal.[19]

But however much he did in these early years, his ministry was limited. He was, after all, just one man. Although he was becoming much better known by the late 1830s, scholars generally agree that he certainly was not the household name that he would become later on. All of this would change when he met Joshua V. Himes in late 1839.

What Was Millerism?

Before venturing into the second, more mature period of the Millerite movement, which began when Miller met Himes, it is important to pause here to answer some basic but perhaps as-yet-unanswered questions about the nature of Millerism. What was Millerism and how did it relate to the larger American society? (In other words, what was new about its theology, and how was it similar to Protestantism in general? What regions of the country and the world did it penetrate? What kinds of people were drawn to Millerism?)

In order to understand such a movement as Millerism, it is important first to understand the man who created it—William Miller. The previous discussion on what made Miller an effective preacher, according to various scholars of Millerism, sheds much light on what kind of man Miller was, but a few things can be added to this portrait.

Miller, of humble origins and lacking seminary training, also embraced his mission relatively late in life (on the verge of entering his fifties) and experienced many debilitating health problems that often sidelined his preaching (sometimes for extended periods), especially in the 1840s. All of this made Miller a self-deprecating man who never seemed to get over the idea that God had chosen him for such a grand mission, as he saw it—warning the world of Christ's imminent return. His letters are filled with expressions of concern about his inadequacies for this job. For example, in one letter to a close friend, he wrote: "It astonishes me, and I can only account for it, by supposing that God is supporting the *old man* weak, wicked, imperfect & ignorant as he is, to confound the wise and mighty. ... Oh my br.

it makes me feel like a worm, a poor feeble creature. For it is God only that could produce such an effect on such audiences. Yet it gives me confidence. ..."[20] He also wrote his son: "I know my own weakness, & I do know that I have neither power of body or mind, to do what the Lord is doing by me as an instrument."[21] These are not the words of someone with an overly positive self-image. His answer, however, was that since he was not capable of doing such things, it must be God. As he says above, that belief gave him the self-confidence that he otherwise lacked.[22]

Although "Father Miller," as he was called by many of his followers, was widely admired and respected, he was hardly perfect and not always successful. He himself was aware of at least some of his failings and noted them often, as have scholars of Millerism. He has been described as kindly and a peacemaker, yet at times he reprimanded himself, as did others, for his anger and sarcasm in responding to his critics. Also, historians credit the urbane, media-savvy Himes with making Miller the nationally known person that he came to be. Miller was too much the product of frontier America—too parochial—and had too limited a vision to have reached the urban masses and national press on his own. The two men formed a productive partnership, each complementing the other—Miller being the better preacher and Himes, the better promoter. Ultimately, they made this relationship work because they both were so dedicated to the Adventist cause, and genuine affection existed between them. However, this union was not without tensions. Miller, with his isolated home (and slow mail service), along with his personality quirks, could be difficult to communicate and work with at times. He could be indecisive in making dates to preach and unreliable in showing up once a date was set. Sometimes he made statements in public that he would come to regret. Himes was all about confident, immediate action, and Miller, who was considerably older than his partner, moved more slowly and never lost his self-doubt about his abilities. These problems were made worse by his deteriorating health in the two to three years leading up to the big year of 1843. His body simply would not allow him to keep up his former pace or meet Himes's demands. Scholars view Miller as important to the movement up to 1844, but somewhat less so by 1843—as various factions arose, advocating ideas and strategies that Miller disagreed with, and as his health deteriorated, increasingly keeping him off the stage. In short, he lost control of the Millerite movement.[23]

It also is important to understand what the movement stood for and what it was trying to accomplish. What exactly was this humble man preaching that stirred up so much controversy? Miller, as a result of years of intense Bible study (especially the books of Daniel and Revelation and parables in the New Testament), came to a conclusion that he had *not set out to prove*—that Jesus Christ would not only personally and visibly return to the earth but would do so in the very near future, sometime between March 1843 and March 1844. Miller concluded that Christ would descend from the heavens and the saved (both the dead and the living), now immortal, would be caught up to meet the Lord in order to reign with him for a thousand years (the millennium described in Revelation 20) over a new earth that had been "cleansed" or destroyed by fire. This fire would consume not only the earth, but also the bodies of the wicked. At the end of the thousand years, the souls of the wicked would be judged and sent to eternal damnation.[24]

Although one of the images of Miller that has come down through the years is that of a fanatic, far outside the mainstream of American, evangelical Protestantism, scholars of Millerism generally describe his beliefs overall as orthodox, having far more in common with his fellow evangelicals than not. Miller's religious beliefs (other than those concerning the Advent, which clearly *were* distinctive) are generally described as examples of conservative evangelicalism, given his belief in biblical literalism, the authority of the Scriptures, and the need to be reborn to God through a physical and emotional experience. This explains something very important about Miller. He was adamantly against sectarianism and never intended to establish a denomination (never mind six). He considered himself a Baptist his whole life and urged his followers *not* to leave their churches. Thus, the Millerite movement was nonsectarian and interdenominational. The orthodoxy of his overall message helped to make that possible, at least up to 1843/1844, when the movement to leave one's church became unstoppable due to the ridicule and hostility of fellow congregants and the consolation Millerites found with one another. And the orthodox nature of Miller's message made it easier for evangelicals to become believers. Once they believed that Christ would return to earth soon, they were in sync with Miller's beliefs. Becoming a believer did not require a great shift in their beliefs as conservative evangelicals.[25]

In regards to the beliefs that made Millerism different from other evangelical churches, it is important to discuss the issue of dating Christ's return. Although by 1842/1843, both a belief in Christ's imminent, personal return to earth *and* the approximate date of that return were increasingly tests of Millerism, before that time, one could be considered an Adventist without believing in the ability to set an exact year or day for the event. A number of people, including some Millerite leaders, did *not* accept the date-setting aspect of Millerism. They simply believed that Christ would come soon. One of the myths about Miller is that he set an *exact* date for the return of Christ. He did not. Miller and virtually all the original Millerite leaders were uncomfortable with setting an *exact* date for the Second Advent. Miller tended to refer to the date for this event as "about the year 1843," usually adding that this date was correct only if his calculations were correct. By early 1843, Miller experienced growing pressure to be more specific so he identified a time period that he had believed in for a while but had not stated publicly. On January 1, 1843, he wrote a letter saying that he believed Christ would come sometime between March 21, 1843, and March 21, 1844. Even being this specific represented a shift in the focus of the Millerite movement. For most of the movement's history, the central focus of the message was simply on the *soon* coming of Christ, but by 1843, the focus shifted to a *specific time*. And after March 21, 1844, this focus on a time element sharpened even more as a new group of leaders (outside of the established Millerite leadership) set a specific date, October 22, 1844, for the Second Advent. A man named Samuel Snow rose at a campmeeting service and announced that he believed that Christ would return on October 22, 1844. This new date caught on immediately among the rank and file. The Millerite leadership, including Miller, did ultimately accept the October 22 date, but they rejected it almost right up to the end. Neither Miller nor Himes publicly acknowledged their acceptance of this date until about two weeks before the 22nd, and the rest of the leadership soon followed suit.[26]

Since Miller's religious beliefs were generally in sync with those of other evangelical Protestants, it seems logical to see Millerism as part of that larger, nondenominational, evangelical movement, the Second Great Awakening. Indeed, Millerism alone brought literally thousands of people to a conversion experience. Scholars of Millerism suspect that many of the souls harvested at the services of Miller and his lieutenants saw themselves as simply coming to God rather than also accepting Miller's Adventist beliefs (a situation that greatly discouraged Miller). But whether Miller's converts accepted his Adventist beliefs or not, they did add to the ranks of evangelical Christians, which was what Great Awakening preachers were trying to do. As mentioned earlier, Millerism scholars see Miller as playing a major role in the later years of the Great Awakening. Ruth Alden Doan argued that "Millerites not only fit into evangelicalism, they also played a significant role in revitalizing it," and she saw "the great revival wave of 1843–1844 as essentially inspired by Millerism."[27] Another historian of Millerism, George R. Knight, argued that "the Millerite crusade ... should not be seen as a separate movement from the Second Great Awakening, but as an extension of it" and that Miller was "perhaps the most successful revivalist of the last phase of the Second Great Awakening."[28] Some scholars have looked at this numerically. Millerism scholar Everett Dick found that in several denominations, their peak church enrollments hit right about the time that Miller expected Christ's return. And another historian, Richard Carwardine, found a similar pattern—that the statistical peak of the Second Great Awakening was in 1843–44.[29]

Millerism drew on and was a part of the Second Great Awakening in other ways as well. As noted earlier, except for the message of Christ's *imminent* return, Miller's conservative, evangelical message was virtually indistinguishable from that of earlier Great Awakening preachers. Both messages emphasized a rebirth experience, Scripture as the ultimate authority, the mission of a Christian to win others to Christ, and living a life of piety. In a discussion of the orthodoxy of Millerism's beliefs, Knight argued that "unlike the Mormons and Shakers and other radical groups of the period, the Millerites were both traditional and orthodox in their theology and lifestyle. ... It was easy for most Americans to accept Millerism once they accepted the premillennial return of Christ, since they did not need to adjust other aspects of their belief structure."[30] Also, both in effect embraced a relatively new idea in American Protestantism in that both Charles G. Finny, the preeminent evangelist of the Second Great Awakening, and Miller preached as if everyone had the ability to *choose* their salvation. In other words, the theological idea of free will replaced the harsh Calvinist idea of predestination—the view that God had chosen, before one's birth, whether one would be granted eternal life or not. And both movements were interdenominational, drawing converts from a number of Protestant denominations, especially from the Methodists and the Baptists. Finally, the Millerites and the preachers of the Second Great Awakening used some of the same methods to win souls. Both used itinerant, lay preachers, who had little theological training, but were called to preach (like both Finny and Miller). They traveled around to lead revivals—special services consisting of singing, praying, and, most importantly, powerful preaching, which ended with an invitation for people to come forward as a sign of committing their lives to Christ. Both also used campmeetings as a part of their evangelistic outreach. These gatherings had been created during the earlier years of the Second Great Awakening and had proven to be highly successful in bringing people to God.[31]

In spite of the many similarities and connections between Millerism and the Second Great Awakening, there were some important differences between them in religious beliefs. Obviously, the biggest difference was Miller's passionate conviction that Christ was coming very soon. Intertwined with the issue of when Christ would return was the issue of when and how the millennium would arrive. Millerites, who were premillennialists, believed that the millennium described in Revelation (a time of peace, love, and harmony on earth) would begin as soon as Christ returned to earth and purified it through fire. In other words, Christ would return *before* the millennium began, and the millennium would come suddenly and abruptly, a view of the millennium that Millerism scholar Doan called "radical supernaturalism." She defined this as "a belief in a divine order outside human history which would break into the lives of men and transform the earth."[32] For many American Protestants, this view of the millennium was heretical and unacceptable because it negated human efforts to bring in the millennium. They believed that God worked *through* people rather than *instead* of them, so the coming of the millennium would be *gradual* rather than *sudden*.[33]

By the eighteenth and nineteenth centuries, a new view of the millennium was emerging and by Miller's time was widely accepted. This was postmillennialism, the idea that Christ would return at the *end* of the millennium, and the millennium would come about gradually, as a result of personal spiritual perfection, social reform, and overall national progress. It was an optimistic, humanist view that saw human beings and their societies as capable of being perfected through human efforts. Thus, for converts of the Second Great Awakening, having a rebirth experience was not the end of a journey, but the beginning. It was now their job to help with the cleansing of society in order to hasten the millennium and Christ's return to earth. Thus, for most Protestants, including evangelicals, Christ would return to earth *after* the millennium, *not before.* Postmillennialism was the newer idea of the two. The early church, like Miller, had believed in the literal return of Christ to earth to judge the wicked and give eternal life to the righteous. Miller was a "restorationist," a person who wanted to return Christianity to the beliefs and behaviors of the apostles and the early Christian church of the first century, and the vehicle for recovering early Christianity was thought to be the Bible. The lines between pre- and postmillennialism were not always clear cut, however. A number of Millerite leaders had been active in reform (especially abolitionism) before their conversion, like Himes, and some, again like Himes, continued some reform activities as Millerites. But it seems that in the end, for most Millerites, Adventism was the ultimate reform. Christ's return to earth and ushering in of the millennium would end all worldly oppressions.[34]

Millerism and the Second Great Awakening also differed in the behaviors exhibited at their revivals. Granted, the Second Great Awakening was a religious movement that spread out over decades, having a number of distinct phases in different regions of the country, and so its revivalism took a number of different forms—from those showing decorum and restraint to those described as wildly emotional, vulgar, and generally unseemly. However, the most successful revivals tended to be on the frontier, where the more extreme behaviors tended to be found, and the predominant evangelist of the 1820s and 1830s, Charles G. Finney, introduced methods to evangelism that tended to emphasize emotionalism. He was especially known for such strategies as "protracted meetings," which went on for days and sometimes weeks; naming specific people in his public prayers; and the use of "anxious seats," seats that were up front where those who seemed to be on the verge of conversion were placed so that they could be specially worked on by the evangelist. These and other techniques, used by Finney and others, raised the emotional level of revival services and often created extreme behavior among people in the audience (especially physical manifestations like shouting, hysterically laughing, dancing, jerking, falling to the ground, writhing on the ground, becoming unconscious, etc.).[35]

The revivals of William Miller in particular and Millerite preachers in general stood in sharp contrast to this. Like most evangelicals of the day, Miller emphasized the Bible in his preaching, but he carried it further than others in that Scripture and carefully reasoned arguments based on Scripture alone were at the heart of his preaching. He compared the various prophetic Scriptures to one another and linked them to historical events that seemed to him to have fulfilled such prophecies. Hewitt described his method of preaching as taking "essentially a scholarly approach."[36] Many contemporaries, including people who rejected his message, commented on the fact that rationalism predominated over emotionalism in his revivals and that was reflected in the restraint and decorum of the people attending these services. He rejected the use of strategies commonly used by evangelists to manipulate people into a conversion experience. It is true that occasionally Adventists did succumb to such things as physical manifestations or other extreme acts, and many critics of the time made these charges, usually in exaggerated form. It is also true that fanaticism did start to grow as the time of Christ's expected return grew near, especially in 1842–43. But it is also true that many contemporaries commented on how relatively quiet and orderly Millerite services were compared to the services and campmeetings of other groups (especially the Methodists). As an example, when a reporter for the New York *Herald* was sent to witness a Millerite campmeeting in Newark, New Jersey, in 1842, he wrote: "Those who think that one of these Millerite meetings resembles a Methodist camp meeting are greatly mistaken; there is much more order, decorum, and argument in these Miller meetings. Up to the present time there has not been a disorderly person upon the ground; all has been quiet and decorous."[37] Not all Millerite preachers stuck as closely as Miller to this emphasis of simply preaching the Bible over trying to stir up emotions, but overall, this seemed to be the pattern. Millerites embraced the Methodist campmeeting—the general idea of informally bringing people together in a rustic setting for a few days in the hope that sinners would be converted and saints would be spiritually replenished—but they also seemed to put their own, more religiously conservative stamp on it, as well as on other types of services.[38]

A final major question remains as part of this attempt to explain the nature of Millerism. Who were the people who became Millerites? What overall patterns have historians found, geographically and demographically?

For the first seven to eight years of Miller's preaching, he spread his message in areas that were relatively close by: upper-state New York; Vermont; across the nearby border, in Canada; and, a bit later, Massachusetts. This geographical small-mindedness changed after Miller created a partnership with Joshua V. Himes, who introduced Miller and the Second Advent message to most of the cities of the Northeast—essentially New England and the mid-Atlantic states. Ultimately, Millerism also penetrated what was described in the 1830s and 1840s as "the West"—the Great Lakes states and the area as far south as St. Louis.[39]

There were also forays into other parts of the world. The work outside the United States tended to be done by native preachers who had been converted to Millerism, usually after reading Millerite literature. Millerism was especially strong in Great Britain. An Englishman, Robert Winter, was converted at Miller's first campmeeting in 1842. He then returned home to spread the word to his countrymen and began a publishing works that reprinted American Millerite literature as well as his own periodicals. This literature, in turn, converted ministers, who then started preaching the Millerite message around Great Britain. A similar thing happened in Canada. A Canadian named Richard Hutchinson also became a Millerite in 1842. He then started to preach and created a newspaper, the *Voice of Elijah*. He distributed it beyond Canada—to the entire, English-speaking world—creating new believers and some new, Millerite preachers, like Thomas Playford, in Australia. Millerite literature also made its way beyond the Anglo-American world—to places near and far. Since the scope of the work was overwhelming, while the number of Millerite preachers was inadequate for such a huge job and time was short, the vehicle for spreading the word was publications.[40]

Note that little has been said about the South. There was minimal activity by Millerite preachers in that region, especially by those from the North. And no major Millerite preacher ever held a revival there. Many scholars have attempted to explain why Millerism seemed to have such little impact there. One approach to addressing this issue is to question the assumption behind it. Robert W. Olson, the major historian of Millerism in the South, says that it is *not* true that Millerism had no impact, arguing that the message of the Second Advent was known in the South. Miller himself once remarked on having received a request from a southern area as remote as Florida. No doubt, at least some historians have overstated the impenetrability of the South, but still, this area lagged way behind northern and western regions in having a Millerite presence. However, having a physical presence in a region is different from communicating a message to it. In the South, as in Great Britain and other countries, Millerite literature did more to win converts than did "foreign" preachers. Not only did southern religious periodicals print articles about Miller and his message, but Millerite publications circulated throughout the South, including the Deep South.[41]

Millerism took hold in the United States when the issue of slavery was heating up in the 1830s/1840s due to the Nat Turner revolt and the increasingly polarizing issue of whether or not slavery could expand to new territories in the West. But the South's hostility toward northern preachers was not just because they were from a non-slaveholding region. The most common explanation given by scholars of Millerism is that virtually all of the major leaders of the movement (including Miller) were either active abolitionists or at least had abolitionist sympathies. Himes is the best example of this, but many others in the top leadership were identified with this cause that was so feared by southerners. It simply was not safe for the major leaders to venture too far into the South, as George Storrs found out. A prominent abolitionist and Millerite, he was mobbed by angry Virginians on a preaching tour. At this time, abolitionists were also unpopular in many parts of the North and were sometimes attacked there, as Storrs had been several years earlier in New Hampshire. How much more hostile the South was to the already unpopular abolitionists was not lost on the leaders of Millerism. One commonly cited story illustrates the assumptions of southerners when they saw northerners coming south to preach. On a preaching tour of Maryland, a Millerite preacher and abolitionist, Joseph Bates, encountered an angry, local leader who accused Bates of coming south in order to steal slaves. Bates responded to this accusation by saying: "Yes, Judge, I am an abolitionist, and have come to get your slaves, and *you too!* As to getting your slaves *from* you, we have no such intention; for if you should give us all you have ... we should not know what to do with them. We teach that Christ is coming, and we want you all saved."[42] Apparently the judge did not understand that the Second Advent would make abolitionism a moot issue.[43]

Not only did southerners hate abolitionists by the 1840s, they also may have feared the *message* of Adventist preachers. One Millerism scholar, David L. Rowe, argued that the apocalyptic message and vivid imagery of Revelation and Adventists' ardent belief in the imminent return of Christ may have caused white southerners to fear renewed slave uprisings. The 1831 Virginia slave rebellion, in which dozens of slave owners and their family members were killed, led by Nat Turner, traumatized the South and contributed to its growing paranoia about slave revolts and hostility toward abolitionists. The year 1831 also happened to be when Miller started to preach about the end of the world, and slaves already tended to focus on the next world rather than the material one, which produced so much suffering for them. Rowe suggests that slave owners may have feared that if slaves started believing that Christ's return to earth was imminent, at which time sinners—i.e., slave owners—would be punished, they might turn to violent rebellion again. Thus, even if one believed the Adventist message, it was best to keep it to oneself. Of course, as many historians have pointed out, reform or sudden change of any kind in a patriarchal slave society, like that found in the South, has generally been viewed as a threat to social peace and political control. In antebellum America, one of the major reform periods in American history (moral reform, temperance, women's rights, abolitionism, and more), the South had little engagement in the numerous reform movements of the era. On the other hand, the very places where antebellum reform was strongest—in New York and New England—were the same areas where Millerism had its deepest roots.[44]

Generally speaking, it was difficult for Millerites to penetrate the South. That changed somewhat in the summer of 1843 as the time of Christ's predicted return drew near. The South began to open up when southerners realized that the Millerites were not there to free their slaves. In 1843 and 1844, northern Millerites preached in Delaware, Maryland, Virginia, Washington, DC, the Carolinas, Kentucky, Tennessee, and even Mississippi, finding interest among African Americans as well as some whites, but overall having limited results. Although Millerism had a larger impact on the South than some have acknowledged, it was considerably less than the grip it had on the North, and the limited efforts that were made were not, for the most part, in the Deep South where slavery had its tightest hold.[45]

Since Millerites were so widely dispersed throughout the North, looking at geography alone does not give a clear picture of who they were as a group. In fact, as Rowe points out, counting the number of Millerites across the country is virtually impossible because it is so difficult to identify them. Unlike some other religious movements of the day (e.g., the Mormons, Shakers), Millerism was a mass movement that was vehemently nonsectarian and thus diverse theologically. Miller constantly urged his followers to put their differences aside and stay within their own churches. The only message that mattered was the imminence of Christ's return to earth. At the same time, except for its Second Advent message, its overall conservative theology and evangelistic style made Millerism look like virtually any other evangelical denomination. All of this helps to explain why the estimated numbers of Millerites (by both contemporaries and scholars) vary so widely—from ten thousand to over one million. Millerites tended to look a lot like their fellow Protestant Americans.[46]

In spite of the problems associated with drawing a collective portrait of Millerites, some generalizations can be made tentatively, based on such things as Rowe's study of 116 Millerites in upstate New York, one of the places where Millerism was strongest. Rowe found that, here, the largest number of Millerites were Baptists, a finding that correlates with some other scholars' findings. However, some scholars, looking in different places, found more Methodists than Baptists. In any case, Millerism drew heavily from both of these groups. It also drew, although less heavily, from the Congregationalists, members of the Christian Connexion (a restorationist group), and Presbyterians. Rowe also found that these followers of Miller were drawn from a broad occupational spectrum—with farmers and laborers at one end and industrialists, ministers, and other professional people at the other. Although, not surprisingly, Rowe's sample is skewed in terms of ministers, it does show that not all Millerites were poor, thus challenging the thesis that millenarianism drew largely from the lower socioeconomic ranks of society.[47] Rowe concluded that there is no evidence that Millerites were predominantly poor or even that the poor accounted for a large minority of Millerites. ... Although no evidence indicates that most Millerites were poor, some suggest that they were often comfortable and sometimes even well-off. ... Nor is there any evidence among Millerites of a widespread perception of social deprivation among our Adventists. More common were concerns about being found with too much hoarded wealth when Christ returns. So if the theory that millenarism generally appeals to the socially dispossessed is true, then Millerism appears to provide a glaring exception. ... The Millerites *were* deprived, but spiritually rather than materially [italics in original].[48]

Rowe is not alone in this kind of finding. Historian Ronald Graybill drew a collective portrait of some 1860 Adventists who were found on a *Review and Herald* subscription list and discovered that these Adventists were "distributed in a wide spectrum of economic statuses, but favoring the upper side of that spectrum."[49] Contemporary witnesses and newspapers also noted the variety of socioeconomic statuses among the people who attended Millerite services, campmeetings, etc.[50] In short, it appears that Millerism drew from a wide spectrum of people in terms of geography, Protestant denominations and theology, and socioeconomic status. Thus, as with their widely embraced conservative theology (except for the Second Advent message) and familiar technique of revivalism, the social portrait of Millerism does not support the view that Millerites were a culturally isolated, socioeconomically deprived group of people. They seemed to be more like their fellow, evangelical Protestant Americans than different.

The Second Stage of Millerism

Throughout the 1831–39 period, the first stage of the Millerite movement, Miller labored virtually alone, in a relatively compact area, and mostly in small towns and villages. Having lived all his life in the frontier area of upper-state New York and Vermont, Miller's personal and preaching world did not include large towns and cities. All of that changed when he met Joshua V. Himes in late 1839 and preached in his Boston church. Himes, who was the minister of Boston's Chardon Street Chapel, an ardent social reformer, and a high-energy person a generation younger than Miller, embraced not only Millerism but Miller himself. It quickly became obvious that Miller needed help in spreading his important, time-sensitive message, and Himes was just the man for the job. They created a productive partnership, which Knight described like this:

> He and Miller formed what can best be thought of as a symbiotic team, with each complementing the other's weaknesses with his own strengths. Miller was a convincing preacher but a poor promoter. Himes … was an excellent promoter, but … only average in the pulpit. Himes was a man of action, while Miller was more of a thinker and theologian. Thus Himes generally deferred to Miller in matters relating to the message to be preached, and Miller to Himes on evangelistic and promotional strategy. … Himes provided the necessary organization and structure to transform Millerism from a one-man show into a genuine social movement; he transformed a doctrine into a cause.[51]

Himes became the day-to-day administrator and the fundraiser/treasurer of the movement. This became more and more important as time passed, not just because it allowed him to greatly expand the movement, but because, in the last few years leading up to the predicted time of Christ's return, Miller's various medical problems seemed to multiply and intensify, keeping him home for extended periods of time. Their closeness continued until the end in a double sense. They were together on the movement's most important day—October 22, 1844—the day on which the world was supposed to end, and on December 20, 1849, the day that Miller's life came to a gentle, peaceful end.[52]

Scholars generally agree that Himes transformed the Millerite movement—extending it to America's largest cities; using cutting-edge public relations and communications techniques to extend the reach of Millerism to the national, and even international, level; organizing the movement, including its finances; developing a core of Adventist evangelists, ultimately hundreds of them, to help spread Miller's message; and putting William Miller onto the national stage. David T. Arthur, a scholar of Adventism, biographer of Himes, and longtime history professor at Aurora College, went so far as to argue that "Himes was one of the truly great publicists in American history. The widespread attention which Millerism received was more the result of his efforts than of the efforts of any other individual, including Miller himself."[53] And, he argued, Himes was aggressive in expanding and transforming the movement, helping to send it on

> a more distinct and independent course. Himes did not wait for doors to open—he opened them. And where they remained closed, he circumvented them by cutting new ones. … Under Himes's leadership Millerism became aggressive. Miller was no longer simply a pleasant and moderately effective revivalist, saving sinners and building up churches. He and his movement became independent forces, capable of disrupting and dividing the churches. With Himes leading the way, Millerism became increasingly self-conscious—a major religious movement with which the churches would have to reckon.[54]

Himes took much greater initiative than Miller ever had, and he made things happen. In short, Himes was more than simply Miller's helper; he was a critically important participant.[55]

Himes was not only Miller's closest confidant. As the movement's main promoter, he was a public relations genius. At the heart of his strategy to spread Millerism's message to the world was publications. In fact, this became the lifeblood of the movement. Shortly after meeting Himes, Miller confided that he had always wanted a publication in which he could state his views. Newspapers often printed the criticisms made about Miller but would not print Miller's responses to them. It seemed that no sooner was Miller's request made than it was done. In early 1840, just two to three months after meeting Miller, Hines, although he had no subscribers, started the first Millerite newspaper, Boston's *Signs of the Times* (renamed the *Advent Herald* in early 1844). This was the first of many publications. The pattern became that, wherever there was a sizable Millerite revival, a paper would be set up for at least the duration of the meetings and often for weeks or months beyond it. These temporary papers helped to publicize the revival and spread the advent message to the many who could not attend the services in the local community.[56]

Some of the newspapers set up for a revival or lecture series, like New York City's the *Midnight Cry*, did not disappear at the end of the meetings. Instead, they became permanent fixtures of the Millerite movement. These newspapers spiritually nourished the new converts, helping them to stay connected, not only to their new spirituality, but also to the Millerite movement—in effect helping them to develop an Adventist identity and community as they wrote letters to the papers, asking questions, commenting on other people's views, etc. The connection that Millerites found through reading and interacting with these early papers was important because they were often isolated from others of like belief. In addition, they gave Millerites a forum in which they could respond to their growing number of critics. Initially, *Signs* went beyond that and published articles on Millerite ideas—both pro *and* con—although eventually it turned to simply refuting charges made against Millerism. The newspapers also served as a forum in which Millerites could air their own disagreements, such as Henry Dana Ward's long letter to the editors in an 1841 issue of *Signs,* explaining why he could not accept Miller's setting of a general time (1843) for Christ's return. As in the South, many people were converted through reading Millerite publications rather than through preaching. Publications, especially Adventist newspapers, would continue to play a critical role in the development of Adventism after the Great Disappointment of 1844, including the emergence of the Advent Christian denomination.[57]

In reference to Himes's innovative strategy of emphasizing publications, Hewitt wrote that "in many respects the most remarkable feature of the entire Millerite movement was its publications ministry."[58] This ministry included many more types of publications than just newspapers, as important as they were. The Millerites published *millions* of pieces of Second Advent writings—single-sheet broadsides, leaflets and tracts, pamphlets, books (including an Adventist hymn book, *Millennial Harp*), and over forty different newspapers. The volume of this literature, which was produced just between 1840 and 1844, is staggering, especially for the time. Himes reported that by May 1844 (just a few months before the anticipated return of Christ), approximately five million pieces of Millerite literature had been produced. And that number kept growing, even after the Great Disappointment. Millerite Isaac Wellcome claimed that by 1854, ten years after the Great Disappointment, Himes had distributed more than ten million pieces, just from his office in Boston. Although scholars of Millerism generally emphasize Himes's genius as a public relations innovator, Knight argues that his innovation lay not so much in devising *new* forms of communication (arguing that he used the standard methods of the era's reform movements, which included the publication of a newspaper for a cause) but in the *intensity* with which he produced his publications. Not only did the Millerite press produce unprecedented amounts of literature in such a short time, the vast majority of this massive output consisted of *original* Millerite writings rather than simply relevant reprints of non-Millerites' works. And some material was even translated into French and German. It is no wonder that one of Himes's critics referred to him as "the Napoleon of the press."[59]

Even more innovative, for its day, than this wide array of publications was the distribution process. Many Millerite materials were sent out to cold prospects—people who had not requested such materials and perhaps had not even heard of Millerism. Literature on the Advent was mailed to clergy and well-known persons across the United States; given to postmasters across the country, who were asked to give the materials away to their customers; handed out at train stations to passengers; and sent to British and American missionaries at their foreign posts. Millerites even put large amounts of their literature in ships leaving from the ports of Boston and New York City, a practice that got writings on Millerism to the other side of the globe. According to one prominent Millerite, Josiah Litch, materials made their way "to China; to Burmah [today known as Myanmar, in Southeast Asia]; to Hindoostan [historical name for India, especially its northern region]; to the East Indies; to Persia, Egypt, Palestine, Syria, Asia Minor, Greece, Constantinople; into Africa, the W. India islands, the Islands of the Pacific."[60] There is also evidence that Millerite materials reached Norway (and other parts of Europe), as well as places farther afield—like Chile, Australia, Hawaii, and the Sandwich Islands. Equally imaginative, not to mention daunting, was the goal of putting what was called a "Second Advent Library" in every town in the United States. These were free, lending libraries.

In Millerite leaders' desperation to get the Adventist message out to as many people as possible before Christ's return, they endorsed the ambitious idea of setting up Adventist reading rooms, where people could go to read Adventist periodicals and borrow other kinds of Millerite literature. Although national coverage was virtually impossible, given the time frame and limited finances that they were working with, the project was begun in 1841 and accomplished much by 1844, although mainly in the northern states.[61]

Another highly effective tactic that Millerites used in the last few years before 1844 was the campmeeting—large numbers of people coming together to camp in the open air of a wooded retreat and attend revival services for about a week. Although Millerite leaders wondered if there were enough potential participants to sustain a single campmeeting when they started in 1842, they successfully organized not just one, but about 30, and in only four months. This number grew to 40 in 1843 and to 54 in 1844 (for a total of 124 campmeetings in those three years). And the number of people at these gatherings was impressive. Attendance for a given campmeeting was estimated on a Sunday (the day with the highest attendance), and campmeeting reports give attendance figures ranging from four thousand to ten to fifteen thousand. In total, Dick estimates that approximately five hundred thousand people attended the 124 campmeetings that were held during the 1842–44 period. The Millerites adopted the Methodist, or frontier, form of campmeeting—a rustic, wooded setting (yet one that was near transportation), in which there was a crude pulpit and benches surrounded by a circle of large tents for sleeping and eating. Generally, there were three services a day, with social get-togethers, prayer meetings, and baptisms in between services. In short, it was a highly informal yet intense few days, the goal being twofold—bringing people to Christ in a conversion experience and bringing already-converted Christians to a belief in the nearness of the Second Advent.[62]

Millerites imitated the form of the Methodist campmeeting, but they clearly put their own stamp on it. The preaching at Adventist campmeetings was less emotional (as discussed earlier about Millerite preaching in general). Their campmeetings also were more orderly in general than those held by the Methodists. The preaching aroused less passion and little fanaticism, while the campmeetings were run with a strict set of rules and often with what would be called today a security person. They also introduced two unique features—the "great tent" (as it was called) and the Millerite charts. The great tent, first pitched in the summer of 1842, was used at campmeetings and for lecture series. Regardless of where or how it was used, it attracted a large, curious crowd because of its unprecedented size, thus drawing people in to hear the Millerites' message. And no wonder. At 120 feet in diameter and over 50 feet in height at its center, it reportedly was able to seat from three or four thousand people and up to six thousand when two later additions were attached to it. It provided the kind of shelter, with the help of stoves, that allowed meetings to be held well into the fall and during inclement, summer weather. It served as a meeting place in large cities where a large hall was needed but where the churches and public halls were closed to Millerites or people kept changing their minds about renting to them. Since it sheltered thousands, it provided a large space in towns where few public buildings or churches could offer ample room. It also saved money by avoiding the substantial rental fees charged for large buildings. However, these savings were somewhat counterbalanced by the cost of transporting such a large tent and the four-man crew needed to transport it, set it up, take it down, and maintain it. And there were other issues. As presumably the largest tent in the country, it had been costly to make ($800) and was difficult to move and repair. It was also vulnerable in high winds. In Rochester, New York, in the summer of 1843, a severe rain- and windstorm brought it down during a service. Fortunately, everyone got out safely, but the tent was damaged. During the repair process, it was reduced in size because it was so unwieldy. Its diameter was reduced to 100 feet and its *seating* capacity to fifteen hundred people, with a *total* capacity of thirty-five hundred. It remained, however, a huge tent and a big attraction, and it was a reflection of the huge crowds that came to listen to Millerite preachers in the last year or two before Christ's predicted return.[63]

Millerite campmeetings and lectures drew many different kinds of people—born-again Christians as well as non-evangelical ones, non-Christians, skeptics, hecklers, the merely curious, and journalists, who had been sent by their newspapers to report on this growing movement. They also drew some people who were well known. Among them was John Greenleaf Whittier, who attended the first Millerite campmeeting, held in East Kingston, New Hampshire, in 1842. Fortunately, and not surprisingly,

Whittier wrote about what he witnessed at that evening service. It gives us a detailed, firsthand account of a campmeeting service, viewed through the eyes of an outsider—one who was just curious, not hostile. Whittier never became a Millerite, but it seems that neither was it his purpose, in attending this service, simply to write an attack on Miller's followers. What he wrote is highly descriptive and neutral sounding—almost like he was an explorer describing an Indian tribe that he had run across:

> Three or four years ago, on my way eastward, I spent an hour or two at a campground of the second advent in East Kingston [New Hampshire, site of the first Millerite campmeeting, in 1842]. ... A tall growth of pine and hemlock threw its melancholy shadow over the multitude, who were arranged upon rough seats of boards and logs. Several hundred—perhaps a thousand people—were present, and more were rapidly coming. Drawn about in a circle, forming a background of snowy whiteness to the dark masses of men and foliage, were the white tents, and back of them the provision stalls and cook shops. When I reached the ground, a hymn ... was pealing through the dim aisles of the forest. I could readily perceive that it had its effect upon the multitude before me, kindling to higher intensity their already excited enthusiasm. The preachers were placed in a rude pulpit of rough boards, carpeted only by the dead forest leaves and flowers, and tasselled, not with silk and velvet, but with the green boughs of the somber hemlocks around it. One of them followed the music in an earnest exhortation on the duty of preparing for the great event. Occasionally he was really eloquent, and his description of the last day had the ghastly distinctness of Anelli's painting of the End of the World. Suspended from the front of the rude pulpit were two broad sheets of canvas, upon one of which was the figure of a man, the head of gold, the breast and arms of silver, the belly of brass, the legs of iron, and feet of clay,—the dream of Nebuchadnezzar. On the other were depicted the wonders of the Apocalyptic vision—the beasts, the dragons, the scarlet woman seen by the seer of Patmos, Oriental types, figures, and mystic symbols ... exhibited like the beasts of a traveling menagerie. ... To an

imaginative mind the scene was full of novel interest. The white circle
of tents; the dim wood arches; the upturned, earnest faces; the loud
voices of the speakers, burdened with the awful symbolic language
of the Bible; the smoke from the fires, rising like incense,—carried
me back to those days of primitive worship which tradition faintly
whispers of, when on hilltops and in the shade of old woods religion
had her first alters [sic], with every man for her priest and the whole
universe for her temple.[64]

The prophetic Millerite charts were equally novel and were so
effective that they continued to be made and used by Advent Christians
into the twentieth century, nearly one hundred years after the demise
of the Millerite movement. The most famous and popular chart of the
time, the "1843 Chart," created and then lithographed in 1842, measured
approximately three by five feet, but others were larger because they were
made to be used as visual tools in large halls, the great tent, and even in
the open air, where they were often hung on trees or poles. Miller and his
lieutenants used the 1843 chart to illustrate the complicated chronologies,
biblical symbolism drawn from Daniel and Revelation, and fulfilled
prophesies that had led to Miller's conclusions about the Second Advent.
And in several columns of numbers, it shows how different sets of numbers,
drawn from prophecies, all add up to the year 1843 for Christ's return to
earth. Millerite charts were largely pictorial, usually showing a large, metallic
man whose various parts represented different great civilizations of the
past. But what really drew people's attention was the colorful portrayal of
animals from the books of Daniel and Revelation, some of them grotesque
and monster-like (such as a multiheaded dragon). Many a child must have
been awestruck by these images. Although the practice of illustrating biblical
prophecies was not original to the Millerites, books on prophecy having been
illustrated for centuries, Millerite preachers innovated by enlarging their
scale so that illustrations could be seen by the whole audience in a large
space. The charts were not just used by preachers in services and lectures.
Even when traveling, a Millerite preacher often hung up a chart while on
a boat or in a public space. The arresting, often frightening images on a
chart would invariably draw a crowd, thus affording a preacher yet another

opportunity to spread the message of Christ's imminent return while in the process of explaining the chart. Millerites believed that time was short and that no opportunities to spread their message should be allowed to slip away. These charts were so intriguing and so frequently used that they became a hallmark of the Millerites. (People find them equally alluring today. Some of the thirty-seven charts that reside in Aurora University's Jenks Memorial Collection of Adventual Materials have traveled to various places in the country to be exhibited. Today, they not only fascinate biblical scholars and historians of religion, but historians of folk art as well.)[65]

Growing Separatism among the Millerites as the "End" Nears

As Miller's partner, Himes took over the management of the movement, increasing not only Miller's reach, and thus his influence, but his own as well. And as Miller's frail body became more and more prone to ailments of various sorts, Himes's guidance of the movement became increasingly important, a development which was reflected in the tendency of critics to lash out at Himes as much as, if not more than, Miller. However, as the movement grew in numbers and approached its predicted "end time," Himes and Miller began to lose some control over the direction of the movement, a process that then was accelerated by the 1843–44 disappointment over Christ not returning to earth in the time frame predicted. Thus, the third and last phase of the Millerite movement, it could be argued, was the 1843–49 period—an era characterized by a decentralization of leadership, a growing variety of theological ideas, greater sectarianism, and increasingly harsh criticism coming from outside the movement. This era ended with Miller's death, which seems to denote the more or less official end of the Millerite movement per se. What little power Miller retained to rally the troops after the Great Disappointment, keep their eyes on the immediacy of the Second Advent, and tamp down any rising sectarianism dissolved with his passing. Although his words remained, they were no match for his presence or for the new leaders who were coming forward to claim his mantle, each major, new leader taking the movement in a different direction toward the founding of a different denomination.

As the end time drew near (1843–44) and the urgency of Millerites' efforts to spread their message grew, tensions increased and deference toward the leadership of Miller and Himes started to break down. One way in which this manifested itself was through the growth of separatism, in defiance of Miller's wishes. In the early years of the Millerite movement, some of the more informal, evangelical churches warmly received Miller and his lieutenants as guest preachers. After all, they produced converts and added to church memberships. However, as the predicted time of Christ's return drew near, Millerism grew in popularity, and its tactics grew ever more aggressive. Many churches became less and less welcoming, ultimately banning the preaching of Adventism altogether. Many churches stopped the practice of allowing Millerites to use their facilities for Adventist lectures, and many Adventists (including ministers who believed in Millerism) were expelled, their membership revoked, or they voluntarily left. Sometimes, if a minister became an Adventist, he left, taking many of his congregants with him, or he stayed and the non-Millerites left. In any case, churches were often divided over Millerism, and sometimes the divisions ran so deep that they split congregations into two different churches.[66]

By late 1843/early 1844, there was a shift in attitude on the part of many Adventists. A milestone in this process was Charles Fitch's sermon, given in July of 1843. Drawn from Revelation and entitled "Come Out of Her, My People," it provided Adventists who yearned to leave their churches with a theological justification for doing so. It draws from the passages in Revelation that urge God's people to flee the corruption of Babylon before it falls. Up until this time, the Adventists had taught that the Antichrist (or Babylon) was the Roman Catholic Church. But Fitch argued that the various Protestant denominations, including Miller's own Baptist church, had become corrupted and fallen away from "pure" Christianity, in that they rejected the notion of the imminent Second Advent, and thus were now also part of "Babylon." By 1844, more and more Adventist preachers were urging other Adventists to "come out of Babylon," and thousands did so. These actions were all taken against the wishes of Miller and Himes and most other established Millerite leaders. For example, the editors of the *Signs of the Times* urged Adventists to remain within their various churches and denominations because that made it all the easier to spread the Adventist message to their fellow church members. However, by 1844, the tide clearly had turned against such restraint. Even Himes changed his position that September, arguing that Adventists should not remain in churches where they were being oppressed and vilified. Miller, however, continued to believe that this was a mistake—both the belief that the Protestant churches were part of Babylon and the idea of embracing sectarianism by leaving one's church. But even he, once in a while, when angry, slipped into that position temporarily.[67]

Thus, as David Arthur states, "Millerism had become separatist in spite of itself."[68] This growing separatism should not have come as a great surprise to Miller or anyone else. By 1844, there were numerous indications that Adventists were developing a separatist mentality. Millerites had their own separate newspapers, hymnbooks, and libraries. They also had established Second Advent Associations in towns all over the North. This was an organization that collected dues, elected officers, and met Sunday afternoons for Bible study, drawing Millerites from their various churches into a separate, church-like setting after they had worshipped in their own churches in the morning. Perhaps most importantly, they organized regional meetings, called General Conferences, which drew Millerite leaders and preachers together to create a communications network, discuss larger issues, develop strategies, make recommendations, and support one another. It could hardly be called a church government, but it did provide the beginning of some national/regional leadership and coordination. Finally, by 1842, some Adventist preachers were being ordained, an action usually done by an organized religious body. All of this, combined with a growing hostility toward Adventists, from both within and outside their churches, ultimately produced separatism. However, this did not mean that Adventists were in a rush to organize a formal denomination with a full array of institutions. They still believed that Christ would return soon, so they retained a bias against formalizing this separatism.[69]

Against this backdrop of expanding hostility from Protestant churches and the larger society, the growing popularity of Millerism, and the increasing separatism of Millerites, the year 1843 arrived—the year that Miller thought would probably bring the end of the world. As 1843 unfolded, everything seemed to accelerate—the pace of Adventist preaching, the number of conversions to Millerism, the attention given the movement by the national press, the joy of Millerites, the anxiety of at least some nonbelievers, and the amount and nastiness of the criticism toward the movement. For Millerites, life as they knew it felt very tentative. When setting a date for a campmeeting (or anything else), they usually added "if time continue." And the Adventist newspaper, *Signs of the Times*, established a policy of extending subscriptions for no more than three months at a time. Throughout 1843–44, various groups of Millerites leaned toward certain specific dates due to their religious significance, but as each one of these passed with no sign of Christ's return, nonbelievers' ridicule and criticism of the movement grew.[70]

The end of the predicted year for Christ's return brought great disappointment, of course, but, surprisingly, it also brought renewed conviction for many Millerites that Christ would still come, and soon. At this point, the fact that Miller had *not* set a specific date and had even qualified the year he predicted worked to the movement's advantage. As Knight argues, "That soft edge on the time issue would serve as a buffer to disappointment as the Millerites approached and finally passed March 21, 1844."[71] Miller led the way in this approach. On May 2, 1844, just weeks after the *end* of the year that he had predicted would see the Second Advent, Miller wrote: "I *confess my error*, and acknowledge *my disappointment*; yet I still believe that the day of the Lord is near, even at the door; and I exhort you, my brethren, to be watchful, and not let that day come upon you unawares."[72] A number of explanations were given for why Christ had not returned when predicted; many of them were biblical. But whether one used the Old Testament story of Noah and his family awaiting the flood for a number of sunny days, while cooped up in the ark, or the New Testament parable about a bridegroom tarrying while some of the waiting virgins slumbered, the theme was that this perhaps was a testing time or "tarrying time"—a term they took from the Bible. God, it was argued, was testing the faith of the believers, but would come soon so they must stay the course and not ease up. So the traveling, preaching, publishing, and praying continued throughout the summer. After all, in Luke 19:13, Christ told his followers to "occupy till I come."Millerite leaders used this commandment many times to keep Millerites at their duties and away from fanaticism as the end time approached. However, the response that the Millerites now received was not the same; there was a distinct lack of enthusiasm. People still responded to the Millerite message, but not like they had earlier. People were more wary and less certain, and this may have even been true of at least some Millerite preachers as well.[73]

The Big Day Draws Near and Then Disappointment

It was in late summer, in the East, while Miller and Himes were on the road preaching in the West, that the movement took a sharp turn in a new direction, with a new group of leaders emerging. At an August campmeeting, Samuel S. Snow, a man who up to this point had played just a minor role in the movement, presented a new and quite specific date, based on a different set of assumptions and calculations. He said that Christ would return on October 22, 1844. This created the seventh-month movement, the seventh month referring to the Jewish calendar. It ignited a whole new level of enthusiasm within the Millerite movement—enthusiasm that rose to considerably greater heights than that preceding Miller's predicted time. It also brought attention to a different set of leaders—Snow and George Storrs, a Millerite preacher who played a large role in publicizing the ideas behind the seventh-month movement. Virtually all of the established Millerite leadership rejected this idea, although some, like both Miller and Himes, reluctantly embraced it at the eleventh hour, given the huge wave of joyful acceptance that it had generated.[74]

There was little time between Snow's early August announcement of a new advent day and the actual day itself—October 22, 1844. Given the nearness of the day and the great enthusiasm with which it was embraced, it would not be unreasonable to expect that many Millerites, after so much waiting and disappointment, might this time drift toward fanaticism in their preparations for the great day. Although some did, scholars have found that, for the most part, Millerites generally obeyed the admonitions of their leaders to prepare themselves spiritually while calmly remaining at their daily work, the leadership often citing Christ's words to "occupy till I come." However, in the fall of 1844, as the day of Christ's predicted return drew near, not everyone "occupied." Some of the newer leaders of the movement did not take the same firm position on "occupying" that Miller did. And there was an uptick in believers who were taking extreme measures as part of their preparations for the last day. Newspapers carried stories of farmers who chose not to harvest their crops, merchants who closed and liquidated their stores, people who held responsible positions resigning from their jobs (like magistrates, custom's officers, county clerks, justices of the peace, teachers), thieves who made restitution for thefts they had committed, debtors who paid back what they owed to others, and people who gave away their money, sometimes to the publishers of Millerite newspapers in support of their work. For example, a tailor in Philadelphia closed his shop in early October and put a sign on the building that read:

> This shop is closed in honor
> of the King of Kings,
> Who will appear about the
> 22d of October.
> Get Ready, friends, to crown
> him Lord of all.[75]

Some stores put their goods on sale or simply gave them away. On a store in Brooklyn hung a sign that read: "This store is closed on account of the near approach of the final dissolution of all things. The articles in this store will be given to those who may call for them on Monday."[76] Once in a while, local government stepped in to help preserve people's property—like probate courts who appointed legal guardians to oversee individuals' financial matters and selectmen who took over people's affairs (including harvesting the crops of farmers who had abandoned them). Nevertheless, most of the believers who took this kind of action were essentially impoverishing themselves and had no backup plan.[77]

As the wait came down to the last few days, a dilemma presented itself. If Millerites gave no outward sign, such as quitting their jobs, that the day of the Lord's return was near, they might be viewed as hypocrites and would not be witnessing for what they believed. On the other hand, if everyone stopped their work and sold their possessions, this might give credence to the world's charges of fanaticism and, indeed, might lead Millerites down that path. Yet if one truly believed that the Lord was about to return, it was natural that people would want time to make themselves right with their God, as well as with their fellow human beings. To deal with this difficult situation, some leaders recommended taking a moderate course between the two extremes of "occupying" to the very end and leaving all work and responsibilities days or weeks before the Second Advent. In the last issue of *The Midnight Cry* before October 22, 1844 (the October 19 one), the editors did this by writing: "Break loose from the world as much as possible. If indispensable duty calls you into the world for a moment, go as a man would run to do a piece of work in the rain. Run and hasten through it, and let it be known that you leave it with alacrity for something better."[78] Another article, in the same issue, gave an example of a middle road that at least one Millerite had taken in the last days: "We cannot all wholly abstain from labor, but we can imitate the example of a brother in this city, who is a wood-sawyer. He said he found that by living temperately, he could sustain his body by laboring half a day, and then he could seek for food for his soul, the other half."[79] Obviously not all Millerites were able to simply work half time without losing their job, but as the time dwindled down to a day or two, that became an option for more and more people. And by then, leaving one's work or selling one's possessions to prepare for the great day looked increasingly practical rather than fanatical.[80]

As the days dwindled to a handful, there was both frenzied activity and a prayerful calm. Adventist presses continued to print, preachers continued to preach, and people continued to come to God. All activities of the movement continued, but at a greatly accelerated pace. Meetings, when not closed because of threats of violence, were held constantly; Millerite presses worked almost continuously; and there was a rush to get baptized before the great day. On October 19, the Philadelphia *Public Ledger* reported that about two hundred people had been baptized in New York City's East River the week before, and there were similar reports elsewhere. All of this, of course, was a result of Millerite leaders' determination to win as many souls as possible before the great day. For individuals, however, preparation was a personal matter—one that was generally done quietly. The records of Millerites and scholars alike generally agree that as October 22 drew near, most Millerites remained calm as they made preparations for leaving this world. Most of them rejected hysteria and fanaticism, although some cases of this kind of behavior have been documented. Sylvester Bliss, a Millerite leader, remembered, in his *Memoirs of William Miller*, that "during the last ten days, secular business was, for the most part, suspended; and those who looked for the Advent gave themselves to the work of preparation for that event, as they would for death, were they on a bed of sickness, expecting soon to close their eyes on earthly scenes forever."[81] And these preparations were generally followed by a calm and prayerful waiting as October 22 dawned.[82]

People quietly gathered in Millerite tabernacles, public halls, and private homes to await their Lord. On that day and those leading up to it, the only hysteria came from nonbelievers who threatened violence to the point that the police closed some public gathering places. Although there were a number of general newspaper reports about Millerites gatherings on October 21-23, Nichol states that only one article written by a reporter who actually *attended* a meeting has been found, this from a Cincinnati newspaper. The reporter observed the following about this October 22 meeting:

> As the consummation of all terrestrial things was expected to have taken place last evening, and being desirous of seeing the effect of such belief upon its votaries at their last earthly meeting, I took the liberty ... of being present. The assemblage, indoors and out, probably numbered 1,500 persons. If rightly informed about the capacity of the house, about 1,200 were inside. ... There was less excitement than I expected, and a great deal more cheerfulness manifested in the countenances of the believers than could have been supposed at the hour of so serious a crisis. ... Considering the crowd, the meeting was very orderly. Two or three attempts were made by a set of rowdies outdoors to raise a breeze by noise and clamor, but the assertion of the preacher, that a strong police was present, calmed the multitude, and he was enabled to proceed with what he at the close said was, in his opinion, his last warning to a sinful world. ... Before nine o'clock the benediction was pronounced, and the people advised to go quietly home and await the awful coming, which not unlikely might transpire at the hour of midnight, while most of us were wrapped in sleep. Notwithstanding all this, daylight, yea, a most splendid day of sunshine, is again upon us.[83]

Thus, not surprisingly, the Millerites gathered together calmly, worshipfully, and joyfully, for they believed that their dearest dream was about to come true. When Christ did not come, the Millerites were stunned, confused, and incredibly sorrowful. One Millerite, Hiram Edson, described the emotions: "Our fondest hopes and expectations were blasted, and such a spirit of weeping came over us as I never experienced before. It seemed that the loss of all earthly friends could have been no comparison. We wept, and wept, till the day dawn."[84] Today, when the Millerites' expectation of Christ's return on this day looks so misguided, it is difficult for us to fully appreciate just how bitterly disappointed they were when October 22 quietly slipped into October 23, with no sign of Christ's return.[85]

With many Millerites absolutely convinced that Christ would return on one specific day, there was no "soft edge" to break their fall when once again Christ did not appear. Not only did they have to deal with this incomprehensible disappointment, they also had to cope with the profound humiliation that they felt, especially since this second and much greater disappointment generated a huge outpouring of ridicule and abuse, both physical and verbal, by nonbelievers. Millerites were accused of being fanatics or just plain crazy. All kinds of charges were made against the movement in general and the Millerite leadership, especially Himes, who was frequently suspected of financially profiting off of the Millerite movement—a charge that Himes denied and historians have found no evidence for. The movement and its leaders had been criticized for years, but this criticism paled in comparison to the tsunami of charges that came after the "Great Disappointment" of October 22, 1844.[86]

Aftermath of the Great Disappointment:
Attacks, Charges of Wrongdoing, Humiliation, and Ridicule

The narrative of the Millerite movement raises some questions that many people, both then and much later, have asked about the Millerites. Was the charge true, made by some contemporaries, that Miller and Himes were con men out to enrich only themselves at the expense of the emotionally vulnerable? How were Millerites treated in the days leading up to and shortly after the Great Disappointment?

Miller, of course, had many skeptics and critics. Many nonbelievers who heard him speak came away convinced that he was sincere, although misguided, in his beliefs. Others made all kinds of personal attacks, especially that he had monetary rather than religious motives, accusing him of making a lot of money from the publication of his books and other things related to the movement. Attacks came from individuals and newspaper journalists, many of whom wrote sensationalist headlines. Historians have found no credible evidence that Miller was anything but convinced that Christ would return soon and was genuinely burdened with a sense of responsibility to warn the world and facilitate the salvation of as many people as possible. After the first disappointment, Miller wrote to Himes: "I hope I have cleansed my garments from the blood of souls. I feel that, as far as it was in my power, I have freed myself from all guilt in their condemnation. ..."[87] Clearly, he had been driven by a deep sense of responsibility for unsaved souls. In terms of taking people's money, Miller was never paid for his ministry. And not only did he *not* receive an income from his preaching, in the early years he paid his own traveling expenses. After 1836, he did get some financial help for his travels from friends, but Miller stated that the costs of his travels always surpassed the amount of money that he received. Miller estimated that he was forced to use about two thousand dollars of his own money to support his preaching tours. This was no small amount in the 1830s–40s, especially for a farmer.[88]

Concerning Himes, historians have also found no ulterior motives or financial corruption. He was often accused by outsiders of financial shenanigans because he was the one who ran the huge publications business and managed the movement's funds. The criticism ranged from simply mismanaging Millerite funds to the outright bilking of Millerites' wealth. By this, the critics meant not just the money that Miller's followers gave to support the cause but also the proceeds from selling their own real estate and many of their earthly possessions. Miller and Himes did *not* support the idea of selling all of one's assets. In fact, Miller could not win on this issue because, while he was criticized by outsiders for actions that he did *not* even approve of—the selling off of one's property—he also was criticized by some Millerites for *not* selling his own farm as the end time approached. They argued that it showed a lack of faith in his own predictions. And not only did Himes disapprove of selling off one's worldly goods, but, within days of the October disappointment, he was leading the charge to organize relief committees around the United States to help those who had sold their possessions and were now destitute. At one point, shortly after the October disappointment, Himes became so frustrated with the endless attacks that he finally asked the Boston *Post*, a newspaper that had published many of these charges, if he might respond to them in the newspaper. The *Post* agreed and published Himes's defense on the first page. In this article, Himes responded to the criticisms one by one and then invited an actual investigation of his activities and even of the movement's financial records. He also stated: "If I have wronged or defrauded any man, I will restore him four-fold; and if any have been thus defrauded, by anything which I have solicited from them, or if I have ever advised them, in public or in private, to any course by which they have become impoverished, they are requested to make their case known to the public."[89] Neither the *Post* nor any other paper made an attempt to refute what Himes had written, and that seemed to tamp down the criticism about him.[90]

Beyond the charges made against the leadership, Millerite followers experienced many kinds of attacks—discrimination, verbal abuse, slander, ridicule, and sometimes even violence—and this grew as the end time grew near and after each disappointment. As the end time approached, anxiety grew, and increasingly Millerites were turned out of their own churches and denied public meeting places, either by churches for religious reasons or by others for fear that Millerite meetings would incite public unrest. Millerites were labeled illiterate, ignorant, and evil, among other things, and were viewed by many as either imposters or lunatics. They also were ridiculed in many ways. They were said to walk around wearing white flowing ascension robes—a charge completely denied by contemporary Millerites and one that scholars have found virtually no evidence for. Newspapers sometimes ran cartoons or caricatures of prominent Millerites or their ideas. One particularly well-known one is of the Boston Tabernacle ascending into the heavens, with Miller sitting on top of it, some Millerites clinging to it for dear life while dangling in midair, some losing their grip and falling to earth, and

Himes left behind with Satan, amid the wealth he supposedly had bilked people out of. Many Millerites were teased, by family, friends, and neighbors, that they were still on earth and why hadn't they ascended yet. This kind of ridicule became especially common after the October disappointment. After describing this kind of taunting in his town after October 22, a devastated Joseph Bates, a Millerite leader, said, "If the earth could have opened and swallowed me up, it would have been sweetness compared to the distress I felt."[91] Ridicule is often as devastating as physical abuse, and Millerites suffered much of it after the Great Disappointment.[92]

And there were many reports of violence, both in the days leading up to October 22 and after. A number of Millerite meetings were interrupted by the attacks of a mob, driving them out of their place of worship, especially after the October disappointment. In Danville, New York, a mob tore down a Millerite tabernacle, and in Ithaca, New York, a Millerite building was set on fire. And they were not necessarily protected if they gathered in private homes, a number of which were attacked—like the one in which a mob wielding guns, stones, and clubs invaded a home where Millerites were gathered. Some of the worshippers received injuries, including some head wounds, and most of the windows in the house's public rooms were smashed. It turned out that the leader of this mob was a former Millerite, who clearly had not coped well after Christ did not return when predicted. As disturbing as physical attacks were, no doubt they,were far less common than the ridicule that Millerites experienced on a daily basis for a while. However, for those who experienced violence, it must have been a truly terrifying experience.[93]

Scholars generally have found the charges against Millerites, both before and after the two disappointments, to be largely unfounded, indefensible, and abusive. However, some, like Arthur, have pointed out that although the Millerites did not deserve the abuse that they endured, they were at least in part responsible for the great hostility toward them that ignited the abuse. As the end time drew near, Arthur argued, many Millerites grew increasingly aggressive and provocative in their tactics and arrogant in their assurance that they had found absolute truth. The movement became narrower, more sectarian, and less tolerant. In fact, by 1842–43, it was not just enough to believe that Christ was coming soon; one had to believe in the time frame specified by Miller and, later, Snow. Those in the movement who *never* believed in setting a specific time no longer felt welcome in the once theologically tolerant movement.[94]

To the end of his life, Miller believed in nonsectarianism and had no regrets about what he had done with the last decades of his life. In May of 1847, he wrote: "If I have any regret, it is because I have done so little, and because I have been so inefficient."[95] His faith that Christ would return soon remained unshaken to the end, as did his belief that God, in choosing him to warn the world of Christ's imminent return, had chosen an inadequate messenger. This crusade of his had cost him much money, when he had so little to begin with, and had put strains on his marriage and family life. Yet he believed that he had done what God wanted.[96]

The Great Disappointment severely injured the Millerite movement, but it continued on, although shaky and greatly diminished in numbers. However, the splintering of the movement, which had started by 1843–44, accelerated after the predicted Second Advent day, because the differing explanations for what had happened on October 22 led down distinctly different, theological roads. Himes tried to keep the movement intact, centered on the original beliefs. Although Miller seemed to want to retire from the movement, Himes pulled him back onto the public stage. By this time, Himes was guiding Miller more than ever. Although Miller was now little more than a figurehead, he was still "Father Miller," and Himes viewed his influence as essential to keep the core of the movement going. And so they both did some traveling and preaching (Miller, when he was physically up to it), but it was not the same. And Miller's physical condition continued to deteriorate. He spent his last year or so almost completely blind, while various other ailments were piling up. What little remained of the movement after October 1844 disappeared completely after Miller's death in December 1849.[97]

Millerism's Impact

In the eyes of the world, Millerism had failed, but its demise did not leave the world unchanged. It provided the Second Great Awakening with its last major wave of revivalism, although this wave was somewhat distinctive theologically. As such, it brought about the conversion of thousands of people. Even though not all of those who accepted Christ as their savior at Millerite revivals became believers in Millerism, this religious rebirth was transformative for them individually, as it, no doubt, was for those who also became Millerites.

It is difficult to estimate how many true Adventists there were before the Great Disappointment. Miller himself estimated 50,000 followers in about a thousand Adventist congregations. (He also estimated that he had preached around 4,500 sermons or lectures to approximately 500,000 different people—although not all of them were or would become Millerites, of course.) A much higher estimate comes from the *Proceedings of the American Antiquarian Society*, which suggests 150,000 to 200,000 Millerites. These figures represent those Millerites who left their home churches to establish Adventist ones so their numbers could be more easily estimated, although, even with them, the estimates vary widely. There is no way of knowing how many Millerites chose to remain in their churches, as Miller instructed. And historian Whitney Cross has added another number to this tally. He estimates that as many as a million, or more, people, though not Millerites per se, were "skeptically expectant." It is equally difficult to estimate the numbers of ministers and lay lecturers who preached the advent message. Estimates here vary greatly as well. Miller conservatively estimated that 200 ministers and 500 lecturers spread his message, while the *Proceedings of the American Antiquarian Society* suggests that about 800 ministers accepted Millerism. Historians have found the estimates for the number of Millerite preachers and lecturers to be even higher, believing that the estimate of Lorenzo Dow Fleming (a well-known Millerite minister and editor) is more likely—1,500 to 2,000 people who preached the advent message.[98]

Regardless of the figure that is accepted, the point is clear. This was not a handful of people receiving Miller's message from a few preachers. At the time, Millerism clearly left its mark on American society and would continue to do so in the form of the six Protestant denominations that grew out of it, one of which was the Advent Christian church. And it was Advent Christians in the Midwest who established Mendota College exactly fifty years after Miller's predicted time for Christ's return.

William Miller

Joshua V. Himes

Miller's Trunk—Inside Were Found Hundreds of Letters of His Correspondence

The Famous 1843 Chart Showing Why Miller Thought Christ Would Return to Earth around 1843

Home of William Miller, in Low Hampton, New York

Miller's Grave—Located in the Cemetery in Low Hampton, New York

A Campmeeting Service Where a Huge Adventist Prophetic Chart Was Used

Advent Christian Minister Standing in Front of a Huge Prophetic Chart Hung on the Side of a Building, ca. 1905

Advent Christian Minister Pointing Out One of the Many Details in an Adventist Chart

A Group of English Adventists Posing in Front of a Huge Prophetic Chart, 1898

Chapter 3
"Occupy till I Come": From Building a Denomination to Building a College

"If the Master comes with the walls of a building half reared; amen: 'we occupied till he came.' "

—Elder H. G. M'Culloch

SPRINGFIELD NATIONAL ADVENT CAMP MEETING
The meeting was held August 24–31, 1868, in Massachusetts. Note J. V. Himes sitting tall in the center of the first row.

National Adventist Campmeeting in Springfield, Massachusetts, 1868—
Held Just Eight Years after the Organization of the Advent Christian Denomination

(Note the tents placed in a circle, as was typical in early campmeetings, and the tall man with a white beard sitting in the middle of the first row—Joshua V. Himes.)

The impact of the Great Disappointment on Millerites was devastating, and, not surprisingly, many fell away from the movement. What *is* surprising is how many of them stayed in it, concluding that they had gotten the time wrong but still believing that Christ would return sometime soon. However, Millerite leaders had a new job to do—their number-one priority became keeping the movement together and viable, given the bitter disappointment, humiliation, and sense of abandonment that came out of the Great Disappointment. Preserving the movement proved to be much more difficult after the Great Disappointment, because the divergent opinions on what happened, or didn't happen, on October 22 added a layer of disagreement on top of those that had already been developing before the Great Disappointment. Not only did Millerite leaders not agree on what had happened on October 22, they also disagreed on what direction to take after that date.[1]

The Diminution and Splitting Apart of the Millerite Movement

Millerism had never been a separate denomination, and that was the way Miller had always wanted it. However, after October 22, although Miller's influence was still important in shoring up Himes's leadership, his involvement in the movement was waning as his body was fading, and in any case, he believed that he had completed his work. This situation, along with the shock of the Great Disappointment, brought to the forefront not only a number of very different interpretations of what had happened, but also new leaders to compete with Himes for the leadership of Adventism. At least before October 22, there had been widespread agreement about Christ's imminent return and even the time element. Now that was gone. And in the wake of this growing disunity, the pre-October 22 sectarianism concerning religious topics other than the Advent, which Miller had worked so hard to keep dormant, now burst onto the scene to increase the amount of disunity. In effect, Adventists were beginning to sort themselves into factions or parties—a process that would eventually lead to the creation of six different denominations. Thus, by early 1845, the Millerite movement had entered what some Adventists called "the scattering time."[2]

As difficult as it was to estimate the number of Adventists/Millerites *before* the Great Disappointment, trying to estimate their number *after* March 22 is even more difficult. Adventists were not likely to publicize their estimates of the people who fell away from Adventism following the Great Disappointment. After all, they were desperately struggling to keep the movement intact. At least some of the estimates of pre–October 1844 Adventists are an undercount because they were based largely on those Adventists who actually left their churches. Many Adventists—historian David Arthur estimated thousands—never left their original churches. Arthur argued that these were the people who were the most likely to have disappeared from the Adventist movement after the Great Disappointment. He likewise suggested that it was the separatist Adventists—those who came out of their churches to form their own Adventist meetings—who were the most likely to have remained within the movement. They had left their churches because of ridicule and hostility toward Millerite beliefs from their fellow church members and, for many Adventists, they had left after labeling their church "Babylon." It was not feasible for them to return to the fold. The humiliation and shame would have been too great, and the memories of how they had been treated too strong. Besides, these hard-core Adventists still believed that Christ would return soon—a belief they were not willing to give up as the price of their return. In any case, although some Adventists quietly remained in their churches, no longer speaking out about Adventism, some of those who had left returned to them, usually after agreeing to some conditions. And some left the movement, and sometimes organized religion, altogether. However, a substantial core of believers, though shaken and humiliated, remained. But they were not to remain a single group for long.[3]

In speaking of the months *before* October 22, 1844, Arthur stated: "Millerism had become separatist in spite of itself. ... Millerite sectarianism furthered Millerite separatism."[4] Citing the divisiveness of the Adventist doctrine, as well as the Adventists' certainty about the truth of their beliefs, their growing desire to be among those of like belief, and their tendency to label those who rejected their beliefs as the "Antichrist," Arthur saw it as a given that separatism would grow, even though Adventists still generally rejected the idea of forming their own denomination. And this was all *before* the Great Disappointment. This trend greatly accelerated after October 22,

1844, but it was no longer *just* a matter of Adventists separating themselves increasingly from non-Adventists. Although there may not be a scholarly consensus on the exact amount of sectarianism that existed before October 1844, scholars do concur that the Great Disappointment generated both additional criticism from outside the movement and greater controversy and fragmentation inside it. Thus, as George R. Knight wrote, "By 1845, that which had held Adventism together [the advent doctrine] was no longer as strong as those beliefs that separated its constituent parts."[5] In effect, the Great Disappointment, followed five years later by Miller's death, ended the Millerite movement and introduced the era of sectarianism, separatism, and denomination building.[6]

Sylvester Bliss, one of the Millerite leaders, identified three distinct groupings of Adventists emerging shortly after the Great Disappointment: First, those who completely rejected Adventism and left the movement (some of them, in their bitterness, rejecting *all* religion); second, those who acknowledged that they had been wrong in their dating of Christ's return but did not give up their Adventist beliefs and continued to preach that Christ's return was imminent; and third, those who believed that, since the seventh-month movement came from God, it could not be wrong, and that included the October 22 date. It was this last group that adopted the most extreme beliefs and practices.[7]

Just two of these groups would matter in the future. No more needs to be said about the first group because they ceased to be a factor in Adventism. The second group was composed of the moderates. It included most of the old leadership, including William Miller. Their point of view was reflected in a letter that William Miller sent to Himes in late 1844: "I have been waiting and looking for the blessed hope, and in expectation of realizing the glorious things which God has spoken to Zion. Yes, and although I have been twice disappointed, I am not yet cast down or discouraged. God has been with me in Spirit, and has comforted me."[8] They believed that they had simply gotten the *time* of Christ's return wrong, counseling hope and patience and encouraging each other to keep preaching to a world that would soon perish. However, although members of this group continued to believe in the nearness of the Advent, and even that the time of Christ's return could be found through careful study of the Scriptures, they differed on the issue of dates. After the Great Disappointment, much of the leadership, including William Miller, believed that there should be no more date setting, but others continued to set dates in the near future.[9]

The third group was defined by their belief that they had *not* been wrong about the date of October 22 and by their radicalism, but it had internal divisions as well. In fact, this group could probably be described as more diverse than the moderates, consisting of a number of distinct factions. Because they believed that they had not been wrong on the date, they had to come up with an explanation for how that belief could gel with the fact that no one saw Christ's personal, physical return to earth, and the explanations differed. One explanation was that Christ had come, but he had come *spiritually* rather than physically. Another related explanation was that Christ had indeed come, but not to receive the righteous *on earth*, an act that remained in the future. Instead he had come as a bridegroom on October 22 to receive his *heavenly* kingdom and had *invisibly* begun his work of preparing his kingdom for the righteous and readying himself for his *visible* return. The proponents of both these positions embraced the "shut door" theory, the idea that since something significant *had* happened on October 22 and that in some sense Christ as the bridegroom had come, the period in which people could be saved was now over. There were a number of explanations—more beyond the two just mentioned—on the spiritualization of Christ's return on October 22 and the "shut door" theory, but they were all in agreement that they had *not* been wrong in setting the October 22 date.[10]

These were beliefs that the moderates, led by Himes, rejected, since they believed that nothing had happened on October 22, and they continued to preach, believing that the door was *still open* to salvation and citing Christ's admonition to "occupy till I come." The more extreme groups were a problem for the moderates, who believed that the radicals were not true Adventists in that they had embraced beliefs and practices that were not part of Millerism before the Great Disappointment. The more radical groups, on the other hand, not only continued to view themselves as Adventists, but they came to believe that *only they* were the *real* Adventists. This group, as they spiritualized October 22, were leaving behind not only their high regard for and deference to Miller, but also the rationalism and biblical literalism that he had always preached. The result was bitter conflict between the moderates and radicals that sometimes sank to the level of personal attacks.[11]

The nature of Millerism, with its core belief that Christ's return to earth was imminent, contributed to conflict between the various factions as well. Millerism, through the death of Miller in 1849, was a religious movement that, for the most part, resisted sectarianism—at least in the sense of forming a separate denomination—so Millerites did not have the unifying factor of consciously and deliberately working to build and maintain a new church. This reluctance was evident even during the "scattering time," as various groups of Adventists went their separate, theological ways. And, of course, at least among the moderate Adventists, the belief that Christ's return was still imminent was a factor. Why build a new denomination when the Second Advent was so near? Clyde Hewitt made an additional observation, noting that this reluctance to create a new denomination was not just an unwillingness to switch one's church loyalty—like Miller's unwillingness to leave his Baptist church. It was also an unwillingness to create an institution that could take on the characteristics of the churches that Adventists had labeled "Babylon"—an attempt to avoid the unchristian-like behavior that was so evident in many formally established churches. I. C. Wellcome, a Millerite and publisher of Adventist materials, explained this antichurch bias among Adventists like this:

> They [Adventists] had seen exhibitions of arbitrary church power in opposing the truth, in abusing and expelling the faithful of the churches, and in exalting and sustaining wicked and unworthy members for sectarian purposes. This had become so fixed in the minds of some they had decided *without* a Scriptural examination, that the Bible furnished no rule for *such arbitrary* government, and finally, no government at all; thus one extreme produced another [italics in original].[12]

This hostility toward establishing churches, or even just organizing certain religious activities, created divisions even among the moderate Adventists. Some Millerite leaders (especially Himes) saw the necessity for greater organization and coordination of activities, were the movement to continue.

They kept denying that they were establishing a church, but others saw such behavior as just that—setting them on the road to church building, and even creating another "Babylon." This bias against denominationalism and institution building made separatism more likely as the bonds among people were much looser and divided the moderates to the point that little organization was able to take place in the late 1840s.[13]

Adventist scholars have identified a number of factors working against Adventist unity. One of these was the ecumenical composition of the Millerite movement. As discussed earlier, Millerism drew people from various Protestant denominations, especially from the Methodists and Baptists, but also from the Congregationalists, Christian Connexion members, Presbyterians, Episcopalians, Dutch Reformed, Lutherans, and Quakers, not to mention Deists and atheists. Before the Great Disappointment, these diverse groups were focused on a common goal—getting themselves and others ready for the imminent return of Christ—so they were able, more or less successfully, suppress, or at least tolerate, their differences in other religious areas. However, after the Great Disappointment, their different beliefs, religious practices, and notions of church government became much more divisive factors. And the time element—their embracing of October 22 as the *specific* day that Christ would return—which was one of the major factors that had united them earlier, became a major source of division and party formation once that day had passed, because differing explanations for what had happened, or not happened, on that date led to whole new and conflicting beliefs.[14]

There were also differences in educational attainment and geographical location. Millerism contained people from many different classes—from uneducated laborers, and even uneducated lecturers and preachers, to highly educated, professional people, including some educated clergymen. In spite of this social heterogeneity, class differences were muted because of their common goal—preparing themselves and others for the Second Advent. However, Arthur found that the post–Great Disappointment period's sorting out of Adventists found many of the better-educated Adventists and movement leaders in the moderate group, whose members still held to Millerism's original beliefs and included Miller and Himes. The fact that the radical factions included more of the less-educated, common people reinforced the existing theological differences between the moderates and radicals. Arthur noted that there were a few well-educated men in the leadership of the radical factions, but most of them eventually left these groups. In addition, he noted that these divisions were also magnified by geographic differences. This is illustrated by which people attended the 1845 Albany Conference—a Himes-initiated meeting whose goal was to consolidate the moderate forces and isolate the new, radical factions. To a large extent, those who attended this conference were from the East—the states along the coast as well as eastern New York and eastern Pennsylvania. No one from Ohio or any state beyond that, or from Maine, attended. In these more remote, sparsely populated, frontier areas, the newer, more radical ideas coming out of the Great Disappointment were more widely embraced. All of this created tension and resentment—especially of the rank-and-file Adventists against the more elitist members of the moderate group.[15]

As with most political and social movements, there were also personality clashes and personal attacks that created deep rifts within Millerism. These conflicts were made worse by the fact that Adventist papers often stood behind a particular person and his set of beliefs over against a rival paper, which supported another person and a different set of beliefs. And these conflicts were not just limited to those between the moderates and radicals. They also took place within the moderate and radical ranks. Probably the best example of this is the movement against Himes, consisting of people who earlier had supported him. Himes had always been the target of criticism, especially from nonbelievers but also from some fellow Millerites. Although many of these accusations were simply untrue, valid criticisms could be made of him. He accrued a lot of power within the movement and much influence over Miller and, like anyone else, had his personal failings. However, after the Great Disappointment, with Miller in retreat and failing in health, the job of saving the original Millerite movement fell to Himes. He fought the shut door theory and consolidated the moderate Adventists. But, increasingly, a younger set of leaders resented his leadership and the amount of power and influence that he had accrued. In short, they wanted a larger voice within Adventism. They started to move secretly against him, which, of course, Himes found out about. At an Adventist conference in Boston, he defended his actions in the movement and asked for an investigation of himself to clear the air and his name. Arthur summed up the outcome of this feud by saying: "During the course of this long, drawn out affair the original issues were lost sight of. Most of the noise was shouted and ink spilled over petty, unworthy matters, and in the heat generated by the participants light was rare and it was easy to lose one's way."[16] In the end, the investigative body found that all of the seven charges made against Himes were unfounded, but it did not end there. The attacks against Himes continued until, in 1852, he ended up in the Rhode Island Supreme Court—brought there by a slander suit against him. The case was so weak that after just a few days of testimony, the plaintiff's own lawyers recommended that their client drop the suit, which he did. However, although Himes was vindicated, this feud took its toll on the Adventist movement, adding to its divisions and aggravating longstanding tensions.[17]

The Albany Conference and the Making of Moderate Adventism

The development of many competing, increasingly radical ideas, all of them labeled Adventist, disturbed not only Miller but rank-and-file Adventists as well. Miller, who claimed at one point to have received sixteen different Adventist publications in a single week, sent them on to an elderly friend and early convert. Shortly after receiving all of these papers, the woman called Miller to her home for an interrogation:

"Have you read all these papers?"
"Why, I have looked them over."
"But are they all Advent papers?"
"They profess so to be."
"Well, then," [said she,] "I am no longer an Adventist; I shall take the
    old Bible, and stick to that."
"But," said he, "we have no confidence in one half there is advocated
    in those papers."
"But," said the old lady, "who is we?"
"Why," [replied Miller,] "we are those who do not fellowship those
    things."

"Well, but I want to know who *we* is."

"Why, all of us who stand on the old ground."

"But that ain't telling who *we* is. I want to know who *we* is."

"Well," said [Miller, in relating the story], "I was confounded, and was unable to give her any information who *we* are [italics in original]."[18]

Scholars often use this story to illustrate the confusion about Adventist identity that led to the calling of the milestone Albany Conference for April 29, 1845, in Albany, New York. The moderates called this conference of Adventists in an attempt to save Millerism from the various new extremist beliefs that were gaining in popularity and to define what they believed in contrast to the more radical factions and in light of the developments since the Great Disappointment. The announcement of the upcoming conference made it clear that those who embraced the new controversial doctrines were not welcome. The hope of unifying Adventists around the original Millerite teachings was exemplified by Miller's presence at the conference as the most important speaker. This was to be a meeting that drew Adventists together, not divide them even more. At the conference, delegates affirmed, among other things, ten principles of belief that largely correlated with Miller's pre-1844 teachings, except for the time element, of course. The beliefs that were affirmed and the decisions that were made at the Albany Conference were then communicated, reinforced, and largely accepted at various regional conferences held the next month—in New York City, Philadelphia, Baltimore, and Boston.[19]

Millerite scholars generally have seen the Albany Conference as an important milestone in Adventist history, and Arthur especially so, writing that "it was ... one of the most important conferences of Adventists ever held, for it was a turning point in the fortunes of the Adventist movement."[20] In supporting this claim, he identified what he saw as four major effects of the Albany Conference.

First, he argued that the conference brought the moderates together based on their reaffirmation of the basic Adventist beliefs coming out of Millerism. In the ongoing storm of vastly different ideas, it also strengthened the moderate group when they clarified and reclaimed their identity. After returning home from the conference, Miller met the elderly woman who had told him that she did not know who "we" are. After the conference, she seemed to have found peace on this issue, telling Miller that "I have found out who *we* is; and I shall still be an Adventist, and stand by the old ship."[21] Second, some Adventists who had taken the radical path returned to the moderate one after the Albany Conference, one of them being O. R. Fassett (who decades later would participate in the debate on whether or not to build a college in the West and then would briefly teach at Mendota College). Third, the Albany Conference contributed to an elitist strain among those who clung most closely to Miller's original teachings. Those who were the best educated among the Adventists tended to align themselves with the moderates and attend, or at least support, this conference's outcomes. The superior socioeconomic standing of these "Albany Adventists" aroused resentments and contributed to already existing divisions within the movement. Finally, the conference created lasting divisions between the moderate and radical Adventists now that the conference had clearly defined what were and were not acceptable beliefs—the unacceptable ones being virtually all of the new ideas that had emerged since the Great Disappointment of 1844.[22]

Other Adventist scholars, like David Rowe, have emphasized another aspect of the Albany Conference that had important ramifications for the future—that the Albany Conference, in spite of its organizers' protests to the contrary, was a milestone on the path to creating an actual denomination. Rowe argues that "the Albany Conference *did* establish a new Adventist sect, and did so in face of the Millerites' continuing confidence that Christ would come at any moment. ... Thus formalization of creed and ritual was more than an expedient to isolate and destroy the radicals. It was a means of keeping faith with God, of continuing the work of Adventism in saving souls and disseminating the Truth."[23] In other words, if the moderate Adventists were going to survive, they were going to have to organize at some level to fight the new radical doctrines, however strong their libertarian bias against organization. Later Rowe qualified the first line above when he stated that "the Albany Conference did not so much create an Adventist sect as give shape and direction to a body that already existed."[24] After all, as a number of scholars have noted, Adventists had already developed a distinctive set of theological beliefs, withdrawn from their home churches, created separate meetings, built their own meeting places, and even started their own publishing arms. However, Knight seemingly agreed with Rowe's earlier statement when he wrote that "Albany was, in effect, the staging ground for the formation of a church organization. ... Albany represents the formation, or at least authorization for the formation, of the first 'Adventist' church."[25] Knight argued that the resolutions made at the conference established, or at least recommended, a congregational type of church organization and the creation of an ordained ministry, along with the exclusion of those who embraced doctrines different from core Millerite beliefs. Significantly, Miller—by attending and agreeing to be a major speaker at the Albany Conference and afterwards, publicly affirming its resolutions—was turning his back on the nonsectarianism that he had preached throughout his entire ministry. Even he came to realize that this was necessary to save traditional Millerism so that they could move on to save more souls before Christ's return, whenever that might be.[26]

The Long Road to Founding a Denomination

Even though the 1845 Albany Conference looked like a gathering of people who were laying the foundation for a new church, it would take another fifteen years before some of the moderate Adventists would allow themselves to finally establish the Advent Christian denomination. The Albany Conference clearly marked a break with those Adventists who had chosen to embrace radical beliefs and practices, although the disentanglement of the moderates from the radicals developed gradually over the next year or so rather than happening abruptly. In any case, by 1846–47, the most radical and fanatical of the groups had faded away. As George Knight noted, "The leaven of Albany was doing its work."[27] However, looking forward, the moderates developed divisions and conflicts within their own ranks—doctrinal, organizational, political, and personal. And many remained reticent about forming their own church—because of both their continuing belief that the Second Advent would come soon and the fear that their own church would become "Babylon." Their religious libertarianism was hard to shake.[28]

What followed in the years after the 1845 conference was a series of smaller regional conferences in different parts of the country. This was now thought to be a better way to keep people within the Adventist fold and preaching the Second Advent than through campmeetings. Continued preaching of the soon return of Christ was also a priority. Preachers took to the road once again, and the big tent was brought back. It was recognized that at least some planning, organization, and coordination were needed to make this mission outreach more effective, now that the date of Christ's return was admitted to be unknown—although a few kept naming dates, especially 1854, and this became a cause of serious disagreement among Adventists. What resulted from this were organizations like the Advent Home Mission—the kind of organization one would expect to find coming from an actual denomination. Even though there was still much denial that they were forming a new church, increasingly, the Albany Adventists were functioning like a denomination.[29]

However, before the moderate Adventists created the Advent Christian denomination, they would experience significant doctrinal disputes among themselves, causing more factions and separations. The battle over whether or not Adventists were or should be organized, which raged on between the 1845 Albany Conference and Miller's passing in late 1849, did not maintain its predominant position in the 1850s. It was still an issue, but by then the focus had shifted to a doctrinal dispute concerning immortality. This disagreement arose just before Miller's predicted year for Christ's return, but Himes and Miller had downplayed it. They simply wanted to save souls and warn sinners that the Second Advent was near. This continued to be their position after the Great Disappointment, and for Himes, throughout the 1850s. However, the topic was revived anyway. At issue was the state of the dead. In other words, was the soul immortal or not? When one died, did the soul survive or did all cease to exist after death until the resurrection? And on the judgment day, did the wicked suffer the fires of hell for eternity, or were they annihilated? The belief that one slept after death until the resurrection was called conditionalism, the idea being that the soul was not immortal and that people achieved immortality on the condition that they had accepted Christ as their savior. On the judgment day, the bodies and souls of those who had not done this would be destroyed once and for all. The early Christian church had embraced conditionalism, but it survived just two hundred years or so. After that, it was replaced with the doctrine of soul immortality, held by Roman Catholic, Eastern Orthodox, and most Protestant churches right up to Miller's time. Although Miller was not a conditionalist, this doctrine fit well with the restorationism that Millerism represented because it was a doctrine that harkened back to the early years of Christianity. There were other doctrinal issues that also divided the moderate Adventists, but even if there had not been, it seems likely that the deep disagreement on immortality and the state of the dead, accompanied as it was by power struggles between newspapers as well as nasty words and vindictive behavior, was enough to separate the moderate Adventists into factions, and ultimately into separate denominations.[30]

This is not the place for an extended theological discussion on this issue but suffice it to say that the debate divided the Albany Adventists into at least two groups. Himes rejected conditionalism, and his newspaper, the *Advent Herald*, refused to publish the writings of people who advocated this belief. This once-civil newspaper started to act in a condescending way and ultimately became sarcastic and even vindictive toward conditionalists, and they responded in turn, thus making the division worse. Interestingly, about 1860, Himes moved away from his belief in natural immortality and embraced the doctrines of conditionalism and annihilationism, which then drew him closer to the Advent Christians. But earlier, this conflict led to a split in May 1858, when Himes and the *Herald* Adventists formed the American Evangelical Adventist Conference, whose stated goal was to spread Millerism's beliefs as defined by the Albany Conference. The conditionalists were represented by a newspaper called the *World's Crisis*, which took the lead in calling for a conference in Providence, Rhode Island. At this July 1860 meeting, in effect, a denomination was created, calling itself the Christian Association. At its first annual meeting, held three months later, it created what was called the Christian Publication Society and changed the name of the new denomination to the Advent Christian Association. (Note the word "Association" in its name, rather than "Church." This was a reflection of continued discomfort about becoming a denomination, the word "Association" suggesting a weaker, more decentralized organization. This, in fact, was the case.)[31]

The Advent Christian denomination remained remarkably weak at its center for many decades. The Advent Christian Association was a legally constituted, incorporated body, which had its own newspaper, the conditionalist *World's Crisis*; its own campmeeting, the Wilbraham campmeeting, the largest among Adventists; ordination of its own ministers; and recommendations sent out to its church members. Yet it failed to meet the definition of a denomination by other standards. The association that was created in 1860 had no national executive apparatus, no full-time national officers, no denominational headquarters, no schools for educating ministers, and no statement of denominational beliefs. Only its Christian Publication Society—publisher of the *World's Crisis*—along with the other regional publication societies that were established over time, had any significant structure or power. This situation was reflected in the fact that Adventists often informally referred to each other as either "Herald Adventists" (Evangelical Adventists) or "Crisis Adventists" (Advent Christians).[32]

It was not until 1893—the year of Mendota College's birth—that the Advent Christian General Conference was organized to replace the Advent Christian Association. It did a bit more by way of coordination among the various conferences and churches, served as a court of appeal for church and conference disputes, published a biennial manual, and held biennial meetings. However, it still lacked critical elements that one would expect to see in a denomination. From 1916 on, the Advent Christian General Conference embarked on an agonizingly slow journey to create a truly national denomination with increased powers and heightened stature. However, although some progress was made, it remained a relatively weak and decentralized organization for quite some time. Until the mid-twentieth century, Boston was, in effect, the informal center of the Advent Christian denomination simply because it was the home of the Christian Publication Society and the *World's Crisis*, as well as several Advent Christian organizations. And before the powers of the denomination were consolidated in the twentieth century, what central power there was continued to reside in the various publication associations, each region of the country having established its own society and newspaper.[33]

It was not until 1968 that the General Conference voted to create a consolidated, denominational budget through which all Advent Christian agencies would be financially supported. What had been *independent*, national, Advent Christian agencies doing work in different areas (men's, women's and youth work, missions, etc.) were now brought together under the management of the General Conference. And this was the body that published the Advent Christian *Witness*—the publication that replaced all of the previous regional and mission newspapers. In the following year, 1969, a denominational headquarters was finally established, located in Charlotte, North Carolina, with a chief executive and staff.[34]

An aversion to centralized power was a longstanding hallmark of Advent Christians. During the 1850s, doctrinal fights among the moderate Adventists predominated over the organization question and ultimately produced several distinct denominations. However, the debate over how much organization to embrace and whether or not to become an actual denomination never went away. Those against organization delayed it for many years, but throughout the 1850s, it became clearer and clearer to some Adventists that at least some organization was needed. To effectively preach Miller's message to save souls, organization and coordination were needed. The group could not be maintained without churches, and churches could not be sustained without permanent ministers, as opposed to the traveling evangelists and circuit preachers of the past. Organization would have had to come at some point, but doctrinal differences provided the push that was needed for the group of conditional Adventists to formally organize themselves in 1860. However, it would take *over one hundred years* for them to consolidate its denominational power, leadership, and agencies into a modern, mature denomination.[35]

This conflict, between religious libertarianism and the belief in the need for greater organization and control, was also reflected in the debate over whether or not the Advent Christians in the West should start a college. Given Adventists' continued belief in Christ's soon return, they debated, up into the 1880s, whether or not they should construct their own church buildings, as opposed to the usual practice of the past—meeting in homes, renting public halls, etc. As a result, many churches did not have their own buildings until the 1880s, and the ones they built were usually quite modest. If there was still a debate over building churches into the 1880s, how much greater the disagreement must have been over establishing a college, and on its own campus, during the years 1890–92.[36]

The Debate Over Founding a College

Mendota College was created in 1893, not by the Advent Christian denomination as a whole, but by the publishing arm of the denomination in the West—the Western Advent Christian Publication Association (hereafter called WACPA) —which published the paper *Our Hope and Life in Christ* (hereafter called *Our Hope)*. Within months of the paper's founding in 1889, a proposal was made by a layman, T. S. Parks (a leading businessman and member of the Advent Christian church in Auburn, Illinois), that a western college be established, a project that he was willing to help launch with a gift of $1,000, if forty-nine other people also gave $1,000. This proposal was made in a letter, which was read at the WACPA convention, held in Aurora, that created (or possibly reinvented) WACPA:

> You meet ... to determine whether our church shall establish a Western paper to defend the doctrines advocated by our people. Now it would probably be a good thing, if we were able to support a Western paper. We now have an excellent paper in the East [the *World's Crisis*], able and willing to defend the tenets of our church.
>
> We have a greater need of a College to educate the rising generation of the church in the doctrines of the same. This is paramount to all other claims; it is the great need, and unless we do something now, we must as a church soon be blotted out from the face of the earth. Our old ministers are passing away; who will take their places unless we prepare for the emergency? ...
>
> Now, I propose to be one of fifty who will subscribe one thousand dollars each to endow a College (one-half payable when $25,000 have been subscribed, and the remainder within one year after the $50,000 is fully subscribed), to be called the Advent Christian College, for the purpose of educating young men and women in the doctrines of our faith, said institution to give a liberal course of instruction, as is given in other Colleges, but to be managed by our church; a committee to be chosen by our Conference, of COMMON SENSE BUSINESS MEN, to locate a site

wherever their judgment may think best; to choose a faculty known for their Christian character, Biblical knowledge, and well versed in classical lore [capitalization in original].[37]

This generous offer initiated the discussion of building a college that would serve the needs of western Advent Christians, especially those in or thinking of going into the ministry. (Sadly, Parks did not live to see his dream come to fruition because he was killed just a year later, on January 28, 1891, in Auburn. While attempting to cross a track on his way to mail a letter, he was hit by a train.) This was a challenging proposal, given the small size of the Advent Christian denomination (not to mention the relatively small number of Advent Christians just in the West); the modest income of most Advent Christians; the fact that the founding institution (the western publications society) itself was brand new and trying to establish itself on a secure financial foundation; and the historical bias of Adventists against forming permanent institutions.[38]

The debate that followed dealt with at least three major questions. The first was simply whether the publication society should establish a college or not. (To what extent was it really needed? To what extent could it be justified theologically?) The second question was for those who wanted a school but disagreed on what kind of school it should be. Was it necessary to create a full-blown, four-year school or was it preferable to build a two-year Bible-training school that would draw students from secular schools or religious schools created by other denominations? The third question concerned where the new school should be located: Mendota, where the campus of Wartburg Seminary was for sale at a bargain price? Or elsewhere, in a larger town with more economic resources? All of these discussions were critically important to the founding of a new western college, but for the purposes of this chapter, it is the first question that is paramount.

Parks's proposal generated a number of newspaper articles and letters from people who seconded his suggestion and then went on to advance their own arguments. These were both educational/social and religious. The educational/social arguments were made by those who took a modernist approach, arguing that they were living in a new society, which required education. Henry Pollard, editor of *Our Hope*, stated: "Our age, more than any preceding it, is one of education and mental culture. We cannot expect to commend the truth to thinking minds unless we can present it intelligibly, forcibly, and ably. ... While God may send us able men, who were educated elsewhere, as long as we are really unable to educate our own ministry, he certainly will not continue to send them after he has given us the power to train them ourselves."[39] There clearly is a religious angle to this argument, presenting the Almighty in the vein of "God helps those who help themselves." Pollard was also acknowledging the reality of a new kind of society—one that was more industrial, more urban, more fast-paced, and more specialized and professionalized, thus requiring greater amounts of education for ministers, among others. To be a good minister in the modern age, he was arguing, one had to be able to communicate effectively. This more-education-is-required-for-a-modern-world argument would be made throughout the Mendota years as a way of recruiting students and the financial support of churches and individuals. Another man, a principal of an academy in New Hampshire, stated the same position a lot more bluntly, writing that "the time has passed when the rantings of the religious idiot are edifying."[40]

However, such modern-sounding arguments were often accompanied by a specific religious argument that considerably lessened the breadth of the educational argument. The concerns took several different forms, but they all dealt with the dangers of giving Adventist young people no option but to attend the schools of other denominations where, it was feared, they would be won over to doctrines that challenged Adventist beliefs or even be drawn into the denomination that founded the school. One of the people who voiced this concern was a young minister by the name of Orrin Roe Jenks, who later would serve as the principal of Mendota College's Bible Training School; head up the fundraising effort that made the 1912 move to Aurora possible; and become the first president of Aurora College, holding that position for over twenty years. He thought a school was necessary *now*. Advent Christians wanted more education and were asking for a denominational college, without which, Jenks feared, they would go to some other denomination's school, and possibly be lost to Advent Christians. He argued that even if the $50,000 college that had been discussed earlier was not financially feasible, one could be set up, for much less money, in an empty or even current church for the time being.[41] These arguments assumed the idea, certainly more accepted a hundred years ago, that absolute truth could be found and that they, Adventist Christians, had found it—although, in all fairness, such a belief was hardly unique to Adventists. One reader of the newspaper wrote a letter that combined both of these arguments. He wrote that "young people in this age will have a college education, and they will get it somewhere and are compelled to decide between a denominational school where religious error is forced upon them, and a secular school where infidelity runs deep, among students, in the fraternities and possibly in the faculty." He also noted the psychological toll it took on an Adventist student to attend the college of another denomination or a non–religiously affiliated school: "I can speak from experience when I say it is hard for one living under the influence of Advent teaching ... to listen to ancient falsehood in a denominational school, or to be sneered at in a secular college."[42]

There were other religious arguments as well. First, there was the position that ministers, and even young people in general, needed to learn to read the Bible in Hebrew and Greek so that they could acquire a greater understanding of the Scriptures.[43] This was very much in the Millerite tradition. Not only did Millerites and, later, Advent Christians, emphasize the importance of the Bible as the foundation of faith, their belief that Christ would soon return to earth had always been based on a careful, systematic reading of biblical prophecies. This emphasis on a biblical-based faith later would be reflected in a Bible Training School requirement that appeared in about 1901–2: that all students working for a degree in that school *must* take multiple courses in Hebrew and Greek.

Not surprisingly, a second argument for educating ministers came from the Bible itself. In late 1892, the editors of *Our Hope* published, without comment, an article from a Baptist newspaper. This short article offered the observation that even Christ's disciples were educated in a sense. After all, the argument went, Jesus taught his disciples for three years, preparing them for their future tasks after he would be gone.[44] (It is very interesting that such an article appeared in this newspaper because in the previous year, the editors had taken the stand that since the paper had just started publication, it was not yet ready for such a challenging venture as founding a school.) Some Advent Christians viewed the apostles as being simple men who were not educated and so wondered why Adventist ministers had to be. This argument was one of the immediate reactions to Parks's proposal in 1890. Parks swiftly responded that the apostles could "read Hebrew, write Greek, and speak Syriac. ... Can your minister do as much?"[45]

The third religious argument was more pragmatic. It was noted by both ministers and lay people that the first generation of Adventist ministers was passing away, and there was a real concern about who would replace them. One woman, who wrote to the newspaper in support of an Adventist school, claimed that "churches are organized, struggle along for a while, and die because there is no one to feed the flock."[46] According to another article in *Our Hope*, this shortage of ministers was at least in part a result of the fact that people wanted educated leaders in this new era. This article stated:

> You think we ought to preach if God has called us, without any training, and yet where are the Advent Christian churches in the West that will agree to take these new beginners as pastors?
>
> There are those in every church who will not come to preaching service unless they can listen to the smartest. ... Now if we are such critical people and must listen to able men or none at all, let us be consistent and have a school where these lacks may be made up, and where the Word of God may be systematically studied.[47]

Some believed that this shortage of educated ministers also had a negative effect on Advent Christians' evangelism at home. Jenks, in an 1891 article, reminded the newspaper's readers of this. He wrote that he knew an evangelist who told him that "he [the evangelist] knew of many places where, with proper work, he could organize Advent Christian Churches; but as we have no pastors to step in and care for such churches, the work is not effectual. ... It is discouraging to our Evangelists to go into new fields and start a good work, and then, because there is no one to care for the work, know that it will all soon be torn down by the devil."[48]

Although the newspaper published many articles in support of a college, there were other articles and letters that voiced some concerns and showed a reluctance to build a school. Some of these anti-school arguments found in the newspaper's articles and letters contained statements of support for a college, but then concentrated on the down side of this venture to such an extent that one had to question their support.

Some people opposed building a college for pragmatic reasons. There was a real and, I might add, reasonable concern about whether such a small denomination, composed overwhelmingly of people of modest means, could realistically afford to build a college from scratch. This concern was often linked to the need for supporting *Our Hope*, the brand-new newspaper of the West, because it was struggling to secure an adequate financial base. One of the leading proponents of this point of view was W. J. Hobbs, the treasurer and business agent of the paper. Hobbs was one of those who said that he supported the idea of a school but then went on to argue against it. In one article, he told his audience about a sizable donation for the newspaper that was dependent on matching funds. This was good news, but he was concerned because he was not convinced that Adventists could donate enough money to support both a fledgling newspaper and fledgling college. His warning to his readers was: "Do not attempt to do so many things at once that you lose all." He then went on to make this suggestion:

> When you take under consideration the cost of competent teachers, and the probable number who could be gathered into a denominational school in the West, I must say I confess to being a little skeptical as to whether we are ready. I hope I am mistaken. Go ahead, brethren, but let us be sure of our foundation support first. ... If we have young men in the ministry among us, or those who contemplate entering it in our church, who desire a more extended education that they may be better prepared for their work; would it not be far more feasible to push the paper to a solid basis and ask through it for special donations to aid such young men to go to institutions now fully prepared to give the instruction they need? I simply suggest this, until such a time, *if the Master tarry* [italics

mine], as will give us reasonable grounds for success in getting an educational institution of our own. If the answer is made that contact with such institutions will draw them from *present truth*; my answer will be: such young men will be of no use to us.

Please understand that this warning is in no sense in opposition to a school, but raises the question: Are we now ready to take hold of the work? Let us make sure of the success of the one thing we *must* have, and without which there will be no hope for other things so desirable [italics in original except where noted otherwise].[49]

(Note in this quotation the phrase "if the Master tarry." This saying, and others like it, such as "if time continues," were frequently used by Adventists when discussing future events and were a legacy of the Millerite movement. No matter how mundane or pragmatic the topic, in the back of Adventists' mind was always the belief that Christ could return at any time.)

Another article also made the case for putting the paper first, over a college, yet also supported the idea that greater education was needed for Adventist youth. The argument centered on the idea that since a college would cost much and directly affect only a few, the paper could be used as a more cost-efficient educational alternative to a college. Speaking of the paper, the proponent of this idea argued: "Now, the ultimate object of both college and paper is to a great extent the same; viz., the conservation and diffusion of truth, especially on those points which are not received by other denominations. And, of the two, the paper is the far more important. For less expenditure, instruction can be given through it, to more people." After detailing how much a college would cost and how few people would benefit from it directly, he told readers that they should "look at the paper. It asks no endowment, salting down a dollar to get six cents a year out of it. This is a weighty consideration, *seeing the Lord is coming soon* [italics mine]. ..."[50] It seems that, for this author, a good part of the appeal of concentrating only on the newspaper was that it was already established and could get on with its work immediately, since, in his mind, time was short and colleges take a great deal of time to fully establish.

Although a number of people hinted at the theological underpinning of their arguments against building a college, one reader, C. A. Meade, who joined the debate fairly late, just a year before the college opened its doors, wrote the most complete and passionate theological argument for why the western Adventists should not found a college:

> I wanted to ask those dear brethren who are so anxious to invest money in the Mendota property, thinking it to be such "a good investment," from a worldly standpoint, if they are aware that Jesus is coming? Yes; *soon* coming! How must it look in the eyes of the world to see us as a people preaching the immediate coming of the Lord from heaven and at the same time laying plans that will take years to complete, or before any returns could be expected. ...
>
> Is there an Adventist in the land ... that does not expect to see the Lord before ten years shall roll around? yes, less than that, by several years? Then why think of locking up the Lord's money in real estate, just because it seems to be a good investment, when there are Holy Ghost men on every hand, working to support their families, whom that same money would enable to go forth in the strength and Spirit of the Lord, proclaiming "Behold the Lord cometh?" Would not money thus spent be "treasure laid up in heaven," a far better investment than the Mendota property—yea, than the whole town, with the state thrown in [italics in original]?[51]

Perhaps the fact that he joined the debate late, after so many arguments had been made in favor of a college, accounts for the ardor of this statement. And he prefaced his remarks by explaining why he had not spoken up before by saying, "Being one of the unknown ones I have thought my words would have no weight. ..."[52] In any case, these were words that would not have been seen as extreme in the years of the Millerite movement, and such beliefs help to account for the fact that the Advent Christian denomination was not formally organized until 1860—sixteen years *after* the date of Christ's expected return. Thirty-two years after the founding of the denomination, in spite of the fact that Christ had not returned, hope still ran high among Advent Christians. This was a belief that could not be ignored when founding a permanent institution like a college.

The response to this issue was not to deny the Adventists' belief in the soon return of Christ. Those who argued *for* a college hoped for and believed in Christ's return as much as those who argued *against* it. They responded by citing Christ's admonition to *"occupy till I come."* As discussed earlier, William Miller and his top lieutenants had used this phrase to keep their followers from fanaticism—quitting their job, selling their property, giving their money away—in the days leading up to the appointed day. Because Miller believed that Christ's return was imminent, he did not advocate the creation of any institutions, not even a new denomination. But the situation was different for Adventists in the early 1890s. Nearly fifty years had passed since Miller's appointed time, yet Christ had not come. This probably helped the younger generation to take this familiar phrase and use it in a way that *promoted* the creation of *permanent* institutions while still believing in the soon return of Christ. For example, Elder H. G. M'Culloch—one of the leading proponents of founding a college, and at Mendota—in responding to this concern, boldly stated that "if the Master comes with the walls of a building half reared; amen: 'we occupied till he came.' "[53] H. Pollard, the editor of *Our Hope*, after admitting that Christ's return could be longer than Adventists had thought, repeated the "occupy till I come" phrase, and then argued that this phrase "justifies his people in pushing every department of their work, up to the very hour of Christ's appearing."[54] He also reminded the newspaper's readers of the consequences of not fully occupying until Christ's return. He stated that "had we so understood our mission as to have begun our work upon the principles of thorough organization, including a college, some twenty-five years ago, it is easy to see we should now be vastly in advance of our present position, numerically, financially, intellectually and spiritually. We should now be doing a work tenfold greater than we are doing. ..."[55] In this article, which was written nearly two years before Meade's impassioned plea not to build a college because of Christ's imminent return, Pollard systematically responded to the various arguments used against founding a school. The fact that one of the arguments that he felt it important to address was the issue of Christ's soon return suggests that a number of people had been making this argument. Meade's letter to the newspaper was the most comprehensive statement of it, but it came quite some time after others had been making it.

In the debate that followed the proposal to establish a college, there was both theological continuity and discontinuity. Much of the Millerite language—like "occupy till I come" —was very much evident in this debate because, even after decades, Advent Christians still believed that Christ would return to earth in the not-so-distant future. However, the larger historical context had changed. In the 1840s, Millerites had used this phrase to *prevent* people from engaging in church and institution building—in short, from becoming sectarian. Time was thought to be short, so Miller and Himes believed that the Millerites' full attention should be aimed at preaching and winning souls. By the early 1890s, however, the "occupy till I come" admonition was being used as an argument to *do* just what Miller had warned against—building a permanent institution— because time had gone on and most Adventists had given up on date setting. Those who argued against a college reflected the old Millerite bias against institution building, and for the same reason—the expected soon return of Christ—but now it was the people who wanted to establish a college who were taking up Christ's plea to "occupy till I come."

The debate that took place over establishing a college is a reminder of the line of continuity that stretched from the 1840s Millerite movement to the founding of a small, denominational college fifty years later. The Adventists' belief in their "blessed hope" survived and continued periodically to resurface. Throughout the Mendota years, there were articles in *Our Hope* and other Advent Christian periodicals that used the "occupy till I come" verse in making their argument that people should support Mendota College. This suggests that there were still Advent Christians in the denomination—although, I suspect, increasingly fewer in number as the older generation died off—who held on to Miller's dictum to *not* build permanent institutions.

In the end, of course, the college was built, and in Mendota, and in the minds of many Adventists, this was reconciled with their belief in Christ's soon return. These modernizers understood that society had been transformed since the days of Miller, and so the Advent Christian denomination, to be effective, also had to change. Time had taken its toll, and building a college no longer seemed like a waste of time or a distraction from the business of preparing for Christ's return. In fact, they now argued, a college was *essential* to prepare the way for the Lord.

Chapter 4
The College Campus and Mendota: Not Enough Space, Too Much Insularity

"Our College building is getting too small for the work which we can easily see is before us."

—*Our Hope and Life in Christ*, 1894

"The growth of the college urgently demands a doubling of the room and facilities of the school."

—Elder B. Forester, 1907

The Main College Building on the Tree-Covered Mendota College Campus

A school is first and foremost about people—the people who created it and keep it running, those who teach, and, most importantly, the students themselves. However, the place where this education takes place *does* matter. A campus that is attractive and has good facilities helps to bring people to a college as well as keep them there. A campus that is well maintained and safe also provides assurance to worried parents that their children will not be harmed and will have good living and learning conditions. We not only believe that today, but this was an argument made throughout the Mendota years, especially by those who were advocating for moving the college to Aurora. But even early on, Dr. J. W. Emmons made this argument in 1895 while raising money to repair and redecorate the Old Main.[1] This chapter introduces the town of Mendota and highlights the campus itself—how it was acquired, what it looked like, what facilities it had, how it evolved over time, and its chronic shortage of space.

Acquiring a Beautiful Campus

During the debate about whether or not to have a college, those who believed that further education for Advent Christian ministers was needed suggested several different options. One was to have a three-month Bible course, given at one or more of the western churches, but others wanted a school on its own property—separate from any Advent Christian church. The latter group of course won, but it took a while. In July of 1890, Elder William McCulloch proposed a location for a *permanent* school. He suggested that the new college be located in Illinois to honor a man named T. S. Parks, the Advent Christian banker from Auburn, Illinois, who had proposed the idea of founding a college to the Western Advent Christian Publication Association (hereafter referred to as WACPA), just a few months earlier. This had seemed like a radical suggestion because it came just a few months after the association's founding of the newspaper, *Our Hope and Life in* Christ, when it was trying to get up on its feet and become financially viable, if not secure. A February 1890 *Our Hope* article reported on the meeting of the General Western Advent Christian Convention, at which a letter from Parks, in which he suggested the founding of a college, was read. The article reported: "He offered to be one of fifty to give one thousand dollars to establish a college. A vote of thanks was extended to

Bro. Parks for his generous offer; and that steps be taken by us to secure this offer by setting on foot measures to establish a Pastor's College."[2] And within Illinois, McCulloch suggested not just a town—Mendota, Illinois—but a specific property within that town. The matter lay dormant for a while, but the issue of founding a college in Mendota resurfaced a year and a half later when J. August Smith reported that the cost of McCulloch's proposed land had been reduced— from $2,500 to $1,800—and that he had obtained the right of refusal on the site, at the reduced price, for sixty days. He noted that the site might also be used for the annual western campmeeting and the headquarters of WACPA.[3]

Mendota was praised as a good location because it was about eighty miles from Chicago, with easy access to that metropolis and many other towns by way of two great railroads—the Chicago, Burlington, and Quincy and the Illinois Central Railroads. The proposed northeastern Mendota site itself also was praised for its good location, as it was just three-fourths of a mile from the railroad station, which was in the center of town. In their 1890 and 1891 *Our Hope* articles, both McCulloch and Smith mentioned the beauty of the five-acre site—its many mature trees creating a park-like setting for the college building, which was set back from the street, in the center of the lot. In his article, McCulloch described the property and his first visit to see it.

> We found one of the nicest plats of ground containing five acres of
> nice grove, large trees, with the college building, four story, brick;
> with well of water and outbuildings, and all the appurtenances
> thereof; which can be bought at the wonderfully low price of $2,500.
> The building was built for a school, and is now owned by
> the Iowa Synod of the German Lutherans, of Dubuque, Iowa. They
> now offer to sell it at that remarkably low price, having moved
> their college to that place. They have an agent on the premises,
> who gave me the facts in regard to the place; and thinking what
> an opportunity it would be for our people to step in and occupy
> at once, without waiting to build and rear the beautiful trees that
> adorn the collegegrounds. ... I asked permission to go through the
> college building, which is four stories high, and of brick, 40 X 50 on
> the ground. The basement, or lower floor, is kitchen, pantry, dining
> room, etc.; the three other stories are recitation and sleeping rooms,

etc. It has accommodated 60 pupils at a time, and is situated in the northeast part of the city, a little retired from the noise of the streets, and none too much so; a most beautiful situation for a school.

The building needs some repairs, as it has not been used for school for some time. My brother-in-law, Mr. David Rude, who lives near it, said $500 would put it in good condition for use, making the sum total for a college building and two blocks of land in a good city within 80 miles of Chicago, only $3,000, all ready for occupancy! ...

Altogether it looks to me that if our people mean business and ever intend to have a school for our rising ministry and others, this is an opportunity that only offers itself [once] in a lifetime.[4]

Clearly, McCulloch was impressed not only by the beauty of the site but also by its attractiveness in terms of finances and timeliness. The college could get off to a much faster start if it purchased a property like this, which already had a building, utilities, and mature landscaping, and for a bargain price.[5]

In 1891, after Smith visited the property, he wrote a similar description of it, except that he went into more detail about its facilities and how it would accommodate the annual campmeeting:

The college building is of brick, four stories high, and is in fair condition. The lower story contains a dining room, 20x45, two kitchens, two pantries; and there is a good cellar. The second story contains a large lecture-room, a large reception-room, a library room and three bed-rooms. The third and fourth stories each contain nine bedrooms. I believe the cost of necessary repairs could be nearly all raised by donations from the citizens of Mendota.

The building is located in the center of the grounds, which contain five acres; about an acre being garden, an acre apple orchard, and three acres of as beautiful park as any one wishes to see. This park would accommodate 150 tents for families, and have two large openings for large tents for worship, or for the building of a tabernacle.

There is a bake-house, with an oven capable of baking 150 loaves. There are two cisterns, which will hold 180 barrels of water. There is also a good well, closets, etc. The grounds are within the city limits, about three-fourths of a mile from the depot, which is in the center of the city. Sidewalks go up to, and beyond the grounds; electric lights are situated at the two corners; and electric light can be conducted to any part with little expense.[6]

A week after Smith's article on the new price of the Mendota property appeared, McCulloch rejoined the discussion, advocating for both a college in a *permanent* location and, in particular, for the Mendota property. Apparently, there were still those who were pushing for a college that would be held in various churches. McCulloch acknowledged and commended all the enthusiastic suggestions from churches in various states that a school be located in *their* town/church, but then he presented the disadvantages of such a plan: "To think of opening schools in the various chapels in the different states which are anxious to have them, seems to me to be the height of folly; the interest would necessarily be scattered and weakened, and no permanent results would follow."[7] Having knocked down this option, McCulloch returned to the Mendota one:

> To avoid sectional interest, and to awaken a general interest and thus concentrate all our labors in this greatly needed work among us as a people, I propose once more to call the attention of our people to the Mendota College, which I reported through *Our Hope* something over a year and a half ago, and which received so little encouragement that it was finally dropped altogether (and perhaps it was best for the time), until our brethren became more fully awake on the subject, and opportunity was afforded for the discussion of the matter through the paper.
>
> That discussion has been had ... ; and now we are nearly all agreed as to the necessity of a School. ...[8]

After once again describing the property, he laid out the finances for purchasing it:

> Brother J. August Smith has secured option of it for sixty days, for the trifling sum of $1,800; which is much below its real value; and

he proposes to form a stock company, and buy the property at once; placing the shares at $10, each, every share to represent a vote in the company; which plan I fully endorse, and I think that within the sixty days we will raise Iowa's portion to secure the college building, with all its appurtenances; and, with the consent of the Association, to locate its Publishing House, and General Western Campmeeting there.

I will take at least five shares in the stock; and I understand that the ball has been actually set in motion, and that quite a number of shares of stock have been pledged already.[9]

With an option on the property for just sixty days, action had to be taken quickly to purchase it. In February 1892, a meeting was held in Mendota for the purpose of forming a legal body to which the property could be deeded. At this meeting, the stock company was organized as the Western Advent Christian Association. A board of directors was established, and the association applied for a charter from the State of Illinois. This new legal body then bought the old Wartburg Seminary building and the five acres of land on which it sat. It cost $1,800 and was paid for on a stockholder basis. About eight months later, the Western Advent Christian Association gave the Mendota property to WACPA, which itself had become a corporate body (with education as one of its major missions). At its annual meeting, held in August 1892, the publication association voted to proceed with the formation of a school. By then, it had already created an Educational Committee, which would serve as the college's board for a number of years.[10]

Interestingly, this was not the first Mendota College on this campus. The main college building, commissioned in 1857, was built to house what was called the Mendota Female College, which was run by the Evangelical Lutheran Synod of Northern Illinois for thirteen years. The citizens of Mendota, who wanted this type of educational institution in their town, had initiated this school. One man donated the land, and people in Mendota raised the $5,000 needed to construct the college building. They also went to the Synod of Northern Illinois and asked them to run it. In 1865, the school's name became Mendota College, because it began to admit men as well. In 1870, this college closed down, due to financial problems, and the campus sat empty for three years, until the Evangelical Lutheran Synod of Iowa purchased it in 1873. This religious group had run a school called Wartburg Seminary in Dubuque, Iowa, but it needed more space by 1873, so the school was moved to Mendota. Wartburg Seminary was run on the Mendota campus until 1889, when the school was moved back to Dubuque. Again, the campus sat vacant for several years until the property was purchased by a group of Advent Christians and some Mendotans in order to start an Advent Christian school.[11]

Mendota—the Town

The actual site for the new college seemed to be good, but what kind of place was the town of Mendota? It was a relatively new town, having been founded in 1853—just forty years before the founding of Mendota College. It lay within a large swath of open land, inhabited by small farms and scattered farming villages. As noted earlier, its promoters emphasized its good transportation links, due to the fact that two major railroads—the Illinois Central and the Chicago and Aurora (soon to become the Chicago, Burlington, and Quincy) ran through it. In fact, Mendota was created as a result of the Illinois Central Railroad and the Chicago and Aurora Railroad passing through that location. A station was established at that junction and was named "Mendota"—a Native American word meaning "where two trails or paths meet." The creation of these two railroads opened up much of the state to further economic development—bringing in people to settle the land and making commercial farming for distant markets possible. Although Mendota, about eighty miles from Chicago, seems to have been somewhat remote and isolated, this was not exactly the case. It was a small place, having around thirty-five hundred people in 1890 (with about three hundred more by 1910—shortly before the college moved to Aurora), and it was some distance from larger towns like Aurora, Galesburg, Peoria, and Rockford. No doubt it also lacked some of the urban amenities and work opportunities of those larger towns. However, the two railroads were a lifeline for Mendota in the 1890s and early 1900s. They could get goods out to Chicago and its suburbs quickly and also served the large farming area of north-central Illinois. Thus, businesses could set up shop in Mendota, knowing that they could ship their goods out easily, and the farming communities could send their crops there for storage and transportation. The more the countryside developed, thanks to the railroads, the better it was for Mendota's economy.[12]

This transportation nexus also proved to be important to both Mendota College's students and its many visitors. They could easily reach Mendota by rail from far-flung places or just nearby towns. For example, the whole time that Orrin R. Jenks served as principal of the Bible Training School, in the first decade of the twentieth century, he also had a pastorate in Chicago. It would have been unthinkable to travel the eighty miles or so between Chicago and Mendota by horse and buggy, riding on rough country roads, on a regular basis. The railroad made his work at Mendota College possible.

During the Mendota College years, Mendota also had a few industries, many of them, not surprisingly, related to agriculture. One produced corn shellers and other farm equipment; another one, grain weighers; and yet another, soil cultivators and pulverizers. The storage of crops was important to commercial farmers in an agricultural region like that surrounding Mendota, and that need was met through a company that dealt in and stored grain, feed, fertilizer, coal, and lumber. Mendota also had some industries that were not related to agriculture. One long-lasting business produced machinery that applied a uniform finish on furniture and millwork. Another one produced carriages and wagons. There was also, early on, a Mendota Bottling Company. And, of course, Mendota had all of the usual small businesses needed to meet the requirements of everyday life—grocery stores, hardware and dry goods stores, banks, restaurants, saloons and breweries, hotels, blacksmiths, liveries, funeral homes, and more. No doubt the college people frequented virtually all of these businesses—with the exceptions of the saloons and breweries, of course. But it was Mendota's three banks that were especially important to the college because they contributed to its survival. The school struggled to pay its bills most years, but there were several especially bad periods when it had to take out loans to make ends meet. Over the years, after the college had moved to Aurora, Mendota acquired some larger industries: Del Monte, arriving in 1948; at least two large feed companies, in 1949 and 1961; a trucking and fertilizer company, in 1958; a chemical company, a subsidiary of Standard Oil, in 1967; and more. However, in the 1890s and 1900s, Mendota was still a railroad and farming community. Even later in the twentieth century, many of the new, larger industries were related to agriculture, although there also were several large, manufacturing plants.[13]

Mendota, although small, was ethnically diverse from its earliest years. The largest ethnic group during the college's time there was the Germans, and the fourth largest was the Irish, both of whom were early arrivals and brought Catholicism to Mendota. St. Mary's Catholic Church was organized in the 1850s, getting its first resident pastor in 1858. It was hoped that Mendota's German Catholics, who were being served by German-speaking priests who traveled to Mendota to offer mass in various homes, would join the Irish immigrants in the English-speaking St. Mary's, but they wanted a German-speaking priest of their own, which they soon acquired. Between 1859 and 1861, they acquired their own church building and their own resident, German-speaking priest. This is not surprising. Ethnic groups wanting their own churches, whose services would be in their own language, was a common occurrence among nineteenth- and early twentieth-century immigrants, something the hierarchy of the Catholic Church disliked, since it typically organized its parishes by neighborhoods and not by ethnicity. Ultimately, in 1931, the Diocese of Peoria declared, in essence, that Mendota was too small to have two Catholic churches and combined them. And by then, presumably there was no longer a need to have a German-speaking priest. Not all the Germans in Mendota were Catholic, however. German Protestants also lived in Mendota, and they established St. John's Lutheran Church in 1858.[14]

Other ethnic groups as well were represented in LaSalle County (the rural county where Mendota is located and the governmental division for which the federal census gives statistics on ethnicity and race in 1910). After the Germans, they were, in descending order according to size: Austrians, the English, the Irish, Italians, Norwegians, Russians, Swedes, Scots, Canadians, Hungarians, the French, and a smattering of other groups. However, looking at the figures of just those people born outside of the United States does not give an accurate picture of the ethnic character of Mendota and its surrounding area. For example, while the 1910 census found 6,004 German immigrants living in LaSalle County, it also found 10,185 native-born people whose parents were born in Germany. Since Germans had been coming to this area since the 1850s, in 1910, many families were in at least the second generation, and some, no doubt, were beyond that. But these families were probably still very German in culture, especially since they attended their own churches. If you add the county's overall percentage of white immigrants (25.3 percent in 1900 and 21.4 percent in 1910) and native-born whites of foreign or mixed parentage (41.2 percent in 1900 and 39.8 percent in 1910), you see that LaSalle County had a high degree of ethnicity in 1900 and 1910 (66.5 percent in 1900 and 61.2 percent in 1910). In short, a substantial majority of the people living in LaSalle County during the Mendota College years were immigrants or were ethnics—native-born but having immigrant parents and so still immersed in German culture. The numbers of African Americans in this area were quite small, representing just .03 percent of the county's population in both 1900 and 1910.[15]

Ethnic groups are often identified as much by their religion as their national origins. For example, German Catholics and German Protestants were two distinct groups, and the Irish were closely associated with Catholicism. And much of the bigotry and discrimination exhibited toward Germans and the Irish in the 1850s and 1860s was really about Americans' fear of and prejudice toward Catholicism in what was still a predominantly Protestant nation. Anti-Catholicism, although not as virulent as in the 1850s and 1860s, continued in the post–Civil War period and beyond. In late 1891, when the possibility of starting a college in Mendota was being discussed and both pro and con articles appeared in *Our Hope*, one person declared that he was against locating a college in Mendota. He gave several reasons, one of them being that it was a "Catholic center,"[16] due to the many Germans and Irish people living there. Ostensibly he was not against the German Protestants living in Mendota since he seemed to be more concerned about the religion of the Germans and Irish rather than their national origins. However, while Advent Christians, like virtually all evangelicals at this time, were anti-Catholic, some saw the German presence in town as a good thing. Smith, in an *Our Hope* article published the same month, wrote—after citing the large number of Germans in Mendota: "I hope our German brethren in Chicago, Minonk, and throughout the states of Illinois and Wisconsin in particular, will aid in this and secure a place where they, too, can hold a campmeeting of their own, or hold services in the German language at our regular meetings."[17] Apparently, he saw the German population as an opportunity rather than a hindrance.

Protestant immigrants and white native-born Mendotans had their Protestant churches. In addition to the German Lutheran church, there were two Methodist churches, a Baptist church, and a Presbyterian one—all of them founded in the 1850s and 1860s. And when Mendota College was established, an Advent Christian church was started, adding to the evangelical presence in town. It was needed for faculty and students as well as to support and build on the work of the annual campmeeting held on the campus every summer. These churches had a common bond of evangelicalism and periodically joined together for special services and events, like the annual, union Thanksgiving service, held on Thanksgiving Day. The churches (including the Advent Christian church) took turns hosting this service, as did the local ministers preaching at it. Also, Mendotans periodically spoke at the college's daily chapel service, especially the town's ministers, and, at least once, a Mendotan was the main Commencement speaker (the minister of Mendota's Presbyterian church). In other words, the religious leaders at the college and the Mendota Advent Christian Church were easily integrated into the town's Protestant establishment.[18]

There were a few cultural amenities in Mendota during the college's years there. The two most important ones for the school were the library and the opera house. In 1870, local people organized the Mendota Library Association, which started with $100 in capital. Three years later, as contributions dribbled in, the library was put on a much more secure footing when a local citizen, Willard H. Graves, made a substantial donation, approximately $6,000, to the association. This gift, along with several others, made the library a reality. After the purchase of 1,700 books, the new library opened the next year, in 1874. In 1894, when the library was turned over to the town, it was named the Graves Public Library. Partway through the college's years in Mendota, in 1904, the town received funds from Andrew Carnegie to build a new library building. It turned out to be an elegant one, which today houses the Mendota Historical Society. The Graves Public Library was a great asset for the college. Since the school could only afford to build its library slowly, it relied on the public library for many years to supplement its small holdings. And after 1904, the students got to enjoy a beautiful, new building. The college also used the opera house, which was home to many different kinds of performances and activities—plays, movies, concerts, dances/balls, graduations, lectures, meetings, sports classes and events (calisthenics classes, fencing, wrestling matches, etc.), and private parties. In short, for nearly thirty years, the opera house was at the center of Mendota's cultural and social life. It closed the year after the college's Mendota years ended, in 1913, due to financial problems. Although some of the activities at the opera house, like dancing and movies, were shunned by Mendota College students as being too worldly, even sinful, they did receive some benefit from it. Concerts and lectures were given there, two activities that Mendota College people and the town's Advent Christians readily attended. In fact, President Twining gave several of his stereographic lectures on Europe there.[19]

Mendota may very well have been the right location for the college in 1893. Locating a college in a small town, in a rural area, was a longstanding tradition in the United States, one which emulated English universities. Although not all American colleges were located outside of cities, many of the ones founded in the eighteenth and nineteenth centuries were. Since so many of the college's students came from rural areas, this must have made them feel more at home. Attending a college in a large city like Chicago, or even Aurora at that time, probably would have required a greater adjustment for these first-generation college students, many of whom had lived at least somewhat isolated lives on farms. And, clearly, the town valued educational institutions, for it was Mendota's own citizens who had initiated the construction of the college building in 1857 and brought in the Lutherans to run a school in it. And in January 1892, a year before the college opened, a Mendota newspaper published a welcoming article on the coming of the Advent Christians to town (which then appeared in *Our Hope*). It stated: "We are glad to note that we are going to have an addition of citizens of so desirable a character, and they will find that they are making a good move in coming to our beautiful city."[20] Years later, in May 1909, the Mendota *Reporter* published an article that showed great appreciation for the college:

Every intelligent well wisher of our city is interested and
ready to encourage whatever advances the wellbeing of Mendota.
It can easily be shown that Mendota College adds no little to the
financial, intellectual, moral and religious development of our city.
It has brought into our midst a large number of permanent and
transient citizens of high moral and religious worth, who spend
their incomes here, while those connected with the college, whether
as students or as professors, are almost invariably intellectual and
religious people whose influence is ennobling. ... Plan to go [to the
upcoming college commencement address] for your own good, and
for the encouragement of this valuable and growing institution.[21]

However, given the effusive nature of this article and its date—May 1909,
just months before the decision to move the college to another town—one
can only wonder whether Mendotans had gotten wind of the growing
unhappiness of many college people with their campus, especially the college
building, and with Mendota itself.[22]

Mendotans tried to get the college to stay, but to no avail. Unfortunately,
at least some Mendotans did not believe that Mendota was seriously considered
as an option for the college's future. Shortly after the decision was made, in
January 1910, to move the college to Aurora, the Mendota *Reporter* wrote
about the decision and the process by which it was made—one that apparently
engendered some resentment, due to the belief that Mendota had not been
treated fairly or been taken seriously in the deliberations.

The Mendota Development Association was—in the light of
events, for no practical purpose—given the privilege to address the
meeting Friday forenoon, and representative members, together
with several ministers and the city council, were present, and made
short speeches, the burden of which was the desire to retain the
college, and to satisfy all reasonable demands of the meeting in
relation to a money subvention to be raised by the citizens. The
air was rather chilly, however, to a careful observer. They left with
the understanding that the conference, after having met and heard
the propositions of Aurora and Zion City, would formulate their

demands and that the Development Association would then be given a reasonable time to comply.

It was, therefore, no small surprise to them to learn Saturday morning that Mendota had not been accorded even this consideration and courtesy. They feel now that the majority of the conference never intended to give Mendota a show, and that the brusqueness with which they expressed this fact by their action, was rather a blessing in disguise, as it has saved them a lot of work and trouble which evidently would have been to no purpose.

As to the decision of the conference, that is a matter of their own, and we have no right to judge of its wisdom or folly. We hope, in a true Christian spirit, that their high anticipations for the future of Mendota College may be realized in Aurora. ... Mendota will not don sackcloth and ashes now that the college is to be removed, although all good citizens regret that fact, not so much on account of the material loss, as from their appreciation of the ideal value of any educational institution.[23]

Of course, there are at least two sides to every disagreement. The citizens of Mendota were sorry to see the college leave and believed they had supported it. At least some Advent Christians, however, believed that they had not gotten a lot of support from the town, especially financial aid, and that Aurorans would be more forthcoming in that regard. By 1910, when the decision was made to leave Mendota, the college people were ready for more—more classroom and dormitory space, more opportunities for growth, more financial support from the local community, and more jobs for students.[24]

Dressing Up the College Building

The Adventist leaders who bought the Mendota property acknowledged that some repairs would have to be made in the college building and, no doubt, they did make some repairs and improvements, especially because the building had not been occupied for several years. But either they did not do as much as necessary or their standard for what was necessary in such a building was low, because just three years later, in 1895, Dr. J. W. Emmons, a future member of the Educational Committee, found the condition of the building to be so poor that he immediately began a campaign to raise the funds to improve it. After visiting the school for the first time, he wrote an article for *Our Hope* in which he described the disrepair of the college building as well as his efforts to bring about repairs, cost being the big issue:

> I looked all over the inside of the building and found the rooms in great need of repairs. All of them needed painting, and that right away before being occupied. I also found many of the rooms sadly in need of papering. I went through the halls and found the floors nearly worn out, and in such a condition that I said to myself, "These shall be put in new before another month goes by."[25]

Emmons also found the windows to be in bad shape—their putty falling out and their panes rattling in the wind, admitting much cold air. [26]

Apparently Emmons got things going very quickly because just two weeks after this article appeared in *Our Hope*, President Clum wrote an article for that newspaper to update people on what had been done so far and what remained to be done in the project to repair and redecorate the college building. The list of accomplishments, after just two weeks of work, is impressive:

—Maple floors were laid in the "school-room," chapel, and hallways of the first and second floors.
—Worn step coverings on one staircase were replaced.
—The chapel was enlarged by nearly a third (by removing a partition and enclosing part of the hall)
—The "boys" (presumably the male students) worked on six to seven rooms—removing the old calcimine from the walls and ceilings, filling nail holes, restoring walls with water damage from the leaking roof or damage from hard and long use, and sizing the walls—all in preparation for the paper hangers.
—Some rooms were painted.
—A new roof was installed.

A few jobs remained to be done as of the writing of Clum's article—painting and wallpapering more rooms as well as painting hallways and floors. (Those jobs were to be performed by the students in order to save money for the college.) But a lot had been accomplished in a few weeks. Even if the decision to do this work had been made a week or so before Emmons's article in *Our Hope*, to have this much done in two to three weeks was stunningly fast and totally uncharacteristic of how quickly other improvements over the years got done. The big problem was always raising the money to make any changes in the physical plant. There is no indication of where the money came from for some of this work. However, during campmeeting, several individuals pledged to put a new floor in a room or porch; donations came in for paint, wallpaper, and repairs; and five churches each pledged to furnish a student room. And after campmeeting, a couple pledged to pay $80 for a new roof. However, two other improvements remained to be done, and these jobs *did* require some fundraising: replacing windows in the college building and buying new chairs for the chapel.[27]

To help in the campaign to raise funds for new windows, J. W. Emmons wrote to a number of people personally to ask them to cover the cost of a window, which was $3.50. He also urged Adventists, any and all Adventists whether of great or limited means, to pay for the cost of one window. In one fundraising article in *Our Hope*, Emmons urged people simply to say, "I will do it," which is a quotation from a woman of modest means who made the decision to give the $3.50. And he promised that he would draw up a list of the people who gave money to buy a window and then frame it and hang it in the main hall of the college building's first floor for all to see. This fundraising technique is, of course, still used today by Aurora University and many other institutions and organizations.[28]

In asking for money for new windows, the college leaders referred to them as "memorial windows." Apparently, this caused some confusion among enough Adventists to motivate one of the fundraisers to write an article for *Our Hope* in which he tried to clarify what was meant by the word "memorial." It seems that some people read it as meaning that Mendota College was raising money for "an *unnecessary expense* to put in some kind of a merely *ornamental* window in the college in memory of some friend, living or dead."[29] One of these confused persons had even written *Our Hope* about the memorial windows, saying that it was "idolatry and hero-worship."[30] An unidentified author, probably the editor, explained that "the memorial windows are simply new window sash of modern style, replacing the old sash, which were many of them worn and broken, and *needed replacing*. They are called 'memorial windows' because each one thus given will serve as a memorial of its giver or of someone in whose name it may be donated."[31] That appears to have settled the matter, but this incident illustrates what college leaders were up against when trying to raise money for improvements. At least some Adventists were quick to criticize what they thought were unnecessary, frivolous, or religiously suspect changes. Cost was certainly an issue for such people, but there often seemed to be a religious critique in their protests, like the person who viewed memorial windows as being idolatrous.

A month after the repairing-redecorating project began in September of 1895, another fundraising campaign was launched to purchase new chairs for the college chapel. Ninety-one chairs were needed for a total cost of $75. To raise this amount, Emmons came up with a clever fundraising idea:

> We will say that I buy three chairs ... and give them to our college for the chapel room, with the proviso that when we go to campmeeting, I shall be entitled to use those chairs during the campmeeting. There will be a record kept at the college, of all who have bought chairs, and when they go to campmeeting they can go to the college clerk and draw the number of chairs that they have bought. ... I will arrange to have the names of those who buy these chairs, plainly lettered on the back of the chairs each one furnishes. Then each one will know his or her chair anywhere, and this will also show who the donors are.[32]

So under this plan, not only could donors be altruistic, but there also was something in it for them—their very own guaranteed chair for campmeeting week.[33]

President Clum explained why new chairs (and additional chairs) were needed in the chapel so badly:

> There are about two and a half dozen common wooden chairs—the same that were used in the dining room at campmeeting, and also

two of the long campmeeting benches. Whenever there is a demand for more chairs they must be carried in from the commercial department, down stairs and from the recitation rooms and students' dormitories. Since we have enlarged the chapel there are not near chairs enough to seat it. Every time there is any special meeting the chairs must be gathered from every room in the college, thus causing much labor, besides the rough usage of the chairs.[34]

The president also could have added what Emmons, and probably many other people at the college, thought—that to attract and keep students, the college needed to provide a pleasant, comfortable, well-equipped, living and working environment.[35] In an *Our Hope* article, Emmons elaborated on Clum's point that chairs were needed now that the chapel had been expanded.

This is the only room in the institution that can be used for lectures or meetings of any kind, when there is a necessity for seating more than twenty-five persons. It is absolutely necessary to have a room that will seat at least one hundred; and such a room will be used and well filled many times during the college term. The work of the college has been seriously crippled by not having a room that would accommodate a fair audience. The chapel room has been enlarged during the course of repairs, neatly painted and papered, and now all it needs is to be well seated.[36]

The lack of a space that could hold large groups of people on campus for special events—like Commencement, lectures, student programs, etc.—would remain a problem for the rest of the Mendota years. The expansion of the chapel certainly helped but did not solve the problem. Commencement continued to be held at the Mendota Advent Christian Church, as did other Mendota College events that drew a large number of people. The chapel was enlarged in 1895, but in 1902, a student, after attending a student recital held in the chapel, wrote: "Few friends can be invited to the college because there is not room in the chapel to seat many. We hope that in a day not far distant Mendota College will be housed in buildings that are better adjusted to school purposes."[37]

In the end, more than enough money was raised. The windows were replaced, and before winter set in. And they provided a bonus—additional light. One student reporter wrote that "being only two lights to a window they afford a perceptible increase of light, besides having a much neater and more modern appearance."[38] All the needed chairs were purchased as well. Emmons urged people to send in their pledged money for new chapel seating, even if more money came in than was needed to buy the ninety-one chairs, because the extra money could be used to improve other rooms. And he promised that people who had sent in what turned out to be surplus funds for the windows would be contacted to ask them what project they would like to put their money toward.[39]

Emmons expressed appreciation for how quickly money was raised and projects completed and then added:

> I shall ever bless the day when I first stepped on the Mendota College campus. Never was there more necessity for immediate action than there was to put Mendota College in a condition fit for occupancy. Never were our people more interested in the welfare of the institution than at this time. I am fully persuaded that as a people we are determined that our college *shall be a success*; and that failure shall never be written on its doors [italics in original].[40]

In another *Our Hope* article, Emmons wrote what was hinted at in this quotation—that the renovation project benefited the *donors* of the funds as well as the *recipients* of the funds. This argument would be used time and time again in Mendota College's history. College leaders believed that people who donated money to the school would have greater ties to and interest in the college, another belief that colleges hold today. And the faculty and students would feel renewed and more hopeful. There also was a behavioral dimension to putting the college building back into good shape. As President Clum argued, "When everything is old, worn out and dirty, habits of carelessness are easily acquired. On the other hand when everything is neat, clean and tasty, carefulness is sure to follow. These improvements will end in culture and refinement as much as in comfort and pleasure."[41] This was a take on the adage that "cleanliness is next to godliness" and reflected the belief that when you provide people with pleasant surroundings, they will behave in a more civilized, refined way.[42]

One seemingly minor change also was made to the college in 1895, although it, no doubt, was *not* minor to the students. Someone donated a bathtub to the dormitory—apparently the school's *first*. Emmons's description of it makes clear that it was not what we would think of as a bathtub. In an *Our Hope* article, Emmons stated: "It is a first-class portable bath-tub, which heats its own water with gasoline at the rate of twenty gallons in the same number of minutes. The tub is made of the best tin-lined copper plate. It folds up into a cabinet and can be set into one corner of the room, or it can be set so it will be stationary and connect with the sewer."[43] However primitive such a tub seems to twenty-first-century people, it was definitely an upgrade from washing oneself using a bowl and pitcher, and with cold water, or using a metal tub to which gallons of water, heated on a cook stove, had to be carried. In 1895, many, if not most, Americans would never have seen such a tub as the one that Emmons described.[44]

Another household necessity that was even more urgent than a bathtub was a stove for the college kitchen. A new stove was desperately needed in 1900, given all the cooking it had to do, for both students and campmeeting attendees. The college bought a commercial-grade stove for $125, which was acquired fairly quickly, in about three to four weeks, although it was not completely paid for in that time. However, the school was not able to simply recognize this need and then buy a replacement. It had to ask for donors to supply the necessary funds. As proof of the hard use that the 1900 stove received, just four years later it needed some new parts, including a new top. Although this clearly was a fairly urgent matter, it took *five months* for someone to step forward and purchase a new top for the old stove. Here, as with so many things, the college ultimately got what it needed to function, but it often took time, patience, and a can-do attitude, because money had to be raised for even the most mundane items.[45]

Ten years later, in 1905, it was time for another round of improvements, especially on the exterior. The biggest project was painting the college building. This was desperately needed because the last time it had been painted was 1892, thirteen years earlier and the year the property had been purchased for the college. The college had begun a campaign to raise money for painting the college building the previous year, but then it was thought more prudent to delay the painting project because the roof so badly needed to be replaced. By 1905, with a new roof installed, college leaders thought it time to return to the fundraising campaign for tuck-pointing and painting the college building. It was painted a dark, brick-red color, while the window frames and porch pillars were painted white. Other architectural elements, like the window caps, sills, and cornice were painted a color that was not named, but was said to be "different and appropriate."[46] It was customary for buildings in the Victorian era to be painted in more than one or two colors, so this was in keeping with the times, although it was probably more expensive to do that.[47]

Generally, painting a four-story building is, and must have been then, fairly expensive, but the college managed to get it done as inexpensively as possible because every penny counted. The painting job cost considerably less than if the college had contracted the job out, because the people who were doing it were Mendota people. The job was under the direction of Bro. J. E. Derham, who was a painter and had been a supporter of Mendota College from its beginning. He was helped by D. J. Costly, a current Mendota College student who was also a painter. The cost of painting the college building was around $254, with the college probably getting about $15 back by returning unused paint. As inexpensive as it was, it represented a large amount of money for Mendota College, which had to raise every penny of this amount.[48]

Once again, the college turned to Advent Christians, especially those who subscribed to *Our Hope*. One article in the newspaper made it clear how dependent the college was on the Advent Christian people to keep the college up and running in a satisfactory way: "All are aware that the maintenance of our school comes directly upon our people. We have no surplus funds, and if we take money from the educational funds to paint the building we must replace it later. The better way is thought to be to invite donations, with the understanding that any surplus will be turned over to the college funds."[49] Ultimately, enough money was raised among the Adventists. What must have been the largest donation came from the Helpers' Union—an Advent Christian women's group created to raise money for and donate gifts to Mendota College. These women raised $80 for the painting project, one of many major contributions that they made to the college over the nineteen years of its existence.[50]

Campus Tour, 1902–1903

About ten years after the college opened, Ophelia Bennett, a prominent supporter of Mendota College and a soon-to-be member of the college's Board of Education, decided that she would "attempt ... a 'free hand' pen picture"[51] of Mendota College for those who had never been there. She, too, made a point of mentioning the beauty of the campus, describing it as a "college campus of lofty trees, with a winding path, leading to a good sized four story brick building, in the center of a broad grassy block. It is a pleasant spot even in winter, but when the trees are out in full foliage it is a most cool, refreshing place."[52]

In her description of the campus, however, she noted the presence of something that the purchasers of the Mendota property would not have seen—the college cow—which grazed on the school's large lawn. In April 1901, the board "voted that Dr. Emmons buy a cow for the college boarding house."[53] Emmons, rather than buying a cow with the school's precious dollars right away, sent out a request, via an *Our Hope article*, asking if anyone among the readers would be willing to donate a cow to the College Boarding Club. Clearly, financial considerations were behind this request. Emmons wrote that "it [the cow] would be gratefully received, and the boarding club would have milk enough at less than one-half the expense and yet have twice as much milk to use. ... We have grass enough on the ground by mowing it to keep a cow, and also a stable to keep her in. It would be a saving of about $80 per year to have a good cow."[54] It is unknown whether someone donated a cow or Emmons had to buy one, but it is certain that by the next year, and probably before, the college had its very own cow because of Bennett's mentioning it in her description of the campus: "All feel a great regard for the good old college cow. ... If we had plenty of money we would have a fence built around the north half of the grounds for the benefit of the cow. We think she would do better, and the fence would save much running for some one. She is staked out whenever the pasture is good, and has been a great help and convenience to the college boarding department."[55] This experiment of having a college cow must have been a successful one because, in 1906, the board authorized a board member to acquire another one. Finally, in the spring of 1910, Bennett's wish for a fence for the college cow became a reality when the board voted to fence the empty lot where once had stood the women's dormitory (even though by this time, it was clear that the college would soon be relocating to another town). These college cows, without a doubt, played an important role at perennially cash-strapped Mendota College and apparently were well loved.[56]

Bennett not only described the campus but went on to give a verbal tour of the college building, the women's dormitory, and even off-campus housing. These tours were presented in seven articles for *Our Hope*, in which she described what she saw so that readers who had never visited the college would get a better feel for it. It is fortunate that she did this; not only is it the only room-by-room description of the college building that exists, but she did it right in the middle of the Mendota era, after the biggest changes had been made to the campus (the major remodeling of 1895, the acquisition of the new women's dormitory that replaced the one that burned down, etc.).

Upon entering the first floor of the south-facing college building, under the front porch, one encountered the rooms used by the Commercial Department—the two rooms in front. These were probably not the best classrooms in the building, being in what was, in effect, a raised basement, but the commercial courses were clearly secondary to the Bible Training School. Behind these two front rooms, to the northwest, were three rooms for cooking, and, to the northeast, the dining room. This room had two long tables, which together seated around thirty people. This kind of seating, as opposed to many separate small tables, not only saved space but promoted conversation among more people. A student reported at the beginning of the 1897–98 school year that the dining room had moved into the basement/ground floor of the Old Main. His explanation for this was that "this change saves extra expense for house rent, as well as making it more convenient for the students, as they will not have to leave the building for their meals."[57] (This young man seems to have momentarily forgotten that women also attended the school, because what he said in this quotation was true only for the male students. The female students never lived in the college building. Their dormitories were always off campus, so they had to walk to the dining hall, no matter what the weather.) It is not known exactly where the cooking/dining facilities were located before this move, other than in some house.

Moving the dining hall to the college building must have squeezed further what were already tight quarters there.[58]

The next tour was of the second floor—the first one that was completely above ground. Because the first, or basement, floor was raised, entering the building required a rather sizable staircase. Bennett noted that the front staircase had recently been rebuilt. The new one was different in that it had a landing halfway up, where there was a trap door that opened to reveal a baptistery for use at campmeeting and at other times. (Advent Christians practiced adult baptism via total immersion in water, using baptisteries in churches or other buildings and even lakes and rivers, especially at campmeetings.) Having ascended one high staircase, upon entering the front door, one encountered a good-sized hall with another staircase leading to the two upper floors.[59]

At the front of the second floor, to the immediate right, was a large room where the Bible Training School resided. Students must have enjoyed a lot of light in this room because it faced both south and east, with two windows on each wall. Behind the Bible Training School room, to the north, was the college museum, containing many artifacts of nature, like stuffed birds and animals, fossils, minerals, and the like, for use in studying the scientific world. At the front of the building, to the left, was the library. It, too, was a bright and sunny room, with its two windows on each wall facing south and west. Due to a lack of space, the library was a multifunctional room, serving as both a classroom and a meeting room. To the north, behind the library, were three small rooms where Mrs. Clark, head of the Boarding Department, and her son lived.[60]

On the third floor, in the northwest corner of the building, was the music room. Bennett wrote this charming description of it: "This room is of good size, lighted by west and north windows having green shades, and white sash curtains. The floor is carpeted, and a stove, table, chairs, and pictures on the walls make it comfortable and pleasant. The piano in one corner does not stand there simply for ornament. ... As you enter the building snatches of melody greet your ear, that make the walls seem gayer and put a refreshing, lively feeling into your veins."[61]

Directly over the library, in front of the music room was the south- and west-facing, sunny chapel, which contained folding chairs and an organ. Like the library, the chapel had to be multifunctional. Using folding chairs—the ones purchased in 1895—made it easier to remove and store the chairs for those times when the room had uses other than religious services or performances. Among its many uses were a late-morning chapel service, held every weekday; an evening prayer meeting, held every weekday; the Literary Society meeting, held every Friday afternoon; many open meetings of various sorts; and the Physical Culture class. In other words, the chapel was always being used, and its size was inadequate for these activities. One student noted: "It is quite well filled when all the students are seated. So when friends are invited many of the students are obliged to accommodate themselves as best they can in the hall or music room adjoining."[62] One sad note was that hanging on the wall of the chapel was a picture of Herman Corliss, the first student to die at Mendota College. He had died around two years before this tour was taken. This is further evidence of the strong bonds in this community (as well as, perhaps, the Victorian sentimentalization of and obsession with death).[63]

Directly across from the chapel was the Ames Laboratory, facing south and east. This laboratory provided students with a place where they could actually conduct chemistry experiments rather than just read about the science. The lab was created in 1896, shortly after Emmons asked President Clum what the college needed. Clum replied that, aside from students, it needed a "chemical laboratory," which would cost at least $100. The president asked some people he knew, the Ames brothers—Zimri and Marsden Ames, of Rutland, Illinois—who were capable and, hopefully, agreeable to providing the requisite $100. They were, and the necessary equipment and supplies were quickly ordered, just a few weeks after Emmons had asked the president about the college's needs. And just a year later, the Ames brothers furnished the capital to set up a "physical laboratory." Space for this was found by removing the wall between the chemical laboratory and the room behind it, thus creating a sixteen-by-eighteen-foot room that was large enough to accommodate a combined chemical and physical laboratory. Given how important the Bible Training School was to the college and the lack of extra space in the college building, this allotment of both funds and space to a discipline that was part of the classical curriculum but was *not* needed for a degree from the theological arm of the college, is impressive.[64]

At least two more spaces were on the third floor. Behind the laboratory, facing north and east, was located what was called the "recitation room." This was the term used for what is called a classroom today. The word "recitation" gives insight into the prevailing teaching method of the day. In good part, class sessions consisted of students reciting facts about the course material. And at the end of the third-floor hall was a storeroom. Bennett noted that "not even the ends of the halls here are permitted to go unoccupied or of no use."[65] The lack of space in the college building was a common theme, brought up by students and faculty alike, time and time again throughout the Mendota years.[66]

The college building had a fourth floor, but it was the men's dormitory. This, along with the women's dormitory—a college-owned, off-campus house with house parents—and off-campus housing, is discussed in chapter seven, on student life.

A Tornado Hits Mendota and the College Campus, 1903

Mendota, of course, is located in Illinois and so, as a midwestern town, it was and is vulnerable to tornado strikes during its hot, humid summers. In July of 1903, a serious one hit Mendota, and in the northern part of town, where the college was located and many Advent Christians lived. It struck on Friday, July 17, at about 5:20 in the evening, delivering a blow to the campus and especially its surrounding area. A few days later, an article in *Our Hope* described it like this:

> Its path was narrow, perhaps two or three hundred feet in width. ... In a very few minutes all was over and twenty or more residences were either completely demolished or badly shattered, besides many barns and outbuildings. Mendota College was almost or quite in the path of the storm but was not seriously damaged. The chimneys were blown off, the cupola partly demolished, and many windows shattered, but the building itself appears uninjured, except the breaking loose of an inside partition in the upper story. The campus suffered severely and the trees were badly broken and blown down.[67]

It was immediately evident that the college building had suffered some damage, but it remained standing. However, the land was another story. The most obvious damage was that many, if not most, of the beautiful, large shade trees on the campus were completely broken or badly damaged. In effect, the tornado (or cyclone as it was called at the time) essentially destroyed the bucolic, park-like setting that so many had commented on and enjoyed for ten years and that had provided a lovely setting for the campmeeting every summer. It would take many years to grow trees to the luxuriant size and lushness of the trees that had been destroyed.[68]

After the overall campus was assessed, a more detailed list of the damages to both the college building and other parts of the property was provided:

—More than fifty large panes of window glass were shattered.
—The cupola and roof of the college building were damaged.
—All the chimneys were blown down.
—The kitchen roof was damaged by the falling chimneys.
—The storehouse was seriously damaged.
—The barn and the outhouse were destroyed.

However, in spite of this substantial damage, it could have been so much worse. The college building was not flattened, and no one at the school was killed or seriously injured. [69]

The same cannot be said for the rest of the neighborhood. Seemingly all around the campus, houses were destroyed or severely damaged. More importantly, four people in Mendota were killed, including a nineteen-year-old woman who was a member of the Mendota Advent Christian Church. Around twelve people were severely injured, including a woman who also was a member of the Mendota church. Many others in Mendota were injured, but less seriously. An estimated $100,000 in damage was done. Seventeen buildings were destroyed, while fifty were damaged. And in the town as a whole, it also could have been much worse. Many people were saved because they had gone to their cellars, where they would not have been had the storm hit during the middle of the night. And the storm would have caused even more damage, and probably even more injuries and loss of life, had the tornado set down in the southern end of town, where the downtown was located.[70]

Some members of the Mendota Advent Christian Church were seriously impacted by the tornado, probably because a number of them lived in the college neighborhood, where the church was located as well. Although many more houses were hit than those of Advent Christians, this is what happened to some church members:

—One church member, Samuel Wilson, who lived just across the street from the college, lost everything—his house, barn, and outbuildings.

—A house next to Wilson, that of Louis Richard, was turned on its side. The family was unhurt, as they were in the basement.

—S. G. Baker lost his barn and a portion of his house roof.

—Brother Cowell's house was moved off its foundation, by six to eight feet, and his barn was destroyed.

—Brother Emery had his barn roll away across the street, coming to rest partly on the grass and partly in the road.

—The Boisdorf house, barn, and outbuildings were all blown away, and the fifteen-year-old daughter in the family was killed.

—The Wirschem home was completely destroyed, and Ora Lundy was instantly killed as a result.

—F. E. Roberts, a student at the college, lived in a small apartment with his family. During the storm, Roberts, his family, and a couple of neighbors were sheltering in the apartment's living room when the entire house blew into pieces. Miraculously no one there died or was even seriously injured. An *Our Hope* article reported that, for the Roberts family and their neighbors, "the shock came, the house left its foundations, there was a moment in which all expected death, and then they found themselves crawling out of a pile of rubbish, scratched and bruised, but not seriously injured."[71] Elder F. A. Baker (minister of the Mendota Advent Christian Church and principal of the Bible Training School) took in Roberts and his family, bringing them to his home to stay until they could find housing.[72]

Immediately after the storm, people leapt into action to help their friends, neighbors, and fellow Mendotans. There were immediate needs to tend to that evening—finding food and housing, for at least the next few days and perhaps weeks, for the people who had just lost everything. There was no federal emergency agency to rush in with aid. Mendotans had to take care of their own, and they did. Since only a part of town was hit severely, those who were outside the tornado's path were able to help their less-fortunate townspeople. After the storm victims' needs for immediate food, shelter, and clothing were met, Mendotans turned to the task of helping their fellow citizens rebuild. A relief committee was created and ultimately $10,200 was raised for repairs and rebuilding. The local effort went beyond that, however. Many people donated in-kind gifts—workers who gave days of their labor, dealers of various sorts who sold supplies just at cost, and people who donated furniture and clothing. In short, they did everything they could to get people back on their feet and provided for before winter set in. One member of the relief committee wrote that "the last thing we did was to put groceries, potatoes, and cured meat enough in each house to last them till spring."[73] Even a railroad got involved. It bought a number of houses and sold them to the relief committee at bargain prices—for just $125 and up. The houses were measured, as were the foundations of houses that had blown up. Then the two were matched up, and a local house mover transported the houses onto foundations at a special, low rate.[74]

Others, many of them Advent Christians who lived elsewhere, also quickly rushed to help. In the first *Our Hope* issue following the tornado, an article on the disaster ended by asking its readers to send household goods and clothing to Mendota to help those whose houses and possessions were destroyed. The Mendota Church's Helpers' Union was put in charge of collecting the items and seeing that they were properly distributed to the needy. People responded quickly with help. By the time the next *Our Hope* issue came out, just a week after the July 22 request for aid, nearly $5,000 had been raised toward a goal of $10,000, and many household goods had been donated to the victims of the storm. And a few weeks later, some Advent Christians brought goods for the tornado victims with them when they came to Mendota to attend campmeeting.[75]

The college needed financial aid as well. What was called the Emergency Fund was set up to help the college recover. Although the campus suffered minor damage compared to the utter destruction around it, the damage was such that college officials determined that $1,000 would be needed immediately to repair the damage. The campaign to raise funds for repairs was kicked off, less than two weeks after the tornado hit, when the following appeared in the July 29 issue of *Our Hope*: "In view of the emergency caused by the recent tornado at Mendota, Ill., and as a thank-offering to God that our college building, and young ladies' dormitory have been spared us, and many precious lives that were in great peril were marvelously preserved, we whose names are appended pledge as a special contribution to be used to repair the damage by the storm upon the college property."[76] Six names were listed as donors who had already given to this fund, and the article asked that others contribute as well. For the rest of the summer and beyond, *Our Hope* listed the names of people who had donated to the fund and what they had given.[77]

Although no one at the school was killed or seriously injured and the college building was not flattened, the college community was hit hard—not just by the loss of its beautiful trees but by the loss of life, serious injuries, and substantial destruction of property experienced by its immediate neighbors and fellow members of the Mendota Advent Christian Church. In fact, given the amount of devastation all around it, it was nothing short of a miracle that the campus survived as well as it did. The people at the school realized this and thanked God for their deliverance. A few weeks later, an article in *Our Hope* expressed their thankfulness: "How easily our college building might have become a heap of ruins. This would probably have stopped our educational work, perhaps permanently. But our college is intact and we trust not seriously damaged. Had this storm come four weeks later, during our campmeeting, what a disaster it would have been and what a terrible blow!"[78] Not only had the tornado *not* hit during campmeeting week, when tents (many of them located near or under the campus's large trees) were used for sleeping, dining, and holding meetings, but had the campus and college building been destroyed, the school would have suffered a severe, and perhaps fatal, blow. And such a blow would have been delivered to the college just a year and a half after the president's home/women's dormitory had burned down. The school's finances were always fragile, so coming back from two such closely spaced events of total destruction would have been difficult, if not impossible.[79]

Advent Christians Move to Mendota

Advent Christians contributed to the town of Mendota in another way—by moving there. A number of Advent Christian families moved to Mendota after the college and church were established. It is not possible to know how many people uprooted themselves, but there is some evidence of this in *Our Hope* articles. They often were the parents of students at the college. As early as 1895, it was reported in an *Our Hope* article that the college "has brought to the town several very fine and substantial families, who have purchased property and made it their permanent home, in order to place their children in school without sending them away from home. This has greatly aided in building up a strong church. ..."[80]

Over the years, both the college and church tried to persuade Advent Christians to move to Mendota. In 1897, a piece in *Our Hope* urged retirees to come: "Many of our people all over the West are retiring from their farms and moving into town. Why not move to Mendota? It would help strengthen the work there, and give to you privileges you will find in no other western town; and then our General Western Campmeeting will come to you every year."[81] Two years later, an article making a plea for students also sent out a special invitation for Advent Christians to move to Mendota: "Our church and college both need the help and encouragement that a few more Adventist families could afford. Our numbers are small, and we are not strong enough to sustain a pastor and afford to our education work the resident care that is needed."[82] And as late as 1908, Advent Christians were still being urged to move to Mendota to support the Adventist mission: "We must rally around the work directly conducive to the Advent Message. Mendota College is such a work."[83] The author then went on to say what Adventists' duties to the college were—sending their children to the college rather than to "worldly" schools and even moving their family to Mendota to join in the church and college work, saying that at least twenty families were needed to do this. Urging people to move to Mendota was one thing, but saying that it was people's "duty" to come was another. That sounds a bit like desperation, and somewhat puzzling in that, by 1908, complaints about the campus and the town were growing.

It appears that not only the college but the church, and even the town, *really* wanted and needed other Advent Christians to come to Mendota. The church, created by the college people when the school was founded, was small and dependent on the college for its members. To become more independent, it needed members from the larger, noncollege, Mendota community. It was not entirely successful in this in that, after the college moved to Aurora, the church remained small and struggling. However, the church did continue to exist for about one hundred years after 1912, so clearly it drew in some Mendotans. And the fact that the college brought people beyond its students and faculty to town was good for Mendota as well, and the town knew it. More people were good for business, in that more goods, services, and houses would be sold. It was also good for the town's civic events and cultural organizations, which needed all the support they could get, given Mendota's small size. And as noted earlier, Mendotans viewed the people that the college and church brought to town as being both intellectual and morally upright—exactly the kind of people they wanted.[84]

A Constant Lack of Space

When the Mendota campus was purchased, the main college building seemed adequate to the needs of a fledgling school and even the headquarters of WACPA, along with the annual Advent Christian campmeeting. However, WACPA's residency in the college building was incredibly short-lived. Just two and a half months after the college opened on January 9, the Educational Committee (the early name for the college board) ordered that the business staff and editor of *Our Hope* leave the college building because the school needed the rooms on the third floor. After leaving the college campus, the publication association rented rooms in buildings in various downtown Mendota locations until it built its own building in 1906–7, also in downtown Mendota. This removal of the WACPA offices from the college building so soon was indicative of the space problem the college would have throughout its years in Mendota.[85]

Just a year after the college was founded, an editor of *Our Hope* noted that the college was already outgrowing its space: "Our College building is getting too small for the work which we can easily see is before us. Although it has formerly accommodated more students than we now have, it was because other buildings were then occupied which are not now available. We shall soon have to plan to enlarge our quarters in order to take care of the pupils who seek our instruction. It is none too early to begin to think of this and pray over it."[86] And just a few months later, an *Our Hope* article noted that the main college building had so many people in it already that a boarding house adjoining it or a new wing might be necessary in the near future, if someone would provide the requisite funds.[87]

Everyone, including students, board members, and visitors, realized that space was a problem. In 1902, a student wrote that not many people could be invited to attend a program at the college because the chapel, which did double duty as a performance space, could seat so few people. It was clear by 1908, and probably before, that the college needed more space for everything—for classrooms, dormitories, and dining. In 1909, a college board member informed *Our Hope* readers that "Mendota College has outgrown its present quarters."[88] (Given how long the Mendota College community had been struggling with the issue of space, many a college person must have found this comment to be a bit of an understatement.) This same board member had also stated this two years earlier, but in stronger words: "The growth of the college urgently demands a doubling of the room and facilities of the school."[89] Even visitors could see the problem, especially if they were attending events on campus. One woman, after attending Commencement, wrote a very positive article about the college for *Our* Hope, urging young people to come and attend the college. But, supporter of the college that she was, even she noted the school's need for more space. People visiting the college to attend Commencement and the College Day programs especially saw this problem, because any event that drew a large number of people always had to be held in the Mendota Advent

Christian Church. There was simply no place to have an audience of any significant size. By at least 1906, there is evidence in *Our Hope* that people were throwing around various ideas about how to expand the college's facilities—among them, doubling the size of the *Our Hope* building that was being constructed downtown so that the college could have an annex there and putting up a new building on the campus. Neither happened, of course, and the college kept spinning its wheels, probably for lack of funds.[90]

The college building was never really adequate. The faculty and student body grew over time, but even in the college's last full year in Mendota (1910–11), both faculty and students were few in number—13 faculty members and 104 students. And yet, throughout the Mendota years, space remained a concern. College officials improved the college building, inside and out—painting the interior and exterior, wallpapering rooms, getting new furniture and rugs, and rebuilding the front, exterior staircase. They reworked spaces to make them more functional and used many rooms for multiple functions. Still, there was not enough space or good functionality, either for daily activities or for large gatherings. And the quality of the facilities, in what space there was, was not great either. More books, more and better laboratories, better-equipped classrooms, among other things, were needed. By the time the controversy was ignited over whether the college should move to another town or remain in Mendota, even those who advocated staying knew that at least one additional building had to be constructed. The inadequacies of the college building and campus would be the major factor that drove the college to another location—Aurora, Illinois.[91]

Postscript: Selling the College Campus

Once the decision to move the college to Aurora was made, a new problem arose for the board to wrestle with—what to do with the Mendota campus. In 1912, the building, now fifty-five years old, was long past its prime and lacked some modern amenities. Who would buy such an old-fashioned property in a small, farming community? The answer to that question at first seemed to be "no one." Then, in 1913, a group of Mendotans purchased the property, intending to put a hospital on the site. However, for some unknown reason, the hospital never materialized at this location. But fortunately for the college, the property had been sold. It was then someone else's problem. In 1916, Mendota's citizens voted to build a consolidated high school building on the former site of Mendota College. The college building itself was purchased by George Moore & Co. for $250. Moore prepared the way for the new high school by razing the old college building. He took its bricks, which were then used to build houses in Mendota. Interestingly, B. J. Dean, former president of Mendota College, had decided not to move with the school to Aurora, instead becoming principal of Mendota's high school (1913–17). He then presided over the new high school, which had been built on the campus of the college that he had once led. Thus, in a sense, the legacy, history, and influence of Mendota College lived on through him for a few more years.[92]

A Close-up of the Main College Building in Spring

Gardening on the Campus — Probably by Students

The Destruction of the Park-like Setting of the Mendota College Campus after the 1903 Tornado

College Park

Aerial View of the Devastation on the Mendota College Campus after the 1903 Tornado

Aerial View of Downtown Mendota and its Rail Lines

Chapter 5
The Intertwining of Academics and Religion

"We pray constantly the Lord of the harvest to send forth more laborers into his harvest. Does he not do it? Yes, he does, but he leaves the training of the laborers to us. He calls them into the work, we must equip them and send them forth."

—Our Hope and Life in Christ

A Class in the College's Commercial Department

At Mendota College, general academics and religion were inextricably intertwined. To discuss the academic side of the school, one *must* also discuss religion—the Bible Training School (hereafter referred to as BTS) of course, but also all the ways that religion shaped the experiences of teaching at and attending the college. This religious emphasis included many things beyond academics—daily student prayer meetings, daily chapel, students serving in various churches as substitute preachers, faculty and students participating in the Mendota Advent Christian Church, and college people preparing for and participating in the Great Western Advent Christian Campmeeting, held on the Mendota College campus for a week each August. Even courses that seemed to have little to do with religion were sometimes rationalized by showing students the religious implications and how they would help future pastors.

The school's *first* name, Mendota Seminary, reveals the major reason the school was founded. Its original and always primary purpose was to prepare future ministers and other Christian workers for Advent Christian churches and mission fields. Just two months after the college arrived in Aurora, President Jenks wrote that "our school stands for aggressive evangelistic work and for the proclamation of the message of the Advent Christian people in all the world."[1] This was not a new idea; in the end, that was always what Mendota College was about.

Yet the name "Mendota Seminary" was short-lived. On March 23, 1893, just two and a half months after the school opened, the Educational Committee (later known as the Board of Directors) changed the institution's name to Mendota College. The committee's minutes indicate that President Campbell initiated the change, but no explanation was provided for why it was done. In August 1893, a report from the Educational Committee gave one explanation: "In view of the fact that this is an age of education and that we are surrounded by educational institutions with which we must compete, and in order to be successful, it was the judgment of your committee that the course of study should be advanced and enlarged as per the present curriculum for 1893–94 ... and that the name should be changed from seminary to college."[2] This explanation emphasizes broadening the school's curriculum because of the increased importance of education in a modern age and to compete more effectively with other schools.[3]

Those are sound reasons, but it could also be argued that the most important reason was finances. The education and competition ideas were just as obvious when the school was named "Mendota Seminary" a few months earlier. What changed, however, was that the school had opened, and administrators must have already seen how difficult the finances of the school would be. It was probably not a coincidence that the same report that mentioned the name change also mentioned this: "After the opening of the school it very soon became apparent that a commercial department was not only a necessity but would be a decided advantage. It was therefore added to the institution. ... There was also a strong demand for instruction upon the violin and banjo. To meet this demand Miss M.R. Fuller was engaged as teacher."[4] School leaders recognized that there was a demand for commercial and musical courses, but this was not a demand that a seminary would generally feel compelled to meet. The critical word in this quotation is "necessity." A broader curriculum would bring in more students, many of them local young people wanting to take some practical courses, and more students meant greater financial support for the institution.

Preparation for a New College

After many months of on-and-off discussion dating back to 1889, the Western Advent Christian Publication Association (hereafter referred to as WACPA) acquired the Mendota campus in February 1892. Although it had taken years after the first proposal for a college was made, once the property was acquired, things happened quickly—perhaps too quickly. It is a great endeavor to start a school of any kind, requiring much money and long-term planning. When it opened its doors on January 9, 1893, Mendota College was not even close to being ready, certainly by today's standards and probably even by the standards of 1893.

There was minimal preparation before the opening of the school—both academic and financial. It was not until the August 1892 meeting of WACPA that its Educational Committee, which had been created just the previous month, was "instructed to at once begin the preliminary work for the establishment of an academical and theological Seminary at the place already named,"[5] and it also was stated "that the said Seminary begin its work as soon as the necessary funds are raised for its support."[6] Whether said money would actually materialize was unknown at the time. *Less* than *three weeks* before the opening date of January 9, 1893, school leaders were saying that the college might not open unless it had enough money. And the president was not even hired until November 14—just two months before the school's opening.[7]

The lack of preparation is also evident in the curriculum. Clearly, much of the curriculum was developed *after* the college opened. The coursework laid out in the first catalog is skeletal and quite different from that in succeeding catalogs. The Commercial Department did not begin its courses until a month later, on February 9. The Bible Training School did not exist at all in January of 1893. An Advent Christian minister was hired in November 1892, for just a term of six months, his job being to draw up plans for the Bible school, which then opened in late June of 1893, two terms after the opening of the college. And there was no library. That had to be built gradually over time, as donations, both financial and in kind, allowed. In March of 1893, a call went out in *Our Hope*, asking people to donate books to start a college library.[8]

This lack of preparation was not unintended. At the August 1892 WACPA meeting mentioned earlier, delegates passed a resolution which admitted their desire to put speed before preparation, resolving "that this society purpose to build this Seminary up and improve it as fast as the means may be provided, not attempting to begin with a fully equipped college necessitating a costly endowment fund for its support."[9] The founders felt a religious call to do this, and as quickly as possible, so academic and financial preparation was secondary. This rush to open as quickly as possible reflected their belief that Christ's return was near and the urgent need of Advent Christian churches for ministers. However, this rush to open did not provide a substantial foundation for the fledging school.

The Preparatory Department

In nineteenth- and early-twentieth-century America, public schooling was often inferior in quality and sometimes even nonexistent beyond the elementary grades, depending on where one lived and one's socioeconomic level. Leaving school prematurely was another problem. Quitting school to help support one's family, provide labor on the family farm, or help with an ill family member was a common occurrence at both the secondary and college levels, including among Mendota College students. As a result, many students and even practicing ministers arrived at Mendota College unprepared to do college-level work. This was a problem for many colleges at this time, and they often solved it the same way—through what they called the Preparatory Department—to provide courses that were the equivalent of high school work. These departments provided high school–level courses for those who did not or could not attend high school, and they prepared students for college work. Preparatory Departments were important to colleges because they provided much-needed tuition and prepared for college those students who, they hoped, then would go on directly to enroll in *their* college courses.[10]

Not only did Mendota College have a Preparatory Department throughout its years, Aurora College had one as well—throughout the 1910s and into the 1920s, finally disappearing in the mid-1920s. (The 1927 Aurora College catalog was the first one that did not list a preparatory program. By the 1920s, the United States had more and better high schools outside of urban areas, so preparatory work at colleges was much less needed.) Charles Sowder was one of many who came to Aurora College academically unprepared because of a lack of an accessible high school. He lived in a California logging camp. Since it was difficult for him and his brother to get from the camp into town to attend the local high school, his mother sent them to Aurora College. They came to the school in the 1920s and started by taking coursework in the Preparatory Department. Such situations were even more common in the Mendota years. Since rural areas and small towns were most likely to lack or have inferior high schools and many Mendota College students came from such places, the college's Preparatory Department performed a necessary service.[11]

Attending the BTS and working on a college degree required a high school diploma (or its equivalent knowledge based on testing). Without that, students had to do coursework in the Preparatory Department. However, students could take courses in the Preparatory Department and in college-level courses *at the same time*. President Twining explained it like this in

1904: "It is not insisted that the student must accomplish this four year's [*sic*] course, before he enters upon a Bible Training course. He may carry one or two studies in the Preparatory courses, and two or three in the Bible Training, thus making them stepping stones and helps to each other."[12] Some students did exactly that. In the 1910–11 school year, there were fourteen students in the BTS, and all of them were taking from one to three courses in the Preparatory Department. And college catalogs show that six students received a certificate of completion in the Preparatory Department in the same year that they received a certificate of graduation from the BTS.[13]

This overlapping of courses did not work at the other end of preparatory work. Students could not take any of the courses in the preparatory program until they had demonstrated that they had mastered the coursework of the elementary grades. Even so, as the 1909–10 catalog stated, "Ample provision will be made to assist such applicants as have not completed the [elementary-level] work required."[14] It is not clear how such low-level students were accommodated, but it was probably through individual tutoring and then testing. Testing was done at least some years to determine if new students had the requisite elementary knowledge to do high school–level work in the Preparatory Department.[15]

Throughout the Mendota years, except for 1893 and 1893–94, the preparatory program had two tracks—classical and scientific. (The academic year of 1893–94 had two tracks as well, but they were called English-scientific and classical-scientific). In spite of having two tracks, the differences between them were fewer than a two-track system might suggest. Students in both tracks took many of the same courses—a variety of English, literature, history, geography, math, and science courses. In fact, they shared more courses than not. Where they differed was that the classical track had some classical literary courses, like one on Cicero, and much more Latin, while students in the scientific track took more advanced science courses. In short, the preparatory program was a liberal arts program, similar to what high schools offered. It was tweaked from time to time, but its focus remained on the liberal arts.[16]

The time required for completion of work in the Preparatory Department changed over the years. Starting in the 1908–9 school year, the preparatory program went from three years to four, making it conceivable that a student in the Bible Training School (three years for completion) could be at the college for seven years, and a student getting a college degree (four years for completion), eight. However, that possibility was somewhat mitigated by the fact that based on testing, some students did not need all four years of preparatory work. While many students left before completing any program, there were a few students who were at the college for at least more than the minimum three or four years required for a degree, especially if they started in the Preparatory Department. Milton Livingston and John Keepers remained at the college for the longest period—at least six years. Both of these young men started in the Preparatory Department, and then moved on to college-level work. And once there, Livingston even earned two degrees—a college degree and one from the Bible Training School.[17]

This Preparatory Department was considered to be a vitally important part of the college. One student publication, the 1910 *Epitome*, described not only how it prepared students for more advanced work, but also how it supported the various other college departments—the Science Department by providing math courses; the Music Department by supplying work on the structure of poetry as well as theories of accent, harmony, rhythm, and clear expression; and the Commercial Department by giving courses in English and political economy. It also helped the Bible Training School, the student arguing that "the Bible Training Department depends upon it for students, even [sic] if students do take preparatory work before coming, the Preparatory Department must instruct them and give them a polishing touch before the Theological Department can pronounce them a finished product."[18] This 1910 *Epitome* even was so bold as to make the following claim: "How could Mendota College survive without the Preparatory Department? It is the strong foundation of our institution. The College Department depends upon it for students, and without the College Department there would be no Mendota College."[19]

The Bible Training School / Theological Department

Over the years, it was stated time and time again that the BTS was *the most important* part of Mendota College. This is evident from the fact that for the first few months of its existence, the school was called "Mendota

Seminary." In 1894, just over a year into the college's life, an *Our Hope* editor wrote: "Remember, this is a practical missionary training institute, organized and adapted to develop Scriptural mission workers for all fields, as rapidly and at as low a personal expense as possible. We are essentially a missionary people. We are ready for this work."[20] More than ten years later, a 1905 article in *Our Hope*, referring to the BTS, stated that "this is a department of Mendota College, and really the leading department, of which we are most careful as to its conduct and most anxious for its success. It is the department for which our college was established, and all the other departments are really subsidiary and contributory to this."[21] Sometimes the claim of the BTS's importance was made in the context of explaining that the college offered coursework in other areas as well. In 1904, a student wrote in *Our Hope* that "the Bible Training department is kept in the fore front of this institution. The President says it is for this department that the college exists. Other things taught here could be learned elsewhere, but we are fortunate as a denomination to have the two, a college and Bible training combined."[22]

On the other hand, college faculty and students frequently pointed out that Mendota College was more than just a Bible school. Its preparatory program, college-degree programs, and music offerings all broadened and enriched a minister's education, making him a better pastor. The fact that the college offered liberal arts courses, both at the high school and college levels, seemed to be a point of pride for many people at the college, although they never saw them as the most important courses or departments at the school.

Given how many times throughout the Mendota years the college faculty and others argued for liberal arts courses to supplement the religious curriculum, it appears that there were still some Advent Christians who did *not* see the need for any courses beyond those in the BTS. This had been an issue in the discussions leading up to the founding of the college, but it seems that even years later, it was not entirely resolved for some Advent Christians. Ten years after the college's founding, an *Our Hope* article stated: "To those who think a college for all branches of instruction exceeds our privilege, who regard a Bible Training School as all we should establish, on the ground that good secular schools abound everywhere; we kindly suggest: Our young ministry need all branches of learning, as well as Bible knowledge. ... And if we can wisely have a college for this class, have we no duty toward all who look to us or will come to us for secular education?"[23] And in 1905, in an *Our Hope* article, President Twining used his presidential authority to argue for the importance of providing courses beyond religious ones, stating that "we study very much here preparatory to the greatest of all studies, the Bible. In order to be a theological school, we must be a commercial, a classical, a scientific, a music school as well."[24] Twining's justification for offering liberal arts courses—that a broader array of courses made BTS students better current or future pastors—was a common one given by the college. Seldom, if ever, were liberal arts courses justified in terms of their own, inherent value for all students, no matter what their future occupation. And, of course, it did not hurt that the college charged tuition for such courses, unlike those in the BTS.[25]

Twining also pointed out that offering supportive courses in the liberal arts set Mendota College apart from some Bible schools. He was correct. Many Bible schools were unwilling to teach underprepared students much more than reading, writing, and arithmetic because they feared that too many liberal arts courses would take time away from Bible courses, and such courses were viewed as too worldly and therefore a threat to some of their core beliefs. Virginia Lieson Brereton, in her pathbreaking book on American Bible schools, describes these threats:

> The social sciences ... posed the greatest threat to the Bible school view of the world, for they tended to place humanity and human concepts in the foreground, and offered naturalistic explanations of human behavior, with little or no reference to divine activity and divine history. Furthermore, they employed the language of gradual development not favored by fundamentalists, who preferred to speak of discontinuities and crises in the individual life, world history, and in geology and biology; they also depended heavily on historical relativism. Then, too, the habit of "separation from the world" ... discouraged extensive exploration of political, social, or economic phenomena.[26]

However, Mendota College *did* offer liberal arts courses, making the opposite argument. A 1905 *Our Hope* article stated:

It is necessary to have departments for scientific, literary and classical studies, because the Bible student needs to have a well-rounded education in all these branches; and it is far better to have him get it in connection with his Bible training, and in harmony with it, than somewhere else and possibly antagonistic to the truths of the Bible. Some have feared that Mendota College would get away from the intention of its founders and soar in the direction of worldly wisdom and mere secular knowledge, but it has not done so yet and we very much hope it never will.[27]

Clearly Mendota's leaders were willing to take the risk with liberal arts courses. It was argued throughout the Mendota years, as this writer did, that it was better for students to take coursework beyond Bible training at the college than to take it in secular schools, where they would be taught material that conflicted with the teachings of the BTS.

Even though the BTS was Advent Christian in its teachings, it was open to all people. In July 1892, nearly six months *before* the school opened, this statement was published in *Our Hope*: "The Mendota Seminary shall be open to all applicants, and the profession of no particular religious faith shall be required of its pupils."[28] Some non–Advent Christians *did* attend, given the number of students from Mendota. Some of these Mendota students were, no doubt, members of the Advent Christian church in town, but it had a small membership, so it is also likely that some local non–Advent Christians attended as well. And, just as in most Bible schools, this inclusiveness included women. In 1894, William Sheldon, an early principal of the BTS, wrote that "THE BIBLE TRAINING SCHOOL has now one commendable feature in it over last year, aside from having a larger attendance, that is: the *sisters* are also attending, two joining the class at the opening of the school, and others intending to join. And still there is more room for both sexes."[29] Clearly, women were welcome to attend because of the college's mission of educating Christian workers in general, not just ministers. But it also seems likely that they were welcome for financial reasons as well. Like the men, women sometimes needed to take courses in the Preparatory Department and/or chose to take college-level, liberal arts courses, especially music. Mendota

College needed every student it could get to survive. Many women attended the college over its nineteen years, contributing to its financial sustainability.

The BTS first opened on June 26, 1893, six months after the college's opening. For a while, its calendar was distinct from that of the college's other departments. Although it opened in June of 1893, after that it began in April and ended in June or August. However, just two years later, *Our Hope* explained that "this course of study] is now short, beginning April 1ˢᵗ and closing with the college year in June. ... This is because the attendance does not at present justify a longer and more thorough course of study. However, it is the settled purpose to have, as soon as possible, a Bible training school running all the year round for those who can attend."[30] This purpose was achieved in the following fall. Starting with the 1895–96 academic year, the calendar of the BTS became the same as the calendar for the college— spanning three terms in nine months. The attendance numbers for the BTS were disappointing in the first few years, but eventually they grew to support year-round courses.[31]

(NOTE: The following paragraph begins a discussion of the BTS curriculum. In analyzing the curriculum in the BTS, and in each of the other academic areas at Mendota College, some tentative language is used at times [like saying "at least by a certain date" something new had happened, appeared in the catalog, etc.]. That tentativeness is usually because two catalogs, for the years 1897–98 and 1900–1901, are missing from the university's archives. Thus, any curricular change in those years is unknown. But it is also sometimes the case that catalogs are vague or give incomplete information on a topic—especially the earlier ones.)

What was the BTS's curriculum like? It, of course, changed over time, dropping this and adding that, but overall becoming more expansive and challenging in its content. In addition to the syncing of the BTS and college calendars, the 1895–96 academic year brought two other changes. First, two categories of courses were created—"elementary" and "advanced." Second, the creation of these two divisions suggests that this was the year that the curriculum went from one to two years for completion of the program. With the creation of these two categories of courses, it is likely that the coursework in each category took a year. The 1898–99 catalog makes this crystal clear in that, unlike the 1895–96 catalog, it lays out the coursework by term—showing the elementary courses taken in the first year and the advanced in the second. The 1901–2 catalog reveals another change. Instead of having two "classes"— "elementary" and "advanced"—there were now three "classes"—"elementary," "junior," and "senior"—indicating that the BTS program had gone from two years to three. As in the 1898–99 catalog, each of these new categories was laid out by term, each category requiring a year.[32]

There were specific areas of study that were in the curriculum in most, if not all, the Mendota years. An important part of the curriculum was biblical studies—the study of both the Old Testament (with an emphasis on prophecy, which was so important to Millerites and Adventists) and the New Testament (especially the life of Christ and apostolic history). The curriculum also included what the catalogs call "systematic theology." This was the study of doctrines as found in the Bible and interpreted through the Adventist lens— the nature of God, Christ, and the Holy Spirit; the nature of sin; immortality; future punishment for the wicked, etc. This area also included eschatology (doctrines concerning the end times) and apologetics (the defense of traditional Christianity and biblical doctrines against modern thought, in both its religious and secular forms). Another area was church history—a study of the Christian church from the birth of Christ up to contemporary time. The last two areas addressed the job of educating people on how to be a minister. One area—homiletics—was all about preaching. It included the history of preaching and, more importantly, the study of how to preach well. The second area was called "pastoral theology." It was not really theology but a practical study of how to perform the duties of a pastor—teaching future pastors how to lead a prayer meeting, serve communion, baptize people, and other pastoral duties.[33]

BTS students took additional courses as well. In later years, they were required to take a course in "expression" or "elocution," which was essentially a public speaking course. Its goal was the development of naturalness and directness in public speaking—in both preaching and conversation. The Department of Expression first appeared in the 1904–5 catalog as an area of coursework open to anyone; it was first listed in the 1905–6 catalog as an area of study in the BTS program, with the requirement that all its students pass an examination on the subject. It was not explicitly stated to be a requirement for BTS students with a length of time attached to it—one term—until 1906–7. Elocution was then required for the rest of the Mendota years. It began as a one-term requirement, but by the 1909–10 school year, two years (six terms, two hours a week) of elocution were required. The last few Mendota College catalogs were quite explicit about why elocution was a requirement for BTS students and why so many terms of elocution were considered necessary. The 1907–8 catalog claimed that "it may be safely stated that in seventy-five per cent of the cases where ministers fail of acceptance with their audiences their failure is due to lack in delivery rather than deficiency in education."[34] It probably was *not* safe to state that statistic, whose source was unknown and its content debatable (and that was the only catalog that gave that statistic), but it was an attempt to illustrate the value the college put on this area of study. In the last three college catalogs, another tack was taken: "There is a prejudice in the public mind that ministers, as a class, are the poorest speakers we have. The minister should be the best speaker, as he has altogether the best field for the cultivation of effective public address."[35] Clearly, the faculty believed that an effective preacher was one who could deliver a sermon well.[36]

Another way in which the BTS curriculum expanded beyond the areas discussed in the previous paragraph was through electives, which first appeared in 1905–6. Although they were added to that catalog, they appear to have been voluntary. It was not until the next year—1906–7—that electives became an ongoing graduation requirement for the BTS. Students had to take eight electives, each requiring twenty hours of what was called "recitation work" (i.e., hours in class). The electives offered came from just two major areas—biblical studies (the Old and New Testaments) and church history. They included some ancient language courses, coursework on the Epistles to the Hebrews and Romans, missions courses, and a course on Adventist doctrine, among others. These electives fleshed out the BTS curriculum by giving students the opportunity to be introduced to new topics and explore other topics in greater detail than given in the required courses.[37]

The idea of adding electives to a curriculum was a modern one, first pioneered at Harvard in the 1870s through the 1890s. Harvard took the idea of electives replacing prescribed courses the farthest. By 1897,

Harvard students were required to take just one year of freshman rhetoric; all other courses were electives. Although implemented gradually, this was a radical change, and it created an uproar—one consisting of countless, passionate arguments and the hurling of charges and countercharges between academic conservatives (advocating holding tight to the prescribed, classical curriculum) and academic modernists (advocating opening up the curriculum to allow greater choice for students and adding new courses to the curriculum, typically more practical ones found in newer disciplines). Most other schools tended to opt for a more conservative approach—combining the two curricular models in varying proportions. Inserting electives into a rigid, traditional curriculum was a blow to the classical curriculum and encouraged serious scholarship in that it allowed students to take more specialized courses in their preferred areas of study. However, adding electives to the curriculum meant that a college had to supply additional faculty and resources.[38]

Small, traditional, sectarian schools were among the last to embrace electives, and Mendota College was no exception. The BTS was mainly the area where electives were added to a curriculum at the college. In the classical and scientific, college-degree tracks, there were hardly any. It was not until the 1904–5 catalog that the word "elective" appeared in the scientific track's course list, but there was just one course labeled that—Mechanical Drawing—and this elective lasted for just four years. In the classical track's course list, starting in the 1901–2 school year, several options were given as electives—German/German Composition or French/French Composition. And students could opt to take Hebrew. However, by the 1906–7 school year, those choices had disappeared altogether. In both of the college-degree programs, it does *not* appear that students *had* to take any electives per se. The closest they came to this was having to take a course chosen from just two specific ones. It appears that they had to take one of them but could choose which one they wanted. These were not the kind of electives that the elective movement was advocating. The Mendota curriculum, when it even mentioned electives, gave students an either-or choice, or a student could opt to take a single course labeled "elective" or not. In all of the Mendota years, there was just one such elective in each of the two tracks, and both of these lasted for just a few years. And in both of these cases, an "elective" was in the main subject area of the track—the classics or science. That is different from a curriculum that *mandates* multiple electives, requiring students to choose from an array of courses *outside* of their major. Instead of this, as was typical of traditional nineteenth-century curricula, there were no majors per se at Mendota College. Instead, it had tracks that focused on a general subject area—the classics or science—and these tracks also included some prescribed, liberal arts courses. In other words, the *entire* curriculum, for each of the two college-degree areas, was set and taken as a whole. There was no set number of electives that needed to be taken; a student could choose to take none of the single courses labeled elective. And the few that existed were listed *within* a specific track's main subject area.[39]

One can only speculate as to why the elective movement in higher education was hardly visible at Mendota College. Perhaps introducing courses from the new social sciences was perceived as a threat to Adventist beliefs. Perhaps the cost of this reform was too great. In any case, the price was paid for the BTS, the college's most important department. However, the nature of this department was such that the electives added did not have the effect of introducing new and more practical areas of study outside of a major to students. These electives, drawn from short lists, allowed Bible students to study a subject at a deeper level, but they all still were traditional religion courses.

A final way in which the BTS curriculum was expanded was through the study of languages. Courses on Aramaic, Syriac, and Assyrian were offered as electives in the Old Testament area. These courses were probably taken by relatively few students, but there were other languages that came to be required of *all* BTS students—Hebrew and Greek. Greek was mentioned as a requirement in the 1894–95 catalog, but then was dropped for a number of years. By at least 1901–2, BTS students were required to take both Hebrew (all nine terms) and Greek (six terms) so that they could do some work with original sources in their study of the Old and New Testaments. Then, starting with the 1904–5 academic year, the Hebrew requirement went down to six terms, making that requirement a match to the six terms of Greek. That remained the language requirement for the rest of the Mendota years.[40]

Requiring Hebrew and Greek, while also offering other ancient languages as electives, set the BTS apart from many Bible schools and, increasingly, even from seminaries, where liberal theologies prevailed. The Bible schools democratized their teaching by having no language requirements, instead having students read the Bible only in English. Without a language barrier, this opened up the study of the Bible to more students. This was very much in line with the overall democratizing tendencies of the typical Bible training school. Ironically, the proponents of modern religious thought ended up on the same page as the fundamentalists, believing that students could not possibly master Greek and Hebrew enough in the time allotted to make this all that helpful in studying the Bible. They argued that just those who intended to become biblical scholars should invest the many years of language studies that it would take to read the Bible in its original languages. Nevertheless, the BTS persisted in offering Hebrew and Greek, thus bucking the trend at both ends of the theological school spectrum. One can only wonder whether the BTS would have graduated more students had there not been this language requirement.[41]

No matter how the curriculum of the Bible Training School changed over the years, one thing remained the same—starting with the 1895–96 academic year, every catalog stated that the Bible was the *main* textbook of the school, although others were used to supplement it. Not only was this printed in these catalogs, it was highlighted by putting it in a separate section with the title, "THE BIBLE—THE TEXT BOOK," even though this section was usually quite short, as illustrated by the wording in the 1901–2 catalog: "And since this department is known as the Bible Training School, the Bible above all other books will be the text book, and the reading and study of the Bible, beyond the reading and study of all other books, will receive special consideration."[42] Future ministers studied difficult languages so they could go back to original sources, but the English Bible also was studied by all, and the BTS's interpretations of it affected the teachings in disciplines outside of this department, such as science. And, of course, reading and discussing the Bible was at the very heart of the college people's various religious services, at the Mendota Advent Christian Church and on campus—in the Sunday services, prayer meetings, and Bible study groups.[43]

The College-Degree Programs Curricula

Unlike many early Bible schools, Mendota College also had programs that led to a college degree. The Bible Training School, after the first few years, offered a three-year, stand-alone program, which, if completed, provided a "Diploma of Graduation" (on the condition that the student had completed the preparatory program or given evidence of having had its equivalent). The college also offered three programs that led to a bachelor's degree—an AB degree (today's BA), for students completing the classical program; the SB degree (today's BS), for those completing the scientific program; and, from 1907–8 on, a DB (bachelor of divinity degree), for those *completing* BOTH a collegiate program (the classical or scientific) *and* the theological program of the Bible Training School. Only two people ever completed the two programs required for the divinity degree, both in 1904— Milton M. Livingston and Roby C. Robbins, both of whom went on to teach at the college for many years. However, there is no indication that the college offered this divinity degree until several years after they both graduated.[44]

As with the BTS curriculum, either the missing 1900–1901 catalog or the 1901–2 catalog brought substantial changes to the classical program. Probably the biggest change was eliminating the study of Greek and Latin. The new curriculum focused on reading classical texts in translation—the changing list of courses included Aristophanes, Cicero, Demosthenes, Herodotus, Homer, Horace, Livy, Ovid, Tacitus, Thucydides, Virgil, etc. Greek and Latin were dropped, but the curriculum still included some languages— German or French and Hebrew (as an elective) were added. These languages lasted just five years. Starting with the 1906–7 academic year, no languages were required for the classical program. The curriculum became more purely classical because of all the new, classical literary and historical courses that were added and all the nonclassical courses that were dropped. However, the advanced rhetoric, English literature, and composition courses remained, as well as some science and mathematics courses. In fact, there continued to be a fair number of mathematics courses—certainly more than most students not majoring in the sciences or information science would take today: Analytical Geometry, College Algebra, Differential Calculus, Integral Calculus,

Trigonometry, etc. Although the more purist classical curriculum endured to the end of the Mendota period, its classical nature was modified somewhat in 1906–7, when some of the courses dropped earlier returned, including some science and social science courses. The dropping of the languages this same year made the return of these courses possible.[45]

The year 1900–1 or the year 1901–2 was one of curriculum reform for the scientific program as well, representing an increase in quality. It was more college-like and challenging. Mathematics especially saw an increase in courses—from essentially Algebra and Trigonometry to an additional five courses—Analytical Geometry, Differential Calculus, Integral Calculus, Conic Sections, and Quaternions (although the last two courses were dropped just three years later). Science saw fewer changes, although Geology was increased from two to three courses, "Botany" was now called "Advanced Botany," and all three courses in zoology were gone. The 1904–5 catalog brought more significant changes to science. Three "Advanced Physics" courses were added, and what had been called "Chemistry" was now called "Advanced Chemistry." Why was the word "advanced" added to various science courses over the years? Unfortunately, the catalogs do not explain this change. One possible theory is that the addition of "advanced" to the name of a science course indicated that it had been upgraded to the college level.[46]

One interesting characteristic of the science curriculum, no matter what the catalog or the changes made, was that the further students went in the program, the fewer science courses they took. By the senior year, there were virtually no science courses—other than the thesis course in later years. This was mostly true of the classical curriculum as well. It looks like the senior year was a time to take general education courses, not to do the most advanced work in the science or classical curriculum. This, of course, is the opposite curricular pattern of today's colleges and universities.

One thing that the BTS degree and both of the bachelor-degree programs came to share was the requirement of a thesis. In 1904–5, a course titled "Thesis," was added to each of the three terms of the senior year, for both the classical and scientific degrees. Until 1907–8, the catalogs are silent on the nature of this thesis. The 1907–8 one includes a description of the thesis requirement for these bachelor-degree programs, fleshing out what was required in the paper as well as the process behind it.

> The subject for thesis must be selected and approved not later than the close of the student's Junior College Year [sic].
>
> It is expected that the student will confer with the instructor in charge, and that the subject of thesis will be chosen from that department in which the major portion of the student's work has been done.
>
> It is not required that the subject matter or even the arrangement be entirely original, but the thesis must be well written and of such a character as to indicate a thorough acquaintance, on the part of the student, with the literature available on the subject.
>
> Before the student will be permitted to graduate two type-written copies of the thesis must be filed with the secretary of the college.[47]

By 1906–7, the college offered a third bachelor's degree—a divinity degree. Since this one required the completion of not just the theological program, but either the classical or scientific program as well, this meant that a thesis was required to earn this degree. Starting in 1909–10, those students who wanted a bachelor of divinity now had to write an additional thesis—this one on a topic in biblical studies. This catalog explains what was required for the divinity degree's thesis: "The candidate must present a thesis on some Biblical theme, the thesis not to contain less than 6000 words. The subject of the thesis must be chosen with the approval of the faculty of the Biblical department. The thesis must be type-written, neatly bound, and must be presented to the faculty and accepted, before the degree can be granted."[48] Adding a thesis requirement to the three bachelor programs was an important step, indicating that more in the way of scholarly work was being asked of students. Not only did they have to do research on a topic, the paper itself had to be well written to be approved.[49]

The Music Program and Music's Role in the Life of the College

Music played a prominent role at Mendota College—not just as an area of study, but beyond the classroom as well. The 1911 student publication, *Epitome*, describes the important role of music on campus: "The Music department though small this year, is of more than small importance. It furnishes music for all public programs of the school, it enlivens the Literary Society, and in every department of school work where music is demanded it never fails."[50] These musical presentations included the College Day service, the end-of-the-year recitals for music students, Commencement, and on-campus entertainment, as well as services and concerts at the Mendota Advent Christian Church, among other events. At virtually any formal college gathering, there was at least one musical presentation, and often more—both vocal and instrumental. At various times in the Mendota years, special musical groups were formed—a college chorus class (1897), a college male quartet (1906), a college orchestra, with ten instruments (1908), a choral club (1908), and a brass band (1909).[51]

Music was considered important for all of the usual reasons. For those who created it, it was a form of individual accomplishment, and for those who created or just listened to it, it was a most pleasurable entertainment. It also had a very important religious role—one, it was believed, that helped bring people to God. Musical training for those working in the Christian ministry was viewed as an important supplement to religious education, if not an outright necessity. Long-time head of the Music Department at the college, J. A. Wallace, advised those studying for the ministry to be able to sing well enough to lead congregational singing and to play church music on the "Cabinet organ." Why? Wallace argued that "singing not only forms an important part of our worship, but is one of our best ways of presenting the truths of the Gospel."[52] In an 1896 issue of *Our Hope*, "A Musician" wrote an article on this topic that stated this argument more passionately: "What a grand help it is to a minister of the gospel to not only be able to sing and to play with the spirit and understanding, but with all the sweetness and power, and grandeur, that training can give to nature! You have seen such preachers—seen how they held their audiences spell-bound; by singing the songs of Zion. You have seen sinners turn to God in meetings where music is given its place, by either preacher or people."[53] Although many students took music lessons and nothing else at the college, developing musical knowledge and skills was viewed as especially important to ministers and other Christian workers. Thus, the music program was viewed as supplementing, not competing with, the biblical program.[54]

Throughout the Mendota years, the music curriculum, like that of the classical, scientific, and theological programs, evolved. Some courses came and went—the organ, cabinet organ, banjo, and violin courses—but some remained throughout the Mendota years. Courses on and lessons in piano and voice were always offered, no matter what the music curriculum looked like in any given year.[55]

Starting in 1893–94 and continuing for the next several years, the music curriculum had two tracks of study—the Academical Program (three years long) and the Collegiate Program (which went two years beyond the academical track). Within each track were three programs—Piano (up to five years), Vocal (up to five years), and Violin (up to four years). This was the only year in which a violin program was offered. Each graduate in music had to have completed work in harmony. By 1896–97, the academical and collegiate tracks had disappeared, and there were now four areas of study—piano, cabinet organ, voice culture/singing, and harmony/composition.[56]

By the turn of the century, as with other areas, some substantial changes were made to the music program. The number of programs had shrunk to three—piano, voice culture/singing, and the science and theory of music. *Each* of these three programs had two tracks. The first was introductory and required no prerequisites. It simply served as an introduction to music or as preparation for more advanced work. It led to a certificate rather than a diploma. The second track was more advanced and was open only to students with a qualifying background in musical education. Each student had to take harmony and musical history along with one of two programs—piano or voice culture. This track led to a diploma. No specific time period was set for completion of a track's program because each student was viewed as unique and so was allowed to work at her own pace.[57]

The last significant change made to the college's music program came in 1904–5. A teaching-certificate-in-music program was added as an option.

In each of the two major areas of study—piano and voice—there were two tracks. The first one led to a teaching certificate in music for the elementary grades while the second one led to a college diploma in music. A minimum of one year's study in harmony was also required.[58]

Music was a distinctive area of study from the others at Mendota College for several reasons. First, it had a relatively large number of students, but very few graduates. Over the span of sixteen years (not counting the two years of the lost catalogs and the one for the 1911–12 school year, for which no regular catalog was produced), only four students graduated in music—all four with a teaching certificate. And no one graduated with a diploma. Yet looking at fifteen of the Mendota years (excluding the two missing-catalog years plus 1911–12 and 1893–94, when the curriculum was in a state of flux), catalogs show that 494 people were listed in music, an average of 33 students a year. Clearly people were taking music courses and lessons, not to get a diploma or even a certificate, but to learn a bit about music and improve their singing or piano-playing skills. This suggests that many of these students lived in Mendota, and that was true. A perusal of the music students' names and their hometowns shows that a substantial majority of those registered for music classes were from Mendota and its surrounding towns.[59]

Second, music students were counted differently. Many times, when the enrollment for a given term or year was announced, there would be a qualifier which would say that the number given did not include music students. Why was this done? A Mendota College board member explained it like this in a 1902 *Our Hope* article: "There are now 40 students in regular attendance and in regular courses, exclusive of music students. Our reason for omitting the music students is that many of them receive their instruction at home instead of at the college."[60] Such students must have been just those living in the Mendota area who were taking individual music lessons and were not registered for any preparatory or college courses. The large numbers of enrolled music students versus the tiny number of graduates suggests another possible explanation. There were large numbers of students coming and going in virtually all of the college programs, but this was especially true for the Music Department. Perhaps it was believed that listing *every* music student, even though she might be just taking individual lessons for a brief time and had no intention of working toward a certificate or diploma, would give a misleading picture of the college's enrollment. If so, the college was being honest about this, perhaps to its detriment, in that adding these names to the official numbers would have made the college look larger and more prosperous.

Third, from time to time, especially in the earlier years, the Music Department felt the need to defend its very existence at Mendota College to outsiders, along with some of what it taught. A March 1893 *Our Hope* article announced that a person had been hired to teach the violin and banjo at the college. Then it was reported, in an article appearing just two weeks later, that an Advent Christian minister had sent a letter to both the college and *Our Hope,* saying that he was "shocked" to hear that the school was teaching the violin and banjo and that the Music Department was giving a concert (which it did—its *first* choral concert, held on April 7, at the Mendota Opera House). The minister saw this as a sign of "a terrible falling away." An unnamed person, probably an *Our Hope* editor or school official, used this article to respond to the minister's letter. This author wrote that it did not occur to people connected with the school that teaching the violin and banjo would be viewed by others as any less acceptable than teaching the piano, organ, or other instruments, noting that the violin and banjo are found "in many refined, cultured and Christian homes."[61] This defender of the music being taught at the college suggested that the Bible be the guide for what was acceptable, arguing that people should not make sinful those behaviors that are not deemed such by the Bible. And he made clear what was considered unacceptable: "We certainly should shun teaching the young under our charge anything unchristian, or necessarily and dangerously worldly in character or in tendency. We regard the dancing school, and the theatrical and stage training, often given in professed Christian schools under the name of Elocution as coming properly under this prohibition."[62] He also reverted to the "occupy-till-I-come argument: "We sincerely believe with the fullest faith that Jesus is soon coming ... , but we do not believe this faith obligates us to cease, in any degree whatever, the everyday secular, but no less *sacred duties* of life, of which the education of our children is one. We are fully justified by our Lord himself in continuing these duties up to the very day and hour of his appearing, for He bids us 'Occupy till I come.' "[63] In regards to the concert and the type of music performed, he argued that it was nothing more than a recital, given periodically, to show parents and others the progress that students had made. He assured this minister that the music performed would be of high quality: "It is not designed for one moment to pander to a taste for the frivolous, the foolish, or the merely worldly. The music chosen will be of the highest character, adapted to elevate the taste as well as please the ear, and will also show the skill of the performers and the high quality of the instruction given."[64] In short, the author made every argument he could think of to defend the teaching of music at Mendota College.[65]

The letter objecting to the teaching of the violin and banjo at the college was certainly an extreme case, but it was not the only example of people objecting to the teaching of music. From time to time throughout the Mendota years, *Our Hope* would publish an article whose author felt compelled to defend the teaching of music at the college. Sometimes this defense of music was clearly in response to a letter; at other times, it is not clear whether authors were arguing for the teaching of music at a Christian college in general or were directly responding to a letter or a specific, spoken criticism.

Periodically, an Advent Christian would raise the issue of why Mendota College should teach something as frivolous as music if, as Adventists believed, Christ's return was imminent. As with the 1893 response cited above, an 1896 *Our Hope* article used, among others, the "occupy-till-I-come" argument to defend the college's Music Department:

> I was somewhat surprised that any of our brethren should think it a waste of time and money to hire competent music teachers for our college at Mendota. "But, can any good come of it," inquires some dear, earnest soul. "If the coming of the Lord is indeed so near, should we not be very careful how we expend the Lord's money?" Yes, truly, we should avoid foolish expenditure of *all* our means, for it is *all* "the Lord's money" if we are truly his stewards, and it is just as wrong to spend it foolishly at one time as another, and whether the Lord's coming is impending or not. ... But let us look at this whole matter fairly and candidly. What can more glorify God in our day than to help those whom he has called to preach the gospel of the Kingdom, to deliver their message as well as possible during these brief closing years of the age? ... Now, certainly there is no better way to do this

than to teach our young men and young women to sing our beautiful Adventist hymns and gospel songs, sweetly and harmoniously, to the heart-heavy, groaning world around us. It is worth having a musical department in our college *just to attend to this important duty.* ... This cannot fail to do great good sooner or later, when at all our campmeetings and conferences we have first-class singing and plenty of it by those who have learned to sing and who know how to use expression, purity of tone, distinct enunciation ... to both charm the ear and instruct the heart [italics in original].[66]

This author used other religious arguments to defend the teaching of music as well. It brought people to the college, where, he argued, they would hear about God and possibly have a conversion experience, thus saving souls that might otherwise be lost. (The author, no doubt, knew that the music program brought in many non–Advent Christian students from the local area.) And this author, like the one in 1893, argued that studying music is *not* inherently sinful. He compared the study of music to learning how to read. One can play or sing frivolous music and read trashy books, but that does not make playing an instrument, singing, or reading a bad thing and something not to be taught. Ultimately, he viewed music as a gift from God, arguing that musical talent should be developed so that it could be put into service to glorify God.[67]

He also made some arguments that had a religious veneer but were actually pragmatic and probably driven, at least in part, by financial concerns. Since music was by then part of a standard education, especially for women, if Mendota College did not teach it, people would go elsewhere—to non–Advent Christian schools—to get it. These were religious concerns, but there also was a financial one underlying them. He pointed out that students going elsewhere or leaving the school because there were no music courses meant a loss of students and the money they brought to the college coffers. Music courses and lessons required tuition, so they would bring money into the school that would help support the Bible Training School, where tuition was *free.*[68]

As criticisms were made about teaching music, defenders came forward. These proponents of music showed that the critics did not have a monopoly on religious arguments. Religion in general, and Adventist beliefs in particular, were used to defend the inclusion of music in the curriculum of

Mendota College. Music, of course, can be defended in its own right, but for a college whose most important area was its Bible Training School, music was also a useful supplement in preparing students for Christian work.

The Commercial Department

The Commercial Department was born of necessity, and its creation seems to have been related to the changing of the school's name from a seminary to a college. Comments in various sources link the two things, such as this one: "During the very first days of work after the opening of Mendota Seminary ... there was a strong local demand for commercial instruction. Accordingly, the next February 1893, the first class in that department was organized. At the next annual meeting of the Association this work was encouraged. The name was changed at this meeting to Mendota College, and the Commercial Department was fully installed."[69] According to the author of this quotation, George Dewing, the first principal of the Commercial Department, this was needed because there was "a strong local demand" for business studies. However, had it not been needed or wanted by the college, that demand could have been resisted. The building of a commercial department/program happened quickly. The department began its first classes on Thursday, February 9, 1893, exactly one month after the school opened. One would expect that a new department, whose necessity was realized only *after* the winter 1893 term had begun, would open no earlier than the next term. The rush to get this department up and running so quickly suggests how badly it was needed. It is likely that college leaders saw this as a necessity because, like the college-degree and music programs, its tuition would bring in much-needed revenue and help support the Bible Training School. And according to Mendotans, there was a ready-made market for such courses. Offer them, and they would come.

At various times, faculty and other people related to the college made a case for the importance of business classes for *everyone*. Some students wanted to complete the program to prepare them for acquiring a job in business. But it was argued that even a few business courses could better prepare any person to more effectively manage his own finances. One

Advent Christian minister wrote: "We consider it one of the most important departments of our college. Those who cannot afford the full college course can here obtain, at but small cost, a thorough, *practical business* education, such as every man *needs*. It affords a grand opportunity for all our young people to fit themselves for the every-day, business demands of life."[70] It was viewed as especially important for ministers to take some business courses because of their small salaries, it being more important for them than for the wealthy who could better afford to misuse or lose some money. Commercial skills could also help students earn their way through college. Not surprisingly, a religious connection to business was made as well. One proponent of commercial education argued that every church needs at least one person with a good business sense and knowledge of business practices, claiming that failing churches often lacked a good understanding of such things.[71]

Unlike the other programs at Mendota College, the courses available in the Commercial Department changed only minimally over the years, although stenography came and went at various times. At the heart of the program were courses in bookkeeping (various methods and for different types of businesses) and office work. They were accompanied by studies in business arithmetic, commercial law, commercial geography, civil government, and political economy, along with supplemental areas like penmanship, spelling, and English grammar (if you did not come into the program with such basic courses). It took approximately one school year to complete the program, depending on what work had been done previously. Completion of the required courses led to a "diploma of honorable graduation." Much, if not most, of the work in this program was hands-on and done individually, which allowed students to work at their own pace.[72]

In an age when business schools were popping up everywhere and colleges were adding commercial courses to their curriculum, the college tried to differentiate itself from the others. Mendota College catalogs, especially in the later years, noted that while some schools were improving the quality of commercial education, many of the new business schools were more interested in numbers of students, and the income they would bring in, than in a quality education. These schools recruited students, it was argued, by requiring just a minimal number of courses, thus making possible a short time for completion of the program. The Mendota catalogs promised thoroughness and high standards, which required a year of training, as opposed to three months in the inferior schools. These sections in the catalogs ended on a confident note and a challenge: "Believing that the standard of commercial work should be high, we have provided a very complete and thorough course of study for our Commercial department. All of the subjects usually taught in commercial schools and colleges will be found in the list given below, and some besides. We invite comparison with the lists published in the catalogues of other schools."[73] To its credit, the college chose not to take shortcuts in its commercial program, even though it may have lost people to schools with shorter programs.[74]

Besides selling the notion of a thorough, quality education, another recruiting method, which schools still use, is evident: telling potential students what kinds of jobs previous students had acquired, thanks to their commercial education at the college. They went on to work as bookkeepers in large manufacturing enterprises, bankers, realtors, accountants, managers for various businesses, stenographers, and more. When the catalogs discussed the subject of finding jobs, the impression was given, of course, that students would be in a better position to find a good position. The college also promised that it would do what it could to help "worthy" students find a job, but it also stated candidly that it could not guarantee this. In any case, the Commercial Department gave students, especially Mendotans who were not necessarily Advent Christian, the opportunity to find better jobs and probably more upward socioeconomic mobility than would have typically existed in a small, rural community without a college.[75]

Academic Facilities

Academic facilities were limited at Mendota College, because of both money and space, but they did improve over time. When the school opened in 1893, it had no science laboratory. This was remedied in 1896, when two brothers—Zimri and Marsden Ames, both of Rutland, Illinois—gave the college the requisite $100 that it would take to get such a laboratory up and running. The next year this space was expanded by removing a wall, creating a sixteen- by eighteen-foot room that was to serve as both a chemical and physical laboratory. The Ames brothers also provided the funds for this project. After 1897 the room was called the Ames Chemical and Physical Laboratory. Over the years, more and more equipment was added to the laboratory. And the study of physiology was enhanced when the college acquired a human skeleton in 1895.[76]

The library, always in need of more books from friends of the college, started with virtually nothing. There is no mention of a library until the 1894–95 catalog, which urged people to give books or money for books: "A valuable nucleus for a library has been formed, around which it is hoped the friends of the College will form a collection of books that will be an honor to the College. Donations will prove very acceptable for this department."[77] Advent Christians did donate to the library—both as individuals and as churches. In 1896, President Clum, in an *Our Hope* article titled "Books—an Urgent Need—a Good Example," explained how Sunday schools could help supply books to the college library:

> Bro. Brown, pastor of one of the Chicago churches, gave the choice to his Sunday school to have their usual Christmas treat, or instead give one book each month to Mendota College. They unanimously voted to give us a book each month. The Mendota Sunday school, following the example of Bro. Brown's Sunday school, has decided to take one extra collection each month for the purpose of buying a book for the library. Their first collection was $1.68, and we already have a nice large book for the library. Why cannot every Sunday school help us? The book will be recorded in your name, will be an honor to you and a help to us.[78]

The college also purchased book collections from two Advent Christian ministers, each of them a substantial benefit to the Bible Training School. The first minister, D. T. Taylor, offered to sell his collection to the college because he was ill and no longer physically able to use the books. He also had doctors' bills that could be paid with the proceeds from selling them. He stated that he was willing to sell $200 worth of materials for $100 or $400 for $200. The collection contained about fifteen hundred books and one thousand pamphlets and tracts, some of them quite old. He described his collection like this: "I have rare and valuable books now out of print ... rare works on Revelation, and on Daniel, and many works on prophecy that our young preachers should have access to. ... I have also forty or fifty volumes of tracts, mostly well bound—tracts and pamphlets of great interest to Adventists; now long out of print, and many that can be found nowhere else in the world. Some of these reach back to 1820, and many to 1843 and '44.''[79] He asked *Our Hope* readers to consider purchasing his materials: "Why not raise money to buy these books for Mendota College, and also help me? These books should *never* be scattered. They have cost so much pains and money to collect them, I cannot bear to think of scattering them again. Are there not some Adventists of means, who know the value of such books, who will buy them of me and place them in the college?"[80]

A number of *Our Hope* readers responded to this proposal, virtually all of them in the affirmative. One woman went beyond, saying she approved of his proposal, suggesting that forty people send five dollars to Elder Taylor, she herself pledging $5. And she followed up this proposed plan with an emotional plea: "Think how severe a trial it must be to him, to part with those silent but loved companions of years. How great the sacrifice, above what ours can possibly be. Let us arouse and hasten quickly to help while we yet have time and opportunity."[81] Another woman, also empathizing with Taylor's plight, made another suggestion about Taylor's books:

> Of course they would be very useful there [the college], but to think of their selling at such a sacrifice, to procure the necessities of life for Bro. Taylor and his loved ones, this seems to be a hard necessity, that we should not take such an advantage of. Is it possible that as a people we can permit this? Shall we suffer this time-honored Christian soldier and pioneer of the great truths we hold so dear, to make this really great personal sacrifice? Nay, brethren and sisters, let us rather bestir ourselves and raise the means to pay our brother something near the real value of the books he has collected so lovingly. We certainly owe him this.[82]

In the end, no *Our Hope* article was found that gave a *final* report on the money raised for Taylor's proposal. People sent their donations directly to Taylor with the understanding that he would send whatever materials the donations purchased directly to the college. Taylor sent a list of the donors and the amounts they gave to *Our Hope*, which published the figures in a May 1896 article. However, more money may have come in after that. It might seem that the college received only part of Taylor's collection, except that in this same article, Taylor was quoted as saying that "the books must go West. It is God's will. If brethren and sisters cannot purchase them for Mendota College, or do not wish to, I now think I will send all I can, anyway, to the West, by freight, and give them myself. trusting [*sic*] God for whatever recompense is right. Our father will take care of all who obey and trust him."[83] In spite of his desperate need for funds and too little money coming in, it looks like he may have given his whole collection to the college anyway. It is likely that at least some, and perhaps all, of Taylor's books and pamphlets are now part of Aurora University's Jenks Memorial Collection of Adventual Materials.[84]

The second collection came from another minister—Norman P. Cook—who served as the principal of the Bible Training School from 1895 until his death in 1899. He became sick in November 1898, soon had to give up his teaching duties, and died in March 1899. His death was not completely unexpected, given the length of his illness, but it was still shocking and left a large hole in the Mendota College community. Cook, who was just in his forties, was a beloved professor and known as a masterful teacher. Shortly after his death, a proposal was made to purchase his two-hundred-volume library for the college library—at a cost of $125 for the books and a walnut bookcase to hold them. The books were to be kept separate in the new bookcase and called the N. P. Cook Collection. As one *Our Hope* article stated, "It was thought much wiser to save this collection intact, for the college, rather than have it *scattered* among many different purchasers."[85] The college had a fundraising drive that was publicized in the pages of *Our Hope*. In one article concerning the purchase of these books, readers were told that "probably no use of them could be more in harmony with Bro. Cook's feelings and wishes while alive than to have them all in the college as a *perpetual memorial* of him. ... Sr. Cook is not able to present them to the college, and it would be cruelly unkind, in view of the past services of both Bro. and Sister Cook to pay her less than the low valuation now set upon them."[86] Those books, too, ended up in the Jenks Collection.[87]

The college library grew slowly over the years. No catalog even reported the size of the library's holdings until the 1901–2 one, which noted that the school had more than eleven hundred volumes. By the 1909–10 academic year, the number of books in the college library had more than doubled—to about twenty-five hundred volumes. There was one other source of books nearby that supplemented the small college library—the Mendota Public Library. In 1901–2, it had more than four thousand volumes and by 1909–10, more than seven thousand. Between 1901–2 and 1909–10, the town's library grew by around three thousand volumes as compared to about fourteen hundred for the college. The importance of the Mendota library to the college was reflected in the fact that most of the school's catalogs cited the number of volumes in it, even in most of the years when no numbers were given for the college's library. No doubt the inclusion of the public library in the college catalogs was meant to help promote the school by highlighting an important academic and cultural institution in the town, but in doing so, it also was a virtual acknowledgment of the college library's inferiority.[88]

The People of Mendota College: Faculty

The faculty at Mendota College was one of the school's best recruiting tools. It was small, but loyal and dedicated to the institution. Faculty pay was low, even by the standards of the day, and the demands put on them were great—going beyond simply teaching and attending meetings. For example, Benton A. King (a 1901 alumnus) taught in the Commercial Department for seven years and worked as the college treasurer for at least four of those years. Even presidents did double duty. Virtually all the presidents taught classes, and B. J. Dean also served as head of the Science Department for the entire five years of his presidency.[89]

Some had additional jobs *outside* the college. All the principals of the BTS were Advent Christian ministers, which at the very least meant that they preached now and then and performed other tasks for the denomination. Some simultaneously served as both the principal of the BTS and the pastor of an Advent Christian church. When N. P. Cook served as the BTS principal (1895–99), he also pastored the Mendota Advent Christian Church for the first two years of his tenure at the college. He ultimately gave up the pastorate, because it was too much on top of his college duties. Principal F. A. Baker (1899–1904) did the same thing and learned the same lesson. After four years, he resigned both positions somewhat abruptly and without another job in hand, suggesting perhaps a burnout factor. The last principal, Orrin Roe Jenks, pastored one of the Advent Christian churches in Chicago at the same time that he headed up the BTS (1904–11). He resigned his pastorate only in 1910, in order to devote all of his time to heading up the fundraising effort to relocate the college to Aurora. And even before the idea of moving the college came up, Jenks performed other duties for the school, like his December 1905, eight-day trip to visit churches in Indiana and Michigan in order to talk face-to-face with Advent Christians about Mendota College.[90]

Most faculty, who generally lived close to campus, were very much involved in campus life. They served as advisors to clubs, attended student social events, and frequently entertained students in their homes. The close ties that developed between faculty and students were reinforced by the fact that most of them attended the Mendota Advent Christian Church. Mendota College students got to know most of their faculty quite well, especially those who taught at the college for many years.

With all the extra things they were doing at the college, faculty had heavy loads. Add in all the religious services and school activities faculty were expected to participate in, along with constant interactions and even entertainments with students, and one can only conclude that working there must have left very little personal time. One reason that faculty shouldered so many different responsibilities was that their numbers were small, especially in the first half of the Mendota era. In 1893–94, there were nine faculty members, but the next year this number was cut to seven. By 1897–98, there were only five—the number of faculty for the next four years. Initially, the founders of the college thought they could support a larger faculty than what turned out to be financially possible. The big financial crisis of 1896–98 (when the college almost closed) was a harsh lesson—that they should not try to build beyond what the number of students could support. In the second decade of the Mendota era, the number of faculty crept up. The 1903–4 school year—an entire decade after the college's founding—was the first to have nine people on the faculty again. By 1908–9, there were twelve faculty members, followed by eleven in 1909–10, and twelve in 1910–11. However, even in some of these later years, when numbers were a bit higher, one or two of the faculty listed in the catalog were part-timers, usually students. Even counting part-time students who were teaching, the number of faculty did not reach more than ten until the very end of the Mendota era, in 1908–9. Even though there was an upward trend in the number of full-time faculty in the second half of the Mendota era, faculty numbers were still relatively small.[91]

How well prepared, academically, were the members of Mendota College's faculty? Such a question has to be answered with care because what were generally seen as acceptable academic credentials at the turn of the twentieth century were quite different from today. Thus, it is important to judge the Mendota College faculty, not by those at Aurora University today, but by similar schools in the Mendota era. In the late nineteenth century, few college professors had PhDs. As late as 1884, even Harvard had only 19 professors with doctorates, out of a faculty of 189. However, by the 1890s, there was a substantial increase in the number of PhD professors, at least at larger and Ivy League schools, which had the financial resources to pay higher salaries for such people. At smaller, Christian schools with limited resources, it was not unusual for at least some college instructors to teach after earning just a bachelor's degree. And in an era when many faculty members did not have degrees beyond the bachelor's degree or, at most, the master's, they tended not to have specialized teaching areas and often taught a broad array of subjects. There were a number of examples of this at Mendota College.[92]

The professors in the BTS, the most important department in the school, were a group apart from the other professors. They were all Advent Christian ministers and, most of them, mature men. For the oldest men, this means that their younger years dated back to a time when higher education was not a prerequisite to becoming a preacher or even becoming an ordained minister. Their many years of Bible-centered preaching and pastoring churches were their credentials. Clearly, they believed in higher education for ministers, unlike some in their generation, even if they had not received one themselves. However, they were not just any Adventist ministers. They were prominent men in the Advent Christian denomination who had taken leadership roles or pastored many Advent Christian churches. And they had a scholarly bent. Much of their education had been self-learning, but they had done a lot of it. Two of the four BTS professors lacked a formal higher education in theology.

William Sheldon, who taught in the BTS during its first three years (although he never served as its principal), epitomized the kind of professor described in the previous paragraph. Born in 1830, he spent most of his childhood in upper-state New York, not far from William Miller's home. He was so impressed by Miller and his preaching that in 1842, at age twelve, he was converted and joined the Adventist movement. The Great Disappointment came the next year, when he was thirteen, but like others who became Advent Christians, he was undeterred by it, probably assuming that the date was wrong, not the message of Christ's imminent return. He began preaching in 1849, at age eighteen, and was ordained two years later. Sheldon had no formal higher education, yet he was a giant in the Advent Christian denomination. He was a pioneer, traveling evangelist in the Midwest, the Far West, and the South. He was a church builder, helping to establish many churches in Wisconsin and neighboring states through tent meetings. He was a writer, producing at least three books and countless numbers of tracts. He was a denominational journalist, editing the *Advent Christian Times* for a term; partly owning and editing the *Bible Banner*; serving as the western correspondent (i.e., reporter) for the *World's Crisis* for many years; and serving as associate editor of *Our Hope* for most of the 1890s. As a denominational leader, he helped establish the first Advent Christian western conference (including Wisconsin, Minnesota, and northern Iowa), served as the presiding officer for many years at the General Western Campmeeting on the Mendota campus, and was president of WACPA from 1890 to 1898—the years of Mendota College's founding and early struggles. In spite of his lack of higher education, he was an effective preacher and church builder, and, given his writing and work with Advent Christian newspapers, a highly literate man. It is not at all surprising that he was tapped to teach in the BTS early on.[93]

Frederick A. Baker, who was the principal of the BTS from 1899 to 1903, also was called to the ministry but had no formal higher education. He was well known, though not for the same reasons as Sheldon. Baker was widely known, not because he held a number of denominational positions, but because he pastored so many churches. He was Canadian, born in New Brunswick, so his first pastorates were in three Canadian provinces. Early in his career, he moved to the United States, first to Maine where he had three pastorates (Frankfort, Levant, and Bangor). He then moved to the West, where he pastored churches in Minnesota (Rose Creek, Minneapolis, Rockford, and Independence), Illinois (Mendota and DeKalb), California (Santa Cruz), and Washington (Seattle), where he celebrated his fiftieth year in the ministry. He also preached widely over the course of his career: at Mendota College, campmeetings, other churches, etc. Given his longevity as a pastor and all the churches that gave him a call to be their minister, Baker must have been an effective preacher and a knowledgeable student of the Bible. He certainly would have had much to offer by way of teaching aspiring ministers what the ministerial profession entailed—not just in terms of biblical study and preaching, but the nuts and bolts of the job as well.[94]

Two of the principals of the BTS, the two youngest ones, had experience as preachers and pastors but had also earned at least one theological degree. **Nathan P. Cook** was relatively young when he served as the BTS principal and was better educated than Sheldon and Baker. Cook initially trained for the Baptist church, but in 1876, he was converted to Advent Christian beliefs and, in 1878, was ordained by the Adventists. Cook graduated from State University at Ann Arbor (later known as the University of Michigan), with a BA, in 1875 (before his conversion to Adventism). He also graduated from New York City's Union Theological Seminary in 1878 (the year he was ordained by the Advent Christians). He wrote a book on William Miller and pastored two churches before he went to Mendota to teach. At that point, he had seventeen years of pastoral work behind him. He did not bring the decades of experience to the BTS that Sheldon and Baker did, but he was better trained, and it appears that he was an impressive teacher. Sadly, after an unidentified illness of four months, Cook died, on March 21, 1899—at the young age of forty-eight. Given the deeply grief-stricken reaction of Mendota College's faculty, students, and board members to Cook's premature death, one can only conclude that he was a beloved teacher and pastor and a highly respected colleague in both the college and the denomination. His excellent teaching was often mentioned, as in this heartfelt memorial article: "It is not too much to say of Prof. Cook, that if he had a specialty it was the training of young men and women for the gospel ministry. His whole soul was in this work, and to continue it was his daily prayer. His interest in the students of the college was intense, and to hear of their success was his great joy. Mendota College has suffered an irreparable loss, but his lecture course and work will continue in charge of Pres. Gordon, which fact affords us great consolation."[95] During the last two years of his life, Cook had his lectures put in a more permanent form for future use. They served as a textbook in the BTS for some years after his death. They and he must have been viewed as so excellent as to draw students to the BTS because, even before his death, in an *Our Hope* article reporting on his illness, the chair of the college board attempted to reassure students that standards were being upheld even though Cook was not in the classroom (having been replaced with President Gordon):

> While we deeply regret the enforced absence of Bro. Cook from his classroom, and the loss of his personal force and inspiration upon his pupils, yet we are confident that they are in good hands, and their work will not materially suffer. We hope that no one who may have planned to attend the Bible Training School the coming term will be deterred or led to change his plans on account of present circumstances. President Gordon has the entire confidence and esteem of the students and of the Board of Education.[96]

Cook's theological studies and experience as a pastor, along with his strong interest in the BTS students, held him in good stead in the classroom and made him a beloved figure. His untimely passing left a large hole in the fabric of the college, but his influence continued for years through the use of his lectures in the BTS.[97]

Orrin R. Jenks, having joined the faculty while in his thirties, was younger than Cook and Baker and also, initially, was a self-taught minister. However, unlike his predecessors, he later earned several divinity degrees—a bachelor of divinity (1905), from the Chicago Theological Seminary (majoring in Semitic languages and graduating at the top of his class) and a bachelor of divinity (1908) from the University of Chicago's Divinity School. He served as pastor to five churches before resigning his last position to work full-time for the college. And he was well known in the denomination *nationally*, not just in the Midwest, so he was the right person to head up the Finance Committee—a job that was all about raising money for the Aurora campus and that required Jenks to travel all over the country to do this.[98]

What were the academic credentials of the Mendota College professors teaching outside of the BTS? It is hard to say because the catalogs list the degrees of faculty by their names in a seemingly haphazard, random way—both within a catalog and from one catalog to the next. However, more is known about the longest-serving professors—Bert J. Dean, Roby C. Robbins, George Dewing, Nathan Twining, and Orrin R. Jenks. Both Dean and Robbins graduated from Mendota College (Dean in 1903, with a bachelor of science, and Robbins in 1904, with a bachelor of arts in Ancient Classical and a Bible Training School diploma, as well as in 1906, with another theological degree—perhaps the equivalent of the bachelor of divinity, which appeared in the college catalog the very next year). Thus, they were both products of the college. Dean did some additional work, attending Iowa Normal School and receiving a master's degree in 1909 (in what area and from what school is unknown). Since Dean became president of the college in 1906, he must have been working on this master's degree while running the school.[99]

George Dewing was in a category all his own. He was a Renaissance man who fit the portrait of the early- and mid-nineteenth-century professor—short on formal higher education and a generalist. He held many different jobs in his life. He was an ordained Advent Christian minister, serving several churches; taught in a Vermont public school system; and worked as a surveyor, a printer, and a newspaper editor. He worked at Mendota College in two different periods—during 1893–95 and then from 1906 straight through 1915, ending his career at the college in Aurora. In the early period, he served as the principal of the Commercial Department, but in the later years, he taught a wide array of topics—English and history primarily, but also rhetoric, economics, and, when he was needed, an occasional course in the BTS.[100]

What prepared Dewing for college teaching? Little in the way of formal degrees. The two that he acquired were a bachelor of science from Mendota College (1909) and a bachelor of arts from Aurora College (1912).

However, the second degree was bestowed on him by the college's board of directors. The faculty had urged the board to do this because, despite Dewing being weak in Greek and Hebrew, he knew so much about everything else. However, these degrees came toward the end of his teaching career. Earlier, he had taken two correspondence courses—a three-year course of study with the University Association of Chicago (in economics, history, political science, sociology, and "universal literature") and a shorter course of study in Greek at the University of Chicago. Dewing's colleague at the college, Roby Robbins, wrote of Dewing in 1908:

> Prof. Dewing has been a life-long student, constantly searching for knowledge. ... While he felt keenly the misfortune of being deprived of a college training in his youth, he did not let this serve as an excuse for not obtaining a higher education; but by association with educated men, by reading and study, by experience and observation, he set himself to acquiring in another and more difficult way that which he had failed to obtain from college. To successfully hold the position which he now occupies is a sufficient indication of the success of his efforts.[101]

In short, Dewing was, to a large extent, self-educated for most of his teaching career. He was a lifelong learner whose teaching also benefited from a number of his jobs—especially in journalism and the ministry.[102]

And he was revered, so much so that the class gift for 1931 was the creation of a reading room for students in Eckhart Hall, which was named for him and was thereafter called the Dewing Room. This honor came sixteen years after Dewing had retired from teaching at the college. Those 1931 graduates explained their choice like this: "The class of 1931 has come to know and to love Dr. Dewing. We shall always remember him for his kindly counsel and cheerful assistance. We deem it a rare privilege to perpetuate in this way the name and memory of one who has taken such an active part in the life of Aurora College from those early days at Mendota."[103] This citation does not mention Dewing's teaching ability, and he was not credentialed in the modern sense, but it appears that he performed acceptably in the classroom, because faculty were let go by the board if they did not, and in 1910, the college, although always tight on money, raised his salary after he received an offer—at a much higher salary—from another college. Perhaps, in part, the wording of the students' 1931 statement honoring Dewing was a product of nostalgia for the good old days, but it was also a show of appreciation for someone who played an important role in the life of the college.[104]

The three best-educated faculty members in the Mendota era were Twining, Dean, and Jenks. All of these men held multiple degrees. Twining and Dean each earned a bachelor's and a master's degree, while Jenks earned two bachelor of divinity degrees. The only one of these three men who has not yet been mentioned is **Nathan C. Twining**. He attended Milton College, both before and after he fought in the Civil War. He also had a master's degree and a doctorate (which may or may not have been an honorary one). He was the cousin of Arthur Twining Hadley, president of Yale from 1899 to 1921. Although he did not reach such an exalted academic height as that, his credentials were good, given the era in which he lived. He spent his life teaching and following other scholarly pursuits. His jobs previous to his Mendota College years included teaching at Milton College, which he did both as a student and after graduating; heading up one of Chicago's largest public schools; and working in public schools in Monroe, Wisconsin. He also worked in the public-school system in California and began teaching at the college level there. In a biographical article that Roby Robbins wrote on Twining for *Our Hope*, he quotes what Wisconsin public-school records say about him:

> Among the most prominent of Wisconsin's educators and teachers in [is, *sic*] Prof. N. C. Twining, of Monroe, Wis. Having received ... a collegiate education, he stands second to none in his profession. He has wielded a great influence in the state in all public-school matters, engrafting his ideas not only on the minds of teachers, but he has been influential in giving shape to their ideas, thus making himself felt throughout the length and breadth of the state.
>
> He has been regarded for years as the best mathematical teacher in the state, having held for eight years the chair of mathematics in Milton College, Milton, Wis. ...
>
> He has given his life energies to the schools of the state, having spent his time from September 1873 to June 1886 in the public schools

of Monroe, Wis. He raised them to the highest rank, his school of fourteen hundred pupils being regarded at the State University as the very best public school of the state, for fitting young men and women to enter upon an advanced course of university education. ...

As an author and writer he stands foremost with his associates. His published papers on astronomy, language and pedagogics, science and current topics, ocean currents and also finance, have been well received and widely copied.[105]

Twining's extensive work in public schools, although mostly not at the college level, no doubt helped prepare him for the presidency at Mendota—shaping his thinking about teaching and learning as well as helping him to develop some important managerial and organizational skills. And throughout this period, he also published in quite different areas. In this regard, he too was a product of the earlier, generalist school of college teaching. As was so typical of that kind of professor, he was a broadly read, lifelong learner. He had a six thousand–volume personal library and read around two hundred books a year.[106]

Twining's academic preparation and years of work with schools bore fruit at Mendota, because he was Mendota College's best-prepared president and its first truly successful one. The four presidents preceding him had short tenures, two of them staying for just one year. Twining served as president for five years, from 1901 to 1906, and when he left, it was his own decision based on a family issue. (His wife had moved to California to care for her ailing, newly widowed father, and he ultimately decided that he needed to join her.) His departure was a sad event for the campus community. When his father-in-law's health improved, he was able to return to Mendota a year later. However, a new president, Bert Dean, had been chosen in his absence, so Twining could not be reinstated as president.[107]

Although several Mendota College students began teaching at their alma mater *after graduating*, a few started teaching at the college *while still students*. There were, of course, important differences between these two situations. Those who joined the faculty after graduation worked full-time and usually taught in an area that was related to the degree that they had earned. Students who taught or "assisted" classes could not work full-time and did not always teach in an area in which they were doing coursework. Only nine people ever taught at the college while still registered as students there, and of those, only two seem to have had their own, college-level classes. Those two students (one teaching Greek and Latin and the other, English and Hebrew) were seniors who graduated at the end of their teaching year, and one of them—Roby C. Robbins—joined the full-time faculty immediately after graduating. The rest of the student teachers either taught a nonacademic, skill course—like typewriting—or were listed in the catalogs as "assistants" in an academic area, suggesting that they were not teaching a course on their own.[108]

At least three of the nine teaching students taught typewriting in the Commercial Department while taking classes in other areas. For example, in the 1905–6 catalog, Winfield W. Giberson is listed as a faculty member who was teaching typewriting, while this same catalog also lists him as a preparatory, BTS, and music student. In the next academic year (1906–7), he is listed as an assistant in English and mathematics, while also identified as a freshman in the college-degree classical program and a music student. It would seem that he was still a student, yet he is also listed as having graduated the previous June, in 1906, receiving diplomas from the Preparatory Department and the BTS. The fact remains, however, that he was still teaching while simultaneously taking coursework. In the 1907–8 catalog, his name is not to be found, except as a 1906 graduate. In that same catalog, however, another student, Howard Bingham, is listed as teaching typewriting, while also being registered as a student in the BTS and in the college-degree classical and music programs.[109]

This practice of using students to teach was not unique to Mendota College. In fact, as just noted above, decades before Mendota College was founded, Twining had taught at Milton College while still a student. A century after Twining did that, in the post–World War II era, students began teaching in larger numbers than ever before. As both undergraduate populations and graduate programs grew, large universities increasingly turned to graduate students to teach undergraduates. Of course, they were graduate students, whereas Mendota College used undergraduates to teach, but there is probably a blurred line between the teaching expertise of academically excellent upperclassmen and first-year master's students. And, at Mendota, there was a limited use of students for this job. For more than a third of the Mendota years, there were no students teaching, whereas it has been argued that large, modern universities use graduate students to teach undergraduates far too much—to the detriment of the younger students.[110]

Among both regular faculty and students assisting in and teaching classes, there were women, and they were present every year of the Mendota era, although they were never a majority. Out of the nineteen years in Mendota, there was only one year (1911–12) when women constituted half of the faculty and only six years when they made up under 50 percent but more than 25 percent of the faculty. The category with the most years—eleven—was fewer than 25 percent women faculty members but more than 10 percent. And there was one year (1907–8) when women accounted for 10 percent or less of the faculty.[111]

However, these percentages need to be looked at with caution, because the numbers of faculty overall were so small. In a year when there were just five faculty members, like in 1900–1901, one woman constituted 20 percent of the faculty. Thus, not counting the one year when women were 50 percent of the faculty—in 1911–12—all six of the years that had the largest percentages of women faculty (under 50 percent but over 25 percent) were in the first decade of the Mendota period. As the faculty grew a bit in the second decade, the percentages of women faculty members tended to drop. Also, the female teaching assistants inflate these percentages a bit. There were female assistants/teachers in three of the years in Mendota's first decade, but in just one year in the second. Removing these assistants from the count would decrease the percentage of faculty women in the early years more because the faculty was smaller then.[112]

It certainly is *not* surprising that in virtually every year of the Mendota period, there were more men on the faculty than women. What *is* surprising is that, in a small, Christian, coeducational college of this era, there were as many faculty women as there were. Women's education took great strides after the Civil War, thanks to the creation of coeducational, land-grant/state universities, and all-women's colleges. However, in the late nineteenth century, women faculty (and administrators) were few in number and mostly clustered in all-women's colleges. When they were found in coeducational universities, they were usually in positions that were segregated because they were gender specific—i.e., deans of women, professors of home economics, etc. In 1880, women composed 36 percent of faculty members in the United States, but from 1890 to 1910 (almost exactly the years of the Mendota era), that percentage plummeted by almost half—going down 16 points to 20 percent. And these statistics are misleading, reflecting the clustering of faculty women at all-women's colleges rather than a more equal distribution of women throughout academia.[113]

Who were the women of Mendota College? What were their characteristics as faculty members? First, they had less longevity as faculty members than the men. The faculty woman who stayed the longest was Jennie Twining. She taught at the college for a total of eight years, but she was also well connected, as she was the wife of President Twining. In fact, at least six of the sixteen female faculty members were related to men working at the college, and all but one of them, to faculty men. This figure includes three out of the four women who were on the faculty the longest—Jennie Twining, Mary Robbins, and Ethel Shatto. These connections may have contributed to their greater longevity. The longevity numbers for the female faculty plummet after Jennie Twining. They go from eight years for Twining to four years for the next-longest, working woman. This *overall* pattern is similar to that of the men, whose longevity numbers were halved from sixteen to fifteen years straight down to eight years for the next-longest, working man. However, the number of years for the women versus the men are quite different—at both the highest level and the level after the sharp decline. There were four women (25 percent) who worked at the college for three years or more (and 50 percent of these four worked for just three years), whereas there were sixteen (44 percent) men in that category (and just 25 percent of these sixteen worked for three years). Only one woman, Jennie Twining, worked at the college for more than five years (less than 10 percent), whereas eight men (22 percent) did.[114]

It is impossible to know all the reasons why women left, but there are a few that are known and a few about which an educated guess can be made. Four of the women listed as faculty were actually students who were teaching, so naturally their tenure would be brief (a reason that applied to men as well). At least one woman left because her program disappeared—in this case, the art program (which only existed for the first two full years of the college's existence and whose students had *all* been women). At least one was called away by a family responsibility—to care for her ailing, elderly father. One woman left to pursue a master's degree. And one woman resigned in the middle of her third year for a reason that is less transparent but can be guessed. Although she resigned in December, it does not seem that she left in the middle of the school year. The April college board minutes of the next calendar year report that she came before the board to make a statement about the college's president. She charged him "with using disagreeable language to herself and others; with an unpleasant manner of handshaking; and with too frequent visitation of the rooms of lady students and with harsh language towards herself."[115] The board held several hearings and listened to the testimony of four women students who had been mentioned in the complaints against the president. It then unanimously renewed the president's contract, although he left a year later. It is difficult to know exactly what the board minutes' vague language in describing the charges meant, although they certainly raise questions. But the minutes, at the very least, suggest that the woman was unhappy because she thought the president was acting rudely and inappropriately. Clearly, the reasons for women leaving the faculty were mixed, with some connected to traditional gender roles and being a female faculty member, while others were not.[116]

What subjects did women teach at Mendota College? They taught in areas where female professors continue to predominate today—mostly in the humanities. Out of the sixteen female teachers at Mendota through 1910–11, the teaching area of three of them is unknown. Out of the remaining thirteen women, twelve taught humanities courses—art, music, English, history, elocution/speech, and languages (Latin, German, and French). At least two of these women also taught mathematics, and one woman taught mathematics as a student, which was her major. No woman taught in the Bible Training School, and none taught science or business courses through 1910–11. These areas were still very much the preserve of men—especially the area of religion—both at Mendota College and at schools around the country. Women were virtually always rejected by seminaries in the nineteenth century, and there was just a handful of female preachers among Advent Christian ministers. Without higher education in religious studies or practical experience as pastors, it is no surprise that women were not hired to serve on the BTS faculty.[117]

Lastly, how many women faculty at Mendota College (through 1910–11) were married? Out of the sixteen faculty women, the marital status of four of them is unknown. (The catalogs are somewhat inconsistent in whether there is a Miss or Mrs. in front of a woman's name on the faculty list, and this inconsistency can sometimes be found within the same catalog.) There were three married women and nine single women. All three of the married women were related to faculty men working at the college. The single women were either once students who now taught at the college as regular faculty members; women who taught at the college just as students; or women hired from outside the college, with no previous ties to it.[118]

The small number of married women on the college faculty fits a pattern that was prevalent in the nineteenth and early twentieth centuries—that generally *married* women did *not* teach. In this era, marriage and a career for women were viewed as incompatible and generally unacceptable. A related pattern was a rise in the percentage of single women in the late nineteenth century, especially in the middle class. This was due to the massive loss of young men fighting in the Civil War; rising expectations about marriage held by women; and the growing opportunities for women to get educated and acquire professional jobs, although those jobs were largely found in what were deemed women's professions. More specifically, *college-educated* women were more likely to be single than other women. This was especially true of graduates from the Ivy League and women's colleges. Just a bare majority of female college graduates embraced matrimony, and when they did, it happened later in life than it did for non-college-educated women. It appears that many, if not most, of the single women who worked at Mendota College were young. This fits the national pattern as well. Opportunities for women's education and professional jobs expanded greatly only after the Civil War, so not enough time had passed to have many professional women of advanced age. And because many of Mendota's single, female teachers were young, no doubt some of them got married eventually, but this also fits the overall pattern that those who married did so later in life than was the norm.[119]

Perhaps the married women working at the college were viewed as more acceptable because every one of them was related to men working on campus, and at least one of them, Jennie Twining, had no children. Also, because the college was small, lacked prestige, paid low wages, and was created by a tiny denomination, women, whether married or not, were probably needed. If the college wanted to hire academically qualified Advent Christians who could afford to work long hours for little pay, the pool of such workers was small. Even though Advent Christians held traditional views of women, places like Mendota did not have the "luxury" of denying positions to all women just because they were married, and sometimes, as with the Twinings, a married woman came to the college as part of a package deal. However, in the end, these women taught largely just in areas that were considered to be part of women's traditional academic sphere.

The People of Mendota College: Students

Students at Mendota College generally worked hard—at their studies and at working their way through school. In addition, if one factors in internships, especially the preaching jobs for BTS students, as well as participation in school clubs and other college social activities, it becomes clear that students had little free time. Mendota College was *not* a party school where affluent young people came to sow their wild oats. Like virtually all small Christian colleges and Bible training schools at this time, it attracted youth from the lower and middle echelons of the middle class—serious young people, most of them from farming families and small towns, who came to college to build better lives for themselves, not to party.[120]

Before proceeding any further, a word of explanation about the data is needed. The information about students was taken from the Mendota College catalogs, each of which listed the names of registered students by area of coursework, and, for most years but not all, listed their hometown and state as well. Since students were listed by program, some were listed more than once. For example, a BTS student who also took a music course would be listed twice, or even three times if he took coursework or lessons in two different music areas. While the lists of registered students are helpful, simply adding up these numbers creates an inflated view of the student population because of this overlap. However, although the exact numbers of enrolled students are a bit inaccurate because of this inflation, they do illustrate overall trends, like when enrollment rose and fell. And many students, probably a majority, were listed only once in any given catalog.[121]

The annual numbers of registered students are misleading in another way. They would lead one to believe that many more people graduated over the nineteen years of the Mendota era than actually did. The truth is that many more students attended the college than graduated from it. There were only 111 graduates in the *entire* Mendota era. By way of comparison, considerably more students were enrolled in the college's first two years than graduated in all of the Mendota years. The college reported that there were 46 students enrolled in 1893–94 and 110 in 1894–95. (Note that this second enrollment number is just one short of the number of all graduates combined.) Also, it should be noted that 14 out of a total of 20 preparatory diplomas ever awarded by Mendota College (which is also to say—13 out of the grand total of 111 diplomas) were *not* accompanied by any other diplomas. In other words, those 14 students who received only the preparatory diploma had completed the high school–level work of the Preparatory Department, but no college program, so actually the college only produced 97 graduates in its nineteen years of existence.[122]

Clearly, Mendota College had a graduation problem. Many students attended for just a year or even less. Some stayed longer than that but left before completing a program. Students' ability or desire to stay in school was dependent upon such factors as their finances; family issues like being needed to work on the family farm or nurse a sick loved one; the desire to get married to a classmate as soon as possible, even if it meant not graduating— an issue that was especially impactful for women; their own health issues; and the impatience of, and sometimes the pressure on, BTS students to not wait three whole years to get their own church. Some of these students were able to return to the college eventually, but many did not.

Sometimes outsiders persuaded students to cut their education short. At times, churches liked a student interim pastor so much that they tried to talk him into becoming their full-time pastor immediately, a move that would require him to leave the college before completing the BTS program. This became such a problem that eventually articles appeared in *Our Hope*, asking churches *not* to give any BTS student a call to come and pastor their church before he completed his education. One such article mentioned a church that wanted a BTS student to do just that. When he declined the offer, a church member criticized him, charging him with putting his education before the ministry. This article went on to beg churches not to call BTS students before their education was complete, saying that ultimately, these young men would not be grateful to them because they would realize that their opportunity for a more complete education was now gone.[123]

Some students, like the one just mentioned, refused to take on a church before they had earned their diploma, but many did leave school prematurely to take on a pastorate. One such student, Edward Lubke, left the college in 1903, his BTS diploma *not* in hand, so that he and his family could move to Magnolia, Wisconsin, where he became pastor of the Advent Christian church there. Perhaps the fact that he had a family made it too difficult to remain in school. At least some of the students who left school prematurely regretted their decision and wanted to take up their studies again. In 1898, George Cooprider, who was then ministering to *two* churches, wrote, in *Our Hope*, that he wanted to return to Mendota for further study. His words to current students suggest regret over his decision to leave school: "Perhaps some of you are anxious to get out into the work, like some of us were. You will *then* realize the value of *thorough* preparation ... [italics in original]."[124] In 1903, E. L. Pettus, an Advent Christian minister and former BTS student, wrote a brief article for *Our Hope*. He said that his time at the college was one of the happiest periods of his life, and he deeply regretted leaving without finishing his program. A few years later an *Our Hope* column announced that William Sheldon Bowden, grandson of the revered former professor William Sheldon, was hoping to return to the college. He had recently been a student but then took a pastorate in Ohio. Now he was hoping to return for winter term of that school year. Whether or not these men ever got back to Mendota, they never finished the BTS program. Their names appear nowhere on the graduation lists.[125]

Some students came for just a few months or a year, never even intending to pursue a degree. This was especially true for BTS students, whose numbers sometimes included working pastors who could not afford to leave their churches for three years to complete the whole BTS program.

They typically came for a short time, sometimes for as short a period as a term, to expand their understanding of biblical studies and then returned to their home churches. It also appears that people were welcome to attend the college for even shorter periods of time—for even a few weeks. A March 1899 *Our Hope* article encouraged schoolteachers to come and attend classes at the college for their April break: "Even *one month's* stay at the school will help you to *know yourself*, to find out your *weak* points, to measure your *capabilities*, and 'size yourself up'. ..."[126] And at the very end of the fall term of 1905, it was reported that "Miss Isabel Wright is attending college for a few weeks, to perfect some studies she has found needful in her work."[127] The studies she came for were not identified, but the brevity of Wright's attendance at the college and the claim that she needed this help for her job suggests that she was probably doing some work in the Commercial Department.

Whether students planned on pursuing a diploma or not, there was a surprising number of them who arrived at the college late. *Our Hope* articles, especially the column written by students, frequently mention these latecomers. Students sometimes arrived on campus way past the beginning of a term—in some cases, in the second half or even just a few weeks before its end. Mendota had a nine-month academic year of three terms, rather than two semesters, so the terms were short. This meant that if you arrived many weeks into the term, you had little time to catch up with the class. In *mid-October* of 1905, a student reporter mentioned that "new students are still constantly arriving, to join our happy ranks."[128] This was allowed but constantly discouraged. Found in many *Our Hope* articles and even the college catalogs are pleas that prospective students enter the college at the beginning of a term—or, better yet, the beginning of the school year—because it would benefit them academically. This issue was a concern as early as 1895, because the 1895–96 catalog was the first to include a statement on it: "Students can enter at any time, but experience has fully demonstrated that it is greatly to the advantage of the student to be present at the beginning of the term. This is important for several reasons: the student can then receive the proper classification, be on equal footing with his classmates, and pursue studies which are continuous through the year and cannot be repeated."[129] And catalogs still included this advice at the end of the Mendota era. Even current students warned prospective students against late arrivals, as Orven H. Loomis did in a 1904 *Our Hope* article:

> Your year's work depends very largely on a good beginning. Come at the opening of the term, in September, and lay your foundation. Start in at the beginning of your textbooks, on an equal footing with your classmates, and there will be no trouble in keeping up, nor in mastering the study.
>
> Some get discouraged and leave school, all on account of a late beginning. They find their work doubled and trebled, because the class they join has gone over the first part of the textbook and mastered the first principles, which are indispensable to progress.[130]

However, given the number of students who continued to arrive late throughout the years, it would seem that such warnings fell on deaf ears.[131]

Aside from strictly personal issues, there were two major factors that affected when students could attend classes—the nature and rhythms of farm life and religious activities. Mendota was located in a rural area, and many students from away came from rural areas as well. In such places, farming was not just an occupation but a way of life, and it shaped many of the life patterns of the people who engaged in it, including dictating when young people could attend school. For example, the harvest season required that all family members be available to work. A November 1893 *Mendota Bulletin* article acknowledges this when it casually mentions that "now that the fall work is finished on the farms many new accessions are expected."[132] An equally casual-sounding announcement ten years later informed readers that "Mr. Moorehouse has dropped his work in the Commercial department to resume farm work."[133] In January 1896, President Clum even used the rhythms of farm life as an argument for young people to attend the college. He argued that since it was winter, a time when little farm work could be done, parents should send their idle children to Mendota for three or four months of coursework. This back-and-forth movement because of farm duties probably affected largely students who lived in the Mendota area or, at most, northern Illinois and its surrounding states, because of the cost of travel.[134]

Also, students would sometimes up and leave for a few days or weeks to do some kind of religious work. For example, in 1906, J. W. Neslund took several weeks off from classes to lead revival services at the Mifflin, Wisconsin Advent Christian Church, where he was filling in as pastor. A few months later, J. F. Whitman, who had been pastoring a church in Minnesota, was reported to be returning to take his final exams before graduating from the BTS. The fact that he was taking exams suggests that he was a registered student for that term, yet he was pastoring a church in Minnesota—too far away for commuting. It was not unusual for a BTS student to pastor a nearby church, whose minister had moved on, while continuing his studies or, at least, to preach at various churches on Sundays. But sometimes, ministerial responsibilities, like revivals, took him away from classes for more than a day or two.[135]

Students who were not pastoring churches also periodically left their classes for religious reasons, but for briefer periods of time—several days or a week. Generally, they did this to attend various denominational conferences, the most common one being the Northern Illinois Advent Christian Conference, which met in different towns. Whether student trips required extensive preparation or not, students lost time in the classroom. And the burden of this lost time and extra work must have been especially hard for ministers-in-training. As one BTS student, J. L. Irvin, pointed out in his column, "It requires extra hard work for a student, of no great experience in the ministry, to carry on a course of study at college, make good standing in the class room and also preach twice every Sunday."[136] No doubt his peers would have agreed with him.[137]

Leaving school prematurely, arriving late for the term, and the missing of classes for multiple days or weeks were all part of a larger pattern—erratic attendance. College officials seemed fairly flexible concerning students missing classes, or even terms, for religious and farming activities. But they, and even some students, tried to convince people, especially BTS students, not to leave the college before finishing their program. Given the number of graduates, those appeals were not terribly successful. Neither were their arguments for students to arrive at the beginning of a term. Given that even the last regular catalog (1910–11) of the Mendota years continued the practice of warning students against late arrivals, and *Our Hope* articles mentioned this issue time and time again, it appears that this continued to be a problem throughout the Mendota era. If, as student Orven Loomis claimed, students who did not arrive at the beginning of a term were apt to leave the college quickly because they could not catch up, it is no wonder that college leaders constantly warned new students about this issue. Yet unlike universities today, which generally do not allow students to add classes beyond the first week or so, Mendota College never adopted any limits on when a student could enter classes. To modern educators, this seems like a strange policy to hold on to and a recipe for student failure.[138]

However, this attendance pattern was not unique to Mendota College. Bible training schools as a whole tended to have erratic attendance, their students casually coming and going at times other than the beginning and end of terms. The 1903 catalog of the Advent Christian denomination's other educational institution—the Boston Bible School—contains a statement that sounds similar to the one that appeared in Mendota College's catalogs. It states: "It is very desirable to begin the year and stay till it ends. But, when this is impossible, students are welcome to begin the year and stay as long as they can."[139] Outside the denomination, other places, like the Boston Missionary Training School, had the same issue. Its 1892 catalog states: "It is desirable that students remain, if Providence permits, for two years. Yet numbers have found themselves greatly benefited by one year's training."[140] The emphasis in the Mendota catalogs is a bit different from this in that they emphasize the importance of entering classes at the beginning of a term, and even, hopefully, the year. However, the college also stated many times that, although it was desirable for students to stay long enough to complete a program, it too welcomed students who could only stay for shorter periods if that was all they could do, believing that they would benefit from any amount of time spent in classes. Whether talking about students leaving prematurely or arriving late, the larger issue was irregular attendance patterns. And this phenomenon was not just a trait of Christian colleges and BTSs. Research done on a range of colleges between 1890 and 1910 shows an overall pattern of high dropout rates and relatively low rates of graduation—including at such schools as Amherst, Brown, and Harvard.[141]

Who were the students of Mendota College? Religiously, they were fairly homogeneous. The college, in particular its most important department—the BTS—was very much Advent Christian. Because Mendota College was first and foremost an Adventist school whose primary mission was to train Christian workers, especially ministers, for the denomination, it was not surprising to find that it attracted students from at least thirty-two states. The top states sending students—not including Illinois—were Iowa, Wisconsin, Minnesota, California, Nebraska, and New York. The denomination was small, as was the number of Advent Christians living in the Mendota area. And Mendota College was the denomination's first school of higher learning and its only one for four years. Its second school, the Boston Bible College and Ransom Institute, was founded in 1897, but it was located far from the Midwest. That meant that Mendota College was the place for many Advent Christian youth to go, especially if they lived in the Midwest or Far West, although some students from the East attended as well.[142]

Also, the communications network through which most prospective students heard about the college was Advent Christian. They knew about the school because they had heard someone speak at their church or campmeeting, their parents read *Our Hope* or another denominational newspaper, a friend or family member had attended, or their minister was an alumnus. The college had no formal admissions department or recruitment strategy beyond writing articles about the college for the denomination's newspapers, especially *Our Hope*; sending faculty and others out to summer campmeetings; and having individuals occasionally go out on a tour of churches to preach and talk about the college. Outside of the Mendota area, virtually all the ways that a person could learn about the college went through the Advent Christian denomination.[143]

Local people, of course, knew about the college firsthand, and large numbers of students also came from Mendota and its environs, suggesting that a fair number of local, *non*-Advent Christians attended the college. As a group, they would have been more religiously diverse. The membership of the Mendota Advent Christian Church was small, so it could supply just a small number of young people. And because of the significant German presence in Mendota, some of the local students may very well have been Catholic. Many local people were members of various Protestant denominations. However, even though they were not Advent Christian, at least some of them were evangelical in nature. Thus, they would have shared many religious and cultural beliefs with Advent Christians. Even so, the local people who were not Advent Christian tended not to be attracted to the BTS. Instead, they benefited from both the Commercial and Music Departments.[144]

Numbers compiled from the Mendota College catalogs confirm this. Although individual numbers are somewhat inaccurate, the overall trends are unmistakable. Overwhelmingly, students in the BTS came from outside Illinois, and those in the music and business programs tended to be local people. (The numbers of out-of-state students in the Music Department are somewhat inflated because some BTS students also took some music courses or lessons on the side, but music was not their main area of study.) For example, the 1895–96 catalog lists 13 BTS students, 8 of them from out of state, whereas 28 students were listed for the Commercial Department with only 3 of them from out of state, and 22 students were listed for the Music Department, with just 7 from out of state. In no year did the number of Illinois-Mendota students in the BTS outnumber the out-of-state students, and the difference was often substantial. In the second decade of the Mendota era, the difference between the two sets of students widened. In Mendota's first decade, before 1903–4, the largest gap between out-of-state and Illinois students was 10, but in the second decade, it was 23. In this era, student numbers were rising, but that was not increasing the local enrollment in the BTS.[145]

The reverse can be argued for enrollment in the Commercial and Music Departments. Except for just one year (and then it was a difference of just one student), more Illinois students enrolled in business courses than out-of-state students. And whereas the BTS enrollment numbers grew in the second decade, they were generally lower in that period for the Commercial Department. Since more local people enrolled in business courses than in the BTS, perhaps the lower enrollment numbers in the Commercial Department meant that, as time went on, the pool of people who had not attended the college, but wanted to, had shrunk. There was a more limited supply of potential students for business courses because Mendota was a small town in a rural area that contained other, equally small or smaller towns. Perhaps the market for such courses was simply drying up a bit. The pattern of many local people taking business courses is backed up by anecdotal evidence as well. Just a month after the college started up in 1893, President Campbell noted, with pleasure, how many students Mendota was contributing to the college's enrollment. He added that "if Adventists would but duplicate the quota of pupils already contributed by Mendota, our spring term would show an enrollment of over thirty matriculants."[146] These students could not have been enrolled in the BTS because it had not yet begun operations. It only began offering classes in June of 1893. And several years later, in 1897, a student wrote in his *Our Hope* column: "The city of Mendota ... is quite well represented this fall in our Commercial Department."[147] Enrollment patterns in the Music Department were similar to those in the Commercial Department in that local people predominated—and usually in substantial numbers.[148]

The student body of Mendota College also included substantial numbers of young women. They dominated in numbers overall in at least eight out of fifteen years at Mendota College (not counting the first, full year; the two years for which the catalog is missing; and the year of the move to Aurora). In the years when there were more men, all the years but one (which had 37 percent women) saw the percentage of women in the 40s (ranging from 47 percent down to 42 percent).[149]

Women's numbers were bolstered by their dominance in the Music Department, where they constituted a majority every year. But men's overall numbers were also bolstered—by their dominance in two departments, the BTS and the Commercial Department, areas in which men were the majority every year for which there is data. Yet even in the BTS area, the percentages of women students were substantial—the highest percentage being 39 percent and the lowest being 0 percent (This was for one year only; every other year had percentages for women in the 30s and 40s). The Commercial Department was different. In that area, men dominated more thoroughly, the women's highest percentage being 36 percent and the lowest being 6 percent. All but three of the percentages for women in this area were in the 20s and 30s.[150]

More men than women were enrolled in the collegiate program, but they were less dominant there than in the BTS. For the twelve years for which there are data (there were three years in which no one was enrolled in the college-degree programs), men constituted a majority of students in eight of those years. In two other school years, there were equal numbers of men and women enrolled, and for two years, more women were enrolled than men. Looking at the male majority years, six of the eight years saw the percentages of women's enrollment in the 30s and 40s. Thus, women did attend Mendota College, and in substantial numbers. And they were welcome. One BTS faculty man wrote in an 1894 issue of *Our Hope*: "THE BIBLE TRAINING SCHOOL has now one commendable feature in it over last year, aside from having a larger attendance, that is: the *sisters* are also attending, two joining the class at the opening of the school, and others intending to join. And still there is more room for both sexes."[151] Women were welcome at the college because the Advent Christian denomination needed them to be trained for work in its churches and mission fields and also because they pushed up enrollment figures and brought in tuition money. Schools like Mendota College could not afford to ignore them.[152]

Significant numbers of women attended Mendota College, but they were hardly on an equal footing with their male classmates. They clustered in traditional areas, like music and art (where, for the two years that the program existed, there were *no* male students), while fewer women took business courses. But there were more opportunities for women in the business world in that day than in the ministry. Substantial numbers of women took courses in the Bible Training School, but it was the men who became ministers. Women, who were the backbone of American Protestant churches in the nineteenth century, were generally viewed as workers in the Sunday schools and mission and temperance societies, and, of course, as ministers' wives, but not as ministers. Those views were evident at the college, especially the BTS, as well. The denomination had a handful of female preachers, but almost none had their own church, except for a tiny number of couples who co-pastored churches. There were few role models of female ministers, and, as religious fundamentalists, Advent Christians embraced traditional gender roles. Although women were welcome to attend the BTS, there were few, if any, expectations that they would go into the ministry. In spite of the not-insignificant number of women who attended the BTS, at least by the end of 1910–11 (the last full school year in Mendota), not a single woman had graduated from that program.[153]

Although the late nineteenth century saw the appearance of what historians call "the new woman," there was little evidence of this on the

Mendota campus, except for one major thing—they were attending a college, and however basic we would today view that college as being, most American women in the 1890s and the 1900s were *not* doing that. Education has a broadening effect—one that is probably magnified when one comes from an insular place and the traditional sphere of women. There is no evidence that Mendota College's women went on to create new careers for women, as the women from the new all-female colleges were doing at this time. Nevertheless, the study of literature, history, mathematics, science, music, and more must have broadened their view of the world, even if they did not graduate. And some women did complete their programs, including three women who earned a bachelor's in science—a liberal arts area dominated by men.[154]

As with its attendance and graduation problem, Mendota College was not unique in having many female students. Bible training schools in general were characterized by substantial numbers of women. In the late nineteenth century, women were still rejected by most seminaries, and so Bible training schools had a readymade pool of potential students. Seminaries were interested in educating future ministers, not in providing the kind of training that would help women do the many different kinds of jobs they had been doing in churches and religious causes for decades— organizing women's societies to recruit, train, and support missionaries as well as women's temperance societies and serving as Sunday school teachers and superintendents, Bible teachers, church secretaries, musicians, and—for a handful of women—even as evangelists. It was not until after 1910 that an increasing number of seminaries ventured beyond their traditional curriculum of ministerial studies and began to offer programs for laypeople, including women.[155]

The Intertwining of Academics and Religion at Mendota College

Early on, it was stated publicly that Mendota College welcomed *all* students, and this was mentioned periodically throughout the Mendota years. In July of 1892 (five months before the opening of the school), the Educational Committee, while still engaged in setting up the college, wrote in *Our Hope* that "the Mendota Seminary shall be open to all applicants, and the profession of no particular religious faith shall be required of its pupils."[156] Eight years later, as part of his January 1900 College Day address, A. J. Bolster, a minister and college board member, stated that "pupils of all faiths—or no faith—will be guaranteed respectful treatment and the advantages of this college untrammeled by any sectarian intrusion. Still, we desire it to be understood as Christian in tone and conduct."[157] And college people may have viewed students who were not evangelical Christians as presenting an opportunity to convert them. In a 1904 *Our Hope* article, J. W. Neslund, a current Mendota student and practicing minister, happily reported that "many young people have accepted Christ after coming here who could not be persuaded to do so while at home. ... There are three who have done so since the opening of this fall term."[158] A policy of religious inclusiveness was smart, given the reality that the college never got the number of Advent Christian students that it wanted and thought its facilities and staff could handle. However, other than local people, it is unlikely that many students from away who were not Advent Christians or evangelical Christians came to Mendota, although a few did.

Nonbelievers would have found that the college *was* an unambiguously Christian and Advent Christian school. This was reflected in the BTS curriculum, certainly, but also in the science curriculum, the religious background of its faculty, and the curricular and extracurricular activities that students participated in. The 1908–9 catalog makes an interesting distinction between the BTS and chapel: "The daily Chapel exercises are not especially intended to form a part of the work of the Biblical department of the school, and students whose religious belief is not in accord with the teachings for which this department stands need have no fear that the Chapel service will be used as an opportunity to indoctrinate them. Work of this kind will be confined to the Theological department."[159] Most of the students who attended the BTS were already Advent Christian, so if chapel, which was mandatory for students and faculty alike, was not a venue for "indoctrination," the local people, many of whom were not Advent Christian and attended the Commercial School, were then perhaps a bit sheltered from the full-blown message of Adventism. However, venturing outside of the Commercial Department meant running into the beliefs of conservative, evangelical Protestantism in general, and Advent Christian doctrine in particular.

These religious beliefs were reflected in the school's curriculum—especially that of the BTS. One former student claimed, in an *Our Hope* article, that the Bible Training School was based on the *Bible* rather than *science*:

> The Bible is *the* text-book in the *theological* department. ... [O]ur theological seminary is not propped up by "science falsely so called," nor does it attempt to reconcile the book of God, with the charming (?) vagaries of the nebular hypothesis, or the atomic theory, neither does it limp along on the crutches of the "higher criticism," but it *does* rest on this one infallible truth. "In the beginning, *God* created the heaven and the earth. Gen. 1:1 [italics in original]."[160]

At least one course in the BTS curriculum dealt with apologetics—teaching students how to defend their religious beliefs, especially against modernist views in religion and science. A student, Sylvester Nokes, wrote about the importance of this for ministers:

> The advanced students will soon complete a course of exegetical study upon the first three chapters of Genesis, intended to fortify the mind against the arguments of modern infidelity and so-called higher criticism, and to settle the question of the inspiration of the Bible. These are fundamental questions which all ministers of the present day are called to meet, and the ability to meet them upon a safe scriptural basis is important to a young preacher of the Kingdom message.[161]

The influence of religion on other parts of the curriculum was strong as well, including the area of science. As Orven H. Loomis, an Advent Christian minister and Mendota College alumnus, wrote about his alma mater: "In many colleges where other courses are taught in connection with a Bible Training course the sciences are not taught in harmony with God's word as they should be. There is no disagreement between true science and the Bible. In Mendota College the Bible comes first then science."[162]

The supremacy of the Bible over scientific principles was especially evident whenever there was a discussion of evolution. Faculty and students alike rejected this theory because it seemed to them to contradict the account in Genesis of how the world and human beings were created. The best example of this is a 1909 two-part article, titled "The Educational Field: Decline, Decay and Death of Darwinism," written for *Our Hope* by Nathan P. Twining (who had earlier served as president but who, in 1909, was a faculty member). He started the article with the provocative statement, "Darwinism is dead!" yet the rest of what he wrote suggests otherwise. He presented Darwinism as having infiltrated many areas of life in a blatant, even overpowering way, stating that "this same Darwinism had become a fabric of huge bulk and vast proportions, having insinuated itself into our language, our literature and even into our text books, designed for public and private schools. It is poison, bereft of bitterness; deleterious, yet sweetly perfumed; very fascinating, at the same time as subtle as satanic advice," ultimately declaring it "the most dangerous cult of modern times."[163] These are not the words of someone who believes such a titanic battle is over and won. In reality, the battle against Darwinism continued in the Mendota College classroom.

Religion played an important role in extracurricular activities as well, taking up much of the limited free time that most students had. Chapel, mandatory for faculty and students alike, was held on campus daily—in the morning, for about half an hour. Chapel services were first mentioned in the 1895–96 catalog, making it clear that chapel was required for students, but with some qualifications: "All students living in the College or near it, and all other students whose duties require them to be at any college exercises during the hour immediately preceding or following chapel services, are required to attend these exercises."[164] Thus, off-campus students who did *not* live near the college were given some wiggle room, but technically this exemption must have affected just a few students. Most of them lived in the school's dormitories or boarded near the college. However, off-campus students may have had a definition of "near" that differed from college authorities. Human nature being what it is, this definition may very well have been manipulated by at least some of these students, who, after all, were the least likely to be Advent Christian. Not surprisingly, there is no direct evidence of students doing this; it is not the kind of thing that was likely to make it into the historical record. But the catalogs did provide a loophole for off-campus students. And there *is* some evidence that faculty attendance at chapel was *not* what was expected by the powers that be. Why else would the college board feel compelled to make this motion at a June 1894 board meeting: It was "moved that the Professors in all depts. be required to attend chapel exercises."[165] Faculty were expected to model a high level of Christian piety, and that included attending daily chapel, no matter how busy they were. Apparently, they had to be reminded of that.

Chapel speakers included guests who were *not* necessarily Advent Christians, including such people as local ministers from other denominations and officials from the National Intercollegiate Prohibition Association, among others. This limited ecumenicalism buttressed the school's claim that "indoctrination" happened in the BTS, not in chapel. However, there were plenty of Advent Christian speakers—ministers traveling through the area; missionaries on furlough; and other prominent people in the denomination, like Henry Pollard (editor of *Our Hope*) and Charles Eckhart (speaking multiple times on different topics, one of which was temperance), as well as faculty and students (both former and current ones). Thus, chapel was a mini-religious service, with a devotional part (prayer, hymn singing, Scripture reading, etc.) and a speaking part on a religious, but also, occasionally, a current, secular topic.[166]

Another major extracurricular religious activity was student prayer meetings. Organized by the students themselves, they were held during most, if not all, of the Mendota years. They took place at least every weekday, generally in the evening after supper—except for prayer meeting night at the Mendota Advent Christian Church. In the 1911 student publication, the *Epitome*, one author identified what students prayed for at their prayer meetings: "We pray for former students in their work, and a continual subject for prayer is the prosperity of our school. ... Thoughts often go to homes that are far away and frequent prayer is made in behalf of the folks at home who miss us and who are sacrificing that we may be here."[167] Based on this description, students were concerned about the college's alumni as well as its future, but they also used these prayer sessions as a means of combatting homesickness. According to another student, they also prayed for the sick and the unconverted. The latter seem to have been never far from their thoughts, as *the* mission of the college was to send out Christian workers to bring people to Christ before it was too late. Praying for the "prosperity" of the school and the work of its former students was also about saving souls before Christ returned to earth.[168]

The Off-Campus Religious Activities of Faculty and Students

Students and faculty also played an active role in religious activities *off* campus. They were especially involved in the Mendota Advent Christian Church. It was a virtual extension of the college in that it was organized and a building was purchased for it in 1892 because an Advent Christian college was coming to Mendota. The founders of the college had no choice but to organize an Advent Christian church—to support the work of the college and, of course, to provide an Adventist house of worship for the many Advent Christians at the school. And since one of the arguments used *against* locating a college in Mendota had been that there was no Advent Christian church there, they had to do it to respond to that issue and answer that need. This all made for a unique situation. The college people did not join a church that had formed naturally; initially, the college people *were* the church, although over time additional people joined the church who did not work at the college. It was the first "college church," and, because it was, it had some special issues. After the college moved to Aurora, the Advent Christian church there became the "college church," while the Mendota church lost a large number of its members. The college did not have to establish a church in its new hometown. The Aurora church had existed since the early 1860s and so was an experienced, stable institution that was financially supported by Aurorans. The college people simply joined it and added to its strength and stability.[169]

By 1904, the church building was in desperate need of extensive remodeling and expansion. Originally a basic, single-room building with just two stoves for heat and oil-burning lamps for light, the remodeling included some excavation to put in a partial basement for a heating plant; an addition that housed some Sunday school classrooms as well as an assembly hall; a new, higher pulpit; a raised ceiling in the sanctuary; more modern lighting, and new windows. The church raised $1,800 of the $3,000 that it needed but then hit a wall in its fundraising. Due to its limited number of paying church members, it sent out a plea for financial help, via *Our Hope*, to Advent Christians elsewhere. This article's author made an argument for why the Mendota Advent Christian church should get help from people outside of its membership, saying that it is "a central and important church to our Western cause, being our college church, and as such have some claim, they think, upon denominational sympathy and help. It is important that our college church should present a neat appearance, and have regular, well conducted services for the benefit of students, who attend, but cannot be expected to contribute toward church expenses."[170] Being a college church established simultaneously with its college had its perks, like a built-in membership, but it had its downside as well, especially financially. Students were a transient population and lacked the funds to support a church. Many, if not most, students were working their way through the college or came with very limited funds that had to be stretched to last the school year. They could not be counted on to help maintain the church or contribute to special projects like enlarging the church.[171]

However, there were multiple ways to contribute to and support the Mendota church, even for students. They could contribute their presence and their labor to the church and did so. They, of course, attended the church's various services—the midweek prayer meeting, the two Sunday services (both morning and evening), and special services (like those for multi-evening revivals). They not only attended revival services, they worked for them as well. In 1904, the Aurora Advent Christian Church's minister, who was a former Mendota College student, invited the minister of the Mendota church, along with some of the college's students, to come to Aurora to hold some revival services. When the Aurora minister reported on these services in *Our Hope*, he noted that "we called these consecrated workers from Mendota College, 'The Pentecostal Band,' and while many colleges were sending out a foot-ball team, Mendota College sent out a band of earnest happy Christians, to hold a revival meeting."[172] And in 1908, the Mendota church had a revival that was so fruitful, it was extended. Not only did the students attend the nightly services—which was a challenge on weeknights, given the work they had to get done for classes the next day—they also did what they could to help out with the revival, including distributing flyers in Mendota to advertise the services.[173]

Students contributed to the church in other ways as well. They joined various groups within the church, especially an organization called Loyal Workers. In 1904, a former student, writing an *Our Hope* article, noted the extensive participation of the college's students in the Mendota Advent Christian Church, especially the Loyal Workers: "The church meetings and Sunday school are quite well attended by the students generally. The church Loyal Workers' Society of young people, composed largely of college students, is another source of spiritual help, growth, and development. ..."[174] And students sometimes provided music for services—both vocal and instrumental. One student group that provided music was a male quartet, which was asked to play at both Memorial Day services and Mendota tent meetings in 1906. In short, on many occasions, church members benefited from various college musical groups performing for services, recitals, and special events.[175]

Faculty, local board members, and staff also contributed to the Mendota church—in financially supporting the church, which was especially important given the number of student members who had virtually no money to contribute to its support, and in providing leadership. For example, as mentioned earlier in this chapter, two of the four principals of the BTS—N. P. Cook and F. A. Baker—served as pastors of the Mendota church in addition to their work at the college. Both faculty and local board members served in other church leadership roles as well, including fundraising.[176]

This relationship was not a one-way street. Yes, college people had created the church, and it depended on the school for much of its membership and leadership. However, the church helped the college in various important ways as well. It occasionally served as a place where groups of BTS students could practice what they had learned by taking over the Sunday evening service to give presentations or mini-sermons. From time to time, a BTS student preached at the Mendota church, which gave him an opportunity to practice and improve his sermon-writing and preaching techniques in the real world. Church people who did not work for the college sometimes socialized with the students, occasionally having them over to their homes for a social gathering of some kind. And the women in the Mendota church's chapter of the Helpers' Union were especially active in working to provide for the needs of the college. They raised money for specific college projects, like refurbishing the library and president's office, in 1906. They also prepared the dormitories for the new academic year. In 1902, they did such a good job that they were applauded for this work in a 1902 *Our Hope* article. The author wrote that they "cleaned, painted, papered, laid carpets, and placed furniture *throughout* the dormitory, beside making the boys' rooms in the college cozy, comfortable and home-like; and that in a way that has been replete with self-sacrifice; not hesitating, when some article seemed to be especially needed, to go into their own homes and *deprive themselves* that others might be more pleasantly environed [italics in original]."[177] In short, they provided services and goods for the college, some of these products made by the women themselves. Even the church building was an extension of the college. Because the school had no assembly hall, it used the Mendota church as its auditorium anytime more than a few people were expected at an event. It was used for the College Day service, Commencement, the annual recital of the Music Department, and special concerts and lectures, like President Twining's famous stereopticon lectures based on his travels in Europe.[178]

There seems to have been recognition of how each institution—the church and the college—supported the other on this two-way street. In February 1907, a student reporter for *Our Hope* wrote that "two college students, and two members of the faculty speak Sunday evening on what the Mendota AC church should do for the college and college students. Last week we were told by members and the pastor what the students and college could do for the church."[179] Despite this recognition of each other and talk about what each could do for the other, the church and the college were not fully distinct entities. They were mutually dependent and overlapped substantially, so that the lines between them must have blurred at times, making it difficult to know exactly where the college left off and the church began.[180]

Mendota College students also were involved with local evangelical activities. They helped out at revivals and performed home missionary work. In 1908, as just noted, college students helped publicize a revival in the Mendota Advent Christian Church by distributing flyers to advertise it around town. Then their work, and attendance at the nightly services, were extended by another whole week because the revival was doing so well. But it did not take a big event like a revival to get students out distributing material. In 1906, some students spent part of a Saturday participating in a systematic distribution of religious tracts all over Mendota. At times, students even entered the homes of Mendota residents—presumably with the owner's permission. In 1907, a student reporter for *Our Hope* identified a similar activity—students traveling around the town knocking on doors: "Our students have now organized among ourselves one or more mission bands, who will devote Sunday afternoon to calling at Mendota residences for the purpose of brief religious services."[181] Six weeks later the student updated this report, saying that "the students' singing bands are making good use of our Sunday afternoons. People seem glad to have them come into their homes for a short session of singing, prayer and Scripture reading."[182] For the college's students, weekends, and sometimes weekday evenings, were not always times when they could catch up with their school work because religious services and activities were calling.[183]

Students not only worked at revivals, they were emotionally and religiously affected by them. A 1904 *Our Hope* article details how one particular revival affected the students. It is not clear where the impetus for this originated—a revival in the Mendota Advent Christian Church, another Mendota church, a city-wide revival, or the college itself. But it does seem to have had a direct effect. References to a religious awakening among the college's students appear in *Our Hope* throughout the 1904–5 school year. The author of one such article claimed that there were "very remarkable outpourings of God's spirit among the students. Several have received a regular Pentecostal baptism of Holy Ghost power, and the only unconverted student in the college has confessed her sins and claims to have received pardon. This latter occurred at an impromptu meeting held unexpectedly at the dormitory one evening. The others occurred generally or entirely at meetings held at the home of Bro. F. E. Roberts. ..." And, as proof of the intensity of the religious revival that was sweeping across the campus at this time, the author added, "The young ladies have cast aside their finery—rings, jewelry, etc., of their own free will. Misunderstandings have been cleared up, apologies made, and debts paid. A decided change has come over the actions of many."[184] This particular revival at the college may have been especially transformative, but it was one of many that students worked at or attended.

The fact that Mendota College students did so much religious work beyond the campus is not surprising. During their time at the college, students had little to do with the secular world—except perhaps their jobs, although some students worked on campus. Religious influences could be found throughout the curriculum, students played an important role in the Mendota Advent Christian Church, they spent much time attending religious services and performing evangelistic tasks of various types, and their social activities were overwhelmingly centered on the college and the church. There were social activities and places for socializing in the town of Mendota, but they did not hold much allure for the students because they often involved doing things that were viewed as sinful by Advent Christians and were forbidden by the college—dancing, drinking, smoking, card playing, etc. For the most part, they lived in a religious and social cocoon, which was what many parents and faculty wanted.

The Annual Great Western Campmeeting Held on the Mendota College Campus

A campmeeting is an annual, usually weeklong gathering of people from a Protestant denomination, located in a rural setting. The days are filled with religious services of various kinds, with an evening, revival service capping off every day. The goal of these meetings is to win new souls for Christ (i.e., have a conversion experience, be "born" again) as well as to renew and nourish the religious lives of those attendees already in the fold. The Methodists invented the campmeeting, and then other evangelical groups, including the Millerites and Adventist Christians, copied this model. In fact, Advent Christians and some other denominations still have campmeetings. Early on, tents were used at these gatherings—a larger one to house the services and smaller ones to provide sleeping places. Over the years, tents were replaced with small, wooden cottages.[185]

The major campmeeting in the Midwest was called the Great Western Campmeeting. When the decision was made to buy the five-acre property in Mendota to start a college, it was also decided that both the campmeeting and the publication society would move there too. The first campmeeting was held on the Mendota campus before the college even opened its doors—in August of 1892. Following that schedule, the campmeeting continued to be held annually in August. No cottages were ever built on the Mendota campus, although at times people were urged to do that. Even before the college opened, the publication association voted to recommend to the Campmeeting Committee that it lay out lots on the north side of the campus—lots on which cottages could be built. However, tents were used throughout the Mendota years and even on the Aurora campus for the few years early on that the campmeeting was held there. Although many, if not most, campmeeting attendees slept in tents, anyone who preferred not to sleep on the ground could rent a room in the college building since most of the students were gone at that time of year. The campmeeting also used the college kitchen to feed the crowds, usually consisting of several hundred people.[186]

Statistics from the early years give a good indication of the scope of the campmeeting and how it worked. In 1892, around 350 people attended; in 1893, there were over 400 attendees (from fifteen states); and in 1894, more than 330 worshippers came. From the first year on, there was a huge tent to hold the services—seating 600 to 800 people—and it was lit with electricity. People could rent rooms (in the college building or even in nearby homes), tents (from $2.50 to $5.75, depending on size), cots (35 cents each), mattresses (35–40 cents), and chairs (10–20 cents each). In 1892, there were fifty-five tents and in 1894, forty-five. In 1892, twenty-four rooms were rented A meal could be had for 15–20 cents, and other food was available on the campus. In 1895, a "grocery" was available for those who wanted to prepare their own food, and there were multiple stands on the grounds, which sold bread and butter, fruit, ice cream, and lemonade. In at least 1893, there was a photographic gallery. There must have been photographers at other campmeetings as well, given the number of photographs of the campmeetings and the people who attended them that are in Aurora University's Jenks Collection. And at least in some years, if not all, the campmeeting association was able to successfully negotiate with the major railroads to get a reduced train fare for attendees coming from specific states. For example, in 1895, people who traveled to Mendota from Illinois, Iowa, and Wisconsin paid, for a round-trip ticket, a full fare for one way, but just a third of the cost for the trip back home.[187]

Not surprisingly, many ministers and Advent Christian lay leaders attended the campmeeting. Out of the 350 people who attended the 1892 campmeeting, 60 of them were ministers. About 60 ministers also attended the next year, and 35 to 40 the year after that. And everyone was kept busy with many services to attend. With so many ministers in attendance and working at the urgent business of saving souls before Christ's return, one might think that campmeeting week was a somber time. At times, no doubt, this was true. Yet there also was a fun, holiday aspect to it. People got to retreat to a beautiful place where they could enjoy nature's beauty for a week. Although the Mendota campus was in a town rather than a more rural area, it provided a beautiful, park-like setting with its many, large, shade trees. Attendees also got to reunite with relatives and friends. Often whole families came in what was for them a kind of vacation. One woman, who attended the Mendota campmeeting for the first time in 1893, was pleasantly surprised, given the seriousness of the Adventist religious message, at the happy tone of the encampment, describing it like this: "Children, young and old people everywhere were lying in hammocks, walking or visiting in groups, singing, etc., occupying the time between services. ..."[188] In short, many Advent Christians viewed campmeeting as a special time when God's work was done, but also when bonds of Christian fellowship were built and strengthened.[189]

Such positive feelings were good for Mendota College. Creating an association in people's minds between the inspiration and camaraderie of campmeeting and Mendota College was better than any public relations campaign. A goodly number of people came to the college from places that the school drew its students from. Parents got to see the college for themselves—meeting the people who ran it, seeing what the accommodations were like, and, most importantly for them, being reassured that it was a place where their children could study in a Christian environment, protected from worldly ideas and temptations. A board member, reporting on the 1893 campmeeting in *Our Hope*, noted that "the school question came in for a large share of attention, which showed the great interest our people have in that important feature of our work."[190] Perhaps there was a lot of buzz about the college because this campmeeting was held in the first year of the college's existence and was just the second one held on the campus. But having the campmeeting there any year was good for Mendota College. The school got to showcase itself and raise funds for its work.

Most important to the future of the college, since so many midwestern Adventists were gathered together for this one week, was that the college, in effect, had a captive audience, making campmeeting week an excellent time to raise money for the school. At the first campmeeting, in 1892, money was raised via pledges for the new college, which was just then being organized and was in desperate need of funds. The next year the huge sum of $2,500 was raised for the school in cash and pledges. This amount was so impressive because typically throughout any given year, contributions trickled in (except for a few weeks right after College Day), and in small amounts. And, during the campmeeting week of 1901, a special fund to finance repairs on the college campus was created and then $1,200 was raised for it. In some years, the college carried debt from the preceding school year through the summer, only to pay it off suddenly in time for the next academic year. This was usually because the required amount of money had been raised at the Mendota campmeeting. One of these years was 1908 (one of the college's high-debt years), when the school's current debt was paid off, in cash and pledges, after $440 was raised among the attendees. It clearly was easier to raise money at the campmeeting than through pleas for funds in *Our Hope*, which seemed to produce relatively little. In Mendota, during that week, college leaders could speak to their fellow western Advent Christians in services and individually. The pressure put on attendees, both from college people and their peers, was considerably more direct. Another factor that made fundraising at this time effective was that the annual meeting of the Western Advent Christian Publication Association was held then, at which the financial state of the college was discussed. As a result, the campmeeting attendees came to the rescue of the college on a number of occasions.[191]

Another advantage for the school of holding the midwestern campmeeting on its campus was that it allowed people to see the college facilities for themselves, and usually attendees visiting the campus for the first time were impressed. However, the campus, especially the college building, did have serious issues at times. Seeing the problems of the physical plant firsthand could lead to greater, more immediate action to fix them, and sometimes this happened. In 1895, J. W. Emmons attended the campmeeting for the first time and was dismayed to see the sorry condition of the college building. He immediately sprang into action and led a campaign to raise money to remodel and redecorate it. He also oversaw the project and made sure that it was done promptly. This extensive job was completed and paid for in just three months. He saw this project through with tremendous enthusiasm, and the experience created another ardent supporter of the college. This is reflected in the article he wrote for *Our Hope* at the end of the project:

> I never have commenced a work that I have felt so intense a desire to bring to a finish, as I have this work of repairs and furnishing the rooms for the students to occupy. I shall ever bless the day when I first stepped on the Mendota College campus. Never was there more necessity for immediate action than there was to put Mendota College in a condition fit for occupancy. Never were our people more interested in the welfare of the institution than at this time. I am fully persuaded that as a people we are determined that our college *shall be a success*; and that failure shall never be written on its doors [italics in original].[192]

It was most fortunate for the college that Emmons made the decision to attend campmeeting that year. Emmons, who was a medical doctor, joined the college board around 1898 and remained on the board until the end of the Mendota era. He was an active board member who involved himself in fundraising. It is not unreasonable to wonder whether Emmons would have done all that he did had he not attended campmeeting in 1895, seen the poor shape of the college building, and demonstrated his leadership skills in leading a campaign to fix it up.[193]

Attendees of the campmeeting also were given an opportunity to better understand the work and needs of the college in a more formal way. In 1902, there was a College Day program on one day of that week, put together and presented by college faculty. Campmeeting provided an opportunity for college leaders to educate people about the work that the college was doing and why the school was so vital to the denomination and their own churches. The message of this program was then reinforced by the presence of the audience themselves on the campus, where they could explore the facilities, ask questions, and talk to faculty and students.[194]

Campmeeting also provided a time when the members of college-related organizations could get together to do business. Since so many Advent Christians attended the campmeeting, a number of the denomination's organizations held their annual meeting right before, during, or after campmeeting week. This made sense because it saved people a trip, and probably fewer people would have attended at another time. At least two of the groups that met then were especially important to Mendota College. One of them was WACPA. Their large meeting was different from either that of the WACPA board or its Educational Committee/Board of Directors. It was the annual, general meeting of the publication association, attended by delegates from fifteen different conferences in the Midwest. This group did not run the daily affairs of the organization. Instead, the publication association's directors and the delegates voted on the big issues—like their vote in 1910 on whether or not the college should relocate to Aurora. Another group important to the college that met during campmeeting week was the Helpers' Union—the organization of women that did so much to supply the material needs of the school and help its students. In fact, it was at the 1894 campmeeting that a group of women formed this organization. Thus, much business was conducted on the Mendota campus—just before, during, and right after campmeeting week—by a number of different Advent Christian organizations, and much of it concerned the college.[195]

How Credible Was Mendota College Academically?

From this historical distance, it is difficult to evaluate the quality of Mendota College. We cannot observe the teachers' performance and grading processes or look at the textbooks they used. We can look at the curriculum and how it changed over time in the college catalogs, but we cannot know what the course content was beyond a course title. Nor can we easily gauge the level of difficulty in any given course. And because the nineteenth century was a long time ago—in effect a different world—colleges then were quite different. There is evidence that can be evaluated, however. Scholars of higher education who have done so state that the academic level at this time was generally low. It has been estimated that in 1900, almost halfway through the Mendota era, probably no more than 20 percent of the approximately five hundred schools of higher learning in existence could be considered true colleges or universities.[196]

The amount of education needed for someone to teach at the college level in the late nineteenth century was far less than today, often just a bachelor's degree, if that. Older faculty were sometimes largely self-educated and taught in many different fields—like George Dewing. Graduate education began in the late nineteenth century, and by the 1890s, growing numbers of professors had PhDs. However, as late as 1884, Harvard had just 19 out of 189 professors who had earned a PhD, while the University of Michigan had just 6 PhDs out of 88 professors. And it was the larger, wealthier, more prestigious schools which first acquired those with PhDs to teach at their institutions. Having many faculty members with a doctorate came much later for small schools, with their limited, financial resources. At such colleges and BTSs, some faculty had a bachelor's degree, but some did not even have that. This was the case at Mendota College for most, if not all, of its years. In a 1905 *Our Hope* "College Notes" column, a student reported, as evidence of how much the college had advanced in quality, that now *nearly* all Mendota College faculty had a degree. Only one person had a PhD—Nathan Twining— and it is not clear whether that was an earned degree or an honorary one.[197]

For the most part, Mendota College had a traditional academic program, even for the era. The BTS taught typically conservative religious doctrines; other than the Adventists' distinctive beliefs about Christ's imminent return, these were largely what other conservative, evangelical denominations were teaching at their schools. And the Bible was always said to be the main textbook of the program. The curriculum reform that took place at the college around the turn of the twentieth century, in both the classical and the scientific programs, did not introduce any innovative curricular ideas, although apparently it did make at least some of the coursework more challenging. At a time when national reforms were pushing colleges away from the classics and providing a more pragmatic curriculum that was grounded in the modern world, the curriculum at Mendota College almost looked like it could have served as the course of study for an antebellum-era college.[198]

However, even though the college's curriculum was traditional and its academic programs weak by today's standards, it was not completely immune to curricular change. Starting with the 1901–2 school year, the BTS program went from two years to three, requiring a greater commitment from students in time, money, and intellectual effort. By at least 1904, in order to graduate from the BTS, students had to demonstrate that they could read the Old Testament in Hebrew and the New Testament in Greek. When the bachelor of divinity degree came along in 1906, earning it required that a student have at least an 80 percent grade average in all coursework, on the college-degree thesis paper, on the pre-graduation exam for elective coursework, and, by 1909, on an additional thesis paper, in biblical studies. By 1909, the vast majority of BTS students—those just pursuing a diploma of graduation rather than the divinity degree—had to achieve at least a 70 percent average in their coursework. Also, nearly from the beginning, the college had two parallel tracks—classical and scientific—which was a bow to the growing importance of science and mathematics, at a time when most colonial and antebellum colleges had mainly classical curricula. These two college-degree tracks became more challenging when a senior thesis paper became a requirement for graduation in the 1904–5 academic year. In the science curriculum, the biggest change was that a number of science course titles had the word "advanced" added to them, suggesting, perhaps, that they were now courses that were more genuinely at the college level. And although the college did not have a curriculum requiring majors and general education courses per se, it did add a few electives over time, although mainly in the BTS.[199]

There was also a mixture of the new with the traditional in teaching methods. Generally speaking, they were typical for the nineteenth century. Many classes included daily "recitations." In fact, what we would call "classes" were usually referred to as "recitations" in the Mendota years. Reciting is not looked upon favorably today, and rightfully so, because it is generally defined as a student simply memorizing material and then regurgitating it in class. But there was, no doubt, a spectrum in recitations—from a mindless recitation of simple, memorized facts at one end over to a presentation requiring at least some understanding of the material. There is some evidence that the daily recitations were not always a regurgitation of facts but demanded some understanding of class readings and application of knowledge, especially in the BTS, where learning the practicalities of being a minister was emphasized. For example, in a 1901 *Our Hope* article, a minister provided an example of this:

> In this department, students are taught the fundamental truths of Christianity, drilled in conducting meetings, instructed upon the divine call to the ministry, prophecy, church ordinances, sermon preparation, pastoral and evangelistic work, mission work, and Bible exegesis. There is also a pulpit drill each morning, a sermon being delivered by one of the students, and then discussed by the class.[200]

What was called a pulpit "drill" was far more than spouting facts about how to do a sermon; students had to actually *give* a sermon, which then was "discussed." That had to have included, at least to some degree, a critique of the student's sermon, requiring an understanding of what principles constituted a good sermon and critical thinking to see whether or not the sermon met these standards. This was what today would be called "hands-on" or "student-centered learning." This was not mindless regurgitation.[201]

Lectures were also given in classes, including in the BTS. Associated with the new, large universities whose professors were becoming more and more specialized, lectures were viewed as a more modern and, given the larger classes, more efficient way of teaching. Mendota College, of course, had much smaller classes, and its professors were not as specialized in teaching areas, but lectures were still sometimes used. However, there was a difference. Due to small class sizes, lectures could be given that allowed for some student input. Early on, in 1894, an *Our Hope* editor wrote: "The method of instruction in our Bible Training School is mainly by oral lectures upon the principles of Bible Truth. These lectures are adapted to the capacity and needs of the class and are quite free and informal, to draw out each student and develop individual thought and expression."[202] This does not sound like the kind of lectures that were being given at universities—those having virtually no student input. Years later, the 1902–3 catalog gave a similar description of BTS lectures: "The instruction in these classes will be given, for the most part, by means of lectures (upon which students will write theses), with frequent references, however, to the authorities, and accompanied by various drills in which the students will put the theories they have learned into actual practice."[203] This quotation suggests that BTS students were processing the lectures by immediately writing about them and applying their material in class "drills." Again, this stands in contrast to students simply listening to lectures and passively taking notes on them.[204]

Because the student body, and thus class size, was small, faculty were better able to have some student-centered activities in class, giving more individual attention to their students than would have been feasible at a large university. The college's students acknowledged this from time to time, expressing their appreciation. For example, one noted that "all students get the benefit of individual instruction, and are called upon to recite every day, and a large share of every lesson. ... In small classes students can ask questions freely upon the lesson—an important privilege."[205]

Another form that student-centered learning took in the BTS was what were essentially informal internships. They were not required for graduation, and students earned no course credits for engaging in them, but virtually all students preparing for the ministry took on preaching jobs—as one-day jobs or even short- or long-term ones. Aspiring ministers often preached at various local churches during the school year and at churches some distance away when on a school break or over the summer. Students sometimes filled in for a pastor who had to be away on a Sunday, but sometimes a student, in effect, became a church's pastor when it had none, filling in for months or even longer, until the church found a new minister. There were always many, small Advent Christian churches that had no minister, so generally, opportunities to preach were not lacking. In a 1908 *Our Hope* column, a student reported that there were so many requests from churches for Mendota College students to supply their pulpit during the summer that it was feared that some requests would have to be turned down.[206]

It seems more than likely that the college played at least some role in helping students find placements and approving them. Starting in the 1909–10 catalog, this was made explicit: "Theological students adjudged competent will be assisted as far as possible in securing pastoral, evangelistic or mission work; but all students wishing to engage in such work must do so with the advice and approval of the faculty."[207] This was, no doubt, to protect both the students and the college. School officials surely did not want their students to get into a bad situation, and they also knew that the BTS students going out to preach were advertisements for the school. To recruit more students and raise more money, these students needed to make a good impression. And it was no easy thing to do. One BTS student wrote that "it requires extra hard work for a student, of no great experience in the ministry, to carry on a course of study at college, make good standing in the classroom and also preach twice every Sunday."[208]

At times, students outside of the BTS also engaged in hands-on learning and experiences outside the classroom. This obviously happened in the area of music, with its performance-based classes and lessons, end-of-the-year recitals, and extracurricular choirs, orchestra, singing groups, etc. It also took place in the Commercial Department, which focused on concrete, pragmatic, business skills rather than more general topics like economic theory. This is obvious from the courses offered over the years—bookkeeping, business arithmetic, English grammar, penmanship, rapid calculation, spelling, stenography, typewriting, etc. Most of these courses required students to perform operations of various sorts, and they often worked individually in class doing this. Students also went on field trips, especially in the sciences. Be it a gathering at a faculty member's home to watch an eclipse of the moon, a trip by a physics class to the Mendota Electric Light plant, or geology classes' daylong trips to Starved Rock to look at that location's distinctive rocks, students periodically left the classroom to engage in experiential learning. In the sciences, this happened on campus as well. In 1907, it was reported, in *Our Hope*, that students in President Dean's Geology and Mineralogy class were busy classifying specimens of rocks and minerals, then arranging them for the college museum and laboratories. In doing this, students performed a valuable service for the college while, at the same time, they had an opportunity to apply what they had learned in the classroom.[209]

While the educational experience at Mendota College included a number of things that would be applauded today, the college also engaged in practices that would *not* be as acceptable. One of these was the hiring of students to teach classes. Granted, the number of students who did this at the college was not large, and just over a third of those who taught did so in the Commercial Department, where they taught only skill-based courses like typewriting and shorthand. And this practice was not unheard of. Many colleges used students in the classroom in the nineteenth century. In fact, President Twining, while still a student at Milton College, taught there several years, in the 1860s. However, what was perhaps less common was appointing a student—a senior in the BTS, Roby C. Robbins—to serve as interim principal for the BTS after Baker suddenly resigned in August 1903. He served in this position for several months, into 1904, when Jenks became principal.[210]

Eleven students taught at the college in the Mendota period. Of these, there were eight men and three women. Four out of the eleven taught in the Commercial Department—at least three of them teaching just typewriting or typewriting along with shorthand. Two students taught in the high school–level Preparatory Department—both of them listed as "assistants." Four students taught more weighty courses, among those at least two of the women. One man—Milton M. Livingston—taught Greek and Latin, while the other man—Roby C. Robbins—taught Hebrew and English; one woman—Ethel Fry—taught English, while the other woman—Ethel Shatto—taught mathematics and science (but was listed as an assistant in these areas). At least three of the four students teaching college-level, liberal arts courses appear to have been superior students. Both men—Livingston and Robbins—completed not one but two programs, graduating with a classical bachelor's degree and a BTS diploma. They were the only two in the Mendota years to complete these two programs. A handful of other people graduated with two diplomas, but the second one was either from the Commercial Department or the Preparatory Department. Both men taught at the college after graduating—Robbins, from 1904 to 1910, and Livingston, in the 1910–11 academic year, as did one of the women—Shatto, from 1907 to 1909. Shatto left the college in 1909 to pursue graduate studies. However, although she graduated with a bachelor's degree in science, she taught German and English Literature at the college after graduation.[211]

Hiring students to teach is certainly not ideal by today's standards, especially if the student has the course all to himself rather than being an assistant to a regular faculty member. However, this practice is not as far removed from today as one might think, given how many first-year graduate students teach undergraduate courses as graduate assistants. They, of course, have college degrees, but in their first year of teaching, they are just a few months to a year ahead of those students who taught at Mendota College. And nearly half (five) of the Mendota students who taught were listed in catalogs as being an "assistant" in a particular area, suggesting that they did not teach courses by themselves. No doubt, the major reason that students were used was to stretch the meager college budget. Rather than earning a salary, some of these students received their tuition, room, and board or were paid a nominal fee of $5 or $6 a month for each class taught. One student, who taught in the Commercial Department, was given the tuition collected for his shorthand class but not for his typewriting class. Another student received 75 percent of the tuition for both shorthand and typewriting. Over the years, students were paid in different ways, but most of these different forms of remuneration had at least one thing in common—they were cost effective for the college in that it paid the students in kind or at least did not have to pay the students *directly*, as in the case of the typewriting and shorthand classes.[212]

Another area where Mendota College's policies look less than desirable was admissions. They differed from the standards of Aurora College/University, but they very much reflected the standards of the nineteenth century, as they were more moralistic and not very selective. A prospective student had to be at least fourteen years of age. This low minimum age existed because the college had a Preparatory Department, and fourteen was the age of freshmen entering high school. They also had to be of good moral character. Evidence for the latter could come in the form of a letter of recommendation from one's minister, former teacher, etc. or a certificate of honorable dismissal from a previous school. This emphasis on being of good moral character was characteristic of most colleges, even state institutions, in the early nineteenth century and of church-related colleges later in the century. However, by that time, the large universities that were developing rejected the moralism and paternalism of earlier schools. The major thing that concerned them was the academic life of their students.[213]

The college's methods of certifying whether a student was ready to attend the school were also behind the times. Prospective students for the Preparatory Department had to give proof of having completed the work of elementary school. Testing also was given before a student was allowed to take "advanced" or college-level courses. An alternative to testing was presenting a certificate confirming that work was satisfactorily completed at another school. It was not until the 1909–10 school year that the college catalog defined more explicitly, for those entering the college based on credentials from an accredited school, what qualified as a full four-year high school program. This represented movement in a more modern direction. However, adding the credentialing of high schools to testing was an admissions trend that was well underway at American colleges and universities by 1909–10. Mendota College was hardly on the cutting edge in this area.[214]

One of the policies that stands out the most as reflecting weak standards was the school's willingness to allow students to come who did not academically qualify for even the Preparatory Department. Catalogs stated that if prospective students fell short of having an elementary-school education, college faculty would work with them to bring them up to that level, although they would not be officially admitted to the preparatory program until they reached that goal. Perhaps the college did this out of a sense of altruism and/or recognition that many Advent Christian students lived in places where educational institutions were poor or nonexistent. It also brought in some additional, much-needed funds. However, it means that the college, in one way or another, took in virtually anyone, if not officially. However, Mendota College was not alone in having low admission standards. This was typical of many colleges around the turn of the century— not just small, church-related colleges but also some larger schools, like land grant colleges. For example, the admissions criteria for the Connecticut Agricultural College (later, the University of Connecticut) did not require students to have a high school degree until 1914.[215]

Another policy—concerning the time of registration—was in this category as well. Although the college constantly urged students to show up at the beginning of a term, throughout the Mendota era many did not. In fact, some showed up astonishingly late—at times just weeks before the end of a term. And whenever students arrived, no matter how late, the college took them in. Most of the catalogs stated this as an actual policy, although always within the context of it being highly desirable that students arrive at the beginning of a term. Starting in 1895–96, the majority of catalogs included this: "Students can enter at any time, but experience has fully demonstrated that it is greatly to the advantage of the student to be present at the beginning of the term. This is important for several reasons: the student can then receive the proper classification, be on equal footing with his classmates, and pursue studies which are continuous through the year and cannot be repeated."[216] This phenomenon also was not unheard of in the nineteenth century, especially in Bible training schools. However, just because it was done elsewhere did not make it a good practice, and constantly trying to get students caught up could not have made for a good classroom situation nor for a quality education for the late students themselves. Why was the college so tolerant on this subject? There is no direct evidence to answer this question. However, an educated guess is that it had to do with finances and with actually getting students to the college. Even late students brought in badly needed funds, and perhaps once there, if only for a short time initially, students would make friends and get enough of a taste of college life to bring them back the next term.[217]

What is the overall academic evaluation of Mendota College? The school was woefully deficient by today's standards and deserves mixed reviews when judged by the standards of its day. It was certainly better than most stand-alone BTSs and some colleges of the late nineteenth century, but it suffered in comparison to other schools, especially because of its financial woes. The college's financial weakness affected its academic resources and the number of faculty it could hire, as well as the academic level of its students, many of them not having yet acquired a high school degree.

Its close relationship to the Advent Christian church brought in many of its students, but its Adventist beliefs affected the quality of the education provided. When religious beliefs conflicted with evidence-based facts, as with Darwinism, Adventist religious beliefs prevailed. Advocates for the college would talk about finding truth through education, but Advent Christians, like other fundamentalist, evangelical groups, believed there was just one TRUTH. This belief that there was such a thing as a single truth was very much a nineteenth-century idea. But scholars of the day argued that truth could be found through the accumulation of facts—which they talked about almost as if they were concrete things that could be collected, and, upon collecting them all, truth would be revealed. To modern scholars, there are many things wrong with this view of how scholarship is done, but at least it was based on the idea of the need for empirical evidence. Mendota College, like many Christian schools and virtually all Bible training schools, saw everything through the lens of their distinctive religious doctrine. This must not have posed a problem for most students because they came to Mendota to attend the Bible Training School or came from Advent Christian families who adhered to such religious beliefs. The areas least affected by religion were the various business concentrations, and it was in these courses where locals, who were more likely *not* to be Advent Christian, were concentrated. This hostility of evangelicalism to modernist thought in religion, the sciences, etc. prevented students from considering cutting-edge ideas in any context other than a negative one, hardly a sign of a quality education.

However, the importance of religion at Mendota College had a positive side. The college's reason for existence was religion—the desire to produce ministers and other Christian workers for Advent Christian churches. This mission was clear and frequently discussed. There was a religious bond among most of the students. And there was a level of dedication among faculty and other staff members that, given the low salaries, can only be explained as mission driven. And while the force of religion was strong, college leaders always argued for the importance of the liberal arts, although their importance was often explained in terms of how they served those in the BTS. They argued that ministers should have a broad education because they needed to be able to speak and preach like educated persons, especially as the educational level of their church members was going up over time. It was argued that times were changing, and church members now expected more from their ministers— knowledge and skills that went beyond simply knowing the Bible.[218]

This chapter has not only described the academics of Mendota College; it also has put them into a larger national context. It cannot be reasonably argued that Mendota College was anything but academically inferior, especially when compared to the standards of today. Many people have pointed this out. But what few have added is how the college stood in relation to other schools of the time, especially small, Christian colleges and BTSs. The academic characteristics of Mendota College—being small and fiscally needy, having educationally unprepared students with erratic attendance and low graduation rates, along with at least some classes that were not at the college level—was the norm at this time.

However, the college slowly improved itself over its nineteen years in Mendota. The campus was groomed and also restored after a devastating tornado, the college building was remodeled and painted, the library grew, more and more faculty had college degrees, and its admissions policies started to look more like the national trends. The curricula also became more challenging—a few electives were added, individual courses were beefed up, and both college-degree programs and the BTS added a requirement for what essentially was a senior-capstone research paper.

When the college moved to Aurora in 1912, it still had a long way to go academically, but it kept improving, so that in 1938, standards had been raised to the point that the school was certified by the North Central Association. Certification required that much more money be found to improve campus facilities, academic resources, faculty salaries, etc. That President Stephens was able to accomplish this by 1938—in the decade of the Great Depression—is impressive.

In the end, the foremost mission for Mendota College was to prepare Christian workers, especially ministers, for service in the Advent Christian denomination. Many churches were without pastors and desperately wanted one, but college leaders always argued that the era in which people simply became a minister because they were called by God to preach was now over. They still believed that ministers needed to be called by God to the ministry, but they also believed that it was the college's God-given duty to prepare those people before they went into the field, even if Christ was returning soon. Only then could they be truly effective in a rapidly modernizing world. In 1910, shortly after the decision was made to move the college to Aurora, an *Our Hope* editor wrote:

> We pray constantly [to] the Lord of the harvest to send forth more laborers into his harvest. Does he not do it? Yes, he does, but he leaves the training of the laborers to us. He calls them into the work,

we must equip them and send them forth. ... If we fail to equip and send forth our ministry, whose fault is it if they are not acceptable to the people and fail to attract and hold intelligent audiences? Do you not see that preacher and people must both suffer when the church of Christ fail[s] to equip its ministry for the work committed to them.[219]

As fundraising began for the college's move out of Mendota, this commitment to educate current and future pastors for a new world was as firmly held in 1910 as it was in 1892, when the college was created. There continued to be a few echoes of criticism from some Advent Christians about not needing such preparation at all, or at least not needing courses beyond those offered in the BTS. But the tide had turned. A new generation of young men had gone out from the college to serve as ministers, believing, whether they ultimately graduated or not, that at least some education had to go hand in hand with a divine calling, and that it should go beyond a narrow religious training. Liberal arts courses may have been secondary to religious study at Mendota College, but they were there and would move with the college to Aurora, where, over time, they would grow in student numbers as well as areas of study and become valued in their own right.

The College Chemistry Laboratory

Bible Training School Students, 1910–11

Jennie Twining—She was the longest-serving woman on the Mendota College faculty, a house parent (along with her husband, N. C. Twining) in the women's dormitory, and a strong role model for the female students.

Ethel E. Fry—She taught some courses as a student at the college and wrote the student column in *Our Hope* for a time.

Library and Classrooms—Science

Laboratories in the Mendota College Building

Mendota College Band, 1909

Ready for Some Exercise—Perhaps in the Physical Culture Class that Began in 1901

(1)

(2)

(3)

A Glimpse Into

1. Not Lincoln he who first you see,
   Tho him he some resembles,—
   Before his tread, with looks of dread,
   Each lad and lassie trembles.

2. That dear old soul with full-orbed features—
   Who can he be?
   He knows all heavenly bounds and creatures
   From Mars to Phoebe.

3. "Just so"; there's some degree of satisfaction
   knowing "where you're at."

4. It's Dewing doing all the while—
   Not being done but doing.
   When doing Dewing's in the style
   Well done will be the Dewing.

5. Money? nay! Nor matri-money—
   The goal of this young prof.
   He plans to marry the dictionary—
   Wouldn't it make you laugh!

6. "Some grow short and some grow tall,
   But he grows on forever."
   For room to grow he Hopes next fall
   To settle on Peace River.

7. The reason why professor J.
   Has features quite so placid—
   Because he bathes them every day
   In strong hydraulic acid.

(4)

(5)

( )

Comical Sketches of Mendota College Faculty Members

the Hall of Fame

(13)

8. This little prof with his big machine
    Is often heard but seldom seen
    Drilling it into some obtuse head.
    Thus he earneth his daily bread.

9. Choose well thy words when I'm around,
    And guard thy manners well;
    Be neat, be dignified, profound—
    Or feel my spell.

10. Altho my praise is seldom sung,
    Yet some think I'm a "Beaut."
    I make my living with my tongue:
    I. e., I elocute.

(12)

11. Oh see! oh see! —Oh see who?
    O. C. Dickerson, kind and true.

12. Pan Kost Kollects Kash,
    Kounts Kosts,—Kredits Klash.

13. I deal, sir, if you please,
    In terms somewhat like these:
        Allegretto decresendo,
        Larghetto dimenuendo;
        Andante moderato,
        Sostenuto marcato;
        Allegro grazioso,
        Vivace furioso;—etc.

(11)

(7)

(8)

with profuse apologies

(9-10)

The Mendota Advent Christian Church—Located Just a Few Blocks from the College Campus

Yourself and friends are cordially invited to attend the

Sixteenth Annual Advent Christian

CAMP MEETING!

at MENDOTA, ILL., AUG. 16=26, 1907.

Preaching services each Sunday at 10:30 A. M., 2:30 and 7:30 P. M. Sunday school each Sunday 9:30 A. M. Preaching each week day at 2:30 and 7:30 P. M.

Special programs will be rendered on the following days:

Monday A. M.
Sunday School Day.

Tuesday A. M.
Association Day.

Thursday A. M.
Helpers' Union Day.

Friday A. M.
Loyal Workers' Day.

Saturday A. M.
"Our Hope" Day.

Saturday P. M.
Students' Reunion.

Sunrise Prayer Meetings each morning at 6 o'clock.	Loyal Workers' Prayer Meeting each Sunday at 4:30 P. M.
Mission Study Classes each morning at 8 o'clock.	Helpers' Union Prayer Meeting each Sunday at 4:30 P. M.
Children's Meetings every day at 1 o'clock.	Song and Social Service each evening at 7:30 o'clock.

Evangelistic Services every evening at 8 o'clock,

Reduced rates on railroads. Ample accommodations at reasonable prices. For full particulars see page 13 of this paper. For further information address the Secretary, Eld. Fim Murra, 1212 24th Ave. N., Minneapolis, Minn.

Come.   EVERYBODY WELCOME!   Come.

Flyer Announcing Details of the Annual Campmeeting Held on the Mendota College Campus, 1907.
(Pictured here is the large preaching tent used for services.)

Several Families Posing in Front of a Sleeping Tent at a Mendota Campmeeting
(On the far left is Ophelia Bennet — the first woman to serve on the college board.)

Long View of the College Campus during Campmeeting Week Showing
Sleeping Tents Lined Up by the College Building

People Attending a Campmeeting Service in the Preaching Tent on the Mendota College Campus

Close-up of Campmeeting Sleeping Tents Lined Up on the Mendota College Campus

Chapter 6
Student Organizations and Social Activities

"We have no time for foolishness, but plenty of time for doing that which gives us a joy and peace the world knows not of. We do not play baseball and football here, for we have something better, something that gives more joy—the glad service of our God, and the indwelling of the Holy Spirit."

—Student O. H. Loomis, *Our Hope and Life in Christ*, 1905

"There has been in the past a prejudice among some of our people against Athletics, but this we feel is now wearing away and we hope in future to be able to engage in more of the sports."

—1910 *Epitome*

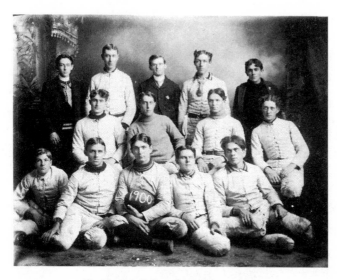

The Mendota College Football Team, 1900.
(It was not an intercollegiate team but instead played a few games against Mendota High School's football team.)

Mendota College students worked hard—at their studies, their jobs and their extracurricular activities—but they also seemed to find time for the traditional college-student organizations and a social life. These things helped to break the tedium of fast-moving schoolwork and, no doubt, helped students get to know each other better.

STUDENT ORGANIZATIONS

The student organizations that existed at Mendota College, at one time or another, were: the Art Club; the Literary Society; the College Prohibition League; two debating clubs; Greek Club; various musical groups, especially the College Choral Club; and YMCA activities. Many of these groups were very much a product of their time, especially the prohibition groups. And, of course, there were many fewer organizations than one would see in today's colleges and universities, or even in the early decades of Aurora College.

Literary Society

The *first* student organization to form was the Literary Society, in the fall of 1893 (which was just the first calendar year and the first full school year of the college's existence), with about thirty charter members. Not only was it the *earliest* student organization, it turned out to be the *longest-lasting* of the student groups, surviving not only through the rest of the Mendota College years but decades into the twentieth century. It is not surprising that this was the first extracurricular organization to appear on campus. Literary societies were a longstanding tradition on American campuses, dating back to the colonial period, in the mid-eighteenth century. One historian called it "the first effective agency of intellect to make itself felt in the American college," arguing that

> nowhere else was reason so fully enthroned in the college as in the activities of the literary societies. ... The literary societies ... owed their allegiance to reason, and in their debates, disputations, and

literary exercises, they imparted a tremendous vitality to the intellectual life of the colleges, creating a remarkable contrast to the ordinary classroom where the recitation of memorized portions of text was regarded as the ultimate intellectual exercise.[1]

Also, literary societies, although often supervised by faculty, were run by students, who planned and put on the programs. As such, there was probably a bit more independence of thought, although students at Bible colleges, already religious conservatives, probably hewed more closely to the prevailing social and religious views at their school.[2]

The meetings were held weekly and operated according to parliamentary rules. Each term new officers were elected, thus providing students with more of an opportunity to have a leadership position and learn how to lead meetings. Membership was mandatory—*except* for those in the Commercial Department and resident students in the music program. Often, meetings having special programs were advertised as being open to the public, so it was not at all unusual to have visitors in attendance.[3]

Programs varied from week to week, but generally were on literary or current affairs topics, along with occasional musical pieces or full-blown recitals. There were recitations, orations, readings, debates, reviews, and music. On a number of occasions, the students had a mock trial. In one of them, a charge of larceny was made against a student for taking the school colors out of the chapel. Evidence was offered by student litigators on both sides, and then the student jury found the defendant "not guilty" because of insufficient evidence. This trial consisted of all student actors, but another one had adults in the major roles—Mr. Wicks, a lawyer in Mendota, serving as the judge; Professor R. C. Robbins playing the prosecuting attorney; and Mrs. A. C. Adams acting as the defense attorney. Occasionally the Literary Society program had a debate. One was "on the question whether the railroads should be owned and controlled by the national government or not."[4] (The idea that the federal government should take over, or at least regulate, the railroads, an industry that farmers saw as exploiting them, was one of the goals of the late-nineteenth-century Populist Movement.) And in 1908, there was a program consisting of talks on the Panama Canal (which was being built at this time, during the term of the then-current president, Theodore Roosevelt.)[5]

Faculty and students were right when they said that such programs were educational. Students learned about current affairs and literature, along with developing their debating skills. In fact, in 1896, one student wrote that developing such skills was the major idea behind the Literary Society: "Someone has said, 'The best way to learn to speak in public, is to speak in public.' And we think this is not simply the best way, but also the only way. This is the purpose for which the Literary Society is intended, that is, to furnish opportunity for public speaking, either in the line of speeches, recitations, essays, or debates, and then the benefit of friendly criticism, which makes improvement an easy matter."[6]

However, whatever educational benefits accrued from participating in the Literary Society, students also must have had some fun in sparring with one another. The 1894–95 *Annual* sets a serious tone when it states that the Literary Society "affords excellent opportunities and facilities to the students for the acquirement of rhetorical and elocutionary accomplishments, besides obtaining a knowledge of parliamentary usages in deliberative bodies."[7] But by the end of the Mendota era, there was an admission in the college catalog that Literary Society meetings were not completely serious. The 1908–9 *Annual* states that "the topics presented in these programs are either of current or educational interest, but endeavor is made to make every program entertaining as well as instructive."[8] This trend of entertainment at Literary Society meetings would continue and even grow during the Aurora College years.

The Literary Society not only enriched and entertained students, it also provided services to both the college and the students. For example, every year the society subscribed to a number of magazines for the college library. In 1910, the society spent nearly $14 doing this. (Although this may look like a small amount of money, $14 in 1910 is the equivalent of about $371 today, in 2018.) And the society created an *annual* tradition—a reception for new students, held sometime during the first weeks of the school year. The reception generally consisted of a program, games, and refreshments. This event welcomed new students, and many of them joined the society then and there. The reception probably helped retention by making students feel welcome early on, but another service performed by the Literary Society probably helped student recruitment. During the 1910–11 school year, the society formed a "Booster Committee." Its purpose was basically to publicize the college—to arouse Adventists' interest in the school by educating them about it and the work being done there. And in its later years in Mendota, the Literary Society sponsored an oratorical contest, which dovetailed nicely with the work of the debating clubs, because being able to speak well obviously enhances a person's debate performance. The 1910 contest included five orators, with the first-place winner receiving $15 and the second-place winner, $10. At a time when Mendota College's tuition for a year in the regular college program was $40, dining hall meals were $2 a week, and furnished college rooms were 40–50 cents a week, these prizes represented serious money, which must have greatly helped students with their bills. Thus, the positive effects of the Literary Society rippled throughout Mendota College, going beyond that of most student clubs. It was the core student organization, out of which came other student groups and new activities. Two of the new groups birthed by the Literary Society were the men's and women's debating clubs.[9]

Debating Clubs

In the later years of Mendota College, the various student debates that had taken place in an ad hoc way became institutionalized with the formation of debating clubs. First, the men organized the Young Men's Debating Club in the fall of 1902. In a "College Notes" column in the newspaper *Our Hope and Life in Christ*, a student announced that "the boys of the college have now organized a debating club, auxiliary to the College Literary Society, for the purpose of training in parliamentary law, and for practice in debating."[10] The club membership grew so that by 1910 the club had enrolled twenty-two students. It met every Saturday evening. It is a bit less clear when the women founded their debating club. The 1904–5 catalog mentions that *both* the men and women had created debating clubs, but the 1910 *Epitome* (a student annual) says that the Young Ladies' Debating Club was organized in the fall of 1908. Apparently that plain, but descriptive, club name did not have the gravitas that the women desired, so a year later they chose a more distinguished one— "Adelphia Rhaetorias"—meaning "Sisters of Oratory." Although several names were proposed, ironically, it was a male student who put forth the winning name.

However, the name must have been considered a mouthful because they came to call themselves the "Alpha Rho's." Originally, the club was supposed to meet every other Saturday evening, but in 1910, the women decided to meet every Saturday evening, as the men had always done. The women also had a healthy membership by 1910—twenty members. Not every meeting was devoted just to debating. Clearly, these clubs were also about teaching students *how* to debate. In the 1911 *Epitome*, the men gratefully acknowledged the help of Professor George Dewing in talking to them about debating from time to time, and the women thanked Professor Jennie Twining for helping them by giving talks on the art of debating, providing exercises on reasoning and argumentation, and donating books on argumentation to both the women's and men's clubs.[11]

The arrival of formal debating clubs was *not* the first time that students debated. The *first* debating was done in connection with the college's Literary Society. In the spring of 1902, the Literary Society accepted a challenge from Mendota's Excelsior Debating Club, which was connected to Mendota's YMCA, to debate the question, "Shall the United States annex more territory?"[12] (The Spanish-American War of 1898 had brought new territories to the United States—in effect its *first* colonies. Becoming an imperialistic nation was quite controversial at the time.) The college's men were to take the affirmative position in the debate. Sadly, they lost, although by today's standards, they, of course, were on the wrong side. The following year, 1903, the college's men, now organized into a debating club, redeemed themselves by beating the Excelsior Club, arguing the affirmative case for the question: "Shall the U.S. government prevent extended strikes by compelling immediate arbitration?"[13] (The late nineteenth–early twentieth centuries were periods of great labor turmoil and many strikes.) Note that the Excelsior Debating Club's challenge was given to the *Literary Society*. The debating clubs, at least in part, began because of the debates done under the auspices of the Literary Society. And when the first debating club was founded in 1902, it was considered to be an auxiliary of the Literary Society. It wasn't until 1904 that the debating clubs were listed in the college catalog separately from the society.[14]

The fact that the men and women were divided into two debating teams was probably a remnant of the nineteenth century, when the genders were separated for many roles and activities. It would not be until 1924, in Aurora, that the two debating teams would combine into a single club. Strange as this separation may seem to modern sensibilities, it provided extra incentive to do one's best when the men's and women's teams debated each other. In 1910, a series of debates between the men's and women's debating clubs was announced. They debated the following questions: "Resolved, that the influence of the pulpit is declining,"[15] which the women, arguing for the affirmative side, won on both points and general delivery; "Resolved, that irrigation is doing more for the West than the mining industry,"[16] which the men, arguing for the negative side, won but only by one point; and "Resolved, that trusts are favorable to the progress of the nation,"[17] which the women, arguing for the negative side, won. A fourth joint debate was held at the very end of the 1909–10 school year, the question being: "Resolved, that the entrance of woman into business and professional life is detrimental to the best interests of our country."[18] Interestingly, the women took the affirmative side in this debate. And they won—for the third time—thus earning the coveted silver cup for winning the majority of debates in the series of four. I found no direct evidence showing how the men took these three defeats and one, slim victory. However, it may not be coincidental that in the following school year, the men changed their constitution to allow men who were in no way connected to the college to join their debating club. It certainly looks like they wanted to strengthen their team, perhaps with some of the Mendotans from the YMCA whom they had debated earlier. In any case, the women's wins certainly proved that they could compete at the men's level.[19]

Most of the topics that the students debated were quite serious and were often about current affairs. And sometimes they simply discussed, in a non-debate format, current topics, like the Adelphia Rhaetorias women discussing women's suffrage in a 1910 meeting. They contributed to the students' educational enrichment and knowledge of the world, not to mention developing their argumentative skills. The 1911 *Epitome* described, in an article on the women's debating club, what its members saw as the benefits of their club: "To some the Debating Club may appear to be simply an organization formed for its social features and for pleasant intercourse, but it is something more. ... It is an important part of an education to learn how to appear before an audience, how to talk clearly and forcibly, and how to govern and be governed by parliamentary laws."[20] But every debate, no doubt, had its moments of levity, one of which was recorded. A student reported, in his "College Notes" column, the following exchange: "The Young Men's Debating

Club had an interesting question up Saturday evening of last week—'Resolved, That the Western states are more beautiful than are the Eastern states.' The affirmative speaker, a New Englander, stated that New England had plenty of natural gas, a fact his Western opponent said he was very ready to concede."[21] And an article in Mendota College's 1910 *Epitome* sarcastically reported that "the meetings are enthralling, holding the members entranced from seven until ten o' clock, and leave then with evident reluctance. The debates are sometimes so interesting that the marshal loses his senses—in sleep—and responds to an applicant for admission by rapping on the door himself."[22] Wherever there are college students, there will be humor.[23]

Prohibition Societies

Much of the nineteenth century saw some type of temperance/ prohibition movement in the United States. Reformers in this movement denounced the drinking of large amounts of alcoholic beverages, a practice which had characterized the colonial period. Although many early reformers worked for temperance—urging people to limit their alcoholic intake—early on, some reformers worked for the outright outlawing of all alcohol consumption. By the late nineteenth–early twentieth centuries, the movement was more about prohibition than temperance. National prohibition was achieved, via the Eighteenth Amendment, in 1919, just seven years after the college had moved to Aurora, so it was very much a controversial, national issue during the Mendota College and early Aurora College years. The leaders and followers of this national movement were overwhelmingly white, Protestant Americans, especially evangelicals, who tended to vote Republican. Since the Advent Christian denomination was socially conservative and evangelical, it is not surprising that both Mendota College and Aurora College students were attracted to the cause of prohibition.

The college's Prohibition League was founded at Mendota College in 1907. However, this first organization did not last. It was disbanded at the end of the 1908–9 school year. In the fall of 1909, the prohibition society was reorganized, by a representative of the Intercollegiate Prohibition

Association, with a membership of seventeen. This national organization was headquartered in Chicago and had a membership of around 150 colleges in 1910. A student writer described the college's league in the 1910 *Epitome*:

> The local League ... conducts meetings every three weeks on Thursday evenings, when league study is done on all phases of temperance work. These are given in the form of debates, papers, recitations, music, etc. At intervals various outside speakers are obtained. The League has thirty-one members. Mr. Harley H. Gill, vice-president of the National League, visited the League one evening and gave a stirring address, at which meeting fifteen new members were added.[24]

The 1909–10 catalog was the first that listed such an organization and described it in more general terms:

> This is a temperance society under the supervision of the National College Prohibition Association. Its purpose is to educate college young men and women in the various phases of the liquor problem, and to interest them in the fight against the saloon. The society is not political in any sense, but only educational, having no party significance. Each year, local, state and interstate contests are held, at which prizes in oratory are offered; members of the local society are eligible to try in these contests.[25]

And Mendota College students did debate temperance/prohibition, both before and after they organized their own prohibition organization.[26]

The students educated themselves on the liquor issue through having guest lecturers on campus, debating temperance in its various forms, and taking courses on the subject. The first oratorical contest on the topic of prohibition, under the auspices of the college's own league, took place in 1909. However, this was not the first time that students debated the prohibition issue. As early as 1896, there was something called the Demorest Medal contest. That year the subject of the debate was temperance. The student writer of *Our Hope*'s "College Notes" column described it like this: The contest "consists of essays on the rum traffic and its abolishment, the best speaker to receive a medal. There are seven contestants at the college, and this speaking, interspersed with good music, will make a very interesting evening's entertainment."[27] Rather than being a temperance/prohibition event per se, it was a fundraiser for the college library. The ten cents admission fee went toward the purchase of library books. The fact that this debate was held long before the founding of the college's Prohibition League shows that the prohibition issue was out there and being discussed early on in the college's Mendota years. The college league's first, official oratorical contest, in 1909, was held in Mendota's Presbyterian church. Five students participated. H. F. Bingham won first prize ($15), while F. E. Warman won second prize ($5). Bingham went on to the state level, where he won third prize. This was typical of these local contests. The local winner moved on to the state level and that winner to the national level. The 1910 contest came with even more prize money: $20 for first prize (plus $10 to go toward attending the state convention), $10 for second prize, and $5 worth of temperance books for third prize. And at least two courses were offered on temperance/prohibition during the first three years on the Aurora campus. In 1914, Professor Robbins offered the first temperance class, using a book titled *Social Welfare and the Liquor Problem*. That was followed by a similar course in 1915, having twenty-one students and using as the textbook, *A Century of Drink Reform in the United States*. In a variety of ways, students were educating themselves on the liquor issue, as students would do fifty years later when they debated and took college courses on the Vietnam War.[28]

Students would become even more active in the prohibition movement in the first few years at Aurora College, especially in 1915. This is worth noting because there is a straight line of continuity in the students' prohibition work from the Mendota era to the Aurora College years. Discussion of the students' prohibition activities in Aurora also is relevant because much of it happened so early in the Aurora era that it must have involved some of the same students who had done this work in Mendota.

Most of the April 1915 *Pharos* was devoted to the topic of prohibition, containing articles on the movement at both Aurora College and the national level. Also, the growing involvement of Aurora College students with the movement, by 1915, was symbolized by the Illinois Intercollegiate Prohibition

Association (IIPA) choosing Aurora College as the location for its 1915 convention and oratorical contest—an honor that multiple colleges vied for. The school had tried to get the convention in 1914, but Augustana College got the nod from the IIPA instead. Undeterred, the students got to work to prepare for another run at it. The college that was chosen as the location for the next IIPA convention had to provide entertainment for the delegates as well as seventy-five dollars in prize money, so, along with hard work, some financial investment was also required. The students left for Augustana College in 1914 with enthusiasm and high hopes that at this convention, Aurora College would be chosen as the location for the next one. They left Aurora with the faculty, students, and President Jenks cheering them on. The students had even given a nearly unanimous vote of moral support. And they had some reason to believe that Charles Eckhart, one of the largest donors to Mendota College and an ardent prohibitionist, might give the college the financial support it needed to host the convention. This hope was not unfounded, because ultimately, Eckhart gave the students $50 for the event. And so, as the students later wrote: "All these forces combined to give irresistible impetus to our delegates who no sooner arrived at Rock Island than they began making strenuous efforts to secure the following Convention for Aurora. Full representation, with a previous application and a prospect of financial backing, put up a strong plea. The president recommended and the Convention unanimously voted that the 1915 Convention should go to Aurora College. Aurora had won."[29] Hopefully, winning the state convention for 1915 helped to dull the pain of losing a local election on prohibition that same year—one that students had put their heart and soul into.[30]

In 1915 Aurora had an election on whether Aurora should become dry or not. Aurora College students took an active role in this, working long and hard for the "drys"—the prohibition side. They performed such tasks as addressing envelopes; typing and doing other kinds of clerical work; giving out placards, handbills, and circulars on the street, in front of factories and theaters, and on Sundays, in front of the few churches in town that did not publicly endorse the local option for dryness; helping to "tag" every house in town the night before the election; canvassing and interviewing potential voters; delivering public speeches on the liquor problem—including one student who actually did this in a saloon; and serving at the polls on election day as poll watchers, distributors of campaign materials, guards, challengers, checkers, messengers, and chauffeurs to bring people to the polls. Almost every polling place in town had at least two Aurora College students working in some capacity for the "dry" side. Their help was so extensive that Dr. T. Harley Marsh, pastor of the First Baptist Church and a prominent figure in the campaign, said publicly that "Aurora College has done more to help the opponents of the saloon than any other organization in the city."[31] The "dry" side lost, but the students plowed on.[32]

They wrote about the campaign in the 1915 *Pharos*, explaining how and why they thought they had lost, as well as what would come next in their fight:

> In spite of all the precautions taken by the opponents of the saloon against illegal voting their efforts seemed almost entirely in vain and their representatives at the polls soon found that the lists of legal voters were of little use. The judges were almost without exception in favor of license and did not repeat the names of voters, so that the "dry" checkers could not check them off on their lists. The west side of the city gave a majority in favor of Local-Option, but in the returns from the east side the number of votes far exceeded the number of voters and Aurora went "wet" by a heavily padded majority.[33]

However, it seems that the students' youthful optimism and can-do attitude helped them to keep their spirits up and remain determined to fight on because they also wrote in the 1915 *Pharos*:

> The students of Aurora College are proud of the city of Aurora and will do their utmost to help free it from the grasp of that brewery and those forty saloons which are doing their best to change the "City of Lights" into a City of Darkness. They are getting tired of seeing drunks on the street and hearing the incessant tooting of the patrol automobile. They think it is about time that Aurora quit the job of being the Sewer of Kane County. Above all they earnestly hope that an ordinance will be adopted making registration necessary in a Local-Option election. Nothing could be designed which would be more favorable to crookedness and fraud than the present system of voting. We hope that all the voters will get tired of seeing their city

polluted by the saloon and that when election day comes around in April 1916 the saloon gang and their repeaters will be buried up with an overwhelming landslide.[34]

Prohibition work held the interest of Aurora College students even after the 1919 Eighteenth Amendment outlawed the manufacture and transportation of alcoholic beverages. The Prohibition League continued to be listed in the college catalog as a student organization through 1920–21. Perhaps this was an oversight, but probably it was not. Prohibition was still an issue for some anti-alcohol people after 1919 because they wanted to make sure that it was actually *enforced*.[35]

Miscellaneous Groups

There were other student groups organized in the Mendota years. The organizations discussed in this section were either founded shortly before the move to Aurora, short-lived, or an auxiliary to an outside group. There was a Greek Club, organized in the fall of 1909. It was open to any faculty member or student who had studied Greek or was currently studying it. The 1910 *Epitome* states that "the object of the club is to acquire the art of conversation, and leaders at each meeting introduce the subject and all discuss freely and ask questions. The topics relate to some form of Greek life and are very interesting as well as instructive."[36] The group met every two weeks, at the home of a club member, the location constantly changing and thus adding additional interest to the meetings. The Choral Club was organized in the fall of 1908. Organized and conducted by the head of the Music Department, Professor Wallace, it gave a number of concerts and sang at special events during the year. What was called "a small tuition charge" was required of each member, something that was not asked of other club members. The fee was needed to cover the cost of the music. One group that seemed to come and go and had at least two different names was the Reading Circle / Reading Club. The Reading Circle existed in at least the 1895–96 school year and was quite different from the Literary Society in that students gathered to discuss a book that they all had read. By 1902, the "College Notes" column mentions a Reading Club. It is not clear whether this was an entirely new group or the same group with a new name. In any case, for a few years, some students gathered to discuss books that they had read in addition to those they had to read for their classes.[37]

In the fall of 1901, the female students organized a group called the Hammer and Thimble Society. It was short-lived by definition because its purpose was to raise money to improve the public spaces of the women's dormitory. The women not only had fundraisers to raise money to purchase items for their parlors, they also made items themselves. They did not waste any time, because at their *first* meeting, they made a "lounging seat," footstool, and pillow. And just days after they organized the group, they had a fundraiser—an illustrated lecture, titled "Our Navy," by President Twining. The small admission fee for this event was put toward decorating the women's parlors. With the money they raised overall, the women were able to buy two chairs, some framed pictures, a rug, and curtains. The group also raised the consciousness of people about the need to improve the parlors, for they were also given some items—a lamp and sofa, as well as money. It appears that the young women accomplished their goal because two months after the group was formed and began its project, mention of it in the "College Notes" column stopped completely. It seems that the college could not spare any funds to fix up the women's living quarters, so they had to do it themselves.[38]

One last group that needs to be mentioned was the college YMCA and YWCA. Each college "Y" group, of course, was an auxiliary to an external institution, but one that had similar goals to those of a conservative, evangelical Christian institution like Mendota College. The college YMCA was founded during the 1893–94 school year but was reorganized in 1898. The college YWCA must have been organized about the same time as the college YMCA—around 1893–94—because the 1894–95 catalog makes reference to the excellent work done by the YWCA the previous year. However, it, like the college YMCA, was reorganized in 1900, two years after the men did it. The YMCA and YWCA met on campus, and their memberships consisted of just Mendota College students. Occasionally the two "Y" groups had joint meetings. These two groups were perceived as organizations that would help shield young, innocent college students from the bad influences of the world that were so tempting to young people, as well as train them to become religious leaders. The college YMCA met weekly for what was essentially a

Bible study. Although it met on campus and seemed to be somewhat insular, it did have contact with the YMCA in town and at higher levels. On more than one occasion, college YMCA students had joint meetings and services with members of the Mendota YMCA, and students sometimes attended state YMCA conventions. At least twice—in 1899 and 1900, the college YMCA sent one of its own to attend the YMCA summer training school, located in Lake Geneva, Wisconsin. Little did these students know that one day, in the distant future, their alma mater would acquire this lakeside campus.[39]

STUDENT PUBLICATIONS

Students produced several publications during the Mendota years. Although there was no specific journalism club, producing a student newspaper was an organized, official school activity. Mendota College students produced three papers, each from a different period: *The Exponent* (first published in 1896), *The Collegian* (first published in 1903), and *Epitome* (first published in 1910). Unfortunately, they were all short-lived.[40]

The Exponent was a monthly, subscription newspaper, published during the school year. The cost was 25 cents for nine issues. If student Sylvester Nokes was accurate in his "College Notes" column, its purpose was primarily public relations and advertising: "We would urge that those who wish to help Mendota College and keep themselves informed as to its progress should subscribe for this little monthly. ... It is hoped to make it an effective help to advertise the college. Friends should help us scatter them widely, where they will reach the young and attract attention."[41] This is a good example of how the current students did their bit for the cause of recruiting new students, something they did in many different ways. This publication was extremely short-lived. The very next year after it appeared, the board voted that it be discontinued. The board minutes do not give an explanation for this action, but it was probably financial, because 1896–97 was the period when the school almost closed due to financial difficulties.[42]

The Collegian, a monthly newspaper produced by the students, began in August 1903. It was financially supported through both advertisements and subscriptions, the latter costing 50 cents a year. Like *The Exponent*, this newspaper also had the goal of both informing people about Mendota College and recruiting students. However, as of the November 1903 issue, the paper had only forty subscriptions and the students reminded *Our Hope* readers that they were publishing the paper for them, not for themselves. Two months later, the cost of the subscription for the rest of the 1903–4 school year had fallen to just 25 cents. It appears that it did not last beyond the 1903–4 school year.[43]

Epitome was first published in 1910 and was edited by the Literary Society. It cost 25 cents. In a 1911 *Our Hope* article, *Epitome* was described as "an annual magazine entirely original with the students of Mendota College," and it goes on to say that "we are rather proud of the work, and doubt if any college annual wholly original with the students, including arranging, editing, designing, planning, and proof reading, can make any better show than this, especially when it is remembered that it was necessary to consult close economy of expenditure."[44] Like the previous two publications, *Epitome* was written for the friends of Mendota College as well as its students—both current and former ones. However, this one seems more personal, more revealing of student life at the school, and more completely a product of student labors. All three of the publications have serious articles, and some of them were written by the president and faculty members, but *Epitome* has more humor— jokes and gossip about students, faculty, classes, and student life; humorous illustrations; and even cartoonish drawings of faculty members.[45]

Student publications came and went fairly quickly during the Mendota College years. It is hard to say why each one did not last longer. Mention of them appeared in the historical record when they were inaugurated, but not always when or why they stopped publication. But since they all were largely subscription-based, and the college's finances were often unstable, money might have been the main issue. It would not be until the *Borealis* was begun at Aurora College, in 1930, that the students would have a newspaper that would last for many decades (until 2002).

SOCIAL ACTIVITIES

When reading about all the things that Mendota College students did every day, one is likely to wonder how they found the time for any kind of social activities. But, like busy college students today, they did. Students sometimes acknowledged that the daily grind could get tedious, and so they enjoyed their time off and made the most of the occasional fun activity or evening social event. And the students, who, for the most part, were young and energetic, enjoyed any activity that they could do outdoors. Given the lack of a gymnasium, they appreciated anything that could get them moving in the fresh air, even in winter.

When the weather was good, they went on picnics, often accompanied by long hikes in the countryside. One Saturday in 1899, a group of students took a trip to Deer Park, Illinois. Describing Deer Park as "one of the most picturesque spots in Illinois," a student wrote that "provided with breakfast, dinner, and supper, the merry crowd started at early sunrise, and with the birds sang the early hours away."[46] Six years later another student reported that on the previous Saturday, some students "drove three miles into the country and spent the day in a large and beautiful grove. We rambled over hills and across creeks and beneath beautiful foliage and shade. At noon we partook of a sumptuous picnic dinner, and toward evening returned home feeling well paid for our trip."[47] And in the fall of the next school year, a student reporter wrote about a trip that a group of students took to Starved Rock—picnicking, boating, and rock climbing. Picnic food, of course, was provided. He noted that "we did not intend to starve, even though at Starved Rock" and also vividly described the day's activities:

> The scenery was certainly grand as our launch went up the Illinois River. The high rocks were pierced by deep canons [sic] and caves, and in the river were beautifully wooded islands, all of which have seen historic events. Having reached our destination we abandoned the boat and spent the forenoon in climbing steep canyons leading back to beautiful arched caverns formed by terrific rushing waters in time long past. There was ample enjoyment for geologist, botanist, zoologist, artist and all. We went back to Starved Rock in a rowboat, following closely the magnificent walls of rock with their variously colored strata richly covered with vegetation; and returned to Mendota ... to resume study with fresh vigor and zeal.[48]

One time the students even went on a snipe hunt. The student who reported this did not give any details, but one could guess that it consisted of upperclassmen taking the new, very green and gullible freshmen in search of that elusive, imaginary animal.[49]

When winter hit, they did what young people do today; they went ice-skating, had snowball fights, etc. Sometimes, even faculty got involved in the snowball wars. A 1906 student column in *Our Hope* reported on a faculty member who acquitted himself quite well when faced with bad odds: "One of our college Faculty [*sic*] held in check, last week, thirteen able-bodied students in a snowball contest. Our readers can draw their own conclusion as to the ability of our Faculty, mental as well as physical."[50] However, they also did something that few people experience today. They periodically went on sleigh rides. A student reported on one of these sleigh rides in his column: "Last Tuesday evening two sleighride [*sic*] parties were organized, and an enjoyable evening spent in the open air. To close the evening's outing, a nice, appetizing luncheon was served at the home of Professor and Mrs. Wallace."[51] It is not clear whether the Wallaces organized this whole event or just fed them afterwards, but the practice of students being entertained in the home of a Mendota College faculty or staff member was not at all uncommon.[52]

Students must have enjoyed socializing with faculty members, the college's presidents, and other employees because they seemed to do it often, usually in their homes. Mendota College was a small, tight-knit community— one that was reinforced by the fact that almost everyone attended the Mendota Advent Christian Church. These social gatherings celebrated birthdays, weddings, and the arrival of babies, as well as welcomed new arrivals and bade farewell to dear friends who were moving on. The affairs were usually held in faculty homes and sometimes in those of church members. Since so many students and faculty were Advent Christian, the social activities for the college and church were frequently intertwined, and often a church social or meeting looked like a gathering of the college's students. More than one Advent Christian pastor in the Mendota church was surprised with a party, like the one that F. A. Baker was given in February 1900. Around 6:00 pm, more than sixty of the Bakers' friends, both church and college people, suddenly appeared at their house, bringing both supper and gifts—two rocking chairs.

It was a great surprise, and it was reported that everyone had an enjoyable evening of fellowship. In May 1907, another pastor, B. Forester, and his wife hosted Mendota College students in their home. The evening's entertainment consisted of games, songs, readings, etc. and, of course, the students were fed. On a Friday evening in November 1900, the Loyal Workers, an Advent Christian organization, met at the home of Baker for both a business meeting and a social gathering. Most of the college students were at this event. One student reported in *Our Hope* what transpired that evening: "At a previous meeting it had been requested that as many as could, should earn a quarter, and in rhyme should tell their stories at the next meeting. These poems, interspersed with piano, piano and cornet, piano and violin duets, and the swinging of Indian clubs, made a very entertaining program. The remainder of the evening was spent in playing games and charades."[53] Swinging Indian clubs is an ancient workout regimen using long, wooden clubs which look like elongated bowling pins and are swung around and around to develop strength and flexibility. One can only wonder what function swinging the Indian clubs served at a social gathering in a crowded room. Fortunately, the student reporter made no mention of any casualties.[54]

There also were showers of various sorts, especially wedding showers. Like many small institutions, Mendota College produced many marriages. Newly married couples sometimes waited to complete their schooling before marrying, but many did not, especially since many young men got a call from an Advent Christian church to be its pastor before they had even graduated. Some of them left school to answer this call and usually did not go alone. One of these showers took place in November 1908 when some college students and young people from the church gave "a tin shower" to a recently married couple.[55]

Some social events were for women only. There were occasional teas just for the women, such as the one given by the Bakers on a Friday evening in October 1900. In January 1907, Professor J. A. Wallace and his wife invited the women students to come to their home for an afternoon social event. Their daughters acted as the hostesses, which may explain why only the women students received invitations.[56]

Although sometimes the social events were for young women or men exclusively, mostly they were coed. However, one party, in October 1907, although coed, certainly reflected traditional gender roles. After a Saturday Literary Society program had ended, the men surprised the women with a program and refreshments. A male student reporter described the surprise party for the women like this: "Though not leap year, the young ladies had the privilege of choosing partners for the occasion and waiting upon them. Then the 'girls' thanked the 'boys' for the enjoyable entertainment afforded."[57] He gave no indication in his report that he saw the irony in this "party for the women." In December 1899, the students enjoyed a coed activity that one would expect to see in this time period—a taffy pull. A student reporter wrote that "we have not had a more pleasant time this year. There were some games of an interesting and uplifting character, and that tired feeling that always comes to both the teacher and student by Friday evening, was lost in the mirth and enjoyment of the hour."[58] President and Mrs. Gordon as well as Professor Vaudry attended the pull. This was typical. Most of the student activities included both men and women, but they were closely supervised. Mendota College was, after all, a socially as well as theologically conservative school where gender roles were traditional and fears about the sexes getting too intimate no doubt existed. The supervision was thorough enough that some parties even took place in the women's dormitory parlor.[59]

Some social events were educational as well, primarily musical programs (student recitals, concerts, etc.) and lectures. Students encountered extracurricular lecturers in different places—a guest speaker in one of the daily chapel services, a guest lecturer in the town of Mendota, and, most famously, President Twining's stereopticon lectures on various places in Europe. After doing preparatory reading on Europe for years, Twining finally went there for three months in 1903, visiting Italy, Switzerland, Germany, France, England, and Scotland. While in France, he purchased stereopticon views of the various places he had visited for the purpose of sharing what he had seen and learned in Europe with the college community. Once he was home, he bought, at his own expense, a stereopticon, and gave a series of six lectures over the next year. As described in an *Our Hope* article on Twining's slide-lecture series, "The stereopticon employed is a double lantern of the latest pattern with a powerful electric light, producing very brilliant and life-like pictures."[60] In other words, it was a slide projector of some kind. These lectures were given every year, except one year when he was living in California. They were on London,

Scotland, Paris, the Rhine, Switzerland, and Italy. They must have been quite popular, given where the early ones were held—in the largest auditorium in town, the Mendota Opera House; the praise they received in *Our Hope*; and the fact that they were given virtually every year. Some people even attended these lectures multiple times over the years.[61]

An important facet of the college's social life for all students, then and today, is humor. Although it may seem that Mendota College students led strict, regimented, somber lives, filled with work with little time for play and laughter, they had their fair share of laughs—often at each other's expense. It is hard to capture such things in a historical record, but a few sources offer some glimpses of student fun and humor—photographs of students fooling around on campus and their own publications.

The jokes that appeared in *Epitome* were often bad—bad probably even by the standards of the day: " 'Why is Mendota college like the brewery?' Answer—'Because it makes Bud wiser.' "[62] It is amusing that the students would put a joke about beer in their publication, because Advent Christians in general and Mendota College faculty and students in particular were very much against the drinking of alcoholic beverages. Sometimes the humorous pieces revealed some "issue" that a student had. In a column-long, faux advertisement titled "Wanted, For Sale, Lost, Found, Etc.," various students posted something that they kiddingly had lost or wanted.

> —Wanted—A new Ladies Dormitory, non-burglar-proof and farther removed from the wood pile. Must have patent entrances and escapes at the windows and all modern conveniences for smearing windows while the occupants are away. W. G. Bird & R. A. Watkins
> —Wanted—For the chemical laboratory, instruments made of unbreakable glass. I am at present compelled to use glass that breaks like rash promises. Will give half my kingdom for a good supply. C. R. Smith[63]

Sometimes an item told of a funny thing that happened in class: "Perhaps Miss Dewey has been wondering why, on certain occasions the girls in her

Ancient History class persist in sitting on the same row of seats, and with such an attitude of innocence and attention, but with faces turned slightly to the left—and up. Could she see an enraptured face of a tall young man peering over the transom her curiosity would be satisfied."[64] Of course, the students loved to zero in on others' peculiar habits and personality traits or odd circumstances. One column, titled "Wouldn't It Surprise You to Know That," did just that:

> "In one of his conversations, Mr. Hodges failed to mention Boston?
> "Mr. Decker stayed home one Sunday afternoon?
> "All was quiet in the library for five minutes?
> "The Chapel leader closed on time?
> "Mr. Peterson forgot his dignity for a minute?
> "Mr. Keepers came to class on time?
> "Ruth Stephens studied her Ancient History lesson?
> "Miss White got up one morning before she was called?"[65]

In spite of the titles "Mr." and "Miss" used in this item and elsewhere, the people mentioned were all students, such formality being quite different from how students would refer to each other today, especially when kidding around. And, at times, students produced humorous artwork—sometimes simply illustrating the various pieces in their publications, but also, in at least one instance, drawing caricatures of their professors.[66]

ATHLETICS

Mendota College students worked hard. They were taking classes and doing schoolwork outside of class—and in a term system rather than a semester system, which meant that the classes were more concentrated because the time was shorter in an academic term. As noted already, many worked, did what amounted to internships in various churches, and attended and had responsibilities in the Mendota Advent Christian Church on multiple days, along with other activities. One student wrote: "If any think attending college is an easy job, just let them come to Mendota, and see how we put in our time here. Athletics? Not much, except hustling to class, and then hustling back to study for the next recitation."[67] This student busyness, plus the small student population and its religiosity, inadequate to nonexistent sports facilities, and the perpetual financial strains that the college seemed to experience, worked together to inhibit the establishment of official, intercollegiate sports teams at Mendota College.

Some students seemed not to miss having a vital, intercollegiate sports program on campus. After stating that the college's young people were experiencing "a continual Pentecost," one student added: "We have no time for foolishness, but plenty of time for doing that which gives us a joy and peace the world knows not of. We do not play baseball and football here, for we have something better, something that gives more joy—the glad service of our God, and the indwelling of the Holy Spirit."[68] Another student proudly wrote that "one purpose of Mendota College is to turn out gentlemen as well as graduates from our college course. The partiality shown by some colleges to football and similar rowdy sports seems to us to put a premium on precisely the wrong type of man."[69] This rationale for not having athletics was less overtly religious, but still had a moralistic tone. It is impossible to know whether these statements, and others like them, represented sincere beliefs or whether religion and morality provided a convenient rationale for not having sports on campus. Certainly, such statements did not represent the views of everyone in the student body.

Other students missed athletics very much and saw no problem with combining religious studies and sports. By late 1899–early 1900, they were asking for a gymnasium, which simply did not exist in the college building. (It appears that in saying that they wanted a "gymnasium," students did not mean a whole building, as that term would be used today. They meant some exercise equipment and some space to use it.) In a December 1899 issue of *Our Hope*, student Milton Livingston summarized the problem as students saw it:

> The boys still talk of a college gymnasium, and are pushing the matter by appealing to the immediate friends of the college living in Mendota. It is too far to go to the Y. M. C. A. rooms, downtown, every time a little exercise is needed; and besides we could not have the

liberty there we would have in a place of our own. Of course nothing very large or expensive is anticipated, but a small gymnasium would be of great benefit to the students, when schoolwork goes hard.[70]

Student H. H. Corliss added another reason to acquire a gymnasium: "Many of the young men who room in the dormitory scarcely leave the building from Sunday night until Friday night and often not till Sunday morning. This, of course, will soon ruin one's health."[71] Corliss also argued that having a gymnasium was important for recruiting and keeping students when he recounted an exchange between two of them:

> We overheard a conversation between two students, one of whom does not expect to come next year. He said, "I don't know as I would come another year if I could." The other, somewhat surprised, asked the reason, and the answer, in substance, was this: "I could not stand it, and am doubtful if I can complete this year. What we want is a gymnasium, where one can keep up his strength." The rest of the conversation was about experience in schools where they had the use of a suitable gymnasium, and how much easier it was to study when the proper amount of exercise was taken.[72]

There was some pushback on this from at least one reader, a man named Fred Newberry, who thought that Mendota College students did *not* need a gym for exercising: "I noticed a request in *Our Hope,* by a student, for funds to help furnish a gymnasium for the college. I think that students belonging to our people could get their exercise in a better way than that."[73] He then suggested using what he termed the "Pingree method" to get exercise— acquiring a vacant lot near the college to farm and thus getting exercise, learning botany, and perhaps making a profit. If students did this, Newberry wrote, "the Adventist body would thus be saved the additional burden of furnishing the means for a gymnasium, as it seems to be enough for them to support the college proper. I hardly approve of any college students, much less Adventist students, getting exercise through the medium of a gymnasium." He then ended his article by asking: "If it is wrong to exercise the mind by reading fiction, why is it not just as wrong to exercise the body in useless performances in a gymnasium?"[74] It is difficult to tell which concern was uppermost in this man's mind—the issue of cost to supporters of the college or the perceived, morally suspect nature of a gymnasium.

In the same issue of *Our Hope* as the letter by Newberry, student H. H. Corliss, who wrote the "College Notes" column at this time, responded in an exemplary fashion—his argument a cogent, point-by-point response to Newberry's letter. In response to Newberry's point about farming a vacant lot, Corliss argued that working to prepare the campus grounds in the spring would provide students with much good exercise, but that putting in a garden would not work because when the spring term ended in early June, most of the students would go home and the garden would go untended. And, of course, for obvious reasons, gardening would not work for the fall and winter terms. A gymnasium was needed in those periods in order for students to get regular, systematic exercise. He added that students are so busy that they do not have an abundance of time to get exercise so, when they get it, it needs to be gotten efficiently. "Exercise ... is far more adapted to the needs of student life than any form of work, as it calls into play more sets of muscles, and being thus superior in quality, it requires less in quantity. ..."[75] As to Newberry's cost argument, Corliss responded that renting a vacant lot every year would equal or even surpass in a few years what it would cost for a gym. He added that a gymnasium should not be considered an extra burden for Adventists to support but, instead, a part of the college's equipment—no different from the library or laboratory. Corliss ended by stating that a gym "is a convenience, promoting the *efficiency, usefulness* and attractiveness of the school. Physical culture is *just as important to a student as is mental culture* [italics in original]."[76] This is a modern stance to take on exercise. His argument went beyond emphasizing students' desire to have equipment for personal use to work off excess energy. The concept that importance should be placed on the physical development of students equal to their academic development is a modern idea and reflects a more sophisticated, holistic view of the body.[77]

The reasons behind having no intercollegiate sports teams or even a gymnasium—a lack of money and space—were formidable obstacles, but some progress was made, although it was minimal. There is evidence, in *Our Hope* and in photographs, that by 1900, there was a football team, and by 1911, a baseball team. However, they were not intercollegiate ones. The evidence for their existence, found in *Our Hope*'s "College Notes" columns, makes reference to the football team playing a local high school and winning both of the games mentioned, as well as the baseball team playing it and losing the game 17 to 7. In 1901, a physical culture class was initiated. The student who reported this in *Our Hope* thought it noteworthy, saying, "This gives the students an opportunity to obtain the systematic exercise which is necessary for the development of highest manhood and womanhood. An active mind seldom if ever dwells in a sluggish body."[78] In 1906, it was announced that "by permission of the Faculty the students have recently purchased a fine tennis set, and laid out a tennis court, which will be made use of with due discretion."[79] It is unclear what was meant by the phrase, "with due discretion," but whatever was meant, it did not seem to slow down the use of the new court. Four years later, the *Epitome* reported that "great pleasure and benefit is [*sic*] derived by our students from tennis. The court is usually occupied from morning till night, excepting school hours, when the weather is good."[80] And in 1900, following months of discussion about a gymnasium in *Our Hope*, H. H. Corliss reported in his "College Notes" column that "a committee has been appointed to purchase some of the most needful gymnasium supplies. The means on hand will not allow very extensive purchases, but they are sufficient to warrant the securing of what will serve as a starter for next year. Donations have been received quite recently for which the association wish to express very sincere thanks."[81] All of these developments represented a fairly minimal improvement in athletics, given the fact that Mendota College existed for nineteen years. However, as the move to Aurora increasingly looked like a reality, there were hints of better things to come.[82]

One good omen for the future of athletics was the creation of the Athletic Association in 1910. The students described the birth of this organization like this:

In view of the fact that Athletics have been neglected in this College, and seeing the need of action, an Athletic Association has been organized by the students. Up to this time the athletic work has been left to the management of one or two, and, in case they withdrew from school, the work was crippled from lack of a leader. Under the new system the responsibility is placed upon all interested in Athletics. ... The society was formed under the advice of the Faculty and all its workings are open to their inspection.[83]

Its purpose was described as being "the development of the physical and moral manhood of the students and the general good of Mendota College."[84] The association was open *only to male* students, and even beyond that—*only to those male students of "upright character."* Given the nature of Mendota College students, it seems unlikely that any of the men were excluded, at least initially. One of the first things that this group did was to bring back the men's baseball team. The creation of this association was a hopeful development, because it promised better organization and continuity of athletics at the college. However, it did not do anything for the women students. They would not get any kind of team until the early Aurora years. Given the comments made by students over the years about how important physical development was to mental development, one can only wonder how they would have explained why that premise did not also apply to women.[85]

Some students used their religiosity to argue *against* sports at the college, or at least to rationalize the lack of them. Other students argued and worked *for* athletics, or at least exercise equipment, and used moral phrases and arguments to do so. For those who were *against* collegiate sports, they represented "foolishness," in sharp contrast to the peace and happiness brought by religion and, they believed, would produce "the wrong type of man" rather than "gentlemen." For the students who *wanted* athletics on campus, sports produced a "physical and moral manhood," so they too used a moralistic argument to make their case.[86]

Clearly, by 1910, with the creation of the Athletic Association, the tide had turned in favor of those who wanted sports and exercise equipment on campus. However, it was equally clear that many college people, including students, were still a bit wary of what they perceived to be the dark underbelly of sports. In 1910, less than two years from the end of the Mendota era, students went out of their way, in *Epitome*, to show their readers that *their* athletics would remain pure. An article on athletics made it clear that the Athletic Association was under the supervision of the faculty and also assured people that "the use of tobacco, intoxicants, or profane language will not be allowed during any game or meeting of the Association." In this same article, the student writer was even more blunt: "Often times in College teams the members are profane and immoral men. It is our desire to put out athletes who are pure-minded and intelligent men. The true object of Athletics is lost if, in developing the physical man, the moral man is degraded. Therefore, if we eliminate, as we believe we shall, the rowdyism of the sports and replace it with clean manhood, we feel that our Association shall not have been in vain."[87]

To be fair, the writer had a point in that athletes at many colleges and universities at the turn of the century were known for their "rowdyism" and generally bad behavior. However, the language is strongly moralistic here. Young college athletes were not necessarily immoral; they and their teams were unregulated. The sports they were playing were growing more quickly than the regulations governing them. For example, in football especially, there was much cheating and other questionable behavior going on—by both individuals and teams as a whole. School administrations had discovered that athletics promoted greater giving from alumni, and the game had become so popular that winning became everything. It was so important that student athletes were not always taught ethical behavior and good sportsmanship, and football was an especially brutal game at this time. In 1905 alone, eighteen young men died playing football for their schools. Since Mendota was a small, conservative, Christian college, what was probably fairly common behavior on large, secular campuses and *did* need to be changed was viewed as the sinful behavior of individuals rather than a social problem that needed to be addressed.[88]

As the students looked toward Aurora, they had the Athletic Association and the prospect of a gymnasium. They also saw a changing attitude about collegiate sports among Adventists. In the 1910 *Epitome*, students wrote that "there has been in the past a prejudice among some of our people against Athletics, but this we feel is now wearing away and we hope in future to be able to engage in more of the sports."[89] And the move to Aurora did bring a new day for sports at the college, although in a limited way. Early on, there were both men's and women's teams. However, although the men's teams were intercollegiate, the women's teams were intramural. They would not have intercollegiate teams for decades to come. Also, Eckhart Hall would have a gymnasium—an actual room whose main purpose was athletics, which was more than what students had at Mendota. However, it was not regulation size, and by the 1920s students were adamantly asking for a new one. In the 1940s, the gymnasium would be moved to a Quonset hut that was purchased after World War II. That too was small and generally inadequate as a gymnasium. It is probably for the best that these Mendota College students did not know that the college would not get a stand-alone, full-size, modern gymnasium until 1970.

The student organizations and social activities at Mendota College were probably fairly typical for a small, religious college around the turn of the century. The biggest differences between the student organizations at Mendota College and those of today's students are how few organizations existed and how educational most of them were—like the Literary Society and the debating clubs. And reform activities and organizations, so often associated with students today, were largely absent. The one reform organization on campus, the Prohibition League, although working for a nationally popular reform at the time, ultimately was conservative in nature and closely linked to evangelicals' religious beliefs. There is no evidence of students working for any of the other reforms of the day that became part of the Progressive Movement under Presidents Roosevelt, Taft, and Wilson. Debating various reform issues seems to have been the closest that students and faculty came to engaging with them. This makes sense, because many of the young people at Mendota College were there to become trained for Christian service, especially the ministry. Participating in the Literary Society programs and debates helped to develop good speaking skills that would be so important in Christian service careers, and that was their focus—preparing for these careers and for the return of Christ to earth. After all, for them that was the ultimate reform—the creation of Christ's kingdom on earth. Even athletics could be sacrificed to those goals, although the students complained about the lack of resources and opportunities for exercise and sports participation. No doubt, to a large extent, a lack of funds explains the lack of athletics at Mendota College, but it was also the view of at least some Adventists, and even some students, that the young people attending the college should focus on higher, less secular concerns.

Men's Debating Club

Women's Debating Club

Mendota College Students Spending the Day at Starved Rock

Play Time, 1901–2 (Orrin R. Jenks is at the bottom of the pyramid, in the center.)

Snowball Fight!

Fence Sitters, 1901–2

Ready to Go on a Hike

Women Students Posing in a Tornado-Ravaged Tree

Students Mugging for the Camera Next to the College Building

Students Posing on the Campus's Large Front Lawn (The college building is in the left background.)

Mendota College's Young Men

Student Play in Honor of Washington's Birthday, 1894

Chapter 7
Student Life and Culture

"The character, moral conduct, and social relations of the students in the College will be kindly guarded by the president. Great care will be taken that the minds of the students are not distracted by frequent or objectionable entertainments."

—*Catalogue of Mendota College for 1898–99*

Male Students Are Sprawled on the Ground and Piled on Top of One Another While the Female Students Stand Demurely behind Them Looking Amused—Victorian Gender Roles Remained Intact.
(Orrin R. Jenks is at the bottom of the pile, on the left.)

The previous chapter discusses how students spent their time, both in organized groups and social activities. But anyone who has lived in a college dormitory will tell you that there is much to college life beyond these activities, specifically the daily life and interactions that come from group living in a dormitory and on a campus. Once again, it is difficult to describe this life because generally it leaves little evidence behind, even less than that for organized activities. But a few hints penetrate the historical fog when we look at where and how students lived, ate, and worked, as well as the rules they lived by. The historical record even gives some hints about women's roles in an era when women's rights in general, and especially the fight for the vote, were beginning to surge.

Student Housing

From its earliest days, the dormitory accommodations at Mendota College were described in home-like and religious terms. It was no small matter for parents to send their children, especially their female children, some distance off to college in 1893, and many assurances were made in *Our Hope* and elsewhere that their children would live in a protected environment. For example, in the article, "Supervision of the Hall," dormitory life was described like this:

> It is the aim of the Seminary to furnish in the Boarding Hall a comfortable and orderly Christian Home.
>
> The management is in the hands of Professor and Mrs. J. H. Nichols, who will endeavor so to direct its life that good health, happiness, and success in the schoolwork shall be secured for its inmates. The regulations will be few and simple, such as commend themselves at once to the judgment of the well-disposed. It is believed that the regularity and the punctuality of the Hall life, the cheerful freedom within safe limits, the atmosphere of refinement and culture, the unobtrusive but real religious influence, will tell in their own way for the highest interests of the students.[1]

The word "inmates" would seem to be at odds with the term "cheerful freedom," at least as these words would be used today. And students today would not consider the rules of collective living at Mendota College to be "few and simple," nor the "religious influence" to be "unobtrusive." However, this was a very different era in college living arrangements and rules. Paternalism and regimentation ruled supreme, especially for women students and especially at small religious colleges—in both academics and campus life. This can be clearly seen in the regulations set out in the 1894–95 catalog:

1. Students are permitted to govern themselves, so far as is deemed consistent with their welfare and the best interests of the College.

2. Regular attendance at all College exercises is required of every student. Realizing, however, that detention in some cases is unavoidable, the Faculty will accept satisfactory reasons for a limited number of absences. All excuses must be submitted to the President, or to a member of the Faculty acting in his place, for approval. All absences not satisfactorily explained will stand as unexcused; when any student has two such absences charged against him, he will be required to appear before the President. A third absence without excuse will be reported to the student's parent or guardian; and on the occurrence of a fourth without reasons satisfactory to the President, he will be considered as no longer having college standing.

3. Students must abstain from indecent or disorderly behavior; from profane or unbecoming language.

4. No student shall enter or leave the class of any department except by permission of the President.

5. Every student is required to pass a satisfactory examination in each study pursued, before entering a succeeding class.

6. Permission for absence from the College during the school sessions must be obtained from the President.

7. Whenever in the judgment of the Faculty a student's attendance is no longer profitable to himself or is in any way detrimental to the school, he may be dismissed.

8. Students are required to attend Chapel services daily, except Saturdays and Sundays, unless excused for special reasons.

9. Any regulation or rule adopted by the Board of Education and announced to the students, shall have the same force as though printed in the catalogue.

10. A faithful record of scholarship and attendance upon school duties is kept, and a card will be sent each term to the parents or guardian of each student if they so desire.

11. Any student who proves insubordinate, vicious, or idle, can be expelled at any time and shall forfeit all right to the tuition paid; nor can he be re-admitted save with the consent of the President.[2]

Note, in the above list of regulations, how many times the president is cited as the authority who makes the final decision concerning both academics and students' behavior. This is very much in keeping with the role of the college president in the antebellum period, before the specialization of administrative functions developed later in the nineteenth century. The *pre*–Civil War college president was, as one historian put it, "an authority unto himself."[3] He, of course, was accountable to some type of board, but he wore many hats, wielding his power in a paternalistic fashion. Although Mendota College was founded well *after* the Civil War, it resembled this paternalistic model.[4]

An undated list of rules at Mendota College is even more specific about student behavior—both on and off campus—and illustrates the many ways that the college regulated the lives of its students in a paternalistic way. Of course, it was a profoundly different, historical era from today, and the college's students were pious and not inclined to question any power structure, although once in a while a request was made for some kind of minor change. Most of the following rules would not be tolerated by students today:

1. Quiet must be observed at all times in the building.
2. Students must keep their rooms in order for both reception and inspection by teachers, at all seasonable hours.
3. Students must be in their rooms during all study hours, excepting when reciting in their classes, or when excused. Students are free to consult the libraries at all hours.

4. Study hours will be uniform throughout the year, except Sundays, and Wednesday and Friday evenings.

5. No student will be permitted to lodge away from the dormitories, except when excused.

6. Students must prepare all their lessons for recitation during study hours.

7. Students are expected to be courteous and respectful at all times, and in all their communications with both teacher and fellow student.

8. Study hours begin at 7 A. M. and continue until 4 P. M., the noon hour excepted; and at 6:45 P. M. for evening study, Sundays excepted.

9. On Sunday and Wednesday evenings students are expected to be back from service, and in their rooms by 9 P. M., but from social gatherings Friday evenings, by 11 P. M.

10. Students are urgently requested to be seen on the public streets as little as possible; not to dissipate non-study hours in aimless talk, but to employ such golden opportunities by select and choice reading.[5]

If these Mendota College rules are any indication, one of the goals of collegiate paternalism was to strictly limit the ability of students to move around—to keep them safe, pure, and studious. It probably comforted parents that their children were being so closely supervised and limited in where they could go and when, but such a system also may have hindered students' maturation process and ability to think for themselves.

The cost of living in a Mendota College dormitory certainly looks absurdly low by twenty-first-century standards, but it was still often an obstacle to attending the college, even for students in the Bible Training School, whose classes were tuition free. On-campus furnished rooms cost around 40 to 50 cents a week (the difference in price relating to the size and location of a specific room), while renting rooms in private homes near campus generally cost a bit more—50 to 60 cents a week. The cost of a room remained virtually unchanged—at least up through 1906–7, the last year that the college catalog included a figure for room rent. For the first few years, board was $2.50 a week, but it went down to $1.60 for the 1895–96 school year. This reduction in cost was perhaps a product of creating what was called the "College Boarding Club"—an organization that was mentioned for the first time in that year's catalog. Then the cost of board did go up over time, but gradually and not by much. In 1896, it inched up to $1.65; in 1897 or 1898, to $1.75, and in 1902–3, it was $2.00, where it stayed for the rest of the Mendota years. However, this was still less than the $2.50 it had been originally. Board for students renting rooms off campus ran about $2.50 to $3.00.[6]

In return for their rent, students could expect to find a room with the basics. An 1893 announcement for Mendota College states that "a furnished room contains stove, chairs, table, mirror, bedstead, springs, mattress, coal-scuttle, bucket, wash-bowl, and pitcher. Students should bring from home napkins and ring, towels, toilet-soap, sheets, pillow-cases, coverlets, blankets, spread, shoe-brush and blacking, a piece of carpet, and such articles of bric-a-brac as will make a room cheerful and home-like."[7] Students also had to pay for light and fuel, although just at cost.

However, improvements were made in the dormitories and the boarding operation throughout the Mendota years—largely due to the benevolence of Advent Christian women, who were organized into what they called the Helpers' Union. This Advent Christian organization, created in 1894 at the Mendota campmeeting, was organized and controlled by women, its initial purpose being to raise funds for the Bible Training School and other college-related needs. (Its focus later expanded to support other Adventist interests, but Mendota College was always important to the organization.)[8]

Helpers' Union women, both as individuals and as members of their own church's branch of the organization, provided necessary items for the college. They both raised money for the purchasing of these things and contributed items themselves—like sheets, pillowcases, quilts, blankets, towels, soaps, rugs, curtains, and furniture for dormitory rooms and public spaces. Many of these things were made by the women themselves. Sometimes the donation of a single, local branch was quite impressive. For example, the Buchanan, Michigan, Helpers' Union sent an entire "bedroom suite consisting of bedstead, dresser, commode, springs, mattress, table, chair, and rocker, comforts, quilts, spread, mattress cover, sheets, pillows and slips, towels, dresser covers, etc., pail, wash-bowl, two pitchers, also eighteen yards of carpeting." They "also made provision for papering and painting the room; also for Memorial windows for Eld. D. R. Mansfield and Mrs. M. S. Mansfield (deceased), the founders of Buchanan Church."[9] And some of the gifts were quite unique, such as a "crazy quilt" made by several women from the Baraboo, Wisconsin, Advent Christian Church. It was not only colorful, it was "autographed with names, dates, and restful Scripture quotations."[10] Many contributions of food also were made to the boarding operation—especially fresh or home-canned fruit. This helped to keep the cost of dining hall food down, a savings that was passed on to the students whenever possible. They also paid for some repairs on campus and did work on the campus themselves—especially the Mendota church's Helpers' Union. A September 1902 *Our Hope* article noted all the hard work done by this group in both the men's and women's dormitories in preparation for the arrival of students: Helpers' Union members "cleaned, painted, papered, laid carpets, and placed furniture *throughout* the dormitory, beside making the boys' rooms in the college cozy, comfortable and home-like; and that in a way that has been replete with self-sacrifice; not hesitating, when some article seemed to be especially needed, to go into their own homes and *deprive themselves* that others might be more pleasantly environed [italics in original]." This article also mentioned the work done by Mendota's Helpers' Union at other times of the year, like right after school ended: "Every year all the bedding is examined, repaired, washed if need be, or discarded, if too far gone, and replaced by others."[11] And they helped students who were in need of financial aid, even going so far as to announce in 1895 that anyone who was interested in attending the Bible Training School, but lacked funds, should contact them. One grateful student wrote in *Our Hope*:

> Having received aid from the Helpers' Union of Mendota, to attend our Bible Training School, I feel it a sense of duty as well as of pleasure to say a few words in a public way ... thanking them for their kindness, liberality and the interest they have taken in me during my stay in Mendota. It was only through their help that I could attend and enjoy the great advantages which our school affords, and receive the instruction which so many of us need. ...I shall always feel

indebted to them for their uniform kindness and hospitality. Though coming here a stranger to all, they have kindly ministered to my wants and have done for me all they agreed to. ...[12]

In short, the Helpers' Union was critically important to the finances of the college and to the comfort of the students as well as their ability to attend the school.[13]

Although dormitory living was generally quite basic, eventually the students got the luxury of a bathtub, or bathing-tub as it was called in 1895, when they received it from a generous donor. In the nineteenth and early twentieth centuries, bathtubs were not the large, gleaming, permanent fixtures we know today. For many people, their bathing vessel was a metal wash tub set in the kitchen. The tub was filled with water that had to be hauled from the stove where it had been heated. Bathing was a long, laborious process. The bathtub that the Mendota College students acquired was clearly an upgrade from that kind of simple tub. It was described as "a first-class portable bath-tub, which heats its own water with gasoline at the rate of twenty gallons in the same number of minutes. The tub is made of the best tin-lined copper plate. It folds up into a cabinet and can be set into one corner of the room, or it can be set so it will be stationary and connect with the sewer."[14] This kind of tub made bathing in a dormitory possible, since dormitory rooms were either several floors from the kitchen or not even in the same building.[15]

Mendota College's men and women had living situations that were quite different from one another. The men's dormitory experience was considerably more stable than that of the women. Whereas the men had one dormitory, the women, for various reasons, had multiple ones over the years. And for the women who lived in the women's dormitory in 1901, their residence hall experience even included some trauma.

The Men's Dormitory

Throughout the span of the college's existence at Mendota, the men's "dormitory" was on the fourth floor of the college building. This space was described by Ophelia Bennett, the woman who wrote about the campus and the college buildings in a series of *Our Hope* articles in 1903. Bennett, a prominent supporter of the college and soon-to-be college board member, took readers on a tour of the campus, as well as off-campus housing. She described the layout of the men's top-floor dormitory space like this: "After two flights of stairs from [the] main hall we find ourselves in a short hallway, and following this southward we come to the hall running east and west dividing the upper floor, into which all the sleeping rooms open. Part are on the north side of building, and part on the south side."[16] It had nine bedrooms for the men, some having one occupant and some, two. The east end of the hallway was partitioned off to create a bathroom, but it only had cold water piped in. To get hot water, one had to go to the kitchen. By 1903, we know that the young men finally had some long-awaited exercise equipment up there, because she reported that the west end of the hallway had been turned into a mini-gym—with pullies, ropes, and weights. The floors had carpets on them, but in her article, Bennett expressed hope that someday soon the carpets could be taken up and replaced with hardwood floors because the carpeting did not last long and was dirtied by the soft coal heating stoves that were used. She suggested that now that the college had an adequate supply of bedding, perhaps the Helpers' Union could work toward providing hardwood floors.[17]

The First Women's Dormitory

Over the nineteen years that the college was located in Mendota, the women had several dormitories, all of them off campus. Initially, the female students had to rent rooms in nearby, private residences, which was a concern because under such an arrangement, the young women had no oversight from the college. Some of them also had to travel longer distances to get to the college than others. That situation changed in 1898, when the college acquired a house. President Gordon and his wife lived on the first floor while the young women lived on the second floor, thus providing them with the ultimate in supervision. The women must have loved this new place, not only because they were now living together under one roof, but also because the house was probably an improvement over earlier residences. It was only three years old and came furnished with new carpets and furniture. Along with the young men, the women took their meals in the college dining room because their new dormitory was practically next door to the college. This new living situation, no doubt, made both parents and college officials happy, but what made it even sweeter was that, ultimately, this house was *given* to the college. Someone described it in an *Our Hope* article:

> The large roomy house built by Bro. Nash about three years ago, within a few steps of the college building, has recently been purchased by a few liberal brethren who saw the need of a young ladies' dormitory, and they have *made a present* of the property to the W. A. C. P. Association, the deed being made out to our general body as above designated. Six rooms have been nicely furnished for young ladies by these brethren in addition to the purchase of the property [italics in original].[18]

This seemed to be a good solution to the women's housing issue, but unfortunately it did not last long.[19]

The Women's Dormitory Fire

Just three years later, the women, as well as President Twining and his wife, were abruptly uprooted from their residence when a fire destroyed their house one cold night. The fire, originating in the basement of the house, broke out around 2:30 in the morning on December 14, 1901. That night saw subzero temperatures, and it was windy as well. The house was warmed by a steam heating unit, installed just a year earlier. That evening, President Twining checked the unit and found a problem. He located the janitor, and together they worked for about an hour to fix it, after which the fire was banked, and the doors of the unit were closed. The Twinings went to bed around 11:00, shortly after which they heard a sound in the basement but did not check it out because they thought it was their shovel falling to the basement floor.[20]

The safe escape of all the residents from the burning house was due to Mrs. Twining's light sleeping and quick thinking. An article in *Our Hope* describes it like this:

Mrs. Twining awoke about 2:00 A. M. and thought she smelled smoke in the room. Arousing Prof. Twining with some difficulty, he got up, opened the door and found the next room full of smoke. He at once gave the alarm and Mrs. Twining roused the young ladies on the floor above, but the combustion was so rapid that nothing could be saved only what each one could carry as they fled from the building. Had Mrs. Twining slept but a few moments longer it is probable that some, if not all, would have been overcome by the smoke and have perished in the flames.[21]

The house was completely destroyed, as were virtually all of its residents' possessions. The students, of course, owned few of the things in their rooms, but they lost even their clothes as they had to run into the bitterly cold night with just their nightshirts on. The loss that President Twining and his wife sustained was substantial—about $2,200 worth of property, which included Twining's large library; his stereopticon slides and "magic lantern," which he had used for years to illustrate his public lectures; a valuable violin; and all their clothes and household goods. Perhaps hardest of all for the president was that he lost all of his writings. The monetary loss for the Western Advent Christian Publication Association—the legal owner of the house—was $3,000 to $4,000. Sadly, the house was only *partly* covered by insurance. However, miraculously no one died or was even injured in the fire, and the Mendota College people thanked God for this.[22]

The fire was a hard blow for such a small, struggling college and, of course, affected everyone. It was a blow that affects even Aurora University today, due to a gap in its archives, because the college records, which had been stored in the president's home, were also destroyed. However, the college bounced back relatively quickly. Since the fire happened in mid-December, this meant that the term was virtually over. Just final exams remained before students left for the holidays, and they all took them—even the women who, just a few days before, had run for their lives and lost virtually all of their possessions, including their schoolbooks. This timing was fortunate in that it gave college officials a few weeks to process what had happened and decide where the returning female students would reside when they returned in January. It was decided that the women would be placed in private homes until a new dormitory could be provided, and this was successfully done. This was the second kindness of neighbors in that they also had taken the homeless women into their homes and given them clothes and other necessities right after the fire, before the Christmas break.[23]

When the new term began in January 1902, all of the previous term's students returned—except one who had graduated—and seven additional students arrived as well. This was wonderful news because college officials had clearly worried that the destruction of a dormitory might have kept potential students away for the time being. An *Our Hope* article in the issue dated January 1, 1902, assured readers that the college was in fine shape, in spite of the fire, and urged all who were interested to come, telling them that accommodations had already been found for the female students. Perhaps one reason for the college's resiliency was the recognition that this could have been so much worse. If even one person had been killed in the fire, profound grief, added to the loss of so much property, would have made coming back so much more difficult.[24]

The Second Women's Dormitory

As soon as early January 1902, the Educational Board met and decided unanimously to build a new dormitory. Given the college leaders' raised consciousness about fire, this time they wanted a dormitory built of brick—not wood. A fundraising campaign was initiated right away. Since time was of the essence, donors were asked to pay at least half of their pledge by March 1 and the second half by July 1. However, in the end, the college did *not* build a new dormitory. The 1902–3 Mendota College catalog states that "a new ladies' dormitory, of brick, commodious, with steam heat, and but a few steps from the College, is expected to be finished in time for the beginning of the school year. Pupils rooming there will be under the personal oversight of the President and Mrs. Twining."[25] This sounds like a new building *was* being constructed and would soon be finished. However, just weeks into that school year, a student writing for *Our Hope*, while mentioning the women's dormitory, referred to it as "lately purchased."[26] And then months later, in 1903, the 1903–4 catalog came out, confirming what that student had written the previous fall, stating that "a large and conveniently arranged brick building near the College grounds has recently been purchased and fitted up for a ladies' dormitory."[27] Perhaps the time needed to build ran out because of the need to have a dormitory by the beginning of the school year, or perhaps it was less expensive to buy an existing house. In any case, the college got its brick dormitory.[28]

By mid-1903, two additional changes had taken place in connection with the women's dormitory. In 1903, the women named their dormitory "Maple Hall." Why? A student wrote in the *Collegian* that "the girls of the College thought that the Dormitory possessed sufficient dignity to be worthy of a name. So, after due deliberation, the pretty and appropriate name of 'Maple Hall' was selected."[29] Also, starting that year, the president and his wife no longer lived in the women's dormitory. Instead a married couple—the Shattos—lived in the house, serving as dormitory "parents." From that point on, the women's dormitory would have a couple, brought in from the outside, living there to supervise the women students. The president and his wife no longer served that function.[30]

A little more than a year after the fire, in April 1903, Ophelia Bennet, a future board member, reported to *Our Hope* readers on her tour of the new women's dormitory. She began with a description of the brick house, with its large porch stretching across the front and down one side, and its location: "The house . . .is two blocks south and a few steps east of the college. The building is of good size, two stories, a brick structure, newly painted a pleasant drab color, and faces the south. It is well in from the street upon a large lot. Just across the street is a full block, well covered with trees, that has been set apart for a park but is not at present open to the public."[31] She then moved on to the first floor. This was the one occupied by President Twining and his wife, Jennie, who would only live there a few more months. Upon entering the house, one stepped into a hall running north and south, the first room on the right being the parlor, which was used by the student residents:

> This we find a pleasant room with south and east windows. The floor is covered with a pretty matting, on which is laid a nice large rug in the center, furnished by the Dormitory Fund. The

couch in one corner was given by the Helpers' Union. The rest of
the furniture was secured by Miss May Pine, ... one of our college
teachers. She does not room in the dormitory, but was one who lost
heavily in the dormitory fire of last year, and she was so interested in
the new home for the girls, that she collected donations from friends
for this room's furnishing, so they have a very nice cozy parlor. There
is one more really necessary piece of furniture needed in one corner
of this room, and that is a piano. The girls need it for practice, to say
nothing of the pleasure they would enjoy by having it here for purely
musical entertainment.[32]

There was a small room in the back, which in 1903 served as a student
bedroom—one that could have been used by Mrs. Twining as her study,
but had been relinquished by her to house a student. On the west side,
the Twinings shared a small bedroom, which Mrs. Twining also used as
her study. Behind the Twinings' bedroom and the student bedroom was
the president's study—a large, long room lined with books. North of the
library was a small kitchen, where the girls could do their own washing
and ironing. Doors on the east and west sides of the kitchen led to porches,
providing good ventilation.[33]

On the second floor, there were four small rooms, which served as
student bedrooms. The hallway was narrow and covered with a "cheerful"
oil cloth, while the stairs were covered in wool stair carpeting. While
acknowledging that the students' bedrooms were small, she noted that "they
are very nice and light, warm, and comfortable, with new carpets furnished
by the Helpers' Union last year, just after the fire, with new furniture."
It is a good thing that the women had a dormitory that was "warm and
comfortable" because Bennett also noted in this article that "they are
not expected to leave the building, except for meals and classes, without
permission."[34] Given the few bedrooms in this house and their small size, it
was not long before it was viewed as inadequate. Orrin R. Jenks expressed
this sentiment in 1910—just eight years after the young women moved
in and just weeks before the final vote was taken on where to relocate
the college—saying that this second dormitory was *never* supposed to be
permanent, was old, and held only seven girls. He believed that turning

it into an acceptable living space would cost what it would to build a new dormitory. He concluded that "a new dormitory must be secured, if we succeed in getting self-respecting and desirable young women to attend our school."[35] Of course, a new dormitory could have been acquired in Mendota, but he saw this new one as part of the overall plan for an Aurora campus.[36]

In this article on the dormitory's second floor, Bennett gratefully acknowledged that the Helpers' Union had supplied carpets for the new dormitory. But that was not all that this group did in the wake of the fire. Two days after it happened, Mrs. E. S. Mansfield, president of the General (National) Helpers' Union, arrived in Mendota to survey the damage and determine exactly what her organization could do to help the college get back on its feet. In an *Our Hope* article published right after the fire, she told her troops that "what we *will* say to all our local societies, is this: We each owe it to our dear young sisters and to the school to do what we can."[37] And so they did—collecting sheets, pillows, pillowcases, towels, table linen, rugs, furniture, and cash donations from local Helpers' Union groups as well as from individuals. In short, once again these Advent Christian women proved how important their efforts were to sustaining Mendota College.[38]

Off-Campus Housing

Most Mendota College students lived on campus, but not all of them did. Over the years, it was noted in a number of publications, including college catalogs, that they were *required* to live on campus, and could only live elsewhere if they had special permission from college officials. The 1906–7 catalog states this clearly:

> All students are expected to room in the college dormitories or in places approved by the college faculty. Students whose homes are in the city or who wish to room with relatives or friends of their family, are excepted from the above requirement.
>
> Changes in rooming or boarding places should be made only with the consent of the faculty.[39]

And the 1907–8 catalog noted that "students rooming outside of the College dormitories are subject to whatever regulations may be adopted for the government of those rooming in the dormitories."[40] How this particular admonishment could be enforced when students lived blocks or even miles away from the college is not clear, but perhaps the college was relying on the honor system, given the pious nature of its students. Some off-campus students rented rooms from residents nearby, many of them connected to the school, while some lived at home. Along with single students renting just a furnished room, some students came as part of a family and required more than one room. Either they were married or were married with children and so were likely to rent an apartment or house.[41]

College Housing Versus Home

For most students, attending college is their first time away from home, so homesickness, at one time or another, is a part of the college experience. Some Mendota College students must have had a fair bit of that, because they spent more time away from home than students do today. For those who lived far from home—on one of the coasts, for example—going home for school breaks was not feasible. Depending on where one lived, trips home could be long and arduous, but more importantly, long trips required money that many of these students did not have. That meant that there were usually students living at the college during Thanksgiving, Christmas, spring breaks, and even during the summer. Sometimes the number of students remaining in Mendota over breaks was greater than that of the students fortunate enough to go home. One writer, whose column appeared in the April 1904 *Collegian*, noted that two young women spent their week of spring break at home, but that "the rest of the young ladies at the Dormitory, unfortunately, were too far away to go home, so they were obliged to content themselves at Maple Hall."[42] The college allowed such students to stay in the dormitories and tried to make holidays festive for them. They celebrated holidays with a special feast prepared by the college cook, served in the dining hall. Usually this meal consisted of items donated to the school especially for the holiday celebration.[43]

Individual supporters of the college, churches, and especially the Helpers' Union also tried to make the dormitories as comfortable and homey as possible. Improvements were made over the years, often with donated items, including from the home churches of students attending the college. In 1902, the Mendota's Helpers' Union upgraded the men's dormitory space—to make it more "home-like"—wallpapering, painting, laying carpet, and adding furniture throughout the rooms. And the next year, a local druggist donated enough wallpaper to cover the walls in all the men's rooms. In 1907–8, the women's dormitory was greatly improved when some individuals and some church groups donated wallpaper, rugs, linoleum flooring, and muslin curtains. And the requests for donations were not just for necessities. In 1901, the student author of the "College Notes" column in *Our Hope* listed some things that people could donate to the college dormitories. Along with furniture and rugs, he mentioned pictures to hang on the walls and anything else that would contribute to a homey look. Over the years, more than one piano was donated to the women's dormitory, contributing to a homey-looking parlor. Of course, the reason a piano was requested was to enable music students to practice, but it also served a social function, as many gatherings were held in the women's parlor. That too contributed to a home-like atmosphere. The women could entertain individually or in groups in the parlor, just as if it was their own home. But there were restrictions. The women could only entertain in the parlor and during certain hours—on Friday evenings, from 7:00 to 10:00, and Saturday afternoons, from 2:00 to 5:00. However, had they been living at home, they probably would also have had some limits on when they could entertain, especially if the guests were men.[44]

The women's dormitory parlor was a much-needed space for social gatherings. The college building had no assembly hall and even the chapel was small. Religious services and small events could take place there, but classrooms and the women's parlor also had to be used. Gatherings did not take place in the men's dormitory because it was simply the fourth floor of the college building. Just the men's rooms were there; there was no gathering place. The women's parlor saw small performances like college music recitals, but it was also a spot for social gatherings of various kinds. Receptions were held there, as were parties—like a Halloween party in 1905.[45]

Employment and Financial Support for Students

Many Mendota College students attended the Bible Training School, which had free tuition, and in 1896, the Educational Board decided to charge just half the tuition rate for the children of Advent Christian ministers. This was a way of thanking the denomination's poorly paid ministers "who have so generously contributed of their time and means to the work of the Lord and building up of the church."[46] However financially unsound this policy was, it was a nice gesture because Advent Christian ministers typically were paid abysmally low salaries. However, students still had to live somewhere, eat, and buy school supplies and textbooks, and some students did have to pay tuition and at the full rate. These financial realities kept many young people from attending the college. As a group, Advent Christians were not an affluent people, although there certainly were some wealthy individuals among them who supported the college—like Charles Eckhart—but for the most part, money was an issue for students, just as it was for the college itself. This meant that in addition to attending classes and studying, many students had to work and/or seek financial aid of some kind, and in an era that had no government loans for students.[47]

One possibility for work was employment by the college. A September 1895 *Our Hope* article announced that the college was in need of a cook and housekeeper for the college's Boarding Club and was looking for an "Adventist sister" to fill the position. But more help was needed because it also advertised for "any young lady desiring to attend the College and willing to assist in kitchen work in part or full payment for board."[48] And at times, a student was hired to serve as a janitor at the school. In fact, the two major areas where students seem to have worked were the dining hall and maintenance. However, that does not necessarily mean that they were always paid a wage. As with the kitchen worker, they sometimes worked for tuition, room, and/or board. However, there is little evidence that the college was able to furnish very many jobs to students. Its labor force and budget were small, and although students did perform a fair amount of labor for the college, much of it appears to have been voluntary. Since the school was always struggling financially, other ways had to be found to help students pay their college bills.[49]

One other source of employment was the residents of Mendota. Because Mendota was a small town, located in a rural area some distance from Chicago, it could not supply the number of jobs for students that Aurora would later provide. However, its inhabitants were always in need of workers to do odd jobs. During the 1908–9 school year, the students created an employment bureau, described in the 1910–11 catalog like this:

> For the benefit of students desiring to work to help pay expenses, an Employment Bureau has been organized and is being successfully conducted. The results already obtained demonstrate the desirability of such an organization and insure its continuance and success. Through its agency employment has been secured for every student desiring it.
>
> The management of the bureau is in the hands of the students and all of the work is conducted by them. In addition to securing employment for those who desire it, the bureau affords some opportunity for the exercise and development of business ability.[50]

One student, in a December 1908 *Our Hope* column, put it more succinctly: " 'The Mendota College Employment Bureau' is a business proposition. Students want work during spare hours. They are willing and capable. Who wants odd jobs done in good shape, to help a young fellow through college? Please let us know promptly. We hope to please patrons."[51] Apparently the Mendota townspeople responded positively because, toward the end of the same school year, this student column reported that "our town's people are finding out what good workers we have, and how handy it is to have them around, and so there are more calls for help than the boys are able to fill."[52] However, the creation of this employment bureau came relatively late in the day, and, no doubt, did not completely solve the problem. Also, the fact that the last quotation refers to "the boys" suggests that much of the work provided through this employment bureau was of the type that was viewed as men's work, not women's.

And so the college turned to the Advent Christian people to help support students financially, and the vehicle for communicating student financial needs and raising money to meet them was the *Our Hope* newspaper. One way that Advent Christians could help was to donate money to the Bible Training Students' Fund, as they were urged to do in many *Our Hope* articles. This existed as early as 1895 and appears to have been set up by the college. Pleas for donations to this fund typically read something like this example from 1895:

> There are worthy young men and young women, whom God has called, whom it is the duty of the church of Christ to send forth to their work as efficiently and promptly as the time and means at our command will permit. They need help. The fields are white unto the harvest. Can we pray in faith to the "Lord of the harvest" to "thrust forth laborers into his harvest," unless we give for that purpose? We set apart a fund for that purpose and will gladly credit all sums large or small sent us for this purpose from time to time.[53]

Whether trying to raise money for the Bible Training Students' Fund or funds for the running of the school, Mendota College officials and their surrogates tried to show Advent Christians how contributing money to the school and its students connected to their religious beliefs. As Advent Christians, they still believed in the imminent return of Christ to earth so there was often a tone of urgency to the pleas for funds. Financially supporting students at Mendota College, it was argued, would create ministers and other Christian workers, whose presence was so urgently needed in the field now "white unto the harvest."

Sometimes student aid was requested and given more directly. From time to time, *Our Hope* published appeals from students seeking financial aid as well as from churches and individuals seeking students to support. Even letters written to the president were often published, like the letter below, written to President Sibley in 1894:

> April 1, 1894
>
> Dear Bro. Sibley: In *Our Hope* of Mar. 28 ... , I read the following: "If you would attend [the Bible Training School] if the way was open, write and let him (Pres. Sibley) know."

Now, Bro. S. this means me. I have been preaching the Gospel for three or four years as the way has opened but have always keenly felt my lack of education. When we began talking of a Bible Training School, I thought: "Now I shall get help," and although I have tried very hard I have not yet been able to obtain money enough to attend even a single term. But God knows best and I shall keep on praying and trusting. I shrink from anything which seems like begging but, oh, if some of the Lord's stewards would open their hearts and pocketbooks! I say the simple truth when I say that there are many young men like myself whose hearts are overflowing with love for God and his truth, and who would delight to proclaim the blessed tidings, but lack Bible training and the time or means to obtain it at present. There are a few of us here who love the "blessed hope" and I have a regular appointment in a schoolhouse. Pray for us that our light may not be hid. Your waiting brother.[54]

This letter received at least two responses, both of which suggested help coming from multiple people. One respondent, believing that $100 would pay the expenses of two students, wrote that he would donate a quarter of that amount. This potential donor also said that he thought he could find three other people to do the same. The other respondent suggested two kinds of help for the student. In addition to direct financial aid from multiple donors, she suggested that local landlords help out. She stated that if this young man would send her a letter in which he gave his name and address and explained his situation, and if he did attend the program this coming term, and if, after July 1, 1894, she received a letter from someone in that department assuring her of this person's worthiness as a minister and in continuing need of financial help, she would send him $5 to go toward his expenses. She then asked if others would do the same. She also requested that the people in Mendota give a week's free board to the young man, arguing that if four people were to give one week's free board, the young man's financial obligations would be greatly lessened. This was a typical response to these kinds of requests—offering help but wanting to make sure that the recipient of such aid was "worthy" and urging others to chip in some money as well. A collective approach was often necessary because the cost of a term's board was too much of a financial stretch for many donors.[55]

Sometimes the collective approach to supporting students was taken by organizations rather than by random Adventist individuals. This was especially true of two important Advent Christian groups that existed in many, if not most, churches—the Loyal Workers Society and the Helpers' Union. These groups in the Mendota Advent Christian Church were especially active in raising money for students, but other churches did so as well. At the Loyal Workers' 1900 annual meeting, it was voted to raise $400 to help support students to attend the college's Bible Training School. This large amount of money, of course, was one that only an organization at the national or regional level could collect, but raising such a large amount required much hard work and even sacrifice from countless Loyal Workers members in individual churches. In 1896, a member of the Mendota Loyal Workers mentioned that over the past year, one local branch had raised more than $70. This gave her an idea about using the collective power of Loyal Workers to support Mendota College students:

If all our young people's societies would adopt some similar plan as that of the Mendota society, and take what we call a penny collection at each meeting, for the same cause, it would not only interest the young people of our faith in the only institution of learning in our denomination, but also provide means whereby many could secure a course of training that would fit them in a short time for active service in the Master's cause, should he tarry a little longer. ... If all of our young people would take hold of this, and adopt some plan whereby they could raise at least one cent per week from each member, we could easily keep ten young men each year in Mendota College.[56]

(It is interesting that an organization composed of so many women should make reference to supporting "ten young *men*," when it was perfectly obvious that young *women* attended the college and needed financial support as well.) Helpers' Union chapters also supported students. In 1896, the Mendota chapter decided to provide board for one Bible Training School student, and an *Our Hope* article asked if there were others who would agree to do the same. Readers were told that if they decided to support a student by supplying board, the college would tell them about "their" student. For those who were unwilling or unable to pay all of a student's board, the article asked who would be willing to pay a month of board for a student.[57]

Many times over the years, an *Our Hope* article suggested a more personal approach to supporting Advent Christian students than either simply giving money to a fund or even supporting some unknown student directly. Churches were often urged to educate their own—to seek out a young person in their congregation who seemed especially spiritual and suited for the ministry and then make it financially possible for him to attend Mendota College.[58]

The college, although chronically short on funds, did its part to help students financially, often through articles in *Our Hope*, in which it attempted to recruit even needy students by helping them to find the required funds. In the fall of 1896, J. W. Emmons—a man who would soon be on the college board—wrote that he wanted "to correspond with good Christian young men and women in Wisconsin, that wish to attend Mendota College; especially if they want to attend the Bible training department." He added: "If you do not feel able to pay all your expenses, then be sure to write to me and your case will be carefully considered. ... We are now entering upon a new era in our work, and hope to be able to do much for those that are not fully able to pay their own way."[59] One way that the college helped students was through the Bible Training Students' Fund (mentioned earlier) and, starting in 1901, the $500 H. H. Corliss Memorial fund, which was set up to honor a student who died that year. Both of these were funds from which Bible Training School students could borrow. The college managed these funds and tweaked the policies concerning their use when necessary. But the most important thing that the school did was to publicize the financial needs of current and potential students, matching them up with individuals, churches, organizations, and college funds that could help them afford to stay in or start attending college.[60]

There was even an attempt to get students and alumni, though small in number, to contribute funds that would help support students. Milton Livingston—a prominent student at Mendota College in the late 1890s who later became an Advent Christian minister—wrote an *Our Hope* article in 1898. Stating that a year's board at the college is $75, he asked if each graduate would give $5 to apply toward this $75. He even asked those who attended, but did not graduate, to contribute whatever they could. And he asked the same of himself, saying, "Can't we as students give five dollars each? I will give five dollars. Who will be next?"[61] If anyone knew how greatly financial aid was needed, it was current and recent students. However, many graduates had limited incomes, especially if they had gone into the ministry, so this plan was not entirely successful. Only $25 was pledged as a result of Livingston's proposal, but he was determined to use the promised funds to help a student anyway. He suggested that since currently there was a worthy student who needed just $25 more to get through the school year, those who had pledged money for his recent proposal should now send it to President Gordon for this person.[62]

Sometimes the desire to attend college, in spite of financial limitations, made some students turn to rather creative solutions. As little as board was, it was a lot of money for many students, so a few managed to eat for even less money. Two students did this by renting a private room together and doing the cooking themselves. (Since this era was long before microwaves, fast food, and packaged meals, one can only wonder what they ate.) The *Our Hope* article that reported this did not mention whether their cooking was done in the landlord's kitchen or in their room. *Our Hope* never reported any fires in the home of the landlord renting to these students, so presumably they made it through the school year without incinerating themselves or others.[63]

In the end, students received financial aid from a variety of different sources, and, no doubt, they were grateful. Whether they received outright donations of money, board, etc. or were able to borrow from funds at the school, this help often made the difference between attending and not attending the college. Sometimes students publicly expressed their appreciation for this, like a young man who wrote an article in a June 1897 issue of *Our Hope* expressing his gratitude to the Mendota church's Helpers' Union and urging others to come to the college. In thanking them, he wrote:

Having received aid from the Helper's Union of Mendota, to attend our Bible Training School, I feel it a sense of duty as well as of pleasure to say a few words in a public way … thanking them for their kindness, liberality and the interest they have taken in me during my stay in Mendota. It was only through their help that I could attend and enjoy the great advantages which our school affords and receive the instruction which so many of us need. Truly their society is well named, for during the five months I have been here, I have experienced ample proof of their helpfulness. ... I shall always feel indebted to them for their uniform kindness and hospitality. Though coming here a stranger to all, they have kindly ministered to my wants and have done for me all they agreed to. ... [64]

His statement of thankfulness shows that the Helpers' Union had helped him financially, but also in many other, more personal ways, aiding him in his adjustment to college life away from home and contributing to his feeling of belonging to a larger, welcoming community.

Sense of Community

A major part of the campus culture was a sense of community. This was a product of many things—the small size of the student population, faculty, and campus; the ethnic, cultural, and religious homogeneity of all the people at Mendota College; the small size of the Advent Christian denomination and its close ties with faculty and students alike; and the isolation of the college from the larger world, given its location in a small town surrounded by farming communities. There is much evidence that Mendota College was a tight-knit community. Earlier chapters discussed the close relationship between faculty and students and between students and the Mendota Advent Christian Church. Much of the students' social life revolved around these relationships, as they socialized in faculty homes and at church events. The Mendota church was created *at the time of* the founding of the college and *because of* the college coming to Mendota, so its congregation was filled with college people. Thus, there were two closely knit, homogeneous, greatly overlapping communities—each reinforcing the other.

There were many acts of selflessness that speak to this sense of community at the college. Sometimes these actions were relatively small—

like when students gathered on a Friday and a Saturday evening in 1898 to address envelopes for the College Day offering coin cards that were being mailed out. They managed to address five hundred envelopes each evening— an impressive number. Sometimes the actions were more physically taxing and ongoing—like when students volunteered their labor to improve the college building and campus. In 1895, when the college building underwent a large-scale remodeling, male students helped in the redecorating of it— especially preparing the many walls for papering by scraping off calcimine, filling nail holes, repairing water-damaged plaster, etc. This was a large task that required hard, manual labor, but students were willing to do it because it eliminated a large part of the labor cost for the college. Even breaks provided time for some students to volunteer their labor to the school. In December 1895, some of the students who could not go home for Christmas used their spare time to build a large bookcase for the college library. During the 1904 spring vacation, it was reported that "some of the boys were busy topping the few remaining trees in the campus that the cyclone of last summer spared us. When this work is finished and the limbs taken away, the trees will be more uniform in size to top out again and the general appearance will be better."[65] This was not an isolated event. Many mentions are made in *Our Hope* of students doing maintenance work on campus—pruning trees, raking leaves, preparing flowerbeds and planting flowers, and shoveling snow. All of this activity suggests that either the college had no maintenance staff for the campus or had such a small one that it needed to be supplemented with student labor. Although most references to the campus work mention the male students, women contributed their labor as well—working on flowerbeds, washing windows, etc.[66]

Doing this work for the school had benefits for the students, not just the college. Participating in fundraising, like addressing envelopes, helped to keep the college alive, as well as keep costs down for students. Engaging in physical labor on campus was good exercise. Not having a gymnasium, the students seemed to welcome some physical activity, especially outdoors, and no doubt, doing this work also helped keep costs down for students, along with improving their living environment. And at times, there were more immediate, tangible results. One student columnist noted that the "boys" shovel the sidewalks in winter so that the "girls" can get to the college building early in the morning to serve pancakes. However, in the end, it was *voluntary* labor done by students who already carried heavy academic loads and workloads to pay for their education. Nevertheless, they continued to provide unpaid labor throughout the Mendota years. And they seemed to do it gladly. In 1896, one student columnist for *Our Hope* wrote that "we think, from what we have heard said, that a number of our students are going to try this year to show appreciation for favors extended to them by extra good care of the college building and grounds. The morning and evening exercise hours have lately been largely devoted to chopping and burning some unsightly old stumpy hedges and trimming shrubbery."[67] And they did it with humor. In 1908, another student writer for *Our Hope* told his readers that if they could only see the young men working, "they would see that we can be useful as well as ornamental."[68] In short, students' willingness to voluntarily work so hard to help maintain the campus, and to do so with good humor, is evidence of the sense of community that they enjoyed. [69]

How do we know that the work done by the students was largely voluntary and unpaid? The recognition, in print, of the students' on-campus labor, often accompanied by profuse thanks for this work, confirms that this was unpaid work. Also, one "College Notes" column mentioned that members of the Literary Society worked on the campus flower beds in the spring. Work by a school club suggests that this was unpaid labor. And sometimes, an *Our Hope* article made it crystal clear that the students' on-campus labor was voluntary. One 1905 article consisted of a report by the College Campus Committee, a group created in 1904 whose purpose was to take in donations for the maintenance and improvement of the campus, dispersing funds where needed. The report noted that 142 trees were planted on campus—as part of a multiyear recovery from the 1903 tornado. It then thanked the students and others for supplying the labor to clean up the campus and plant so many trees. As a result of this voluntary work, about twenty days of labor were donated to the college.[70]

One event illustrates how this sense of community manifested itself at a time of tragic loss—the *first* death of a student at the college. On the evening of Saturday, February 2, 1901, a student named Herman Hayward Corliss, of Milltown, Maine, died at the home of his theology professor, just two weeks after taking sick. He was twenty-three years old. Two weeks earlier, when he had not shown up for class, Elder Baker, principal of the Bible Training School, went to his dormitory room and there found him sick in bed. Baker immediately took him to his home so that he could be nursed. A student reporter wrote that "from the first, fervent prayer was offered in his behalf, by students, faculty and many of the church, as Bro. Corliss was a general favorite. His physician was with him both night and day, and his fellow students nursed him with the most affectionate solicitude, but in spite of prayer and every care death prevailed."[71] This young man, who had planned on going into the ministry, had been at the college for just a year and a half.[72]

One of the things that this story illustrates is how widespread and personal the sense of community at the college was. The communal bonds at Mendota College were such that not only Baker and the doctor took care of Corliss, but students nursed him as well. Corliss's parents, who lived in one of the more remote parts of Maine, were not there during his short illness or at his deathbed. But the Mendota College community was, and in a rather touching and intimate way. And this sense of community, which manifested itself in a very hands-on way, did not end with Corliss's death. After his funeral, which was held at the Mendota Advent Christian Church, "the dear one was borne to the station by his fellow students, twelve of whom served as bearers, the faculty of Mendota College acting as honorary pall bearers, and the whole school and church following as mourners."[73] The students chose to perform this arduous task. It was five long blocks to the depot, and they were walking through snow, but they did it by taking turns carrying the casket. This description of Corliss's exit from his college and Mendota paints quite a picture—virtually the whole school either carrying the casket or walking with his body to the train depot, and in the depths of winter. And Baker's commitment to Corliss did not end with his death, because he and his wife got on that train that would take Corliss all the way to Milltown, Maine. Once Corliss was home, there was another funeral, for family and friends in the Milltown Advent Christian Church, and Baker spoke at it.[74]

Corliss's passing was a terrible shock to the people at the college, not just because his sickness and death happened so quickly—within about two weeks—but also because he was an active and popular student. The student columnist in *Our Hope* wrote that "our hearts are deeply saddened by the death of Mr. H. H. Corliss, our beloved brother in Christ and fellow student. None but those of you who have known him can realize how deeply we feel our loss, nor how much we shall miss him. ... We shall miss his pleasant smile, his kind words, and merry ways, but we hope that we may all so live as to meet him again in that great day, and enter together the glorious heavenly city to come."[75] And he was not forgotten. Two years later, when Bennett wrote about her tour of the campus for *Our Hope*, she pointed out his portrait, which was hanging on the wall of the chapel, noting how well loved he had been by his fellow students.[76]

Women Students

Looking at a college's sense of community raises the question of whether there were any students who were viewed as different from the norm. Today's colleges are concerned with making sure that they represent diversity— ethnic, racial, gender, and sexual orientation—not only of their students but of faculty and staff as well. This is not a concept that any college would have addressed or even fully understood more than a century ago. There were almost no racial minorities at Mendota College, although there may have been a few in the later Mendota years. In 1908, the college board created a policy that provided for the admittance of any students from Sanderlin Academy (an Adventist school for African American children in Memphis, Tennessee) who wanted to attend the school.[77] Given the near invisibility of racial minorities at the college, there was just one group that was viewed as a distinct subgroup of the student population. Not only was this group viewed differently, its members even had some different rules, and yet they attended Mendota College in substantial numbers. This group was women.

The Mendota College years (1893–1912) happened to correlate with a time period which saw a new type of American woman emerging—what historians call the "New Woman." This phenomenon was particularly evident in more urban areas and among educated, middle-class women. The late nineteenth and early twentieth centuries saw a host of social reform movements, many of which were led by women, and others in which women participated: the kindergarten movement; the education movement; the playground movement (creating safe places for poor children to play in American cities); the juvenile justice movement (the movement to treat children accused of crimes differently from adults); the movement to beautify American cities (including the park movement); labor reform for working women and children; the anti-lynching movement, along with a movement for greater racial justice in general; and what became the two largest ones by the World War I era (1914–18)—the prohibition movement and the women's suffrage movement. There was a rise in women attending college as well as a rise in women going into professional areas. Although many of these women remained in traditional women's areas, whether they were involved in reform or the professions, still, they were more visible and more vocal than they ever had been in American history.

How much impact all of this had on the young women of Mendota College is difficult to measure with any precision, but there are a few hints. On the one hand, these female students were attending a somewhat isolated, insular college founded by a religious denomination that, in spite of the female preachers evident in its earliest years, held to a traditional view of gender roles, like most evangelical churches of the day. There continued to be some female preachers, but they were few and far between, and the ones that did exist tended to be preachers rather than pastors of a church—except for a few couples who pastored a church together. Whereas many of the Advent Christian missionaries were women, they typically served as nurses, teachers, and helpmates to husbands and seldom, if ever, had the title of "Reverend," which most of their male counterparts had acquired. And as they lived in an era that predated radio, television, films, the Internet, and social media, and probably had only limited access to newspapers from large cities, the college's female students were more insulated from reform ideas than young women who attended larger, secular schools in urban environments. On the other hand, there is some evidence that Mendota College's female students did have some exposure to these new ideas, and because of this, they were different from most American women at the time.

First, the very fact that they were attending college—higher learning of any kind, however humble—made them exceptional. Although more women were attending college in this era, the vast majority of women never did. And the fact that most of Mendota's college women came from small towns or even rural areas made their attendance even more unusual, although the religious nature of the college probably explains a good part of this in that Bible Training Schools in general were known for having many women students. From its earliest years, Mendota College not only allowed women to matriculate, it encouraged their attendance. An 1894 article in *Our Hope* makes that clear: "THE BIBLE TRAINING SCHOOL has now one commendable feature in it over last year, aside from having a larger attendance, that is: the *sisters* are also attending, two joining the class at the opening of the school, and others intending to join. And still there is more room for both sexes."[78] Mendota College women may not have flocked to the ministry per se, but many attended the Bible Training School, and they were welcome to do so. According to the college's catalogs—each of which listed its students and the program(s) they were enrolled in—overall, there were more women enrolled in eight of the Mendota years and more men in only seven. The theological program was more dominated by men, so there was never a year when women outnumbered them. However, there was just one year when no women were enrolled in it. In short, Mendota's female students were living in an environment that preached the importance of higher education for *both* sexes. Because of the Adventist belief that Christ's return to earth was *imminent*, everyone's contributions—including those of women—were needed to prepare people for this world event. And it was argued that both men and women had to be educated to do this work effectively.[79]

Second, when these young women arrived at Mendota College, they then had a whole new set of female role models. The faculty was always small because the student body was small, and funds were limited. However, over the eighteen years that the college spent in Mendota—not counting the partial 1911–12 school year in Mendota before the move to Aurora—sixteen women taught at the college, and there was *not a single year* when at least one woman was not on the faculty. These female professors were mostly single, a common trait of career women at the time, but a handful, like Jennie Twining, were married. The female members of the faculty interacted with students outside of the classroom as well. They advised clubs—like Jennie Twining, who helped the women's debating club—giving talks on how to debate, providing books on argumentation, and supplying exercises to help the students develop clear and logical reasoning. In a few cases, faculty women even lived with female students. Jennie Twining, along with her husband, President Twining, served as a house parent in the women's dormitory in the 1901–3 period. And during at least the 1901–2 school year, L. May Pine, a history instructor, lived in the women's dormitory. It was no small thing for a sheltered, young woman from a conservative religious background to see that some women had chosen to have a profession—a career in academe—and to get the chance to informally interact with them. Another type of role model for Mendota's female college students was provided by the women who served on the college's Board of Directors— Ophelia Bennett (1903–6) and Mary E. Smith (1906–9). Even though they were often given assignments that were traditionally feminine in nature and they probably did not get to interact with students as much as the faculty, they were important role models. They were examples of women holding some power—having a voice and a vote in the top governing body of the college.[80]

Even the female missionaries who visited the college over the years, while on furlough, served as role models. Yes, they had entered a traditional field for women—religious work—and often did not have the titles or the authority of their male counterparts. However, they were women who had chosen lives that were lived outside the parameters of traditional womanhood— women who embraced education, often lived outside of marriage and the traditional nuclear family, had at least some authority over people, and gave up the comforts of a middle-class home for what were usually more primitive living conditions. Although religiously motivated to become a missionary for an evangelical denomination that generally saw woman's place as being in the home and submissive to her husband, these women had, in effect, chosen a career over the home, and one that brought them many adventures as they navigated cultures that were completely foreign to them, lived their daily lives with few comforts, and had to deal with all kinds of emergencies—accidents, natural disasters, epidemics, revolutions, and wars. To be a missionary, one had to be able to think quickly on one's feet and embrace a life of action in the larger world that few women at home experienced.[81]

When furloughed missionaries—including single women—visited the college, they usually preached and mingled with students. For example, in 1906, Miss Alice Spence, an Advent Christian missionary in India and the daughter of Captain James Spence, who founded the Advent Christian Indian mission, visited the college for nearly a week. She spoke at a chapel service and visited with students. One evening the college had a reception for her. Seventy people attended, no doubt many of them students who got to interact with her once again. The student *Our Hope* columnist reported that "Miss Spence described her work and answered questions. She also showed many photographs of the India work and its workers. Refreshments were served of a curry with rice, prepared and served as in India."[82] Spence and other missionary visitors to the college sometimes inspired students to go into the mission field themselves. But whether that happened or not, the female missionaries who visited the college—preaching and talking with students— provided Mendota's young women with an example of a different kind of life. It was one in which women, whether wives and mothers or not, were able to expand their field of action and independence.[83]

Third, the female students enjoyed competing with men in at least some areas and showed competence and confidence in doing so. One of these areas was debating—an area long considered to be for men only. As noted in the previous chapter, there were four debates between the men's and women's debating clubs in 1910. The women won three of them and lost the other one by just one point. These debates apparently did not intimidate the women, given their number of victories. In fact, the competition between the sexes seemed to have had a galvanizing effect, especially for the men. They must have seen the women as worthy opponents, because the section on the men's debating club in the 1910 *Epitome* states that "the last two years joint debates with the Ladies' Club have spurred all members to renewed energy."[84] And the topics up for debate in these clubs very much reflected current events, including those affecting women. In 1910, the women's debating society, Adelphia Rhaetorias, had a meeting at which they discussed women's suffrage. The female student journalist who reported on this wrote that "needless to state, the cause of woman's suffrage received the support of the judges."[85] There were certainly areas in which men and women did not compete at all, the primary one being sports, but academics and extracurricular activities like debating provided male and female students with more or less equal settings in which they could compete, building their self-confidence, skills, and knowledge.[86]

Having said all of this, however, it is *not* true that the college's female students were liberated from the social norms and gender distinctions of the day. They were not. They enjoyed greater freedom and more opportunities for self-improvement than most American women, but they still were college women who were attending a socially conservative school and living in an age in which traditional gender roles—outside of small colonies of artists, writers, and other members of the intelligentsia located in large cities—were very much intact. In the end, most of Mendota's young women embraced traditional marriage and gender roles that limited the activities of women and demanded that women not go too far beyond men, remaining deferential to them. And by and large, only women who remained single had a professional career.[87]

For example, even though women were admitted into the Bible Training School, this education rarely led to a career as a church pastor or evangelist. In 1908, Orrin R. Jenks, then principal of the Bible Training School, noted this phenomenon:

> Someone may ask why we have ignored the young ladies as prospective ministers. For the simple fact that of all the young ladies who take work in our Biblical department but few ever enter the public work of the ministry. They become Sunday school teachers, minister's wives, missionaries, and so forth, and are thus useful in the Lord's work, but do not become preachers, except in rare cases. The writer knows of but one young lady who has taken a course of study in our Biblical department who is now in the active ministry in the Middle West. And she has now returned to our school to take a further course of study. This writer would not put one obstacle in the way of young women becoming ministers. However, it is evident that our supply of ministers must come from the ranks of the young men.[88]

Jenks seemed resigned to this situation, perhaps seeing it as the natural order of things. In this article, he raised the question of why more women, who were studying religion at the college, were not becoming ministers. He went on to say that the ministers for the denomination must come from the male students, given how few women appeared to be interested. He stated that he was not against women becoming ministers but gave no hint that he or anyone else would take any kind of action to recruit female students for the ministry. This, after all, was not an era of affirmative action. The fact that he was not opposed to the idea of women becoming ministers was fairly enlightened for the day. However, Jenks's willingness to see women enter the ministry did not change the fact that gender norms were powerful and that the ministry in virtually all Christian churches was overwhelmingly male. He seems not to have understood the cultural and religious barriers that stood in the way of women entering the ministry. Few people, especially men, did in this era. And most feminist women were mainly focused on just winning the vote in 1908; women's career issues would remain dormant until the 1960s and 1970s and the emergence of a new women's movement. Historian Nancy Woloch went so far as to say that in the late nineteenth and early twentieth centuries, the ministry was "nearly impenetrable" for women.[89]

Several examples of ways in which the lives of women—both students and faculty—differed from the men's, simply because they were women, can be found in the historical record. The *first* one comes from an event in 1915, in Aurora. Although this was three years after the college moved to Aurora, it was close enough in time that some of the students involved had no doubt started their education at Mendota. Also, it seems highly unlikely that there would have been *fewer* restrictions on the behavior of women students at Mendota College. In the spring of 1915, Aurora College students played a significant role in an election campaign to outlaw alcohol in Aurora. The proposal to make Aurora dry, of course, failed, but what is interesting about this event is not only what the students did for this cause, but who did what jobs. The students performed many of the tasks that you would expect to see in a campaign—both clerical work (addressing envelopes, typing, etc.) and field work—spending much time interacting with the electorate in various ways. Leonard T. Richardson, in reporting about this campaign for the April 1915 *Pharos*, made a point of writing that it was the *male* students who handed out materials on the street and served on election day, which involved a host of jobs. They included serving as poll watchers, distributors of campaign materials, guards, challengers, checkers, messengers, and chauffeurs to bring people to the polls—all of which were performed out in the public space. Women were restricted to working in a more protected environment.[90]

A *second* example concerns a young woman who appears to have restricted her own actions along traditional gender lines. Upon winning *first* prize in a 1910 oratorical contest at the college, she was not only allowed but also expected to go on to compete at the state level. Instead, she deferred to a male student who had come in *second*. By way of explanation, the 1910 *Epitome* said that the first-place and second-place scores were close and having the second-place winner going to the state level was "desired" by the first-place winner. It is interesting that she had enough self-confidence to compete in and win an oratorical contest in Mendota but was unwilling to do so at the state level. It is hard to imagine a male debater doing this.[91]

A *third* example is about a single, female faculty member—Martha Dewey. The students had a good laugh at her expense as they jokingly portrayed her as an unhappy woman desperate for a man, in an item titled "A Serious Case," in the humor section of the 1911 *Epitome*. The item reads like this: "Miss Dewey was seen searching around the library, halls and Bible Training room, and when asked what the object of her search was, replied that, she was looking for a man."[92] Obviously this was a joke and not true, but it must have been embarrassing for Dewey, as this was an age in which women were still seen as incomplete without a husband and children. And however much female students may have laughed when they read this, it must have registered with them, if only subconsciously, that women who remain single are objects of ridicule. Many of them left Mendota College either engaged or married, sometimes even before finishing their education.

At a time when American college students were perceived to be running wild, both the social life and organized activities of Mendota College students looked pretty tame. The students realized that and were proud of it. One former student, writing in *Our Hope*, praised the wholesome, moral and religious atmosphere at Mendota College, citing the weekday chapel services and evening prayer meetings and noting that "there were no tobacco users, no card players, no profanity, no idle habits that he could see, and no one appeared to have any desire for these objectionable practices."[93] No doubt this statement was truer for some than others, but nevertheless, parents *could* send their children to Mendota College and worry much less than if their children attended a large university. The smallness and insularity of both the town of Mendota and the college; the strong, conservative, religious atmosphere on campus and the piety of the students themselves; the heavy academic load, sometimes accompanied by jobs or internships; the organizations whose meetings took up many evenings, even Saturday nights; and the strict rules and close supervision of dormitory life left little room for crude behavior or wild social events. And the paternalism at the college meant that the president himself was the overseer of student morals. The 1898–99 catalog lays this out pretty clearly: "The character, moral conduct, and social relations of the students in the College will be kindly guarded by the president. Great care will be taken that the minds of the students are not distracted by frequent or objectionable entertainments."[94]

No doubt, there were a few students who broke the code of behavior at the college. We will never know how many because such cases would not make it into the historical record. But indications are that the number of youthful indiscretions was small. Many, if not most, of the students came from pious, Advent Christian families who themselves probably had strict rules of behavior for their children. And once on campus, the students were enveloped in a socially conservative, pious, Christian, campus culture. They had many good times together, both on and off campus, but their activities were quite wholesome—even by the standards of their day, given the behavior of students at many large, secular universities.

For the most part (aside from the woman's issues), this student and campus culture, with its strong sense of community and common religious purpose, served students and faculty well, especially in dark days. The people at Mendota College, however isolated or pious, were not immune to hard times or even outright tragedy, as the dormitory fire, tornado, and death of a beloved student show. But in such times, the religious faith that permeated the campus culture and academic life shored them up, as they always turned to their "blessed hope" for that "great day"—when, they believed, Jesus would return to earth and those saved through Christ would rise from the dead.

The First Women's Dormitory

The Ruins of the First Women's Dormitory after the December 1901 Fire

The Second Women's Dormitory, its Residents, and Mr. and Mrs. White—the Dorm Parents

Two Students Socializing in a Women's Dormitory Room, 1901–2

Women's Dormitory Room, 1901–2

Candid Photo of People Gathered in the College Dining Hall

Mendota College's Young Women, 1901–2

RULES AND REGULATIONS

for students rooming in the
dormitories of Mendota College.

1. Quiet must be observed at all times in the building.

2. Students must keep their rooms in order for both reception and inspection by teachers, at all seasonable hours.

3. Students must be in their rooms during all study hours, excepting when reciting in their classes, or when excused. Students are free to consult the libraries at all hours.

4. Study hours will be uniform throughout the year, except Sundays, and Wednesday and Friday evenings.

5. No student will be permitted to lodge away from the dormitories, except when excused.

6. Students must prepare all their lessons for recitation during study hours.

7. Students are expected to be courteous and respectful at all times, and in all their communications with both teacher and fellow student.

8. Study hours begin at 7 A. M. and continue until 4 P. M., the noon hour excepted; and at 6:45 P. M. for evening study, Sundays excepted.

9. On Sunday and Wednesday evenings students are expected to be back from service, and in their rooms by 9 P. M., but from social gatherings Friday evenings, by 11 P. M.

10. Students are urgently requested to be seen on the public streets as little as possible; not to dissipate non-study hours in aimless talk, but to employ such golden opportunities by select and choice reading.

"Lost, somewhere between sun-rise and sun-set: Sixty golden minutes, each with sixty diamonds set. No reward is offered, for they are gone forever!"

BY ORDER OF THE
BOARD OF EDUCATION.
COMMITTEE.

Dormitory Rules and Regulations

Chapter 8
A Shoestring and a Prayer: The Difficulties in Financing a Small College

"Now shall a people like ours, that pretend to be a reading, thinking class of Christian believers go back on the first and only institution that has been founded by us during our history of fifty years? If we can't support this at this time of our history as a people, what could and would we do in fifty years to come? ... What kind of a history could be written of us as a body of Christian believers, not even to cherish and keep up one small institution. ..."

— J. W. Emmons, *Our Hope and Life in Christ*, 1896

SUMMARY OF ACCOUNTS
Of Mendota College from August 1st, 1896, to August 1st, 1897.

RECEIPTS.

Cash on hand August 1, 1896	$ 64.95
Endowment Fund and Donations	2701.93
Donations to Bible Training department	595.00
Tuition from all departments	388.43
Books and Stationary sold	98.05
Room Rent	63.00
Ledger accounts	9.18
Total	$3920.56

EXPENDITURES.

Books and Stationery bought	$ 49.35
Salaries	1860.20
Fuel and Light	108.58
Current Expenses	478.13
Bible Training Dept. (salaries and board of students)	568.89
Bills Payable, canceled	600.00
Miscellaneous accounts	73.45
Cash on hand August 1, 1897	181.96
Total	$3920.56

ASSETS.

Furniture and Fixtures	$1500.00
Books and Stationary	163.72
College Library	400.00
Ledger accounts	77.62
Bills receivable	101.99
Repairs and Improvements	1000.00
Ames' Chemical Laboratory	100.00
Cash on hand	181.96
	$3525.29

ELLA M. MOORE, Treas.

Having examined the accounts of Ella M. Moore, Treasurer of Educational Board of the W. A. C. P. Association, we find them correctly kept and properly vouched, with a balance in the treasury of $181.96.

J. AUGUST SMITH, } Auditors.
A. J. BOLSTER, }

Summary of Accounts, 1896-97, Showing the College's Financial Status at a Time of Financial Crisis

Mendota College was *always* in need of funds to support its work. That is hardly surprising because virtually all colleges and universities say that they need funds to operate and/or to fund special projects and capital improvements. But Mendota College *really* needed money, so much so that looking back at that period as a whole, one wonders how the school ever survived for nineteen years. But it did, and by the end of the Mendota era, it was raising money to build a new campus in Aurora.

The leaders of Mendota College were an optimistic lot, because they often gave *Our Hope* readers a low figure as the cost of running the college. Although this number gradually went up over the school's nineteen years, it was never quite enough to keep the school out of debt for any significant period of time. Even after bringing the college out from under an especially large debt in the mid-1890s and swearing that the college would remain debt free, Mendota College's leaders virtually always waged an urgent campaign toward the end of the school year to raise money to pay off that year's operating expenses. Often that debt was *not* paid off by the end of school and lingered into the summer. And in the very last few years at Mendota, the college went deeply into debt again, in large part because the fundraising was focused on building the Aurora campus and not on current operating expenses.

Acquiring a College Property

In December 1891, before Mendota College was established and while discussions about a future college were going on, an article appeared in *Our Hope*, written by an unidentified author. This person offered some good advice:

> A College—a real College—will cost a great deal. The late Brother Park's proposal to raise $50,000 to found one was not at all extravagant. That sum, invested at 6 per cent., would yield $3,000 a year; which is a very moderate figure for running expenses of a "College," over receipts from students.
>
> I do not know that it would be consistent for Adventists to "salt down" a principal for the sake of using its interest only—and

I cannot see why the body should not do it as well as individuals; but it is certain that something like that amount of income must be provided for *every year*, for anything to be properly called a "College," and to attract students from all over this great territory, and to unify and give character to the denomination. Enquire, if you please, what other Colleges have cost, and do cost, and how they are supported [italics in original].[1]

It is unknown what effect this article had on the leaders of the college movement, but it was a reality check and a warning of sorts. They would quickly find out how expensive it is to establish and then operate a college. But at least the December 1891 cost of the five-acre campus and the one major building on it was a bargain. Even by 1891 standards, $1,800 for such a property was an excellent price, especially since in 1890, it was selling for $2,500, and that had been a good deal because originally it had cost $12,000. To buy the property quickly, instead of the much slower process of raising the $1,800 through donations, it was decided to form a stock company and sell its stock at $10 a share. Each share subscribed was to represent one vote in the company. About a month after the proposal to form a stock company and sell shares, an article appeared in *Our Hope*, which said: "Please do not send any more pledges for stock for the Mendota property, as we will have $3,000 pledged by the time this notice appears in *Our Hope*."[2] Probably the college movement leaders were limited to just selling enough shares to purchase the land and building, but if that was not so, it seems odd that they would tell people to stop buying shares when so many things beyond the property would have to be paid for before the college could open.[3]

A few weeks later, on February 3, 1892, an important meeting took place, at a church in Mendota. A corporate body was created—the Western Advent Christian Association. This organization then gave the property to the Western Advent Christian Publication Society—its Educational Committee, General Western Campmeeting Committee, and Publishing Board. (Shortly later "Association" replaced the word "Society" in the title. Hereafter, the Western Advent Christian Publication Association will be referred to as WACPA.) The report for this meeting stated:

First. That we organize and constitute ourselves a corporate body.

Second. The name of this corporation shall be The Western Advent Christian Association.

Third. The object for which this association is formed, shall be for Religious and Educational purposes without individual profit.

Fourth. That we purchase the property known as the "Wartburg Seminary" and grounds, containing five acres of land, for eighteen hundred dollars.

Fifth. That the books for subscriptions of stock be now opened and subscribed to.

When, upon the following conditions, the money was pledged and paid; viz., "We, the undersigned, hereby severally subscribe for the number of shares set opposite our respective names to the capital stock of The Western Advent Christian Association; and we severally agree to pay the said Association the sum of ten dollars for each share, at such time or times as shall be required by the Board of Directors of said Association. Said shares shall be non-assessable; and transferable only on the books of the Association at par value.

In case of a transfer of stock the offer shall be first made to the Association."

[The report then goes on to list each of the stockholders and the number of shares purchased by each.]

Sixth. On motion, it was voted to elect seven Directors, in whose name the property shall be vested and controlled. The following persons were elected as that Board of Directors: H. M. Robbins, W. McCulloch, I. H. Carpenter, J. A. Smith, D. Rude, J. W. Finn, and L. H. Davis.

Seventh. A committee of three, consisting of H. M. Robbins, J. H.

Nichols, and D. R. Mansfield, was elected to draft By-Laws of the Association, and to report at the next meeting.

Eighth. The following preamble and resolution was [sic] passed. Whereas, having examined the before mentioned property, we find it in the condition as reported by Brother J. A. Smith, it is suitable for the purposes suggested, and we are pleased with it. And, whereas, in the providence of God we have come in possession of the afore mentioned property, located in the city of Mendota, Ill., suitable for a General Western Campground, an Academy, and a Publishing House; therefore be it,

> Resolved: First. That we hereby tender the said property
> to the General Western Campmeeting Committee, the
> Committee on Education, and the Publishing Board of the
> A. C. brotherhood of the West, for them to occupy. ...[4]

Some months later, in August 1892, at multiple meetings of WACPA, additional important business was conducted concerning the transfer of the Mendota property and the startup of the college. WACPA's Educational Committee presented the following resolutions there, which were adopted:

RESOLVED: That the college property, purchased by the W. A. C. Association at Mendota, Ill., and offered to this Society, is, in our judgment eminently suitable and desirable for such a school as is needed among us.

That the Educational Committee is hereby instructed to at once begin the preliminary work for the establishment of an academical and theological Seminary at the place already named:

That the said Seminary begin its work as soon as the necessary funds are raised for its support; and that it be named in honor of N. W. Wait, Esq., of New York.

RESOLVED: That this society purpose to build this Seminary up and improve it as fast as the means may be provided, not attempting to begin with a fully equipped college necessitating a costly endowment fund for its support.

RESOLVED further: That it is the judgment of this body, that of the fund yet to be raised equal to the value of the property offered, one-half should be appropriated to the school-fund, and expended by the Educational Committee for school purposes.

RESOLVED: That the Educational Committee be empowered also to receive subscriptions to the school fund . ...

RESOLVED: That ... we extend our hearty thanks to the owners of this property, The W. A. C. Association, for granting us the use of these beautiful grounds for this our annual meeting.[5]

The Relationship between WACPA and Mendota College

The fact that the college was founded by a publication association created an unusual financial and legal situation. It was not until December 1899 that the Mendota College board applied for a separate, corporate charter for the school. It was granted, and Mendota College became a corporation. Up until this time, the college had been the child of WACPA in that the publication association was the entity that established the college, and the school's legal existence was under the umbrella of WACPA's own corporate charter. This was reflected in the fact that for the first year and a half of the school's existence, what would normally be called a board was titled the Educational Committee; it was simply one of several committees under WACPA's authority. After that this group was called the Educational Board or Board of Education. It was not until 1903–4—four years after its incorporation—that it took the name of Board of Directors, the title one generally associates with a corporate board. The school's lack of a legal identity before 1899 was also reflected in the fact that in 1893 and 1894, WACPA passed some motions to give the Educational Committee the legal authorization to wield some financial powers—to appoint a treasurer to handle the school's funds and to secure loans to pay down college debts.[6]

It is impossible to say why the college became incorporated when it did, and what exactly its corporate charter said is unknown. Perhaps the school took this step because the child of WACPA had become a teenager. By 1899, the college had passed through some tense times, especially the years 1896 and 1897, when it looked like the school might fail. But it had survived, and by 1899, it appeared that it had become an ongoing enterprise (although still financially vulnerable). It does not seem that the college had an immediate expansion of powers after it incorporated, so perhaps that process simply provided a legal basis for what the college had already been doing—things like hiring and firing faculty, making purchases, etc. Whatever incorporation meant for the college, it did *not* mean complete independence from WACPA. It appears, based on the minutes of WACPA's Board of Directors and its annual meetings, that the college *never* owned the property associated with it—not the campus, the buildings on it, or the women's dormitory, which sat on a separate lot. It was WACPA that sold the Mendota campus once the college moved to Aurora, and it was WACPA that deeded the off-campus, dormitory property over to Aurora College, presumably so it could benefit from its sale. And WACPA's authority was such that the two votes to move the college to Aurora happened in two special, publication association meetings—the decision being made *not* by the college board, but by the fifteen members of the WACPA board, along with delegates representing fifteen different conferences in the Midwest.[7]

Throughout the Mendota years, WACPA owned the property and made the decisions concerning it, while college leaders ran the school itself—hiring and firing presidents and faculty, writing and revising the curriculum, building a library, gathering academic materials and other resources, etc. However, this division of ownership and authority was not as clear-cut as it sounds. It appears to be true overall, but the minutes of the college and WACPA board meetings, along with the publication association's annual meetings, present some conflicting evidence. For example, in 1908, the college board asked WACPA to give the college a deed for the school's property, and that same year WACPA voted to do just that at its annual meeting. However, in spite of these two votes, the transfer of the deed for the school property from WACPA to the college appears *not* to have taken place because in the end, as noted above, it was WACPA, not the college, that sold the Mendota campus after the school's relocation to Aurora. To confuse matters further, for years the college property was listed as an asset on WACPA's financial statement. This changed in 1905–6, when it appeared as such on the *college's* financial statement instead. And in 1909, the college board created a committee to write a constitution and by-laws for the college corporation, which seems to have been fairly late in the day to be doing this, given the fact that the college acquired a charter in 1899. Gaps and contradictions in the documentary evidence are not just confusing to historians; it appears that the college board was sometimes confused as well. In 1908, late enough in the college's history to assume that any fuzziness in the WACPA-college relationship had been worked out, the college board authorized President Dean to investigate the school's legal relationship with WACPA. Unfortunately, since the minutes of the boards and annual meeting are often incomplete and cryptic, they do not generally supply explanations for contradictions in the historical record, thus leaving the exact nature of the WACPA-college legal relationship somewhat murky.[8]

Whatever the exact nature of the legal relationship between WACPA and the college over time, it remained a close and entangled one—so close that the lines between them remained blurred throughout the Mendota years. For example, the two entities borrowed money from each other. One might think that, given the chronic financial problems that the college had, borrowing money would have been a one-way street—the college borrowing from WACPA. However, the publication association had its own financial issues and at times needed additional funds. In April of 1911, WACPA asked the college board for a $2,200 loan at 6 percent interest, the money to come from the school's endowment fund; the college board then voted to do this. Interestingly, the funds were needed to pay "college notes," which were payable on demand. The minutes do not explain this, but one possibility is that WACPA had borrowed money to go toward college operating funds, and when the loans were due, it did not have the money to repay them. In 1908, WACPA became the lender, the college board voting to borrow $1,000 from what was either the college's own endowment, which was then still controlled by WACPA, or WACPA's endowment. And sometimes a staff member was borrowed. In 1909, the college board voted to hire H. E. Pancost as school treasurer. However, he apparently worked for WACPA, as the college board agreed to pay it $100 for Pancost's services. And this was not just a short-term situation; Pancost retained this job until May 1911, when he left the treasurer position for both the college and WACPA. These lines were blurred even more by the fact that many of the same people served on the board of directors of the two entities, although usually not concurrently. However, B. Forester did. According to the college catalogs, starting in 1896–97, he was on the college board virtually every year, serving as its secretary for most of those years and its chair during the last two, full years at Mendota. He also served on the WACPA board. Starting in 1893–94, he was a board member for many years, serving as association secretary early on and then taking the position of association president during the second decade of the Mendota era. And sometimes the college and WACPA boards held joint board meetings, although it is not known how often that happened.[9]

In spite of the fact that incorporation did not mean the college's full independence from WACPA, incorporation was, no doubt, a significant milestone in the college's legal and financial history. WACPA's child was growing up and needed more independence and legal authority, which the corporate charter must have supplied. However, there was no sharp break with the past; rather, the changes evolved over the next decade or so. Only in 1905 did the college board ask WACPA to transfer all college funds to the school, which the publication association then voted to do. And not until 1908 did WACPA transfer at least the *management* of the college's endowment fund over to the school.[10]

Although the college was gradually maturing and becoming more independent throughout the Mendota years, its bonds with WACPA (beyond WACPA's continued ownership of college property) were never severed—not suddenly or even gradually. The young adult remained close to its parent, and this parent did everything it could to contribute to the growth of the college's student population and its financial well-being. It went beyond loaning money and personnel to the college. *Our Hope* was the college's main avenue of communication and a major fundraising and recruitment tool. Hardly an issue went by that it did not have an article—and almost always there were multiple ones—about the college. Most articles urged readers either to send their children to the school or to donate money to it. Even the editor of *Our Hope* for many years, Henry Pollard, taught Latin at the college, from the 1907–8 school year through 1910–11, while also retaining his position as editor. And WACPA's and Pollard's helpfulness to the college was especially important in 1896, when the school was experiencing the worst financial crisis of its life. The WACPA board voted that Pollard be granted a two-month "vacation" to travel and raise funds for the college. WACPA continued to pay his salary, as well as his expenses on the road. Pollard had to be replaced for this period of time so another salary had to be paid also. WACPA, like the college, had chronic financial problems, so freeing Pollard from his duties on the newspaper, while still paying him, must have been a sacrifice. The parent was doing what it could to help its struggling offspring.[11]

Preparing to Open the New College

Purchasing the Mendota property—and so quickly—was an impressive achievement for this small group of educationally oriented Adventists. However, a college is more than a piece of property, and even that had to be repaired. Faculty and support staff had to be hired, a curriculum had to be drawn up, students had to be recruited, and furnishings had to be provided for the college building, among other things.

Given all these impending costs, fundraising had to begin right away, but it did not start as early as one might think. In November and December of 1892, several *Our Hope* articles asked that subscribers send in money to help in the setting up of the college. In a December 7, 1892, article—written *about a month before the opening of the college*—President Campbell wrote that "there is now in the hands of the treasurer a fund of over $14,000 in pledges: of this 10 per cent, or $1,400, is now overdue and must be paid in at once."[12] The figure of $14,000 doesn't sound bad, but only half of it was earmarked for the college. The other half was to go to the publishing effort. Also, it represented the amount *in pledges*, 10 percent of which were overdue. In a December 28, 1892, *Our Hope* article—*less than two weeks before the college's opening*—President Campbell reported on the progress of the college and made an urgent plea for funds, saying, "We shall need considerable more money than we have on hand now. I have engaged to open the school at the date named, and it will depend upon you to keep it progressing."[13] These were not reassuring words for those who supported the educational experiment that was about to begin under the auspices of WACPA.[14]

The opening date of the college was fluid for some time. In July of 1892, the projected opening date was October 3, 1892, but that deadline passed. Then the November 23, 1892, issue of *Our Hope* gave the projected date as Monday, January 9, 1893. But even that date was not entirely certain, because in that same issue, an article written by the Educational Committee stated that the opening of the school was *contingent* upon two things—raising enough money and acquiring enough students. Clearly, even after the final date was announced, college leaders were worried that there might not be enough money or students to go forward. The upshot of this is that when the school finally opened on January 9, it had both a money and a student problem. From day one, the college had a financially shaky foundation and a student population that was too small to provide any degree of financial stability. Only three students matriculated on the first day—perhaps explained by the facts that there was a big snowstorm on that day, that the weather was colder than it had been in some time, and that Mendota had enough illness in town (scarlet fever and measles) that some of its public schools were closed. Fortunately, registration was extended to about February 6, and by the end of the spring term, in June, there were fifty-one students enrolled. Still, it was *not* an auspicious beginning. Nevertheless, Mendota College was open for business—based on little more than faith, hope, and prayer.[15]

Running a Small College—Dollars and Determination Yet Debts

Mendota College always struggled with debt, although to varying degrees. By the mid-1890s, a period of national economic depression, it had dug itself into a financial hole. It not only needed to raise about $700 for the current school year, it had a debt of nearly $400 from the recent past as well.[16] To get back on track, during the 1896–97 school year, there was a campaign to pay off this debt. As a part of this fundraising effort, the college announced what was no doubt a dubious yet earnest pledge:

> There will be no more begging for old college debts if you will pay up the present indebtedness. We can now see how the school can be run so economically and carefully that our people need have no fears for its future management. ... We have figured closely to run the college within the limits of $1800 annually, and yet to do our duty in the line

of educational work. ... We are sure of what we are talking about. Our machinery ... is in good running order. The college is in good repair and well furnished for our work.[17]

By March of 1897, the college announced in *Our Hope* that "the $600 note held by the bank against the college is paid."[18] Since some bills and financial commitments *had* to be paid, the college leadership had been forced to take out a bank loan. More debt remained, but the substantial debt owed a local bank was eliminated. Paying off such a large part of the college debt must have produced a great sense of relief for college leaders, but the school was not out of the woods yet. A much greater sense of relief must have appeared when, in late June, J. W. Emmons, fundraiser and soon-to-be Mendota College board member, announced in *Our Hope* that "there was money on hand to pay all indebtedness up to August 1, 1897. ..."[19] And in early September, things looked even better when *Our Hope* readers were told that "all debts incumbent upon our college have been lifted and a handsome donation of a cool $1000, received during the campmeeting, with other large donations in prospect, has gladdened the hearts of our Educational Board. ..."[20] This was good news indeed. The college had climbed out of its financial hole and would not be in debt as badly as it had been in the mid-1890s until 1912—the year it moved to Aurora. But according to Emmons, this debt had been a serious challenge for, and even an outright threat to, the college. In April 1897, Emmons wrote, about paying off a major part of the school's debt, that "we were obliged to do this or sink."[21]

Emmons was right. The college board minutes of late 1896 and 1897 reveal a desperate financial situation. The December 1896 minutes show that the board voted to shorten the spring term by two weeks, while both the president and principal of the Bible Training School agreed to "throw off" part of their salaries. At the April 1897 meeting, there was even a discussion about eliminating programs at the college (although that did not ultimately happen). In short, the college almost failed in this period. However, at the April 1897 meeting, board members decided to fight for the college, voting "that in the name of the Lord we maintain the college."[22] This was a close call.[23]

The promise of college leaders, that once the school got out of the 1896–97 debt, it could operate on a mere $1,800 a year and remain in the black, was overly optimistic. True, the 1890s was an era of deflation rather than inflation, but over time, faculty ranks would have to be expanded, salaries would have to see some increase, and unexpected repairs and replacements of equipment would have to be made. Since the college had so small a financial cushion, such needs would inevitably send college leaders scrambling to raise money beyond what it received from tuition and the usual donations.

The reality for most years was an *annual*, urgent-sounding, spring campaign to pay off the debts of the school year—hopefully before the academic year ended, which often did not happen. This campaign sometimes lasted beyond Commencement, into the summer, and occasionally into September. This certainly was an improvement over the debt that had piled up in the mid-1890s, but it was not an indication that the college could easily operate on such limited funds without at least going into short-term debt. Even in years when college leaders claimed that the college had come out in the black, they were sometimes stretching the truth a bit. When such claims were made, they had to have been based on the financial year of the WACPA, which ended in late summer. Since the college was created by WACPA and so was under its supervision, these claims were not exactly untrue. However, in raising funds in the spring to balance the budget for the school year, Adventists were usually told that the money was needed by the end of the school year in June. That deadline was seldom met.[24]

As hard as the college tried to stay out of debt (at least trying to balance the budget by September of the following school year), it *did* accumulate significant additional debt several times after the 1896–97 campaign. Each of these periods of extra high debt correlated with competing projects that needed money—projects of either the college or WACPA. This is further evidence of the college's persistent and precarious financial situation. The national and local environments were always changing, and there would be times when they would not be great—a financial panic, a depression, competing fundraising projects, etc. In short, the lack of a substantial financial cushion meant that the college would go from financial crisis to financial crisis.

By 1902, the college had accumulated debt from the previous year while trying to raise funds for current operating costs. The college treasurer wrote in a December 1902 *Our Hope* article that "the donations have not been such as to meet the expenses during the last term, and a debt has been contracted in addition to the two hundred dollars left unpaid at the close of the last school year."[25] Two things contributed to this deficit. One was the dormitory fire of December 1901, which necessitated a fundraising campaign to build or buy a new building to serve as the women's dormitory. (The college was underinsured so it could not simply rebuild with the insurance money.) In May 1902, an *Our Hope* article notified readers that cash and pledges for the new dormitory were coming in slowly, a phenomenon that some earlier articles had noted as well.[26] But as slowly as these funds came in, this special fundraising effort was still seen as harmful to the regular fundraising campaign. Just two months after the fire, Mendota College's board chair reported that once the dormitory fund was created, the money being donated in the College Day Offering began to decline. He reminded *Our Hope* readers that "these two funds should not interfere one with the other; the burning of the dormitory was an unavoidable misfortune, and must be met as such; what is given to that fund should be in addition to what was expected to be given to the college."[27]

The fire's financial consequences came on top of a somewhat earlier, but continuing, financial commitment. In the summer of 1901, substantial money was spent on campus repairs and improvements. To pay for these repairs, a fund was created at that year's Mendota campmeeting. About $1,200 was raised, in cash and pledges, at the campmeeting, leaving around $400 to be raised. By late November, just several months after the campmeeting and just a few weeks before the fire, around $1,300 had been raised in cash and pledges. However, the debt for these improvements had *not* diminished; instead it had *grown* to nearly $500.[28] This meant that the college would not be well positioned financially when the fire struck. Not only would fundraising for operating expenses be hurt because of the campaign to raise funds for a new dormitory, the college had a significant debt to pay down on top of raising enough funds to run the college currently. A March 1902 *Our Hope* article reported that nearly $1,000 had been raised for the college through the College Day Offering, but then it went on to say that "it is not enough to carry our school through the year. On account of the large expense for repairs last summer, amounting to over $1800 dollars, not a dollar was raised for the support of the school at the last campmeeting nor until the College Day offering arrived. It has required all the offerings sent in to meet current expenses, and at this writing *less than a dollar* remains in the treasury [italics in original]."[29] Little did college officials know when they made costly campus repairs in the summer of 1901 that just a few months later they would take a huge financial hit because of the fire. But that was life, and Mendota College was not very well prepared financially for life's ups and downs.

Another significant debt was accumulated during the 1907–8 school year. When it began in September 1907, the college was free of debt and had $177.16 in the treasury. Between September 4, 1907, and March 31, 1908, fall and winter terms, there was a shortfall of $1,410.00—an amount the board was forced to borrow to keep on operating with its bills paid. The shortfall for the spring term was estimated to be $566.60 for a total debt of $1,976.60. The situation was so serious that $700 had to be borrowed to help cover the bills early in the year. By way of explaining this dramatic shortfall, the author of an *Our Hope* article mentioned the current "financial depression that is affecting all institutions that depend upon public benevolence for their support."[30] Another reason was especially important, however. Many monetary contributions, which ordinarily would have gone to the college, were diverted to the *Our Hope* Building Fund campaign, which raised $10,000–$12,000 in order for WACPA and its press to move out of rented space and into its own, newly constructed, Mendota building. These two fundraising campaigns—for the college and the publication building—were aimed at virtually identical audiences, the relatively small, scattered group of Advent Christians in the Midwest—especially those who subscribed to *Our Hope*, most of whom were of limited means. An October 1906 *Our Hope* article, whose topic was the new publication building, urged readers not to give to the building fund at the expense of the college, but clearly that happened anyway. Many Advent Christians had only so much surplus income to donate to an Adventist cause, so the college did suffer.[31]

By the end of the Mendota era, the college had amassed another large debt—again because another major project was diverting money away from the regular fundraising to cover the school's operating costs. The school was hardly beyond paying off the 1907–8 debt when fundraising for the new campus in Aurora began in earnest in 1910. In June 1912, two months after the college had moved to Aurora, *Our Hope* readers were told that there was a double debt owed—$3,000, to pay off the new college buildings in Aurora, needed right away because bills were coming due, and $6,000, needed to pay off operating costs for the two previous school years. The $10,000 that needed to be raised, and quickly, also included $1,000 to get the school up and running on the new campus.[32]

Jenks explained this debt by saying that he had been off traveling for fourteen months to raise money for the Aurora campus, so fundraising for operating costs suffered. He also blamed it on a smaller-than-usual number of students in the recent past, saying that potential students were waiting for the new campus to open. Both of these explanations, no doubt, were valid, but this debt problem also had another explanation that fit an earlier pattern, one that Jenks acknowledged—when there were competing fundraising campaigns, Mendota College accrued a larger-than-normal debt. Advent Christians seemed to be unwilling, or perhaps unable, to give to more than one campaign at a time.[33]

Although Mendota College had much debt over its nineteen years, it also had some financial assets, which was especially important because it so often needed to take out bank loans. In 1902, about halfway through the Mendota years, *Our Hope* published some financial data, including its monetary assets, as a way reassuring its readers that even though the president's home / women's dormitory had burned down, all was not lost financially. The loss from the fire, after insurance was deducted, was about $2,400. (This figure did not include the significant property loss of individuals.) However, the campus itself was intact, and the existing property of the college and its monetary worth was given as follows:

　　—College Building (& 5 acres of land) - - $10,000
　　—Dormitory Lot & Barn - - $450
　　—Ames Chemical Laboratory (in the college building) - - $520
　　—College Library (in the college building) - - $2400
　　—Museum (in the college building) - - $800
　　—Boarding Department (Dining) - - $400
　　—Other Rooms (in the college building) - - $1200
　　—Total Valuation - - $15,770 [34]

It was good to have property that had gained in market value. The campus, with the college building on it, had cost just $1,800 in late 1891. The $10,000 market value of the campus in 1902 represented a nice boost in equity, but this asset was *not* liquid, and although 1902 was in the era when the college had its own charter, WACPA was still the owner of the actual real estate and the manager of the school's endowment fund. And a look at the percentages of the various revenue streams six years after the fire, in 1908, shows a high reliance on donations and little help from the endowment:

—Tuition (for those not in the Bible Training School) & Room Rent - - 20.26%

—Endowment Fund / Interest - - 6%

—Monetary Donations - - 72%

—All Sources except for Donations & Interest on Endowment - - 22%[35]

Thus, even in the good years, when there were no other projects competing for the dollars of *Our Hope* readers and other Adventists, and the bills were paid by the end of the school year or at least by the beginning of the next school year, Mendota College had the burden of raising a substantial majority of its revenue through fundraising. To do this, the college had to employ a variety of fundraising strategies.

Fundraising Strategies

To raise money for the support of the college, its leaders used several different strategies, some of which they would emulate in the fundraising campaign of 1910–12 to raise funds for the new Aurora campus. But no matter what the strategy, it was usually implemented by using the weekly newspaper of WACPA—*Our Hope and Life in Christ*. As mentioned earlier, the majority of the paper's articles on the college had to do with fundraising, either directly or indirectly, along with the recruitment of students. The paper's subscribers resided in different regions of the country, but the bulk of them lived in the "West," a term loosely construed to include mainly the Midwest, but also a few parts of the South and Far West. Of course, the subscriber base was overwhelmingly Advent Christian. Not only was *Our*

Hope the publication arm of the organization that had founded Mendota College, one 1893 article referred to the paper as the "organ" of the college. Thus, it was reasonable to assume that *Our Hope* readers would have a special interest in supporting it. The school was a place where they could send their children with little worry, and it provided the ministers that their churches so badly needed, especially the small, rural churches. Thus, *Our Hope* was the place where campaigns and strategies were introduced, explained, encouraged, and reported on.[36]

As with most fundraising campaigns today, Mendota College sought large donations, but it also encouraged small ones, if that was all someone could give. The large donations got the school to its goal more quickly, and the few that it received were gratefully accepted. But over the years, article after article in *Our Hope* emphasized the importance of small donations. Not only did many, small gifts amount to substantial sums over time, they connected the donors to the college in a way that simply reading about the college in *Our Hope* did not do. Receiving many small donations told the college that *Our Hope* readers were truly interested in and supported the college, not only financially but in other ways as well. They provided a wide base of support for the school. Milton Livingston, the college treasurer in 1902, noted that the school had recently received two $50 donations, but most of them had fallen within the range of $1 to $10. By way of encouraging even more small donations, he said that "one thousand dollars from one thousand friends is vastly better as an evidence of widespread interest than the same amount from one person."[37] This was not the only time that Livingston emphasized the importance of small donations. As treasurer, he especially understood their importance to the financial viability of the college.[38]

Livingston was just one of many college officials who broadcast this message, because they all knew that to a large extent, their subscribers were not affluent. Their message was often the same as the one that Livingston gave—although most people could not give much, giving something was a sign of interest in and commitment to the college. However, this was not the only reason that small donors were considered important. In 1910, while trying to raise money for the Aurora campus, Jenks provided another one:

No one man is going to give liberally to erect our buildings, unless there is quite a general response from all our people. It would be foolish thus to do. For if our people are not interested sufficiently to arise and do their part, then they have no interest in what is their own, and what is a vital factor in the advance of the cause they profess to love. We must all have an interest in our school, else it will be shorn of its power and absolutely fail to accomplish the end for which it was established.[39]

This statement by Jenks is very modern sounding. Fundraisers today know that many big donors like to see that others are supporting a cause as well.[40]

To encourage small donations in the campaign to pay off the large debt of 1896–97, one strategy that college officials used was to launch a dollar campaign—asking everyone to send in at least a dollar. The rationale for this was laid out in an 1896 *Our Hope* article: "The talk has always been that those who had but limited means, were not contributing to our college work. Now we have made the sum asked for so small that almost anybody can contribute, and that without much delay."[41] To inspire readers, and perhaps to make them feel some guilt, another 1896 *Our Hope* article told the story of two, multiple–$1 contributors, women of very limited means: "I received a letter to-night from Sister Mary A. Tibbets with her third donation of one dollar towards our 'College debt,' and also one from Sister Lizzie S. Wallace, a daughter of Sister Tibbets', with her second donation of one dollar for the same purpose. The latter donor earns her money by sewing with her needle, but she says she expects the Lord will send her more work to make it all up."[42] Tibbets responded to this praise with a call for others to give, making a suggestion about how young farm girls with little money could contribute to the cause: "Save up a certain portion of the eggs, butter, or poultry you sell every week, and though it may be small, it will soon amount to one dollar."[43] Like the man who sang her praise, she was not letting anyone off the hook. Thus, the fundraising message across the years can be summed up with this quotation from a 1901 *Our Hope* article: "Who is so poor among us that he or she cannot afford a small College Day offering? *No one* [italics in original]."[44] *All* donations were welcome, and college officials were not too proud to beg for even the smallest ones.

These are not the only examples of individual poor people giving to the college over the years and at great sacrifice to themselves, yet the constant pleas for funds and the chastising tone of many articles in *Our Hope* suggest that such people were in the minority. Donations were slow to come in even for the dollar campaign. The frustration of one fundraiser was evident when he wrote:

> Our people are very slow and have to think a long time to make up their minds that it is the best thing to do to pay the small sum of one dollar each to raise money to pay the college debts. When I asked them to pay it within thirty days, I truly thought it was time enough for each one to make up his mind what he could and would do. But I find that only a small part of all our people in the West have decided as yet that it is their duty to help pay an honest and just debt.[45]

One-dollar donations did come in, but not in the volume that one might have expected, given the small size of the request.

Another strategy used by the college was to make special appeals to Advent Christian churches and their pastors, as opposed to just general appeals to *Our Hope* readers. Churches were seen as collection vehicles. Sometimes congregations *as a whole* contributed money to the college, and sometimes subgroups, like the Loyal Workers Society, the Helpers' Union, etc., collected money from their members or had their members raise it through various projects. For example, in the fall of 1897, having just paid off a large debt, the college's leaders asked that churches take up collections for the school's operating costs. They were trying to pay their bills as they came in so as to avoid accumulating another substantial debt. In an *Our Hope* article urging churches to take the *second* of such collections, the author notes that "this is the plan that has been devised for raising money this year for College expenses."[46] Sometimes the churches needed no urging to do this and spontaneously sent funds to the school, much to the surprise and delight of college officials. But mostly churches had to be urged to do this. In 1910, such a request was even accompanied by some rather specific instructions.

The week of Jan. 2d to 8th has been appointed for a week of self-denial, with special reference to the current expenses of Mendota College. Jan. 8th is Mendota College Day, on which it is hoped that as many of our churches as can will take up an offering for Mendota College, in connection with a special program devoted to College interests. Every church ought to send in an offering, at least to equal twenty cents each for each enrolled member, and we hope, far in excess of this. Do not ask for a penny collection![47]

Apparently the college had received many a "penny collection" and was trying to head off any future ones in hopes of receiving a more substantial response from the churches. It was fine to welcome any donation from individuals, however small, but it was also important to urge groups to aim higher.[48]

The success of this strategy, no doubt, depended on several variables, one of which was how well the church understood the necessity of a denominational school for its own well-being—how the work being done there related to them. College leaders tried to educate Advent Christians about the college's mission and work through the celebration of College Day and Educational Week. But a more direct way that a church could see this was through the work of the Bible Training School students who went out to various churches to preach—either a few times or on a regular basis. One example of this was a small church in Tecumseh, Nebraska. In 1903, it wrote a letter to the *Our Hope* editors, saying that two Mendota College students had preached at their church. It appears that the students did a fine job because the church then decided to take up a *monthly* collection for the school, saying that they saw the need for such a place and thought that everyone should support it. There was a fair number of churches without pastors at any given time, so Mendota students were in high demand. And each single visit or longer stay at a church was an advertisement for the support of the college.[49]

Another variable in determining a church's support for the college was the pastor's degree of interest in the school. Pastors were viewed as being particularly important in the process of raising money through the churches. Fundraisers generally did not explain why they thought this, but some reasons stand out as an educated guess. Parishioners usually looked up to their pastors and viewed them as authority figures so it probably was assumed that their endorsement of Mendota College would have some persuasive power. Ministers also were more likely to be educated than their congregations and so might have a greater appreciation for how important ministerial education was in producing better ministers and providing an adequate supply of them. And they knew their parishioners well and would best know how to approach them for donations. One fundraiser even referred to ministers as the school's "special agents."[50]

Thus, because of the pastor's leadership role and personal influence over parishioners, he, as the leader of the *entire* church, was often called upon to see that a congregation-wide collection was made. Asking Advent Christian ministers, specifically, to take up a collection for the college, instead of making a request for funds from churches in general, put the responsibility squarely on ministerial shoulders, and, one might reasonably assume, was a more efficient way of collecting college funds from church members. In June 1908, one of the periods of larger debt, an *Our Hope* article included such a request: "We hope each A. C. pastor will do his best to aid us in raising this needed sum. If each of our pastors will send in a church collection for this purpose, soon, we believe there will be no further need of our appeals for aid in this case."[51] And in the early days of fundraising for the new Aurora campus, Jenks expressed a similar hope: "If our ministers would carefully canvass their members and secure the pledges, it would relieve the committee of much work and expense. If the members of your church would pledge, and then the pledges be sent in in a bunch, it would show what the church as a whole is ready to do in this work. Try it and let us know the result. It may inspire other pastors and churches to do the same."[52] At least one fundraiser sensed that ministers might fear that raising money for the college would take funds away from their own projects. He tried to reassure them by saying: "Don't any of you think by so doing it will lessen the interests in your home work. Remember that your home work is somewhat dependent upon our college work. ... Some churches to-day would be without pastors if it had not been for Mendota College."[53] This was not just reassurance, but another reminder of how dependent the churches' well-being was on the college.[54]

Asking for church collections and receiving them, however, were two different things. College administrators were often disappointed by the lack of response to such requests (as well as other types of pleas for money). While individual churches or one of their organizations sometimes took it upon themselves to take a collection or raise money in some other way for the college, the majority did not. Many of the widely scattered and often isolated churches in the Midwest apparently did not see the connection between themselves and the distant Mendota College and so did not support it financially.

And ministers could not always be depended upon to help raise money for the college. Some reports on the College Day offering, published in *Our Hope*, suggest that even pressure applied specifically to ministers did not always work. In 1908, one of the periods of larger debt for the college, the school treasurer complained that "a few weeks ago we made an appeal to our ministers, asking them to take up church collections each for our college. But few have taken up such a collection."[55] Virtually all the Advent Christian churches, to varying degrees, had relatively small memberships and little money, and many of their ministers lived in poverty. But college leaders continuously emphasized that even the smallest donation was welcome.[56]

Appealing to churches and ministers as a way of raising money for the college must have seemed like a good idea in theory, and it certainly did produce some revenue that might not have been raised had all the pleas for money just been aimed at individual Advent Christians. It centralized the giving by church in that the school received one lump sum representing the collective effort of a congregation rather than multiple, smaller donations, each from a different church member. This approach also provided a leader, the minister, to organize the giving and prod the potential givers. And one could hope that group giving would produce more money through a spirit of camaraderie and shared purpose, not to mention peer pressure. However, the results were mixed at best.

Another way of raising money for the college in Advent Christian churches was the use of Educational Day. As early as 1897, the WACPA board voted that the fourth Sunday in November be designated as the Sunday to learn about Mendota College and take up a collection for it. By at least 1903, the second Sunday in January had been set aside as "Educational Day," its close proximity to College Day on January 9 *not* being a coincidence. Some version of this special Sunday existed throughout the twentieth century—later known as Aurora College / Aurora University Sunday. And before 1903, at least one church was setting its own date for such an event (and probably more were as well). In 1897, the Sparta, Wisconsin, Advent Christian Church designated Sunday, May 30, as "College Day." A sermon was preached that was appropriate for the special occasion, and a collection for Mendota College was taken up. The *Our Hope* article announcing this urged other ministers in the West to have such a day at their church. A January 1912 *Our Hope* article, as part of its report on the day, described it as "the day set apart for presenting before all our A. C. churches the value and needs of our General Educational Work, and then giving the people an opportunity to respond with their pecuniary offerings."[57] In short, this day was both a student-recruiting tool and a fundraising event.[58]

What eventually became the *major* tool to raise money to support the college was the College Day Offering. This offering was part of the College Day celebration. In a January 1894 issue of *Our Hope*, just one year after the opening of Mendota College, the secretary/treasurer of the Educational Committee announced that "it is proposed by the Educational Committee and management of Mendota College to set apart January 9th as a Memorial College Day, this date being the natal day of our college work."[59] This anniversary was named College Day. January 9 remained a special day of celebration throughout the Mendota years and for most of the twentieth century in Aurora, where eventually it became known as Founders Day. This was a time for the people of Mendota College to celebrate the school's founding, but there were always multiple, enthusiastic invitations to others—to Mendotans and Advent Christians in general—since one of the major purposes of the day was to show off the college and educate people about the work that it was doing.[60]

The purpose and program of College Day was laid out in the first few years, creating a template for this day that essentially remained in place for the rest of the Mendota period. The purpose of College Day was often described as having three parts: to publicly thank God for all the school's blessings and pray for blessings in the coming year; to educate Advent Christians about what Mendota College was like and what it was doing, urging people to come and see for themselves; and to generate greater financial support for the college as well as additional students. For the majority of Advent Christians in the West who could not participate in the public prayers in Mendota on that day, it was suggested that they pray for the school in their own homes. They also were encouraged to make a College Day donation to the school. The schedule for the day was generally in three parts as well. Typically, in the morning, there was a special service at the Mendota Advent Christian church, at which there was a guest speaker who gave the College Day address. In the afternoon, there usually was an open house on the college campus. Visitors were invited to walk around to see the facilities and work of the college for themselves. The day generally ended in the evening with a program on campus, given by students in the Literary Society, the program being literary and/or musical in nature.[61]

Attendance at College Day events was often good, but given the time of year that it occurred, some years saw low attendance, due to either sickness or the weather. However, on at least one occasion, in 1905, College Day had a decent turnout in spite of the weather. This was surprising because the weather that day was truly horrible—sleet, snow, and very cold temperatures, which froze the ice and snow hard on the sidewalks so that it was difficult to walk. Of course, such terrible weather actually was quite fitting for this particular celebration because on opening day, January 9, 1893, the weather was bad also. It, no doubt, kept some people away, but not the three intrepid students who showed up for classes.[62]

From the first College Day in January 1894 to the last one in Mendota, in January 1912, school leaders urged Advent Christians to give a monetary donation of gratitude and support for Mendota College as part of this celebration. However, what changed over time was that the College Day offering went from a suggestion and hope in 1894, existing alongside other appeals for funds during the year, to a more organized campaign, with the message that this was to be the *single* fundraising effort of the year. As early as 1898, one fundraiser was saying such things as "if all give $1.25 each there will be no necessity for asking further contributions" and "we hope that there will be enough given so that we shall not have to ask for one dollar more after this collection is all reported."[63] By at least 1902/1903, college fundraisers were stating that they viewed the College Day offering as the school's *only* fundraising campaign—to raise all the money necessary for the support of the college beyond what tuition brought in. Eventually college leaders began setting a specific amount of money as the stated goal of the campaign, as fundraisers do today. At least by 1902, college fundraisers stated the monetary goal on the coin cards being mailed out, and this amount went up over time—from $1,500 in 1902 to $2,000 in 1904. But as late as the 1908 campaign, the goal was still $2,000.[64]

Since around 1897, the college, to further encourage broad-based giving for the College Day offering and probably to make giving as easy as possible, mailed what were called "coin cards" out to all the *Our Hope* subscribers and other friends of the college. Initially, the cards were perforated in such a way as to hold $1.25 in coins—or more if you stuffed them in or added a bill. College fundraisers believed that $1.25 was a manageable amount of money for most people to donate, and they wanted to encourage giving from the many, not just the wealthy few. However, by 1903, cards were no longer designed to hold $1.25. Believing that many people could give more, college officials decided to let people decide for themselves how much to send in. They must have believed that having a $1.25 figure on the cards was suppressing what at least some people could afford to give. On the other hand, they continued to say that if everyone who received a card gave, on average, just a dollar, the college would not have to ask for any more money. This idea of *everyone* giving $1 or $1.25 was one that fundraisers would use time and again. One fundraiser called the $1.25 request "a small tax upon the many"[65] and a year later added that "this is a way by which *all may help a little* [italics in original]."[66] They encouraged those who could give more than $1 to $1.25 to do so, but they also wanted those who could not give as much—even less than the requested amount—to send in whatever they could afford as a sign of their commitment to the work of the college. Perhaps this was another reason that a requested amount was removed from the coin cards—so that people who could not afford to give a dollar would not feel that therefore they could not give anything.[67]

In theory, this was a smart strategy in that Adventists, it was argued, would *not* be bombarded with numerous and various fundraising appeals throughout the year—just those for the College Day offering. Sadly, it did not work out that way. Greater effort was put into the College Day offering campaign, but there were other necessary campaigns—to upgrade the college building and to fulfill basic maintenance needs. The College Day offering barely covered operating expenses for any given year, and sometimes not that, so there had to be other campaigns to pay for anything extra. In their appeals for funds, college leaders usually said that the money was needed by the end of the school year in early June, and it was, because bills and faculty had to be paid by then. However, many times the school was not rid of its red ink until the rest of the needed money was raised at the campmeeting, held in mid-to-late August on the college grounds. When that happened, it was usually the result of many donations. But at the 1897 campmeeting, an unnamed person paid off the school's debt with the incredible donation of $1,000. Unfortunately, however, the college could not count on that happening every year. And sometimes the debt even lingered into the fall. As long as the bills were paid off by the end of WACPA's financial year, which came right after its annual campmeeting, the college claimed that it had balanced the budget. Technically that was true, but the impression left by the appeals in *Our Hope* was that the funds had to be sent to the college by Commencement, because bills needed to be paid and the *timely* paying of faculty was in jeopardy—facts that were also true.[68]

Even though this was supposed to be the one major campaign to support the college, fundraising continued to go on throughout the year, just like it did before the College Day offering was deemed the major fundraising campaign for the school. College Day offerings, which were requested in January, usually trickled in until late summer and sometimes even into the fall of the next school year. The reason that the campaign went on and on was because not enough money was being raised in a month or two to pay the bills for the school year. There usually would be a spurt early on and then just a trickle. In the years having specific monetary goals, few to none of them were met. That made it necessary to continue making College Day offering appeals, in *Our Hope* and elsewhere, for much of the school year.[69]

The amount raised through the College Day offering did grow over time. In 1900, about $300 was raised, and the next year the amount was doubled—to about $600. Over the next four years (1902–5), the amounts raised were similar—in 1902, about $1,100; in 1903, more than $1,100; in 1904, more than $1,200; and in 1905, $1,071. Then, by 1907, the amount raised had taken a substantial jump to over $1,500. However, over this same span of years, the campaign's goals ranged from $1,500 to $2,000, so even in 1907, when the offering was substantially larger, that year's $2,000 goal was not reached. And these goals were not fanciful. They were based on what college officials believed was the actual cost of running the college—without even factoring in capital improvements or emergencies of any kind.[70]

People had to be persuaded, cajoled, and even shamed to give, and often even that did not bear much fruit—either in numbers of donors or amount donated. Year after year just a small percentage of the cards sent out were returned with money. These were not cold mailings; the people who received these cards were a select group. They were mostly *Our Hope* subscribers and other known friends of the college, so one might reasonably assume that they had a special interest in the denomination and its educational work. Yet the college received, on average, only about six hundred donations per year, even though for most years, it mailed out numbers of coin cards that were several times that—from fourteen hundred to thirty-five hundred. And when one looked at the percentage of *all* Advent Christians in the Midwest who gave to the college, the percentage of donors shrunk considerably. In 1908, the college treasurer stated that the college "has always been largely supported by the free-will offerings of probably less than one-tenth of our Adventist people of the middle West."[71] In addition to its ongoing *Our Hope* appeals aimed at people who had never contributed to the school before, the college tried other strategies to get a broader base of support. For example, in 1904, *Our Hope* readers were told that the college had deliberately sent out an unusually large number of coin cards—thirty-five hundred—in the hope that more would be returned. After 1905, the number of cards being mailed out declined so that by 1908, just twenty-five hundred were mailed. Apparently, the college fundraisers had concluded that mailing more coin envelopes out did not produce more revenue; it just raised their mailing cost. Thus, the trend continued that a relatively small group of people supported the school, some of them giving multiple times. And the donations that were received were usually small. For example, in May 1902—four months after the College Day offering campaign was launched—the school treasurer reported that the college had received two $50 donations, but that most of the less than six hundred donations fell within the range of $1 to $10.[72]

The College Day offering was probably better than having many miscellaneous campaigns throughout the year, and the amount given did grow over time. But in the end, it failed to adequately support the college, even if one just counts the college's annual operating costs. The amounts raised for the College Day offering improved over time, but the college budget went up as well, especially as faculty had to be added. For example, in 1901, a college fundraiser told *Our Hope* readers that $325 a month ($3,900 a year) was needed to run the school, but that year only around $600 was raised in the College Day offering. And although the amount raised by this offering had leapt forward by 1907, surpassing $1,500, the college budget by then was $6,000. To make matters worse, the very next year, the college had serious debt again because of fewer donations, due to people giving money for WACPA's new building instead of to the school.[73]

One of the most important groups of people for a college or university is alumni—as a source of moral support and school spirit, future students, and, of course, money. What role did the alumni of Mendota College play in fundraising? The answer to that is "mostly unknown, but probably not much." The college generally did not appeal to alumni as a distinct group, nor were their contributions listed separately. However, many, if not most, of them would have been *Our Hope* subscribers and seen the many fundraising appeals there. During the Mendota years, there was a hint of recognizing this group for fundraising purposes, but only a hint. At the 1905 campmeeting, held on the college campus, a reunion of former students was held one afternoon; about sixty people attended. Many of those who had graduated the previous year were there, but also some from as far back as 1898. The next year, at the campmeeting, another reunion was held for former students. They had been urged to attend this one, not just for the social aspect of it, but also because the college wanted to form an Alumni Association, seeing this organization as the "means of which we shall be able to keep in closer touch with each other and with the college."[74] Although this quotation makes no mention of fundraising, that hope, no doubt, lay behind this effort at organization.[75]

By 1908, this hope was made a bit more explicit when a board member wrote that "the alumni of Mendota College have not forgotten her, but we are hoping that the time is at hand when they will become one of her strongest sources of support."[76] Again, this support was not described as financial, but there is little doubt that this was what was meant. In 1908, the college was trying to pay down one of its larger debts and was in desperate need of expanding its donor base. And since the college had been in existence for fifteen years, it probably looked as if it was the right time to start looking at alumni "support" to a greater extent than in the past. Given that former students were mostly Advent Christians who probably felt affection for their alma mater, and who often went into some kind of Christian ministry, one can reasonably assume that donations had already come from at least a few alumni. The two alumni get-togethers, in 1905 and 1906, suggest that by the later Mendota years, the college was starting to think of alumni as a potentially important source of donations.

However, alumni giving in the Mendota era was not the financial pillar of the college that it would become in Aurora. Aside from a comment made in an *Our Hope* article, there is no evidence that an alumni association was ever formed at Mendota. Alumni were becoming increasingly important to their colleges and universities across the country in the late nineteenth and early twentieth centuries, but their influence was dependent on several things that Mendota College's alumni did not yet have—substantial numbers and wealth. Because the college was so young and attendance was so small, there were not very many alumni, even if those who attended but did not graduate were counted—as some colleges in this era were starting to do. Many, if not most, of the students came from humble backgrounds, and even if their education created some upward social mobility, they often did not have many extra dollars that they could spare for the college. Alumni working in Christian service areas, especially Advent Christian ministers, generally worked for low pay. The only academic area at the school whose graduates may have had a higher income was the Commercial Department. However, these students tended to be local people who were more likely to live at home and less likely to be Advent Christian. And, along with the college's lack of an admissions office, it also did not have one devoted to alumni affairs. Developing and then implementing such ideas as formally organizing alumni and rallying them to raise substantial sums of money would take years, not reaching fruition until the Aurora era. As late as 1910 and beyond, while Jenks was raising funds for the new, Aurora campus, no special effort was made to solicit alumni. He developed special appeals for specific groups—ministers, laymen, young men, young women, and even people who lived in isolated places with no nearby church. And yet, the group known as alumni was not among the specific ones called on for donations. Alumni were a part of some of the groups that were solicited, of course, but they were not seen as a distinct group whose rosy college memories would spur them to give to the school.[77]

Some fundraising strategies were initiated by individuals. One of these was the promise to contribute a certain amount of money if a set number of other people each gave the same amount, a strategy used in the 1896–97 campaign to save the college. H. M. Robbins, a member of the college's board, pledged to donate $100 if five other people pledged to do the same. A different, but related, strategy did not require matching donations. It involved a donor promising to make a substantial contribution if and when a certain amount of money was raised, sometimes giving a specific date by which this needed to happen. In building the new campus in Aurora, the largest donors—Charles Eckhart and D. A. Davis—used this method. Eckhart did this at least twice, promising $10,000 if $30,000 were raised by November 1, 1910, and later offering another $10,000 if $60,000 were raised by December 31, 1912. Davis offered $2,000 on the condition that $50,000 be raised by April 1, 1911. Although probably just a few Advent Christians could have matched Robbins's $100 gift to the college, the approach taken by Eckhart and Davis was geared toward galvanizing many Adventists into giving smaller donations, thus showing that there was a broad base of financial support for building the Aurora campus. It is not known whether the earlier strategy worked. It probably did not because after *Our Hope* reported that, not counting Robbins's pledge, a second one for $100 had been made, there were continued requests for three more $100 pledges, but the newspaper never reported that they had come through. Fortunately, the second strategy worked—the more ambitious monetary goals of both Eckhart and Davis were met and so their large donations were made.[78]

One of the more interesting fundraising schemes from an individual came from a man named William A. Burch, an Advent Christian minister. In 1911, when college leaders were busy raising money for the Aurora campus and the college debt for operating costs was growing by leaps and bounds, he reported that he had discovered a great fundraising opportunity and urged others to join him. The money raised would go into what he called a "maintenance fund"—a fund to help pay down the growing debt for operating costs rather than the Aurora campus building fund. The money-making opportunity consisted of selling a laundry detergent, called CAMEO. It is not entirely clear how this worked, but Burch found out that the CAMEO company would donate some money to the college—probably a percentage of the proceeds from selling their product. Over a number of months, the company had contributed, as of November 1911, a total of $221.30 to Mendota College's treasury. Two months later this amount had climbed to $279.80, and this included just the proceeds from what Burch himself sold.[79]

Burch was not the only Advent Christian who was involved in this endeavor. In one of his *Our Hope* articles on this subject, he included the CAMEO testimonials of two prominent Advent Christians. Emma Dennin Jenks, the wife of Orrin R. Jenks, said that "it is excellent and I would not like to do without it."[80] Mary E. Smith, a member of the college board of directors from 1906 to 1909 and a leader in the Helpers' Union, not only used this soap, she sold it. She testified that "there is no trouble in disposing of it, if one could get out and tell the people about it. As it is, everyone who uses it tells a neighbor, and so it spreads along the street till all are using it."[81] Burch also mentioned that a ninety-three-year-old man had already sold five cases of the soap. This person must have been a persuasive salesman because it is doubtful that he could personally recommend it, based on his own experience in doing the wash. And Burch loved to sing the praises of this soap. He wrote that this laundry detergent saved a woman much time and strength on washing day because no rubbing is required.[82]

Burch seemed very proud of himself for having found out about this sales opportunity and getting it going. But as a good Advent Christian, he expressed his gratitude to God, noting his "thankfulness to our heavenly Father who brought to my attention a way in which I could do something for the current expenses of Mendota College. ... "[83] It is unknown how long he and others continued selling this soap and donating its proceeds to the college. In any case, the $280+ that he raised himself and the amounts raised by other Advent Christians who were selling the soap were sizeable contributions to the coffers of Mendota College, given the fact that the school had been trying for years to get people to send in a dollar.

Advent Christian women often took the initiative to raise money for the college as well, both individually and in groups. Sometimes these *individual* donations were quite inspirational. In 1898, a college fundraiser reported that a woman named Mary A. Bloom, a seamstress, sent in two dollars. The fundraiser remarked that this was probably more than she earned in two days. The *groups* of women who donated funds were able to raise even more money. The largest and most productive of these groups was the Helpers' Union (discussed in chapter 7), a regional organization with local chapters in churches throughout the Midwest. They not only supplied many items to the men's and women's dormitories, they raised a lot of money as well. There also were groups affiliated with a single church, such as a Minnesota church's "Busy Gleaners," whose members decided that they wanted to do more and give aid beyond their own congregation. In 1904, they decided "to send to Mendota College the proceeds of the last meeting in each quarter for this year."[84] Whether as individuals or groups, women were active donors to Mendota College, often putting to shame other Advent Christians in giving.[85]

Making Arguments for Giving to Mendota College and Chastising Those Who Didn't Give

Whether it was a good year or a bad one in terms of debt, raising money was a continuing struggle that required college leaders to make constant pleas for funds. To do this, they made an array of arguments for why people should financially support the college and even chastised them when the donations were only trickling in or there were none at all. Throughout the Mendota years, there were also constant pleas for students—especially from presidents. These pleas were not always attached to those for funds, but whether they were or not, college leaders were quite aware that getting more students was essential to the college's survival. Acquiring more students was financially important because, it was noted, the college could handle many more students without having to expand the faculty by much, if at all. And Advent Christians were periodically reminded that they had said that they wanted a college and would support it.[86]

Not surprisingly, the most common arguments made were religious in nature. Prominent among them was the one based on the core belief of

Advent Christians—that Christ would return to earth *soon*, so time was short to do the Lord's work of winning souls. People were told that their earthly treasures would soon do them no good, so now was the time to use their money for God's work. One *Our Hope* writer urged readers to show their love of God in word and deed "by making the year to come more full of loving sacrifice and labor than ever before. ... We have but a brief time to work. ... This is no time for hoarding up treasures upon earth, to be devoured by the soon coming judgment fires."[87] Thus, using one's money to support young people in training for Christian work was deemed more important than ever.[88]

But what if Christ did *not* return soon? There was an argument to be made in that circumstance as well. An early board member, M. A. Stevens, after calling Advent Christians "a most highly favored people"— given their great task from God to preach Christ's imminent return— provided an argument for this situation that was used by many others as well. He said that "there are two reasons why every Adventist in the land should contribute to this cause. 1st. If the Lord comes soon, as we expect and as there is every indication that he will, you will *not need* your money. And you had better have it where the rust of it will not be a swift witness against you. 2nd. If he should tarry longer than we now expect or think, then *we* will certainly *need* this institution, which can and must be made a mighty power for the advancement of his cause, to the glory of his name."[89] Such arguments about monetary donations in what Advent Christians believed were the end times essentially amounted to "use it or lose it." If Christ "tarried," their job was to occupy till Christ returned, and part of occupying was financially supporting God's work.

In 1890–91, when the idea of building a college in the West was being discussed, some people argued that if Advent Christians truly believed that Christ's return was *imminent*, they should be out preaching *now*, not spending years in college, so that they might save as many souls as possible. It appears that this anti-college argument never completely went away because pro-college responses to it were made throughout the Mendota years, those responses taking the form of reciting Jesus's own words: "Occupy till I come." In regards to relocating the college to a new campus in Aurora, one author in *Our Hope* suggested that some may ask "why" when Christ's return is *imminent*. (No one had yet asked this question, but he expected that it would be asked.) His answer to this question was about what he thought it meant to occupy:

> If we have the Kingdom message, beloved, prepare to sacrifice to the utmost to herald it widely. We must have a ministry equipped for the work. ... What does it matter if our Lord comes and finds us planning still greater things for him than ever before? Is it not better to be thus united in His work than engrossed with worldly cares and the deceitfulness of our small measure of riches, and so that day come upon us unawares? ... Just as well be building and equipping a college with the Lord's money as doing any other work, if this is His will.[90]

Another common religious argument concerned the children of Advent Christians, and this was a concern shared by many different Christian groups, not just Adventists. The argument went this way: Adventist Christians should send their children to Mendota College rather than to a secular state school or even to another denomination's college, the reason being fear that they would lose their Advent Christian faith, becoming completely secular or leaving their childhood denomination for another one. During the Mendota years, the college used this argument many times. It was one that probably reflected at least some parents' fears about what might happen to their children while away in college. The response to this fear was the argument that Mendota College provided a protected, more purely Christian moral environment, where the faith of Advent Christian students would be nurtured. It had Advent Christian and active Christian faculty and, outside of Mendotans, most of the students were Advent Christian. And it was argued that living and learning so closely with fellow Advent Christians would help to keep students' Adventist faith intact because they were likely to meet an Advent Christian spouse at Mendota College, which actually did happen frequently.[91]

Virtually all Protestant denominations wanted to protect the faith of their people, especially their young people, and so most of them built church-related colleges of some sort. What irked Mendota College leaders so much was that it seemed that other denominations did a much better job of supporting their colleges (and often they had multiple schools). Advent

Christians had just *one* college and, after 1897, a Bible school, the Boston School of Theology, and they struggled to keep them going. Mendota College leaders *must* have realized that in at least one sense, this comparison was a bit unfair to Advent Christians because the denomination was much smaller than many of the others. Still, from their perspective, this comparison did not favor them. Advent Christians did have many fewer people than most other Protestant denominations, but they also had just two, small institutions to support. College fundraisers frequently mentioned what other denominations were doing for the education of their people, perhaps hoping that a sense of guilt or competition would kick in and spur Advent Christians to start giving or continue to give, but more generously, to the college.[92]

Often when these comparisons were made, fundraisers had a passionate or even testy tone, no doubt a reflection of their frustration at seeing other denominations do a better job of educating their people than Advent Christians were doing. Milton Livingston—who graduated from Mendota College, served as the school's treasurer for several years, and entered the ministry—periodically wrote letters and articles for publication in *Our Hope*. He remained a strong and vocal supporter of the college and tried in different ways to encourage giving to his alma mater. He too used the theme of comparing Mendota College to the schools of other denominations. "Has Mendota College no friends? ... Where is that Adventist brother that is hoarding up his treasures? If people will give so much to these other institutions where so many errors are taught (and of course some truth) what ought we to do, who have the best message the world affords? ... Why not endow a chair, one of you good brethren who are so anxious for our young men to preach doctrine?"[93] And as late as 1911, when Jenks was desperately trying to raise money for the Aurora campus, his frustration sometimes revealed itself in his pleas for donations, and in the following case, he brought out the well-worn theme of comparisons between the Advent Christians and other denominations. After citing a number of other denominations that had built and supported *multiple* colleges, he wrote in *Our Hope* that "we are asking our people to help us build just ONE college, and this ONE will cost only a small sum in comparison of what other people have paid for their schools [underlining in original]."[94]

Another major argument for supporting Mendota College financially was religious, but also utilitarian—that both individual churches and the

Advent Christian denomination as a whole were dependent on Mendota College for their well-being. During the Mendota years, many Advent Christian churches were small and located in rural areas or small towns. There was stiff competition among churches for ministers because there were more churches than ministers. Many congregations lacked a minister, a serious condition because without ministerial leadership it was difficult to survive for long, and some did not. (As noted in chapter 5, this minister shortage actually provided numerous opportunities for Mendota College students to preach and even serve as pastors on weekends and school breaks.) The answer to this shortage, college fundraisers argued, was to support the school and students who wanted to attend or were already attending, especially those who wanted to enter the ministry.[95] J. W. Emmons, a board member and major fundraiser for the college, put it like this: "We could promise every church among us a good efficient pastor, so far as education and college training are concerned. We do not claim, however, that this would take the place of a divine call, but it would add to that call the efficiency that study gives. ... If we had not had a college to draw upon for trained ministers, seventy-five per cent of our churches would now be without pastors or preachers. We are filling up the vacant pulpits as fast as our facilities will allow."[96]

The minister shortage went beyond the concerns of individual churches, however. It was also seen as bad for the denomination as a whole. F. A. Baker, an Advent Christian minister and principal of the Bible Training School, made this clear in an article he wrote for *Our Hope* in 1900: "Our existence as a denomination, or at least our continuation and growth, depends upon the education of our ministry. We cannot live, as a people, without ministers. We cannot have ministers unless God gives them to us. God will not give us ministers if we do not think enough of them to equip them for their work."[97] The point of such articles was obvious: Mendota College was the major producer of Advent Christian ministers. Individual churches and the denomination would get back from the college many benefits if they supported it, they were told, and their very future depended on them doing so.

Mendota College leaders and supporters also argued that not only did the school supply ministers, it provided *educated* ministers who would be prepared to work in a new, modern world. In an era of growing education, specialization, and professionalization, churches now expected more of their pastors. If ministers wanted to acquire a pulpit and then *retain* it, it was argued, they needed to have some formal higher education—to know the Bible and Adventist doctrine in greater depth, to know something about the larger society, and to communicate well.[98] Although college leaders argued this over and over, church members also realized this. In 1898, a Mrs. Emery made this case in the pages of *Our Hope*: "The time was when one could go into the sacred desk without an education, and be received, although he did great violence to the 'Queen's English.' But that time has past [*sic*]. Old men may be excused, but when a young man goes out to preach and teach the people, his heart should be full of the Spirit and his head should not be empty."[99] Times had changed, and people now expected more of their pastors. The era of the uneducated, pioneer preacher was over.

A more secular argument viewed Mendota College from the perspective of an investment. Future college board member and fundraiser, J. W. Emmons, who was a medical doctor, *not* a minister, often made more secular arguments in his *Our Hope* articles. In one 1896 article, after reminding Adventist readers of all that had been done to provide a college—buying the college property, extensively renovating the Old Main the previous year, hiring good teachers, etc.—Emmons asked *whether*, given the substantial amount of money already invested in the school and what it had to offer the denomination, they would really let it fail by not paying their debts and for such a small amount of money. (He noted that the *current* amount of debt was only $1,200 but that $500 was due at the bank immediately.) In another 1896 article, Emmons wrote passionately that "the college *must be sustained*. Just think of it; a large number of people like ourselves to give up for a bad investment such an institution as we have established at Mendota, Ill, all paid for and fully equipped for the work that we now have on hand, with the exception of raising less than $400 on old debts, and about $700 on current running expenses [italics in original]."[100] Since 1896 was the year that the college *almost did fail*, the urgency of Emmons's tone was genuine. Failure was a possibility so, from his more secular perspective, it made no sense monetarily to let all that had been invested in Mendota College simply slip away because of an amount of money that, he and others believed, the Advent Christian people should be able to pay.[101]

Another secular argument concerned the legacy that Advent Christians would be creating if they failed to keep the college alive. Once again, it was Emmons who made this secular argument, saying that

> now shall a people like ours, that pretend to be a reading, thinking class of Christian believers go back on the first and only institution that has been founded by us during our history of fifty years? If we can't support this at this time of our history as a people, what could and would we do in fifty years to come? … What kind of a history could be written of us as a body of Christian believers, not even to cherish and keep up one small institution. …[102]

In making their arguments for giving, fundraisers often mentioned large versus small donors and one-time versus multiple-time donations. As discussed earlier, it was important to the college leaders that as many small donors as possible give—for monetary reasons, but also as a show of support for the college. Most of the donations that the school received *were* small. Some donors even gave multiple times, which fundraisers loved to point out in *Our Hope*, no doubt to inspire others to do the same. Their words concerning the donations, or lack thereof, of more affluent Advent Christians, however, were often less than complimentary. They were sometimes chastised for giving donations that were too small or for not giving at all. In an article titled "Have You Paid Your Taxes?" Emmons referred to donations as a school tax that individuals and churches owed the college. Given Americans' antipathy towards taxes of any kind, this was probably not the best tactic to use, but perhaps he did so to tell Adventists that the school needed something more than random donations—that as Advent Christians they owed the college ongoing, regular support, given what it was doing for individual students, churches, and the denomination as a whole. He wrote that people were supposed to be giving according to their means, but that some of the wealthier Advent Christians were not paying their fair share, leaving the slack to be picked up by the people with less money. He reminded readers, especially the wealthier ones, that paying versus not paying would matter when one's final, earthly account is drawn up someday.[103]

Given the annual scramble to pay off the year's operating expenses by the end of the school year, the periodic large debt that the college accumulated, and the frequent pleas for money, it appears that Advent Christians in the West were *reluctant* donors. It was not at all unusual for Emmons to put out a call for funds in *Our Hope*, only to be followed weeks later by another article saying that just a handful of donations had come in and sometimes absolutely nothing. It must have been discouraging, and that comes through in some of the *Our Hope* fundraising articles, especially those by Emmons. In 1898, he wrote that "there has been very little given by our people this year for school purposes."[104] In 1900, he expressed this concern a bit more forcefully: "All we ask from year to year so far is less than $3000 a year to support this institution, and yet we have to do a great deal of writing and begging to get what we have."[105] Ten years after the first complaint referenced here, he expressed a similar frustration even more forcefully:

> Why is it that our people are so slow in paying the actual running expenses of Mendota College? ... the few ... pay the bills, and the rest go on and never heed the urgent calls for funds, and these very parties often complain that they can't get a minister ... , and they know that if they did get one, someone else had to pay their money to enable these poor boys to get an education so they would be acceptable speakers, even before an ordinary country congregation. ...[106]

Emmons was not the only fundraiser; other board members, the treasurer, some ministers, and some faculty members also wrote fundraising articles for *Our Hope*. But for most of the Mendota years, he was the major one. He gave great service to the college in performing this discouraging task for so long, and, at times, it strained his patience, his words revealing irritation, frustration, incomprehension, and discouragement about why more people did not financially support the college. He did everything he could think of to get people to give, including one odd promise that "every one that sends money for this work, if they want it, I will send them my photograph, free of charge, at my own expense."[107] There is no record showing who, if anyone, took him up on this [italics in original].[108]

Mendota College fundraisers generally put on a happy face in their *Our Hope* articles, saying that they were sure the Advent Christian people would continue to support the school adequately, as they had done in the past. But because raising adequate funds for the running of the college was painfully slow, the regular fundraisers—like J. W. Emmons and later Orrin R. Jenks— sometimes revealed great frustration in their pleas for money and let it show through angry chastisements and shaming as well as humor and sarcasm.

A good example of the chastising of Advent Christians comes from Emmons, in a 1901 article. After stating that it took $325 a month to run the college, he launched into a bit of a tirade:

> What can be done *without* the necessary funds to pay our bills as we go along? Do you realize the load it places upon your Educational Board to run such a school as ours without means to pay our bills as we go? ... Do you know that the raising of funds for Mendota College occupy more of my reserve force than all my other duties put together? and simply because it takes so much planning and urging. ... The time I give to my practice I get pay for, but my time spent for our school I do not get one cent for, nor do I expect pay for it in the future. All I expect and want is your money, to run your school with, and your good will to go with it [italics in original].[109]

But Emmons was not alone. In addition to Jenks, the college treasurer and the *Our Hope* editors did the same. In 1901, a fundraiser asked these unsettling questions: "Is it possible that over *a thousand* cards out of 1400 sent out have met no response? What! *Not a word or a nickel in reply?* We cannot believe this is intentional neglect. It is just carelessness. These were selected names. ... Who is so poor among us that he or she cannot afford a small College Day offering? *No one* [italics in original]."[110]

At other times, some fundraisers, especially Emmons, tried their hand at humor and even sarcasm. Because Emmons was a doctor, he sometimes used his medical knowledge in a humorous way, as in the following 1901 piece:

I can see that the eyesight and hearing of many of *Our Hope* readers must be improving by the way the "college day offerings" are coming in.

I am sure that some of the deaf ears ought to have been looked after, to see what was the cause of such profound inability to hear. I had feared that cataracts were forming in the eyes of many, so that they could not read *Our Hope* or they would have seen that we have a "college day offering" that they had ought to have a share in. ...

To those who still fail to see or hear, I will say, that if you will write to me I will send you a prescription, free of charge, that will cause you to have your eyesight and hearing restored, so that you won't forget what you read and hear.[111]

The next year Emmons used another medical analogy in a fundraising article. After urging people to stop acting as though they were dead and wake up to help support the school, he told his readers that if they were experiencing spiritual degeneration, they should "send us a few dollars and I will guarantee that your condition will improve for the better, and you will feel that you are not among the dead but among the living."[112] Two weeks later Emmons published a response to his plea. The humorous letter was from Byron N. Meigs, a minister who was president of the Wisconsin Advent Christian Conference. Meigs delightedly continued the medical analogy: "I am going to try your prescription. Enclosed find $2 to help fix up that College expense. I feel the force of your diagnosis and know it is all right, and if my spiritual condition improves from this dose you may expect to hear from me again on the same line. ... Wake them up, Doctor, and give them a dose, not of morphine but of something that will nerve them up for future usefulness."[113] Emmons continued the fun in this same article:

Don't you forget now, and go to sleep, and compel me to ring you up again, out of a dead sound sleep. It costs money and time to wake you up so many times, besides it might injure your health to be too often disturbed out of a sound slumber; but I tell you it will do you good to get *thoroughly waked up*. ... I expect that some would be pleased if we would not ask for any more funds for the school but you are all aware that the only way we have of getting money is by asking for it; and we shall keep *asking you for it*. If there are any who have such delicate nerves that it makes them sick to read in *Our Hope* that Mendota College needs money, then please write to me and I will send you a prescription that will fortify your nervous system so you will survive the shock [italics in original].[114]

It is not clear which approach worked better—chastising and shaming or humor and sarcasm. Since fundraisers probably did not know which worked better, both approaches were used. No doubt the approach used varied according to the personality of the fundraiser. Come time to raise money for the Aurora campus, Jenks also would use a lot of blunt language when funds were just trickling in, but very little humor. He left that to others, like Emmons.

Living on a Shoestring and a Prayer

Mendota College perpetually lived on a monetary diet. There were virtually no extras, and the school was thoroughly dependent on the help of Advent Christians in Mendota and across the West, not just for monetary donations, but also for free labor, books and other academic materials, food, and furnishings for the dormitories.

When anything outside of regular operating expenses was needed, the college had to ask for it. In the case of bigger projects, the school had to launch a separate fundraising campaign, like the one Emmons led in the fall of 1895. As discussed in chapter four, after visiting the campus for the first time, he was appalled by the shabbiness of the College Building and immediately started raising money to replace windows, paint and wallpaper classrooms, lay new floors, and buy new furniture. In succeeding years, there were more repairs and redecorating that would need to be done, although on a smaller scale than the 1895 job, and they too would require additional requests for money.[115]

Colleges generally need to raise money for capital improvements, but Mendota College also had to raise money even for mundane things and some maintenance issues. The college dining room operation was especially needy because it always had a barebones budget so as to keep board to a minimum for students. At least twice, when a new stove for the college kitchen was needed, the school asked for donations. It even asked for funds several years later when the stove had to have some replacement parts. When kitchen utensils and dishpans were needed for the dining hall operation, the call went out for money to purchase them. When someone donated $5 to go toward the purchase of something for the college kitchen, the student column in *Our Hope* reported that "Ma," the cook, was ecstatic, the student saying that "any woman who has to cook with a lot of leaky pots and pans that have seen about six years in constant service, and must be kept stuffed with rags to be serviceable, will appreciate her feelings. 'Ma' says she has often looked outwardly calm when she inwardly boiled."[116] When the college board decided that the school needed a cow to offset costs, readers of *Our Hope* were asked if someone would donate one. Emmons wrote that "it [the cow] would be gratefully received, and the boarding club would have milk enough at less than one-half the expense and yet have twice as much milk to use. ... We have grass enough on the ground by mowing it to keep a cow, and also a stable to keep her in. It would be a saving of about $80 per year to have a good cow."[117] And food donations came in frequently—at times even without the college asking—but sometimes *Our Hope* readers were reminded that the college always needed donations of food. In 1907, the student-written "College Notes" column made such a plea: "We trust our good sisters will continue their generous help as heretofore, in the line of eatables for our college boarding club. 'Ma' Clark says she finds it pretty hard to make ends meet in her department, as fruit is very high priced, and college young people are pretty fond of good things. A box now and then will be greatly appreciated. ..."[118] Donations of food came in from Advent Christian individuals, churches, and women's groups, as well as Mendota neighbors, and from states as far away as New York, although mostly they came from the Midwest. Often donors would send a barrel, filled with apples or assorted foodstuffs. Aside from fresh fruit of various sorts, the college often received chickens and other fowl as well as homemade items like butter, jellies and jams, canned fruit and vegetables, maple syrup, and sausage, along with such staples as eggs, flour, sugar, molasses, potatoes, beans, and coffee. Sometimes packages contained special treats, like candy, popcorn, etc., for the students—the kinds of extras that mothers supplied their children with at home and were sorely missed by Mendota students.[119]

There were other types of things that the college asked for—things that one might reasonably expect a college to have the funds to supply for itself. But Mendota College needed all the help it could get, in all areas, in order to take some pressure off its tight budget. One major type of donation was linens—everything from sheets, pillowcases, quilts, bath towels, and facecloths to table linens—both tablecloths and cloth napkins. Furnishings for the college building rooms and the dormitories were also donated—bureaus, chairs, tables, curtains, and especially rugs. The academic areas also received items that you would expect a school to furnish. There were many donations to the library and the school's geology collection. Multiple people also bought equipment for the laboratory. At several different times, the college requested a piano for students to practice on. And even painting the college building in 1905, although a maintenance issue, required a substantial sum—about $100—so a fundraising campaign was started to cover that. The previous year the college had begun a campaign to raise money for painting the College Building, but then it was thought more prudent to delay the painting project because the roof so badly needed to be replaced. Once a new roof had been installed, it was time to return to the campaign for raising money to tuck point and paint the college building. In one fundraising article for this project, the author stated that the college needed the help of the western Advent Christians to keep up the campus: "All are aware that the maintenance of our school comes directly upon our people. We have no surplus funds, and if we take money from the educational funds to paint the building we must replace it later. The better way is thought to be to invite donations, with the understanding that any surplus will be turned over to the college funds."[120] In short, the acquisition of anything beyond the most basic things required outside financial help.[121]

If things were tight even in the better financial years, they became dire in the periods when the college was trying to dig itself out of a financial hole or when projects other than raising operating funds were competing for donor's contributions. At those times especially, the college sometimes had to take out loans to make it through the school year. Fundraisers often warned *Our Hope* readers that if the required funds were not raised very soon, a loan would have to be taken out. Even when they ultimately did not have to borrow money, they sometimes came very close to having to do so. And sometimes there were frighteningly close calls. In a 1911 *Our Hope* article, Jenks reported that ten days earlier, on the day the school was going to borrow money to cover operating expenses, an unexpected check for $500 arrived from a "brother." There was even the worry that these loans could piggyback, one on top of another. In 1908, the college treasurer wrote that "in addition to paying our current expenses for the remainder of this school year we have a debt of $700 that should be paid in a few weeks. This money was borrowed in order to pay bills that were due at the time of borrowing."[122] On a number of occasions, college articles in *Our Hope* bluntly stated that there was virtually no money in the treasury. In March 1902, it was reported that nearly $1,000 had been raised in the College Day offering to date, but that it was "not enough to carry our school through the year. On account of the large expense for repairs last summer, amounting to over $1800 dollars [*sic*], not a dollar was raised for the support of the school at the last campmeeting nor until the College Day offering arrived. It has required all the offerings sent in to meet current expenses, and at this writing *less than a dollar* remains in the treasury [italics in original]."[123] Five years later the treasurer made a similar assertion. After writing in *Our Hope* that the school needed $600 just to meet the *current* bills, he candidly stated that "the fact that we have no funds on hand with which to pay bills places your treasurer in a very embarrassing position."[124] Mendota College truly lived hand to mouth. Some years were better than others, but every year was a struggle to raise the necessary operating funds.[125]

This financial precariousness seems to have impacted the faculty especially hard. It appears that paying the faculty was often one of the last financial obligations taken care of in times of financial need. In December 1896, one fundraiser noted that the college had less than $400 in old debt and also needed $700 for current operating expenses dating back to August of that year, adding that the $700 was for faculty salaries and a bit of coal. In April 1897, this same fundraiser informed *Our Hope* readers that the college's debts had been paid and that all that remained for that school year was to pay the faculty. In the previous issue of *Our Hope*, he had written that "our teachers must have their pay on or before the end of the school year."[126] Comments about faculty needing to be paid as the school year, or even a term, was drawing to a close were especially common, leaving one to wonder just how regularly faculty were paid. A low or empty treasury that especially hurt the faculty remained an issue right up to the end of the Mendota era. In May 1912, the month after the college moved to Aurora, Jenks noted that fundraising for operating expenses had suffered during the fundraising campaign for the Aurora campus. "The result," he stated, "is that there is not a dollar in our treasury with which to meet the salaries of our teachers, for the two months closing our school year."[127] And this was sometimes a problem much earlier in the school year, like at the end of the fall term in December and several weeks before the annual College Day offering campaign began. In mid-December 1905, the college treasurer wrote that "as funds are getting low, we find it necessary to ask a few more donations soon, so we may be able to meet the teachers' salaries and a few other bills that must be paid at the close of this term."[128] Even worse, at least once, faculty paid down a substantial debt with their own money. In January 1897, a time of financial crisis for the college, a fundraiser wrote, in *Our Hope*, that "the expenses of the college for the coming year have been reduced about $600; and that all this saving was caused by the instructors of our school giving the college this amount out of their wages. ... When this proposal was made to our teachers it was on the ground that we should do our best to pay them every dollar we now owe them, and that the coming school-year wages should be paid at the end of the school-year and as much sooner as we could."[129] Given how meager faculty salaries were to start with, this was a remarkable sacrifice on their part.[130]

Because the college's budgets were always so lean, the board had to find creative ways to get things done. This often meant paying students in kind—be it students who taught in exchange for room and/or board or students doing other jobs on campus. Some male students, like Sylvester Nokes, tended the college property. Nokes was hired as a janitor for the 1895–96 school year. In return, he received tuition, room, board, and even fuel for lighting his room. The female students were more likely to be found doing more conventionally female jobs, like working in the college kitchen or dining hall. One September 1895 *Our Hope* article advertised for a "young lady desiring to attend the College and willing to assist in kitchen work in part or full payment for board."[131] Thirteen years later, the board minutes note that the matron of the dining hall was authorized to hire two girls, presumably students, who would work in exchange for their board—the same in-kind pay that was offered in 1895. Another way to accomplish things was to have faculty and even board members do jobs that would be done by paid workers in a specialized college office today. Recruiting new students was as important as raising money, yet there was no admissions office or even an individual whose paid position was to serve as a recruiter. For example, J. W. Emmons, a board member, played an active role in both fundraising and student recruitment over the years, and at no pay. To do both these jobs, he wrote innumerable articles for *Our Hope*. In an 1899 one, he explained the approach he took: "We have not as yet felt able to put a man on the road in the interest of the institution, and pay all the expenses it would necessitate; and therefore we shall try to work up the matter through correspondence."[132] In this same article, he asked readers to write him with the names of prospective students and also to ask prospective students to write him. If their parents were not in favor of them going away to college, Emmons promised that he would write them and see what could be done. The various presidents also encouraged this kind of correspondence. Writing articles for *Our Hope* and individual correspondence, along with occasionally sending out someone to travel among Advent Christian churches to discuss the college, remained the major strategies for fundraising and recruiting students throughout the Mendota era.[133]

On a lighter note, sometimes these assignments were quite unusual. In 1901, the board appointed Emmons to buy a cow for the college boarding operation. And in 1906, another board member, Mary E. Smith, was authorized to buy a cow for the college. The cryptic board minutes do not say whether this was a second cow or the first one had died. Once acquired, the cow apparently was well cared for, even over the summer, when the students were gone. In 1903, the college treasurer, Milton Livingston, was entrusted with the cow for the summer. And in 1909, the cow's summer caretakers had an even higher status—the secretary of the board, B. Forester, and President Dean were given the responsibility of caring for it.[134]

Why Did the College Struggle So Much Financially?

At least some of the reasons for the college's financial problems are now, no doubt, fairly obvious, but the question is worth considering in a more deliberate, systematic way.

First, during the Mendota years, there were economic forces at work that created an unstable national economy. In short, in approximately fourteen of the college's nineteen years (1893–1912), the American economy experienced an economic downturn of some sort—either a financial panic or economic recession or both. The two worst economic periods during the Mendota years were the financial panic of 1893, along with the depression that followed, lasting until 1897, and the Panic of 1907. In fact, much of the nineteenth-century and pre–World War I eras saw a boom-or-bust economy. After President Jackson destroyed the Second Bank of the United States in 1836, there was no central bank in the United States until the creation of the federal reserve system in 1912. It was this problem that led to the passage of federal economic and banking regulations in both the Progressive Era and during the Great Depression, in the 1930s. But these reforms came too late for the Mendota era.[135]

The worst economic downturn of the Mendota years started the same year that the college was founded, in 1893. The Depression of 1893 was the worst economic crisis in American history up to that point and was superseded only by the Great Depression of the 1930s. The college leaders knew very well that they were starting their educational endeavor at an economically precarious time. An August 1893 *Our Hope* article, announcing that the first fall term would be starting in a few days, acknowledged the poor economic situation of the nation currently and admitted that it would have some impact on the school. Nevertheless, it expressed hope that Advent Christian parents would send their children to the college anyway. It is perhaps no accident that the school almost failed in 1896–97. Although there were certainly factors related to the college and the Advent Christian people that contributed to that, it could not have helped that 1896 and 1897 were the two last years of the 1893–97 downturn—the worst depression to date. Likewise, another especially difficult financial time for the college, 1907–8, were the years of the Panic of 1907. In a 1908 *Our Hope* article, a college fundraiser identified two things contributing to the school's current, large debt. One was the fact that too many Adventists had temporarily moved their donations over to the *Our Hope* Building Fund. The second was identified as the "financial depression that is affecting all institutions that depend upon public benevolence for their support."[136] In other words, the two worst economic periods of the American economy during the Mendota years corresponded with the two periods in which the college had the largest debt before it started fundraising for the Aurora campus in 1910.[137]

A second factor explaining Mendota College's financial woes was its location in a small, isolated town, surrounded by a large agricultural area containing other small, isolated towns. Mendota's situation was unlike Aurora's, which had more railroad lines and sizable towns north, east, and south of it. Many of these towns were joined by trains, which connected them to one another and to Aurora and Chicago in an efficient and timely manner. Thus, when the college was in Mendota, it had a much smaller population to draw students from—about four thousand inhabitants, as opposed to Aurora's size of thirty thousand to thirty-one thousand residents. And even though several rail lines went through Mendota, the distance to Chicago and its suburbs was much greater. Compared to Aurora, Mendota was more than twice the distance from Chicago.[138]

Aurora was superior in terms of fundraising as well. The Aurora business community supported Aurora College to an extent that Mendota's business people seem not to have done for Mendota College. In both towns, the business community initially invested financially in getting the college to their town, although Mendota's monetary contribution was considerably smaller and shorter in duration than Aurora's. Among the group of around seventy people who bought shares in the Western Advent Christian Association to raise the $1,800 needed to purchase the campus were many of Mendota's leaders and business people. Aurora's business leaders, in order to bring the college to their town, pledged to donate $15,000 to the school, and the president of a local bank donated five acres for its campus. In terms of ongoing support, it is difficult to know how much money Mendotans gave to the college. At least one indirect source suggests that it was not much. In one of the few 1910 *Our Hope* articles arguing that the college should remain in Mendota, the point was made that Mendota's citizens would probably give money to the college, and just as liberally as other places, but no one had asked them to do so—in other words, Mendotans had *not* been giving to the college. And in a *Mendota Reporter* article written right after Aurora was chosen as the new college location, a journalist, who clearly believed Mendota had not been given a fair and complete hearing, noted that at the meeting where Mendota presented its case for the school staying in town, "the Mendota Development Association ... made short speeches, the burden of which was the desire to retain the college, and to satisfy all reasonable demands of the meeting in relation to a money subvention to be raised by the citizens."[139] Mendotans said that they were trying to raise $10,000 for the college. However, this offer of funds to keep the college in Mendota was both too little and too late. The advocates of leaving Mendota believed that its people had not done much financially over the years to support the college. An offer that came this late probably did not instill much confidence, given the town's history of not doing much to help the school financially after the first year. Instead, advocates for Aurora were convinced that the town's citizens would do a better job at that. That belief was confirmed when, in February 1910, Jenks reported that Aurora had promised the college *annual* donations amounting to $2,000 to $3,000 to help with *operating expenses*, in addition to the money being raised to help build the new campus.[140]

A third explanation for the college's financial precariousness was its endowment. It was always too small to be of much help in supporting the college. It had another use, however. Because of its small size, it was more useful as a separate cache of money that could be used to pay bills when operating funds ran low or dried up altogether and debts had to be paid. In short, it really served as an emergency fund rather than an endowment. This proved to be helpful, given how often the college struggled to pay its everyday expenses. And this situation was sometimes used as a fundraising argument. For example, in June 1898, fundraiser Emmons reported that the college needed to repay itself $300, which it had borrowed from its Endowment Fund recently to pay off some debts. Technically, all debts had been paid, but Emmons made it clear that the college was not really out of debt until the borrowed money was returned to the Endowment Fund. The fact that the school's endowment was so small was also used to raise money. In 1903, the college treasurer argued that "since the endowment of Mendota College is small and does not furnish sufficient means of support for our school, let us as friends of the college, make the College Day Offerings answer for the income of an endowment."[141] The endowment enabled the college's creditors to get paid back in a more timely fashion and its small size was used as a rationale for people to give in the College Day offering, but the college still had to raise money to pay itself back when it borrowed from it and did not enjoy the financial benefits of an adequately large endowment. Even by the end of the Mendota era, the endowment was way too small. In December 1911, Jenks told *Our Hope* readers that the college's endowment was less than $6,000, earning around $300 of interest annually. He said that the endowment needed to be around $200,000 to put the college on a more secure financial footing.[142]

A fourth contributing factor to the college's shaky finances was the mindset of the college leaders. They were not as business oriented as they probably should have been. Many of the school's leaders were ministers, and so, of course, focused on the religious mission of the college. The Bible Training School was the most important part of the institution for them. The denomination had a desperate need for more ministers, and the college was determined to supply them, so, to encourage as many people as possible to enroll in this department, no tuition was ever charged. Students in the Bible Training School had to pay for room, board, and books, but not tuition. This put all the greater burden on the other areas of the college to subsidize the theological department. It also mattered in fundraising, and the school's leaders sometimes reminded Adventists that some students paid no tuition. In a 1901 *Our Hope* article on the College Day offering, an editor wrote that "it is impossible to sustain a school like this by its earnings, since a large share of its pupils—all the Bible Training classes—receive tuition *free*. This is right, and is the custom of all theological schools and colleges."[143] Seven years later, a 1908 article made the same point: "As Mendota College has been established for the purpose of educating young men and women for the Christian ministry, and giving them free tuition in that course, it was not expected to continue without the liberal support of the Adventist Christian people."[144]

The decision to have free tuition for theological students was made a couple of months before the college even opened, but other tuition-reduction policies were developed later—ones that generously helped the denomination's ministers but further hurt the college's bottom line. Early on, in 1896, WACPA's Educational Committee decided that the children of ministers would be able to attend Mendota College for *half* the tuition of the advertised rate. Two explanations were given—to raise the school's attendance and to help the ministers in the Advent Christian denomination "who have so generously contributed of their time and means to the work of the Lord and building up of the church."[145] Years later, in 1910, the same thing was done for the wives of ministers who were also students. They too would have to pay just half the tuition rate. These policies were certainly commendable, because Advent Christian ministers generally were paid abysmally low salaries, but financially they hurt the college. And unlike the rationale for free tuition in the Bible Training School, there was no payoff for the denomination in terms of producing additional ministers. If a student was paying half tuition because his or her father was a minister, it meant that they were *not* going into the ministry. Anyone who wanted to enter the ministry would have to enroll in the Bible Training School, where students got an even better deal—no tuition at all. What is especially interesting about the 1896 decision concerning the lower tuition rate for ministers' children is that 1896–97 was one of the most financially precarious times in the college's history. The article announcing the new policy was dated September 30. Just a few weeks earlier, at the college board's August meeting, it had been reported that there was a debt of $1,120. Perhaps the thought was that since there was room for more students without hiring more faculty, getting half the tuition rate was better than getting nothing, because without this reduction, at least some ministers' children could not afford to attend.[146]

A fifth problem that contributed to the college's financial instability was the population it was drawing from—for both students and monetary donations. Advent Christians as a whole were not affluent. Many of them lived in small towns and rural areas, scratching out a living as farmers. This meant that many families did not have the surplus income to pay for their children's education or give anything more to the college than small donations, if anything. And because of their limited funds, when another denominational need (like the construction of a new building for WACPA and *Our Hope* in 1907–8) or an out-of-the-ordinary college need (like acquiring a new dormitory after the old one burned down) came along, the College Day offering usually suffered, which meant that the school's operating funds declined and debt started to grow. In 1910, during the fundraising campaign to build the Aurora campus, one supporter of the school wrote an *Our Hope* article after reading in this paper that some people were feeling discouraged because of the significant percentage of donations and pledges coming into the Building Fund that were small. He urged people not to be discouraged about this situation, saying that in the denomination's mission work, similar numbers of small donations ($1–$5) were given, with an occasional, large one—a pattern similar to the college's donations. He then added that Advent Christians are "people of limited means, who cannot afford to give very much at a time,"[147] a reality he knew that Jenks understood as he traveled around from church to church raising money and so was not pressuring people to donate as he might were the conditions different. He thought that this was the right approach because he saw benefits to Jenks's trips other than donations (although he admitted that they were important also): "The largest results that will come from his sojourn in the East will be an intelligent interest on the part of our people in our college, which is a fundamental essential before parents will send children and money to any institution of learning."[148] People had to be educated about the college's work and be convinced that their children and their precious, few dollars were going to a worthwhile institution.

Some people wanted to give to the college, but simply were too poor to do so. Sometimes such people wrote to *Our Hope*, expressing their desire to send their children and/or make a donation to the school and explaining why they could not do it. Their stories were sometimes heartbreaking. What follows are excerpts from two such letters, each written by a different farmer in 1896 and appearing in the same *Our Hope* article—the first from a farmer living in South Dakota and the second from one in Kansas.

> #1 – I have noticed appeals for help, and would be glad to contribute, but am almost helpless myself as to obtaining money. Crop prospects are not flattering here. Have been hoping to get our boy to Mendota

to school this fall but now see no way to do so. I have a three-year-old colt, broke to ride only, also a five-year-old. If there are brethren in Dakota that can come and get either of these, they will be freely donated to the work. There is no sale for them here at any price, and my health and circumstances forbid my taking them away at present.

#2 – I have been hoping for some possible way to help the work at Mendota, but at present cannot see my way out. My children need schooling, and two of them have done about all they can at the public school here. Would like so much to send them to Mendota but cannot now. My pension has been stopped. Had two horses killed by lightning last year. Crops have been light for two years, hardly paying the hired help. Oats are worth but eight cents per bushel, potatoes twenty cents, and other produce corresponding prices. A horse that cost me $65, I sold for $15. Another that cost $80 four years ago, I sold for $10 on credit. Taxes are high and the prospect discouraging. But I am not complaining. I have more blessings than I deserve. Let us hope for better times.[149]

These letters give some insight into the hard life of a farmer at the turn of the twentieth century. In the best of economic times, farmers' incomes were at the mercy of the weather, insects, and plain old luck. A windstorm or tornado, an invasion of thousands of grasshoppers, and the simple bad luck of a farmer getting seriously injured, losing many animals to disease, etc. could mean economic disaster for a farm family. And the 1890s were not the best of times. As mentioned earlier, there was a four-year depression in this decade. However, the problems of late-nineteenth-century farmers had arrived much earlier than the 1890s. High costs for farm machinery, high railroad fees for transporting crops, growing debt with high interest rates, and declining crop prices were longstanding complaints among farmers in the last third of the nineteenth century. By the 1890s, farmers' unhappiness with railroads, banks, and other institutions they thought were exploiting them produced the Populist Movement—the only American reform movement whose origins and center lay in rural areas.

Not only did many Advent Christian people have little surplus income to give to the college, what little they had needed to go to their own churches, many of which were small and struggled financially as well. The smaller the church, the harder it was to keep it going, both religiously and financially. It was less likely to have a minister, and the financial burden of maintaining a building and paying a minister or temporary preacher fell upon too few people. Many of these small churches lost the battle and disappeared. On top of the strains of keeping a small church going, there were other denominational causes that needed funding as well, like missions.[150]

Because of this focus on the local level and perhaps because many Advent Christians had minimal education, they did not fully appreciate what was happening at the college and what it was doing for the denomination. College fundraisers sometimes reminded *Our Hope* readers how important the college was to individual churches. It was probably easy to forget that, because their own church's financial state was often so challenging, and the college seemed like a distant institution that did not directly impact their lives. That is why Jenks took a year off from his college duties and ended his pastorate: it had become apparent to him that only a limited amount of money could be raised by appeals made in the denominational newspapers. He believed that he must meet people in person to raise more substantial amounts of money. So he reported that he intended "to visit every church in the nation that will open its doors to him for one service" and argued that "our people must learn what our school stands for, what it purposes to do, and what are its pressing, present needs. The best way to impart this information is to go to the people."[151] Only traveling around the country, going from church to church, talking to people face-to-face would spur them on to give to the Building Fund. Simply writing *Our Hope* articles, no matter how humorous or chastising they were, was not enough to raise the amount of money that was needed to build a whole new campus.[152]

Overseeing the finances of Mendota College—raising funds for operating expenses as well as anything extra, trying to build up the endowment, maintaining a campus with its aging building, and making sure the bills were paid in a timely fashion—was not for the fainthearted. Some years were easier than others, but keeping the college going and financially stable was always a struggle. Not only was the annual fundraising always a long, hard road, so was student recruitment. Many more students attended the school than its anemic graduation rate would suggest, but college leaders still said that the school could handle many more students at minimal cost, because the current faculty was large enough to teach increased numbers.

College finances did seem to stabilize somewhat by the turn of the century, but even so, there was a financial crisis in 1907–8 because the donations of many Adventists were temporarily diverted to the new WACPA building, and then again, in 1910–12, because virtually all the fundraising attention was put on raising funds for the new campus. In its earliest years, the college received the message that finances were going to be a challenge. Perhaps this challenge can be summed up best by the words in the minutes of WACPA's Educational Board in 1894—less than two years into the college's life: **"The financial situation gave much perplexity."**[153]

SUMMARY OF ACCOUNTS

Of Mendota College, from Aug. 14, 1906 to Aug. 2, 1907.

RECEIPTS.

Books and Stationery..............................$	465 81
Donations	2098 22
Key Deposits..	4 75
Bible Training Fund for Salaries....................	4 00
Interest..	292 98
Repairs...	65 00
Bible Training Fund General.........................	5 00
Tuition...	730 87
Library Fund..	34 55
Piano Rent..	37 70
Room Rent...	376 08
Laboratory Tickets..................................	11 50
Expense...	3 65
Laboratory Fund.....................................	113 27
Fuel and Light......................................	116 72
Sanderson Loan Fund.................................	10 00
Lindsey Loan Fund...................................	5 00
Teachers' Copies, Books.............................	2 36
College Endowment Fund Bills Receivable.............	1210 00
H. H. Corliss Loan Fund Bills Receivable............	75 00
Diplomas..	17 50
Piano Fund for buying a new piano...................	2 00
Bills Payable.......................................	1141 94
College Supplies, for anything needed...............	1 00
Dormitory Bills Receivable..........................	125 00
Dormitory, for anything needed......................	5 00
N. C. Twining Donation..............................	20 00
College Endowment Fund..............................	1 00
Bills Receivable....................................	12 52
Personal Accts.....................................	31 49
Cash Balance Aug. 14, 1906..........................	217 53
	$7237 44

EXPENDITURES.

Books and Stationery................................$	437 03
Key Deposits..	4 00
Interest..	2 15
Repairs...	133 72
Tuition refunded....................................	11 57
Library Fund..	7 60
Piano Rent..	20 70
Room Rent refunded..................................	6 61
Laboratory Tickets..................................	3 23
Expense...	765 87
Laboratory Fund.....................................	126 50
Fuel and Light......................................	421 12

Summary of Accounts, 1906-07, Showing the College's

Teachers' Copies, Books...........................	16 86
College Endowment Bills Receivable.............	1200 00
Diplomas	4 50
Bi ls Payable.....................................	266 94
Special Fund by vote of the Board	228 40
N. O. Twining Donation............................	5 50
Salaries for Teachers and Treasurer...............	3460 00
Personal Accts....................................	34 71
Cash Balan e Aug 2, 1907..........................	85 43
	$7237 44

RESOURCES.

Cash on hand...............................$	85 43
Books and Stationery.............................	74 90
Teachers' Copies, Books..........................	76 16
Col ege Endowment Fund Bills Receivable........	5405 00
Students Aid Fund Bills Receivable..............	445 00
H. H. Corliss Loan Fund Bills Receivable........	801 00
Diplomas..	41 50
College Roof Fund................................	56 77
Real Estate.......................................	10,000 00
Dormitory Bills Receivable........................	698 55
Bills Receivable..................................	59 87
Personal Acct....................................	23 20
	$17,271 38

LIABILITIES.

College Stock...............................$	8460 38
Key Deposit......................................	75
Bible Training Fund, General.....................	184 35
Library Fund.....................................	63 95
Laboratory Fund..................................	21 67
Sanderson Loan Fund.............................	113 50
Lindsey Loan Fund................................	40 60
Piano Fund for buying a new piono...............	2 00
Bills Payable....................................	875 00
Special Fund, balance for maps...................	1 60
College Supplies for anything needed.............	1 00
Dormitory Fund..................................	823 55
Dormitory, for anything needed...................	5 00
N. C. Twining Donation..........................	14 50
Students Aid Fund...............................	487 00
College Endowment Fund.........................	5676 10
H. H. Corliss Loan Fund.........................	500 00
Personal Acct...................................	1 13
	$17,271 38

B. A. KING, Treas.

Having examined the books of B. A. King, Treasurer of Mendota College, we find them correctly kept and properly vouched, with a balance of cash in the treasury of $85.43.   Geo. H. Dewing,) Auditors.
          Mabel E. Dean, (

Chapter 9
The Rocky Road from Mendota to Aurora

"New things must come. Through the generous gifts of noble men and women we are provided with three splendid buildings in Aurora. We enter them with joy and hopefulness, believing that a great door of opportunity is open before us and that our school is entering a new period of usefulness."

—Orrin R. Jenks

Welcome-to-Aurora Parade on the Day the College Arrived in Aurora—April 3, 1912
(Orrin R. Jenks is sitting in the front seat beside the driver, while the mayor of Aurora is sitting in the back seat behind the driver.)

April 3, 1912 was an historic day for both Aurora College and the city of Aurora. Around 8:20 A.M. a train, with a special car attached to it, pulled out of the Mendota station. Stretching the entire length of this passenger car, on both sides, were huge banners, which proclaimed in big, brightly colored letters, AURORA COLLEGE! Inside the car were about sixty-five students, professors, and guests.[1]

About an hour later the eagerly awaited train pulled into Aurora's train station. The Mendotans were met by prominent Aurorans, including Mayor Thomas Sanders and the Board of Education. The new Aurorans then piled into flag-draped automobiles and were taken on a tour of the city. *Our Hope* described the scene like this: "The cavalcade took its way through various business streets of the city, past the High Schools, and in and out of residential localities, causing some attraction to sightseers. ..."[2] After what must have seemed like an eternity, the group arrived at the new campus. What they saw there did not look conventionally inviting. The site had virtually no trees, the grounds were muddy and lacked sidewalks, and the rooms were not yet fully furnished, but it must have been a beautiful sight to those who had waited so long for this day.[3]

The on-campus events began with an opening service in Eckhart Hall. Around two hundred people gathered in the chapel, listening to President Jenks's opening remarks and then to speeches of welcome from Mayor Sanders, clergy, school superintendents, and some Aurora businessmen. On the Aurora College side, Charles Eckhart and an Advent Christian minister responded to the warm welcome. They then adjourned and had the very first meal ever served in the new dining room, prepared by women from the Aurora Advent Christian Church.[4]

Since they could not see into the future, these faculty and students probably did not fully appreciate the symbolism of this occasion, which brought town and gown together in celebration of a successful, cooperative effort. Although for the next twenty years, the college would be somewhat detached from the Aurora community—located on the western boundary of town and largely attended by Advent Christians from other towns and states—the seeds of a much closer college-community relationship had been sown and would start bearing fruit in the 1930s.

However, all of this lay in the future. Although certainly what they were looking at that day were the future opportunities that this new location would bring to the college, they also must have been looking backward—back at the long, hard struggle that had brought them to this day. They had done it, against great odds, raising more money than had ever been raised for a single Advent Christian cause or institution.[5] They also had mended the wounds resulting from the college location controversy—at least enough to create the necessary unity to get the job done. It was something of a miracle, and on that first day, as these newly transplanted people wandered around the campus exploring their brand new, beautiful buildings, they must have been pinching themselves to make sure that this was really happening.

Why Move the College?

Mendota College had space problems from the beginning, so much so that WACPA was asked to move its offices out of the college building just a few months after the school opened. There was a barn and a few other small service structures on campus, but there was just one college building. Virtually all of the school's functions had to fit into that one, four-story structure, which was smaller than Eckhart Hall. It contained *all* the classrooms plus faculty offices, a library, a museum, a chapel (which also served as a room for various student activities and classes and as a small assembly room), a kitchen, a dining room, and two laboratories, along with space for the men's dormitory. The building had so many functions by 1910 that there were just three rooms left for classes. With forty to forty-five "recitations" a day, this meant that some classes had to start as early as 7:30 and some as late as 5:00. Even with that, sometimes there were two to three classes meeting in a single room simultaneously. In June 1910, President Dean wrote about the school's space problems and catalogued the additional spaces that were needed: two office areas, an assembly room, a library room (the current library was also the president's office), a third laboratory, a minimum of eight classrooms, two rooms for the Commercial Department, one or two classrooms for stenography, two "society rooms" for the meetings of the Literary Society and debating clubs, two "toilet rooms," a dark room, one or more storerooms, a furnace room, and a coal room. It is no wonder that at, least by 1908, there was talk of constructing an additional building on the Mendota campus.[6]

Another serious problem was the *quality* of the space and the educational resources. When the college began operations in 1893, the college building was already around thirty-five years old, and so it lacked the modern conveniences of the day. (By the late nineteenth century, many new conveniences had come along that greatly improved the quality of life in newer buildings—central heating, electricity, indoor plumbing, etc.) And there was barely enough money for maintenance, never mind remodeling. In 1910, President B. J. Dean admitted that although the campus itself was beautiful, the buildings were sadly lacking in both attractiveness and modern conveniences. He went so far as to say that "Mendota College has failed to secure more students because of a lack of attractive surroundings than through any other cause. ... Time and again parents have told me that they would not think of sending their children to a school where they could not have better surroundings and conveniences than they find here."[7]

First Steps toward Relocation of the College

The origins of the decision to relocate the college date back more than three years before the move to Aurora. In the fall of 1908, Charles Eckhart, the wealthy owner of the Auburn Automobile Company, made a wonderful offer—he would give $10,000 for a new college building. He was a well-known visitor to Mendota who had heard the talk about, and even witnessed for himself, the crowded, inadequate conditions in the college building. There had been discussion about constructing a new building for years, but in 1908, Eckhart offered to provide the means to actually accomplish this. Then in 1909, WACPA, at its annual August meeting, voted to construct a new building for the *Mendota* campus, at a cost of at least $40,000. However, just two months later, the WACPA board called for a general meeting on January 5, 1910, to decide on the location of the college. Clearly something had changed; it appears that Eckhart's generous offer of money and a formal vote to construct a new building caused people to think more broadly. It was time to consider whether or not to set down deeper roots in Mendota through an additional investment of funds for a new facility. Was Mendota still the right place for the college? Would it do better in a different location? By 1909, two schools of thought had developed on the question of how to use Eckhart's money—build a new facility on the Mendota campus versus leave Mendota and build a whole new campus elsewhere. Thus, a critical debate was ignited. On January 5, 1910, a special meeting of WACPA was held at Mendota to decide the future location of the college. An *Our Hope* article reported that this topic

> received protracted and quite full discussion. Three locations were proposed (1) Mendota as at present, (2) Aurora, Ill., and (3) Zion City, of Lake county, Ill. The advantages of each location were very fully discussed, and on Friday, Jan. 7th, delegations of businessmen from Mendota, from Aurora, and also from Zion City were received by the Association, at appointed hours, and heard as to their wishes and proposals relative to the college and its location. ... After much balloting and discussion of the advantages and disadvantages of the various proposed places of location, the wish of the body was indicated by a large majority to be in favor of Aurora, Ill. ...[8]

The "large majority" mentioned in this quotation was actually huge, Aurora getting nineteen votes, while Zion City received just three and Mendota only one. An attendee wrote afterwards: "We hope this important question ... is now settled. It is impossible that it should have a more impartial, careful and prayerful consideration than it has just received."[9] Unfortunately, soon it became apparent that the matter was *not* settled. Staying in Mendota was no longer considered an option, but some people believed that Zion City was, or at least should still be, considered one. As this debate continued beyond the vote for Aurora, the next few months would be the ultimate test of these Adventists' Christian love and harmony.[10]

The Aurora–Zion City Debate

In the weeks and months following the January meeting at which the location decision had been made for Aurora, some WACPA board members, voting delegates, and others increasingly believed that the investigation of Zion City had been given short shrift because there had not been enough information about it available at the time of the vote. Also, while at the meeting, they had thought that the association could not remain in session for the time it would take to thoroughly investigate Zion City and that it would mean additional cost and uneasiness if the meeting ended without having made a decision. They also came to believe that the vote had been based on a false premise about Aurora—that its people would contribute as much as $60,000 to $65,000 to the project, after which it became clear that it would be closer to $20,000.[11]

Therefore, some leading Advent Christians went to Forester, chair of the WACPA board, to ask him to create a committee that would visit Zion City and investigate its possibilities further. He decided not to do that or call a board meeting, because the decision had *just* been made for Aurora, and he thought that only the best of reasons could warrant reopening the question. However, he told the men to visit Zion City themselves, and if what they saw was compelling, they could ask the leading men, like Eckhart, to ask for a reopening of the question by the board. Nothing was said about this quarrel publicly at this early stage because no one wanted to undermine the fundraising effort. So a small group of men quietly visited Zion City on their own, finding what they perceived to be an excellent situation there. At that point, the Zion City supporters decided to push the issue. An *Our Hope* article later reported that these advocates of Zion City "wished to present the facts through 'Our Hope,' but it was feared that such a course would cause friction and impede the canvass for funds. As time passed on these brethren declared that they would lay the facts before our people. If not allowed access to the columns of 'Our Hope' they would print and circulate the facts in some other way. Finally it became evident that the question would NOT down."[12] With this kind of pressure, it was decided to call together the WACPA board members and arrange for them to go to Zion City.[13]

They visited Zion City on May 18 and 19, 1910, just over four months after the supposed final decision had been made. They toured the city and the main college building, talked with officials, and had long discussions among themselves. Before leaving, a motion was made that the location of the college be reconsidered and that a meeting of the entire WACPA be called in the near future to decide the issue once and for all. The motion passed with just two dissenting votes, one of which was cast by Orrin R. Jenks, the chair of the Finance Committee for the relocation project. (As its chair, he served as the top fundraiser for the new campus, which required him to travel extensively for over two years.) Those who supported *reconsidering* the location question included the WACPA board chair, the current president of Mendota College, and Charles Eckhart. Of course, many of the people who voted to reopen the matter or were not on the WACPA board, but supported the decision to do so, did not necessarily support Zion City in the end. They simply thought that there were enough good reasons to at least look at Zion City again. Forester's comments in an *Our Hope* article suggest that now unhappiness existed on *both* sides. The pro–Zion City people were upset already, and then after the vote to reopen the location debate, those who supported the Aurora choice also felt aggrieved, first among them—Jenks. He said that the voters at the January 5 meeting had agreed beforehand that they would abide by whatever the majority decision of the group was. He also stated that reopening the location question was an affront to majority rule. Clearly Jenks was not alone; there also was more general complaining about the nullification of the January vote. Forester responded to these complaints and resentments by saying that

> it would seem that those who have never investigated the facts from firsthand should be SLOW in criticizing this call. ALL that is desired by the friends of the Zion City proposition is that the most THOROUGH INVESTIGATION be had. They ask for no repression of facts, no sentimentalism, nothing but BUSINESS-LIKE INVESTIGATION. These men are as warm friends as Mendota College possesses, and as prominent and trustworthy men as there are in the denomination.[14]

And so a great debate began—one that dwarfed the one leading up to the January decision in intensity, politicking, and shenanigans.[15]

To better understand the debate about the location of the college, a few words about Zion City are in order. Zion City (today called Zion) was incorporated in 1902. It is located forty-one miles north of Chicago's Loop. It was founded by a Scotsman, John Alexander Dowie, who, in 1896, had already founded a church, the Christian Catholic Apostolic Church (no connection to the Roman Catholic Church). Beginning his ministerial career as a Congregational preacher, he evolved into an independent evangelist who believed in divine healing. Dowie immigrated to the United States in 1888, and in 1890 moved to the Chicago area, where he started a healing ministry. Eventually, he had several healing tabernacles scattered around Chicago, including a large complex on the South Side. Over time, his religious beliefs grew more and more bizarre. He argued that both the Anglo-Saxons and the Celts were the lost tribes of Israel, and by 1902, as people were arriving to make their home in the new town of Zion City, he claimed to be another Elijah—"Elijah the Restorer"—and began wearing priestly robes and vestments.[16]

On New Year's Eve, 1899, Dowie announced that he planned to build a holy city in the Chicago area. Like George Pullman's town of Pullman on the South Side of Chicago, Zion was one of the few towns in the United States that was planned as a single integrated community before being built. Dowie intended that it would be a Christian utopia that would be characterized by communitarianism, racial peace, and strict moral values. In reality, Dowie *owned* the town and was the authoritarian ruler of a theocracy. The first settlers in Zion did not own their land, but instead had eleven-hundred-year leases from Dowie (one hundred years for Christ's return / creation of His kingdom and one thousand years for Christ's reign on earth). Dowie also controlled society in that he banned alcohol, tobacco, gambling, theaters, circuses, dancing, and swearing. This is not very surprising in a fundamentalist religious community. But Dowie also banned pork, oysters, spitting, whistling on Sundays, politicians, doctors, and tan-colored shoes! And Zion police officers carried both a club and a Bible.[17]

At his most powerful, Dowie was thought to have millions of dollars and around fifty thousand followers (six thousand of whom resided in Zion

City). But after founding Zion City, things went downhill quickly for both Dowie and his town. He lost followers as a result of his priestly airs as Elijah the Reformer, as well as rumors of extravagant spending and even sexual misconduct in the form of polygamy. Also, during these years, his daughter died, and his wife left him—twice. Then, in 1905, he had a stroke. While recovering, he was deposed by his right-hand man, Wilbur Glenn Voliva, whose actions were backed by a court ruling. Dowie died just a few years later, in 1907, a bankrupted, broken man. His estate went into bankruptcy, and his many properties were sold for a small fraction of their worth, which is why buying his college building looked so enticing to some Advent Christians.[18]

Exactly what in Zion City impressed so many members of the WACPA board that they were willing to reconsider the college location, even though the school had already been promised to Aurora? There were at least two major reasons that were given time and time again.

First and foremost was the *finances* of the move. It was estimated that the Zion City property would cost around $200,000 to build at that time (with the original cost being $125,000), yet the asking price was only $45,000. Not only was that considerably cheaper than the $70,000 price tag for the Aurora property, but in addition to the building, the price included the furniture, the fixtures, and the grounds. And the building was large—large enough to accommodate around six hundred students. It also was quite grand when compared to what could be built at almost twice the cost in Aurora. It was a sturdy building made of wood, brick, cement, and stone, having a steel frame. With its tile roof, the building was considered to be fireproof. And it was new enough that it had such modern conveniences as steam heat throughout, conduits for electrical wiring, "toilet rooms" and "washing facilities." The first, second, and third floors had ten to twelve rooms, while the fourth and highest floor had fewer rooms because one of them was a grand assembly hall that could hold eight hundred to twelve hundred people. It also had a basement with twelve large finished rooms. And it had enough room for a kitchen, a dining room, individual offices for every faculty member, and dormitory space for all the students.[19] In short, it had so much room that the college would have to grow into it. One Zion City advocate got so carried away that he actually said that "there would be no necessity of ever building larger for our purposes."[20]

The second major pro–Zion City argument was meant to go to the hearts of the religiously conservative Advent Christians—the argument being that Zion City was vastly superior to Aurora in terms of *morality*. For this argument, the Zion City ban on alcohol, tobacco, gambling, etc. was often compared to the more worldly city of Aurora, with its "forty-five saloons, and 2000 majority for whiskey."[21] (The 2,000 figure refers to the number of votes the "drys" in Aurora had lost by to the "wets" in a recent election.) As one minister wrote, "We are commanded to live soberly, righteously, and godly in the present world. I know of no other city in the country that comes nearer to that requirement than Zion City."[22] This same clergyman added to the pressure by noting that five hundred *mothers* in Zion City were praying that the college would come to town. And, it was argued, parents would be more comfortable sending their children to the cleaner, more morally upright Zion City.[23]

Orrin R. Jenks was, it could be argued, the most ardent proponent of relocating in Aurora. He was against Zion City from the start and was one of only two people who voted against even reopening the issue of location. His views were not all that obvious in his *Our Hope* articles, but a perusal of his correspondence in June of 1910 reveals a bone-weary man who was angry that a small group had, he thought, manipulated the situation to try to undo a fair election. He also feared for the future of the college if Zion City was chosen as the new location. He wrote Eckhart that "if they were to give us the building it would be a calamity to go there with the tremendous prejudice against the place and that movement."[24] Although there was much talk about how, after the final vote, everyone had to come together to work for the common cause, Jenks made it clear that he could not be a part of any college residing in Zion City. A few weeks before the final location vote in June 1910, Jenks wrote this to a friend: "I CANNOT GO THERE. But if our people vote to go there, I shall then be silent. BUT NO ZION CITY FOR ME [capitalization in original]."[25] On the day before the final location vote, Jenks wrote a letter that shows the toll that the Aurora–Zion City debate had taken on him. He bitterly wrote: "I BELIEVE IN HONESTY. And the men [pro-ZC men] are not honest." Then he stated: "I wish you would not mention the Zion City matter to me again. It has about broken me down in health," and further down the page, again, he wrote, "DO NOT MENTION ZION CITY TO

ME, please. I know so much of the place that I do not wish even to think of it [capitalization in original]."[26]

Jenks, of course, was not alone in his view of Zion City. After all, in the end, the Aurora location was chosen, and for a second time. A church leader in Minnesota wrote in *Our Hope* that Zion City being a bargain did not necessarily mean that it was God's will and reminded his readers that "the present building at Mendota, which we are now ready to abandon, was supposed to be a great bargain."[27] J. August Smith, the other person who had voted against reopening the issue of location, quoted, in *Our Hope*, from a letter sent to him just a few weeks before the final vote: "Are you going to put the knife into the heart of your denomination by erecting your only college on the rotten pillars of Dowie's defunct work? Every dollar invested in the Dowie-Voliva Zion City location will be lost to the cause. Better leave the college at Mendota a thousand times. ... Brethren, be careful what you do."[28]

It is clear that Zion City was a troubled place under Dowie's rule, but Dowie had died three years earlier. Why was Jenks, along with some others, so adamant about *not* going to Zion City? First and foremost was the *political and religious situation* there. After Dowie's removal and then death, the town was fiercely divided between those who supported Voliva and the anti-Voliva faction, known as the "Independents." While the pro–Zion City people argued that Voliva's power was waning and, in any case, the college could remain neutral in this fight, Jenks completely rejected this idea. He noted that in a recent election, every one of Voliva's candidates had been elected. He also argued that the Independents were urging the Advent Christians to come so that they could help them bring down Voliva, and that the battles and bitter feelings would not end any time soon. And he did not want the college associated with the national notoriety that Zion City now had, thanks to Dowie's bizarre teachings and the iron-fisted, theocratic rule of both Dowie and Voliva. Jenks's comments in a letter sum up his feelings on this: "The QUARREL there is TERRIBLE. The most disgraceful of anything in the world. It is simply DEVILISH. ... It means the sidetracking of our work, and for all the world I would not willingly take my family into such a town."[29] In short, Jenks's unwillingness to go to Zion City was less sour grapes and more a gut-level belief that Zion City was not just the wrong choice, but one that could kill the college and harm his family.[30]

Not only was Zion City a hotbed of notoriety, divisiveness, and fear, Jenks argued that Advent Christians simply were not wanted there. Yes, the opponents of Voliva wanted the college people to serve as a counterweight to his power, but Jenks estimated that a minimum of half of the Zion City residents did *not* want the college to move there and would oppose it if it did. Chief among those who opposed the college was Voliva, and that was a serious problem. In an *Our Hope* article published just before the final vote on the school's location, Jenks described Voliva as "a strong man, powerful in mind and body." He then described the situation with Voliva like this:

> I know him and have talked with him more than once over this matter. At least half of the people in Zion City are dominated by his influence. ... General Overseer Voliva looks upon our people coming to Zion City the same as he would view the coming of saloons and brothels. Listen to this from their official paper: "A temperance town cannot be built with a lot of whisky-bloats and beerpots; nor can a Zion City be built with Methodists, Baptists, Presbyterians, Adventists, etc." [*Zion Herald*, June 8, 1910]. Now Mr. Voliva does not believe that we are as bad as drunkards, but he maintains that we have no moral right in his town, and that we would stand in the way of his people realizing their ideal of the kingdom of God, the ideal for which Zion City was founded, just the same as "whisky-bloats and beerpots" would stand in the way. I for one cannot for a single moment lend my influence to a movement to locate our educational and publishing interests, a number of our families and many of our choice sons and daughters, in a place where they would be looked upon with the same degree of tolerance with which good men view drunkards and harlots! Overseer Voliva told me with his own lips, no longer ago than on June 12th, that he has nothing against our people as a people, but if they come to Zion City it will be his duty, and that of his people, to fight us first, last and all the time.[31]

For Jenks, moving the college to Zion City would bring a never-ending struggle with half the population and the powers-that-be.[32]

Zion City's notoriety, political and religious divisiveness, and opposition to the college seem to have been Jenks's greatest concerns about Zion City, but there were several other ones, although they were probably secondary. First, he was afraid that going to Zion City would create a deep, long-lasting division among the Advent Christian people, one that could take years to disappear. And, he argued, no other place under consideration would create that kind of division. Second, these divisions would make college fundraising more difficult for a Zion City location than elsewhere, as many Advent Christians would not donate to a college there. And it would be difficult to raise money among the inhabitants of Zion City itself. Many of its inhabitants were poor, or at least had modest incomes, and the business that had the resources to give to the college, Marshall Field's, refused to do so as it did not want to upset Voliva. Third, as Jenks informed his readers, "the College Property in Zion City is, probably, ALREADY OUT OF OUR REACH."[33] It appeared, he explained, that the likeliest scenario for the Dowie estate was for it to be sold as a whole, probably to Voliva:

A brokerage company of Chicago has already offered $700,000 in cash for the Zion Estate, which includes the college. This company is under contract to sell the property to Mr. Voliva for $900,000 on eight years' time, if the company secures the estate. Early in June this proposition was placed by the Receiver before the six thousand stockholders. They have forty days in which to reply. Both the Receiver and Judge Landis believe it to be a good offer. It is probably more than the estate is worth. But as the brokers will receive from Mr. Voliva two hundred thousand dollars more than they pay for it, they are safe, and so are willing to finance the deal. Judge Landis will probably instruct the Receiver to accept the offer of $700,000 in cash, and close the receivership. ... The stockholders are not going to accept $45,000 from our people for a parcel of the property when they can close out the whole estate for a cash offer of $700,000. Now the twelve Directors [of WACPA] knew that this bid was in when we met in Zion City in May, though we did not know the price offered. This was one reason, though not the chief one, why I voted against a reconsideration.[34]

Thus, for all these reasons and more, Jenks, along with others, believed that Zion City was absolutely the wrong place to locate the college.[35]

Given the fact that Jenks's concerns about Zion City were quite serious, what was driving so much support for Zion City? It was the *financial argument*—that such a big, beautiful building could be purchased for so little money, thus giving the college a much larger building for considerably less money than in Aurora. Jenks acknowledged that the building was nice, but he did not accept this financial argument. In fact, he made the opposite one—that there was not much difference in cost between Zion City and Aurora. The Zion City building was being offered at around $45,000, and Jenks thought it would take another $5,000 to fix it up. But there was still a need for dormitories. Even if the men could be housed in the main building, he did not think it would be acceptable to house the women there as well. So at least one dormitory would have to be built, at a cost of about $10,000, for a total of $60,000. In Aurora, he argued, they would get three new buildings, designed specifically for their needs—a main building and two dormitories—all for $70,000. Since Aurora citizens had promised to contribute no less than $15,000, this put the expenses for Aurora in the same ballpark as the costs for Zion City.[36]

One of the fascinating things about the pro–Zion City people is how irrational—even bizarre—their behavior was at times. As Jenks noted, it was not entirely clear that the property there was even available, because Voliva had already taken some preliminary steps to buy Dowie's *entire* estate, and they knew that. And then two Zion City proponents told Jenks that they were thinking about putting a $500 deposit down on the property, and this was *before* the meeting at which the final location vote would be taken. The $500 was not refundable, and Jenks urged them not to do this. Also, at least one of the college directors left the receiver for the Dowie estate with the idea that the college *would* purchase the property. He was later brought to court after it had become clear that this was not going to happen. It is no wonder that Jenks viewed at least some of the pro–Zion City people as being dishonest and underhanded. At least some of them acted like they were so desperate to acquire the Zion City college building that they were in denial about certain facts and willing to gamble with a substantial amount of their own money.[37]

Thus far, little has been said about Aurora and what it had to offer the college. What exactly made Aurora the obvious choice for Jenks and many others? At that time, Aurora was not really a suburb of Chicago. It was an independent, industrial and market town of about thirty-one thousand people, located about forty miles from Chicago, with a rail line connecting it directly to the city. Between Aurora and Chicago was a large population of suburbs. Thus, the area offered the potential for many more students than Mendota could provide, since Mendota was a much smaller town that was a long eighty-six miles from Chicago and surrounded by farmland rather than towns.[38]

Aurora's largest industry was the railroad—the large shop complex for the Chicago, Burlington, & Quincy Railroad. But the railroad was not the only big employer in town. Since the 1880s, Aurora had been diversifying its industrial base, so a wide array of businesses had developed in or moved to Aurora. Thus, jobs were much more plentiful than in either Mendota or Zion City, and this was confirmed by the large numbers of immigrants who had been migrating to Aurora in search of work since the mid-1800s. Unlike Mendota and even Zion City, Aurora offered a wide spectrum of jobs for students trying to work their way through college, and they were jobs in businesses that were not entangled in major political disputes, as in Zion City.[39]

These businesses served another function as well—support for the college. One of the complaints about Mendota was that the town and its businessmen had shown little interest in and support for the school—in terms of both money and students. And in Zion City, many businesses were owned by people who did not even want the college, especially Voliva. In Aurora, it was a very different situation. The leading businessmen of the town, led by William George, the president of the Old Second National Bank, not only wanted the college to come but worked to make it happen, including giving monetary support. George *gave* the school its first five acres of land—an entire city block—located just outside the town's western boundaries, and Aurora businessmen collectively proposed to donate a substantial amount of money—$15,000. And this much larger business community held the potential for much greater financial support for the college in the years to come. In fact, Jenks claimed in one letter that Aurorans had promised the college at least $2,500 annually for its operational expenses.[40]

In short, Aurora provided a good location with excellent transportation, a dynamic and supportive business community, a growing population that was pushing the physical boundaries of the town outward, and political and religious peace that would allow businesses to thrive and people to live and worship in a setting of much greater religious diversity and tolerance. Even the proposed site for the school was advantageous. Unlike the situation in both Mendota and Zion City, the Aurora site was located on the edge of town, so it offered a larger campus and one with the potential for growth since open land extended westward as far as the eye could see. To the east lay the best residential neighborhood in town, which would help make the college neighborhood an attractive place to live. And the streetcar ended just one block away, on LeGrande Avenue, so although the college was on the edge of Aurora, it would be connected to the rest of the town.[41]

Much of this chapter has been spent on the topic of the Aurora–Zion City debate because this was such a critically important issue. The outcome determined the future of the college. The towns were so different, and what they offered would mean a very different day-to-day life for the school. This topic is also important because the final decision would, as Jenks and many others firmly believed, determine the future viability of the college. Jenks and other supporters of Aurora were convinced that it would be considerably easier to raise money for Aurora than for Zion City. And a considerable amount of the money pledged by Advent Christians, on the premise that the college would be in Aurora, would, it was believed, not materialize for a Zion City college. And then, of course, even if the money could be raised, there was the question of whether or not the college could even survive in such a hostile and contentious environment.[42]

Fundraising Strategies

In the end, the *second and final* vote, on June 28, 1910, was almost anticlimactic in that Aurora won by a healthy margin. Once that decision was finally safely behind them, college leaders had to return to another, huge problem—how to raise enough money among a people who were small in numbers and of modest means. Ever since the January 1910 meeting had named Aurora as the location, Jenks had been working feverishly to raise money, and people were donating funds based on the understanding that the college would be built in Aurora. When the Aurora–Zion City debate returned, Jenks ceased all fundraising activity until the final decision was made. As soon as the second vote was taken, *again* going for Aurora, Jenks quickly returned to the task of raising money, and he did very little of it from Mendota. From the summer of 1910 until just before the move in the spring of 1912, much, and probably most, of Jenks's time was spent in the "field," as he called it, visiting churches and campmeetings all over the country to talk up the college and raise money for the new buildings. Fundraising articles in *Our Hope*, especially Jenks's "Bulletins," helped to raise money. The Bulletins reported on the progress of the college project and tried to cajole its readers into donating to the building fund, but that route produced insufficient funds. Jenks believed that what was *really* required was to go out among the Advent Christian people and talk to them face-to-face about the college. And so, at great expense to his other work, his family life, and his health, that is what he did. Of course, along with this, he was cultivating, through copious correspondence, a number of large donors, especially Charles Eckhart.[43]

The leaders of this college movement tended to be ministers, and virtually none of them, including those who were not clergymen, had professional experience as fundraisers. Yet they, and the Advent Christian people themselves, managed to come up with a number of creative strategies to raise money for the new campus. First, for well over two years, every issue of *Our Hope* contained a numbered article (his "Bulletin"), which Jenks wrote from the field, and these columns often had distinct themes. For example, in the months between the first and second decision for Aurora, various Bulletins were aimed specifically at ministers, lay people, young men, young women, and even people living in remote, rural areas.[44]

After the second location decision, the Bulletins took on a more general look of being a project update, but they were never just informational. No matter what was discussed, it was always tied to fundraising. For example, one Thanksgiving, the Bulletin suggested that if you were truly thankful for life's blessings, one way to show that was to give to the college building fund. And the Bulletins were important for other strategies that were used. Some of these fundraising methods are still common today, such as a donor agreeing to give a specific amount (in this case, $10,000 from Charles Eckhart) once the public raises a specific amount (in this case, $30,000, and later $60,000 for another $10,000 donation from Eckhart) or setting a series of smaller objectives to achieve what would otherwise seem like an overwhelming single goal. This became especially important after the price tag on the project rose from $70,000 to around $100,000—due to the purchase of additional acreage for the campus, the completion of the top floor on each of the three buildings, furnishings, etc. However, these fundraising techniques would not have worked without *Our Hope*. It was in this *weekly* newspaper that Jenks and others pushed these matching and small goal strategies. It was especially in Jenks's Bulletins that Advent Christians were urged on to meet each new goal. It was also here that Jenks celebrated when each goal was reached.[45]

Our Hope readers also came up with some creative fundraising ideas, and there was one that was particularly interesting. A female supporter of Aurora College wrote to *Our Hope*, suggesting that Advent Christian women start an Anti-Hat Club. Instead of buying a new hat for the season, church women should, she suggested, take that $3 (which she saw as the least amount of money one would have to spend for a respectable hat) and send it to the college fund. She got this idea because her husband, not being an Advent Christian, was not likely to give to the college, yet she was an ardent supporter of the school. So, she came up with the idea of sacrificing something personal that she would ordinarily buy and sending the price of it to the building fund. She wrote a letter to *Our Hope* in order to tell other women about her idea and urge them to do this as well.[46] A number of readers did just that, such as the woman who wrote in that, although she had not been planning on buying a new hat this season, she thought she would give up something that she did want to buy and send the $3 to the college. And she urged others to do the same, writing: "How many others will join us? Are there not three hundred women who could give three dollars each, and so raise almost another thousand dollars? Don't say 'we can't afford it.' We can't afford not to give."[47] Another woman wrote in to say: "I am heartily in favor and will gladly do all I can to help. I have been an anti-hat believer for many years, and would now propose that we join for life instead of for a season or two. The money can be used for something more uplifting than a hat and the price will be needed, even after the college is built."[48] An even more ambitious woman wrote in to say: "We want one thousand women to enroll as members of our Anti-Hat Club." That was a pretty tall order for such a small denomination, but, as she said in explaining her motivation, "There is inspiration in numbers and we can encourage each other in the sacrifice. ... The college is to be ours and if possible should be built with our money."[49] This certainly was not an overtly feminist message, but it was one that indicated that women, especially those who did not work outside the home, could make a personal sacrifice and contribute to the cause, making a contribution that was truly their own.

Another Bump in the Road

Less than three months before the spring groundbreaking in Aurora, there was yet another bump in the road. A Mr. Virden, president of Dixon College, in Dixon, Illinois, contacted WACPA, offering to sell the college property to them. A group of board members and a contractor went to look at the property, which included multiple buildings. The buildings were old, and the contractor estimated that it would take around $26,000 to modernize them, and, of course, the college felt committed to Aurora at this late date.[50]

The problem was that at almost the same time, the Aurora people, including William George, seemed to be doing little to make the school's move possible, and some of the college leaders were becoming frustrated. There was disagreement about the $15,000 figure that was promised to the college from Aurora's businessmen, some of them thinking that it was closer to $5,000. Then, suddenly, the college was being told by the city engineer that the city could only bring water to the campus if it was brought within the city limits, and even then, it would cost the college $2,000. He also said that although the college site had a sewer, it was probably inadequate for the college, so a larger one would have to be put in at a cost of $2,000.[51]

The board member who reported this to Jenks, who was in California at the time, wrote: "I have had the utmost hopes of Aurora doing her part until within the last two weeks. I thought sure that when I told them that they would certainly lose the college unless they got busy; but I think they take at [it] as a joke and think that we will come anyway as we have no other place to go and they will do as little as possible."[52] After writing that, the board member then started to tell Jenks all of the things that he liked about the Dixon property, no doubt as an antidote for the frustration that he was feeling about Aurora. In his reply, Jenks dismissed the notion of locating in Dixon because of the renovation cost, the fact that Eckhart was against it, and what he called "other very SERIOUS difficulties [capitalization in original]," which he did not identify in his letter. Yet he also said: "As to Aurora, ... we should yet do all that we can, and if we do not locate there throw the responsibility upon the citizens of Aurora."[53] No one seemed to take the Dixon proposal seriously, but it was yet another issue to deal with. It required taking a trip to Dixon and making yet another location decision, and so late in the day, at precisely the time that Aurora seemed to have dropped the ball. Of course, the deal with Aurora did *not* fall through—Aurora businessmen *did* raise an adequate amount of money to make the deal viable, and the campus *did* get water and a sewer, but this situation must have produced a great deal of stress so close to the groundbreaking.[54]

Building the Aurora Campus

Early on, college leaders stated that they did not intend to start building the Aurora campus until the money for it had been raised. No doubt, learning from their financial problems at Mendota, they wanted to start life in Aurora debt free. Therefore, at the first annual WACPA meeting after the final vote for Aurora, the Building Committee was "instructed not to close any contracts for the actual erection of the new college buildings until the necessary funds be paid in or subscribed by responsible contributors."[55] In the end, this did not exactly happen. Two months later, Jenks now said that construction could begin after just $40,000 *in cash* was raised, but he also stated what he said many times over in the two and a half years of fundraising for the Aurora campus: "We cannot incur debt. We are to pay as we go, or else we don't go."[56] When ground was finally broken, far more than the $40,000 had been raised—around $70,000, although some of this was in pledges rather than cash. At a May 23, 1911, meeting of the college board, Building Committee, and Finance Committee, it was agreed to begin construction. Although not all the money had been raised, college leaders felt compelled to act, as they explained in an *Our Hope* article: "Two brethren felt it would be best to wait a few months longer. In fact the Finance Committee would like six months more for its work. But the need is urgent. If school is held in Mendota next fall, the building there must be repaired at considerable expense. It was felt that to spend another year where our buildings and equipment are so inadequate would be a needless delay. So, the command is FORWARD."[57] So onward they went in faith and with hope that the entire cost would eventually be covered. Jenks would continue his fundraising for more than a year, his goal being to have all the money raised by the dedication of the campus in October 1912, and it mostly was.[58]

And so, on May 31, 1911, ground was broken. Jenks, holding a simple plow pulled by a horse, broke ground first. Other milestones quickly followed. Just a week later, the excavation for Eckhart Hall had been completed. And then on Saturday, July 22, 1911, the ceremonial laying of the cornerstone took place. This was a very special day, with a ceremony befitting the occasion and a large audience of four hundred to five hundred people. It was, in part, a religious service, with prayer, the reading of Scripture, and music. And several people gave speeches, including Aurora's Mayor Sanders. Then Jenks spoke a few words and the cornerstone was laid. A large copper box was put in amid the stones, in the southeast corner of Eckhart Hall. It contained quite a few items: "college catalogues, copies of all our denominational papers, copies of the Chicago 'Record-Herald' and Chicago 'Tribune' of that date, a few coins of 1893, the year Mendota College was founded, also 1911, the year of removal to Aurora, also a small Bible and a brief type written account of the circumstances bringing about the erection of the buildings at Aurora, with some other articles."[59] After so much hard work to get to this day, the laying of the cornerstone must have been an exciting and joyous occasion for everyone there. Even the weather cooperated, because it was a beautiful day.[60]

During this summer of 1911, when exciting first steps were taking place, Jenks took time out to move his family to Aurora. The problem was that they had no place to stay, so for a while, they lived in a tent on campus. Since Jenks

was away fundraising so often, this meant that his wife and daughters lived on
their own much of the time, roughing it in a tent on a construction site, with
no running water. Apparently, the Jenks family members were a hardy lot,
and they were there in the summer, but still, it had to have been unpleasant
at times, especially when a violent thunderstorm swept through the area.
Presumably, they were able to get out of this flimsy shelter before cold weather
set in, but it could not have been easy for them. In addition to having minimal
income coming into the family coffers during Jenks's fundraising days, this is
another way in which the family sacrificed for the college.[61]

Compared to the bumps in the road experienced thus far, the
actual construction of the campus buildings went relatively smoothly. It was
predicted that it would take about a year to construct the three buildings, and
that was close to what it took. However, because that is what college officials
believed, it is perplexing that they kept setting dates for occupancy that were
way too early. Even though the ground had just been broken on May 31, Jenks
still wrote in mid-August that classes would start in Aurora, on October 4. In
the same article, he also said that the walls of Eckhart Hall were nearly up, and
the roof would be on by early September. Jenks seems to have been in serious
denial here. He was allowing three to four weeks between the time the roof
would go on and the start of classes. Even if he meant that just a few rooms
would be ready to hold classes, which he did, this would still involve all kinds
of extensive interior work—plastering walls, laying floors, installing heat and
lights, etc., because most of such work can be done only after there is a roof. As
it turned out, the roof did not go on until at least mid-October. The prematurity
of Jenks's August announcement was recognized by early September; an
article published on the sixth of that month announced that classes were now
scheduled to start in Aurora at the beginning of the *second* term, in January.
Several months later, Jenks explained to *Our Hope* readers why the occupancy
date had changed. In June, the contractor was asked to have some rooms
ready for an October 1 school start date. That did not happen because of several
difficulties, especially heavy rains that made it difficult to get materials on the
site. Unfortunately, this had not been explained at the time, so people had read
the October opening date as meaning that *all* the buildings would be finished
by then. They then wondered why they were not, so more than two months

later, in December, Jenks had to explain that college officials never expected all the buildings to be completed by then and why even a few rooms had not been finished. The date of occupancy would change one more time. In late February, it was announced that the move would take place in early April, and on March 6, that it would happen no later than April 15. As time went on, the occupancy date became later and vaguer. It seems that Jenks and the other Building Committee members had to learn, through hard experience, the art of promising the completion of a job farther out than expected and in vague terms so that if and when it is completed early, people are pleasantly surprised.[62]

Of course, there were the usual construction issues—cost overruns, bad weather delaying work, doing more than originally planned, etc. One of the additional costs came from the fact that college officials believed that the college needed more land. It was offered an adjoining block of land to the west, which would nearly double the original five acres donated by George. It could be had for $6,000 but would add $10,000 to the value of the property. If the option on the block at this price was not accepted within a few months, the same piece of land would then cost $10,000. This was a good deal for the college, and it was a good time to buy for another reason. Since there was nothing but empty land west of the college, the time to expand the campus was right away rather than years down the road after that land had been developed.[63]

Once the college broke ground, it was committed to Aurora once and for all, which must have eased some of the college leaders' anxiety. Of course, for Jenks, as chair of the Finance Committee for the move, the strain of raising money for the building fund continued right up to the move and beyond. His constant refrain in 1911 and 1912 was to have the debt paid off by the October 1912 dedication of the buildings. But in spite of the continuing stress about money, he was moving the college forward. A photograph of the partially constructed Eckhart Hall, published in the September 13, 1911, issue of *Our Hope*, symbolizes what was happening. Some workmen are standing on top of the first floor while a group of people stands below. On the left is a horse and carriage, and on the right, an early automobile. The college was moving from the old-fashioned, limited past of the horse and buggy to the vastly more modern future, symbolized by the car, with its seemingly limitless possibilities.[64]

Not only was a campus being built, the neighborhood surrounding it was as well. The reason that the streetcar had recently come out to LeGrande Boulevard, which was just a block from the college, was because some of Aurora's finest homes were being built there. So, even at the time of the campus's construction, it was clear that the college would reside in a beautiful neighborhood. And that neighborhood came even closer when a friend of the college gave it an option on twenty lots located on the west side of the two blocks immediately north of the campus, on Calumet Avenue. The owner was selling these lots for $425 each—either for cash or $25 down and then $10 a month with a 6 percent interest rate. It was a good deal for buyers and the college alike, because the owner gave $200 from each sale to the school. Shortly after the move to Aurora, Jenks noted that the option on these lots had been very helpful in paying for the college buildings. This would become the area where Jenks and other college people built their homes.[65]

Pulling Off a Small Miracle

One final question remains—given all the trials and tribulations along this journey, how, in the end, did the college leaders and the Advent Christian people pull off what was nothing short of a small miracle? Obviously, there were many factors: the creative fundraising of the college leaders and the people themselves; the generosity of several large donors, especially Eckhart; and the boosterism of Aurora's business people, who, in the end, provided the college with excellent incentives to locate in their town. However, the one person who stands out in this saga, the one whose labors were so intense and diverse that one can hardly imagine this success without him, was Orrin R. Jenks. What emerges from his published articles and personal correspondence was a picture of a leader who was *the* driving force behind the entire relocation process. In spite of some shortcomings, he was the right person for this job and was the single most important person in terms of making the college a reality. Many other people aided the cause of building a new campus in Aurora, and some in a big way, like Charles Eckhart, but no one virtually put his personal life on hold for over two years in order to raise funds for the project or pushed his physical limits through nearly constant, often difficult travel the way Jenks did. He also was well known and liked by Advent Christians across the country, not just in the Midwest, and this national profile must have helped in the fundraising.

Hopefully, this praise of Jenks will not be viewed as simply sentimental hero worship. The evidence shows that as a person and even as a leader, he, like the rest of us, was far from perfect. At times, he was overly sensitive and jumped to conclusions, which often resulted in his getting angry and saying or writing things that he would later regret. There was no doubt that Jenks had a temper, and he was not afraid of being blunt (although it should also be said that people knew where they stood with Jenks, and he certainly exhibited enough diplomacy to turn Eckhart into a very generous donor). And in his letters while on the road fundraising and during the debate over location, he complained so frequently about being physically done in, his nerves shot, that it starts to sound a bit like whining.[66]

However, although he probably should have talked less about his exhaustion and illnesses, he was doing so many things at once that even by today's multitasking standards, it was impressive. He held onto his pastorate at an Advent Christian church in Chicago until as late as July 1910, which means that he was still working as a pastor throughout the months of the Zion City debate. He also taught part-time at Mendota College, and he had the *huge* task of raising the required funds for the new campus. To raise the funds needed for relocation, he had to nurture potentially large donors, like Eckhart, through an extensive correspondence; negotiate with Aurorans about funding to bring the college to Aurora; and travel around the country to visit innumerable churches and campmeetings. He believed that the most effective way to raise money was to talk to people face-to-face about the college, and this required that he be gone for long periods, sometimes months at a time.[67] In a January 17, 1911 letter to Eckhart, while already on the road, he wrote: "I had thought of going to the Pacific Coast in the summer but as this trip will take me into Oklahoma and Texas, I am thinking of going direct from Texas to California, and then into Oregon, Washington, Montana, Minnesota and Wisconsin, and reach Chicago about the first of April. By so doing, I will have visited most of the churches west of the Mississippi without any unnecessary travelling."[68]

When on the road, the traveling was sometimes primitive and long because the churches were few and far between, and when at a place, he was constantly preaching and visiting people to tell them about the college. At times he was literally so busy all day long that he had no time to write his weekly Bulletin for *Our Hope*. And, of course, he had family responsibilities. He had four daughters, all of them young enough to still be at home, so his wife had a heavy burden as well. For all practical purposes, she was a single parent during the more than two years of Jenks's fundraising. In February 1911, after a long time away fundraising, Jenks wrote, in *Our Hope*, what must have been viewed by many readers as a great understatement: "Having been away from home for more than five months, I feel it only right to go home a few days."[69] Indeed. Not only was he not seeing his family for long periods of time, he also was not getting paid for this work. The only money he received to cover his traveling expenses and support his family came from what he called "loose collections," which did not begin to cover his expenses. (In one of these "loose collections," he received 27 cents.) So perhaps some complaining about physical ills was needed to get him through the huge task before him. [70]

In fact, Jenks had a number of strengths that served him well as leader of this college-building movement. He showed great leadership, insight, and wisdom when it came to the debate over Zion City. The college building there was so impressive and seemingly inexpensive that it would have been very easy to be swayed by it and go into denial about the hostile environment and dictatorial government that would have come with it. But he was able and willing to see the larger picture.

And, as it turned out, Jenks revealed himself to be a real political animal. Throughout the fundraising process, and especially during the debates over location, he was quietly writing to a number of influential people to make his case either for leaving Mendota or for not going to Zion City. Some of these people, before hearing from Jenks, had looked upon Zion City favorably, mainly because they knew little about the actual conditions there and only saw what a supposed bargain it was. To win them over to his point of view, he wrote them in a politically nuanced way, clearly making a case for why the college needed to leave Mendota or that Zion City was a bad, if not evil, place to be, but doing so in a subtle, low-pressure manner that was less likely to offend people or let them think that he was beating them over the head with his arguments. As early as 1909, he wrote a letter to Eckhart that exhibited this talent. After making his case, he wrote: "Of course, you will understand that this is not written to influence you … , but simply to let you know how matters stand here."[71] In a letter to a prominent Advent Christian couple, after making his case, he wrote: "Well, you must, of course, do as you think best; but I felt that I must write to you. I know you desire what is for the best interests of our people."[72] Of course Jenks *was* trying to influence people, in spite of his denials to the contrary, while attempting to make them think that they were making up their own mind. And a couple of weeks before the final vote on location, Jenks took direct, politically shrewd action, which he hoped, no doubt, would pull the blinders off the eyes of the pro–Zion City people. He wrote to Voliva, asking him to write back on whether or not he wanted the college to move to his town. This was a brilliant political move to counteract the Zion City supporters who still held out hope that the college could coexist with Voliva. Jenks always believed that Voliva hated the idea of the college relocating in his town and would fight the college to the death. Jenks clearly was hoping to get indisputable evidence that a belief in peaceful coexistence with Voliva was an illusion.[73]

Another strength was Jenks's willingness to talk tough, not just in private letters, but also in published articles. His tough love talk served an invaluable purpose whenever the money for the building fund was coming in too slowly. He was willing to write publicly about people's apathy in a way that most other people would have felt uncomfortable doing. In one article, he wrote: "Now is the time to give. If you ask me WHO is to give the money needed, my answer is YOU. If the pledges are coming in slowly, YOU are partly the cause. If the movement fails, YOU are one part of the failure."[74] In early 1912, he wrote in *Our Hope* that only twelve hundred people out of a denomination of twenty-five thousand had given something to the cause. Saying that he was interested not just in raising money but in awakening people's sense of responsibility to the denomination, he ended with these provocative words: "We would rather make you angry than to be quiet at this time. Indignation is preferable to stagnation. Who dares to read this bulletin and say, 'This does not hit me.'"[75]

In several different letters, Jenks remarked that if the college moved to Aurora, he would be willing to give the next twenty years of his life to serving the school.[76] Little did he know how closely this promise would come to match reality. He served as president from 1911 to 1933, a little over twenty years. By the time he turned the presidency over to Theodore P. Stephens in 1933, the school had come upon another bump in the road—the Great Depression. Stephens would have his own rocky road to navigate, but his journey would also be successful, at least in part because of the foundation that Jenks had helped to build in Aurora.

Aurora at Last—Gratitude for the Past and Hope for the Future

Jenks's parting thoughts on April 3, 1912—moving day—first showed gratitude to Mendota, saying that "we shall always love and revere the place of our birth." But then he quickly looked to the future, saying that "new things must come. Through the generous gifts of noble men and women we are provided with three splendid buildings in Aurora. We enter them with joy and hopefulness, believing that a great door of opportunity is open before us and that our school is entering a new period of usefulness."[77]

By the day of the move, faculty and students alike had already commemorated their time at Mendota. Now their thoughts were focused on the years-long journey that had brought them to this day and on the future, with all of its untold possibilities. They could not have possibly imagined the extent to which Aurora College would grow and develop over the next one hundred years. But looking back on that day, we can see that their journey was only *just beginning*, and it was going to be another very interesting ride!

The Main Educational Building in Zion City that Some People Wanted to Purchase for the College

John Alexander Dowie Dressed as Elijah the Restorer

Wilbur Glenn Voliva—Dowie's Successor as General Overseer of Zion City Who Was
Adamantly Opposed to Mendota College Moving to Zion City

William George—President of Aurora's Old Second National Bank, Facilitator of the College's Move to Aurora,
and Donor of an Entire City Block of Land to the College

Architect's Rendering of Eckhart Hall

Breaking Ground for the New Aurora Campus, May 31, 1911

Eckhart Hall Cornerstone Laying Ceremony, July 22, 1911

The Past Meets the Future as a Horse and Carriage Faces an Automobile, Each Bringing People to
See the Progress of the College's Future—Eckhart Hall

Construction Workers in Front of Eckhart Hall

The Tent in which the Jenks Family Lived on Campus in the Summer of 1911
(The Jenks's new house, near the campus, on Calumet Avenue, was not ready when the family moved to Aurora, so they lived in this tent for a while, often without Orrin Jenks, who was frequently on the road raising money for the new campus. Mrs. Jenks [standing] and her girls are pictured here with a few friends.)

Aurorans Greet the Mendota College People as They Arrive in Aurora, on April 3, 1912,
to Move onto their New Aurora Campus

The Biggest Donor—Charles Eckhart—after Whom Eckhart Hall Was Named

D. A. Davis—the Benefactor after Whom
Davis Hall Was Named

William Wilkinson—the Benefactor after Whom
Wilkinson Hall Was Named

Chapter 10
"Occupy till I Come": "Occupying" in Mendota and Aurora

It was moved "that in the name of the Lord we maintain the college."
—Mendota College Board of Education, 1897

President Nathan Twining, 1901–6

In the end, Mendota College was a hybrid—an amalgamation of a bible training school, a type of religious school that appeared in the late-nineteenth century, and a college, one based on the nineteenth-century model of a small, Christian college. It drew heavily from both types of schools, whether consciously or not. It was more than a Bible training school or Bible school. In one of the few scholarly books on the American Bible School, Boston School of Theology, the other Advent Christian school, is listed, but not Mendota College, and rightfully so. As important as the college's religion department was, it did not comprise the entire school; it also offered liberal arts degrees and a few practical programs, like business. But neither was it a modern college. As with many other, small, Christian schools in the late nineteenth century, it resembled, in many ways, the college of the pre–Civil War era. State and Ivy League colleges and universities, with their larger student populations, campuses, academic resources, and donations, were able to modernize earlier and more quickly than small colleges. Turning away from an emphasis on the liberal arts and teaching to a focus on professional programs and research was costly, so smaller schools, like Mendota College, had to make a virtue out of the former.[1]

In what ways was Mendota College similar to the "old-time" college of the antebellum period? First and foremost, religion was at the heart of the school—having mandatory, daily chapel; frequent, student prayer meetings on campus; religious doctrine taught in the theological department; and some ministers serving on the faculty and college board. In short, religious beliefs and everyday piety were evident throughout the college. This was reflected in the school's paternalism, another similarity. The president was a father figure, who wore many hats on campus, including that of disciplinarian. Part of this paternalistic, pious approach to students was to create a strict code of behavior for them and to require that students live in dormitories, unless a student was given permission to live elsewhere, which meant it had to be a proper place with some authority figure in residence. Dormitory living was important in this paternalistic environment because it was a way of keeping a tight rein on students and providing a protected, Christian living space.[2]

Academically, the college also shared many characteristics with the old-style college. Both offered liberal arts courses that were almost completely literary (classical) and scientific, although Mendota evolved a bit in that area over the years. Faculty at both tended to be generalists rather than specialists who had advanced degrees, and they often used recitations as a teaching method. The patterns of students also were similar. They tended to be underprepared for college, which lowered admissions and academic standards, and many more people attended than graduated, with much coming and going of students. Because there were so many underprepared students, preparatory departments were common.[3]

Financially, antebellum colleges suffered from many of the problems that Mendota College did. Tuition was kept low to attract students, many of whom did not come from affluent families. Thus, Mendota College, like other small, Christian colleges in the nineteenth century, served as an avenue of upward social mobility for students coming from humbler backgrounds, thanks to their low tuition rates. Low tuition meant that costs had to be kept down, so budgets were generally lean, with little to no fat to cut when a fiscal crisis hit. A major way of keeping costs down was to keep faculty salaries low. Endowments also were low and fundraising difficult. Most alumni were neither wealthy nor donors to their alma mater. Fundraising and student recruitment were made more difficult by the lack of bureaucracy—specialized offices whose personnel worked full time to raise money, develop engaged alumni, and recruit students. At Mendota, as with early colleges, these tasks were performed by the president and faculty on top of their other duties.[4]

In many ways, Mendota College seems like an institution from decades earlier, yet in other ways it was quite different from antebellum-era colleges. Times were rapidly changing by the late nineteenth century, including in religious education. As discussed in chapter one, Bible schools, Bible training schools, and Bible institutes were modest institutions—both academically and financially. (Until about 1920, there was no hard and fast distinction among these institutions, but by the 1920s and 1930s, the last two types of schools were dying out as stand-alone institutions.) They were fundamentalist and evangelical and admitted many women, at a time when almost no seminaries did. Modeled on the old missionary training schools, they emphasized practical training over theological knowledge and getting people into Christian service as quickly as possible. At least initially, they were not created to prepare ministers, but to train lay people for Christian service. And they were underfunded as well as academically weak.[5]

Much of this sounds similar to Mendota College—being fundamentalist and evangelical, having academic and financial challenges, admitting many women, educating lay people rather than just ministers, etc. But there were distinct differences as well. Mendota College was clearly superior to the Bible training schools. Although the religion department at Mendota College was often called the Bible Training School, it was academically better than a stand-alone Bible training school of the 1890s. The major goal of Mendota's theological department was to prepare ministers—to educate them through the teaching of theology, the Bible, ancient languages, etc., as opposed to quick, practical training. It also wanted to educate lay people for Christian service, but first and foremost was the need to produce more ministers for the denomination. It was superior also because it provided liberal arts courses and encouraged theology students to take some, even if they were not working for a bachelor's degree in addition to their Bible Training School diploma. This took time, and the Mendota faculty and supporters argued for *thorough* preparation over quick training. Initially, it seemed like quick training was the way that the school might be going. There certainly were Adventists around the country arguing that if ministers needed education, it should be quick and strictly religious. And early on, in 1895, an *Our Hope* editor wrote that "the object of this school is not to put its pupils through a routine course in theology, requiring several years study, but to take those whom God has called to gospel work, and by a course of study *adapted to their needs*, fit them passably for work, in as short a time as possible, and send them out. This is essentially the principle upon which the D. L. Moody Bible Schools are successfully conducted, in Chicago. ..."[6] Dwight L. Moody's school in Chicago, the Moody Bible Institute, was probably the best known of the early, stand-alone Bible training schools. Although this 1895 quotation suggests that the Bible Training School was going the route of the Moody Bible Institute, that turned out *not* to be the case. Initially, the religion program was much shorter—just a year. However, in a short time, the program went from one year to two, and eventually to three. And the religion students were frequently urged to stay the course and complete the program before taking on a pastorate.[7]

The Weaknesses and Challenges of Mendota College

A number of the weaknesses and challenges of the college have already been discussed in this book—especially its at times mediocre academic programs (along with its low admission standards, underprepared students, inability to recruit or graduate enough students, etc.) and its financial instability throughout the nineteen years of its existence. There were other weaknesses that were not recognized initially, but which became increasingly visible over time—the school's lack of ongoing monetary support from Mendota's citizens and the town's isolation from larger population centers, thus limiting the number of students who could be recruited, the number of jobs available for students, and the cultural resources available. These too were discussed earlier in this book. However, there were at least two problems that have not yet been discussed.

One of these problems was presidential weakness and turnover. Seven presidents served in the *nineteen Mendota years*. By way of contrast, seven people have served as president in the *more than one hundred years* since the move to Aurora. The first eight years at Mendota were especially problematic. Each of the first four presidents—J. Oscar Campbell, Abial B. Sibley, George V. Clum, and M. L. Gordon—was essentially let go by the board, Campbell and Sibley after each had served just a year and Clum and Gordon after each had served three years.

It is probably not a coincidence that these men served in the early years, when the school's financial status was especially difficult. College board minutes make it clear that Sibley was not asked to serve a second year because he was not raising enough money. The issue for Campbell may very well have been financial as well, but there was more than that, although it is not clear what. The board minutes state that "Dr. C. was called before the Com. and Bro. White stated to him that owing to the lack of friends they had accepted his resignation."[8] They do not explain what was meant by "the lack of friends." However, in an article published in *Our Hope*, in which Campbell announces his resignation, he wrote:

I have had the great pleasure of organizing, in the face of considerable opposition, an institution of learning. ...

My duty has been faithfully performed and I have notified the Educational Committee that I can no longer serve them and the College, in the capacity of President, but have accepted another position at a very much larger salary and very much less opposition.[9]

When he wrote of "opposition," perhaps he meant opposition from people who did not think that Advent Christians needed their own college. However, that would have been an issue for a number of the presidents. It sounds more like he was being opposed by the board for some reason. In 1898, Clum was given the opportunity to turn in his resignation. He took it and resigned, but there is no explanation in the board minutes for why he was let go. However, there might be a hint in the *Our Hope* article that announced both the resignation of Clum and the hiring of Gordon as acting president. It made a plea for cooperation with the new president, urging "the *warm, cordial co-operation* of all friends of Mendota College. Do not handicap him with distrust or criticism. He is our brother in Christ, and a co-helper in this great work. He comes to help us, and brings all the strength and ardor and resolve of a consecrated heart and an educated, well-trained mind and brain [underlining mine]."[10] The underlined sentence in this quotation could be interpreted several different ways: people were being urged to cooperate with Gordon, because many had not done so with Clum; or some people were unhappy about Clum's dismissal and still supported him; or a number of people were unhappy about Gordon himself ascending to the presidency, thinking him unqualified, too divisive, etc. Clum's fundraising ability could also have been a factor. Without an Advancement Office, the president played a major role in fundraising, and Clum's abilities in this area may have been viewed as flawed, as he presided over one of the worst financial crises in the college's history. We will never know what the issue was, but it almost doesn't matter. This was not a good way for Gordon to start his presidency. However, with the financial crisis over, one would have thought that Gordon would have had clear sailing, but he too was relieved of the presidency after just three years, probably because of some inappropriate behavior toward a faculty member and some students. He was called before the board to explain his behavior, as were the recipients of his actions. In spite of the complaints against him, the board hired him for another year. However, he left long before completing this contract. The meeting in which the board renewed his contract was held in April of 1901, but he was gone before the next school year opened a few months later. The 1901–2 catalog lists Twining as "Acting President." There is no mention of Gordon leaving in the board minutes.[11]

The presidents that followed provided greater stability and less contentiousness. After a year serving as acting president, Twining was given the title of president, serving for another four years. There is much evidence that Twining was held in high regard. When he left, it was not because the board wanted him to leave, but because he was following his wife, who had moved to California to take care of her elderly, recently widowed father. In fact, the board was so sorry to see him go that they wrote a tribute to him and had it published. Dean became president in 1906, remaining in that position until 1911, when Jenks was elected president. It is not entirely clear why that happened. Perhaps because Jenks was such a fundraising dynamo and was literally making the move to Aurora financially possible, the board thought he should be the one to lead the college in its new location. Dean was offered a teaching position, so the board did not want to get rid of him altogether. However, the fact that he turned down the position and remained in Mendota rather than moving to Aurora with the college, suggests that there was some unhappiness on Dean's part.[12]

Presidential instability and frequent turnover were certainly weaknesses of the college, especially in its early years when it was such a fragile institution struggling to put down roots and survive. A situation in which presidents came and went relatively quickly was not a good advertisement for the college, and it probably created new divisions among Adventists, as well as college people, as individuals took sides. And even if there was a consensus among faculty and students that a president must go, however unlikely that might have been, it had to have been unsettling to try to get to know yet another new president—his personality and way of working with people, his policies, etc.—in a short period of time.

Another problem was the mindset of at least some Advent Christians. Many Adventists came from rural areas—the kinds of places that provided minimal educational opportunities. They also tended not to have much money. With this kind of background, they often were not in favor of spending anything but the absolute minimum at the college and did not always understand the needs behind some of the requests for funds or what constituted an adequate education for a minister. For example, as discussed in an earlier chapter, in 1900, students were campaigning for a gymnasium, by which they meant exercise equipment. An *Our Hope* reader wrote in, expressing his disagreement with the students' request. He argued that instead of using exercise equipment, they should get their exercise by raising some crops on a vacant lot and that

> the Adventist body would thus be saved the additional burden of furnishing the means for a gymnasium, as it seems to be enough for them to support the college proper. I hardly approve of any college students, much less Adventist students, getting exercise through the medium of a gymnasium. ... If it is wrong to exercise the mind by reading fiction, why is it not just as wrong to exercise the body in useless performances in a gymnasium?[13]

Fortunately, the students had a more expansive and holistic view of education than some Adventists, and ultimately they got some exercise equipment.

And, as Adventists, some people saw the imminence of Christ's return as a reason *not* to educate pastors or to provide just a Bible Training School rather than a college. Not only did they believe that there was not enough time for ministers to get an education before Christ returned, they often sounded defensive, usually saying that the old-time preachers had not been educated and they had done just fine. They believed that all that was needed to preach was a call from God and a fire in the belly. They seemed to think that getting an education became a replacement for a call from God. College people always denied this, saying that both were needed. Nevertheless, some opponents of education for Adventist ministers called a school like Mendota College a "preaching factory." Not surprisingly, many of the people who sounded defensive about ministerial education were themselves older preachers who had not gotten one. One eighty-five-year-old man wrote, in *Our Hope*, that "our young preachers must not get it into their heads that because they come from Mendota they must do all the preaching, and break themselves down in a few years, or that no one has a right to speak unless he hails from Mendota College. They must not think that our old veterans are old fogies, who must keep back and let the Mendota boys take the stand."[14] This man was not a preacher himself, but he had helped to build a number of churches in Wisconsin. Although he wrote some good things about the college in this piece, they had an edge, and at times, this edge revealed his resentment toward young, college-educated ministers, as in the quotation above. Another man, even before the college opened, wrote to *Our Hope*, objecting to an Advent Christian college. After making the Christ-is-coming-soon argument, he too revealed his bias against educated clergy in general when he stated, "Is it not a fact that unlearned men, all on fire with the Spirit of God, are more successful as evangelists than the 'College bred' preachers?"[15] College supporters found themselves occasionally responding to these arguments throughout the Mendota era.[16]

Also, some Advent Christians disliked anything that looked too secular or worldly. For example, when it was announced, just months into the college's life, that the music department would be teaching the banjo and violin as well as giving a concert, a man wrote to *Our Hope*, stating just how shocked he was by this. College leaders then had to reassure people that such things were not sinful. Then, in 1895, when Emmons was raising money for a remodeling of the college building, including new windows, he referred to them as "memorial windows." Apparently some people read this term as meaning that Mendota College was raising money for "an *unnecessary expense* to put in some kind of a merely *ornamental* window in the college in memory of some friend, living or dead."[17] One person, reacting to the term "memorial windows," even said that they represented "idolatry and hero-worship."[18] An *Our Hope* editor had to clear up the confusion by writing that the windows were simply new, inexpensive, windows that were needed to replace the old, broken and worn-out ones. He explained that "they are called 'memorial windows' because each one thus given will serve as a memorial of its giver or of someone in whose name it may be donated."[19]

It also appears that there was some overall opposition to Mendota College, although it is impossible to determine exactly how much. The school was seen by some Adventists as somehow suspect, especially religiously. Hints of that are sprinkled in *Our Hope* articles over the years. One minister, who had spent a term studying at the college, wrote an article praising it but also noted this problem: "I am aware that there has been some feeling of distrust regarding the college and its work, on the part of some of our brethren in Minnesota. As one who has seen its work and been benefited by its advantages, I wish to speak in its favor and interests."[20] Another man had a similar experience. After visiting the college, he declared it "a grand success" and urged people to go and see it for themselves. He then gave some advice: "Do not heed disparaging reports from those who think no good can come from Mendota. It is wiser and safer to examine for one's self."[21] And another student heard a negative remark about the college, which proved not to be true when he got there, and so he mentioned this in an *Our Hope* article in hopes of debunking such erroneous ideas about the school:

> Shortly before coming [to Mendota] I was told that Mendota College was not what it should be, and I hardly knew whether to come or not, and I would never have known what I do had I not come and seen for myself. Now I wish to say to anyone who may be hesitating, that Mendota College is all right. I have lived in many different places, and have seen a few churches. ... If all church people would show the godliness and love one for another that is shown among the students of Mendota College this world would be a much pleasanter place to live in than it is.[22]

At least some of the opposition came from those who believed that Mendota College was not teaching purely Advent Christian doctrine. In 1909, Jenks mentioned in passing that some Advent Christians in Wisconsin had doubts about the college for this reason until he preached at their campmeeting:

> If I mistake not, before the campmeeting began some of our brethren were somewhat fearful that Mendota College was not strong on Adventual doctrines. After I had preached each evening and taught a large class in Bible study every day, even the "old hands" concluded that I had not departed from the faith. ... Wishing to express this feeling, and to publish to our people their confidence in our college, the resolution referred to was written and adopted.[23]

Not only had Jenks changed their minds about the college, he had done this so completely that the campmeeting decided to state their support for the school formally and publicly.

At times the suspicions that some Adventists had about Mendota College were expressed more concretely. Some people were questioning the fact that the school was teaching science, fearful that scientific knowledge would conflict with and undermine Adventist beliefs. The president, B. J. Dean, pushed back on that in one *Our Hope* article, posing the kinds of questions that people were asking and then answering them. The questions he asked and then responded to were: "Are things taught in Mendota College that an Adventist does not need to know? ... Are there not things taught in our school that an Adventist would be better off without knowing? ... Is there not danger in studying some of the scientific subjects, such as Geology, for instance, that our young people will be led to doubt the Bible and perhaps become infidels? ... What textbooks do you use, and are there not errors in them?" Dean defended the teaching of science in each of his responses and then wrapped it up with a religious reason for studying the sciences. He noted that the sciences most likely to be objected to by Adventists are those concerning nature—geology, astronomy, etc., yet "these very studies are of the highest importance to one who is to be a minister" because they enriched ministers' understanding of God's wondrous creation. However, he also reassured people that the college was not embracing all that modern science had to offer. Some subjects were unacceptable: "There need be no fear as to consequences of studying any of these subjects in Mendota College. *Science and the Bible are not in conflict.* Of course there is a great deal of so-called science that is not science, and much of this is not in harmony with the word of God. None of these false sciences have a place in Mendota College, and we trust they never will have."[24]

Some Adventists even expressed concern about the textbooks that were being used in the school's courses. Dean addressed this concern in at least one *Our Hope* article: "Our text books are not written by Adventists, and so occasionally something may be found in them not in accord with our views, but if such things are in all our text books, where would you prefer to have your son or your daughter meet them, in a school like ours, where the false teaching can be, and is, pointed out and corrected, or in a school where nothing would be said to discourage its acceptance?"[25] Six years later, in 1909, the textbook issue was still alive. An *Our Hope* article appeared that was about the publication of Jenks's latest two books, which, due to the lack of Advent Christian texts, he had written for use in the Bible Training School. He had even borrowed money to pay for their printing himself, in hope that there would be enough sales to reimburse him. The article's author urged people to buy the books:

> If several hundred of our people would send in their orders for
> the books, our brother would feel justified in preparing copy for
> another book, to be published early next summer, thus adding to
> our literature and helping to keep our presses busy. Here, also, is an
> opportunity for those brethren who have been criticizing the books
> used by the college and the Correspondence Course, to help our own
> publishers to bring out books unobjectionable to us.[26]

It is not known how many people did this and whether the criticism of textbooks stopped at this point, but in any case, misgivings about the college among some Advent Christians persisted into the last few years at Mendota (and beyond).

How Was Mendota College Able to Survive?

Given all the weaknesses and problems of Mendota College that have been documented in this book, an important question comes to mind—how did Mendota College ever survive long enough to move to Aurora? It did, and that accomplishment is remarkable, especially since so many small colleges founded in the nineteenth century did *not* last beyond a few years. As with any historical question, there are multiple answers, although some are more important than others. But when all is said and done, it came down to people— both individuals and groups. In the end, enough people came forward in various ways to counteract the many obstacles that the college faced.

One of these groups was the school's leaders—the president, the treasurer, and especially the board. Many of them showed that they could deal with a large amount of stress and frustration without giving up on the institution. Fundraising was the most frustrating task of all. Time after time, calls went out for funds to balance the budget, but with disappointing results. Board member J. W. Emmons, a medical doctor and the school's major fundraiser, especially felt the stress of fundraising among a people who seemed reluctant to give to the college. For example, in late May of 1901, he reported in *Our Hope* that a mere three donations had come in since his last fundraising report more than a month earlier, and the next year, he reported one month that there had not been a single donation since his last report two weeks earlier.[27] At times he would get so frustrated that he felt compelled to chastise *Our Hope* readers for not responding to his pleas for funds, and in one article, he even got personal, noting the impact of this on board members, especially himself:

> What can be done *without* the necessary funds to pay our bills as we go along? Do you realize the load it places upon your Educational Board to run such a school as ours without means to pay our bills as we go? ... Do you know that the raising of funds for Mendota College occupies more of my reserve force than all my other duties put together? and [sic] simply because it takes so much planning and urging. ... The time I give to my practice I get pay for, but my time spent for our school I do not get one cent for, nor do I expect pay for it in the future. All I expect and want is your money, to run your school with, and your good will to go with it.[28]

This stress hit Emmons especially hard, but it was difficult for others as well. Treasurers had to pay the bills, so they often spoke up about the need for funds, and sometimes their articles hinted at the stress they were feeling, as with this terse statement written by treasurer B. A. King in 1907: "Your treasurer is now unable to meet pressing demands for accounts already overdue because of no funds on hand."[29] The treasurers' reports were usually short, factual, and to the point, without the arguments or scoldings that Emmons often gave. However, even the treasurers sometimes chastised *Our Hope* readers when they were especially frustrated. In May 1904, Livingston said that if $500 was not raised by the end of the school year, just weeks away, the college would have to take out a loan. His frustration is evident in another part of this article, where he bluntly stated that we have been seriously disappointed since notifying the readers of "Our Hope" of the pressing needs of Mendota College. We really expected that when our good people found out that five hundred dollars are yet needed, they would respond at once. Outside of the College Day Offerings we have not asked for help this year, and we thought, surely since our people have not been annoyed this year with "begging" calls they will be prompt to send the needed help.[30]

And in times of dire financial crisis, the board especially had to have a high tolerance for constant stress over fundraising; in fact, at times they had to have a fierce determination to survive and nerves of steel. One of those times was the 1896–97 financial crisis. After debating what to do and considering such suggestions as cutting the spring term back two weeks (which they did) and stripping the college down to just the bachelor-degree programs and, presumably, the Bible Training School (which they didn't do), they defiantly moved "that in the name of the Lord we maintain the college."[31] The motion passed unanimously. However discouraged they must have felt, they took a leap of faith and continued to push forward, trying to raise more money to save the college.[32]

Also the college's president and board were very much hands-on. Since the college had next to no administrative structure or specialized offices to run the school, the president, treasurer, and board did many things themselves. This, of course, saved money and tied the board members more directly to the everyday life of the college. This was not a board whose members simply attended several meetings a year. As discussed in chapter eight, they wrote fundraising and student recruitment articles for *Our Hope*, and some people even traveled to raise funds for the college, including faculty members, like Jenks—even before the years of fundraising for the new campus. At times, individual board members were charged with doing decidedly un-board-member-like tasks, such as when they were tasked with buying a couple of cows to provide milk for the school's dining hall, and at times, like in the summer, took over the care of the resident cow. Even the more conventional jobs done by the board were tasks that one might expect college employees to do, such as when H. M. Robbins, chair of the college board, "was authorized to buy one rocker, six chairs, three iron bedsteads, and one study table for the dormitory, and a couch"[33] for a new women's dormitory—the house that replaced the one that was destroyed by fire. And in 1907, the board voted that President Dean and board member Forester "be a committee to repair or build a chimney for the kitchen stove."[34] It appears that no job was too small for a board member to do or oversee.[35]

Another group that was just as dedicated to the college and sacrificed more financially than board members was the faculty. The pay of college faculty in nineteenth-century America was notoriously low, and it was at its lowest at small colleges. Such places, especially religious schools like Mendota College, were mission-driven, so people still took these jobs. They wanted to make an adequate living, of course, but many saw a higher purpose for their teaching than just earning a living. And since these colleges often struggled financially, board members often thought that they could not afford to pay the salaries that other professional people received, even though in some cases, the pay was so low that it smacked of labor exploitation. Education historian Frederick Rudolph argued that

> essentially what was happening on the American college campus was the creation of a profession that was not expected, and finally not permitted, to enjoy or to aspire to the material pleasures and living standards that elsewhere defined American goals. An occasional institution revealed what a living salary might be: $1,500 at South Carolina in the 1800's and at Virginia in the 1820's; $2,000 at Harvard in the 1830's and $4,000 in the 1860's. But the overwhelming majority of American college professors knew such salaries as these: $600 at Dartmouth in 1805, $600 at the University of Georgia in 1815, $700 at Bowdoin in 1825, $700 at Williams in 1835, $600 at Wabash in 1845, $775 at Emory in 1855, $600 at Denison in 1865.[36]

An historian of the Christian college, William C. Ringenberg, noted that in the 1860s, Kalamazoo and Olivet paid their professors in the range of $600–$700 a year, while the Kalamazoo president earned $1,500 a year, and this was an improvement on the salaries paid at western colleges just a few decades earlier. However in this same decade, Princeton was paying its professors $2,100 plus a rent-free house to live in. In other words, Ringenberg found great differences in faculty and presidential salaries across the country: "Faculty salaries varied widely from reasonable levels in the better eastern colleges to bare subsistence wages in new, struggling institutions in the West."[37] All of his examples of faculty salaries, like Rudolph's, came from decades earlier than the 1890s, yet most of those salaries were higher than those at Mendota College in the 1890s and 1900s. Another historian of American higher education, John R. Thelin, cited a series of newspaper articles, published in 1905, during the Mendota era. Their subject was exploited workers and the miseries of their lives. It discussed such groups as coal miners, workers in the dangerous meatpacking industry, sweatshop workers in the garment industry, oppressed African American workers in the Jim Crow South, and exploited immigrant workers. Included in this list was a "professor's wife," who had to make do on the lowly pay of a college professor. The series stated that a professor at a small college in the Midwest earned just $1,100 a year and, on such a salary, had a hard time making ends meet. No faculty member's salary at Mendota College ever reached $1,000, not to mention $1,100.[38]

The college board minutes give most, but not all, of the annual salaries, so a comparison can be made with other schools. For the 1898–99 school year, faculty were generally paid $400. This figure slowly inched up for the top people to $500–$550, but no one made $600 or more until 1909–10. The presidents also were underpaid. Campbell and Sibley were paid $1,000 and Clum, $900, which were low for the 1890s. However, after the financial crisis of 1896–97, the presidential salary plummeted. Once Clum left, shortly after this crisis, Gordon became president with a salary of just $600, in 1898. He remained at that figure for the entire three years that he was president. Twining also was paid $600, but in the second part of his tenure, his salary was moved up to $750. Dean entered the presidency with a salary of $700, was moved up to $750, and by 1909–10—the last year for which there are figures, received around $862. That year was the first that faculty were given an across-the-board raise, and presumably the president received it as well. The raise was a healthy 15 percent, but even with that, Dean, in one of the last years of the Mendota era, was paid under $900—less than the salaries of the first two presidents. Also, faculty were not always paid for extra work. In 1897–98, Mary Robbins, probably a relative of board member H. M. Robbins, was paid $400.

She was both a teacher and the college treasurer. The next year, when she was no longer treasurer, she also was paid $400, so it would seem that she had not been paid an additional amount for her work as treasurer.[39]

Was Mendota College the lowest-paying school around? No, it was not. Denominational colleges tended to pay substantially less than state schools and private, nondenominational colleges. In 1908, board member Forester wrote an *Our Hope* article that reported on a recent study of faculty salaries at denominational colleges. H. S. Prichett, chair of the Carnegie Foundation for the Advancement of Teaching, stated in this report that "in more than one hundred of the colleges that have furnished statistical information the average salary of a teacher is less than $1,000 a year, and in seventeen of these the average salary is $500 or less."[40] Prichett went on to argue that denominations should have fewer colleges so that they would be stronger and be able to pay better wages. Forester rejected Prichett's premise that good teachers could be acquired only if they were paid good salaries, responding that "from a secular and business standpoint the contention of Dr. Prichett is certainly true, but it takes no account of the religious zeal and the Christian sacrifice that in all ages have produced much of the noblest educational and religious work." This, of course, was the normal response to low teacher pay—that this profession had a higher calling. Forester then pointed out that this report showed that "not a few institutions are paying even less to its professors than is Mendota College, but that is no reason why we should not more fully compensate our teachers than we are now doing, as soon as possible. I do not believe that our people half understand the competency of the present faculty of Mendota College, nor the deep personal interest in the work and the great labor and pains they are giving to it."[41] That may well have been true, but the bar for this comparison was set pretty low. Even college leaders admitted that faculty were underpaid. In 1907, the year before this report was published, Forester admitted, in an *Our Hope* fundraising article, that the college was run on just $6,000 a year, thanks in large part to the faculty who worked for such low salaries—many of them salaries that were around half what faculty members would be paid at other schools, given their credentials. Sometimes a faculty member knew for a fact that he could earn more money elsewhere. In 1901, Twining accepted a position on the Mendota College faculty even though his previous salary had been nearly three times what he would make at Mendota.[42]

And, as discussed in chapter eight, not only was faculty pay low, it sometimes was delayed, due to a lack of funds, or its delay was threatened if enough funds were not raised soon, especially when the college was in serious debt. On more than one occasion, it seemed like faculty pay was the last financial obligation to be satisfied. This was especially true during the 1896–97 financial crisis. A December 23, 1896, fundraising article noted that the school needed $700 for operating expenses for the fall term, which had just ended. The author added that this amount was mainly for faculty salaries and a bit of coal. Since this article was written in late December and $700 was a large amount of money for the college to raise quickly, it would have taken weeks into the new year and new term before the faculty received all of their pay for the fall. And, as it turned out, they did not receive it right away. In mid-January, an article appeared that explained what had happened:

> You will recollect that the expenses of the college for the coming year have been reduced about $600; and that all this saving was caused by the instructors of our school giving the college this amount out of their wages. I assure you this is no small gift from each one of them. It is far larger than any one of our people has done this year towards paying the college debts. When this proposal was made to our teachers it was on the ground that we should do our best to pay them every dollar we now owe them, and that the coming school-year wages should be paid at the end of the school year and as much sooner as we could.[43]

It is not known whether the faculty ever received their full pay for that school year. In another fundraising article, Emmons stated that "our teachers must have their pay on or before the end of the school year."[44] A week later, Emmons reported that all the school's debts had been paid, except for faculty pay for that school year. This continued to be a problem in periods of substantial college debt. In May 1912, the month after the college moved to Aurora, Jenks reported that due to the emphasis on fundraising for the new campus, fundraising for operating costs had been neglected, the result being "that there is not a dollar in our treasury with which to meet the salaries of our teachers, for the two months closing our school year."[45] Even in years that did not see the worst of the financial crises, uncertainty sometimes existed as to when faculty would receive their final pay for a term or the school year. In mid-May of 1902, Emmons urged *Our Hope* readers to send in donations to pay off the last $200 that was needed that school year, so that the "teachers shall have what is due them."[46] Once again, it would seem, teachers were being paid last. It is not known how often during a term that faculty members were given a paycheck, but it does seem that at times, usually at the end of a term, their pay was delayed.[47]

And faculty at the college worked hard for their pay. If Jennie Twining's schedule is any indication, their workload was heavy. In 1903, she laid out her typical daily schedule for *Our Hope* readers, noting that it left her with just around six hours of sleep:

6:30 — Breakfast

8:00–8:45 — Extra class work done on campus

8:45–9:00 — Chapel

9:00–Noon — Classes

1:00–4:00 — Classes

4:00–5:50 — Extra class work done on campus

7:00–10:00 — Class preparation for eight classes

10:00–Midnight — Grading and catching up with work

In addition, as a wife in this age of polarized gender roles, she had many domestic chores on top of this. Why did she publish her schedule? This becomes clear upon reading what she wrote toward the end of the article: "Yet do some say: 'The teachers receive *such big* pay!' My dear friends, do you realize that the teachers in your college are working for about half of what they can get elsewhere?"[48] It must have been galling to work so hard for so little pay while having acquired a level of education, however limited it seems today, that the vast majority of Americans, especially women, did not have in this era.

It has been stated elsewhere in this book that the faculty of Mendota College were truly dedicated to their work, but it is worth restating it within the context of explaining how the college survived. They knowingly worked for pay that was low, even by the standards of the day. And that paltry sum, at times, was delayed or there was the possibility of not receiving it in a timely manner because of budgetary deficits. This uncertainty about when they would actually get paid must have produced much stress, especially for those with families to support. Also, faculty often had extra jobs at the school, sometimes at no extra pay. This helped the bottom line of the college, but it must have made the financial lives of faculty members somewhat precarious (although perhaps it helped that they lived in a small town where the cost of living was lower). And along with a heavy load of teaching and other responsibilities, they spent a lot of time with students outside the classroom, supervising their various clubs and school activities. These long hours were then rewarded with low pay. The college's tuition had to be kept low to successfully recruit students. To achieve that, salaries had to be kept low. In short, the faculty contributed to the viability and survival of Mendota College with their extensive, underpaid labor, which, in effect, subsidized the college. And their sense of mission and working for a higher power kept many of them working at the college. This is not to say that faculty were always content with their low pay. It is hard to believe that there was not at least some grumbling about their poor compensation. For the 1909–10 school year, one of the last years in Mendota, a 15 percent increase was given to all the faculty members (except one person). This appears to be the only time that this happened, suggesting that there was faculty pressure to do it (although it is impossible to know for certain, since the board minutes just state that the motion to raise the salaries was passed). At least once, a faculty member, George Dewing, pressed the board to raise his salary. At the end of the first full year, Dewing appeared before the board and said that he could not work for less than $40 a month. The board rejected Dewing's request for $40, but decided that he, as the head of the Commercial Department, would receive 95 percent of its tuition. Dewing then stayed another year. However Dewing, as an Advent Christian minister and head of a department, probably had more influence than some faculty. For the most part, it seems that faculty made do with their pay and found psychic or spiritual compensation to complement their low salaries.[49]

Another important group that contributed to the survival of Mendota College was the small donors—those who did not have the means to make large gifts to the college but faithfully gave time and again. Most of the school's donors fell into this category. Sometimes these supporters even sent a small gift to the college multiple times in the same fundraising cycle. The majority of Advent Christians did not give any amount of money to the college, and even the majority of *Our Hope* subscribers did not, but the relatively small group of people who did give, some of whom could even be described as poor, generally could be counted on to faithfully give something to the college every year. No matter how many hundreds or even thousands of fundraising cards for the College Day offering were sent out, year after year, just six hundred cards or so came back with donations, most of them small. College officials realized that this situation existed and sometimes used it in their fundraising articles, like one published in 1906. In this article, board member Forester urged those who had not given anything to the college to send in a donation so that those who had been doing more than their fair share could do a bit less. The sacrifices made by at least some of these small donors were inspirational, so much so that college leaders sometimes showcased them in their fundraising articles, no doubt hoping that such stories would inspire or perhaps create guilt in those with greater surplus incomes who did not support the college. For example, in 1896, Emmons wrote about two people of very humble means who made small donations but made them multiple times. "I received a letter to-night from Sister Mary A. Tibbets with her third donation of one dollar towards our 'College debt,' and also one from Sister Lizzie S. Wallace, a daughter of Sister Tibbets', with her second donation of one dollar for the same purpose. The latter donor earns her money by sewing with her needle, but she says she expects the Lord will send her more work to make it all up."[50] And in 1898, Emmons told readers about Mary A. Bloom, a seamstress, who sent in $2. Emmons thought that this was probably more than she earned in two days.[51]

Ministers were another group of low-income people who gave to the college—sometimes also at great personal sacrifice. As a group, Advent Christian pastors were a poorly paid lot. Many of them headed up small churches whose members could not pay much for a minister, and so some pastors lived in poverty or near poverty. In 1896, Forester, a minister who served on the boards of both the college and its parent, WACPA, wrote a fundraising article to raise funds for the denomination. In this, he mentioned the ministers who were giving from their meager resources to support the church, describing them as "men who receive scarcely any salary, men who have large families, men who have no property upon which to rely in coming years, or in times of sickness, men who had already spent more to get to campmeeting than many people contribute in a year."[52] And in 1910, Emmons wrote about one minister, William C. Churchill from Crouseville, Maine, who gave to the building fund for the new campus in Aurora. Although he earned just $6 a week, he gave $25 to the college—more than a month's salary. And this was not even a pledge, to be paid over several months. He sent the school a check.[53]

Relatively small donors were important to Mendota College, as college leaders pointed out time after time, and throughout the Mendota years those were the people who, by and large, supported the school. Occasionally, especially in a time of financial crisis, a large check would come in, like in 1897, when suddenly it was announced that the college's debt had been paid off: "All debts incumbent upon our college have been lifted and a handsome donation of a cool $1000, received during the campmeeting, with other large donations in prospect, has gladdened the hearts of our Educational Board. ..."[54] But generally it was the middling folks, and even some among the poor, who supported the college. Even the wealthy Charles Eckhart, who donated goods (like a piano) and gave donations for operating costs larger than what most other people could afford, was not writing huge checks for the school before the fundraising campaign for the Aurora campus. Board member Forester noted the role of different types of donations in 1908, writing that "it is desired to meet the current expenses with the smaller contributions, while the larger ones are used in erecting more suitable and much needed buildings, for which we are planning."[55] The big financial need during the Mendota period was for operating funds, not for constructing buildings. It was not until the campaign to raise money for the Aurora campus came along in 1910 that large gifts became especially important. Whether monetary gifts were for the annual operating costs or special-but-limited projects, like remodeling or painting the college building, there were never enough small donors, and some people gave multiple times while the majority of *Our Hope* readers gave nothing. This small base of loyal donors, who could only make small gifts to the college but who could be counted on to do so regularly, was critical to the school's survival, and college officials constantly tried to expand it. The school's operating costs were largely paid for by these people, as individuals and as members of church-organized groups, so their small donations were important. They chipped away at the school's debt and contributed to the gradual amassing of funds for special projects. Furthermore, there may not have been many, if any, larger donors without the smaller ones. No large donor wanted to sweep in and pay for things all by himself, especially on an ongoing basis. He or she wanted to be assured that the college had the financial and moral support of many people.[56]

By and large, it was the smaller donations that kept the college going for nineteen years, but it was a handful of benefactors—Eckhart first among them—who made the move to Aurora possible. But even here, Eckhart was not willing to just write some large checks. He doled out his donations for the Aurora campus only after it was demonstrated that the Advent Christian people were willing to do their part. As early as the fall of 1908, Eckhart offered $10,000 to the college to provide it with more space. That began a movement that culminated in the decision to leave Mendota instead of constructing a new building there. After the decision for Aurora was made for the second time, he promised an additional $1,000. However, he wanted $30,000 raised before he wrote the $10,000 check. The next year, in 1911, he pledged another $10,000, to be paid when the building fund reached $60,000. In 1911, when the school's leaders decided that they would not finish off the top floors of the three Aurora buildings because there was not enough money to do so, Eckhart urged them to completely finish the structures, and ultimately donated $4,000 of the $5,000 needed to do that. And he paid for all of the furnishings for the three buildings, costing him over $10,000. When all was said and done, Eckhart donated around $40,000 to build the new campus. (This is the equivalent of $1,061,212 in 2018 dollars.) It is hard to believe that the move to Aurora could have been made without his generous gifts, something that Jenks and others believed as well. Three weeks after the move, in an *Our Hope* article, Jenks thanked the Eckharts for all that they had done to make the new campus possible: "We hereby publicly thank our Brother most heartily for this generous help. He and Mrs. Eckhart have stood by from the very beginning, and have cheered us on in every right way. Had it not been for their help we do not think that the buildings could possibly have been secured. We give thanks to our Heavenly Father and to them for this excellent co-operation."[57] Eckhart died just three years after the college had moved to Aurora and had health problems in the preceding years—so much so that he made a point of saying, concerning his second $10,000 pledge, that if $60,000 in cash was raised, it would be paid by December 31, 1912, whether he was alive or dead. He clearly knew that he did not have a lot of time left and chose to leave a legacy in the form of a new campus for the college. D. A. Davis was another major benefactor of the college campus in Aurora. He gave around $14,000 to the Aurora building fund, providing more than enough money to build Davis Hall, the women's dormitory. William A. Wilkinson was the other major donor for the Aurora campus. His monetary contributions were impressive as well—$500 plus five thousand shares of mining stocks that were worth about $14,000—and so the men's dormitory was named after him.[58]

In the late Mendota years, Davis and Eckhart gave much smaller donations, like $100 here and there, some of them going toward operating expenses. But their largest gifts, like Wilkinson's, were for the Aurora campus. Therefore, it cannot be said that they helped the college survive in times of financial crisis. It can be argued, however, that their much larger contributions for the move to Aurora did save the college, because if the school had not moved, it may very well have withered and died. Jenks certainly believed this, saying in 1910, during the Aurora fundraising campaign, that "if we cannot provide a suitable school for our young people and for the training of our workers, then we might as well disband, for there is sure to be disintegration among our people and a constant loss from our membership of our brightest and best young men."[59] The implication here is that, looking forward, Mendota could not provide a "suitable school." Aurora, Jenks believed, would give the college a new lease on life and provide the conditions that could produce a bigger and better school.[60]

The smaller, but still substantial, monetary gifts of benefactors throughout the years were important also. Although college leaders wanted many small gifts as a show of support for the school, they urged those who could afford it to give larger ones as well. It must have been frustrating and discouraging to nickel-and-dime their way through the process of raising funds to eliminate a debt or pay for a specific project. One *Our Hope* article noted that just when the school fundraisers were feeling discouraged about all of the small donations that they were receiving for the Aurora campus, along came a large one, a $2,000 gift from D. A. Davis. Such gifts not only helped the college to reach its fundraising goals more quickly, they were morale boosters. Sometimes larger gifts, around $100 or so and, less frequently, around $1,000, came from board members, and sometimes they came from people who were simply friends of the college. In addition to most board members playing a hands-on role, at least some of them were generous in their giving as well. For example, during the 1896–97 financial crisis, H. M. Robbins, who two years later would be chair of the college board, pledged $100 if five other people also made a $100 donation. At least two other people pledged $100 each, one of them being D. A. Davis. Then, of course, the 1896–97 debt was finally paid off by an unnamed donor's gift of $1,000. Probably the best example of donations from friends of the college was the 1896 $100 gift for a new, fully equipped chemistry lab from two brothers—Zimri and Marsden Ames. The next year they provided the funds for what was called the physical laboratory. Before this, there had been no laboratories at all in the college building, so these gifts were important to the science program. These mid-range benefactors were important, in that they often paid for things, like a chemistry laboratory, that the college needed but could not afford to buy, and accelerated the fundraising.[61]

All of the above groups contributed to the financial survival of Mendota College, yet these are groups that all small colleges, to varying degrees, had to support them financially at the turn of the twentieth century. However, two additional groups stand out as being not only critically important in keeping the college going financially, but distinctive to Mendota College—women, especially the Helpers' Union, and the Western Advent Christian Publication Association (WACPA).

Women, both as individuals and in groups, were praised time and again for their tireless work in supporting the college. Three times in 1903, Milton Livingston, the college treasurer, praised women's contributions in *Our Hope*. In February, he wrote that "when I say that Mendota College is largely supported by women, I know whereof I speak. Many are the 'widow's mites' that come in as College Day offerings. ... We feel sure that with the prayers, the sympathy and the general support of the mothers of our Israel our school will not go down. God bless these mothers and sisters in Christ."[62] In May, Livingston wrote an article that had a chastising tone because people had not responded to his earlier pleas for the $500 that the college needed by the time the term ended in just a few weeks. However, women were not the ones he was scolding because he also wrote: "I stated sometime [sic] ago that Mendota College was supported largely by our women. This is true. Look over the list of names in 'Our Hope' of those sending College Day Offerings."[63] Then at the end of that year, Livingston wrote an article specifically on women as supporters of the college, informing *Our Hope* readers that, every year, the College Day offering from the all-women Helpers' Union was the largest one that the college received. And beyond the Helpers' Union contributions, a sizeable portion of College Day offerings came from women. Not only did many women give, they tended not to be among the affluent donors. Livingston noted that "we have learned to depend largely upon women in humble circumstances for the support of our school; women who not only forego luxuries, but many of the necessaries and comforts of life."[64] Livingston even compared what many of these humble women had given to the college to what some affluent men he knew had given, although he mentioned no names. The next year, in 1904, Jenks also praised the women in an *Our Hope* fundraising article, stating that "the Helpers' Union has raised more money for our educational work than any other one society in the middle West. It has been a constant source of help to our school and to students in need of help." He urged those churches that did not have a Helpers' Union to organize one. He then told his readers that "our women can do much that men cannot do, and they will raise money in places where men fail. Give the sisters a chance. 'Help those women.' "[65] Even a student understood the importance of female donors. In a 1907 student column, Harry Hanson, by way of a preface to announcing that a woman had died and left a $200 bequest to the Bible Training School, wrote: "All are aware that Mendota College is sustained by the small donations of many friends. In justice to the sisters of our A. C. faith we must state that these gifts are largely from them."[66] As these *Our Hope* articles illustrate, not only were women doing an impressive job of supporting the college, their praiseworthy efforts were sometimes used in fundraising to inspire others to do the same.

And women's contributions were important from the very beginning. Just a year after the college opened, the Helpers' Union was created, its goal being to raise funds for the Bible Training Department and "other benevolent interests connected with the college."[67] In 1909, the obituary of Elvira S.

Mansfield, the first and longtime president of the General Helpers' Union, noted that "it has been said that without the funds she secured through the H. U., Mendota College in its early struggle would not have been able to meet the expenses of the Bible Training department."[68]

As Livingston noted, many women *apart* from the Helpers' Union gave money and goods to the college. However, the Helpers' Union was an especially effective way to raise funds for the school. The General Helpers' Union was a regional (essentially midwestern, although it was called western) organization, but many Advent Christian churches formed their own branch, so the organization was not some distant group but the parent that gave direction and organized the giving at the local levels. This was an effective way to raise money because the fundraising took place within a structured organization, one that could efficiently rally and organize its members to give. This was important, for it seems unlikely that all of the women who gave to the college through the Helpers' Union would have done so if left to their own devices and, in many cases, would not have given as much. In 1899, the Helpers' Union decided to broaden its mission to include *all* benevolent, denominational work for women in the "West." It also tried to broaden organizationally as well. An officer of the General Helpers' Union wrote that the organization hoped that every Advent Christian church would form a Helpers' Union, and that churches having a women's missionary group and/or sewing circle would take on the name of Helpers' Union, so as to unite western Advent Christian women in their benevolent work. It is unknown how far this centralization process went, but even if not every church did this, some, no doubt, did, adding to the efficiency of fundraising.[69]

A 1908 project of the Mendota Helpers' Union is a good example of how an organization could raise money more effectively than college leaders simply asking people to give individually. At its April meeting, someone suggested that each member earn one dollar for the college cause, and then at the next meeting, each woman tell the group how she raised the money; the women agreed to do this. Apparently, this excited one woman so much that at the same meeting that the proposal was made, she had a brainstorm. Mrs. Forester, wife of minister and longtime college board member, B. Forester, decided that she "could charge Mr. F. for his laundry."[70] (Given Forester's extensive involvement in the running of the college, he probably did not object to being charged for one of his wife's domestic chores, but probably not every woman could get away with that.) Then, at the next month's meeting, the women told their stories: "Some ... began to peddle what they did not care to use themselves. Rags, eggs, cakes, fish, handkerchiefs, carrots, cookies, horseradish, milk, and strawberry plants. ... Others ... remained at home, planting potatoes, pressing clerical suits, washing, ironing, dressmaking, giving facial treatments, setting hens, piecing quilts, and doing general house work. ... One lady felt that she had earned her dollar year by year as a faithful housewife."[71] Members initially had not been very enthusiastic about doing this because it was hard for them to see how a dollar could be earned in just four weeks—a 1908 dollar being the equivalent of $27 in 2018. However, they tried, and the group managed to raise $16—the equivalent of $438 in 2018. This was an impressive amount for one month's work and probably a larger one than if each woman had simply been asked to donate. The fact that this was a group project and that each woman had to report on the amount she was contributing and how she had raised it had to have made a difference. The kind of group project that the Mendota group experimented with must have appealed to others, because it was adopted by the head organization, which notified women that at the 1911 Mendota campmeeting, the Helpers' Union would hold a meeting at which each woman would describe how she earned or saved the money—hopefully, a dollar—that she was giving to the building fund for the Aurora campus.[72]

The fundraising role of the Helpers' Union was critically important to the college. The organization provided a systematic way by which funds could be collected and turned over to the school on a regular basis. Some branches were more active than others, the Mendota branch being the most active and hands-on for obvious reasons. But, collectively, the many Helpers' Union branches, along with the head organization, provided a steady stream of funds from small donors to the college. The women of the Helpers' Union were an important part of the base of small donors discussed earlier in this chapter. Their importance was such that the few times that they did not do what they normally did, people noticed. In September 1910, when the Aurora fundraising campaign was well underway, the president of the General Helpers' Union wrote an *Our Hope* article telling the members that "the officials appealed to us on the campus [probably at the recent Mendota campmeeting], and asked that the Helpers' Union lend a more decided effort to help them this year. The Helpers' Union has really been a mother to Mendota College ever since its foundation, but in the last few years we have not been as united as we might have been."[73] And, donating to the college, even a dollar, could be a problem for women especially, given the fact that many women, if they were housewives, did not have a job outside the home or control the purse strings. One *Our Hope* article quoted a woman who, like Mrs. Forester, had this dilemma: "My husband carries the pocketbook. I can't give money, but if it might be butter, fruit or anything I have to deal with, I would gladly give it."[74] Her assumption seems to have been that her husband would not be willing to make a donation, so she would not even ask him to make one. Instead, she came up with a way to donate that was open to her because it came from her domestic realm. Because women often did not have their own money, they had to get creative, which makes their numerous monetary donations all the more impressive.[75]

The fundraising role of the Helpers' Union was probably most important, but the organization also helped the college in other ways as well, providing both goods and services. Helpers' Union women donated all kinds of things, especially to the dormitories and the food operation. They donated goods or raised money to buy them—furniture and other furnishings for the dormitories and the college building; various kinds of linens for student rooms and the dining hall; and food, which they usually grew and/or processed themselves. Women were precisely the right group to supply such items because, with their skills in baking, canning, and sewing, they could make many of these things themselves. They also provided services for the college, like upgrading rooms in the dormitories and the college building. Sometimes they upgraded rooms themselves and other times they raised money to help pay for services that others would do, like making repairs on the college building and painting its exterior. One example of such an upgrade took place in 1906, when the Mendota Helpers' Union took on the job of improving the appearance of the library, which also served as the president's office. This involved laying a hardwood floor, painting, and wallpapering. Another service was taken on, from time to time, by the Mendota Helpers' Union, mainly because it was the branch that was local to the college. This service was to collect funds for special events or projects, like in 1905, when the school was raising money to paint the college building. People were told to send their donations to the treasurer of the local Helpers' Union, not to the college treasurer. The reason for doing that is not clear, but whatever the reason, it was a service performed for the school. The goods and services that Helpers' Union women provided for the college were important because each item and service given was one less thing that the college had to purchase or do itself.[76]

The Helpers' Union provided another important service—helping the college recover from disaster. After a tornado struck the college neighborhood in 1903, people in Mendota and elsewhere rushed household goods and clothing to Mendota for those who had lost their homes and possessions. The Mendota Helpers' Union was put in charge of collecting these items and seeing that they were properly distributed to the people who really needed them—a large task. An even larger task came after the 1901 dormitory fire. Since the Twinings and the women living in the dormitory fled the rapidly moving fire wearing nothing but their nightclothes, they needed everything. Two days after the fire, Elvira Mansfield, president of the General Helpers' Union, took a train to Mendota to look over the situation for herself in order to see what the Helpers' Union could do to help. Under her leadership, Helpers' Union branches all over the Midwest sprang into action, collecting and sending linens and other necessities. And she appointed Mary Robbins Dillon to serve as the Helpers' Union Superintendent of College Supplies—her job being to "look after the needs of the rooms in the college and also of out-rooming students, especially those who have suffered loss from the fire."[77] In addition to its fundraising for the College Day offering, whose campaign was about to start, the Helpers' Union also took on the job of collecting funds for the school's fire-recovery effort. In fact, after the initial few weeks, Mansfield urged Helpers' Union members to send money rather than things so that the college could purchase exactly what was needed. In short, in times of disaster, the Helpers' Union was a hugely important support network that served as a kind of Adventist Red Cross. When crisis struck, the Helpers' Union took over whatever jobs they could do, like collecting goods and money, thus freeing up college officials to deal with all the other critical issues emanating from these terrible events.[78]

Another important way in which the Helpers' Union supported the college was its work with students. Of all the things that these women did in this area, the most important was helping to support students financially. At the core of the Helpers' Union mission was supporting the Bible Training School and its students, so aside from raising money for that program, the Helpers' Union members periodically took students under their wing, helping to support them financially as well as aiding in their adjustment to life away from home. Students in the religion program paid no tuition, but they had to live, and paying room and board was sometimes an obstacle to people attending the school. Generally, a Helpers' Union branch would offer to pay the board of one or more Bible students. But in 1896, the Mendota's Helpers' Union offered a more homey solution to providing board—it offered to feed a student in members' homes. This help for Bible Training School students was even offered publicly, not just through word of mouth. An 1895 quarterly report of the General Helpers' Union was published in *Our Hope*. It included this invitation—that anyone who was interested in attending the Bible Training School, but lacked funds, should contact the Helper's Union, and it would be glad to help. The college needed to acquire and retain as many students as possible to survive financially, so this support of Bible Training School students was an important contribution, both to the college and the denomination, which desperately needed more and better-educated ministers. In at least some cases, this support made it possible for students to attend and stay in school.[79]

It is not altogether surprising to see the crucial role that women played in supporting Mendota College and its religious mission. Women were closely associated with Protestantism in nineteenth-century America. Although they were not likely to be ministers, they often worked closely with them in various benevolent activities. For at least some women, raising money for the college meant not only soliciting funds from others, but giving of their own, meager resources as well. In other words, it required of them a certain amount of sacrifice. But their religion not only gave them a cause to work and sacrifice for, it gave them hope for a future reward. Shortly after the 1910 Mendota campmeeting, Ella Pullen, president of the General Helpers' Union, wrote an *Our Hope* article. Although this was a period of strained resources because of the fundraising for the Aurora campus and the school's growing deficit in operating funds, she noted that the Helpers' Union could probably take on the project of supporting one or more Bible Training

School students (by which she meant, presumably, *again*, since this had been happening for years). That would involve sacrifice on everyone's part, so she reminded her members of their coming reward: "We will all need to cut corners closer, although I noticed at campmeeting that others as well as myself were wearing garments several years old. We may wonder where we can scrimp any more. Never mind, sisters, we will have new garments in the Kingdom, and something new for our head, too. Best of all, it will be after Christ's own fashioning, if we *occupy till He comes* [italics mine]."[80]

The other major support for the college was even more distinctive. It was the fact that throughout the Mendota years, to varying degrees, the college had a "parent" in the form of the Western Advent Christian Publication Association (WACPA)—an entity that not only brought the college into the world but then nurtured and supported it. Over the years, Mendota College became increasingly independent of WACPA, but WACPA was always close by—serving at first as a parent and later a partner. It provided a backup system that most other Bible training schools and small religious colleges did not have. It is true that most small colleges that began in the nineteenth century were founded by a denomination and, no doubt, received support from them, but that is different from Mendota College's origins. It was founded, not by a national denomination whose headquarters were located in some distant city, but by a regional publication society, barely older than the college it created, which moved its headquarters to Mendota when it founded the school there. The relationship between WACPA and the college was close—both structurally and geographically. And WACPA had a stake in the college that went beyond the fact that it always owned the college's real estate, even after 1899, when the college became incorporated, and thus more independent.

The lives of the people in both WACPA and the college were extensively intertwined. They were mostly Advent Christians and so attended the same church—the Mendota Advent Christian Church, which was just a few blocks from the college campus. Probably many, if not most, of them were neighbors since many of the Advent Christians lived in the college and church neighborhood. As fellow church members, they not only worshipped together, they worked and raised money for the church together. Their families socialized, and it seems highly likely that they occasionally married one another. In other words, they had many informal interactions and friendships independent of their institutional connections. These bonds must have enabled them to understand each other's institution and its problems to a greater extent.

Perhaps most importantly, WACPA served as a buffer and a backup for the college when times were tough, especially financially. As discussed in chapter 8, WACPA loaned the college money, provided it with *Our Hope's* mailing list to use in the school's fundraising, and provided the college with its major communication tool—*Our Hope*—which it used to raise money, recruit students, and generally inform Advent Christians in the Midwest about what the school was doing. WACPA was not a perfect parent or, later, partner. It too had serious financial woes from time to time, and it had the same fundraising base as the college, which sometimes created problems, like in 1907–8, when WACPA built its own building in downtown Mendota. Because most Advent Christians in the Midwest did not have deep pockets, this fundraising campaign for WACPA created a serious deficit for the college. However, in spite of such problems, in the end, the WACPA-college relationship was helpful—both financially and in other ways. It was a backup in times of financial hardship. It also drew people to Mendota because not only was its headquarters in town, its annual campmeeting was held on the campus. This drew many Adventists to Mendota, who then got to see the college firsthand and interact with faculty and students. This was useful in educating visitors about the work of both the denomination and the college.

What did Mendota College Accomplish in Its Nineteen Short Years?

Nineteen years is not a long period of time when measuring an institution's overall accomplishments, but some can be identified for Mendota College. Its most important mission, and the reason that it was founded, was providing new Christian workers, especially ministers, for the denomination's churches. The total number of new ministers produced is not impressive. Just twenty-nine people graduated from the Bible Training School. At least three of these graduates were women, and women were far more likely to be workers in the church than actual ministers. And we do not know whether all of the twenty-six male graduates actually went into the ministry, although probably most of them did. However, even if all the graduates had been men who took on a pastorate, twenty-nine is a small number of graduates to produce in nineteen years, in what was considered the college's most important department. Nevertheless, some new ministers were produced by the school, and they were desperately needed by the denomination.[81]

The small number of graduates from the Bible Training School gives a misleading picture of what the college did for the Advent Christian ministry. Many more people attended the Bible Training School than graduation numbers would suggest. In May 1911, President Dean provided some statistics about the college in an *Our Hope* article, noting that over three hundred people had enrolled in the Bible Training School thus far. This figure was somewhat inflated, because it was the sum of each year's enrollment. If someone attended two years or more, they were counted more than once. But even if two-thirds of that number is removed, one hundred students are still a lot more than twenty-nine actual graduates, and Dean's figure did not include the last two terms of the college's time in Mendota. These short-term students came for a few weeks, a month, a year, etc. but did not stay long enough to get a diploma. They simply took specific religion courses that they thought would help them to become better ministers, and then they returned to their congregations. Many ministers were unable to afford to go to college for three years or simply could not afford to take that much time away from their churches, so they did what they could to improve themselves professionally on a short-term basis. The college encouraged this and saw it as part of their mission. It may not have produced more ministers, but it produced better ones. In 1904, board member Forester described the effect that this practice of being even a short-term student had on the Advent Christian ministry: "The College has had a wholesome tendency to stop the practice of licensing and ordaining almost any young man who could be persuaded to submit to it, whether there was any kind of literary qualification or not. It has also aroused a holy ambition on the part of our ministry generally to qualify itself more thoroughly for its great work."[82] Since many ministers did not have much, or any, advanced schooling, this was an important contribution made by the college.[83]

The college also provided what many nineteenth-century colleges provided—a secondary education to those young people who otherwise would not have had access to one or whose town provided an inferior education. Twenty people received diplomas from the Preparatory Department, but again, this number is misleading because many more than that enrolled in the high school program but did not graduate. The ideal, of course, was to prepare young people for college-level work with their completion of the secondary-level program and then funnel them right into the college coursework at the same institution. But even though not everyone could do this or chose not to do it, the college was providing further education to such people.[84]

Another accomplishment of the college was to furnish young people, especially young people in Mendota who were not Advent Christian, with a practical business education via the Commercial Department. Mendota was a small, somewhat isolated town lacking a lot of options to acquire this kind of education. The college provided a way for young people to get an education in the various aspects of business while remaining at home. This then enabled them to get the kinds of jobs that represented some upward social mobility. In fact, the college provided this to students in all the departments, especially if they graduated. For many of the college's students, who came from small towns in rural areas and were often poor, becoming a minister, a teacher, a business person, etc. represented the kind of upward social mobility that they would not have achieved otherwise.

"Occupy till I Come"

In the early 1890s, when the possibility of founding a school was being debated in the pages of *Our Hope*, some people had argued against it because of the core Adventist belief that Christ would soon return to earth. Advent Christians had been slow to organize a formal denomination, and some were reluctant to establish a college because of this belief, arguing that if Christ was returning soon, why spend time and money building institutions. But that was not the only way to look at it. Those who were arguing for a college quoted Christ when he told his followers to "occupy till I come"—to stay in the world, at their work, preparing for his return. They argued that although educating young people to become ministers delayed their entrance into the field, their studies made them better, more effective ministers once they got there. These modernizers, who defended the idea of forming a college, won the day, of course. However, throughout the Mendota years, at various times and in various ways and places, college supporters continued to urge Advent Christians to "occupy" until Christ's return, and for them, this meant educating people to become ministers for the denomination. The admonition to occupy came from board members, faculty, students, and other supporters. It was made in College Day speeches and countless *Our Hope* articles. It was made often enough that one can only wonder why. It suggests that there were still some people in the denomination who clung to the older idea that Adventists should not build permanent institutions and that to do so was proof that one was not a true Adventist.

Not surprisingly, given its prominence in the debate over whether or not to start a college, the "occupy" message was quite evident in the early years of the school. In January 1895, board member Stevens returned to this theme in his College Day address: "Christ is soon coming brethren. He is even now at the door. *He has said, 'Occupy* TILL *I come.'* Let us work as never before, in every department of Christian labor, and not forget to sustain Mendota College [italics in original]."[85] The college had been founded, and so occupying now represented a new job—the formidable task of *sustaining* the college. Students also wrote about "occupying." In 1898, student Fim Murra wrote that "I firmly believe we are near the close of this dispensation, and know we have no time to waste, yet I believe time spent in preparing one's self for the great work of rescuing a perishing world, is time *well spent*; and should the Lord come he will consider such as occupying."[86] And as late as November 1910, an *Our Hope* article, while looking back on the Mendota years, returned to this theme: "We are counting our blessings in thankfulness to God and our brethren, and planning, praying and purposing for larger usefulness while the Master tarries, for which we have His own significant charge, "OCCUPY TILL I COME [capitalization in original]."[87]

And so Mendota College occupied. The occupying argument won the day in 1892 when plans went into motion to create a new college. Then, it was a matter of sustaining the institution. By 1910–12, however, occupying took an even more modern form—making it possible for the college to get bigger and better to attract more students to prepare them for Christian work. Occupying meant moving to a new location.

Occupying and the Secularization of Aurora College

Once in Aurora, how did the meaning of "occupying" change as the college/university secularized over time, its ties to the denomination loosening considerably and then, for the most part, being cut? Aurora College remained a primarily Advent Christian school for its first two decades. By the late 1930s, the Advent Christian influence had declined somewhat as more local people attended Aurora College. School enrollment records show that the percentage of students residing in Aurora edged upward in the 1920s but was still no more than about 25 percent as late as 1927. However, by 1931, the percentage of students from Aurora hit 38 percent and in 1934 and 1936, an impressive 60 percent. This percentage dipped in the late 1930s but was still nearly half. Furthermore, these percentages represent something of an undercount because, in making these calculations, only those students who were listed as coming from Aurora were counted. There were other students listed as residing in Oswego, Yorkville, Geneva, etc., and they may very well have been non-Advent Christian, commuting students also. Although in many ways, the college was still very much an Advent Christian school, at least through the 1950s, it was gradually loosening its ties with the denomination and diversifying, which had become very apparent by the late 1960s and 1970s. The process had accelerated as a result of the GI Bill, which was passed after World War II. It enabled the young men who had served in the military to attend college because the government paid for it. This brought a wave of young men of varying backgrounds into colleges all over the country, including Aurora College, making the student population ethnically and religiously more diverse. And there were other indicators of these loosening ties. Aurora College stopped receiving funds from the Advent Christian denomination around 1970—when the denomination reorganized and brought all its parts together in its new headquarters, located in Charlotte, North Carolina. As time went on, fewer and fewer Advent Christian young people chose to attend the college. And after the retirement of Religion

Department theologians Moses Crouse, in 1978, and Asa Colby, in 1980, there would be no more Advent Christians in that department.[88]

On the surface, it seems like the occupying is over, but I would argue that another kind of occupying has taken hold—one not all that different from the message given by Christ in the Gospels. Among other things, Aurora University prepares students to minister to the social and cultural needs of a diverse America—through its majors in education, history, social work, nursing, the social sciences, and more. Today, Aurora University is far less homogeneous and less insular than Mendota College or the early Aurora College, and it no longer has a single religious stamp on it. But it has become fully engaged with the world, and so whether its students are Christian, Jewish, Hindu, or Muslim, its mission points toward the concept of servants ministering to others. The urgency of and even belief in Christ's imminent return have dissipated, but a major message of the Gospels is reflected in Aurora University's core values—that it is important to engage in lifelong learning and serve others.

However, today's Aurora University would not exist without its founding leaders. Those Advent Christians who established and guided Mendota College led it safely through some serious challenges in its nineteen years of existence—the burning down of a dormitory, a cyclone ripping through its campus, and always the issue of how to keep the college going financially. It was founded during the most serious depression up to that time in American history, students did not appear in the numbers expected, presidents came and went quickly in the first ten years, and, as early as 1894, the board minutes state that "the financial situation gave much perplexity."[89] For years to come, the financial situation would perplex and, at times no doubt, even frighten college leaders, but they held steady.

These leaders occupied, and not just in the sense of arguing that Adventist ministers be educated, even though they believed in Christ's imminent return. They and the faculty also occupied financially—doing multiple jobs for low pay, constantly promoting the college, and spending many hours with students outside of the classroom. For most of these people, Mendota College was their life. Keeping the college alive was a mission and a calling, and one that demanded sacrifices, including financial ones.

Throughout the Mendota years, its leaders argued that Adventist ministers would do a more effective job in bringing people to Christ if they were educated to meet the expectations and demands of a new and modern world. But to do that, they had to keep the college going, and they did. To read the primary sources of the Mendota years, with their many trials, is to wonder how they ever pulled it off. Not only did they keep Mendota College alive, in 1909–10, they embraced the audacious idea of building a whole new campus in Aurora. This they accomplished as well. In 1911, more than a year before the fundraising for the Aurora campus would be completed, Jenks wrote that "we have already raised the largest sum of money ever raised by our people at one time."[90] It seems like such a contradiction—their constant financial challenges throughout the Mendota era, followed by raising enough money to build a new campus. Granted, they had some help along the way, from a handful of large donors and the city of Aurora. Rational explanations can be made, and I have made them. But even for historians, along with evidence, there are usually some intangible factors that can never be "proven." The Advent Christians of Mendota would identify the major factor as faith that God would provide for them. During the financial crisis of 1896–97, Emmons wrote that "the college *must be sustained*."[91] It certainly took faith, as well as a high degree of commitment, determination, and hard work. And, as one Advent Christian minister wrote in a letter to Jenks in 1910, "it takes grit, grace and green-back[s] to build and sustain a College."[92] Jenks would have agreed. In the end, the college was sustained, and even the actors in this drama, although deeply grateful, seemed amazed. A writer of an *Our Hope* article in late 1910, in a nostalgic mood as the Mendota era was drawing to a close, described how difficult it had been to start and sustain the college:

> When we remember that our college started without funds, almost
> without encouragement; that many of our able preachers and early
> pioneers of the Advent movement were strongly prejudiced against
> college educated preachers and theological schools; that even
> the first Board of Directors who started the school were painfully
> dubious as to success, while strong brethren among us predicted a

brief existence and failure for our college; when we recall our own inexperience in college management and maintenance, the mistakes that were made, the difficulties that met us to be overcome, the fact but that a small portion of our people were interested in the work or contributed to its support: and then consider that Mendota College has continued for eighteen years, without lapse and without serious financial embarrassment, and today is in better condition than its founders ever hoped to see, with an excellent reputation for thorough teaching at some of our great universities, we are filled with amazement and gratitude to God.[93]

One might take exception to the exaggerations in this quotation, but the people of Mendota College did have good reason to feel proud of their accomplishments, the greatest of which was surviving a host of difficult problems and tragic events. This same writer, looking back on what the college had accomplished, noted that "what this school has accomplished in the past should teach us its possibilities in the near future, under better conditions, more general patronage, and better support."[94]

The future in Aurora looked bright to the author of this quotation, and rightly so. The decision to relocate and to do it in Aurora proved to be a good one, as was the decision to have Jenks lead the college. Jenks was the major transitional figure between Mendota and Aurora College. He served as the principal of the Bible Training School and personally raised most of the money for the new campus. After the move, he then gave Aurora College twenty-one years of stable leadership—a tenure that was longer than all the previous Mendota presidents combined. He, like so many others at Mendota College, had occupied. And their occupying—doing whatever they could, often at great sacrifice, to keep the college going—was their greatest accomplishment. The school's survival made possible the move to Aurora, where eventually a new kind of occupying would take hold—one which would benefit a wider array of people.

What would the founders of the college and Jenks think if they could see Aurora University today and understand the larger religious and social context of the changes that have taken place since their time? They would probably still mourn the disappearance of the Adventist message that was at the core of Mendota College and reflected in every aspect of its life. But hopefully they would also feel some pride about their role in starting, nurturing, moving, and expanding the school—in short, helping it to survive to become the flourishing institution that it is today.

"It is true that the coming of our Lord is very near but this is an important work, necessary to keep alive the cause of truth by providing an efficient ministry, and Christ has himself commanded us to *occupy* till he comes."
—Student Milton Livingston, 1898

The Presidents of Mendota College

President J. Oscar Campbell, 1892–93 (The Colby Archives has no photo of him.)

President Abial W. Sibley, 1893–94

President G. V. Clum, 1895–98

President M. L. Gordon, 1898–1901

President Nathan C. Twining, 1901–6

President Bert J. Dean, 1906–11

Notes

Chapter 1 – Mendota College and American Higher Education

1. *Annual of Mendota College: Catalogue, 1910–1911* (Mendota, Ill.: Our Hope Print, 1910), 89–91.

2. Christopher J. Lucas, *American Higher Education: A History* (New York: St. Martin's Griffin, 1994), 116–17; William C. Ringenberg, *The Christian College: A History of Protestant Higher Education in America*, 2nd ed. (Grand Rapids, Mich.: Baker Book House Co., 2006), 57; Frederick Rudolph, *The American College and University: A History* (1962; repr., Athens, Ga.: University of Georgia Press, 1990), 47; and John R. Thelin, *A History of American Higher Education* (Baltimore: Johns Hopkins University Press, 2004), 41–42.

3. Lucas, *American Higher Education*, 119–20; Ringenberg, *The Christian College*, 57–58; Rudolph, *The American College and University*, 54–57; and Thelin, *A History of American Higher Education*, 60–61.

4. Rudolph, *The American College and University*, 51–54, 56; Lucas, *American Higher Education*, 118; and Ringenberg, *The Christian College*, 57–59.

5. Rudolph, *The American College and University*, 47. See Donald G. Tewksbury, *The Founding of American Colleges and Universities Before the Civil War* (New York, 1932), 28.

6. Rudolph, *The American College and University*, 47–48. See Frederick. A. P. Barnard, *Two Papers on Academic Degrees* (New York: Macgowan & Slippers, Printers, 1880), 18.

7. Rudolph, *The American College and University*, 241–42, 244, 247–53, 257–58, 260; Lucas, *American Higher Education*, 146–48, 164–65; and Thelin, *A History of American Higher Education*, 74–78.

8. Lucas, *American Higher Education*, 170–72, 174–76, 179–80, 191–93, 210–12; Rudolph, *The American College and University*, 331–33, 335–36, 338–43, 346–47, 349–52, 398–400, 403–5, 417–24; and Thelin, *A History of American Higher Education*, 127–33.

9. Lucas, *American Higher Education*, 180–82, 186–87.

10. Thelin, *A History of American Higher Education*, 153.

11. Rudolph, *The American College and University*, 245, 329–34; and Thelin, *A History of American Higher Education*, 131–33, 151–53.

12. Nancy Woloch, *Women and the American Experience*, 4th ed. (Boston: McGraw Hill, 2006), 275–78, 283–86.

13. Ringenberg, *The Christian College*, 93, 92; Rudolph, *The American College and University*, 307–12; Thelin, *A History of American Higher Education*, 56; and Woloch, *Women and the American Experience*, 70–71, 88–92, 125–26.

14. Lucas, *American Higher Education*, 155; Rudolph, *The American College and University*, 314–18, 325–27; Thelin, *A History of American Higher Education*, 186; and Woloch, *Women and the American Experience*, 275–78.

15. Lucas, *American Higher Education*, 156–57, 205; Rudolph, *The American College and University*, 326; and Thelin, *A History of American Higher Education*, 143–44, 182–83.

16. Thelin, *A History of American Higher Education*, 143.

17. Thelin, *A History of American Higher Education*, 142–45; and Woloch, *Women and the American Experience*, 285–86.

18. Lucas, *American Higher Education*, 158–60; Ringenberg, *The Christian College*, 85–88; and Thelin, *A History of American Higher Education*, 186.

19. Lucas, *American Higher Education*, 162–63; Ringenberg, *The Christian College*, 89–90; and Thelin, *A History of American Higher Education*, 186.

20. Lucas, *American Higher Education*, 163–64; and Thelin, *A History of American Higher Education*, 102–3.

21. Lucas, *American Higher Education*, 162–63, 207, 209; Ringenberg, *The Christian College*, 88–89; Thelin, *A History of American Higher Education*, 186; and Woloch, *Women and the American Experience*, 281–82.

22. Lucas, *American Higher Education*, 204.

23. Lucas, *American Higher Education*, 204.

24. John T. Wahlquist and James W. Thornton, *State Colleges and Universities*, The Library of Education (Washington, D.C.: Center for Applied Research in Education, 1964), 4–5, quoted in Ringenberg, *The Christian College*, 82.

25. Ringenberg, *The Christian College*, 57–59, 67, 80–82, 91.

26. Gary S. Greig, "The History of Seminary Education and Theological Accreditation," http://www.cwgministries.org/sites/default/files/files/books/History-of-Seminaries-and-Accreditation.pdf; Geo. E. Cooprider, "College Bonds," *Our Hope and Life in Christ*, 7 February 1900, 4–5; E. Z. Ellis, "A Fraternal Epistle," *Our Hope and Life in Christ*, 7 January 1903, 10; W. Alford, "An Opinion," *Our Hope and Life in Christ*, 28 January 1903, 5; B. Forester, "Colleges and Education," *Our Hope and Life in Christ*, 11 February 1903, 5; Blanche Dick, "The Need of Education," *Our Hope and Life in Christ*, 6 January 1904, 3; J. Gilpen Byrd, "Should Our Ministry Be an Educated One?" *Our Hope and Life in Christ*, 21 July 1909, 2; and Ringenberg, *The Christian College*, 25–27, 65, 71.

27. Virginia Lieson Brereton, *Training God's Army: The American Bible School, 1880–1940* (Bloomington: Indiana University Press, 1990), 61–68.

28. Brereton, *Training God's Army*, 61–69.

29. Brereton, *Training God's Army*, 60–65.

30. Brereton, *Training God's Army*, 62–64.

31. Brereton, *Training God's Army*, 71.

32. Dale A. Robbins, "What People Ask about the Church: What's the Difference Between Elders, Bishops and Pastors?" The Victorious Network, http://www.victorious.org/cbook/chur42-elders-bishops-pastors; "Organization of the Local Church: The Office of Elders, Pastors, Bishops and Stewards," The Interactive Bible, http://www.bible.ca/ntx-elders-pastors-bishops.htm; Matt Perman, "What Is the Role of an Elder?" Desiring God, https://www.desiringgod.org/articles/what-is-the-role-of-an-elder; Stan Hudson, "Pastoral Roles in Adventism's First Century," *Ministry: International Journal for Pastors*, https://www.ministrymagazine.org/archive/1997/06/pastoral-roles-in-adventisms-first-century; William Abbott, "Nomenclature and Honorific Titles in Ellen G. White's Works," *Adventist Today*, http://atoday.org/nomenclature-and-honorific-titles-in-ellen-g-whites-works/; and Robert Hickey, "Honor and Respect: The Official Guide to Names, Titles, & Forms of Address," Seventh Day Adventism— The Protocol School of Washington, http://www.formsofaddress.info/SDAdventist.html.

Chapter 2 – Origins of a Denomination: The Millerite Movement

1. Ronald D. Graybill, "The Abolitionist-Millerite Connection," in *The Disappointed: Millerism and Millenarianism in the Nineteenth Century*, ed. Ronald L. Numbers and Jonathan M. Butler (Knoxville: University of Tennessee Press, 1993), 141–45; Clyde E. Hewitt, *Midnight and Morning: An Account of the Adventist Awakening and the Founding of the Advent Christian Denomination, 1831–1860* (Charlotte, N.C.: Venture Books, 1983), 84; George R. Knight, *Millennial Fever and the End of the World: A Study of Millerite Adventism* (Boise, Idaho: Pacific Press Publishing Association, 1993), 74, 117; and Francis D. Nichol, *The Midnight Cry: A Defense of the Character and Conduct of William Miller and the Millerites, Who Mistakenly Believed that the Second Coming of Christ Would Take Place in the Year 1844* (Washington, DC: Review and Herald Publishing Association, 1944), 189–90.

2. Everett N. Dick, *William Miller and the Advent Crisis, 1931–1844* (Berrien Springs, Mich.: Andrews University Press, 1994), xx, 84–95, 130–34; Hewitt, *Midnight and Morning*, 62, 71, 86–87, 93–95, 101–2; Knight, *Millennial Fever*, xxvii, 23, 132–34, 138–40, 159–61; Nichol, *The Midnight Cry*, 67, 143, 147, 156, 163–68; and David L. Rowe, *God's Strange Work:*

William Miller and the End of the World (Grand Rapids, Mich.: William B. Eerdmans Publishing Company, 2008), xiii–xiv, 115.

3. William Miller, Wm. Miller's Apology and Defence (Boston: Published by J. V. Himes, 1845), Second Advent Library, vol. 41, Jenks Memorial Collection of Adventual Materials, Aurora University, Aurora, Illinois, 6.

4. Miller, Apology and Defence, 11–12.

5. Miller, Apology and Defence, 16.

6. Miller, Apology and Defence, 17–18.

7. Miller, Apology and Defence, 18.

8. Sylvester Bliss, Memoirs of William Miller, Generally Known as a Lecturer on the Prophecies, and the Second Coming of Christ (Boston: Joshua V. Himes, Publisher, 1853), 140.

9. Dick, William Miller and the Advent Crisis, 13–14; Hewitt, Midnight and Morning, 74–75; Knight, Millennial Fever, 46–49; Nichol, The Midnight Cry, 67, 130; and Rowe, God's Strange Work, 104–5.

10. Hewitt, Midnight and Morning, 46, 71; and Rowe, God's Strange Work, 116.

11. Dick, William Miller and the Advent Crisis, 12; Hewitt, Midnight and Morning, 74; Knight, Millennial Fever, 35, 54–56; Nichol, The Midnight Cry, 130; and Rowe, God's Strange Work, 80–81, 148.

12. Hewitt, Midnight and Morning, 76.

13. Editors, The Fountain, quoted in Isaac C. Wellcome, History of the Second Advent Message and Mission, Doctrine and People (Yarmouth, Maine: I. C. Wellcome, Publisher, 1874), 248.

14. Dick, William Miller and the Advent Crisis, 14; Hewitt, Midnight and Morning, 74–76; Knight, Millennial Fever, 55; Nichol, The Midnight Cry, 67–68; and Wellcome, History of the Second Advent Message and Mission, 248.

15. Editorial, Cincinnati Commercial, August 23, 1844, quoted in Le Roy Edwin Froom, The Prophetic Faith of Our Fathers: The Historical Development of Prophetic Interpretation, vol. 4 (Washington, D.C.: Review and Herald, 1954), 688.

16. Wellcome, History of the Second Advent Message and Mission, 75.

17. William Miller to Joshua V. Himes, "Letter from Mr. Miller, NO 3, on the Return of the Jews," March 31, 1840, quoted in Signs of the Times, Relating to the Second Coming of Christ, April 15, 1840, 14.

18. Dick, Miller and the Advent Crisis, 16; Froom, The Prophetic Faith of Our Fathers, 4:688; Hewitt, Midnight and Morning, 75; Knight, Millennial Fever, 48, 56; Miller to Himes, "Letter from Mr. Miller, NO 3"; Nichol, The Midnight Cry, 127, 130, 303–4; and Wellcome, History of the Second Advent Message and Mission, 75.

19. William Miller to Truman Hendrix, May 19, 1841, Jenks Memorial Collection of Adventual Materials, Aurora University, Aurora, Illinois.

20. William Miller to Truman Hendryx, July 21, 1836, Jenks Memorial Collection of Adventual Materials, Aurora University, Aurora, Illinois.

21. William Miller to Son, November 17, 1838, Jenks Memorial Collection of Adventual Materials, Aurora University, Aurora, Illinois.

22. Hewitt, *Midnight and Morning*, 68–69; Knight, *Millennial Fever*, 50–51; Miller to Hendryx, July 21, 1836, and Miller to Son, November 17, 1838; and Rowe, *God's Strange Work*, 104, 124–27.

23. David T. Arthur, "Millerism," in *The Rise of Adventism: Religion and Society in Mid-Nineteenth-Century America*, ed. Edwin S. Gaustead (New York: Harper & Row, 1974), 155–56; Dick, *Miller and the Advent Crisis*, 10, 34–35; Hewitt, *Midnight and Morning*, 92; Knight, *Millennial Fever*, 53–54, 67, 75, 151, 155–58; and Rowe, *God's Strange Work*, 132–33, 160–61, 164–71, 180.

24. Dick, *Miller and the Advent Crisis*, 7–8; Hewitt, *Midnight and Morning*, 76–77; Nichol, *The Midnight Cry*, 467; and Knight, *Millennial Fever*, 17, 54.

25. Arthur, "Millerism," 154; Dick, *Miller and the Advent Crisis*, 34–35; Hewitt, *Midnight and Morning*, 92; Knight, *Millennial Fever*, 21–22, 36, 56, 151, 155–58; Nichol, *The Midnight Cry*, 39, 99, 143, 149, 179; and David Leslie Rowe, "Thunder and Trumpets: The Millerite Movement and Apocalyptic Thought in Upstate New York, 1800–1845" (PhD diss., University of Virginia, 1974), 177–79.

26. David Tallmadge Arthur, "Come Out of Babylon: A Study of Millerite Separatism and Denominationalism, 1840–1865" (PhD diss., University of Rochester, 1970), 28–29, 32–36, 45–48; Arthur, "Millerism," 160; Dick, *Miller and the Advent Crisis*, 96–98, 139–46; Hewitt, *Midnight and Morning*, 103, 161–63; Knight, *Millennial Fever*, 85–86, 126–30, 188–92, 199–205; and Nichol, *The Midnight Cry*, 96, 99–101, 135–36, 220–21, 225–30, 243–46.

27. Ruth Alden Doan, "Millerism and Evangelical Culture," in *The Disappointed: Millerism and Millenarianism in the Nineteenth Century*, ed. Ronald L. Numbers and Jonathan M. Butler (Knoxville: University of Tennessee Press, 1993), 121, 122.

28. Knight, *Millennial Fever*, 23, 65.

29. Dick, *Miller and the Advent Crisis*, xx, 130; Doan, "Millerism and Evangelical Culture," 121, 122; Hewitt, *Midnight and Morning*, 62; and Knight, *Millennial Fever*, 23, 64–65.

30. Knight, *Millennial Fever*, 22.

31. Arthur, "Millerism," 154; Dick, *Miller and the Advent Crisis*, 37; Doan, "Millerism and Evangelical Culture," 121; Hewitt, *Midnight and Morning*, 55–62, 92, 134–37; Knight, *Millennial Fever*, 21–22, 99–105; Nichol, *The Midnight Cry*, 39, 111–19, 143; and David L. Rowe, "Millerites: A Shadow Portrait," in *The Disappointed: Millerism and Millenarianism*

in the Nineteenth Century, ed. Ronald L. Numbers and Jonathan M. Butler (Knoxville: University of Tennessee Press, 1993), 4, 12–14.

32. Doan, "Millerism and Evangelical Culture," 123.

33. Dick, *Miller and the Advent Crisis*, xxv, xxvii, 8; Doan, "Millerism and Evangelical Culture," 122–23, 125–26, 130; Hewitt, *Midnight and Morning*, 62–64; Knight, *Millennial Fever*, 16–20, 24, 54, 142; and Nichol, *The Midnight Cry*, 449, 455–56.

34. Dick, *Miller and the Advent Crisis*, xxv, xxvii, 8; Hewitt, *Midnight and Morning*, 44–51, 62–64, 84, 114, 146–47; Knight, *Millennial Fever*, 16–21, 24, 38–39, 54, 68–70, 74–75, 116–17, 142, 280; and Nichol, *The Midnight Cry*, 188–90, 448–74.

35. Dick, *Miller and the Advent Crisis*, 43; Hewitt, *Midnight and Morning*, 61, 127, 135; and Nichol, *The Midnight Cry*, 90, 312–16, 333.

36. Hewitt, *Midnight and Morning*, 127.

37. New York *Herald*, November 4–15, 1842, quoted in Hewitt, *Midnight and Morning*, 150.

38. Hewitt, *Midnight and Morning*, 127, 135, 143, 150; Knight, *Millennial Fever*, 102–3; and Nichol, *The Midnight Cry*, 90, 231–34, 327, 332–34, 240–41, 493.

39. Dick, *Miller and the Advent Crisis*, 67–71; Hewitt, *Midnight and Morning*, 68, 86, 93–95; and Knight, *Millennial* Fever, 132–33.

40. Dick, *Miller and the Advent Crisis*, 67, 72–74, 168; Hewitt, *Midnight and Morning*, 128–29, 131; Knight, *Millennial Fever*, 83, 136–37; and Nichol, *The Midnight Cry*, 152, 166–68, 222–23.

41. Dick, *Miller and the Advent Crisis*, 89; Hewitt, *Midnight and Morning*, 96–97; and Knight, *Millennial Fever*, 133–36.

42. Joseph Bates, *The Autobiography of Elder Joseph Bates* (Battle Creek, Mich.: Steam Press of the Seventh-Day Adventist Publishing Association, 1868), 281.

43. Dick, *Miller and the Advent Crisis*, 89; Hewitt, *Midnight and Morning*, 44, 97–98; Knight, *Millennial Fever*, 133–35; and Nichol, *The Midnight Cry*, 196–97.

44. Hewitt, *Midnight and Morning*, 43–44, 97–98; Knight, *Millennial Fever*, 133; and David L. Rowe, "Northern Millerites and Virginia Millennialists, 1838–1847" (master's thesis, University of Virginia, 1972), 37–40.

45. Dick, *Miller and the Advent Crisis*, 92–93, 139; Hewitt, *Midnight and Morning*, 98–99; and Knight, *Millennial Fever*, 133, 135.

46. Dick, *Miller and the Advent Crisis*, 167–68; Knight, *Millennial Fever*, 113–14; Nichol, *The Midnight Cry*, 240, 493; and Rowe, "Millerites," 2, 4, 9.

47. Rowe, "Millerites," 7, 9, 11–12.

48. Rowe, "Millerites," 11, 12.

49. Ronald Graybill, "Millenarians and Money: Adventist Wealth and Adventist Beliefs," *Spectrum*, August 1979, 32, quoted in Rowe, "Millerites," 11–12.

50. Philadelphia *North American*, October 16, 1844, and John Greenleaf Whittier, *Prose Works*, vol. 1, 423, quoted in Nichol, *The Midnight Cry*, 231–32.

51. Knight, *Millennial Fever*, 75.

52. Arthur, "Come Out of Babylon," 8–9, 14–15; Dick, *Miller and the Advent Crisis*, 10, 16, 21, 154; Hewitt, *Midnight and Morning*, 83, 133; Knight, *Millennial Fever*, 72–77, 131–32, 282; Nichol, *The Midnight Cry*, 64, 75–77, 87, 91, 150, 172, 242, 301; and Rowe, *God's Strange Work*, 160–63, 169–71.

53. Arthur, "Come Out of Babylon," 8.

54. Arthur, "Come Out of Babylon," 14–15.

55. Arthur, "Come Out of Babylon," 8–9, 14–15; Dick, *Miller and the Advent Crisis*, 10; Hewitt, *Midnight and Morning*, 83; Knight, *Millennial Fever*, 72–77; Nichol, *The Midnight Cry*, 75–77; and Rowe, *God's Strange Work*, 162–65.

56. Arthur, "Come Out of Babylon," 8–9, 15; Dick, *Miller and the Advent Crisis*, 61, 68; Hewitt, *Midnight and Morning*, 128–30; Knight, *Millennial Fever*, 73–74, 76–80; and Nichol, *The Midnight Cry*, 78–79, 131–33.

57. Arthur, "Come Out of Babylon," 8-9, 15–16; Dick, *Miller and the Advent Crisis*, 63, 68; Hewitt, *Midnight and Morning*, 129; Knight, *Millennial Fever*, 76–80; and Nichol, *The Midnight Cry*, 79–80, 100, 131–32.

58. Hewitt, *Midnight and Morning*, 128.

59. Arthur, "Come Out of Babylon," 8–9, 24; Dick, *Miller and the Advent Crisis*, 60, 64–66, 73–76; Hewitt, *Midnight and Morning*, 128–29; and Knight, *Millennial Fever*, 76–77, 80–84.

60. Josiah Litch, *Prophetic Expositions*, I, 166–67, quoted in Hewitt, *Midnight and Morning*, 128–29.

61. Dick, *Miller and the Advent Crisis*, 26–27, 64, 66–67; Hewitt, *Midnight and Morning*, 128–29; Knight, *Millennial Fever*, 80, 82–83, 88, 133, 136; and Nichol, *The Midnight Cry*, 91, 93, 144, 154, 166–68.

62. Dick, *Miller and the Advent Crisis*, 30, 37–40, 43, 55; Hewitt, *Midnight and Morning*, 134–35; Knight, *Millennial Fever*, 99–101; and Nichol, *The Midnight Cry*, 111–19, 129.

63. Dick, *Miller and the Advent Crisis*, 40–43, 47–50, 53–54; Hewitt, *Midnight and Morning*, 135–40; Knight, *Millennial Fever*, 102–5; and Nichol, *The Midnight Cry*, 113, 116, 122, 125–26, 128–29, 152–53.

64. Whittier, *Prose Works*, vol. 1, 423, quoted in Nichol, *The Midnight Cry*, 118–19.

65. Dick, *Miller and the Advent Crisis*, 30, 39, 52, 65; Hewitt, *Midnight and Morning*, 117–20; Knight, *Millennial Fever*, 112; and Nichol, *The Midnight Cry*, 110, 117–18.

66. Arthur, "Come Out of Babylon," 36–38, 48–57, 72–76; Dick, *Miller and the Advent Crisis,* 33–34; Hewitt, *Midnight and Morning*, 149, 187; Knight, *Millennial Fever*, 65, 142, 147–49, 151–53, 155–56; and Nichol, *The Midnight Cry*, 157, 160, 179.

67. Arthur, "Come Out of Babylon," 57–65, 72–76, 87; Dick, *Miller and the Advent Crisis*, 34–35; Hewitt, *Midnight and Morning*, 149, 187–88; Knight, *Millennial Fever*, 151, 153–58; and Nichol, *The Midnight Cry*, 159–60.

68. Arthur, "Come Out of Babylon," 76.

69. Arthur, "Come Out of Babylon," 15–16, 21, 24, 27–28, 41; Dick, *Miller and the Advent Crisis*, 20, 26–27, 31–32; Hewitt, *Midnight and Morning*, 132–34; Knight, *Millennial Fever*, 81, 84–85, 87–89, 151–53; and Nichol, *The Midnight Cry*, 86, 88, 92–93, 225.

70. Arthur, "Come Out of Babylon," 35; Dick, *Miller and the Advent Crisis*, 98–99, 117–20, 130–35; Knight, *Millennial Fever*, 129–33, 138–40, 142–47, 159–61; and Nichol, *The Midnight Cry*, 135–37, 163–65, 181–83.

71. Knight, *Millennial Fever*, 129.

72. William Miller, quoted in Bliss, *Memoirs of William Miller*, 256.

73. Bliss, *Memoirs of Miller*, 256; Dick, *Miller and the Advent Crisis*, 136–37; Hewitt, *Midnight and Morning*, 159–61; Knight, *Millennial Fever*, 129, 163–68, 206; and Nichol, *The Midnight Cry*, 219–20.

74. Arthur, "Come Out of Babylon," 45–48; Dick, *Miller and the Advent Crisis*, 141–46; Hewitt, *Midnight and Morning*, 161–63, 168–69; Knight, *Millennial Fever*, 169–71, 187–93, 199–205; and Nichol, *The Midnight Cry*, 220–21, 225–30.

75. Philadelphia *Public Ledger*, October 5, 1844, and *Alexanders Express Messenger*, October 10, 1844, quoted in Dick, *Miller and the Advent Crisis*, 150.

76. Portland *Daily American*, October 21, 1844; Baltimore *Clipper*, October 12, 1844; *Eastern Argus*, October 12, 1844; Albany *Atlas*, October 16, 1844; Providence *Journal*, October 22, 1844; and Philadelphia *Enquirer* in Baltimore *American*, October 22, 1844, quoted in Dick, *Miller and the Advent Crisis*, 151.

77. Dick, *Miller and the Advent Crisis*, 149–52; Hewitt, *Midnight and Morning*, 168–69; Knight, *Millennial Fever*, 205–9, 214; and Nichol, *The Midnight Cry*, 246–49, 253–55, 268.

78. "Occupy Till I Come," *The Midnight Cry*, October 19, 1844, 133, quoted in Nichol, *The Midnight Cry*, 251.

79. "Charge of Fanaticism," *The Midnight Cry*, October 19, 1844, 132, quoted in Nichol, *The Midnight Cry*, 253.

80. Knight, *Millennial Fever*, 206; and Nichol, *The Midnight Cry*, 250–53.

81. Bliss, *Memoirs of Miller*, 275–76.

82. Bliss, *Memoirs of Miller*, 275–76; Dick, *Miller and the Advent Crisis*, 152–53; Hewitt, *Midnight and Morning*, 163–64, 168–69, 176; Knight, *Millennial Fever*, 214; and Nichol, *The Midnight Cry*, 234–35, 237–39, 249.

83. Cincinnati *Chronicle*, quoted in *United States Saturday Post*, November 9, 1844, quoted in Nichol, *The Midnight Cry*, 261.

84. Hiram Edson, Fragment of manuscript on his life and experience, 8–9, quoted in Nichol, *The Midnight Cry*, 263–64.

85. Arthur, "Come Out of Babylon," 85; Dick, *Miller and the Advent Crisis*, 156–57; Hewitt, *Midnight and Morning*, 171–73; Knight, *Millennial Fever*, 216; and Nichol, *The Midnight Cry*, 234–35, 237–39, 259–65.

86. Dick, *Miller and the Advent Crisis*, 11, 31, 75, 95, 120–21, 156–57, 161–62; Hewitt, *Midnight and Morning*, 115, 140–46, 173–74; Knight, *Millennial Fever*, 90–92, 129, 142–46, 217, 220–23; and Nichol, *The Midnight Cry*, 95, 266–75.

87. *Advent Herald*, April 10, 1844, 77–78, and *Midnight Cry*, April 18, 1844, 318, quoted in Knight, *Millennial Fever*, 162.

88. Dick, *Miller and the Advent Crisis*, 11, 75; Hewitt, *Midnight and Morning*, 145; Knight, *Millennial Fever*, 90, 143; Nichol, *The Midnight Cry*, 95, 129, 137–38, 269, 274–75, 296; and Rowe, *God's Strange Work*, 132–33.

89. Joshua V. Himes, Boston *Post*, November 2, 1844, quoted in Hewitt, *Midnight and Morning*, 145–46.

90. Dick, *Miller and the Advent Crisis*, 74–75, 160–62; Hewitt, *Midnight and Morning*, 145–46; Knight, *Millennial Fever*, 90–92, 143, 220–21, 219, 229; and Nichol, *The Midnight Cry*, 95, 267–74.

91. Joseph Bates, quoted in Knight, *Millennial Fever*, 222.

92. Arthur, "Come Out of Babylon," 38; Dick, *Miller and the Advent Crisis*, 120–30, 156–57; Hewitt, *Midnight and Morning*, 141–45; Knight, *Millennial Fever*, 142–45, 220–22; and Nichol, *The Midnight Cry*, 95, 140, 255–58, 266, 321, 389–418.

93. Dick, *Miller and the Advent Crisis*, 156–57; Knight, *Millennial Fever*, 146, 213, 222–23; and Nichol, *The Midnight Cry*, 234–39, 267.

94. Arthur, "Come Out of Babylon," 31–33, 36–37; Hewitt, *Midnight and Morning*, 148–49; and Knight, *Millennial Fever*, 142, 147–48.

95. William Miller, quoted in Bliss, *Memoirs of Miller*, 358.

96. Bliss, *Memoirs of Miller*, 358; Dick, *Miller and the Advent Crisis*, 162; Hewitt, *Midnight and Morning*, 216; Knight, *Millennial Fever*, 282; and Nichol, *The Midnight Cry*, 295, 301, 303.

97. Dick, *Miller and the Advent Crisis*, 162; Hewitt, *Midnight and Morning*, 215–16; Knight, *Millennial Fever*, 234–35, 238, 241–42, 281–82; Nichol, *The Midnight Cry*, 290–292, 301; and Rowe, *God's Strange Work*, 119–21, 208–11, 219, 221, 223–24.

98. Arthur, "Come Out of Babylon," 87; Whitney R. Cross, *The Burned-over District: The Social and Intellectual History of Enthusiastic Religion in Western New York, 1800–1850* (Ithaca, N. Y.: Cornell University Press, 1950), 287; Everett N. Dick, "The Millerite Movement," in *Adventism in America: A History*, ed. Gary Land (Grand Rapids, Mich.: William B. Eerdmans Publishing Company, 1986), 34; Froom, *The Prophetic Faith of Our Fathers*, 4:686; and Knight, *Millennial Fever*, 159.

Chapter 3 – "Occupy till I Come":
From Building a Denomination to Building a College

1. David Tallmadge Arthur, "Come Out of Babylon: A Study of Millerite Separatism and Denominationalism, 1840–1865" (PhD diss., University of Rochester, 1970), 88; and George R. Knight, *Millennial Fever and the End of the World: A Study of Millerite Adventism* (Boise, Idaho: Pacific Press Publishing Association, 1993), 220, 224, 229, 230.

2. Clyde E. Hewitt, *Midnight and Morning: An Account of the Adventist Awakening and the Founding of the Advent Christian Denomination, 1831–1860* (Charlotte, N.C.: Venture Books, 1983), 180, 189, 208, 228–29; and Knight, *Millennial Fever*, 224, 228–33.

3. Arthur, "Come Out of Babylon," 87–88, 147.

4. Arthur, "Come Out of Babylon," 76.

5. Knight, *Millennial Fever*, 232.

6. Arthur, "Come Out of Babylon," 76; and Knight, *Millennial Fever*, 231–34.

7. Sylvester Bliss, *Memoirs of William Miller, Generally Known as a Lecturer on the Prophecies, and the Second Coming of Christ* (Boston: Joshua V. Himes, Publisher, 1853), 293–94; Hewitt, *Midnight and Morning*, 180–81; and Knight, *Millennial Fever*, 232.

8. William Miller to Joshua V. Himes, quoted in *Advent Herald*, November 27, 1844, 127–28, quoted in David T. Arthur, "Joshua V. Himes and the Cause of Adventism," in *The Disappointed: Millerism and Millenarianism in the Nineteenth Century*, ed. Ronald L. Numbers and Jonathan M. Butler (Knoxville: University of Tennessee Press, 1993), 52.

9. Arthur, "Come Out of Babylon," 92–93, 95–96, 128; Knight, *Millennial Fever*, 233; and Miller to Himes, quoted in Arthur, "Joshua V. Himes and the Cause of Adventism," 52.

10. Arthur, "Come Out of Babylon," 96–99, 107–9, 112–15, 128; Hewitt, *Midnight and Morning*, 181–83; and Knight, *Millennial Fever*, 236.

11. Arthur, "Come Out of Babylon," 100–101, 105–6, 123–24, 127–28, 137, 139, 374; Hewitt, *Midnight and Morning*, 181; and Knight, *Millennial Fever*, 238–42.

12. Isaac C. Wellcome, *History of the Second Advent Message and Mission, Doctrine and People* (Yarmouth, Maine: I. C. Wellcome, Publisher, 1874), 500.

13. Arthur, "Come Out of Babylon," 123, 156, 159, 161–62, 164, 169, 332; Hewitt, *Midnight and Morning*, 210–11; and Knight, *Millennial Fever*, 228–29, 274–78.

14. Hewitt, *Midnight and Morning*, 211–12, and Knight, *Millennial Fever*, 231–32.

15. Arthur, "Come Out of Babylon," 131–32, 138–39; Hewitt, *Midnight and Morning*, 212; and Knight, *Millennial Fever*, 268.

16. Arthur, "Come Out of Babylon," 241.

17. Arthur, "Come Out of Babylon," 235–61, 271, 273, 276; Hewitt, *Midnight and Morning*, 212; and Knight, *Millennial Fever*, 290–91.

18. *Morning Watch*, June 12, 1845, 189, quoted in Knight, *Millennial Fever*, 265.

19. Arthur, "Come Out of Babylon," 129–33, 136–37; Hewitt, *Midnight and Morning*, 190–93; and Knight, *Millennial Fever*, 267–71, 273.

20. Arthur, "Come Out of Babylon," 132.

21. *Morning Watch*, June 12, 1845, 189, quoted in Knight, *Millennial Fever*, 273.

22. Arthur, "Come Out of Babylon,"137–39; and Knight, *Millennial Fever*, 272–73.

23. David L. Rowe, *Thunder and Trumpets: Millerites and Dissenting Religion in Upstate New York, 1800–1850* (Chico, Calif.: Scholars Press, 1985), 154.

24. Rowe, *Thunder and Trumpets*, 155.

25. Knight, *Millennial Fever*, 272.

26. Arthur, "Come Out of Babylon," 155–56, 159, 161–64, 169, 171–72; Hewitt, *Midnight and Morning*, 192–96, 213; Knight, *Millennial Fever*, 268–73; and Rowe, *Thunder and Trumpets*, 154, 155.

27. Knight, *Millennial Fever*, 278.

28. Arthur, "Come Out of Babylon," 139, 144, 155–56, 169, 172, 233, 276–77, 332; Hewitt, *Midnight and Morning*, 204, 207–8, 210–11; and Knight, *Millennial Fever*, 271–74, 278, 281, 283, 285.

29. Arthur, "Come Out of Babylon," 136–37, 155, 169, 172, 186–90, 193–94, 198–200, 208, 264–65, 282–85, 287–89; Hewitt, *Midnight and Morning*, 204, 207–8, 210–11, 213–15; and Knight, *Millennial Fever*, 273–74, 278–81, 285.

30. Arthur, "Come Out of Babylon," 201–4; Hewitt, *Midnight and Morning*, 219–28; and Knight, *Millennial Fever*, 195–99, 283–84.

31. Arthur, "Come Out of Babylon," 296–97, 304–6, 309–10, 320–23, 331–34; Hewitt, *Midnight and Morning*, 228–32, 235–45; and Knight, *Millennial Fever*, 284–87, 290–91.

32. Hewitt, *Midnight and Morning*, 254–55.

33. Hewitt, *Midnight and Morning*, 254–55, 258, 263.

34. Hewitt, *Midnight and Morning*, 263.

35. Arthur, "Come Out of Babylon," 276, 310, 328–29; and Knight, *Millennial Fever*, 283.

36. Hewitt, *Midnight and Morning*, 256.

37. T. S. Parks, "Letter from Brother Parks," *Our Hope and Life in Christ*, February 5, 1890, 4–5.

38. By Order of Committee, "Western Convention," *Our Hope and Life in Christ*, December 25 1889, 8; B. F., "Report of the General Western Advent Christian Convention," *Our Hope and Life in Christ*, February 5, 1890,

2–3; Parks, "Letter from Brother Parks," 4–5; and A. P. Moore, "A Terrible Accident," *Our Hope and Life in Christ*, February 11, 1891, 9.

39. Henry Pollard, "That Proposed College," *Our Hope and Life in Christ*, March 5, 1890, 11.

40. A. E. Hatch, "The School Question," *Our Hope and Life in Christ*, November 18, 1891, 3.

41. Orrin R. Jenks, "An Advent School," *Our Hope and Life in Christ*, October 7, 1891, 3.

42. R. S. Blinn, "From the Ohio State University," *Our Hope and Life in Christ*, March 19, 1890, 6.

43. Lucy M. Chaffee, "The Paper and the College," *Our Hope and Life in Christ*, April 30, 1890, 2.

44. N. A., "Shall We Educate Our Ministers?" *Our Hope and Life in Christ*, December 23, 1891, 3.

45. N. A., "Remarks," *Our Hope and Life in Christ*, February 5, 1890, 5.

46. Ada Spencer, "An Advent School," *Our Hope and Life in Christ*, October 21, 1891, 11.

47. A. A. S., "Sparta School," *Our Hope and Life in Christ*, March 2, 1892, 3.

48. Orrin R. Jenks, "He Wants the School," *Our Hope and Life in Christ*, October 28, 1891, 13.

49. W. J. Hobbs, "Business," *Our Hope and Life in Christ*, December 16, 1891, 8.

50. N. A., "The Paper and the College," *Our Hope and Life in Christ*, September 17, 1890, 9.

51. C. A. Meade, "From C. A. Meade," *Our Hope and Life in Christ*, January 20, 1892, 4.

52. Meade, "From C. A. Meade," 4.

53. H. G. M'Culloch, "Advent Christian College," *Our Hope and Life in Christ*, March 19, 1890, 3.

54. H. Pollard, "That Proposed College," *Our Hope and Life in Christ*, March 19, 1890, 8.

55. Pollard, "That Proposed College," March 19, 1890, 8.

Chapter 4 – The College Campus and Mendota: Not Enough Space, Too Much Insularity

1. J. W. Emmons, "What We Want," *Our Hope and Life in Christ*, October 9, 1895, 8.

2. B. F., "Report of the General Western Advent Christian Convention," *Our Hope and Life in Christ*, February 5, 1890, 3.

3. B. F., "Report of the General Western Advent Christian Convention,"

3; William M'Culloch, "That Western College," *Our Hope and Life in Christ,* July 2, 1890, 10; J. August Smith, "Our Opportunity," *Our Hope and Life in Christ,* December 2, 1891, 4; and William McCulloch, "That Mendota College," *Our Hope and Life in Christ,* December 9, 1891, 10.

4. M'Culloch, "That Western College,"10.

5. M'Culloch, "That Western College,"10; Smith, "Our Opportunity," 4; and McCulloch, "That Mendota College," 10.

6. Smith, "Our Opportunity," 4.

7. McCulloch, "That Mendota College," 10.

8. McCulloch, "That Mendota College," 10.

9. McCulloch, "That Mendota College," 10.

10. McCulloch, "That Mendota College," 10; J. August Smith, "The Mendota Meeting," *Our Hope and Life in Christ,* February 17, 1892, 9–10; A. S. Calkins, J. F. Adair, and M. A. Stevens, "From the Educational Committee," *Our Hope and Life in Christ,* July 20, 1892, 2–3; N. A., "Report of the Third Annual Meeting of the Western Advent Christian Publishing Society," *Our Hope and Life in Christ,* September 7, 1892, 4–6; N. A., "Founders Motivated by High Purpose," *Aurora College Bulletin* (*Aurora News*), January-February 1968, 2; and *Annual of Mendota College, 1909–1910* (Mendota, Ill.: Our Hope Printing Company, 1909), 6.

11. Mendota Area Chamber of Commerce, *Tracks of Time: Mendota, Illinois, 1853–1978* (Mendota, Ill.: Wayside Press, 1978), 137–38; and Mendota Centennial Committee, *Magnificent Whistle Stop: The 100-Year Story of Mendota, Ill.* (Mendota, Ill.: Wayside Press, 1953), 220–23.

12. Department of Commerce and Labor, Bureau of the Census, *Thirteenth Census of the United States Taken in the Year 1910: Statistics for Illinois,* 586, https://www2.census.gov/library/publications/decennial/1910/abstract/supplement-il-p1.pdf (accessed July 15, 2018); Mendota Chamber of Commerce, *Tracks of Time,* 5, 7–8; and Mendota Centennial Committee, *Magnificent Whistle Stop,* 11–14.

13. J. W. Emmons, "One Debt Paid," *Our Hope and Life in Christ,* March 10, 1897, 10; B. A. King, "College Day Offerings: Received from Dec. 28, '07 to Jan. 18, 1908," *Our Hope and Life in Christ,* January 22, 1908, 10–11; and Mendota Chamber of Commerce, *Tracks of Time,* 50–52, 55–63, 65–68, 71–94, 107–9.

14. Mendota Chamber of Commerce, *Tracks of Time,* 149–53.

15. Department of Commerce and Labor, Bureau of the Census, *Thirteenth Census of the United States Taken in the Year 1910: Illinois,* 624.

16. N. A., "Mendota," *Our Hope and Life in Christ,* December 23, 1891, 9.

17. Smith, "Our Opportunity," 5.

18. N. A., "Editor's Notes," *Our Hope and Life in Christ,* December 6, 1899, 6; N. A., "Personal and General," *Our Hope and Life in Christ,* December 5, 1900, 6; M. B. C., "College Notes," *Our Hope and Life in Christ,* December 4, 1901, 10;

N. A., "Brief Mention," *Our Hope and Life in Christ*, May 29, 1907, 6; College Literary Society, ed., "Theological Department," *Epitome: 1911 Mendota College Annual*, 15; and Mendota Chamber of Commerce, *Tracks of Time*, 151–61.

19. N. A., "An Enjoyable Entertainment," *Our Hope and Life in Christ*, February 3, 1904, 7; N. A., "Brief Mention," *Our Hope and Life in Christ*, March 16, 1904, 6; and Mendota Chamber of Commerce, *Tracks of Time*, 117–20, 177–79.

20. N. A., "Headquarters for Adventists," *Our Hope and Life in Christ*, January 20, 1892, 7.

21. Mendota *Reporter*, May 21, 1909, quoted in N. A., "A Valuable Institution," *Our Hope and Life in Christ*, May 26, 1909, 7.

22. N. A., "Headquarters for Adventists," 7; Mendota *Reporter*, May 21, 1909, quoted in N. A., "A Valuable Institution," 7; Orrin R. Jenks, "BULLETIN NO. 3: What Will Aurora Do?" *Our Hope and Life in Christ*, February 16, 1910, 15; N. A., "A Few Important Facts: Briefly Stated for Careful Consideration," *Our Hope and Life in Christ*, June 22, 1910, 7; and Frederick Rudolph, *The American College and University: A History* (1962; repr., Athens, Ga.: University of Georgia Press, 1990), 87–88, 91–93, 95–96.

23. "Mendota Not Favored: The College Is to Be Removed to Aurora," Mendota *Reporter*, January 14, 1910.

24. "Mendota Not Favored," Mendota *Reporter*, January 14, 1910.

25. J. W. Emmons, "Some Things Seen and Done," *Our Hope and Life in Christ*, September 11, 1895, 2.

26. Smith, "Our Opportunity," 4; and Emmons, "Some Things Seen and Done," 2–3.

27. Emmons, "Some Things Seen and Done," 2–3; and G. V. Clum, "What Is Being Done for the College," *Our Hope and Life in Christ*, September 25, 1895, 12–13.

28. J. W. Emmons, "Waiting! Waiting! Waiting!" *Our Hope and Life in Christ*, October 2, 1895, 7.

29. N. A., "Memorial Windows," *Our Hope and Life in Christ*, October 9, 1895, 8.

30. N. A., "Memorial Windows," 8.

31. N. A., "Memorial Windows," 8.

32. J. W. Emmons, "Those Chairs for the College Chapel," *Our Hope and Life in Christ*, October 23, 1895, 5–6.

33. J. W. Emmons, "What We Want," *Our Hope and Life in Christ*, October 9, 1895, 8; and Emmons, "Those Chairs for the College Chapel," 5–6.

34. G. V. Clum, "How Our Chapel Is Seated," *Our Hope and Life in Christ*, October 23, 1895, 13.

35. Emmons, "What We Want," 8.

36. J. W. Emmons, "College Chapel Chairs," *Our Hope and Life in Christ*, November 6, 1895, 11.

37. M. B. C., "College Notes," *Our Hope and Life in Christ*, March 26, 1902, 11.

38. Sylvester Nokes, "College Notes," *Our Hope and Life in Christ*, November 6, 1895, 10.

39. J. W. Emmons, "The Good Work Goes On," *Our Hope and Life in Christ*, October 16, 1895, 12; Emmons, "Those Chairs for the College Chapel," 5–6; J. W. Emmons, "College Windows All Paid For," *Our Hope and Life in Christ*, October 23, 1895, 13; Nokes, "College Notes," November 6, 1895, 10; and J. W. Emmons, "College Chapel Chairs," *Our Hope and Life in Christ*, November 13, 1895, 7.

40. Emmons, "College Chapel Chairs," November 13, 1895, 7.

41. G. V. Clum, "College Repairs," *Our Hope and Life in Christ*, October 2, 1895, 9.

42. Clum, "College Repairs," 9; Emmons, "The Good Work Goes On," 12; and Emmons, "College Chapel Chairs," November 13, 1895, 7.

43. J. W. Emmons, "Bathing-Tub for the College," *Our Hope and Life in Christ*, November 20, 1895, 11.

44. Sylvester Nokes, "College Notes," *Our Hope and Life in Christ*, November 13, 1895, 10; and Emmons, "Bathing-Tub for the College," 11.

45. N. A., "Help Those Women," *Our Hope and Life in Christ*, November 7, 1900, 7; N. A., "The Boarding Club Range," *Our Hope and Life in Christ*, November 28, 1900, 7; O. H. Loomis, "College Notes," *Our Hope and Life in Christ*, December 21, 1904, 10; and O. H. Loomis, "College Notes," *Our Hope and Life in Christ*, May 24, 1905, 10.

46. Harry L. Hanson, "College Notes," *Our Hope and Life in Christ*, November 15, 1905, 10.

47. N. A., "An Urgent Need," *Our Hope and Life in Christ*, July 6, 1904, 7; N. A., "A Long Needed Improvement on Foot," *Our Hope and Life in Christ*, September 20, 1905, 7; N. A., "College Painting Fund," *Our Hope and Life in Christ*, October 11, 1905, 7; and Hanson, "College Notes," November 15, 1905, 10–11.

48. N. A., "College Painting Fund," 7; and B. A. King, "College Funds Received: From Oct. 23d to Nov. 18, 1905," *Our Hope and Life in Christ*, November 29, 1905, 12.

49. N. A., "A Long Needed Improvement on Foot," 7.

50. N. A., "A Long Needed Improvement on Foot," 7; and King, "College Funds Received: From Oct. 23d to Nov. 18, 1905," 12.

51. Mrs. (Ophelia) Edgar Bennett, "A Visit to Our College," *Our Hope and Life in Christ*, December 31, 1902, 3.

52. Bennett, "A Visit to Our College," 3.

53. Minutes of the Board of Education, Mendota College, April 3, 1901, Jenks Memorial Collection of Advental Materials, Aurora University, Aurora, Illinois.

54. J. W. Emmons, "A Good Chance to Invest," *Our Hope and Life in Christ*, April 24, 1901, 7.

55. Bennett, "A Visit to Our College," 3.

56. Emmons, "A Good Chance to Invest," 7; Bennett, "A Visit to Our College," 3; and Minutes of the Board of Education, Mendota College, April 3, 1901, and Minutes of the Board of Directors, Mendota College, August 27, 1906, and April 5, 1910, Jenks Memorial Collection of Adventual Materials, Aurora University, Aurora, Illinois.

57. Sylvester Nokes, "College Notes," *Our Hope and Life in Christ*, September 15, 1897, 11.

58. Nokes, "College Notes," September 15, 1897, 11; and Bennett, "A Visit to Our College," 3.

59. Mrs. (Ophelia) Edgar Bennett, "A Visit to Our College: No. 2," *Our Hope and Life in Christ*, January 7, 1903, 3.

60. Bennett, "A Visit to Our College: No. 2," 3.

61. Mrs. (Ophelia) Edgar Bennett, "Our College Visit: No. 3," *Our Hope and Life in Christ*, January 21, 1903, 3.

62. Bennett, "Our College Visit: No. 3," 3.

63. Bennett, "Our College Visit: No. 3," 3.

64. J. W. Emmons, "The Ames Chemical Laboratory of Mendota College," *Our Hope and Life in Christ*, September 2, 1896, 3; Sylvester Nokes, "College Notes," *Our Hope and Life in Christ*, September 30, 1896, 7; Sylvester Nokes, "College Notes," *Our Hope and Life in Christ*, September 8, 1897, 10; and Bennett, "Our College Visit: No. 3," 3.

65. Bennett, "Our College Visit: No. 3," 3.

66. Bennett, "Our College Visit: No. 3," 3.

67. N. A., "The Cyclone at Mendota," *Our Hope and Life in Christ*, July 22, 1903, 6.

68. George G. Emery, "A Good Place to Live," *Our Hope and Life in Christ*, June 23, 1897, 9; N. A., "The Cyclone at Mendota," 6; "Tornado Strikes Mendota," Mendota *Sun-Bulletin*, July 24, 1903; and Centennial Committee, *Magnificent Whistle Stop*, 132-134.

69. H. M. Robbins, "An Urgent Appeal," *Our Hope and Life in Christ*, July 29, 1903, 7.

70. N. A., "The Cyclone at Mendota," 6; "Tornado Strikes Mendota," *Sun-Bulletin*, July 24, 1903; Robbins, "An Urgent Appeal," 7; and Mendota Centennial Committee, *Magnificent Whistle Stop*, 133.

71. N. A., "The Track of a Cyclone," *Our Hope and Life in Christ*, July 29, 1903, 1.

72. Emery, "A Good Place to Live," 9; N. A., "The Storm Sufferers," *Our Hope and Life in Christ*, July 22, 1903, 7; "Tornado Strikes Mendota," *Sun-Bulletin*; and N. A., "The Track of a Cyclone," 1.

73. Mendota Centennial Committee, *Magnificent Whistle Stop*, 135.

74. N. A., "Brief Mention," *Our Hope and Life in Christ*, August 5, 1903, 6 and Mendota Centennial Committee, *Magnificent Whistle Stop*, 133–35.

75. N. A., "The Storm Sufferers," 7; N. A., "The Track of a Cyclone," 1; N. A., "Brief Mention," August 5, 1903, 6; and Mrs. (Ophelia) Edgar Bennett, "Special Report," *Our Hope and Life in Christ*, October 7, 1903, 3.

76. N. A., "Emergency Fund," *Our Hope and Life in Christ*, July 29, 1903, 7.

77. N. A., "Emergency Fund," 7; and Robbins, "An Urgent Appeal," 7.

78. N. A., "Closing Words," *Our Hope and Life in Christ*, August 12, 1903, 6.

79. N. A., "Closing Words," 6.

80. E. S. M., "College Day," *Our Hope and Life in Christ*, January 30, 1895, 12.

81. Emery, "A Good Place to Live," 9.

82. N. A., "Something to Think About," *Our Hope and Life in Christ*, April 26, 1899, 7.

83. N. A., "Unrealized Opportunities—No. 6: Mendota College Continued," *Our Hope and Life in Christ*, June 24, 1908, 6–7.

84. N. A., "Editorial Mention," *Our Hope and Life in Christ*, December 28, 1892, 8; N. A., "A Valuable Institution," 7; Mendota Chamber of Commerce, *Tracks of* Time, 161; and Mendota Centennial Committee, *Magnificent Whistle Stop*, 115–16.

85. N. A., "Our Prospective Office," *Our Hope and Life in Christ*, October 10, 1906, 7; N. A., "Brief Mention," *Our Hope and Life in Christ*, March 27, 1907, 6; and Minutes of the Educational Committee, Western Advent Christian Publication Society, March 23, 1893, and September 28, 1893, Jenks Memorial Collection of Advental Materials, Aurora University, Aurora, Illinois.

86. N. A., "Editorial Notes," *Our Hope and Life in Christ*, February 21, 1894, 8.

87. N. A., "Editorial Notes," February 21, 1894, 8; and N. A., N. T., *Our Hope and Life in Christ*, June 6, 1894, 11.

88. B. Forester, "Good News," *Our Hope and Life in Christ*, May 26, 1909, 5.

89. B. Forester, "Mendota College and Its Friends," *Our Hope and Life in Christ*, March 6, 1907, 3.

90. M. B. C., "College Notes," March 26, 1902, 11; Harry L. Hanson, "College Notes," *Our Hope and Life in Christ*, March 14, 1906, 10; N. A., "Brief Mention," *Our Hope and Life in Christ*, March 21, 1906, 6; B. Forester, "Mendota College and Its Friends," 3; Ada Spencer Monson, "About Mendota College," *Our Hope and Life in Christ*, June 19, 1907, 5; N. A., "Brief Mention," *Our Hope and Life in Christ*, September 30, 1908, 6; and B. Forester, "Good News," 5.

91. B. J. Dean, "The Educational Field: Why Do We Need New Buildings?" *Our Hope and Life in Christ*, June 1, 1910, 10–11; N. A., "A Few

Important Facts," 7; Minutes of the Board of Directors, Mendota College, April 6, 1910, Jenks Memorial Collection of Adventual Materials, Aurora University, Aurora, Illinois; and *Annual of Mendota College: Catalogue, 1910–1911* (Mendota, Ill.: Our Hope Print, 1910), 4, 81–84.

92. Minutes of the Board of Directors, Aurora College, August 31, 1913, Jenks Memorial Collection of Adventual Materials, Aurora University, Aurora, Illinois; Mendota Chamber of Commerce, *Tracks of Time*, 138, 144–45; and Mendota Centennial Committee, *Magnificent Whistle Stop*, 223.

Chapter 5 – The Intertwining of Academics and Religion

1. Orrin R. Jenks, "BULLETIN NO. 72: Wanted: TEN THOUSAND DOLLARS," *Our Hope and Life in Christ*, June 26, 1912, 16.

2. Western Advent Christian Publication Society, "Report of the Educational Committee," *Our Hope and Life in Christ*, August 30, 1893, 11.

3. Western Advent Christian Publication Society, "Report of the Educational Committee," August 30, 1893, 11; and Minutes of the Educational Committee, Western Advent Christian Publication Society, March 23, 1893, Jenks Memorial Collection of Adventual Materials, Aurora University, Aurora, Illinois.

4. Western Advent Christian Publication Society, "Report of the Educational Committee," August 30, 1893, 11.

5. N. A., "Report of the Third Annual Meeting of the Western Advent Christian Publishing Society," *Our Hope and Life in Christ*, September 7, 1892, 6.

6. N. A., "Report of the Third Annual Meeting of the Western Advent Christian Publishing Society," 6.

7. A. S. Calkins, J. F. Adair, and M. A. Stevens, "From the Educational Committee," *Our Hope and Life in Christ*, July 20, 1892, 2; N. A., "Report of the Third Annual Meeting of the Western Advent Christian Publishing Society," 6; J. August Smith, "The Mendota Seminary," *Our Hope and Life in Christ*, December 21, 1892, 9; J. Oscar Campbell, "Mendota Seminary," *Our Hope and Life in Christ*, December 28, 1892, 4; and Minutes of the Educational Committee, Western Advent Christian Publication Society, November 14, 1892, Jenks Memorial Collection of Adventual Materials, Aurora University, Aurora, Illinois.

8. J. O. C. (J. Oscar Campbell), "School Notes," *Our Hope and Life in Christ*, February 8, 1893, 9; J. H. Nichols, "Our Seminary," *Our Hope and Life in Christ*, February 22, 1893, 9; N. A., "The Bible Training School," *Our Hope and Life in Christ*, June 28, 1893, 8; Minutes of the Educational Committee, November 14, 1892, and March 23, 1893, Jenks Memorial Collection of Adventual Materials, Aurora University, Aurora, Illinois; and *Announcement of Mendota Seminary, 1893* (Cincinnati: Press of C. J. Krehbiel & Co., 1893), 9–16.

9. "Report of the Third Annual Meeting of the Western Advent Christian Publishing Society," 6.

10. Virginia Lieson Brereton, *Training God's Army: The American Bible School, 1880–1940* (Bloomington: Indiana University Press, 1990), 103; Christopher J. Lucas, *American Higher Education: A History* (New York: St. Martin's Griffin, 1994), 152; William C. Ringenberg, *The Christian College: A History of Protestant Higher Education in America*, 2nd ed. (Grand Rapids, Mich.: Baker Book House Co., 2006), 60, 70–71; and Frederick Rudolph, *The American College and University: A History* (1962; repr., Athens, Ga.: University of Georgia Press, 1990), 281–82.

11. Charles Sowder, interview by Susan Palmer, Dowling Park, Florida, November 12, 1991, Doris K. Colby Archives, Aurora University, Aurora, Illinois.

12. N. C. Twining, "Our Bible Training School," *Our Hope and Life in Christ*, January 20, 1904, 8–9.

13. Twining, "Our Bible Training School," 8–9; College Literary Society, ed., "Preparatory Department," *Epitome: 1911 Mendota College Annual*, 34; and *Annual of Mendota College: Catalogue, 1910–1911* (Mendota, Ill.: Our Hope Print, 1910), 90–91.

14. *Annual of Mendota College, 1909–1910* (Mendota, Ill.: Our Hope Printing Company, 1909), 10.

15. *Announcement of Mendota Seminary, 1893*, 18; *Catalogue: Mendota College, 1907–1908* (Mendota, Ill.: Hope Print, 1907), 41; and *Annual of Mendota College: Catalogue, 1910–1911*, 10.

16. *Announcement of Mendota Seminary, 1893*, 9; *Annual of Mendota College, 1893–1894* (Aurora, Ill.: Copeland & Phillips, Printers, 1893), 12–13; *Annual of Mendota College, 1894–1895* (Bloomington, Ill.: Pantagraph Printing and Stationery Co., 1894), 14–15; and *Annual of Mendota College: Catalogue, 1910–1911*, 21–22.

17. *Catalogue: Mendota College, 1907–1908*, 8–9; *Annual of Mendota College, 1908–1909* (Mendota, Ill.: Our Hope Print, 1908), 8–9; and *Annual of Mendota College: Catalogue, 1910–1911*, 10, 89–91.

18. College Literary Society, ed., "Preparatory Department," *Epitome: Mendota College Annual, 1910*, 23.

19. Literary Society, ed., "Preparatory Department," *Epitome, 1910*, 23.

20. N. A., "Editorial Notes," *Our Hope and Life in Christ*, April 4, 1894, 8.

21. N. A., "The Bible Training School," *Our Hope and Life in Christ*, November 8, 1905, 7.

22. Abby Lee Shatto, "Bible Training at Mendota," *Our Hope and Life in Christ*, January 6, 1904, 3.

23. N. A., "Our Wonderful Privilege," *Our Hope and Life in Christ*, January 7, 1903, 7.

24. N. C. Twining, "The Work in Mendota College," *Our Hope and Life in Christ*, March 29, 1905, 4.

25. N. A., "Our Wonderful Privilege," 7; Twining, "The Work in Mendota College," 4; *Annual of Mendota College, 1894–1895*, 15; and Brereton, *Training God's Army*, 103–104.

26. Brereton, *Training God's Army*, 103.

27. N. A., "The Bible Training School," November 8, 1905, 7.

28. Calkins, Adair, and Stevens, "From the Educational Committee," 2.

29. W. S. (William Sheldon), N. T., *Our Hope and Life in Christ*, May 9, 1894, 10.

30. N. A., "The Bible Training School," *Our Hope and Life in Christ*, February 13, 1895, 8–9.

31. N. A., "The Bible Training School," *Our Hope and Life in Christ*, June 28, 1893, 8; N. A., "The Bible Training School," February 13, 1895, 8–9; and *Catalogue of Mendota College for 1895–96* (Bloomington, Ill.: Pantagraph Printing and Stationery Co., 1895), 11.

32. J. O. Campbell, "Bible Training School," *Our Hope and Life in Christ*, May 17, 1893, 13; *Annual of Mendota College, 1893–94*, 11; *Catalogue of Mendota College for 1895–96*, 11, 12; *Catalogue of Mendota College for 1898–99* (Mendota, Ill.: Western Advent Christian Publication Association, 1898), 16–17; and *Catalogue of Mendota College for 1901–1902* (Mendota, Ill.: Our Hope Printing Office, 1901), 23–25.

33. *Catalogue of Mendota College for 1895–96*, 12; *Catalogue of Mendota College for 1898–99*, 16–17; *Catalogue of Mendota College for 1901–1902*, 23–25; *Catalogue: Mendota College, 1904–1905* (Mendota, Ill.: Hope Print, 1904), 19–23; *Catalogue: Mendota College, 1905–1906* (Mendota, Ill.: Hope Print, 1905), 20–21; and *Annual of Mendota College: Catalogue, 1910–1911*, 46–55.

34. *Catalogue: Mendota College, 1907–1908*, 39.

35. *Annual of Mendota College: Catalogue, 1910–1911*, 67.

36. *Catalogue: Mendota College, 1904–1905*, 27; *Catalogue: Mendota College, 1905–1906*, 21; *Catalogue: Mendota College, 1906–1907* (Mendota, Ill.: Hope Print, 1906), 22; *Catalogue: Mendota College, 1907–1908*, 39; *Annual of Mendota College, 1909–1910*, 53; and *Annual of Mendota College: Catalogue, 1910–1911*, 67.

37. *Catalogue: Mendota College, 1905–1906*, 20–21; *Catalogue: Mendota College, 1906–1907*, 20–23; *Catalogue: Mendota College, 1907–1908*, 30–33; *Annual of Mendota College, 1908–1909*, 31–34; *Annual of Mendota College, 1909–1910*, 47–48, 52, 54; and *Annual of Mendota College: Catalogue, 1910–1911*, 47–48, 52, 54.

38. Lucas, *American Higher Education*, 165–70, 210; Ringenberg, *The Christian College*, 102–4; and Rudolph, *The American College and University*, 290–94, 300–306.

39. *Catalogue of Mendota College for 1901–1902*, 8–9; *Catalogue: Mendota College, 1902–1903* (Mendota, Ill.: Western Advent Christian Publication Association, 1902), 10–11; *Catalogue: Mendota College, 1903–1904* (Mendota, Ill.: Western Advent Christian Publication Association,

1903), 10–11; *Catalogue: Mendota College, 1904–1905,* 9–10; *Catalogue: Mendota College, 1905–1906,* 11–12; *Catalogue: Mendota College, 1906–1907,* 11–12; *Catalogue: Mendota College, 1907–1908,* 10–11; *Annual of Mendota College, 1908–1909,* 10–11; Annual *of Mendota College, 1909–1910,* 23–24; *Annual of Mendota College: Catalogue, 1910–1911,* 23–24; and Lucas, *American Higher Education,* 169–70.

40. *Annual of Mendota College, 1893–1894,* 20; *Annual of Mendota College, 1894–1895,* 16; *Catalogue of Mendota College for 1895–96,* 12–13; *Catalogue of Mendota College for 1896–97* (Bloomington, Ill.: Pantagraph Printing and Stationery Co., 1896), 12–13; *Catalogue of Mendota College for 1898–99,* 16–17; *Catalogue of Mendota College for 1899–1900* (Mendota, Ill.: Western Advent Christian Publication Association, 1899), 16–17; *Catalogue of Mendota College for 1901–1902,* 23–25; *Catalogue: Mendota College, 1902–1903, 22–24; Catalogue: Mendota College, 1903–1904,* 22–24; *Catalogue: Mendota College, 1904–1905, 21–23; Catalogue: Mendota College, 1905–1906,* 20; *Catalogue: Mendota College, 1906–1907,* 20, 22; *Catalogue: Mendota College, 1907–1908,* 30, 32; *Annual of Mendota College, 1908–1909,* 31, 34; *Annual of Mendota College, 1909–1910,* 47, 54–55; and *Annual of Mendota College: Catalogue, 1910–1911,* 47, 54–55.

41. Brereton, *Training God's Army,* 88–89.

42. *Catalogue of Mendota College for 1901–1902,* 22–23.

43. *Catalogue of Mendota College for 1895–96,* 12; *Catalogue of Mendota College for 1896–97,* 11–12; *Catalogue of Mendota College for 1898–99,* 15; *Catalogue of Mendota College for 1899–1900,* 15; *Catalogue of Mendota College for 1901–1902,* 22–23; *Catalogue: Mendota College, 1902–1903, 21–22; Catalogue: Mendota College, 1904–1905, 18–19; Catalogue: Mendota College, 1905–1906,* 19; *Catalogue: Mendota College, 1906–1907,* 19; *Catalogue: Mendota College, 1907–1908,* 29; *Annual of Mendota College, 1908–1909,* 30; *Annual of Mendota College, 1909–1910,* 45; and *Annual of Mendota College: Catalogue, 1910–1911,* 45.

44. *Catalogue: Mendota College, 1905–1906,* 21; *Catalogue: Mendota College, 1906–1907,* 23; and *Catalogue: Mendota College, 1907–1908,* 7, 32, 53.

45. *Annual of Mendota College, 1894–1895, 12–13; Catalogue of Mendota College for 1901–1902,* 8; *Catalogue: Mendota College, 1906–1907,* 11; and *Annual of Mendota College: Catalogue, 1910–1911,* 23.

46. *Annual of Mendota College, 1894–1895, 13–14; Catalogue of Mendota College for 1901–1902,* 9; *Catalogue: Mendota College, 1904–1905,* 10; and *Annual of Mendota College: Catalogue, 1910–1911,* 24.

47. *Catalogue: Mendota College, 1907–1908,* 7.

48. *Annual of Mendota College, 1909–1910,* 56.

49. *Catalogue: Mendota College, 1904–1905,* 9–10; *Catalogue: Mendota College, 1906–1907,* 8, 23; *Catalogue: Mendota College, 1907–1908,* 7; and *Annual of Mendota College, 1909–1910,* 20, 56.

50. Literary Society, ed., "Music," *Epitome: 1911,* 47.

51. E. S. M., "College Day," *Our Hope and Life in Christ*, January 30, 1895, 12; N. A., "Commencement," *Our Hope and Life in Christ*, June 17, 1896, 7; Sylvester Nokes, "College Notes," *Our Hope and Life in Christ*, October 13, 1897, 11; Clara Lindauer, "College Notes," *Our Hope and Life in Christ*, June 7, 1899, 10; O. H. L. [Alven H. Loomis], "College Notes," *Our Hope and Life in Christ*, December 16, 1903, 10; Harry L. Hanson, "College Notes," *Our Hope and Life in Christ*, June 6, 1906, 10; N. A., "Commencement," *Our Hope and Life in Christ*, June 13, 1906, 7; J. L. Irvin, "College Notes," *Our Hope and Life in Christ*, March 4, 1908, 3; N. A., "College Day," *Our Hope and Life in Christ*, December 30, 1908, 7; S. T. Neduts, "College Notes," *Our Hope and Life in Christ*, February 24, 1909, 11; S. T. Neduts, "The Educational Field: College Notes," *Our Hope and Life in Christ*, March 17, 1909, 10; S. T. Neduts, "College Notes," *Our Hope and Life in Christ*, June 9, 1909, 11; Literary Society, ed., "The Choral Club," *Epitome: 1910*, 46; and Literary Society, ed., "Music," *Epitome: 1911*, 47.

52. J. A. Wallace, "The Music Department," *Our Hope and Life in Christ*, May 29, 1901, 1.

53. "A Musician," "Music—Why Teach It?" *Our Hope and Life in Christ*, June 17, 1896, 12.

54. "A Musician," "Music—Why Teach It?" 12; Wallace, "The Music Department," 1; and J. A. Wallace, "Music at Mendota College," *Our Hope and Life in Christ*, January 7, 1903, 5.

55. A. H. Stoddard, "Seminary Notes," *Our Hope and Life in Christ*, March 22, 1893, 9; *Annual of Mendota College, 1893–1894*, 21–24; and *Annual of Mendota College: Catalogue, 1910–1911*, 76–78.

56. *Annual of Mendota College, 1893–1894*, 21–23 and *Catalogue of Mendota College for 1896–97*, 14–15.

57. *Catalogue of Mendota College for 1899–1900*, 19–21.

58. *Catalogue: Mendota College, 1904–1905*, 24–26.

59. *Annual of Mendota College, 1894–1895*, 27–28; *Catalogue of Mendota College for 1895–96*, 30–31; *Catalogue of Mendota College for 1896–97*, 26–27; *Catalogue of Mendota College for 1898–99*, 30; *Catalogue of Mendota College for 1899–1900*, 30; *Catalogue of Mendota College for 1901–1902*, 39; *Catalogue: Mendota College, 1902–1903*, 37; *Catalogue: Mendota College, 1903–1904*, 38–39; *Catalogue: Mendota College, 1904–1905*, 36; *Catalogue: Mendota College, 1905–1906*, 33; *Catalogue: Mendota College, 1906–1907*, 35–36; *Catalogue: Mendota College, 1907–1908*, 50–51; *Annual of Mendota College, 1908–1909*, 55–56; *Annual of Mendota College, 1909–1910*, 8; and *Annual of Mendota College: Catalogue, 1910–1911*, 84, 89–91.

60. Albert J. Bolster, "Our Prospective Dormitory—NO. 2," *Our Hope and Life in Christ*, January 22, 1902, 7.

61. N. A., "No Cause for Alarm," *Our Hope and Life in Christ*, April 5, 1893, 8.

62. N. A., "No Cause for Alarm," 9.

63. N. A., "No Cause for Alarm," 8–9.

64. N. A., "No Cause for Alarm," 9.

65. Stoddard, "Seminary Notes," 9; and N. A., "No Cause for Alarm," 8–9.

66. D. A. Dickinson, "Music in Our College," *Our Hope and Life in Christ*, January 1, 1896, 10.

67. Dickinson, "Music in Our College," 10.

68. Dickinson, "Music in Our College," 10.

69. George H. Dewing, "The Educational Field: Professor King and the Commercial Department," *Our Hope and Life in Christ*, January 6, 1909, 10.

70. J. O. S. (Staats), "The Commercial Department," *Our Hope and Life in Christ*, May 22, 1901, 1.

71. B. J. Dean, "The College Commercial Course," *Our Hope and Life in Christ*, June 27, 1900, 4; Staats, "The Commercial Department," 1; B. A. King, "Commercial Work: What We Are Doing and What We Need," *Our Hope and Life in Christ*, January 7, 1903, 9; and Geo. H. Dewing, "The Educational Field: Professor King and the Commercial Department," *Our Hope and Life in Christ*, January 6, 1909, 10.

72. *Annual of Mendota College, 1894–1895*, 20–21; *Catalogue of Mendota College for 1895–96*, 16–21; *Catalogue of Mendota College for 1896–97*, 16–18; *Catalogue of Mendota College for 1898–99*, 9–11; *Catalogue of Mendota College for 1899–1900*, 9–11; *Catalogue of Mendota College for 1901–1902*, 15–20; *Catalogue: Mendota College, 1902–1903*, 14–19; *Catalogue: Mendota College, 1903–1904*, 14–19; *Catalogue: Mendota College, 1904–1905*, 13–17; *Catalogue: Mendota College, 1905–1906*, 15–18; *Catalogue: Mendota College, 1906–1907*, 15–18; *Catalogue: Mendota College, 1907–1908*, 24–28; *Annual of Mendota College, 1908–1909*, 25–29; *Annual of Mendota College, 1909–1910*, 67–75; and *Annual of Mendota College: Catalogue, 1910–1911*, 68–75.

73. *Annual of Mendota College: Catalogue, 1910–1911*, 69.

74. *Annual of Mendota College, 1909–1910*, 67–68 and *Annual of Mendota College: Catalogue, 1910–1911*, 68–69.

75. Dewing, "Professor King and the Commercial Department," 10; *Annual of Mendota College, 1908–1909*, 29; *Annual of Mendota College, 1909–1910*, 74–75; and *Annual of Mendota College: Catalogue, 1910–1911*, 75.

76. Sylvester Nokes, "College Notes," *Our Hope and Life in Christ*, November 6, 1895, 10; J. W. Emmons, "The Ames Chemical Laboratory of Mendota College," *Our Hope and Life in Christ*, September 2, 1896, 3; Sylvester Nokes, "College Notes," *Our Hope and Life in Christ*, September 30, 1896, 7; Sylvester Nokes, "College Notes," *Our Hope and Life in Christ*, September 8, 1897, 10; and G. V. Clum, "Mendota College," *Our Hope and Life in Christ*, January 5, 1898, 5.

77. "College Library," *Annual of Mendota College, 1894–1895*, 17.

78. G. V. Clum, "Books—an Urgent Need—a Good Example," *Our Hope and Life in Christ*, January 29, 1896, 3.

79. D. T. Taylor, "A Proposal," *Our Hope and Life in Christ*, April 8, 1896, 13.

80. Taylor, "A Proposal," 13.

81. Mrs. H. A. Brower, "Brother Taylor's Appeal," *Our Hope and Life in Christ*, April 22, 1896, 12.

82. Mrs. M. A. Street, "Bro. D. T. Taylor's Proposal," *Our Hope and Life in Christ*, April 22, 1896, 13.

83. D. T. Taylor to *Our Hope and Life in Christ*, May 4, 1896, quoted in N. A., "Eld. D. T. Taylor's Proposal," *Our Hope and Life in Christ*, May 13, 1896, 11.

84. Luther Boutelle, "Secure Those Books for the College," *Our Hope and Life in Christ*, April 15, 1896, 7; Brower, "Brother Taylor's Appeal," 12; Street, "Bro. D. T. Taylor's Proposal," 13; Editor, N. T., *Our Hope and Life in Christ*, April 22, 1896, 13; N. A., "Eld. D. T. Taylor's Proposal," *Our Hope and Life in Christ*, April 29, 1896, 7; and N. A., "Eld. D. T. Taylor's Proposal," May 13, 1896, 11.

85. N. A., "Bro. Cook's Library," *Our Hope and Life in Christ*, May 31, 1899, 7.

86. N. A., "Who Will Help?" *Our Hope and Life in Christ*, May 3, 1899, 7.

87. A. J. Bolster, "Call for Special Prayer," *Our Hope and Life in Christ*, November 30, 1898, 10; N. A., "Sad Tidings," *Our Hope and Life in Christ*, March 29, 1899, 7; N. A., "Brother Cook's Library," *Our Hope and Life in Christ*, April 12, 1899, 10–11; N. A., "Who Will Help?" 7; and N. A., "Bro. Cook's Library," May 31, 1899, 7.

88. "Library," *Catalogue of Mendota College for 1901–1902*, 35 and "Library and Reading Room," *Annual of Mendota College, 1909–1910*, 15.

89. H. M. Robbins, "The Bible Training School," *Our Hope and Life in Christ*, December 21, 1898, 7; *Catalogue: Mendota College, 1903–1904*, 4; *Catalogue: Mendota College, 1904–1905*, 4; *Catalogue: Mendota College, 1905–1906*, 6; *Catalogue: Mendota College, 1906–1907*, 6; *Catalogue: Mendota College, 1907–1908*, 4; *Annual of Mendota College, 1908–1909*, 4; *Annual of Mendota College, 1909–1910*, 4; and *Annual of Mendota College: Catalogue, 1910–1911*, 4.

90. N. A., "Deserved Commendation," *Our Hope and Life in Christ*, September 16, 1903, 7; Orrin R. Jenks, "A Visit among the Hoosiers and Wolverines," *Our Hope and Life in Christ*, December 27, 1905, 4–5; Orrin R. Jenks, "Close of Chicago Pastorate," *Our Hope and Life in Christ*, July 13, 1910, 4; Orrin R. Jenks, "BULLETIN NO. 19: A Word from the Field," *Our Hope and Life in Christ*, August 3, 1910, 15; and J. August Smith, eulogy for Norman P. Cook, quoted in E. A. Stockman, ed., *World's Crisis*, April 19, 1899, 1.

91. *Annual of Mendota College, 1893–1894*, 6; *Annual of Mendota College, 1894–1895*, 5; *Catalogue of Mendota College for 1895–96*, 3;

Catalogue of Mendota College for 1896–97, 3; Catalogue of Mendota College for 1898–99, 3; Catalogue of Mendota College for 1899–1900, 3; Catalogue of Mendota College for 1901–1902, 4; Catalogue: Mendota College, 1902–1903, 4; Catalogue: Mendota College, 1903–1904, 4; Catalogue: Mendota College, 1904–1905, 4; Catalogue: Mendota College, 1905–1906, 6; Catalogue: Mendota College, 1906–1907, 6; Catalogue: Mendota College, 1907–1908, 4; Annual of Mendota College, 1908–1909, 4; Annual of Mendota College, 1909–1910, 4; and Annual of Mendota College: Catalogue, 1910–1911, 4.

92. Lucas, American Higher Education, 124; and Rudolph, The American College and University, 394–96.

93. N. A., "Our Beloved Dead," Our Hope and Life in Christ, February 19, 1902, 6–7.

94. N. A., "Important Change," Our Hope and Life in Christ, July 12, 1899, 7; N. A., "Deserved Commendation," Our Hope and Life in Christ, September 16, 1903, 7; N. A., "Brief Mention," Our Hope and Life in Christ, November 4, 1903, 6; and Editor, "Fifty Years in the Christian Ministry," World's Crisis, May 29, 1912, 1–2.

95. J. August Smith, "In Memoriam," Our Hope and Life in Christ, April 5, 1899, 10.

96. H. M. Robbins, "The Bible Training School," Our Hope and Life in Christ, December 21, 1898, 7.

97. M. A. Stevens, "Our Bible Training School," Our Hope and Life in Christ, March 27, 1895, 9; A. J. Bolster, "Call for Special Prayer," Our Hope and Life in Christ, November 30, 1898, 10; H. M. Robbins, "The Bible Training School," 7; N. A., "Sad Tidings," 7; Smith, "In Memoriam," 10; B. Forester, "A Tribute of Affection," Our Hope and Life in Christ, April 19, 1899, 5; and Smith, eulogy for Norman P. Cook, quoted in Stockman, ed., World's Crisis, April 19, 1899, 1.

98. B. Forester, "Cheering Information," Our Hope and Life in Christ, April 20, 1904, 7; George H. Dewing, "The Educational Field: O. R. Jenks and the Bible Training Work," Our Hope and Life in Christ, March 31, 1909, 10–11; Jenks, "Close of Chicago Pastorate," 4; Jenks, "BULLETIN NO. 19: A Word from the Field," 15; and N. A., "A Faithful Worker," Our Hope and Life in Christ, February 15, 1911, 9.

99. Annual of Mendota College, 1909–1910, 4; and Annual of Mendota College: Catalogue, 1910–1911, 90.

100. R. C. Robbins, "Professor Dewing and His Work," Our Hope and Life in Christ, December 9, 1908, 10–11; Annual of Mendota College, 1893–1894, 6; Annual of Mendota College, 1894–1895, 5; Catalogue: Mendota College, 1906–1907, 6; Catalogue: Mendota College, 1907–1908, 4; Annual of Mendota College, 1908–1909, 4; Annual of Mendota College, 1909–1910, 4; and Annual of Mendota College: Catalogue, 1910–1911, 4.

101. Robbins, "Professor Dewing and His Work," 11.

102. Robbins, "Professor Dewing and His Work," 10–11; Minutes of the Board of Directors, Mendota College, September 27, 1911, Jenks Memorial Collection of Adventual Materials, Aurora University, Aurora, Illinois; and *Annual of Mendota College: Catalogue, 1910–1911*, 91.

103. N. A., "The George H. Dewing Room: Senior Gift," *Pharos*, 1931, 84–85.

104. N. A., "The George H. Dewing Room: Senior Gift," 84–85; and Minutes of the Board of Directors, Mendota College, September 5, 1910, Jenks Memorial Collection of Adventual Materials, Aurora University, Aurora, Illinois.

105. Wisconsin Public School Records, quoted in B. J. Dean, "The Educational Field: Prof. N. C. Twining and His Work," *Our Hope and Life in Christ*, December 23, 1908, 10–11.

106. Dean, "Prof. N. C. Twining and His Work," 10–11.

107. Dean, "Prof. N. C. Twining and His Work," 10–11.

108. *Annual of Mendota College, 1893–1894*, 6; *Annual of Mendota College, 1894–1895*, 5; *Catalogue of Mendota College for 1895–96*, 3; *Catalogue of Mendota College for 1896–97*, 3; *Catalogue of Mendota College for 1898–99*, 3; *Catalogue of Mendota College for 1899–1900*, 3; Catalogue *of Mendota College for 1901–1902*, 4; *Catalogue: Mendota College, 1902–1903*, 4; *Catalogue: Mendota College, 1903–1904*, 4; *Catalogue: Mendota College, 1904–1905*, 4; *Catalogue: Mendota College, 1905–1906*, 6; *Catalogue: Mendota College, 1906–1907*, 6; *Catalogue: Mendota College, 1907–1908*, 4; *Annual of Mendota College, 1908–1909*, 4; *Annual of Mendota College, 1909–1910*, 4; and *Annual of Mendota College: Catalogue, 1910–1911*, 4.

109. *Catalogue: Mendota College, 1905–1906*, 6, 32–33; *Catalogue: Mendota College, 1906–1907*, 6, 33, 36, 39; and *Catalogue: Mendota College, 1907–1908*, 4, 47–53.

110. Dean, "Prof. N. C. Twining and His Work," 10; *Annual of Mendota College, 1893–1894*, 6; *Annual of Mendota College, 1894–1895*, 5; *Catalogue of Mendota College for 1895–96*, 3; *Catalogue of Mendota College for 1896–97*, 3; *Catalogue of Mendota College for 1898–99*, 3; *Catalogue of Mendota College for 1899–1900*, 3; *Catalogue of Mendota College for 1901–1902*, 4; *Catalogue: Mendota College, 1902–03, 4; Catalogue: Mendota College, 1903–1904*, 4; *Catalogue: Mendota College, 1904–1905*, 4; *Catalogue: Mendota College, 1905–1906*, 6; *Catalogue: Mendota College, 1906–1907*, 6; *Catalogue: Mendota College, 1907–1908*, 4; *Annual of Mendota College, 1908–1909*, 4; Annual *of Mendota College, 1909–1910*, 4; *Annual of Mendota College: Catalogue, 1910–1911*, 4; and John R. Thelin, *A History of American Higher Education* (Baltimore: John Hopkins University Press, 2004), 282.

111. *Annual of Mendota College, 1893–1894*, 6; *Annual of Mendota College, 1894–1895*, 5; *Catalogue of Mendota College for 1895–96*, 3;

Catalogue of Mendota College for 1896–97, 3; *Catalogue of Mendota College for 1898–99*, 3; *Catalogue of Mendota College for 1899–1900*, 3; Catalogue *of Mendota College for 1901–1902*, 4; *Catalogue: Mendota College, 1902–1903*, 4; *Catalogue: Mendota College, 1903–1904*, 4; *Catalogue: Mendota College, 1904–1905*, 4; *Catalogue: Mendota College, 1905–1906*, 6; *Catalogue: Mendota College, 1906–1907*, 6; *Catalogue: Mendota College, 1907–1908*, 4; *Annual of Mendota College, 1908–1909*, 4; *Annual of Mendota College, 1909–1910*, 4; and *Annual of Mendota College: Catalogue, 1910–1911*, 4.

112. *Annual of Mendota College, 1893–1894*, 6; *Annual of Mendota College, 1894–1895*, 5; *Catalogue of Mendota College for 1895–96*, 3; *Catalogue of Mendota College for 1896–97*, 3; *Catalogue of Mendota College for 1898–99*, 3; *Catalogue of Mendota College for 1899–*1900, 3; Catalogue *of Mendota College for 1901–1902*, 4; *Catalogue: Mendota College, 1902–1903*, 4; *Catalogue: Mendota College, 1903–1904*, 4; *Catalogue: Mendota College, 1904–1905*, 4; *Catalogue: Mendota College, 1905–1906*, 6; *Catalogue: Mendota College, 1906–1907*, 6; *Catalogue: Mendota College, 1907–1908*, 4; *Annual of Mendota College, 1908–1909*, 4; *Annual of Mendota College, 1909–1910*, 4; and *Annual of Mendota College: Catalogue, 1910–1911*, 4.

113. Mary Hoffschweilie, "Women Professionals," National Park Service, U.S. Department of the Interior, https://www.nps.gov/nr/travel/pwwmh/prof.htm (accessed February 17, 2018); and Nancy Woloch, *Women and the American Experience*, 4th ed. (Boston: McGraw Hill, 2006), 275–78, 280, 285.

114. *Annual of Mendota College, 1893–1894*, 6; *Annual of Mendota College, 1894–1895*, 5; *Catalogue of Mendota College for 1895–96*, 3; *Catalogue of Mendota College for 1896–97*, 3; *Catalogue of Mendota College for 1898–99*, 3; *Catalogue of Mendota College for 1899–*1900, 3; Catalogue *of Mendota College for 1901–1902*, 4; *Catalogue: Mendota College, 1902–1903*, 4; *Catalogue: Mendota College, 1903–1904*, 4; *Catalogue: Mendota College, 1904–1905*, 4; *Catalogue: Mendota College, 1905–1906*, 6; *Catalogue: Mendota College, 1906–1907*, 6; *Catalogue: Mendota College, 1907–1908*, 4; *Annual of Mendota College, 1908–1909*, 4; *Annual of Mendota College, 1909–1910*, 4; and *Annual of Mendota College: Catalogue, 1910–1911*, 4.

115. Minutes of the Board of Education, Mendota College, April 3, 1901, Jenks Memorial Collection of Adventual Materials, Aurora University, Aurora, Illinois.

116. Dean, "Prof. N. C. Twining and His Work," 11; Minutes of the Board of Education, Mendota College, April 3, 1901, and April 9, 1902, Jenks Memorial Collection of Adventual Materials, Aurora University, Aurora, Illinois; *Annual of Mendota College, 1893–1894*, 6, 8; *Annual of Mendota College, 1894–1895*, 5, 28; *Catalogue of Mendota College for 1895–96*,

3; *Catalogue of Mendota College for 1896–97*, 3; *Catalogue of Mendota College for 1898–99*, 3; *Catalogue of Mendota College for 1899–1900*, 3; Catalogue *of Mendota College for 1901–1902*, 4; *Catalogue: Mendota College, 1902–1903*, 4; *Catalogue: Mendota College, 1903–1904*, 4; *Catalogue: Mendota College, 1904–1905*, 4; *Catalogue: Mendota College, 1905–1906*, 6; *Catalogue: Mendota College, 1906–1907*, 6; *Catalogue: Mendota College, 1907–1908*, 4; *Annual of Mendota College, 1908–1909*, 4; *Annual of Mendota College, 1909–1910*, 4; and *Annual of Mendota College: Catalogue, 1910–1911*, 4.

117. *Annual of Mendota College, 1893–1894*, 6; *Annual of Mendota College, 1894–1895*, 5; *Catalogue of Mendota College for 1895–96*, 3; *Catalogue of Mendota College for 1896–97*, 3; *Catalogue of Mendota College for 1898–99*, 3; *Catalogue of Mendota College for 1899–1900*, 3; Catalogue *of Mendota College for 1901–1902*, 4; *Catalogue: Mendota College, 1902–1903*, 4; *Catalogue: Mendota College, 1903–1904*, 4; *Catalogue: Mendota College, 1904–1905*, 4; *Catalogue: Mendota College, 1905–1906*, 6; *Catalogue: Mendota College, 1906–1907*, 6; *Catalogue: Mendota College, 1907–1908*, 4; *Annual of Mendota College, 1908–1909*, 4; *Annual of Mendota College, 1909–1910*, 4; *Annual of Mendota College: Catalogue, 1910–1911*, 4; Brereton, *Training God's Army*, 61; Ringenberg, *The Christian College*, 95; and Woloch, *Women and the American Experience*, 283, 285–86.

118. *Annual of Mendota College, 1893–1894*, 6; *Annual of Mendota College, 1894–1895*, 5; *Catalogue of Mendota College for 1895–96*, 3; *Catalogue of Mendota College for 1896–97*, 3; *Catalogue of Mendota College for 1898–99*, 3; *Catalogue of Mendota College for 1899–1900*, 3; Catalogue *of Mendota College for 1901–1902*, 4; *Catalogue: Mendota College, 1902–1903*, 4; *Catalogue: Mendota College, 1903–1904*, 4; *Catalogue: Mendota College, 1904–1905*, 4; *Catalogue: Mendota College, 1905–1906*, 6; *Catalogue: Mendota College, 1906–1907*, 6; *Catalogue: Mendota College, 1907–1908*, 4; *Annual of Mendota College, 1908–1909*, 4; *Annual of Mendota College, 1909–1910*, 4; and *Annual of Mendota College: Catalogue, 1910–1911*, 4.

119. Ringenberg, *The Christian College*, 96; and Woloch, *Women and the American Experience*, 274–75, 278–80.

120. Brereton, *Training God's Army*, 60–61; Helen Lefkowitz Horowitz, *Campus Life: Undergraduate Cultures from the End of the Eighteenth Century to the Present* (Chicago: Chicago University Press, 1987), 29–30, 59; and Ringenberg, *The Christian College*, 168.

121. *Annual of Mendota College, 1893–1894*, 8–9; *Annual of Mendota College, 1894–1895*, 26–31; *Catalogue of Mendota College for 1895–96*, 29–32; *Catalogue of Mendota College for 1896–97*, 25–28; *Catalogue of Mendota College for 1898–99*, 28–30; *Catalogue of Mendota College for 1899–1900*, 28–30; Catalogue *of Mendota College for 1901–1902*, 38–39;

Catalogue: Mendota College, 1902–1903, 36–37; *Catalogue: Mendota College, 1903–1904*, 36–39; *Catalogue: Mendota College, 1904–1905*, 35–36; *Catalogue: Mendota College, 1905–1906*, 32–34; *Catalogue: Mendota College, 1906–1907*, 33–38; *Catalogue: Mendota College, 1907–1908*, 47–51; *Annual of Mendota College, 1908–1909*, 51–56; *Annual of Mendota College, 1909–1910*, 81–84; and *Annual of Mendota College: Catalogue, 1910–1911*, 81–84.

122. *Annual of Mendota College, 1893–1894*, 8–9; *Annual of Mendota College, 1894–1895*, 26–31; *Catalogue of Mendota College for 1895–96*, 29–32; *Catalogue of Mendota College for 1896–97*, 25–28; *Catalogue of Mendota College for 1898–99*, 28–30; *Catalogue of Mendota College for 1899–1900*, 28–30; Catalogue *of Mendota College for 1901–1902*, 38–39; *Catalogue: Mendota College, 1902–1903*, 36–37; *Catalogue: Mendota College, 1903–1904*, 36–39; *Catalogue: Mendota College, 1904–1905*, 35–36; *Catalogue: Mendota College, 1905–1906*, 32–34; *Catalogue: Mendota College, 1906–1907*, 33–38; *Catalogue: Mendota College, 1907–1908*, 47–51; *Annual of Mendota College, 1908–1909*, 51–56; *Annual of Mendota College, 1909–1910*, 81–84; and *Annual of Mendota College: Catalogue, 1910–1911*, 81–84, 89–91.

123. N. A., "Notes," *Our Hope and Life in Christ*, December 30, 1903, 8.

124. George E. Cooprider, "To Our Biblical Training Students," *Our Hope and Life in Christ*, June 1, 1898, 10.

125. Cooprider, "To Our Biblical Training Students," 10; E. L. Pettus, "Grateful Praise," *Our Hope and Life in Christ*, February 11, 1903, 9; O. H. L. (Orven H. Loomis), "College Notes," *Our Hope and Life in Christ*, November 11, 1903, 10; and J. L. Irvin, "College Notes," *Our Hope and Life in Christ*, October 30, 1907, 3.

126. M. E. S., "Something to Think About," *Our Hope and Life in Christ*, March 29, 1899, 10.

127. Harry L. Hanson, "College Notes," *Our Hope and Life in Christ*, December 20, 1905, 10.

128. Harry L. Hanson, "College Notes," *Our Hope and Life in Christ*, October 18, 1905, 3.

129. *Catalogue of Mendota College for 1895–96*, 6.

130. Orven H. Loomis, "A Word to Prospective Students," *Our Hope and Life in Christ*, July 27, 1904, 5.

131. N. A., "The Bible Training School," *Our Hope and Life in Christ*, April 10, 1895, 8; N. A., "The Bible School," *Our Hope and Life in Christ*, May 8, 1895, 8; Ethel E. Fry, "College Letter. No. 7," *Our Hope and Life in Christ*, October 31, 1900, 10; Orven H. Loomis, "College Letter," *Our Hope and Life in Christ*, October 29, 1902, 7; O. H. L. (Orven H. Loomis), "College Notes," *Our Hope and Life in Christ*, November 4, 1903, 11; N. A., "Brief Mention," *Our Hope and Life in Christ*, February 3, 1904, 6; Loomis, "A Word to Prospective Students," 5; O. R. J. (Orrin Roe Jenks), "Come Early to Mendota

College," *Our Hope and Life in Christ*, August 10, 1904, 8; John Keepers, "Impressions about Our College," *Our Hope and Life in Christ*, August 10, 1904, 9; N. C. Twining, "Mendota College Opening," *Our Hope and Life in Christ*, August 31, 1904, 3; Will S. Trowbridge, "A Good Work at Mendota," *Our Hope and Life in Christ*, November 16, 1904, 4; O. H. Loomis, "College Notes," *Our Hope and Life in Christ*, February 15, 1905, 10; Hanson, "College Notes," October 18, 1905, 3; Harry L. Hanson, "College Notes," *Our Hope and Life in Christ*, November 8, 1905, 3; J. L. Irvin, "College Notes," *Our Hope and Life in Christ*, April 22, 1908, 10; *Catalogue of Mendota College for 1895–96*, 6; *Annual of Mendota College, 1909–1910*, 12; and *Annual of Mendota College: Catalogue, 1910–1911*, 12.

132. Mendota *Bulletin*, November 25, 1893, quoted in N. A., "Kind Words for Mendota College," *Our Hope and Life in Christ*, January 3, 1894, 9.

133. N. A., "Personal Locals," *The Collegian*, February 1904, 6–8.

134. Mendota *Bulletin*, November 25, 1893, quoted in N. A., "Kind Words for Mendota College," 9; G. V. Clum, "Improve the Opportunity," *Our Hope and Life in Christ*, January 8, 1896, 5; and N. A., "Personal Locals," 6–8.

135. Harry L. Hanson, "College Notes," *Our Hope and Life in Christ*, February 14, 1906, 10; and Harry L. Hanson, "College Notes," *Our Hope and Life in Christ*, May 2, 1906, 3.

136. J. L. Irvin, "College Notes," *Our Hope and Life in Christ*, January 22, 1908, 10.

137. Harry L. Hanson, "College Notes," *Our Hope and Life in Christ*, February 28, 1906, 7; Harry L. Hanson, "College Notes," *Our Hope and Life in Christ*, April 11, 1906, 10; and Irvin, "College Notes," 10.

138. N. A., "Notes," December 30, 1903, 8; Loomis, "A Word to Prospective Students," 5; and *Catalogue, 1910–1911*, 12.

139. Boston Bible College and Ransom Institute, 1903 Catalog, 7, quoted in Brereton, *Training God's Army*, 81.

140. Catalogue and Prospectus of the Boston Missionary Training School with Abstract of Third Annual Report, 1892, n. p., quoted in Brereton, *Training God's Army*, 81.

141. Brereton, *Training God's Army*, 81; and Thelin, *A History of American Higher Education*, 176–77.

142. *Annual of Mendota College, 1893–1894*, 8–9; *Annual of Mendota College, 1894–1895*, 26–31; *Catalogue of Mendota College for 1895–96*, 29–32; *Catalogue of Mendota College for 1896–97*, 25–28; *Catalogue of Mendota College for 1898–99*, 28–30; *Catalogue of Mendota College for 1899–1900*, 28–30; Catalogue *of Mendota College for 1901–1902*, 38–39; *Catalogue: Mendota College, 1902–1903*, 36–37; *Catalogue: Mendota College, 1903–1904*, 36–39; *Catalogue: Mendota College, 1904–1905*, 35–36; *Catalogue: Mendota College, 1905–1906*, 32–34; *Catalogue: Mendota College, 1906–1907*, 33–38; *Catalogue: Mendota College, 1907–1908*,

47–51; *Annual of Mendota College, 1908–1909*, 51–56; *Annual of Mendota College, 1909–1910*, 81–84; and *Annual of Mendota College: Catalogue, 1910–1911*, 81–84.

143. J. W. Emmons, "We Are after the Students," *Our Hope and Life in Christ*, February 8, 1899, 10; N. A., "College Day Program," *Our Hope and Life in Christ*, August 13, 1902, 11; Jenks, "A Visit among the Hoosiers and Wolverines," 4–5; and Orrin R. Jenks, "An Evangelistic Mission," *Our Hope and Life in Christ*, August 15, 1906, 2–3.

144. *Annual of Mendota College, 1893–1894*, 8–9; *Annual of Mendota College, 1894–1895*, 26–31; *Catalogue of Mendota College for 1895–96*, 29–32; *Catalogue of Mendota College for 1896–97*, 25–28; *Catalogue of Mendota College for 1898–99*, 28–30; *Catalogue of Mendota College for 1899–1900*, 28–30; Catalogue *of Mendota College for 1901–1902*, 38–39; *Catalogue: Mendota College, 1902–1903*, 36–37; *Catalogue: Mendota College, 1903–1904*, 36–39; *Catalogue: Mendota College, 1904–1905*, 35–36; *Catalogue: Mendota College, 1905–1906*, 32–34; *Catalogue: Mendota College, 1906–1907*, 33–38; *Catalogue: Mendota College, 1907–1908*, 47–51; *Annual of Mendota College, 1908–1909*, 51–56; *Annual of Mendota College, 1909–1910*, 81–84; *Annual of Mendota College: Catalogue, 1910–1911*, 81–84; and Mendota Area Chamber of Commerce, *Tracks of Time: Mendota, Illinois, 1853–1978* (Mendota, Ill.: Wayside Press, 1978), 149–63.

145. *Annual of Mendota College, 1893–1894*, 8–9; *Annual of Mendota College, 1894–1895*, 26–31; *Catalogue of Mendota College for 1895–96*, 29–32; *Catalogue of Mendota College for 1896–97*, 25–28; *Catalogue of Mendota College for 1898–99*, 28–30; *Catalogue of Mendota College for 1899–1900*, 28–30; Catalogue *of Mendota College for 1901–1902*, 38–39; *Catalogue: Mendota College, 1902–1903*, 36–37; *Catalogue: Mendota College, 1903–1904*, 36–39; *Catalogue: Mendota College, 1904–1905*, 35–36; *Catalogue: Mendota College, 1905–1906*, 32–34; *Catalogue: Mendota College, 1906–1907*, 33–38; *Catalogue: Mendota College, 1907–1908*, 47–51; *Annual of Mendota College, 1908–1909*, 51–56; *Annual of Mendota College, 1909–1910*, 81–84; and *Annual of Mendota College: Catalogue, 1910–1911*, 81–84.

146. J. Oscar Campbell, "Mendota Seminary," *Our Hope and Life in Christ*, February 15, 1893, 9.

147. Harry L. Hanson, "College Notes," *Our Hope and Life in Christ*, October 3, 1906, 10–11.

148. Campbell, "Mendota Seminary," February 15, 1893, 9; Hanson, "College Notes," October 3, 1906, 10–11; *Annual of Mendota College, 1893–1894*, 8–9; *Annual of Mendota College, 1894–1895*, 26–31; *Catalogue of Mendota College for 1895–96*, 29–32; *Catalogue of Mendota College for 1896–97*, 25–28; *Catalogue of Mendota College for 1898–99*, 28–30; *Catalogue of Mendota College for 1899–1900*, 28–30; Catalogue *of Mendota*

College for 1901–1902, 38–39; *Catalogue: Mendota College, 1902–1903*, 36–37; *Catalogue: Mendota College, 1903–1904*, 36–39; *Catalogue: Mendota College, 1904–1905*, 35–36; *Catalogue: Mendota College, 1905–1906*, 32–34; *Catalogue: Mendota College, 1906–1907*, 33–38; *Catalogue: Mendota College, 1907–1908*, 47–51; *Annual of Mendota College, 1908–1909*, 51–56; *Annual of Mendota College, 1909–1910*, 81–84; and *Annual of Mendota College: Catalogue, 1910–1911*, 81–84.

149. *Annual of Mendota College, 1893–1894*, 8–9; *Annual of Mendota College, 1894–1895*, 26–31; *Catalogue of Mendota College for 1895–96*, 29–32; *Catalogue of Mendota College for 1896–97*, 25–28; *Catalogue of Mendota College for 1898–99*, 28–30; *Catalogue of Mendota College for 1899–1900*, 28–30; Catalogue *of Mendota College for 1901–1902*, 38–39; *Catalogue: Mendota College, 1902–1903*, 36–37; *Catalogue: Mendota College, 1903–1904*, 36–39; *Catalogue: Mendota College, 1904–1905*, 35–36; *Catalogue: Mendota College, 1905–1906*, 32–34; *Catalogue: Mendota College, 1906–1907*, 33–38; *Catalogue: Mendota College, 1907–1908*, 47–51; *Annual of Mendota College, 1908–1909*, 51–56; *Annual of Mendota College, 1909–1910*, 81–84; and *Annual of Mendota College: Catalogue, 1910–1911*, 81–84.

150. *Annual of Mendota College, 1893–1894*, 8–9; *Annual of Mendota College, 1894–1895*, 26–31; *Catalogue of Mendota College for 1895–96*, 29–32; *Catalogue of Mendota College for 1896–97*, 25–28; *Catalogue of Mendota College for 1898–99*, 28–30; *Catalogue of Mendota College for 1899–1900*, 28–30; Catalogue *of Mendota College for 1901–1902*, 38–39; *Catalogue: Mendota College, 1902–1903*, 36–37; *Catalogue: Mendota College, 1903–1904*, 36–39; *Catalogue: Mendota College, 1904–1905*, 35–36; *Catalogue: Mendota College, 1905–1906*, 32–34; *Catalogue: Mendota College, 1906–1907*, 33–38; *Catalogue: Mendota College, 1907–1908*, 47–51; *Annual of Mendota College, 1908–1909*, 51–56; *Annual of Mendota College, 1909–1910*, 81–84; and *Annual of Mendota College: Catalogue, 1910–1911*, 81–84.

151. W. S., N. T., *Our Hope and Life in Christ*, May 9, 1894, 10.

152. W. S., N. T., May 9, 1894, 10; *Annual of Mendota College, 1893–1894*, 8–9; *Annual of Mendota College, 1894–1895*, 26–31; *Catalogue of Mendota College for 1895–96*, 29–32; *Catalogue of Mendota College for 1896–97*, 25–28; *Catalogue of Mendota College for 1898–99*, 28–30; *Catalogue of Mendota College for 1899–1900*, 28–30; Catalogue *of Mendota College for 1901–1902*, 38–39; *Catalogue: Mendota College, 1902–1903*, 36–37; *Catalogue: Mendota College, 1903–1904*, 36–39; *Catalogue: Mendota College, 1904–1905*, 35–36; *Catalogue: Mendota College, 1905–1906*, 32–34; *Catalogue: Mendota College, 1906–1907*, 33–38; *Catalogue: Mendota College, 1907–1908*, 47–51; *Annual of Mendota College, 1908–1909*, 51–56; *Annual of Mendota College, 1909–1910*, 81–84; and *Annual of Mendota College: Catalogue, 1910–1911*, 81–84.

153. *Annual of Mendota College, 1893–1894*, 8–9; *Annual of Mendota College, 1894–1895*, 26–31; *Catalogue of Mendota College for 1895–96*, 29–32; *Catalogue of Mendota College for 1896–97*, 25–28; *Catalogue of Mendota College for 1898–99*, 28–30; *Catalogue of Mendota College for 1899–1900*, 28–30; Catalogue *of Mendota College for 1901–1902*, 38–39; *Catalogue: Mendota College, 1902–1903*, 36–37; *Catalogue: Mendota College, 1903–1904*, 36–39; *Catalogue: Mendota College, 1904–1905*, 35–36; *Catalogue: Mendota College, 1905–1906*, 32–34; *Catalogue: Mendota College, 1906–1907*, 33–38; *Catalogue: Mendota College, 1907–1908*, 47–51; *Annual of Mendota College, 1908–1909*, 51–56; *Annual of Mendota College, 1909–1910*, 81–84; *Annual of Mendota College: Catalogue, 1910–1911*, 81–84, 89–91; Brereton, *Training God's Army*, 61; and Woloch, *Women and the American Experience*, 115–25, 167–71, 283.

154. *Annual of Mendota College: Catalogue, 1910–1911*, 89–91; and Woloch, *Women and the American Experience*, 269–71, 275–86.

155. Brereton, *Training God's Army*, 61, 69.

156. Calkins, Adair, and Stevens, "From the Educational Committee," July 20, 1892, 2.

157. A. J. Bolster, "College Day Address," *Our Hope and Life in Christ*, January 24, 1900, 4–5.

158. J. W. Neslund, "Mendota College," *Our Hope and Life in Christ*, November 23, 1904, 3.

159. "Chapel Attendance," *Annual of Mendota College, 1908–1909*, 43.

160. L. J. Schaumburg, "Is Mendota College a Benefit?" *Our Hope and Life in Christ*, September 20, 1899, 9.

161. Sylvester Nokes, "College Notes," *Our Hope and Life in Christ*, January 22, 1896, 3.

162. Orven H. Loomis, "My College Experience," *Our Hope and Life in Christ*, February 18, 1903, 11.

163. N. C. Twining, "The Educational Field: Decline, Decay and Death of Darwinism" (Part 1), *Our Hope and Life in Christ*, February 3, 1909, 10–11.

164. *Catalogue of Mendota College for 1895–96*, 23.

165. Minutes of the Educational Committee, Western Advent Christian Publication Society, June 5, 1894, Jenks Memorial Collection of Adventual Materials, Aurora University, Aurora, Illinois.

166. J. L. Irvin, "College Notes," *Our Hope and Life in Christ*, November 27, 1907, 11; Literary Society, ed., "Theological Department," *Epitome: 1910*, 9–10; Literary Society, ed., "Theological Department," *Epitome: 1911*, 15; *Catalogue of Mendota College for 1895–96*, 23; and *Mendota College Annual, 1907–1908*, 40.

167. C. R. Smith, "Students' Prayer Meetings," *Epitome: 1911 Mendota College Annual*, 20.

168. J. J. Schaumburg, "College Notes," *Our Hope and Life in Christ*, October 19, 1898, 10; Warwick, "College Notes," *Our Hope and Life in Christ*,

February 15, 1899, 10–11; H. H. Corliss, "College Notes," *Our Hope and Life in Christ*, April 11, 1900, 10; M. B. C., "College Notes," *Our Hope and Life in Christ*, October 23, 1901, 11; Orven H. Loomis, "College Notes," *Our Hope and Life in Christ*, September 24, 1902, 11; Dan J. Costley, "Our College," *Our Hope and Life in Christ*, July 6, 1904, 9–10; O. H. Loomis, "College Notes," *Our Hope and Life in Christ*, November 23, 1904, 3; Harry L. Hanson, "College Notes," *Our Hope and Life in Christ*, September 20, 1905, 3; J. L. Irvin, "College Notes," *Our Hope and Life in Christ*, December 11, 1907, 3; J. L. Irvin, "College Notes," *Our Hope and Life in Christ*, May 13, 1908, 3; and Literary Society, ed., "Students' Prayer Meetings," *Epitome: 1911*, 20.

169. N. A., "Mendota," *Our Hope and Life in Christ*, December 23, 1891, 9; N. A., "Editorial Mention," *Our Hope and Life in Christ*, December 28, 1892, 8–9; Mendota Chamber of Commerce, *Tracks of Time*, 161; and Mendota Centennial Committee, *Magnificent Whistle Stop: The 100-Year Story of Mendota, Ill.* (Mendota, Ill.: Wayside Press, 1953), 115–16.

170. J. August Smith and George E. Cooprider, "A Church That Deserves Help," *Our Hope and Life in Christ*, July 6, 1904, 10.

171. N. A., "Brief Mention," *Our Hope and Life in Christ*, July 6, 1904, 6; and Smith and Cooprider, "A Church That Deserves Help," 10.

172. George E. Cooprider, "Pentecostal Revival at Aurora," *Our Hope and Life in Christ*, December 28, 1904, 5.

173. Cooprider, "Pentecostal Revival at Aurora," 5; and J. L. Irvin, "College Notes," *Our Hope and Life in Christ*, February 5, 1908, 10.

174. Costley, "Our College," 9.

175. Costley, "Our College," 9–10; and Harry L. Hanson, "College Notes," *Our Hope and Life in Christ*, June 6, 1906, 10.

176. Smith, eulogy for Norman P. Cook, quoted in Stockman, ed., *World's Crisis*, April 19, 1899, 1; and N. A., "Deserved Commendation," *Our Hope and Life in Christ*, September 16, 1903, 7.

177. Mary E. Smith, "How All May Help," *Our Hope and Life in Christ*, September 17, 1902, 3.

178. N. A., "Personal and General," *Our Hope and Life in Christ*, April 17, 1901, 6; M. B. C., "College Notes," *Our Hope and Life in Christ*, February 12, 1902, 10–11; Smith, "How All May Help," 3; N. A., "Brief Mention," *Our Hope and Life in Christ*, June 3, 1903, 6; O. H. Loomis, "College Notes," *Our Hope and Life in Christ*, June 7, 1905, 7; Cornelia Pollard, "Helpful Hints," *Our Hope and Life in Christ*, March 28, 1906, 9; Harry L. Hanson, "College Notes," *Our Hope and Life in Christ*, October 3, 1906, 10–11; Harry L. Hanson, "College Notes," *Our Hope and Life in Christ*, October 10, 1906, 10; N. A., "Mendota College Commencement," *Our Hope and Life in Christ*, May 22, 1907, 7; J. L. Irvin, "College Notes," *Our Hope and Life in Christ*, March 4, 1908, 3; S. T. Neduts, "The Educational Field: College Notes," *Our Hope and Life in Christ*, March 17, 1909, 10; and Literary Society, ed., "Music," *Epitome: 1911*, 47.

179. Harry L. Hanson, "College Notes," *Our Hope and Life in Christ*, February 20, 1907, 10.

180. Trowbridge, "A Good Work at Mendota," 4.

181. J. L. Irvin, "College Notes," *Our Hope and Life in Christ*, October 16, 1907, 10.

182. J. L. Irvin, "College Notes," *Our Hope and Life in Christ*, November 27, 1907, 10.

183. Harry L. Hanson, "College Notes," *Our Hope and Life in Christ*, February 28, 1906, 7; Irvin, "College Notes," October 16, 1907, 10; Irvin, "College Notes," November 27, 1907, 10–11; and J. L. Irvin, "College Notes," *Our Hope and Life in Christ*, February 5, 1908, 10.

184. Trowbridge, "A Good Work at Mendota," 4.

185. Clyde E. Hewitt, *Midnight and Morning: An Account of the Adventist Awakening and the Founding of the Advent Christian Denomination, 1831–1860* (Charlotte, N.C.: Venture Books, 1983), 134.

186. Smith, "Our Opportunity," 4; J. August Smith, "The Mendota Meeting," *Our Hope and Life in Christ*, February 17, 1892, 9–10; H. P. (Henry Pollard), "The General Western Camp-meeting," *Our Hope and Life in Christ*, April 27, 1892, 7; L. H. Davis, "The Mendota Campmeeting," *Our Hope and Life in Christ*, June 29, 1892, 6; N. A., "Report of the Third Annual Meeting of the Western Advent Christian Publishing Society," 4–6; and J. F. Adair, "Camp Meeting Notes," *Our Hope and Life in Christ*, September 6, 1893, 9.

187. N. A., "Report of Mendota Campmeeting," *Our Hope and Life in Christ*, September 14, 1892, 2–3; N. A., "General Western Camp Meeting," *Our Hope and Life in Christ*, July 5, 1893, 9; J. August Smith, "Mendota Campmeeting Committee Report," *Our Hope and Life in Christ*, September 6, 1893, 7; W. S. [probably William Sheldon], "A Camp of the Saints," *Our Hope and Life in Christ*, September 13, 1893, 10; Lora M. Ives, "Reply and Suggestions," *Our Hope and Life in Christ*, May 2, 1894, 5; J. August Smith, "Mendota Campmeeting," *Our Hope and Life in Christ*, August 1, 1894, 14; N. A., "Mendota Campmeeting," *Our Hope and Life in Christ*, August 29, 1894, 8; and F. A. Baker, M. A. Stevens, A. J. Bolster, N. Runquist, E. B. Townsend, M. McCulloch, G. G. Emery, Wm. Watson, and J. August Smith, "Mendota Campmeeting," *Our Hope and Life in Christ*, July 17, 1895, 13.

188. Ives, "Reply and Suggestions," 5.

189. N. A., "Report of Mendota Campmeeting," 2; Smith, "Mendota Campmeeting Committee Report," 7; Ives, "Reply and Suggestions," 5; and N. A., "Mendota Campmeeting," 8.

190. Adair, "Camp Meeting Notes," 9.

191. N. A., "Editorial," *Our Hope and Life in Christ*, September 14, 1892, 12; Smith, "Mendota Campmeeting Committee Report," 7; J. August Smith, "College Repair Fund," *Our Hope and Life in Christ*, September 4, 1901, 9; B. A. King, "College Day Offerings: Received August 8–15, 1908," *Our Hope and Life in Christ*, August 19, 1908, 3; and B. A. King, "College Day

Offerings: Received August 15–Sept. 5, 1908," *Our Hope and Life in Christ*, September 16, 1908, 12.

192. J. W. Emmons, "College Chapel Chairs," *Our Hope and Life in Christ*, November 13, 1895, 7.

193. J. W. Emmons, "Some Things Seen and Done," *Our Hope and Life in Christ*, September 11, 1895, 2–3; G. V. Clum, "What Is Being Done for the College," *Our Hope and Life in Christ*, September 25, 1895, 12–13; G. V. Clum, "College Repairs," *Our Hope and Life in Christ*, October 2, 1895, 9; J. W. Emmons, "What We Want," *Our Hope and Life in Christ*, October 9, 1895, 8; J. W. Emmons, "The Good Work Goes On," *Our Hope and Life in Christ*, October 16, 1895, 12; and Emmons, "College Chapel Chairs," November 13, 1895, 7.

194. N. A., "College Day Program," *Our Hope and Life in Christ*, August 13, 1902, 11.

195. N. A., "The Coming Meetings," *Our Hope and Life in Christ*, June 29, 1892, 8–9; E. S. Mansfield, "The Helper's Union," *Our Hope and Life in Christ*, September 12, 1894, 12; F. F. Boynton, "Helper's Union, Annual Meeting: Mendota Campmeeting, 1897," *Our Hope and Life in Christ*, September 15, 1897, 9; O. R. J. (Orrin Roe Jenks), "Who Decides the Question?" *Our Hope and Life in Christ*, June 15, 1910, 15; and G. E. Pullen, "Special Meeting at Chicago, Ill., June 28, 1910: Secretary's Minutes. Full Report," *Our Hope and Life in Christ*, July 13, 1910, 2–3.

196. Lucas, *American Higher Education*, 204.

197. O. H. Loomis, "College Notes," *Our Hope and Life in Christ*, May 3, 1905, 7; Brereton, *Training God's Army*, 65; Lucas, *American Higher Education*, 124, 170–71, 186–87; Rudolph, *The American College and University*, 334–36, 395–96; and Thelin, *A History of American Higher Education*, 131.

198. *Catalogue of Mendota College for 1901–1902*, 8; Lucas, *American Higher Education*, 131–33, 186; Ringenberg, *The Christian College*, 67; and Thelin, *A History of American Higher Education*, 129.

199. N. C. Twining, "Our Bible Training School," *Our Hope and Life in Christ*, January 20, 1904, 9; *Annual of Mendota College, 1894–1895*, 12–13; *Catalogue of Mendota College for 1901–1902*, 23–25; *Catalogue: Mendota College, 1904–1905*, 9–10; *Catalogue: Mendota College, 1905–1906*, 20–21; *Catalogue: Mendota College, 1906–1907*, 20–23; *Annual of Mendota College, 1909–1910*, 55–56; Lucas, *American Higher Education*, 127, 186; and Rudolph, *The American College and University*, 115–16.

200. J. O. Staats, "Bible Training School—Mendota College," *Our Hope and Life in Christ*, May 8, 1901, 1.

201. Staats, "Bible Training School—Mendota College," 1; Lucas, *American Higher Education*, 128; and Ringenberg, *The Christian College*, 104.

202. N. A., "Editorial Notes," *Our Hope and Life in Christ*, May 16, 1894, 9.

203. *Catalogue: Mendota College, 1902–1903*, 22.

204. N. A., "Editorial Notes," May 16, 1894, 9; *Catalogue: Mendota College, 1902–1903*, 22; and Ringenberg, *The Christian College*, 104.

205. Dan J. Costley, "Our College," *Our Hope and Life in Christ*, July 6, 1904, 9.

206. N. A., "Brief Mention," *Our Hope and Life in Ch*rist, July 29, 1903, 6; O. H. L. (Orven H. Loomis), "College Notes," *Our Hope and Life in Christ*, December 9, 1903, 10–11; O. H. Loomis, "College Notes," *Our Hope and Life in Christ*, November 16, 1904, 3; Harry L. Hanson, "College Notes," *Our Hope and Life in Christ*, November 1, 1905, 3; N. A., "Brief Mention," *Our Hope and Life in Christ*, June 20, 1906, 6; Harry L. Hanson, "College Notes," *Our Hope and Life in Christ*, September 19, 1906, 10; Harry L. Hanson, "College Notes," *Our Hope and Life in Christ*, November 21, 1906, 7; Harry L. Hanson, "College Notes," *Our Hope and Life in Christ*, January 23, 1907, 10; Harry L. Hanson, "College Notes," *Our Hope and Life in Christ*, January 30, 1907, 10; J. L. Irvin, "College Notes," *Our Hope and Life in Christ*, April 22, 1908, 10–11; J. L. Irvin, "College Notes," *Our Hope and Life in Christ*, May 13, 1908, 3; J. L. Irvin, "College Notes," *Our Hope and Life in Christ*, May 27, 1908, 3; and Literary Society, ed., *Epitome: 1911*, 13.

207. *Annual of Mendota College, 1909–1910*, 56.

208. J. L. Irvin, "College Notes," *Our Hope and Life in Christ*, January 22, 1908, 10.

209. Orven H. Loomis, "College Notes," *Our Hope and Life in Christ*, October 22, 1902, 11; Harry L. Hanson, "College Notes," *Our Hope and Life in Christ*, April 10, 1907, 10–11; Harry L. Hanson, "College Notes," *Our Hope and Life in Christ*, June 5, 1907, 10; S. T. Neduts, Et Cetera, "College Notes," *Our Hope and Life in Christ*, May 19, 1909, 11; and S. T. Neduts, Et Cetera, "College Notes," *Our Hope and Life in Christ*, May 26, 1909, 11.

210. Orven H. Loomis, "College Notes," *Our Hope and Life in Christ*, October 21, 1903, 10; Dean, "Prof. N. C. Twining and His Work," 10; Minutes of the Board of Directors, Mendota College, August 21, 1903, Jenks Memorial Collection of Adventual Materials, Aurora University, Aurora, Illinois; *Catalogue of Mendota College for 1895–96*, 3; *Catalogue of Mendota College for 1896–97*, 3; Catalogue *of Mendota College for 1901–1902*, 4; *Catalogue: Mendota College, 1902–1903*, 4; *Catalogue: Mendota College, 1903–1904*, 4; *Catalogue: Mendota College, 1905–1906*, 6; *Catalogue: Mendota College, 1906–1907*, 6; *Catalogue: Mendota College, 1907–1908*, 4; *Annual of Mendota College, 1908–1909*, 4; and *Annual of Mendota College: Catalogue, 1910–1911*, 4.

211. O. R. J. (Orrin Roe Jenks), "Notes," *Our Hope and Life in Christ*, June 8, 1904, 8; N. A., "Commencement," *Our Hope and Life in Christ*, June 15, 1904, 6–7; O. R. J. (Orrin Roe Jenks), "Notes," *Our Hope and Life in Christ*, June 15, 1904, 8; *Catalogue of Mendota College for 1895–96*, 3; *Catalogue of Mendota College for 1896–97*, 3; Catalogue *of Mendota College for 1901–1902*, 4; *Catalogue: Mendota College, 1902–1903*, 4; *Catalogue:*

Mendota College, 1903–1904, 4; *Catalogue: Mendota College, 1905–1906*, 6; *Catalogue: Mendota College, 1906–1907*, 6; *Catalogue: Mendota College, 1907–1908*, 4; *Annual of Mendota College, 1908–1909*, 4; and *Annual of Mendota College: Catalogue, 1910–1911*, 4.

212. Minutes of the Educational Committee, Western Advent Christian Publication Society, August 13, 1893, Jenks Memorial Collection of Adventual Materials, Aurora University, Aurora, Illinois; Minutes of the Board of Education, Mendota College, April 3, 1901, Jenks Memorial Collection of Adventual Materials, Aurora University, Aurora, Illinois; and Minutes of the Board of Directors, Mendota College, April 10, 1907, April 1, 1908, April 6, 1910, Jenks Memorial Collection of Adventual Materials, Aurora University, Aurora, Illinois.

213. *Annual of Mendota College, 1893–1894*, 10; *Annual of Mendota College, 1894–1895*, 9; *Catalogue of Mendota College for 1895–96*, 5–6; *Catalogue of Mendota College for 1896–97*, 4; *Catalogue of Mendota College for 1898–99*, 22; *Catalogue of Mendota College for 1899–1900*, 23; Catalogue *of Mendota College for 1901–1902*, 33; *Catalogue: Mendota College, 1902–1903*, 31; *Catalogue: Mendota College, 1903–1904*, 31; *Catalogue: Mendota College, 1904–1905*, 29; *Catalogue: Mendota College, 1905–1906*, 27–28; *Catalogue: Mendota College, 1906–1907*, 28–29; *Catalogue: Mendota College, 1907–1908*, 41; *Annual of Mendota College, 1908–1909*, 44; *Annual of Mendota College, 1909–1910*, 10–11; *Annual of Mendota College: Catalogue, 1910–1911*, 10–11; Lucas, *American Higher Education*, 168, 180, 182, 186; Ringenberg, *The Christian College*, 61, 80–81, 83, 113–14, 131–32, 160; and Rudolph, *The American College and University*, 346.

214. *Annual of Mendota College, 1893–1894*, 10; *Annual of Mendota College, 1894–1895*, 9; *Catalogue of Mendota College for 1895–96*, 5–6; *Catalogue of Mendota College for 1896–97*, 4; *Catalogue of Mendota College for 1898–99*, 22; *Catalogue of Mendota College for 1899–1900*, 23; Catalogue *of Mendota College for 1901–1902*, 33; *Catalogue: Mendota College, 1902–1903*, 31; *Catalogue: Mendota College, 1903–1904*, 31; *Catalogue: Mendota College, 1904–1905*, 29; *Catalogue: Mendota College, 1905–1906*, 27–28; *Catalogue: Mendota College, 1906–1907*, 28–29; *Catalogue: Mendota College, 1907–1908*, 41; *Annual of Mendota College, 1908–1909*, 44; *Annual of Mendota College, 1909–1910*, 10–11; *Annual of Mendota College: Catalogue, 1910–1911*, 10–11; Lucas, *American Higher Education*, 152; and Thelin, *A History of American Higher Education*, 196.

215. *Annual of Mendota College, 1893–1894*, 10; *Annual of Mendota College, 1894–1895*, 9; *Catalogue of Mendota College for 1895–96*, 5–6; *Catalogue of Mendota College for 1896–97*, 4; *Catalogue of Mendota College for 1898–99*, 22; *Catalogue of Mendota College for 1899–1900*, 23; Catalogue *of Mendota College for 1901–1902*, 33; *Catalogue: Mendota College, 1902–1903*, 31; *Catalogue: Mendota College, 1903–1904*, 31;

Catalogue: Mendota College, 1904–1905, 29; *Catalogue: Mendota College, 1905–1906*, 27–28; *Catalogue: Mendota College, 1906–1907*, 28–29; *Catalogue: Mendota College, 1907–1908*, 41; *Annual of Mendota College, 1908–1909*, 44; *Annual of Mendota College, 1909–1910*, 10–11; *Annual of Mendota College: Catalogue, 1910–1911*, 10–11; Lucas, *American Higher Education*, 204; Ringenberg, *The Christian College*, 160; and Rudolph, *The American College and University*, 260, 282–84.

216. *Catalogue of Mendota College for 1895–96*, 6.

217. N. A., "The Bible School," May 8, 1895, 8; Fry, "College Letter. No. 7," 10; Loomis, "College Notes," February 15, 1905, 10; Irvin, "College Notes," April 22, 1908, 10–11; and Brereton, *Training God's Army*, 64, 81.

218. Geo. E. Cooprider, "College Bonds," *Our Hope and Life in Christ*, February 7, 1900, 4–5; W. Alford, "An Opinion," *Our Hope and Life in Christ*, January 28, 1903, 5; Blanche Dick, "The Need of Education," *Our Hope and Life in Christ*, January 6, 1904, 3; and J. Gilpen Byrd, "Should Our Ministry Be an Educated One?" *Our Hope and Life in Christ*, July 21, 1909, 2.

219. N. A., "Do Not Overlook Page Fifteen," *Our Hope and Life in Christ*, March 16, 1910, 7.

Chapter 6 – Student Organizations and Social Activities

1. Frederick Rudolph, *The American College and University: A History* (1962; repr., Athens, Ga.: University of Georgia Press, 1990), 137, 138.

2. College Literary Society, ed., "College Literary Society," *Epitome: Mendota College Annual, 1910*, 31; *Annual of Mendota College, 1894–1895* (Bloomington, Ill.: Pantagraph Printing and Stationery Co., 1894), 12; and Rudolph, *The American College and University*, 137, 138.

3. Clara Lindauer, "College Notes," *Our Hope and Life in Christ*, November 23, 1898, 10; Dan J. Costley, "Our College," *Our Hope and Life in Christ*, July 6, 1904, 9–10; Literary Society, ed., "Literary Society," *Epitome: 1910*, 31; *Catalogue of Mendota College for 1895–96* (Bloomington, Ill.: Pantagraph Printing and Stationery Co., 1895), 24–25; *Catalogue of Mendota College for 1898–99* (Mendota, Ill.: Western Advent Christian Publication Association, 1898), 24; and *Catalogue: Mendota College, 1904–1905* (Mendota, Ill.: Hope Print, 1904), 30–31.

4. Ethel E. Fry, "College Letter. No. 20," *Our Hope and Life in Christ*, February 13, 1901, 10.

5. Lindauer, "College Notes," November 23, 1898, 10; Clara Lindauer, "College Notes," *Our Hope and Life in Christ*, May 17, 1899, 10; H. H. Corliss, "College Notes," *Our Hope and Life in Christ*, May 30, 1900, 10; Fry, "College Letter. No. 20," 10; J. L. Irvin, "College Notes," *Our Hope and Life in Christ*, March 18, 1908, 10; and *Catalogue of Mendota College for 1895–96*, 25.

6. W. R. Shaw, "College Notes," *Our Hope and Life in Christ*, February 19, 1896, 10.

7. *Annual of Mendota College, 1894–1895*, 12.

8. *Annual of Mendota College, 1908–1909* (Mendota, Ill.: Our Hope Print, 1908), 46.

9. J. W. Emmons, "About Mendota College. Facts for Enquiring Students," *Our Hope and Life in Christ*, July 7, 1897, 7; Harry L. Hanson, "College Notes," *Our Hope and Life in Christ*, September 20, 1905, 3; Literary Society, ed., "College Literary Society," *Epitome: 1910*, 31; College Literary Society, ed., "College Literary Society," *Epitome: 1911 Mendota College Annual*, 44; *Catalogue: Mendota College, 1906–1907* (Mendota, Ill.: Hope Print, 1906), 31; *Annual of Mendota College, 1909–1910* (Mendota, Ill.: Our Hope Printing Company, 1909), 16, 79; and Official Data Foundation, "Calculating Inflation in the U.S.," http://www.officialdata.org (accessed October 4, 2018).

10. Orven H. Loomis, "College Notes," *Our Hope and Life in Christ*, October 22, 1902, 11.

11. Loomis, "College Notes," October 22, 1902, 11; Literary Society, ed., "Young Men's Debating Club" and "Adelphia Rhaetorias," *Epitome: 1910*, 37, 39; Literary Society, ed., "Adelphai Rhetorias," and "Hoi Demosthenioi," *Epitome: 1911*, 49, 51; and *Catalogue: Mendota College, 1904–1905*, 30.

12. M. B. C., "College Notes," *Our Hope and Life in Christ*, April 30, 1902, 10; and M. B. C., "College Notes," *Our Hope and Life in Christ*, May 14, 1902, 11.

13. Orven H. Loomis, "College Notes," *Our Hope and Life in Christ*, January 28, 1903, 11.

14. M. B. C., "College Notes," April 30, 1902, 10; M. B. C., "College Notes," May 14, 1902, 11; Loomis, "College Notes," October 22, 1902, 11; Loomis, "College Notes," January 28, 1903, 11; Orven H. Loomis, "College Notes," *Our Hope and Life in Christ*, February 4, 1903, 7; and *Catalogue: Mendota College, 1904–1905*, 30.

15. Mrs. J. B. Keepers, "College Notes," *Our Hope and Life in Christ*, January 26, 1910, 10; and Literary Society, ed., "The Joint Debates," *Epitome: 1910*, 41.

16. Mrs. J. B. Keepers, "College Notes," *Our Hope and Life in Christ*, February 23, 1910, 3; and Literary Society, ed., "The Joint Debates," *Epitome, 1910*, 41.

17. Mrs. J. B. Keepers, "College Notes," *Our Hope and Life in Christ*, March 30, 1910, 11; and Literary Society, ed., "The Joint Debates," *Epitome, 1910*, 41.

18. Mrs. J. B. Keepers, "College Notes," *Our Hope and Life in Christ*, June 8, 1910, 3; and Literary Society, ed., "Joint Debates," *Epitome: 1911*, 51.

19. Keepers, "College Notes," January 26, 1910, 10; Keepers, "College Notes," February 23, 1910, 3; Keepers, "College Notes," March 30, 1910, 11;

Keepers, "College Notes," June 8, 1910, 3; Literary Society, ed., "The Joint Debates," *Epitome, 1910*, 41; Literary Society, ed., "Hoi Demosthenioi" and "Joint Debates," *Epitome, 1911*, 51–52; *Aurora College Bulletin*, April 1922, 18; and *Aurora College Bulletin*,(April 1924, 17.

20. Literary Society, ed., "Adelphai Rhetorias," *Epitome, 1911*, 49.

21. Edwin C. Hardison, "College Notes," *Our Hope and Life in Christ*, February 1, 1911, 5.

22. Literary Society, ed., "Young Men's Debating Club," *Epitome, 1910*, 37.

23. Mrs. J. B. Keepers, "College Notes," *Our Hope and Life in Christ*, March 23, 1910, 7; Hardison, "College Notes," February 1, 1911, 5; Literary Society, ed., "Young Men's Debating Club," *Epitome, 1910*, 37; and Literary Society, ed., "Adelphai Rhetorias," *Epitome, 1911*, 49.

24. Literary Society, ed., "The Prohibition League," *Epitome: 1910*, 42.

25. *Annual of Mendota College, 1909–1910*, 14.

26. Harry S. Bridge, "Mendota College Prohibition League," *Our Hope and Life in Christ*, October 13, 1909, 5; Literary Society, ed., "The Prohibition League," *Epitome, 1910*, 42; and *Annual of Mendota College, 1909–1910*, 14.

27. W. R. Shaw, "College Notes," *Our Hope and Life in Christ*, February 19, 1896, 10.

28. Shaw, "College Notes," February 19, 1896, 10; S. T. Neduts, "The Educational Field: College Notes," *Our Hope and Life in Christ*, February 24, 1909, 10–11; Mrs. J. B. Keepers, "College Notes," *Our Hope and Life in Christ*, March 16, 1910, 11; and Elizabeth H. Lesuer, "The Aurora College Prohibition League," *Pharos*, April 1915, 123–24; and Literary Society, ed., "The Prohibition League," *Epitome, 1910*, 42.

29. G. E. W., "The State I. P. A. Convention," *The Pharos*, April 1915, 131.

30. G. E. W., "The State I. P. A. Convention," 130–131.

31. T. Harley Marsh, quoted in Leonard T. Richardson, "Aurora College and Local Option: Students Take a Prominent Part in Campaign," *Pharos*, April 1915, 124.

32. Richardson, "Aurora College and Local Option," 124–25.

33. Richardson, "Aurora College and Local Option," 125.

34. Richardson, "Aurora College and Local Option," 125–26.

35. *Aurora College Bulletin*, April 1920, 19; and *Aurora College Bulletin*, April 1922, 18–19.

36. Literary Society, ed., "The Greek Club," *Epitome: 1910*, 46.

37. Sylvester Nokes, "College Notes," *Our Hope and Life in Christ*, November 13, 1895, 10; W. R. Shaw, "College Notes," *Our Hope and Life in Christ*, January 29, 1896, 11; M. B. C., "College Notes," *Our Hope and Life in Christ*, January 22, 1902, 10–11; M. B. C., "College Notes," *Our Hope and Life in Christ*, February 12, 1902, 10–11; Mrs. J. B. Keepers, "College Notes," *Our Hope and Life in Christ*, January 19, 1910, 11; Literary Society, ed.,

"The Greek Club" and "The Choral Club," *Epitome, 1910,* 46; and *Annual of Mendota College, 1909–1910,* 14.

38. M. B. C., "College Notes," *Our Hope and Life in Christ,* October 16, 1901, 10–11; M. B. C., "College Notes," *Our Hope and Life in Christ,* November 20, 1901, 7; M. B. C., "College Notes," *Our Hope and Life in Christ,* November 27, 1901, 7; and M. B. C., "College Notes," *Our Hope and Life in Christ,* December 4, 1901, 10.

39. Shaw, "College Notes," January 29, 1896, 11; J. J. Schaumburg, "College Notes," *Our Hope and Life in Christ,* September 28, 1898, 7; J. J. Schaumburg, "College Notes," *Our Hope and Life in Christ,* October 19, 1898, 10; Milton Livingston, "College Notes," *Our Hope and Life in Christ,* October 18, 1899, 7; H. H. Corliss, "College Notes," *Our Hope and Life in Christ,* February 7, 1900, 10; H. H. Corliss, "College Notes," *Our Hope and Life in Christ,* May 9, 1900, 10; "One of the Students," "A College Letter. No. 1," *Our Hope and Life in Christ,* September 19, 1900, 11; Ethel E. Fry, "College Letter. No. 23," *Our Hope and Life in Christ,* March 6, 1901, 10; Milton Livingston, "Mendota College Y. M. C. A.," *Our Hope and Life in Christ,* May 29, 1901, 11; M. B. C., "College Notes," *Our Hope and Life in Christ,* October 23, 1901, 11; M. B. C., "College Notes," *Our Hope and Life in Christ,* November 13, 1901, 10; M. B. C., "College Notes," *Our Hope and Life in Christ,* February 12, 1902, 10–11; *Annual of Mendota College, 1894–1895,* 11; *Catalogue of Mendota College for 1898–99,* 23–24; and *Catalogue of Mendota College for 1899–1900* (Mendota, Ill.: Western Advent Christian Publication Association, 1899), 25.

40. Sylvester Nokes, "College Notes," *Our Hope and Life in Christ,* November 4, 1896, 7; O. H. L. (Orven H. Loomis), "College Notes," *Our Hope and Life in Christ,* October 7, 1903, 10; *The Collegian,* August 1903–May 1904; Literary Society, ed., *Epitome: 1910,* 1–58; and Literary Society, ed., *Epitome: 1911,* 1–59.

41. Nokes, "College Notes," November 4, 1896, 7.

42. Nokes, "College Notes," November 4, 1896, 7; *The Exponent: In the Interest of Mendota College and the Public Schools,* October 1896, 4; and Minutes of the Board of Education, Western Advent Christian Publication Association, September 23, 1896, and August 24, 1897, Jenks Memorial Collection of Adventual Materials, Aurora University, Aurora, Illinois.

43. O. H. L., "College Notes," October 7, 1903, 10; O. H. L. (Orven H. Loomis), "College Notes," *Our Hope and Life in Christ,* October 28, 1903, 10; O. H. L. (Orven H. Loomis), "College Notes," *Our Hope and Life in Christ,* December 2, 1903, 10; F. E. R. (F. E. Raasch), "College Notes," *Our Hope and Life in Christ,* January 20, 1904, 7; and *The Collegian: Devoted to Our Educational Interests,* August, October, November, December 1903 and January, February, March, April, May 1904.

44. N. A., " '*Epitome*' for 1911," *Our Hope and Life in Christ,* May 17, 1911, 9.

45. N. A., " *'Epitome'* for 1911," 9; *The Exponent*, 1896–97; *The Collegian*, August 1903–May 1904; Literary Society, ed., *Epitome: 1910*; and Literary Society, ed., *Epitome: 1911*.

46. Clara Lindauer, "College Notes," *Our Hope and Life in Christ*, May 3, 1899, 10–11.

47. O. H. Loomis, "College Notes," *Our Hope and Life in Christ*, June 7, 1905, 7.

48. Harry L. Hanson, "College Notes," *Our Hope and Life in Christ*, October 11, 1905, 3.

49. Lindauer, "College Notes," May 3, 1899, 10; O. H. Loomis, "College Notes," *Our Hope and Life in Christ*, April 26, 1905, 10; Loomis, "College Notes," June 7, 1905, 7; and Hanson, "College Notes," October 11, 1905, 3.

50. Harry L. Hanson, "College Notes," *Our Hope and Life in Christ*, January 31, 1906, 3.

51. O. H. Loomis, "College Notes," *Our Hope and Life in Christ*, February 15, 1905, 10.

52. H. H. Corliss, "College Notes," *Our Hope and Life in Christ*, January 31, 1900, 10; M. B. C., "College Notes," February 12, 1902, 10–11; F. E. R. (F. E. Raasch), "College Notes," *Our Hope and Life in Christ*, January 20, 1904, 7; O. H. Loomis, "College Notes," February 15, 1905, 10; Hanson, "College Notes," January 31, 1906, 3; and Edwin C. Hardison, "College Notes," *Our Hope and Life in Christ*, December 14, 1910, 5.

53. Ethel E. Fry, "College Letter. No. 9," *Our Hope and Life in Christ*, November 14, 1900, 10.

54. Milton Livingston, "College Notes," *Our Hope and Life in Christ*, November 15, 1899, 10; F. A. Baker, "A Beautiful Surprise," *Our Hope and Life in Christ*, February 7, 1900, 10; Fry, "College Letter. No. 9," 10; M. B. C., "College Notes," February 12, 1902, 10–11; M. B. C., "College Notes," May 14, 1902, 11; O. H. Loomis, "College Notes," *Our Hope and Life in Christ*, June 7, 1905, 7; Harry L. Hanson, "College Notes," *Our Hope and Life in Christ*, May 30, 1906, 3; and Harry L. Hanson, "College Notes," *Our Hope and Life in Christ*, May 22, 1907, 10.

55. "By Somebody," "College Notes," *Our Hope and Life in Christ*, November 4, 1908, 3.

56. Ethel E. Fry, "College Letter. No. 5," *Our Hope and Life in Christ*, October 17, 1900, 10; and Harry L. Hanson, "College Notes," *Our Hope and Life in Christ*, January 23, 1907, 10.

57. J. L. Irvin, "College Notes," *Our Hope and Life in Christ*, October 23, 1907, 10.

58. Milton Livingston, "College Notes," *Our Hope and Life in Christ*, December 13, 1899, 10.

59. Livingston, "College Notes," December 13, 1899, 10; Harry L. Hanson, "College Notes," *Our Hope and Life in Christ*, November 8, 1905, 3; and Irvin, "College Notes," October 23, 1907, 10.

60. N. A., "An Enjoyable Entertainment," *Our Hope and Life in Christ*, February 3, 1904, 7.

61. A. H. Stoddard, "Seminary Notes," *Our Hope and Life in Christ*, March 22, 1893, 9; Clara Lindauer, "College Notes," *Our Hope and Life in Christ*, June 7, 1899, 10; O. H. L. (Alven H. Loomis), "College Notes," *Our Hope and Life in Christ*, December 16, 1903, 10; N. A., "An Enjoyable Entertainment," 7; N. A., "Brief Mention," *Our Hope and Life in Christ*, March 16, 1904, 6; O. H. L. (Alven H. Loomis), "College Notes," *Our Hope and Life in Christ*, June 8, 1904, 7; Harry L. Hanson, "College Notes," *Our Hope and Life in Christ*, December 13, 1905, 10; Harry L. Hanson, "College Notes," *Our Hope and Life in Christ*, December 20, 1905, 10; Harry L. Hanson, "College Notes," *Our Hope and Life in Christ*, January 10, 1906, 3; Harry L. Hanson, "College Notes," *Our Hope and Life in Christ*, January 24, 1906, 3; Harry L. Hanson, "College Notes," *Our Hope and Life in Christ*, February 14, 1906, 10; Harry L. Hanson, "College Notes," *Our Hope and Life in Christ*, May 23, 1906, 10; J. L. Irvin, "College Notes," *Our Hope and Life in Christ*, November 13, 1907, 7; J. L. Irvin, "College Notes," *Our Hope and Life in Christ*, November 27, 1907, 10–11; J. L. Irvin, "College Notes," *Our Hope and Life in Christ*, December 11, 1907, 3; J. L. Irvin, "College Notes," *Our Hope and Life in Christ*, March 4, 1908, 3; B. J. Dean, "The Educational Field: Prof. N. C. Twining and His Work," *Our Hope and Life in Christ*, December 23, 1908, 10–11; S. T. Neduts, "The Educational Field: College Notes," *Our Hope and Life in Christ*, March 17, 1909, 10; S. T. Neduts, "College Notes," *Our Hope and Life in Christ*, June 9, 1909, 11; and Literary Society, ed., "Music," *Epitome: 1911*, 47.

62. Literary Society, ed., "From the Fun Factory," *Epitome: 1910*, 56.

63. Literary Society, ed., "Advertisements: Wanted, For Sale, Lost, Found, Etc.," *Epitome: 1910*, 56.

64. Literary Society, ed., "The Problem Solved," *Epitome: 1911*, 59.

65. Literary Society, ed., "Wouldn't It Surprise You to Know That," *Epitome: 1911*, 57.

66. Literary Society, ed., "A Glimpse into the Hall of Fame," *Epitome: 1911*, 32–33.

67. S. T. Neduts, Et Cetera, "College Notes," *Our Hope and Life in Christ*, March 24, 1909, 10.

68. O. H. Loomis, "College Notes," *Our Hope and Life in Christ*, January 18, 1905, 10.

69. Harry L. Hanson, "College Notes," *Our Hope and Life in Christ*, February 21, 1906, 10.

70. Milton Livingston, "College Notes," *Our Hope and Life in Christ*, December 6, 1899, 10.

71. H. H. Corliss, "College Notes," *Our Hope and Life in Christ*, February 21, 1900, 10

72. H. H. Corliss, "College Notes," *Our Hope and Life in Christ*, March 7, 1900, 10.

73. Fred Newberry, "The College Gymnasium," *Our Hope and Life in Christ*, April 18, 1900, 9.

74. Newberry, "The College Gymnasium," 9.

75. H. H. Corliss, "College Notes," *Our Hope and Life in Christ*, April 25, 1900, 10.

76. Corliss, "College Notes," April 25, 1900, 10.

77. Corliss, "College Notes," April 25, 1900, 10.

78. W. B. C., "College Notes," *Our Hope and Life in Christ*, October 23, 1901, 11.

79. Harry L. Hanson, "College Notes," *Our Hope and Life in Christ*, April 25, 1906, 10.

80. Literary Society, ed., "Athletics," *Epitome: 1910*, 47.

81. H. H. Corliss, "College Notes," *Our Hope and Life in Christ*, May 9, 1900, 10.

82. Corliss, "College Notes," May 9, 1900, 10; E. E. F., "College Letter. No. 8.," *Our Hope and Life in Christ*, November 7, 1900, 10; W. B. C., "College Notes," October 23, 1901, 11; Harry L. Hanson, "College Notes," *Our Hope and Life in Christ*, October 25, 1905, 3; Harry L. Hanson, "College Notes," *Our Hope and Life in Christ*, November 1, 1905, 3; Hanson, "College Notes," April 25, 1906, 10; Edwin C. Hardison, "College Notes," *Our Hope and Life in Christ*, March 1, 1911, 5; Edwin C. Hardison, "College Notes," *Our Hope and Life in Christ*, March 29, 1911, 5; and Literary Society, ed., "Athletics," *Epitome: 1910*, 47.

83. Literary Society, ed., "Athletics," *Epitome: 1910*, 47.

84. Literary Society, ed., "Athletics," *Epitome: 1910*, 47.

85. Literary Society, ed., "Athletics," *Epitome: 1910*, 47.

86. Loomis, "College Notes," January 18, 1905, 10; Hanson, "College Notes," February 21, 1906, 10; and Literary Society, ed., "Athletics," *Epitome: 1910*, 47.

87. Literary Society, ed., "Athletics," *Epitome: 1910*, 47.

88. Christopher J. Lucas, *American Higher Education: A History* (New York: St. Martin's Griffin, 1994), 176–78; Rudolph, *The American College and University*, 374–76, 381–83; and John R. Thelin, *A History of American Higher Education* (Baltimore: John Hopkins University Press, 2004), 180.

89. Literary Society, ed., "Athletics," *Epitome: 1910*, 47.

Chapter 7 – Student Life and Culture

1. *Announcement of Mendota Seminary, 1893* (Cincinnati: Press of C. J. Krehbiel & Co., 1893), 17–18.

2. *Annual of Mendota College, 1894–1895* (Bloomington, Ill.: Pantagraph Printing and Stationery Co., 1894), 9–10.

3. Christopher J. Lucas, *American Higher Education: A History* (New York: St. Martin's Griffin, 1994), 124.

4. Lucas, *American Higher Education*, 124–25; and Frederick Rudolph, *The American College and University: A History* (1962; repr., Athens, Ga.: University of Georgia Press, 1990), 164–65, 168–70.

5. Board of Education Committee, Rules and Regulations for Students Rooming in the Dormitories of Mendota College, 1893, Mendota College Folder, Doris K. Colby Memorial Archives, Aurora University, Aurora, Illinois.

6. J. O. Campbell, "Bible Training School," *Our Hope and Life in Christ*, May 17, 1893, 13; J. W. Emmons, "About Mendota College. Facts for Enquiring Students," *Our Hope and Life in Christ*, July 7, 1897, 7; *Announcement of Mendota Seminary, 1893*, 19; *Catalogue of Mendota College for 1895–96* (Bloomington, Ill.: Pantagraph Printing and Stationery Co., 1895), 25–26; *Catalogue of Mendota College for 1896–97* (Bloomington, Ill.: Pantagraph Printing and Stationery Co., 1896), 23; *Catalogue of Mendota College for 1898–99* (Mendota, Ill.: Western Advent Christian Publication Association, 1898), 25–26; *Catalogue: Mendota College, 1902–1903* (Mendota, Ill.: Western Advent Christian Publication Association, 1902), 34; *Catalogue: Mendota College, 1906–1907* (Mendota, Ill.: Hope Print, 1906), 31; and *Annual of Mendota College: Catalogue, 1910–1911* (Mendota, Ill.: Our Hope Print, 1910), 16–18.

7. *Announcement of Mendota Seminary, 1893*, 19.

8. E. S. Mansfield, "The Helper's Union," *Our Hope and Life in Christ*, September 12, 1894, 12; and Mrs. E. S. Mansfield, "The Helper's Union," *Our Hope and Life in Christ*, October 3, 1894, 10–11.

9. Anna Whitney, "General Helper's Union Quarterly Report," *Our Hope and Life in Christ*, November 13, 1895, 10.

10. F. F. Boynton, "Helper's Union, Annual Meeting: Mendota Campmeeting, 1897," *Our Hope and Life in Christ*, September 15, 1897, 9.

11. Mary E. Smith, "How All May Help," *Our Hope and Life in Christ*, September 17, 1902, 3.

12. E. E. Denniston, "Grateful Commendation," *Our Hope and Life in Christ*, June 23, 1897, 10.

13. Belle M. White, "The Helper's Union," *Our Hope and Life in Christ*, December 12, 1894, 12–13; Belle M. White, "The Helper's Union: Quarterly Report," *Our Hope and Life in Christ*, March 20, 1895, 12; Whitney, "General Helper's Union Quarterly Report," 10; Anna Whitney, "Helper's Union Quarterly Report," *Our Hope and Life in Christ*, February 26, 1896, 11; Anna J. Whitney, "Semi-Annual Report—Helper's Union," *Our Hope and Life in Christ*, February 24, 1897, 11; Denniston, "Grateful Commendation," 10; Boynton, "Helper's Union, Annual Meeting," 9; and Mary E. Smith, "How All May Help," 3.

14. J. Emmons, "Bathing-Tub for the College," *Our Hope and Life in Christ*, November 20, 1895, 11.

15. Sylvester Nokes, "College Notes," *Our Hope and Life in Christ*, November 13, 1895, 10; and Emmons, "Bathing-Tub for the College," 11.

16. Mrs. Edgar Bennett, "College Visit: No. 4," *Our Hope and Life in Christ*, March 11, 1903, 3.

17. Bennett, "College Visit: No. 4," 3.

18. N. A., "A Handsome Christmas Gift," *Our Hope and Life in Christ*, December 21, 1898, 7.

19. M. L. Gordon, "A New College Dormitory," *Our Hope and Life in Christ*, August 31, 1898, 7; N. A., "Encouraging Prospects," *Our Hope and Life in Christ*, September 7, 1898, 7; N. A., "The New College Dormitory," *Our Hope and Life in Christ*, November 2, 1898, 7; J. Wolfenstetter, "Young Ladies' Home," *Our Hope and Life in Christ*, November 9, 1898, 10; J. W. (Joseph Wolfenstetter), "Our Own," *Our Hope and Life in Christ*, December 14, 1898, 7; and N. A., "A Handsome Christmas Gift," 7.

20. N. A., "A Great Calamity and a Great Deliverance," *Our Hope and Life in Christ*, December 18, 1901, 6–7; M. B. C., "College Notes," *Our Hope and Life in Christ*, December 18, 1901, 10; and N. A., "The Recent Fire," *Our Hope and Life in Christ*, December 25, 1901, 7.

21. N. A., "A Great Calamity and a Great Deliverance," 6.

22. N. A., "A Great Calamity and a Great Deliverance," 6–7; M. B. C., "College Notes," December 18, 1901, 10; and N. A., "The Recent Fire," 7.

23. N. A., "A Great Calamity and a Great Deliverance," 6–7; H. M. Robbins, "Card of Thanks," *Our Hope and Life in Christ*, December 18, 1901, 7; M. B. C., "College Notes," December 18, 1901, 10; N. A., "College Prospects," *Our Hope and Life in Christ*, January 1, 1902, 7; M. B. C., "College Notes," *Our Hope and Life in Christ*, January 8, 1902, 10; and M. B. C., "College Notes," *Our Hope and Life in Christ*, January 22, 1902, 10–11.

24. N. A., "College Prospects," 7; M. B. C., "College Notes," January 8, 1902, 10; and M. B. C., "College Notes," January 22, 1902, 10–11.

25. *Catalogue: Mendota College, 1902–1903*, 34.

26. Orven H. Loomis, "College Notes," *Our Hope and Life in Christ*, September 24, 1902, 11.

27. *Catalogue: Mendota College, 1903–1904* (Mendota, Ill.: Western Advent Christian Publication Association, 1903), 34.

28. A. J. Bolster, "Our Prospective Dormitory," *Our Hope and Life in Christ*, January 15, 1902, 7; Albert J. Bolster, "Our Prospective Dormitory— NO. 2," *Our Hope and Life in Christ*, January 22, 1902, 7; Board Minutes of the Western Advent Christian Publication Association, April 8, 1902, Jenks Memorial Collection of Adventual Materials, Aurora University, Aurora, Illinois; *Catalogue: Mendota College, 1902–1903*, 34; and *Catalogue: Mendota College, 1903–1904*, 34.

29. N. A., "Local and Personal," *The Collegian*, October 1903, 6.

30. N. A., "Brief Mention," *Our Hope and Life in Christ*, August 12, 1903, 6; O. H. L. (Orven H. Loomis), "College Notes," *Our Hope and Life*

in Christ, December 16, 1903, 10; and N. A., "Local and Personal," *The Collegian*, October 1903, 6.

31. Mrs. Edgar Bennett, "College Visit: No. 5," *Our Hope and Life in Christ*, April 1, 1903, 3.

32. Bennett, "College Visit: No. 5," 3.

33. Bennett, "College Visit: No. 5," 3.

34. Mrs. Edgar Bennett, "College Visit: No. 6," *Our Hope and Life in Christ*, April 8, 1903, 3.

35. Orrin R. Jenks, "Help Our Young Women," *Our Hope and Life in Christ*, May 11, 1910, 15.

36. Bennett, "College Visit: No. 6," 3; and Jenks, "Help Our Young Women," 15.

37. Mrs. E. S. Mansfield, "Fire! Fire!: Helpers to the Rescue!" *Our Hope and Life in Christ*, December 18, 1901, 7.

38. Mansfield, "Fire! Fire!" 7; E. S. Mansfield, "Revised Conclusions," *Our Hope and Life in Christ*, January 1, 1902, 7; and Mrs. E. S. Mansfield, "Acknowledgment," *Our Hope and Life in Christ*, January 15, 1902, 10–11.

39. *Catalogue: Mendota College, 1906–1907*, 31.

40. *Catalogue: Mendota College, 1907–1908* (Mendota, Ill.: Hope Print, 1907), 44.

41. Mrs. Edgar Bennett, "College Visit: No. 7," *Our Hope and Life in Christ*, May 6, 1903, 3; *Catalogue: Mendota College, 1906–1907*, 31; and *Catalogue: Mendota College, 1907–1908*, 44.

42. N. A., "Locals and Personals," *The Collegian*, April 1904, 4–5.

43. H. H. Corliss, "College Notes," *Our Hope and Life in Christ*, May 16, 1900, 10; O. H. L. (Orven H. Loomis), "College Notes," *Our Hope and Life in Christ*, December 2, 1903, 10; Harry L. Hanson, "College Notes," *Our Hope and Life in Christ*, December 5, 1906, 10; J. L. Irvin, "College Notes," *Our Hope and Life in Christ*, December 4, 1907, 10; J. L. Irvin, "College Notes," *Our Hope and Life in Christ*, January 8, 1908, 3; and N. A., "Locals and Personals," *The Collegian*, April 1904, 4–5.

44. M. B. C., "College Notes," *Our Hope and Life in Christ*, October 9, 1901, 10–11; Smith, "How All May Help," 3; Bennett, "College Visit: No. 5," 3; Bennett, "College Visit: No. 6," 3; N. A., "College Notes," *Our Hope and Life in Christ*, September 23, 1903, 10; N. A., "Brief Mention," *Our Hope and Life in Christ*, November 11, 1903, 6; and J. L. Irvin, "College Notes," *Our Hope and Life in Christ*, March 25, 1908, 10–11.

45. Orven H. Loomis, "College Notes," *Our Hope and Life in Christ*, September 24, 1902, 11; O. H. L. (Alven H. Loomis), "College Notes," *Our Hope and Life in Christ*, December 16, 1903, 10; O. H. L. (Alven H. Loomis), "College Notes," *Our Hope and Life in Christ*, June 8, 1904, 7; and Harry L. Hanson, "College Notes," *Our Hope and Life in Christ*, November 8, 1905, 3.

46. B. Forester, "Important to Ministers," *Our Hope and Life in Christ*, September 30, 1896, 12.

47. Forester, "Important to Ministers," 12; and J. W. Emmons, "THE FIRST ANSWER: To Help the Bible Training School," *Our Hope and Life in Christ*, November 18, 1896, 11.

48. G. L. Carpenter, "A Good Place," *Our Hope and Life in Christ*, September 11, 1895, 13.

49. Carpenter, "A Good Place," 13; Minutes of the Educational Committee, Western Advent Christian Publication Association, June 4, 1895, Jenks Memorial Collection of Adventual Materials, Aurora University, Aurora, Illinois; and Minutes of the Board of Directors, Mendota College, August 29, 1908, September 5, 1910, April 4, 1911, Jenks Memorial Collection of Adventual Materials, Aurora University, Aurora, Illinois.

50. *Annual of Mendota College: Catalogue, 1910–1911*, 17.

51. "The Students in English," "College Notes," *Our Hope and Life in Christ*, December 9, 1908, 3.

52. S. T. Neduts, "College Notes," *Our Hope and Life in Christ*, April 21, 1909, 3.

53. N. A., "Bible Training Students' Fund," *Our Hope and Life in Christ*, March 20, 1895, 9

54. Editor, "Very Suggestive," *Our Hope and Life in Christ*, April 11, 1894, 5.

55. N. A., "Let Others Follow," *Our Hope and Life in Christ*, May 2, 1894, 3; and Lora M. Ives, "Reply and Suggestions," *Our Hope and Life in Christ*, May 2, 1894, 5.

56. G. L. Carpenter, "Suggestions to Loyal Workers," *Our Hope and Life in Christ*, July 29, 1896, 2.

57. Carpenter, "Suggestions to Loyal Workers,"2; Emmons, "THE FIRST ANSWER," 11; and Lauren Dillon, "Greeting!" *Our Hope and Life in Christ*, September 12, 1900, 2.

58. Josie Lowry, "Mendota College," *Our Hope and Life in Christ*, July 25, 1900, 5.

59. J. W. Emmons, "Wanted! Wanted!" *Our Hope and Life in Christ*, September 16, 1896, 9.

60. N. A., "What Is Our Duty," *Our Hope and Life in Christ*, March 20, 1895, 8; N. A., "Bible Training Students' Fund, 9; N. A., "Encourage the Young Preachers," *Our Hope and Life in Christ*, September 11, 1895, 8; Emmons, "Wanted! Wanted!" 9; Emmons, "THE FIRST ANSWER, 11; J. W. Emmons, "WHAT WE NEED. And What We Must Have," *Our Hope and Life in Christ*, December 16, 1896, 10–11; J. W. Emmons, "Young Lady, Look Here!" *Our Hope and Life in Christ*, December 16, 1896, 11; J. W. Emmons, "Bound for Mendota Bible School," *Our Hope and Life in Christ*, December 23, 1896, 7; J. O. Staats, "Bible Training School—Mendota College," *Our Hope and Life in Christ*, May 8, 1901, 1; J. H. Stuckey, "A Word to Adventists," *Our Hope and Life in Christ*, July 25, 1906, 10; and Orrin R. Jenks, "Attention Churches!" *Our Hope and Life in Christ*, March 13, 1907, 7.

61. Milton Livingston, "A Proposition," *Our Hope and Life in Christ*, May 4, 1898, 10.

62. Livingston, "A Proposition," May 4, 1898, 10; and Milton Livingston, "A Proposition," *Our Hope and Life in Christ*, January 18, 1899, 11.

63. F. Murra, "What It Costs," *Our Hope and Life in Christ*, July 19, 1899, 10.

64. E. E. Denniston, "Grateful Commendation," *Our Hope and Life in Christ*, June 23, 1897, 10.

65. O. H. L. (Orven H. Loomis), "College Notes," *Our Hope and Life in Christ*, April 20, 1904, 10.

66. G. V. Clum, "What Is Being Done for the College," *Our Hope and Life in Christ*, September 25, 1895, 12; Sylvester Nokes, "College Notes," *Our Hope and Life in Christ*, January 8, 1896, 7; Sylvester Nokes, "College Notes," *Our Hope and Life in Christ*, April 22, 1896, 10; Milton Livingston, "College Notes," *Our Hope and Life in Christ*, December 21, 1898, 10; Ethel E. Fry, "College Letter. No. 26," *Our Hope and Life in Christ*, April 17, 1901, 10; M. B. C., "College Notes," *Our Hope and Life in Christ*, April 9, 1902, 11; Orven H. Loomis, "College Notes," *Our Hope and Life in Christ*, May 20, 1903, 11; O. H. L. (Orven H. Loomis), "College Notes," *Our Hope and Life in Christ*, March 2, 1904, 10; O. H. L. (Orven H. Loomis), "College Notes," *Our Hope and Life in Christ*, April 20, 1904, 10; O. H. L. (Orven H. Loomis), "College Notes," *Our Hope and Life in Christ*, May 18, 1904, 10; The Committee (Edgar Bennett, James Skiles and F. E. Roberts), "College Campus Committee Report," *Our Hope and Life in Christ*, July 26, 1905, 3; Harry L. Hanson, "College Notes," *Our Hope and Life in Christ*, April 25, 1906, 10–11; and J. L. Irvin, "College Notes," *Our Hope and Life in Christ*, April 15, 1908, 3.

67. Nokes, "College Notes," April 22, 1896, 10.

68. J. L. Irvin, "College Notes," *Our Hope and Life in Christ*, April 15, 1908, 3.

69. Nokes, "College Notes," April 22, 1896, 10; O. H. L. (Orven H. Loomis), "College Notes," March 2, 1904, 10; and Irvin, "College Notes," April 15, 1908, 3.

70. Orven H. Loomis, "College Notes," *Our Hope and Life in Christ*, May 20, 1903, 11; and The Committee, "College Campus Committee Report," 3.

71. N. A., "Sad News," *Our Hope and Life in Christ*, February 6, 1901, 7.

72. N. A., "Sad News," 7; and F. A. Baker, "Obituaries," *Our Hope and Life in Christ*, February 27, 1901, 13.

73. Baker, "Obituaries," 13.

74. N. A., "Sad News," 7; Ethel E. Fry, "College Letter—No. 19," *Our Hope and Life in Christ*, February 6, 1901, 10–11; Baker, "Obituaries," 13; and Mrs. Edgar Bennett, "Our College Visit: No. 3," *Our Hope and Life in Christ*, January 21, 1903, 3.

75. Fry, "College Letter—No. 19," 11.

76. N. A., "Sad News," 7; Fry, "College Letter—No. 19," 10–11; Baker, "Obituaries," 13; and Bennett, "Our College Visit: No. 3," 3.

77. Minutes of the Board of Directors, Mendota College, April 2, 1908, Jenks Memorial Collection of Adventual Materials, Aurora University, Aurora, Illinois.

78. W. S., N. T., *Our Hope and Life in Christ*, May 9, 1894, 10.

79. W. S., N. T., May 9, 1894, 10; all existing Mendota College catalogs, 1893–94 through 1896–97, 1898–99 through 1899–1900, 1901–2 through 1910–11; and Virginia Lieson Brereton, *Training God's Army: The American Bible School, 1880–1940* (Indianapolis: Indiana University Press, 1990), 69.

80. Mansfield, "Fire! Fire!" 7; College Literary Society, ed., "Adelphia Rhaetorias," *Epitome: 1911 Mendota College Annual*, 49; Board of Directors Minutes, Western Advent Christian Publication Association, April 3, 1901, Jenks Memorial Collection of Adventual Materials, Aurora University, Aurora, Illinois; faculty list in all existing Mendota College catalogs, 1893–94 through 1896–97, 1898–99 through 1899–1900, 1901–2 through 1910–11; *Catalogue: Mendota College, 1903–1904*, 4; *Catalogue: Mendota College, 1904–1905* (Mendota, Ill.: Hope Print, 1904), 4; *Catalogue: Mendota College, 1905–1906* (Mendota, Ill.: Hope Print, 1905), 6; *Catalogue: Mendota College, 1906–1907*, 6; *Catalogue: Mendota College, 1907–1908*, 4; and *Annual of Mendota College, 1908–1909* (Mendota, Ill.: Our Hope Print, 1908), 4.

81. Harry L. Hanson, "College Notes," *Our Hope and Life in Christ*, April 25, 1906, 11.

82. Hanson, "College Notes," April 25, 1906, 11.

83. Harry L. Hanson, "College Notes," *Our Hope and Life in Christ*, January 31, 1906, 3; Hanson, "College Notes," April 25, 1906, 10–11; and N. A., "Miss Spence's Visit," *Our Hope and Life in Christ*, May 9, 1906, 7.

84. College Literary Society, ed., "Young Men's Debating Club," *Epitome: Mendota College Annual, 1910*, 37.

85. Mrs. J. B. Keepers, "College Notes," *Our Hope and Life in Christ*, March 23, 1910, 7.

86. Mrs. J. B. Keepers, "College Notes," *Our Hope and Life in Christ*, January 26, 1910, 10; Mrs. J. B. Keepers, "College Notes," *Our Hope and Life in Christ*, February 23, 1910, 3; Keepers, "College Notes," March 23, 1910, 7; Mrs. J. B. Keepers, "College Notes," *Our Hope and Life in Christ*, March 30, 1910, 11; and Literary Society, ed., "Young Men's Debating Club" and "The Joint Debates," *Epitome: 1910*, 37, 41.

87. Literary Society, ed., "The Alumni or Who-What-Where? of Mendota College," *Epitome: 1910*, 52–54; and Nancy Woloch, *Women and the American Experience*, 4th ed. (Boston: McGraw Hill, 2006), 269, 285.

88. Orrin R. Jenks, "The Number of Biblical Students," *Our Hope and Life in Christ*, December 2, 1908, 10.

89. Woloch, *Women and the American Experience*, 283.

90. Leonard T. Richardson, "Aurora College and Local Option: Students Take a Prominent Part in Campaign," *The Pharos*, April 1915, 124–26.

91. Literary Society, ed., "The Prohibition League," *Epitome: 1910*, 42.

92. Literary Society, ed., "A Serious Case," *Epitome: 1911*, 58.

93. Dan J. Costley, "Our College," *Our Hope and Life in Christ*, July 6, 1904, 10.

94. *Catalogue of Mendota College for 1898–99*, 22.

Chapter 8 – A Shoestring and a Prayer: The Difficulties in Financing a Small College

1. N. A., "The Promised Donation," *Our Hope and Life in Christ*, December 16, 1891, 6.

2. J. August Smith, "Enough," *Our Hope and Life in Christ*, January 6, 1892, 2.

3. William M'Culloch, "That Western College," *Our Hope and Life in Christ*, July 2, 1890, 10; J. August Smith, "Our Opportunity," *Our Hope and Life in Christ*, December 2, 1891, 4–5; William M'Culloch, "That Mendota College," *Our Hope and Life in Christ*, December 9, 1891, 10; D. R. Mansfield and J. H. White, "Camp and School," *Our Hope and Life in Christ*, December 23, 1891, 9; and Smith, "Enough," 2.

4. J. August Smith, "The Mendota Meeting," *Our Hope and Life in Christ*, February 17, 1892, 9–10.

5. N. A., "Report of the Third Annual Meeting of the Western Advent Christian Publishing Society," *Our Hope and Life in Christ*, September 7, 1892, 6.

6. *Annual of Mendota College, 1893–1894* (Aurora, Ill.: Copeland & Phillips, Printers, 1893), 6; *Annual of Mendota College, 1894–1895* (Bloomington, Ill.: Pantagraph Printing and Stationery Co., 1894), 5; *Catalogue: Mendota College, 1902–1903* (Mendota, Ill.: Western Advent Christian Publication Association, 1902), 4; *Catalogue: Mendota College, 1903–1904* (Mendota, Ill.: Western Advent Christian Publication Association, 1903), 4; *Annual of Mendota College: Catalogue, 1910—1911* (Mendota, Ill.: Our Hope Print, 1910), 6–7; Minutes of the Mendota College Board of Education, Western Advent Christian Publication Association, March 24, 1899, Jenks Memorial Collection of Adventual Materials, Aurora University, Aurora, Illinois; Minutes of the Annual Meeting, Western Advent Christian Publication Association, August 22, 1893, August 27, 1894, August 20, 1912, Jenks Memorial Collection of Adventual Materials, Aurora University, Aurora, Illinois; and Minutes of the Board of Directors, Western Advent Christian Publication Association, August 24, 1899, Jenks Memorial Collection of Adventual Materials, Aurora University, Aurora, Illinois.

7. O. R. J. (Orrin R. Jenks), "Who Decides the Question?" *Our Hope and Life in Christ*, June 15, 1910, 15; Minutes of the Board of Directors, Western

Advent Christian Publication Association, January 10, 1913 and August 31, 1913, Jenks Memorial Collection of Adventual Materials, Aurora University, Aurora, Illinois; and Minutes of the Special Meeting of the Western Advent Christian Publication Association, January 5–7, 1910, and June 28, 1910, Jenks Memorial Collection of Adventual Materials, Aurora University, Aurora, Illinois.

8. L. Dillon, "Summary of Accounts of the Western Advent Christian Publication Association, from Aug. 1st, 1905 to Aug. 1st, 1906," and B. A. King, "Summary of Accounts of Mendota College, from August 2, 1905, to August 14, 1906," *Our Hope and Life in Christ*, September 5, 1906, 5; Minutes of the Board of Directors, Mendota College, March 31, 1908, and August 27, 1909, Jenks Memorial Collection of Adventual Materials, Aurora University, Aurora, Illinois; and Minutes of the Annual Meeting, Western Advent Christian Publication Association, August 25, 1908, Jenks Memorial Collection of Adventual Materials, Aurora University, Aurora, Illinois.

9. Minutes of the Board of Directors, Mendota College, March 31, 1908, August 27, 1909, April 4, 1911, May 24, 1911, Jenks Memorial Collection of Adventual Materials, Aurora University, Aurora, Illinois; and Minutes of the Board of Directors, Western Advent Christian Publication Association, April 3, 1901, Jenks Memorial Collection of Adventual Materials, Aurora University, Aurora, Illinois.

10. Minutes of the Board of Directors, Mendota College, April 19, 1905, Jenks Memorial Collection of Adventual Materials, Aurora University, Aurora, Illinois; and Minutes of the Annual Meeting, Western Advent Christian Publication Association, August 11, 1905, August 25, 1908, Jenks Memorial Collection of Adventual Materials, Aurora University, Aurora, Illinois.

11. Minutes of the Board of Education, Western Advent Christian Publication Association, December 29, 1896 (mistake in minutes, giving the year as 1897), Jenks Memorial Collection of Adventual Materials, Aurora University, Aurora, Illinois; Minutes of the Board of Directors, Mendota College, March 31, 1908, Jenks Memorial Collection of Adventual Materials, Aurora University, Aurora, Illinois; and Minutes of the Board of Directors, Western Advent Christian Publication Association, August 3, 1896, Jenks Memorial Collection of Adventual Materials, Aurora University, Aurora, Illinois.

12. J. Oscar Campbell, "The Mendota Seminary," *Our Hope and Life in Christ*, December 7, 1892, 8–9.

13. J. Oscar Campbell, "Mendota Seminary," *Our Hope and Life in Christ*, December 28, 1892, 4.

14. A. S. Calkins, J. F. Adair, and M. A. Stevens, "From the Educational Committee," *Our Hope and Life in Christ*, July 20, 1892, 2; N. A., "From the Educational Committee," *Our Hope and Life in Christ*, November 23, 1892, 4; F. A. Baker, "A Pointed Proposal to All Adventists," *Our Hope and Life in Christ*, November 30, 1892, 4; Campbell, "The Mendota Seminary," December 7, 1892, 8–9; J. August Smith, "The Mendota Seminary," *Our Hope and Life in Christ*, December 21, 1892, 9; Campbell, "Mendota

Seminary," December 28 1892, 4; N. A., "School Matters," *Our Hope and Life in Christ*, January 18, 1893, 8; J. Oscar Campbell, "The Mendota Seminary," *Our Hope and Life in Christ*, January 25, 1893, 9; and N. A., "Report of the Educational Committee" (of the Western Advent Christian Publication Association), *Our Hope and Life in Christ*, August 30, 1893, 11.

15. Calkins, Adair, and Stevens, "From the Educational Committee," July 20, 1892, 2; N. A., "From the Educational Committee," November 23, 1892, 4; J. Oscar Campbell and J. H. Nichols, "Announcement," *Our Hope and Life in Christ*, November 23, 1892, 4; Baker, "A Pointed Proposal to All Adventists," 4; Campbell, "Mendota Seminary," December 28, 1892, 4; N. A., "Editorial Mention," *Our Hope and Life in Christ*, December 28, 1892, 8; N. A., "School Matters," 8; Campbell, "The Mendota Seminary," January 25, 1893, 9; J. Oscar Campbell, "Mendota College President's Report of Progress," *Our Hope and Life in Christ*, April 12, 1893, 8; and N. A., "Report of the Educational Committee," August 30, 1893, 11.

16. J. W. Emmons, "The Conclusion of the Whole Matter," *Our Hope and Life in Christ*, December 23, 1896, 10.

17. J. W. Emmons, "What Do You Say?" *Our Hope and Life in Christ*, January 6, 1897, 10.

18. J. W. Emmons, "One Debt Paid," *Our Hope and Life in Christ*, March 10, 1897, 10.

19. J. W. Emmons, "Out of Debt," *Our Hope and Life in Christ*, June 30, 1897, 7.

20. N. A., "Greeting," *Our Hope and Life in Christ*, September 8, 1897, 6.

21. J. W. Emmons, "Bound to Win—Success Ahead," *Our Hope and Life in Christ*, April 28, 1897, 10.

22. Minutes of the Board of Education, Western Advent Christian Publication Association, April 15, 1897, Jenks Memorial Collection of Adventual Materials, Aurora University, Aurora, Illinois.

23. Minutes of the Board of Education, Western Advent Christian Publication Association, December 29, 1896 (mistake in minutes, giving the year as 1897), and April 14–15, 1897, Jenks Memorial Collection of Adventual Materials, Aurora University, Aurora, Illinois.

24. J. W. Emmons, "No Answer to the Call," *Our Hope and Life in Christ*, April 26, 1899, 10–11; J. W. Emmons, "College Finances, Etc.," *Our Hope and Life in Christ*, May 29, 1901, 12; J. W. Emmons, "To Friends of the College," *Our Hope and Life in Christ*, September 3, 1902, 10–11; J. W. Emmons, "Heed the Call!" *Our Hope and Life in Christ*, June 24, 1908, 10–11; J. W. Emmons, "Read! Read!! Read!!!" *Our Hope and Life in Christ*, May 14, 1902, 10–11; N. A., "Only Three Weeks," *Our Hope and Life in Christ*, May 13, 1903, 7; and O. R. Jenks, "Our Present College Need—Special and Important," *Our Hope and Life in Christ*, May 22, 1912, 9.

25. M. M. Livingston, "College Day Offerings," *Our Hope and Life in Christ*, December 24, 1902, 11.

26. Albert J. Bolster, "Dormitory Fund," *Our Hope and Life in Christ*, May 7, 1902, 11.

27. H. M. Robbins, "College Day Offerings," *Our Hope and Life in Christ*, February 26, 1902, 10.

28. J. August Smith, "College Repair Fund," *Our Hope and Life in Christ*, September 4, 1901, 9; and J. August Smith, "College Repair Fund," *Our Hope and Life in Christ*, November 27, 1901, 7.

29. N. A., "The College Day Offerings," *Our Hope and Life in Christ*, March 12, 1902, 7.

30. B. Forester, "Please Read This!" *Our Hope and Life in Christ*, April 8, 1908, 2.

31. N. A., "Our Prospective Office," *Our Hope and Life in Christ*, October 10, 1906, 7; B. A. King, "Mendota College: Important Monetary Statement," *Our Hope and Life in Christ*, December 4, 1907, 10–11; B. A. King, "College Day Offerings: Received from Dec. 28, '07 to Jan. 18, 1908," *Our Hope and Life in Christ*, January 22, 1908, 10–11; and Forester, "Please Read This!" 2.

32. Orrin R. Jenks, "BULLETIN NO. 72: Wanted: TEN THOUSAND DOLLARS," *Our Hope and Life in Christ*, June 26, 1912, 16.

33. Orrin R. Jenks, "Our College Running Expenses," *Our Hope and Life in Christ*, November 8, 1911, 5; and Orrin R. Jenks, "Our College Operating Expenses: An Appeal from the President," *Our Hope and Life in Christ*, December 6, 1911, 4.

34. Albert J. Bolster, "Our Prospective Dormitory—NO. 2," *Our Hope and Life in Christ*, January 22, 1902, 7.

35. M'Culloch, "That Western College," 10; Smith, "Our Opportunity," 4; Bolster, "Our Prospective Dormitory—NO. 2," 7; and B. Forester, "Please Read This!" 2.

36. J. O. C. (J. Oscar Campbell), "School Notes," *Our Hope and Life in Christ*, February 8, 1893, 9.

37. Milton M. Livingston, "College Day Offerings," *Our Hope and Life in Christ*, May 7, 1902, 10.

38. N. A., "College Day Offering," *Our Hope and Life in Christ*, January 3, 1900, 7; Milton Livingston, "Those Coin Cards," *Our Hope and Life in Christ*, February 20, 1901, 7; Livingston, "College Day Offerings," May 7, 1902, 10; Milton M. Livingston, "College Day Offerings," *Our Hope and Life in Christ*, January 7, 1903, 13; and Milton M. Livingston, "College Day Offerings," *Our Hope and Life in Christ*, December 30, 1903, 10.

39. Orrin R. Jenks, "BULLETIN NO. 9: A Call to Our Laymen," *Our Hope and Life in Christ*, April 6, 1910, 15.

40. J. W., "Our School," *Our Hope and Life in Christ*, January 18, 1899, 10; N. A., "College Day Offerings," *Our Hope and Life in Christ*, February 10, 1904, 11; N. A., "The College Day Offering," *Our Hope and Life in Christ*, January 11, 1905, 7; N. A., "A Little Behind," *Our Hope and Life in Christ*, May 17, 1905, 7; B. Forester, "Another Visit," *Our Hope and Life in Christ*, December 9, 1908,

2–3; Jenks, "BULLETIN NO. 9," 15; N. A., "Page Sixteen," *Our Hope and Life in Christ*, September 28, 1910, 9; and Jenks, "Our Present College Need," 9.

41. J. W. Emmons, "Another Short Talk," *Our Hope and Life in Christ*, November 25, 1896, 10.

42. J. W. Emmons, "A Noble Example," *Our Hope and Life in Christ*, November 25, 1896, 7.

43. M. A. Tibbets, "Many Hands Make Light Work," *Our Hope and Life in Christ*, December 9, 1896, 12.

44. N. A., "Personal and General," *Our Hope and Life in Christ*, February 6, 1901, 6.

45. J. W. Emmons, "What the Doctor Thinks," *Our Hope and Life in Christ*, December 2, 1896, 10.

46. J. W. Emmons, "Attention Ye Ministers!" *Our Hope and Life in Christ*, November 17, 1897, 10.

47. William A. Burch, "Prayers That Count," *Our Hope and Life in Christ*, December 28, 1910, 10–11.

48. J. W. Emmons, "Nearly to the Winding Up," *Our Hope and Life in Christ*, June 9, 1897, 10–11; Emmons, "Attention Ye Ministers!" 10; J. W. Emmons, "Good News! Read It!" *Our Hope and Life in Christ*, December 8, 1897, 11; M. M. Livingston, "A Sample Letter," *Our Hope and Life in Christ*, November 18, 1903, 7; M. M. Livingston, "College Day Offerings," *Our Hope and Life in Christ*, December 16, 1903, 10; M. M. Livingston, "College Day Offerings," *Our Hope and Life in Christ*, March 2, 1904, 10–11; B. A. King, "College Day Offerings: Received June 6–13, 1908," *Our Hope and Life in Christ*, June 17, 1908, 10–11; and Burch, "Prayers That Count," 10–11.

49. Livingston, "A Sample Letter," 7; and B. Forester, "Debts Versus Duty," *Our Hope and Life in Christ*, June 22, 1898, 10–11.

50. J. W. Emmons, "What We Want," *Our Hope and Life in Christ*, December 5, 1900, 10.

51. B. A. King, "College Day Offerings: Received June 13–20, 1908," *Our Hope and Life in Christ*, June 24, 1908, 11.

52. Orrin Roe Jenks, "When Should Pledges Be Paid?" *Our Hope and Life in Christ*, March 23, 1910, 15.

53. Emmons, "What We Want," December 5, 1900, 10.

54. J. W. Emmons, "That Debt Is Melting Away," *Our Hope and Life in Christ*, May 5, 1897, 11; Emmons, "What We Want," 10; King, "College Day Offerings: Received June 13–20, 1908," 11; Orrin R. Jenks, "BULLETIN NO. 6: Good Cheer among Our Ministers," *Our Hope and Life in Christ*, March 16, 1910, 15; and Jenks, "When Should Pledges Be Paid?" 15.

55. B. A. King, "College Day Offerings: Received July 11–18, 1908," *Our Hope and Life in Christ*, July 22, 1908, 10–11.

56. Emmons, "Nearly to the Winding Up," 10–11; Emmons, "Attention Ye Ministers!" 10–11; J. W. Emmons, "We Are Waiting Patiently!" *Our Hope*

and *Life in Christ*, December 15, 1897, 7; and King, "College Day Offerings: Received July 11–18, 1908," 10–11.

57. N. A., "Educational Day," *Our Hope and Life in Christ*, January 17, 1912, 9.

58. J. W. Emmons, "A Word for the Pastors," *Our Hope and Life in Christ*, May 19, 1897, 7; N. A., "Educational Day," *Our Hope and Life in Christ*, December 10, 1902, 6–7; E. B. P., "Educational Day," *Our Hope and Life in Christ*, December 24, 1902, 2; N. A., "College Day," *Our Hope and Life in Christ*, December 31, 1902, 7; N. A., "Educational Sunday," *Our Hope and Life in Christ*, January 7, 1903, 7; N. A., "Educational Day," January 17, 1912, 9; and Minutes of the Board of Directors, Western Advent Christian Publication Association, August 27, 1897, Jenks Memorial Collection of Adventual Materials, Aurora University, Aurora, Illinois.

59. E. L. Whitney, "College Day—Important," *Our Hope and Life in Christ*, January 3, 1894, 9.

60. Whitney, "College Day—Important," 9.

61. Whitney, "College Day—Important," 9; N. A., "College Day," *Our Hope and Life in Christ*, January 16, 1895, 8; E. S. M., "College Day," *Our Hope and Life in Christ*, January 30, 1895, 12; N. A., "College Day," *Our Hope and Life in Christ*, December 11, 1895, 7; N. A., "College Day," *Our Hope and Life in Christ*, December 30, 1896, 6; N. A., "College Day," *Our Hope and Life in Christ*, December 15, 1897, 7; N. A., "College Day," *Our Hope and Life in Christ*, December 29, 1897, 6; N. A., "Conference and College Day," *Our Hope and Life in Christ*, January 12, 1898, 7; N. A., "College Day," *Our Hope and Life in Christ*, December 7, 1898, 7; N. A., "College Day," *Our Hope and Life in Christ*, January 4, 1899, 7; N. A., "College Day," *Our Hope and Life in Christ*, January 3, 1900, 6; N. A., "College Day," *Our Hope and Life in Christ*, December 26, 1900, 7; N. A., "College Day," *Our Hope and Life in Christ*, January 16, 1901, 6–7; N. A., "College Day," *Our Hope and Life in Christ*, January 8, 1902, 6–7; N. A., "College Day," *Our Hope and Life in Christ*, January 14, 1903, 6–7; N. A., "College Day," *Our Hope and Life in Christ*, December 23, 1903, 7; N. A., "College Day," *Our Hope and Life in Christ*, December 28, 1904, 7; N. A., "College Day, 1906," *Our Hope and Life in Christ*, January 3, 1906, 6–7; N. A., "College Day Exercises," *Our Hope and Life in Christ*, January 8, 1908, 3; and N. A., "College Day," *Our Hope and Life in Christ*, December 30, 1908, 7.

62. N. A., "School Matters," *Our Hope and Life in Christ*, January 18, 1893, 8; N. A., "College Day," *Our Hope and Life in Christ*, January 17, 1894, 8; N. A., "College Day," January 4, 1899, 7; N. A., "College Day," *Our Hope and Life in Christ*, January 13, 1904, 6–7; N. A., "College Day and Conference," *Our Hope and Life in Christ*, January 18, 1905, 7; and J. August Smith, "College Day Address," *Our Hope and Life in Christ*, January 20, 1909, 2–3.

63. J. W. Emmons, "College Day Offering," *Our Hope and Life in Christ*, January 5, 1898, 11.

64. Whitney, "College Day—Important," 9; N. A., "College Day," December 11, 1895, 7; Emmons, "College Day Offering," January 5, 1898, 11; N. A., "College Day Offering," *Our Hope and Life in Christ*, December 25, 1901, 6–7; H. M. Robbins, "College Day Offerings," *Our Hope and Life in Christ*, February 26, 1902, 10; N. A., "Brief Mention," *Our Hope and Life in Christ*, March 4, 1903, 6; Milton M. Livingston, "College Day Offerings," *Our Hope and Life in Christ*, December 30, 1903, 10; Milton M. Livingston, "Needed at Once," *Our Hope and Life in Christ*, April 20, 1904, 11; N. A., "Our College and Its Needs," *Our Hope and Life in Christ*, December 25, 1907, 7; and William A. Burch, "Prayers That Count," *Our Hope and Life in Christ*, December 28, 1910, 10–11.

65. Emmons, "College Day Offering," January 5, 1898, 11.

66. J. W. Emmons, "Nothing Like It!" *Our Hope and Life in Christ*, January 25, 1899, 10.

67. J. W. Emmons, "According to My Promise," *Our Hope and Life in Christ*, January 13, 1897, 11; Emmons, "College Day Offering," January 5, 1898, 11; N. A., "College Day Offering," *Our Hope and Life in Christ*, January 11, 1899, 7; Emmons, "Nothing Like It!" 10; N. A., "College Day Offering," *Our Hope and Life in Christ*, January 3, 1900, 7; N. A., "Those Coin Cards," *Our Hope and Life in Christ*, December 26, 1900, 7; Milton M. Livingston, "College Day Offerings," *Our Hope and Life in Christ*, January 7, 1903, 13; Livingston, "College Day Offerings," December 30, 1903, 10; and Forester, "Please Read This!" April 8, 1908, 2.

68. N. A., "Greeting," *Our Hope and Life in Christ*, September 8, 1897, 6–7; J. W. Emmons, "A Good Report," *Our Hope and Life in Christ*, June 29, 1898, 10; J. W. Emmons, "Look Here! Read This!" *Our Hope and Life in Christ*, May 23, 1900, 10; N. A., "College Day Offering," *Our Hope and Life in Christ*, December 25, 1901, 6–7; J. W. Emmons, "Thank You!" *Our Hope and Life in Christ*, June 11, 1902, 11; Milton M. Livingston, "College Day Offerings," *Our Hope and Life in Christ*, August 13, 1902, 11; J. W. Emmons, "To Friends of the College," *Our Hope and Life in Christ*, September 3, 1902, 10–11; M. M. Livingston, "College Day Offerings," *Our Hope and Life in Christ*, December 24, 1902, 11; Milton M. Livingston, "Very Important for All," *Our Hope and Life in Christ*, May 27, 1903, 11; Livingston, "Needed at Once," 11; B. A. King, "Donations for Mendota College: From Nov. 18th, to Dec. 2d, 1905," *Our Hope and Life in Christ*, December 13, 1905, 12; B. A. King, "College Day Offerings: Receipts from May 12 to May 26, 1906," *Our Hope and Life in Christ*, May 30, 1906, 11; J. W. Emmons, "Look Here, See What We Are Doing," *Our Hope and Life in Christ*, May 20, 1908, 3; J. W. Emmons, "It's Got to Be Done!" *Our Hope and Life in Christ*, July 15, 1908, 3; B. A. King, "College Day Offerings: Received August 15–Sept. 5, 1908," *Our Hope and Life in Christ*, September 16, 1908, 12; H. E. Pancost, "College Cash Receipts," *Our Hope and Life in Christ*, October 12, 1910, 10–11; T. L.

S., "Please Note," *Our Hope and Life in Christ*, September 27, 1911, 9; N. A., "A Little Extra Help Just Now," *Our Hope and Life in Christ*, May 22, 1912, 9; and Orrin R. Jenks, "BULLETIN NO. 72," 16.

69. George J. French, "College Day Offerings," *Our Hope and Life in Christ*, February 24, 1897, 7; N. A., "Brief Mention," *Our Hope and Life in Christ*, December 29, 1897, 6; Milton Livingston, "Those Coin Cards," *Our Hope and Life in Christ*, February 6, 1901, 10; H. M. Robbins, "College Day Offerings," *Our Hope and Life in Christ*, January 8, 1902, 7; N. A., "Personal and General," *Our Hope and Life in Christ*, January 22, 1902, 6; Milton M. Livingston, "College Day Offerings," *Our Hope and Life in Christ*, January 14, 1903, 10; B. Forester, "Good News," *Our Hope and Life in Christ*, May 9, 1906, 4–5; and J. W. Emmons, "Rather Slow of Late," *Our Hope and Life in Christ*, June 3, 1908, 3.

70. N. A., "College Day Offering," December 25, 1901, 6–7; Milton M. Livingston, "College Day Offerings," *Our Hope and Life in Christ*, May 7, 1902, 10–11; Livingston, "College Day Offerings," January 7, 1903, 13; N. A., "Brief Mention," March 4, 1903, 6; Milton Livingston, "Ho! For More College Day Offerings," *Our Hope and Life in Christ*, May 6, 1903, 10–11; N. A., "College Day," December 23, 1903, 7; Livingston, "Needed at Once," 11; and N. A., "Our College and Its Needs," 7.

71. B. A. King, "College Day Offerings: Received Dec. 14–26, 1907," *Our Hope and Life in Christ*, January 1, 1908, 12.

72. J. W. Emmons, "College Day Offering," *Our Hope and Life in Christ*, January 5, 1898, 11; J. W. Emmons, "Nothing Like It!" 10; N. A., "Personal and General," February 6, 1901, 6; H. M. Robbins, "College Day Offerings," *Our Hope and Life in Christ*, February 26, 1902, 10; Livingston, "College Day Offerings," May 7, 1902, 10–11; Livingston, "College Day Offerings," January 7, 1903, 13; Livingston, "Ho! For More College Day Offerings," 10–11; N. A., "College Day Offerings," *Our Hope and Life in Christ*, February 10, 1904, 11; M. M. Livingston, "College Day Offerings," *Our Hope and Life in Christ*, March 2, 1904, 10–11; N. A., "Various Matters: College Day Offerings," *Our Hope and Life in Christ*, March 29, 1905, 6; B. A. King, "College Day Offerings: From May 13, to May 27, 1905," *Our Hope and Life in Christ*, May 31, 1905, 7; B. A. King, "College Day Offerings: Receipts from Feb. 17, to March 3, 1906," *Our Hope and Life in Christ*, March 7, 1906, 10; B. Forester, "Mendota College and Its Friends," *Our Hope and Life in Christ*, March 6, 1907, 3; N. A., "How to Sustain Our Cause," *Our Hope and Life in Christ*, March 6, 1907, 7; B. A. King, "College Day Offerings: Received February 8–29, 1908," *Our Hope and Life in Christ*, March 4, 1908, 3; J. W. Emmons, "The College Obligation," *Our Hope and Life in Christ*, June 10, 1908, 10; and Emmons, "It's Got to Be Done!" 3.

73. J. W. Emmons, "Important—Read Carefully," *Our Hope and Life in Christ*, January 9, 1901, 10; Livingston, "College Day Offerings," May 7, 1902, 10–11; N. A., "Our College and Its Needs," 7; B. Forester, "Mendota College

and Its Friends," *Our Hope and Life in Christ*, March 6, 1907, 3; and B. A. King, "College Day Offerings: Received April 11–25, 1908," *Our Hope and Life in Christ*, April 29, 1908, 11.

74. R. C. Robbins, "We Are Counting on You!" *Our Hope and Life in Christ*, July 18, 1906, 3.

75. "A Student," "A Pleasant Reunion," *Our Hope and Life in Christ*, September 20, 1905, 5; Robbins, "We Are Counting on You!" 3; and N. A., "Attention Students!" *Our Hope and Life in Christ*, August 8, 1906, 3.

76. B. Forester, "College Factors," *Our Hope and Life in Christ*, May 6, 1908, 3.

77. Orrin R. Jenks, "BULLETIN NO. 4: A Call to Our Ministers," *Our Hope and Life in Christ*, February 23, 1910, 15; Jenks, "BULLETIN NO. 9," 15; Orrin R. Jenks, "BULLETIN NO. 10: An Appeal to Our Young Men," *Our Hope and Life in Christ*, April 13, 1910, 15; Orrin R. Jenks, "BULLETIN NO. 11: Our Young Women to the Front," *Our Hope and Life in Christ*, May 4, 1910, 15; Orrin R. Jenks, "BULLETIN NO. 12: To Our Isolated Ones," *Our Hope and Life in Christ*, May 18, 1910, 15; Christopher J. Lucas, *American Higher Education: A History* (New York: St. Martin's Griffin, 1994), 190–91; and Frederick Rudolph, *The American College and University: A History* (1962; repr., Athens, GA: University of Georgia Press, 1990), 189, 428–30.

78. J. W. Emmons, "What Do You Say?" *Our Hope and Life in Christ*, January 6, 1897, 10; J. W. Emmons, "Another Hundred for the College," *Our Hope and Life in Christ*, March 3, 1897, 10; J. W. Emmons, "Another Lift for the College," *Our Hope and Life in Christ*, March 17, 1897, 10–11; Orrin R. Jenks, "BULLETIN NO. 20: Help Us to Reach This Goal—Forty-One Thousand Dollars by Nov. 1, 1910," *Our Hope and Life in Christ*, August 17, 1910, 15; Orrin R. Jenks, "BULLETIN NO. 22: We Reached the Goal—and On Time!" *Our Hope and Life in Christ*, November 9, 1910, 16; Orrin R. Jenks, "BULLETIN NO. 29: Victory Again!" *Our Hope and Life in Christ*, March 29, 1911, 16; Orrin R. Jenks, "BULLETIN NO. 30: A Ten Thousand Dollar Pledge," *Our Hope and Life in Christ*, April 5, 1911, 16; and Orrin R. Jenks, "BULLETIN NO. 39: A Re-statement of Our Financial Condition," *Our Hope and Life in Christ*, June 14, 1911, 16.

79. Wm. A. Burch, "Several Things I Want to Say," *Our Hope and Life in Christ*, November 29, 1911, 9; and Wm. A. Burch, "Cameo Progress," *Our Hope and Life in Christ*, January 24, 1912, 10–11.

80. Emma Dennin Jenks, quoted in Burch, "Several Things I Want to Say," 9.

81. Mary E. Smith, quoted in Burch, "Several Things I Want to Say," 9.

82. Burch, "Several Things I Want to Say," 9; and Burch, "Cameo Progress," 10–11.

83. Burch, "Several Things I Want to Say," 9.

84. Mrs. Florence Ritchie, "Minnesota Methods," *Our Hope and Life in Christ*, March 23, 1904, 3.

85. Emmons, "College Day Offering," January 5, 1898, 11; and Ritchie, "Minnesota Methods," 3.

86. J. Oscar Campbell, "Mendota College President's Report of Progress," *Our Hope and Life in Christ*, April 12, 1893, 8–9; N. A., "The Bible Training School," *Our Hope and Life in Christ*, June 28, 1893, 8; M. L. Gordon, "College Work," *Our Hope and Life in Christ*, November 9, 1898, 7; Jenks, "Our College Operating Expenses: An Appeal from the President," 4; and Emmons, "What the Doctor Thinks," 10–11.

87. N. A., "Greeting," 6–7.

88. N. A., "Greeting," 6–7; N. A., "College Day Offerings," *Our Hope and Life in Christ*, February 10, 1904, 11; Orrin R. Jenks, "BULLETIN NO. 6," *Our Hope and Life in Christ*, March 16, 1910, 15; and George E. Cooprider, "That New $70,000 College for Aurora, Illinois," *Our Hope and Life in Christ*, March 23, 1910, 4–5.

89. M. A. Stevens, "Our Opportunity," *Our Hope and Life in Christ*, April 25, 1894, 3.

90. N. A., "Read Page Fifteen," *Our Hope and Life in Christ*, February 23, 1910, 6–7.

91. A. J. Bolster, "College Day Address," *Our Hope and Life in Christ*, January 24, 1900, 4–5; M. L. Gordon, "College Education," *Our Hope and Life in Christ*, May 30, 1900, 9; and Jennie M. Twining, "Plea for Higher Christian Education," *Our Hope and Life in Christ*, November 26, 1902, 4–5.

92. J. W. Emmons, "The Conclusion of the Whole Matter," *Our Hope and Life in Christ*, December 23, 1896, 10–11; Milton M. Livingston, "Donations to Seminaries," *Our Hope and Life in Christ*, March 22, 1905, 3; Orrin R. Jenks, "BULLETIN NO. 8: What Thirty-Five Hundred Persons Could Do—An Appeal from One of Our Sisters," *Our Hope and Life in Christ*, March 30, 1910, 15; and Orrin R. Jenks, "BULLETIN NO. 50: Thanksgiving Is Coming," *Our Hope and Life in Christ*, October 25, 1911, 16.

93. Livingston, "Donations to Seminaries," 3.

94. Jenks, "BULLETIN NO. 50," 16.

95. Emmons, "What We Want," December 5, 1900, 10; F. A. Baker, "Mendota College," *Our Hope and Life in Christ*, December 26, 1900, 10; J. W. Emmons, "Mendota College School-Tax," *Our Hope and Life in Christ*, May 6, 1908, 4; and Emmons, "Heed the Call!" 10–11.

96. Emmons, "Heed the Call!" 10.

97. Baker, "Mendota College," 10.

98. Emmons, "What the Doctor Thinks," 10–11; and Jenks, "BULLETIN NO. 8," 15.

99. Mrs. H. R. Emery, "Our Work," *Our Hope and Life in Christ*, May 25, 1898, 10.

100. Emmons, "The Conclusion of the Whole Matter," 10.

101. Emmons, "What the Doctor Thinks," 10–11; Emmons, "The Conclusion of the Whole Matter," 10–11; and N. A., "A Little Extra Help Just Now," 9.

102. Emmons, "The Conclusion of the Whole Matter," 10–11.

103. J. W. Emmons, "Have You Paid Your Taxes?" *Our Hope and Life in Christ*, January 19, 1898, 10–11.

104. J. W. Emmons, "From Dr. J. W. Emmons," *Our Hope and Life in Christ*, May 11, 1898, 11.

105. J. W. Emmons, "What Will You Do?" *Our Hope and Life in Christ*, February 28, 1900, 1.

106. Emmons, "It's Got to Be Done!" 3.

107. Emmons, "Another Lift for the College," 10–11.

108. J. W. Emmons, "Not Forgotten!" *Our Hope and Life in Christ*, February 9, 1898, 11; Emmons, "From Dr. J. W. Emmons," 11; J. W. Emmons, "No Answer to the Call," *Our Hope and Life in Christ*, April 26, 1899, 10–11; J. W. Emmons, "Friends of Mendota College. Attention!" *Our Hope and Life in Christ*, November 1, 1899, 10; Emmons, "What Will You Do?" 10; and Emmons, "It's Got to Be Done!" 3.

109. Emmons, "Important—Read Carefully," 10.

110. N. A., "Personal and General," February 6, 1901, 6.

111. J. W. Emmons, "For Eyes and Ears," *Our Hope and Life in Christ*, March 6, 1901, 10–11.

112. Emmons, "Read! Read!! Read!!!" 10.

113. Byron N. Meigs, quoted in J. W. Emmons, "Sound Asleep," *Our Hope and Life in Christ*, May 28, 1902, 10.

114. J. W. Emmons, "Sound Asleep," *Our Hope and Life in Christ*, May 28, 1902, 10–11.

115. J. W. Emmons, "Some Things Seen and Done," *Our Hope and Life in Christ*, September 11, 1895, 2–3; J. W. Emmons, "What We Want," *Our Hope and Life in Christ*, October 9, 1895, 8; J. W. Emmons, "The Good Work Goes On," *Our Hope and Life in Christ*, October 16, 1895, 12; and J. W. Emmons, "Those Chairs for the College Chapel," *Our Hope and Life in Christ*, October 23, 1895, 5–6.

116. J. L. Irvin, "College Notes," *Our Hope and Life in Christ*, March 11, 1908, 2.

117. J. W. Emmons, "A Good Chance to Invest," *Our Hope and Life in Christ*, April 24, 1901, 7.

118. J. L. Irvin, "College Notes," *Our Hope and Life in Christ*, October 2, 1907, 3.

119. N. A., "Help Those Women," *Our Hope and Life in Christ*, November 7, 1900, 7; Emmons, "A Good Chance to Invest," 7; O. H. Loomis, "College Notes," *Our Hope and Life in Christ*, December 21, 1904, 10; O. H. Loomis, "College Notes," *Our Hope and Life in Christ*, May 24, 1905, 10; Harry L. Hanson, "College Notes," *Our Hope and Life in Christ*, October 10, 1906, 10; Harry L. Hanson, "College Notes," *Our Hope and Life in Christ*, November 14, 1906, 10; Harry L. Hanson, "College Notes," *Our Hope and*

Life in Christ, December 5, 1906, 10; Harry L. Hanson, "College Notes," *Our Hope and Life in Christ*, January 9, 1907, 10–11; Harry L. Hanson, "College Notes," *Our Hope and Life in Christ*, March 6, 1907, 3; Irvin, "College Notes," October 2, 1907, 3; J. L. Irvin, "College Notes," *Our Hope and Life in Christ*, October 16, 1907, 10; J. L. Irvin, "College Notes," *Our Hope and Life in Christ*, October 30, 1907, 3; J. L. Irvin, "College Notes," *Our Hope and Life in Christ*, November 20, 1907, 3; J. L. Irvin, "College Notes," *Our Hope and Life in Christ*, December 4, 1907, 10; J. L. Irvin, "College Notes," *Our Hope and Life in Christ*, January 8, 1908, 3; Irvin, "College Notes," March 11, 1908, 2–3; Ruth A. Bixler and Gertie M. Bump, "An Appeal," *Our Hope and Life in Christ*, March 18, 1908, 9; and Ruth A. Bixler and Gertie M. Bump, "In Grateful Acknowledgement: From the College Kitchen," *Our Hope and Life in Christ*, April 22, 1908, 7.

120. N. A., "A Long Needed Improvement on Foot," *Our Hope and Life in Christ*, September 20, 1905, 7.

121. G. G. Emery, "A Chance for Some One," *Our Hope and Life in Christ*, June 9, 1897, 11; N. A., "An Urgent Need," *Our Hope and Life in Christ*, July 6, 1904, 7; M. E. Smith, "Notes," *Our Hope and Life in Christ*, July 27, 1904, 3; N. A., "A Long Needed Improvement on Foot," 7; Mary E. Smith, "Encouraging," *Our Hope and Life in Christ*, September 27, 1905, 9; E. R., "Needed," *Our Hope and Life in Christ*, October 25, 1905, 9; Harry L. Hanson, "College Notes," *Our Hope and Life in Christ*, November 22, 1905, 11; Harry L. Hanson, "College Notes," *Our Hope and Life in Christ*, January 17, 1906, 3; Harry L. Hanson, "College Notes," *Our Hope and Life in Christ*, October 31, 1906, 3; Hanson, "College Notes," November 14, 1906, 10; Harry L. Hanson, "College Notes," *Our Hope and Life in Christ*, December 12, 1906, 10–11; Hanson, "College Notes," January 9, 1907, 10–11; Harry L. Hanson, "College Notes," *Our Hope and Life in Christ*, January 23, 1907, 10; N. A., "Brief Mention," *Our Hope and Life in Christ*, April 3, 1907, 6; Harry L. Hanson, "College Notes," *Our Hope and Life in Christ*, April 10, 1907, 10–11; J. L. Irvin, "College Notes," *Our Hope and Life in Christ*, February 19, 1908, 10; and J. L. Irvin, "College Notes," *Our Hope and Life in Christ*, March 25, 1908, 10–11.

122. King, "College Day Offerings: Received from Dec. 28, '07 to Jan. 18, 1908," 10–11.

123. N. A., "The College Day Offerings," *Our Hope and Life in Christ*, March 12, 1902, 7.

124. B. A. King, "Our College and Needs," *Our Hope and Life in Christ*, March 13, 1907, 3.

125. J. W. Emmons, "Look Here! Something for You," *Our Hope and Life in Christ*, October 18, 1899, 10; J. W. Emmons, "Wake Up!" *Our Hope and Life in Christ*, December 19, 1900, 10; H. H. Robbins, "Important: From the College Board," *Our Hope and Life in Christ*, December 25, 1901, 7; N.

A., "The College Day Offerings," March 12, 1902, 7; King, "Our College and Needs," 3; B. A. King, "College Day Offerings: Receipts from March 9–23, '07," *Our Hope and Life in Christ*, March 27, 1907, 10–11; King, "College Day Offerings: Received from Dec. 28, '07 to Jan. 18, 1908," 10–11; Forester, "Please Read This!" 2; King, "College Day Offerings: Received April 11–25, 1908," 11; J. W. Emmons, "First Report Encouraging," *Our Hope and Life in Christ*, May 13, 1908, 10; Orrin R. Jenks, "Help in an Hour of Need," *Our Hope and Life in Christ*, December 13, 1911, 16; and Jenks, "Our Present College Need—Special and Important," 9.

126. J. W. Emmons, "Where Are the Dollar Men?" *Our Hope and Life in Christ*, April 7, 1897, 11.

127. Jenks, "Our Present College Need—Special and Important," 9.

128. B. A. King, "Donations for Mendota College: From Nov. 18th, to Dec. 2d, 1905," *Our Hope and Life in Christ*, December 13, 1905, 12.

129. J. W. Emmons, "According to My Promise," 11.

130. Emmons, "The Conclusion of the Whole Matter," 10; Emmons, "According to My Promise," 11; Emmons, "Where Are the Dollar Men?" 11; Emmons, "What We Want," December 5, 1900, 10–11; King, "Donations for Mendota College: From Nov. 18th, to Dec. 2d, 1905," 12; and Jenks, "Our Present College Need—Special and Important," 9.

131. G. L. Carpenter, "A Good Place," *Our Hope and Life in Christ*, September 11, 1895, 13.

132. J. W. Emmons, "We Are after the Students," *Our Hope and Life in Christ*, February 8, 1899, 10.

133. J. Oscar Campbell, "Mendota Seminary," *Our Hope and Life in Christ*, December 28, 1892, 4; Carpenter, "A Good Place," 13; Emmons, "We Are after the Students," 10; Minutes of the Educational Board, Western Advent Christian Publication Association, June 4, 1895, Jenks Memorial Collection of Adventual Materials, Aurora University, Aurora, Illinois; and Minutes of the Board of Directors, Mendota College, August 29, 1908, Jenks Memorial Collection of Adventual Materials, Aurora University, Aurora, Illinois.

134. Minutes of the Board of Education, Mendota College, April 3, 1901, and April 7, 1903; Minutes of the Board of Directors, Mendota College, August 27, 1906, and March 31, 1909, Jenks Memorial Collection of Adventual Materials, Aurora University, Aurora, Illinois.

135. National Bureau of Economic Research, "US Business Cycle Expansions and Contractions," https://www.nber.org/cycles/cyclesmain.html (accessed November 12, 2018).

136. Forester, "Please Read This!" 2.

137. N. A., "Educational," *Our Hope and Life in Christ*, August 30, 1893, 9; J. F. Adair, "Camp Meeting Notes," *Our Hope and Life in Christ*, September 6, 1893, 9; and Forester, "Please Read This!" 2.

138. Smith, "The Mendota Meeting," 9–10; Orrin R. Jenks, "BULLETIN NO. 3: What Will Aurora Do?" *Our Hope and Life in Christ*,

February 16, 1910, 15; Orrin R. Jenks, "BULLETIN NO. 16: An Account of Our Stewardship," *Our Hope and Life in Christ*, June 22, 1910, 15; and Mendota Centennial Committee, *Magnificent Whistle Stop: The 100-Year Story of Mendota, Ill.* (Mendota, Ill.: Wayside Press, 1953), 222–23.

139. "Mendota Not Favored: The College Is to Be Removed to Aurora," Mendota *Reporter*, January 14, 1910.

140. N. A., "Shall We Move Our College? A Comparison of Conditions at Aurora and at Mendota," *Our Hope and Life in Christ*, December 8, 1909, 2–3, 7; N. A., "A Few Important Facts: Briefly Stated for Careful Consideration," *Our Hope and Life in Christ*, June 22, 1910, 7; "Mendota Not Favored," Mendota *Reporter*, January 14, 1910; and Jenks, "BULLETIN NO. 3," 15.

141. Livingston, "College Day Offerings," January 7, 1903, 13.

142. Emmons, "A Good Report," 10; J. W. Emmons, "Good News," *Our Hope and Life in Christ*, March 22, 1899, 10–11; Livingston, "College Day Offerings," January 7, 1903, 13; and Jenks, "Our College Operating Expenses: An Appeal from the President," 4.

143. N. A., "College Day Offering," December 25, 1901, 6.

144. King, "College Day Offerings: Received February 8–29, 1908," 3.

145. B. Forester, "Important to Ministers," *Our Hope and Life in Christ*, September 30, 1896, 12.

146. Forester, "Important to Ministers," 12; Minutes of the Educational Committee, Western Advent Christian Publication Association, November 15, 1892, Jenks Memorial Collection of Adventual Materials, Aurora University, Aurora, Illinois; Minutes of the Board of Education, Western Advent Christian Publication Association, August 24, 1896, Jenks Memorial Collection of Adventual Materials, Aurora University, Aurora, Illinois; and Minutes of the Board of Directors, Mendota College, April 5, 1910, Jenks Memorial Collection of Adventual Materials, Aurora University, Aurora, Illinois.

147. Fim Murra, "Concerning Brother Jenks in the East," *Our Hope and Life in Christ*, November 9, 1910, 4–5.

148. Murra, "Concerning Brother Jenks in the East,"4–5.

149. N. A., "Appreciative," *Our Hope and Life in Christ*, July 29, 1896, 6–7.

150. Murra, "Concerning Brother Jenks in the East,"4–5; and Orrin R. Jenks, "BULLETIN NO. 24: The Chairman's Report and Plans for the Future," *Our Hope and Life in Christ*, December 21, 1910, 16.

151. Jenks, "BULLETIN NO. 24: The Chairman's Report and Plans for the Future," 16.

152. Emmons, "What We Want," 10; Emmons, "Heed the Call!" 10–11; N. A., "Do Not Overlook Page Fifteen," *Our Hope and Life in Christ*, March 16, 1910, 7; and Jenks, "BULLETIN NO. 24," 16.

153. Minutes of the Educational Board, Western Advent Christian Publication Association, November 22, 1894, Jenks Memorial Collection of Adventual Materials, Aurora University, Aurora, Illinois.

Chapter 9 – The Rocky Road from Mendota to Aurora

1. William A. Burch, "Our College Reception at Aurora, Ill.," *Our Hope and Life in Christ*, April 10, 1912, 5 and N. A., "The College Removal," *Our Hope and Life in Christ*, April 10, 1912, 9.

2. N. A., "The College Removal," 9.

3. N. A., "The College Removal," 9.

4. Burch, "Our College Reception at Aurora," 5; and N. A., "The College Removal," 9.

5. Orrin R. Jenks, "BULLETIN NO. 35: Cash Will Decide," *Our Hope and Life in Christ*, May 10, 1911, 16.

6. B. J. Dean, "The Educational Field: Why Do We Need New Buildings?" *Our Hope and Life in Christ*, June 1, 1910, 10.

7. Dean, "Why Do We Need New Buildings?" 11.

8. N. A., "The Recent Special Meeting," *Our Hope and Life in Christ*, January 12, 1910, 6.

9. N. A., "The Recent Special Meeting," 6.

10. B. Forester, "My Pleasant Visit," *Our Hope and Life in Christ*, November 25, 1908, 3; G. H. Dewing, "The Educational Field: College Building," *Our Hope and Life in Christ*, September 22, 1909, 10–11; N. A., "Notice of Special Meeting of Members of the Western Advent Christian Publication Association," *Our Hope and Life in Christ*, December 1, 1909, 16; N. A., "Here's Your Chance," *Our Hope and Life in Christ*, December 15, 1909, 5; N. A., "The Recent Special Meeting," 6; Orrin R. Jenks, "Which Shall It Be? College or No College?" *Our Hope and Life in Christ*, April 13, 1910, 15; and George H. Dewing, "The Special Association Meeting," *Our Hope and Life in Christ*, April 20, 1910, 4–5.

11. B. Forester and B. J. Dean, "Special Meeting of the Board of Directors," *Our Hope and Life in Christ*, June 1, 1910, 2; and B. Forester, "The Reconsideration of College Removal," *Our Hope and Life in Christ*, June 8, 1910, 2.

12. Forester, "The Reconsideration of College Removal," 2.

13. Forester and Dean, "Special Meeting of the Board of Directors," 2; and Forester, "The Reconsideration of College Removal," 2.

14. Forester, "The Reconsideration of College Removal," 2.

15. Forester and Dean, "Special Meeting of the Board of Directors," 2; N. A., "Official and Important: First Published Notice," *Our Hope and Life in Christ*, June 1, 1910, 7; Forester, "The Reconsideration of College Removal," 2; and letter from Orrin R. Jenks to Henry Pollard, January 31, 1910, and letter from Brother Whitman to Orrin R. Jenks, February 29, 1910, Doris K. Colby Memorial Archives, Aurora University, Aurora, Illinois.

16. Wallace Best, "Zion, IL.," *Encyclopedia of Chicago*, www. encyclopedia.chicagohistory.org/pages/1399.html; Kevin McDermott, "A. J. Christ Dowie and the Harmonial Philosophy," *A Biography of John*

Alexander Dowie (1847–1907), Music in the Works of James Joyce, www. james-joyce-music.com/extras/dowie_bio.html; and Zion Historical Society, "Early History," www.zionhs.com/history.htm.

17. Best, "Zion, IL."; McDermott, "A. J. Christ Dowie and the Harmonial Philosophy"; South Loop Historical Society, "John Alexander Dowie"; and Zion Historical Society, "Early History."

18. Best, "Zion, IL."; McDermott, "A. J. Christ Dowie and the Harmonial Philosophy"; South Loop Historical Society, "John Alexander Dowie"; and Zion Historical Society, "Early History."

19. James Todd, "Four Reasons Why We Should Move to Zion City," *Our Hope and Life in Christ*, June 1, 1910, 7; J. W. Emmons, "Zion City College," *Our Hope and Life in Christ*, June 8, 1910, 2–3; and W. H. Lichty and J. A. Goudie, "The Educational Field: The College Building at Zion City, Ill.," *Our Hope and Life in Christ*, June 8, 1910, 10–11.

20. Emmons, "Zion City College," 2–3.

21. Emmons, "Zion City College," 2–3; and J. W. Emmons, "Location of Mendota College Again," *Hope and Life in Christ*, June 15, 1910, 2.

22. George Erhardt, "A Few Thoughts Relative to Zion City," *Our Hope and Life in Christ*, June 15, 1910, 11.

23. Todd, "Four Reasons Why We Should Move to Zion City," 7; Emmons, "Zion City College," 2–3; Emmons, "Location of Mendota College Again," 2; and Erhardt, "A Few Thoughts Relative to Zion City," 11.

24. Letter from Orrin R. Jenks to Charles Eckhart, n.d., Doris K. Colby Memorial Archives, Aurora University, Aurora, Illinois.

25. Letter from Orrin R. Jenks to H. F. Carpenter, June 11, 1910, Doris K. Colby Memorial Archives, Aurora University, Aurora, Illinois.

26. Letter from Orrin R. Jenks to Mr. Hardison, June 27, 1910, Doris K. Colby Memorial Archives, Aurora University, Aurora, Illinois.

27. W. C. Batdorf, "The Zion City Location," *Our Hope and Life in Christ*, June 15, 1910, 11.

28. "A respected and interested brother," quoted in J. August Smith, "As to Mendota College. A Warning Note," *Our Hope and Life in Christ*, June 15, 1910, 11.

29. Jenks to Hardison, June 27, 1910.

30. Orrin R. Jenks, "Keep Out of Zion City," *Our Hope and Life in Christ*, June 22, 1910, 2; Jenks to Eckhart, n. d., and letter from Charles Eckhart to Orrin R. Jenks, January 8, 1910, and letter from Orrin R. Jenks to Charles Eckhart, January 11, 1910, and letter from Orrin R. Jenks to Charles Eckhart, January 31, 1910, and letter from Orrin R. Jenks to A. C. Adams, February 1, 1910, and letter from Orrin R. Jenks to D. R. Mansfield, April 24, 1910, and letter from Orrin R. Jenks to Brother Whitman, May 22, 1910, and letter from Orrin R. Jenks to Mr. and Mrs. Bixler, May 26, 1910, and letter from Orrin R. Jenks to George E. Cooprider, May 26, 1910, and letter from Orrin R. Jenks to Sister Parks, June 8, 1910, and Jenks to Hardison, June 27, 1910, Doris K. Colby Memorial Archives, Aurora University, Aurora, Illinois.

31. Jenks, "Keep Out of Zion City," 2.

32. Jenks, "Keep Out of Zion City," 2; Jenks to Whitman, May 22, 1910; Jenks to Cooprider, May 26, 1910; and Jenks to Parks, June 8, 1910.

33. Jenks, "Keep Out of Zion City," 2.

34. Jenks, "Keep Out of Zion City," 2.

35. Jenks, "Keep Out of Zion City," 2; Jenks to Adams, February 1, 1910; Jenks to Whitman, May 22, 1910; and Jenks to Parks, June 8, 1910.

36. Jenks, "Keep Out of Zion City," 2; Jenks to Adams, February 1, 1910; Jenks to Mansfield, April 24, 1910; Jenks to Whitman, May 22, 1910; Jenks to Cooprider, May 26, 1910; and Jenks to Parks, June 8, 1910.

37. Letters from Orrin R. Jenks to Brother Whitman, May 22, 1910, June 1, 1910, and Jenks to Bixlers, May 26, 1910, and letter from Orrin R. Jenks to Charles Eckhart, May 27, 1910, and letter from Orrin R. Jenks to Wilbur Glenn Voliva, June 15, 1910, and "Testimony of Mr. C. E. Patten Given In Judge Landis' Court, Wednesday, June 1, 1910, In Connection With Petition of W. H. Lichty, Et. Al. Re. Mendota College Deal," Doris K. Colby Memorial Archives, Aurora University, Aurora, Illinois.

38. Letter from Orrin R. Jenks to Brother Bloom, 1909, letter from Orrin R. Jenks to Charles Eckhart, January 25, 1909, and letter from William George to Charles Eckhart, January 25, 1909, Doris K. Colby Memorial Archives, Aurora University, Aurora, Illinois.

39. Orrin R. Jenks, "BULLETIN NO. 3: What Will Aurora Do?" *Our Hope and Life in Christ*, February 16, 1910, 15; Susan L. Palmer, "Building Ethnic Communities in a Small City: Romanians and Mexicans in Aurora, Illinois, 1900–1940" (PhD diss., Northern Illinois University, 1987), 27–30, 34–36; Jenks to Bloom, 1909; Jenks to Mansfield, April 24, 1910; and Jenks to Bixlers, May 26, 1910.

40. Jenks, "BULLETIN NO. 3," 15; N. A., "A Few Important Facts: Briefly Stated for Careful Consideration," *Our Hope and Life in Christ*, June 22, 1910, 7; Jenks to Bloom, 1909, and Jenks to Eckhart, January 25, 1909, and George to Eckhart, January 25, 1909, and letter from Charles Eckhart to Orrin R. Jenks, January 8, 1910, and letter from Orrin R. Jenks to Charles Eckhart, February 18, 1910, and Jenks to Mansfield, April 24, 1910, and letter from Orrin R. Jenks to Charles Eckhart, May 25, 1910, and Jenks to Bixlers, May 26, 1910, and Jenks to Whitman, June 1, 1910, Doris K. Colby Memorial Archives, Aurora University, Aurora, Illinois.

41. Jenks, "BULLETIN NO. 3," 15; Jenks to Eckhart, January 25, 1909; George to Eckhart, January 25, 1909; and Jenks to Mansfield, April 24, 1910.

42. A. W. Merritt, "To Zion City or Aurora, Which?" *Our Hope and Life in Christ*, June 15, 1910, 10; and Jenks to Parks, June 8, 1910.

43. Orrin R. Jenks, "BULLETIN NO. 24: The Chairman's Report and Plans for the Future," *Our Hope and Life in Christ*, December 21, 1910, 16; Jenks to Eckhart, n.d., and letter from Charles Eckhart to Orrin R. Jenks, January 17, 1910, and Jenks to Eckhart, February 18, 1910, and letter from

Orrin R. Jenks to Charles Eckhart, January 3, 1911, and letter from Charles Eckhart to Orrin R. Jenks, January 5, 1911, and letter from Orrin R. Jenks to Charles Eckhart, January 17, 1911, Doris K. Colby Memorial Archives, Aurora University, Aurora, Illinois.

44. Orrin R. Jenks, "BULLETIN NO. 4: A Call To Our Ministers," *Our Hope and Life in Christ*, February 23, 1910, 15; Orrin R. Jenks, "BULLETIN NO. 7: Our Ministers to the Front," *Our Hope and Life in Christ*, March 23, 1910, 15; Orrin R. Jenks, "BULLETIN NO. 9: A Call to Our Laymen," *Our Hope and Life in Christ*, April 6, 1910, 15; Orrin R. Jenks, "BULLETIN NO. 10: An Appeal to Our Young Men," *Our Hope and Life in Christ*, April 13, 1910, 15; Orrin R. Jenks, "BULLETIN NO. 11: Our Young Women to the Front," *Our Hope and Life in Christ*, May 4, 1910, 15; and Orrin R. Jenks, "BULLETIN NO. 12: To Our Isolated Ones," *Our Hope and Life in Christ*, May 18, 1910, 15.

45. Orrin R. Jenks, "BULLETIN NO. 20: Help Us to Reach This Goal— Forty-One Thousand Dollars by Nov. 1, 1910," *Our Hope and Life in Christ*, August 17, 1910, 15; Orrin R. Jenks, "BULLETIN NO. 30: A Ten Thousand Dollar Pledge," *Our Hope and Life in Christ*, April 5, 1911, 16; Orrin R. Jenks, "BULLETIN NO. 50: Thanksgiving Is Coming," *Our Hope and Life in Christ*, October 25, 1911, 16; and Orrin R. Jenks, "BULLETIN NO. 66: Our New Buildings and the Cost," *Our Hope and Life in Christ*, April 17, 1912, 16.

46. N. A., "Help for Our College: An Anti-Hat Club Proposed," *Our Hope and Life in Christ*, March 9, 1910, 5.

47. N. A., "Let Us All Help," *Our Hope and Life in Christ*, March 23, 1910, 11.

48. N. A., "Editorial Mention," *Our Hope and Life in Christ*, March 23, 1910, 6.

49. "Your Sister in His Service," "That Anti-Hat Club," *Our Hope and Life in Christ*, April 13, 1910, 5.

50. Letter from A. C. Adams to Orrin R. Jenks, March 8, 1911, Doris K. Colby Memorial Archives, Aurora University, Aurora, Illinois.

51. Adams to Jenks, March 8, 1911.

52. Adams to Jenks, March 8, 1911.

53. Letter from Orrin R. Jenks to A. C. Adams, March 18, 1911, Doris K. Colby Memorial Archives, Aurora University, Aurora, Illinois.

54. Adams to Jenks, March 8, 1911, and Jenks to Adams, March 18, 1911.

55. William A. Burch, "Annual Business Meeting of Mendota College," *Our Hope and Life in Christ*, September 14, 1910, 11.

56. Orrin R. Jenks, "BULLETIN NO. 23: The Payment of Pledges," *Our Hope and Life in Christ*, November 23, 1910, 16.

57. Orrin R. Jenks, "BULLETIN NO. 37: Work on New College Begins To-Day," *Our Hope and Life in Christ*, May 31, 1911, 16.

58. Burch, "Annual Business Meeting of Mendota College," 11; Jenks, "BULLETIN NO. 23," 16; Jenks, "BULLETIN NO. 37," 16; Orrin R. Jenks, "A Word Explanatory," *Our Hope and Life in Christ*, February 21, 1912, 9; and E.

B. Arnold and Charles E. Decker, "Minutes of the Annual Meeting of Aurora College, 1912," *Our Hope and Life in Christ*, September 18, 1912, 10–11.

59. N. A., "The Corner Stone Laying," *Our Hope and Life in Christ*, July 26, 1911, 9.

60. Jenks, "BULLETIN NO. 37," 16; Orrin R. Jenks, "BULLETIN NO. 38: Progress of the Work," *Our Hope and Life in Christ*, June 7, 1911, 16; Orrin R. Jenks, "BULLETIN NO. 41: Laying the Cornerstone," *Our Hope and Life in Christ*, July 12, 1911, 16; and N. A., "The Corner Stone Laying," 9.

61. Orrin R. Jenks, "BULLETIN NO. 43: Matters of Interest," *Our Hope and Life in Christ*, August 2, 1911, 16.

62. Orrin R. Jenks, "BULLETIN NO. 44: Progress of the Work and Outlook," *Our Hope and Life in Christ*, August 16, 1911, 16; Wm. A. Burch, "BULLETIN NO. 45: Important Notice," *Our Hope and Life in Christ*, September 6, 1911, 16; Orrin R. Jenks, "BULLETIN NO. 48: Progress of the Work," *Our Hope and Life in Christ*, October 11, 1911, 16; Orrin R. Jenks, "BULLETIN NO. 54: When Will Our Buildings Be Completed," *Our Hope and Life in Christ*, December 20, 1911, 16; Orrin R. Jenks, "A Word Explanatory," *Our Hope and Life in Christ*, February 21, 1912, 9; and Orrin R. Jenks, "BULLETIN NO. 60: Getting Ready to Move," *Our Hope and Life in Christ*, March 6, 1912, 16.

63. Orrin R. Jenks, "BULLETIN NO. 34: More about Aurora," *Our Hope and Life in Christ*, May 3, 1911, 16 and Jenks, "BULLETIN NO. 35," 16.

64. N. A., "New College Buildings," *Our Hope and Life in Christ*, September 13, 1911, 16.

65. Orrin R. Jenks, "BULLETIN NO. 22: We Reached the Goal—and On Time!" *Our Hope and Life in Christ*, November 9, 1910, 16; Orrin R. Jenks, "BULLETIN NO. 40: Lots for Sale," *Our Hope and Life in Christ*, June 21, 1911, 16; and Orrin R. Jenks, "BULLETIN NO. 68: Can We Pay for Our New Buildings? Our Resources," *Our Hope and Life in Christ*, May 1, 1912, 16.

66. Letter from B. Forester to Orrin R. Jenks, February 8, 1909, and letter from Orrin R. Jenks to B. Forester, March 24, 1909, and letter from B. Forester to Orrin R. Jenks, March 25, 1909, and letter from Orrin R. Jenks to H. E. Pancost, February 24, 1910, and letter from H. E. Pancost to Orrin R. Jenks, February 26, 1910, and letter from B. Forester to Orrin R. Jenks, February 26, 1910, and letter from George H. Dewing to Orrin R. Jenks, February 27, 1910, and Jenks to Eckhart, May 25, 1910, and Jenks to Cooprider, May 26, 1910, and Jenks to Eckhart, May 27, 1910, and Jenks to Hardison, June 27, 1910, and Jenks to Eckhart, January 17, 1911, Doris K. Colby Memorial Archives, Aurora University, Aurora, Illinois.

67. Orrin R. Jenks, "BULLETIN NO. 19: A Word from the Field," *Our Hope and Life in Christ*, August 3, 1910, 15; Jenks, "BULLETIN NO. 24," 16; Jenks to Eckhart, May 27, 1910; and Jenks to Eckhart, January 17, 1911.

68. Jenks to Eckhart, January 17, 1911.

69. Orrin R. Jenks, "Contributions of the East to Our College," *Our Hope and Life in Christ*, February 1, 1911, 10.

70. Jenks, "BULLETIN NO. 24," 16; Jenks to Eckhart, May 27, 1910; and Jenks to Eckhart, January 17, 1911.

71. Letter from Orrin R. Jenks to Charles Eckhart, October 22, 1909, Doris K. Colby Memorial Archives, Aurora University, Aurora, Illinois.

72. Jenks to Bixlers, May 26, 1910.

73. Jenks, "Keep Out of Zion City," 2; Jenks to Mansfield, April 24, 1910, and letter from Orrin R. Jenks to Wilbur Glenn Voliva, May 27, 1910, and Jenks to Parks, June 8, 1910, and Jenks to Voliva, June 15, 1910, Doris K. Colby Memorial Archives, Aurora University, Aurora, Illinois.

74. Orrin R. Jenks, "Why They Come Slowly," *Our Hope and Life in Christ*, April 6, 1910, 15.

75. Orrin R. Jenks, "BULLETIN NO. 57: Were There Not Ten Cleansed? But Where Are the Nine?" *Our Hope and Life in Christ*, January 31, 1912, 16.

76. Letter from Orrin R. Jenks to B. J. Dean, December 22, 1909, and letter from Orrin R. Jenks to Charles Eckhart, December 22, 1909, and letter from Orrin R. Jenks to Charles Eckhart, January 12, 1910, Doris K. Colby Memorial Archives, Aurora University, Aurora, Illinois.

77. Orrin R. Jenks, "BULLETIN NO. 64: Moving In," *Our Hope and Life in Christ*, April 3, 1912, 16.

Chapter 10 – "Occupy till I Come": "Occupying" in Mendota and Aurora

1. Christopher J. Lucas, *American Higher Education: A History* (New York: St. Martin's Griffin, 1994), 181–82, 187.

2. Lucas, *American Higher Education*, 124, 126–27, 186; William C. Ringenberg, *The Christian College: A History of Protestant Higher Education in America*, 2nd ed. (Grand Rapids, Mich.: Baker Book House Co., 2006), 63–65, 78, 83–84; Frederick Rudolph, *The American College and University: A History* (1962; repr., Athens, Ga.: University of Georgia Press, 1990), 68, 75, 87–89, 96, 103–6, 164–65, 168–71, 245; and John R. Thelin, *A History of American Higher Education* (Baltimore: Johns Hopkins University Press, 2004), 62, 99, 90.

3. Lucas, *American Higher Education*, 119–20, 128, 131–34, 186, 204; Ringenberg, *The Christian College*, 67, 60, 70–71, 83–84; Rudolph, *The American College and University*, 89, 245; and Thelin, *A History of American Higher Education*, 61, 129, 131, 133.

4. Lucas, *American Higher Education*, 119–21; Ringenberg, *The Christian College*, 65, 72–73; Rudolph, *The American College and University*, 177–78, 193–200; and Thelin, *A History of American Higher Education*, 61–62, 69, 158.

5. Virginia Lieson Brereton, *Training God's Army: The American Bible School, 1880–1940* (Bloomington: Indiana University Press, 1990), 60–65, 69–70.

6. N. A., "What Is Our Duty," *Our Hope and Life in Christ*, March 20, 1895, 8.

7. O. R. Fassett, "An Advent College," *Our Hope and Life in Christ*, April 16, 1890, 1–2; N. A., "Editorial," *Our Hope and Life in Christ*, December 30, 1891, 1–2; N. A., "What Is Our Duty," 8; N. A., "College Day," *Our Hope and Life in Christ*, December 31, 1902, 7; *Annual of Mendota College, 1893–1894* (Aurora, Ill.: Copeland & Phillips, Printers, 1893), 11; *Catalogue of Mendota College for 1898–99* (Mendota, Ill.: Western Advent Christian Publication Association, 1898), 16–17; *Catalogue of Mendota College for 1901–1902* (Mendota, Ill.: Our Hope Printing Office, 1901), 23–25; and Brereton, *Training God's Army*, 52–54.

8. Minutes of the Educational Committee, Western Advent Christian Publication Association, September 28, 1893, Jenks Memorial Collection of Adventual Materials, Aurora University, Aurora, Illinois.

9. J. Oscar Campbell, "A Card," *Our Hope and Life in Christ*, October 11, 1893, 13.

10. N. A., "An Important Change," *Our Hope and Life in Christ*, June 15, 1898, 7.

11. Campbell, "A Card," 13; N. A., "An Important Change," 7; Minutes of the Educational Committee, Western Advent Christian Publication Association, September 28, 1893, and June 5, 1894, Jenks Memorial Collection of Adventual Materials, Aurora University, Aurora, Illinois; Minutes of the Board of Education, Western Advent Christian Publication Association, September 20, 1894, and April 3, 1901, Jenks Memorial Collection of Adventual Materials, Aurora University, Aurora, Illinois; and *Catalogue of Mendota College for 1901–1902*, 4.

12. Minutes of the Board of Directors, Mendota College, April 23–24, 1906, and April 4, 1911, Jenks Memorial Collection of Adventual Materials, Aurora University, Aurora, Illinois.

13. Fred Newberry, "The College Gymnasium," *Our Hope and Life in Christ*, April 18, 1900, 9.

14. O. G. Watkins, "From Bro. O. G. Watkins," *Our Hope and Life in Christ*, February 11, 1903, 11.

15. C. A. Meade, "From C. A. Meade," *Our Hope and Life in Christ*, January 20, 1892, 4.

16. Meade, "From C. A. Meade," 4; W. S., "Denying the Faith," *Our Hope and Life in Christ*, April 12, 1893, 11; J. O. Staats, "Bible Training School—Mendota College," *Our Hope and Life in Christ*, May 8, 1901, 1; N. A., "College Day," *Our Hope and Life in Christ*, December 31, 1902, 7; W. Alford, "An Opinion," *Our Hope and Life in Christ*, January 28, 1903, 5; and Watkins, "From Bro. O. G. Watkins," 11.

17. N. A., "Memorial Windows," *Our Hope and Life in Christ*, October 9, 1895, 8.

18. N. A., "Memorial Windows," 8.

19. N. A., "Memorial Windows," 8.

20. C. F. Whitney, "Our College," *Our Hope and Life in Christ*, June 9, 1897, 11.

21. George J. French, "A Good Word for Mendota College," *Our Hope and Life in Christ*, June 19, 1895, 12.

22. John Keepers, "Impressions about Our College," *Our Hope and Life in Christ*, August 10, 1904, 9.

23. Orrin R. Jenks, "Concerning a Recent Resolution," *Our Hope and Life in Christ*, July 21, 1909, 5.

24. B. J. Dean, "What an Adventist Ought to Know," *Our Hope and Life in Christ*, January 14, 1903, 4–5.

25. Dean, "What an Adventist Ought to Know," 5.

26. B. Forester, "Good Books—Send for Them," *Our Hope and Life in Christ*, December 8, 1909, 3.

27. J. W. Emmons, "College Finances, Etc.," *Our Hope and Life in Christ*, May 29, 1901, 12; and J. W. Emmons, "Latter Day Reports," *Our Hope and Life in Christ*, October 29, 1902, 11.

28. J. W. Emmons, "Important—Read Carefully," *Our Hope and Life in Christ*, January 9, 1901, 10.

29. B. A. King, "College Day Offerings: Receipts from March 9–23, '07," *Our Hope and Life in Christ*, March 27, 1907, 10–11.

30. Milton M. Livingston, "Very Important for All," *Our Hope and Life in Christ*, May 27, 1903, 11.

31. Minutes of the Board of Education, Western Advent Christian Publication Association, April 15, 1897, Jenks Memorial Collection of Adventual Materials, Aurora University, Aurora, Illinois.

32. Minutes of the Board of Education, Western Advent Christian Publication Association, December 29, 1896, and April 14–15, 1897, Jenks Memorial Collection of Adventual Materials, Aurora University, Aurora, Illinois.

33. Minutes of the Board of Education, Mendota College, January 8, 1902, Jenks Memorial Collection of Adventual Materials, Aurora University, Aurora, Illinois.

34. Minutes of the Board of Directors, Mendota College, August 22, 1907, Jenks Memorial Collection of Adventual Materials, Aurora University, Aurora, Illinois.

35. Minutes of the Board of Education, Mendota College, April 3, 1901, January 8, 1902, and Minutes of the Board of Directors, Mendota College, August 27, 1906, August 22, 1907, April 1, 1908, March 31, 1909, Jenks Memorial Collection of Adventual Materials, Aurora University, Aurora, Illinois.

36. Rudolph, *The American College and University*, 193.

37. Ringenberg, *The Christian College*, 72.

38. Ringenberg, *The Christian College*, 72–73; Rudolph, *The American College and University*, 193–200; and Thelin, *A History of American Higher Education*, 158.

39. Minutes of the Educational Committee and Board of Education, Western Advent Christian Publication Association, and Minutes of the Board of Education and Board of Directors, Mendota College, Jenks Memorial Collection of Adventual Materials, Aurora University, Aurora, Illinois.

40. H. S. Prichett, 1908, quoted in B. Forester, "Denominational Colleges," *Our Hope and Life in Christ*, December 2, 1908, 4–5.

41. Forester, "Denominational Colleges," 4–5.

42. B. Forester, "Mendota College and Its Friends," *Our Hope and Life in Christ*, March 6, 1907, 3; Forester, "Denominational Colleges," 4–5; and B. J. Dean, "The Educational Field: Prof. N. C. Twining and His Work," *Our Hope and Life in Christ*, December 23, 1908, 10–11.

43. J. W. Emmons, "According to My Promise," *Our Hope and Life in Christ*, January 13, 1897, 11.

44. J. W. Emmons, "Where Are the Dollar Men?" *Our Hope and Life in Christ*, April 7, 1897, 11.

45. O. R. Jenks, "Our Present College Need—Special and Important," *Our Hope and Life in Christ*, May 22, 1912, 9.

46. J. W. Emmons, "Read! Read!! Read!!!" *Our Hope and Life in Christ*, May 14, 1902, 10–11.

47. J. W. Emmons, "The Conclusion of the Whole Matter," *Our Hope and Life in Christ*, December 23, 1896, 10; Emmons, "According to My Promise," 11; Emmons, "Where Are the Dollar Men?" 11; J. W. Emmons, "What We Want," *Our Hope and Life in Christ*, April 14, 1897, 10–11; H. H. Robbins, "Important: From the College Board," *Our Hope and Life in Christ*, December 25, 1901, 7; Emmons, "Read! Read!! Read!!!" 10–11; B. A. King, "Donations for Mendota College: From Nov. 18th, to Dec. 2d, 1905," *Our Hope and Life in Christ*, December 13, 1905, 12; and Jenks, "Our Present College Need," 9.

48. Mrs. Jennie M. Twining, "A Mendota Teacher's Programme," *Our Hope and Life in Christ*, January 7, 1903, 9.

49. Rudolph, *The American College and University*, 195–200; Minutes of the Educational Committee, Western Advent Christian Publication Association, June 6, 1894, and Minutes of the Board of Directors, Mendota College, April 1, 1909, Jenks Memorial Collection of Adventual Materials, Aurora University, Aurora, Illinois.

50. J. W. Emmons, "A Noble Example," *Our Hope and Life in Christ*, November 25, 1896, 7.

51. Emmons, "A Noble Example," 7; J. W. Emmons, "College Day Offering," *Our Hope and Life in Christ*, January 5, 1898, 11; J. W. Emmons, "No Answer to the Call," *Our Hope and Life in Christ*, April 26, 1899, 10–11; N. A., "A Little Behind," *Our Hope and Life in Christ*, May 17, 1905, 7; B. Forester, "Good News," *Our Hope and Life in Christ*, May 9, 1906, 4–5; N.

A., "How to Sustain Our Cause," *Our Hope and Life in Christ*, March 6, 1907, 7; B. A. King, "College Day Offerings: Received Dec. 14–26, 1907," *Our Hope and Life in Christ*, January 1, 1908, 12; B. A. King, "College Day Offerings: Received February 8–29, 1908," *Our Hope and Life in Christ*, March 4, 1908, 3; J. W. Emmons, "Heed the Call!" *Our Hope and Life in Christ*, June 24, 1908, 10–11; and J. W. Emmons, "It's Got to Be Done!" *Our Hope and Life in Christ*, July 15, 1908, 3.

52. B. Forester, "Amen!" *Our Hope and Life in Christ*, November 4, 1896, 5.

53. Forester, "Amen!" 5; and Orrin R. Jenks, "BULLETIN NO. 7: Our Ministers to the Front," *Our Hope and Life in Christ*, March 23, 1910, 15.

54. N. A., "Greeting," *Our Hope and Life in Christ*, September 8, 1897, 6.

55. B. Forester, "Another Visit," *Our Hope and Life in Christ*, December 9, 1908, 2.

56. N. A., "Greeting," 6; Milton M. Livingston, "College Day Offerings," *Our Hope and Life in Christ*, May 7, 1902, 10–11; M. M. Livingston, "College Day Offerings," *Our Hope and Life in Christ*, February 18, 1903, 7; Charles Eckhart, "Glad to See That Statement," *Our Hope and Life in Christ*, May 6, 1908, 1; J. W. Emmons, "The College Obligation," *Our Hope and Life in Christ*, June 10, 1908, 10; J. W. Emmons, "Heed the Call!" *Our Hope and Life in Christ*, June 24, 1908, 10–11; Forester, "Another Visit," 2–3; and N. A., "Brief Mention," *Our Hope and Life in Christ*, December 23, 1908, 6.

57. Orrin R. Jenks, "BULLETIN NO. 67: Can We Pay for Our New Buildings? Our Resources," *Our Hope and Life in Christ*, April 24, 1912, 16.

58. Orrin R. Jenks, "THE DUTY OF THE HOUR! Our God-Given Opportunity!" *Our Hope and Life in Christ*, February 2, 1910, 15; Orrin R. Jenks, "Which Shall It Be? College or No College?" *Our Hope and Life in Christ*, April 13, 1910, 15; Orrin R. Jenks, "BULLETIN NO. 17: The Voce of Our People," *Our Hope and Life in Christ*, July 6, 1910, 15; Orrin R. Jenks, ""BULLETIN NO. 20: Help Us to Reach This Goal—Forty-One Thousand Dollars by Nov. 1, 1910," *Our Hope and Life in Christ*, August 17, 1910, 15; N. A., "The College Project," *Our Hope and Life in Christ*, October 19, 1910, 9; Orrin R. Jenks, "BULLETIN NO. 29: Victory Again!" *Our Hope and Life in Christ*, March 29, 1911, 16; Orrin R. Jenks, "BULLETIN NO. 30: A Ten Thousand Dollar Pledge," *Our Hope and Life in Christ*, April 5, 1911, 16; Orrin R. Jenks, "BULLETIN NO. 31: Another Ten Thousand Dollar Pledge," *Our Hope and Life in Christ*, April 12, 1911, 16; Orrin R. Jenks, "BULLETIN NO. 39: A Re-statement of Our Financial Condition," *Our Hope and Life in Christ*, June 14, 1911, 16; Chas. E. Decker, "Pledges for New College Buildings," *Our Hope and Life in Christ*, December 27, 1911, 16; Orrin R. Jenks, "BULLETIN NO. 62: Moving Time," *Our Hope and Life in Christ*, March 20, 1912, 16; William A. Burch, "Our College Reception at Aurora, Ill.," *Our Hope and Life in Christ*, April 10, 1912, 5; Jenks, "BULLETIN NO. 67," 16; Orrin R. Jenks, "BULLETIN NO. 69: Can We Pay for Our New Buildings? Our Resources," *Our Hope and Life in Christ*, May 8, 1912, 16;

and CPI Inflation Calculator, http://www.in2013dollars.com/1910-dollars-in-2018?amount=40000 (accessed December 13, 2018).

59. Orrin R. Jenks, "BULLETIN NO. 5: The Outlook of a Western Preacher," *Our Hope and Life in Christ*, March 9, 1910, 15.

60. J. W. Emmons, "Another Lift for the College," *Our Hope and Life in Christ*, March 17, 1897, 10–11; Eckhart, "Glad to See That Statement," 1; and Jenks, "BULLETIN NO. 5," 15.

61. J. W. Emmons, "The Ames Chemical Laboratory of Mendota College," *Our Hope and Life in Christ*, September 2, 1896, 3; Sylvester Nokes, "College Notes," *Our Hope and Life in Christ*, September 30, 1896, 7; J. W. Emmons, "What Do You Say?" *Our Hope and Life in Christ*, January 6, 1897, 10; Emmons, "Another Lift for the College," 10–11; N. A., "Greeting," 6; Sylvester Nokes, "College Notes," *Our Hope and Life in Christ*, September 8, 1897, 10; and N. A., "The College Project," 9.

62. M. M. Livingston, "College Day Offerings," *Our Hope and Life in Christ*, February 18, 1903, 7.

63. Milton M. Livingston, "Very Important for All," *Our Hope and Life in Christ*, May 27, 1903, 11.

64. Milton M. Livingston, "Help Those Women," *Our Hope and Life in Christ*, December 2, 1903, 3.

65. O. R. J. (Orrin R. Jenks), "Help Those Women," *Our Hope and Life in Christ*, August 10, 1904, 8.

66. Harry L. Hanson, "College Notes," *Our Hope and Life in Christ*, November 8, 1905, 3.

67. E. S. Mansfield, "The Helper's Union," *Our Hope and Life in Christ*, September 12, 1894, 12.

68. Mary E. Smith, "Our Beloved Dead," *Our Hope and Life in Christ*, December 15, 1909, 9.

69. Ella Bennett Patten, "Annual Report of the Helpers' Union," *Our Hope and Life in Christ*, November 1, 1899, 9.

70. Mrs. B. F., "Suggestive," *Our Hope and Life in Christ*, April 1, 1908, 9.

71. Edith Adams, "Mendota Helpers' Union," *Our Hope and Life in Christ*, April 29, 1908, 9.

72. Mrs. B. F., "Suggestive," 9; Adams, "Mendota Helpers' Union," 9; and Ella Pullen, "Attention! By the President," *Our Hope and Life in Christ*, September 28, 1910, 7.

73. Pullen, "Attention! By the President," 7.

74. "A Friend of the College," "Some Timely Thoughts," *Our Hope and Life in Christ*, January 8, 1908, 9.

75. "A Friend of the College," "Some Timely Thoughts," 9; Pullen, "Attention! By the President," 7; and Orrin R. Jenks, "BULLETIN NO. 61: Our Women to the Front," *Our Hope and Life in Christ*, March 13, 1912, 16.

76. Belle M. White, "The Helper's Union," *Our Hope and Life in Christ*, December 12, 1894, 12–13; Belle M. White, "The Helper's Union: Quarterly Report," *Our Hope and Life in Christ*, March 20, 1895, 12; Anna Whitney, "General Helper's Union Quarterly Report," *Our Hope and Life in Christ*, November 13, 1895, 10; Mary E. Smith, "How All May Help," *Our Hope and Life in Christ*, September 17, 1902, 3; N. A., "A Long Needed Improvement on Foot," *Our Hope and Life in Christ*, September 20, 1905, 7; Cornelia Pollard, "Helpful Hints," *Our Hope and Life in Christ*, March 28, 1906, 9; Harry L. Hanson, "College Notes," *Our Hope and Life in Christ*, January 9, 1907, 10–11; Harry L. Hanson, "College Notes," *Our Hope and Life in Christ*, April 10, 1907, 10–11; J. L. Irvin, "College Notes," *Our Hope and Life in Christ*, November 6, 1907, 3; J. L. Irvin, "College Notes," *Our Hope and Life in Christ*, November 20, 1907, 3; J. L. Irvin, "College Notes," *Our Hope and Life in Christ*, November 27, 1907, 10–11; J. L. Irvin, "College Notes," *Our Hope and Life in Christ*, December 4, 1907, 10; J. L. Irvin, "College Notes," *Our Hope and Life in Christ*, March 25, 1908, 10–11; and "S. T. Neduts, Et Cetera," "College Notes," *Our Hope and Life in Christ*, May 5, 1909, 11.

77. E. S. Mansfield, "Fire! Fire!: Helpers to the Rescue!" *Our Hope and Life in Christ*, December 18, 1901, 7.

78. Mansfield, "Fire! Fire!" 7; E. S. Mansfield, "Revised Conclusions," *Our Hope and Life in Christ*, January 1, 1902, 7; E. S. Mansfield, "Acknowledgment," *Our Hope and Life in Christ*, January 15, 1902, 10–11; and Mary R. Dillon, "Helpers Union Emergency Report," *Our Hope and Life in Christ*, February 26, 1902, 9.

79. White, "The Helper's Union: Quarterly Report," March 20, 1895, 12; J. W. Emmons, "THE FIRST ANSWER: To Help the Bible Training School," *Our Hope and Life in Christ*, November 18, 1896, 11; J. W. Emmons, "Bound for Mendota Bible School," *Our Hope and Life in Christ*, December 23, 1896, 7; E. E. Denniston, "Grateful Commendation," *Our Hope and Life in Christ*, June 23, 1897, 10; and Pullen, "Attention! By the President," 7.

80. Pullen, "Attention! By the President," 7.

81. *Annual of Mendota College: Catalogue, 1910–1911* (Mendota, Ill.: Our Hope Print, 1910), 89–91.

82. B. Forester, "Educational Day Discourse," *Our Hope and Life in Christ*, February 3, 1904, 4.

83. Forester, "Educational Day Discourse," 4; N. A., "Mendota College Graduates: And Some Things to Be Glad Of," *Our Hope and Life in Christ*, November 9, 1910, 8–9; and Bert J. Dean, "Educational Work and Home Missions," *Our Hope and Life in Christ*, May 17, 1911, 10.

84. *Annual of Mendota College: Catalogue, 1910–1911*, 89–91.

85. N. A., "College Day," *Our Hope and Life in Christ*, January 16, 1895, 8.

86. Fim Murra, "Our College," *Our Hope and Life in Christ*, May 18, 1898, 5.

87. N. A., "Mendota College Graduates," 8.

88. N. A., "Obituaries: Dr. Moses C. Crouse," *Beacon News*, November 10, 1985; Janet Mae Hansen and Alison Lynn Whitehead, co-editors, *1939 Pharos* (N. P.: Williamson Press, 1939), 56; Homer Easley, phone interview by author, April 8, 2015; *Aurora College Bulletin*, April 1920, 68–71; July 1931, 56–59; May 1934, 65–67; April 1936, 53–55; March 1937, 52–54; February 1939, 58–60; *Aurora College Catalog*, April 1927, 67–72; and Invitation to the Retirement Luncheon of Doris and Asa Colby, March 29, 1980, Doris K. Colby Archives, Aurora University, Aurora, Illinois.

89. Minutes of the Educational Board, Western Advent Christian Publication Association, November 22, 1894, Jenks Memorial Collection of Adventual Materials, Aurora University, Aurora, Illinois.

90. Orrin R. Jenks, "BULLETIN NO. 35: Cash Will Decide," *Our Hope and Life in Christ*, May 10, 1911, 16.

91. J. W. Emmons, "The Conclusion of the Whole Matter," *Our Hope and Life in Christ*, December 23, 1896, 10.

92. Letter from William C. Churchill to Orrin Roe Jenks, March 8, 1910, Doris K. Colby Memorial Archives, Aurora University, Aurora, Illinois.

93. N. A., "Mendota College Graduates," 8–9.

94. N. A., "Mendota College Graduates," 8.

Bibliography

Primary Sources

Letters and Minutes

Correspondence of Orrin R. Jenks, 1908–1911. Doris K. Colby Memorial
    Archives, Aurora University, Aurora, Illinois.

Minutes of the Educational Committee. Western Advent Christian
    Publication Association. Jenks Memorial Collection of Adventual
    Materials, Aurora University, Aurora, Illinois.

Minutes of the Board of Directors. Western Advent Christian Publication
    Association. Jenks Memorial Collection of Adventual Materials, Aurora
    University, Aurora, Illinois.

Minutes of the Annual Meeting of the Western Advent Christian Publication
    Association. Jenks Memorial Collection of Adventual Materials, Aurora
    University, Aurora, Illinois.

Minutes of the Board of Education. Mendota College. Jenks Memorial
    Collection of Adventual Materials, Aurora University, Aurora, Illinois.

Minutes of the Board of Directors. Mendota College. Jenks Memorial
    Collection of Adventual Materials, Aurora University, Aurora, Illinois.

Newspapers

"Mendota Not Favored: The College Is to Be Removed to Aurora." *Mendota
    Reporter*, January 14, 1910.

Our Hope and Life in Christ, 1889–90 through 1912–13 (published weekly).
    Western Advent Christian Publication Association. Jenks Memorial
    Collection of Adventual Materials, Aurora University, Aurora, Illinois.

Publications of Mendota College and Aurora College

Announcement of Mendota Seminary, 1893. Cincinnati: Press of C. J.
    Krehbiel & Co., 1893, 1–20.

Annual of Mendota College, 1893–1894. Aurora, Ill.: Copeland & Phillips,
    Printers, 1893, 1–32.

Annual of Mendota College, 1894–1895. Bloomington, Ill.: Pantagraph
    Printing and Stationery Co., 1894, 1–32.

Catalogue of Mendota College for 1895–96. Bloomington, Ill.: Pantagraph
    Printing and Stationery Co., 1895, 1–32.

Catalogue of Mendota College for 1896–97. Bloomington, Ill.: Pantagraph Printing and Stationery Co., 1896, 1–28.

(The 1897–98 catalog is missing from the university archives.)

Catalogue of Mendota College for 1898–99. Mendota, Ill.: Western Advent Christian Publication Association, 1898, 1–31.

Catalogue of Mendota College for 1899–1900. Mendota, Ill.: Western Advent Christian Publication Association, 1899, 1–31.

(The 1900–1901 catalog is missing from the university archives.)

Catalogue of Mendota College for 1901–1902. Mendota, Ill.: Our Hope Printing Office, 1901, 1–40.

Catalogue: Mendota College, 1902–1903. Mendota, Ill.: Western Advent Christian Publication Association, 1902, 1–38.

Catalogue: Mendota College, 1903–1904. Mendota, Ill.: Western Advent Christian Publication Association, 1903, 1–40.

Catalogue: Mendota College, 1904–1905. Mendota, Ill.: Hope Print, 1904, 1–37.

Catalogue: Mendota College, 1905–1906. Mendota, Ill.: Hope Print, 1905, 1–36.

Catalogue: Mendota College, 1906–1907. Mendota, Ill.: Hope Print, 1906, 1–40.

Catalogue: Mendota College, 1907–1908. Mendota, Illinois: Hope Print, 1907, 1–57.

Annual of Mendota College, 1908–1909. Mendota, Ill.: Our Hope Print, 1908, 1–62.

Annual of Mendota College, 1909–1910. Mendota, Ill.: Our Hope Printing Company, 1909, 1–95.

Annual of Mendota College: Catalogue, 1910–1911. Mendota, Ill.: Our Hope Print, 1910, 1–95.

Aurora College Bulletin, April 1920, April 1922, April 1924, July 1931, May 1934, April 1936, March 1937, February 1939.

N. A. "Founders Motivated by High Purpose." *Aurora College Bulletin* (*Aurora News*), January-February 1968.

Aurora College Catalog, April 1927.

College Literary Society, ed. *The Collegian: Devoted to Our Educational Interest*, August 1903, October 1903, November 1903, December 1903, January 1904, February 1904, March 1904, April 1904, May 1904.

College Literary Society, ed. *Epitome: Mendota College Annual, 1910*.

College Literary Society, ed. *Epitome: 1911 Mendota College Annual*.

The Exponent: In the Interest of Mendota College and the Public Schools, October 1896–November 1896.

Pharos, April 1915.

Janet Mae Hansen and Alison Lynn Whitehead, co-editors. *1939 Pharos*. N. P.: Williamson Press, 1939.

Secondary Sources

Anthologies and Monographs

Arthur, David T. "Joshua V. Himes and the Cause of Adventism." In *The Disappointed: Millerism and Millenarianism in the Nineteenth Century*, edited by Ronald L. Numbers and Jonathan M. Butler. Knoxville: University of Tennessee Press, 1993.

Arthur, David T. "Millerism." In *The Rise of Adventism: Religion and Society in Mid-Nineteenth-Century America*, edited by Edwin S. Gaustead. New York: Harper & Row, 1974.

Brereton, Virginia Lieson. *Training God's Army: The American Bible School, 1880–1940*. Bloomington: Indiana University Press, 1990.

Cross, Whitney R. *The Burned-over District: The Social and Intellectual History of Enthusiastic Religion in Western New York, 1800–1850*. Ithaca, N.Y.: Cornell University Press, 1950.

Dick, Everett N. "The Millerite Movement." In *Adventism in America: A History*, edited by Gary Land. Grand Rapids, Mich.: William B. Eerdmans Publishing Company, 1986.

Dick, Everett N. *William Miller and the Advent Crisis, 1931–1844*. Berrien Springs, Mich.: Andrews University Press, 1994.

Doan, Ruth Alden. "Millerism and Evangelical Culture." In *The Disappointed: Millerism and Millenarianism in the Nineteenth Century*, edited by Ronald L. Numbers and Jonathan M. Butler. Knoxville: University of Tennessee Press, 1993.

Graybill, Ronald D. "The Abolitionist-Millerite Connection." In *The Disappointed: Millerism and Millenarianism in the Nineteenth Century*, edited by Ronald L. Numbers and Jonathan M. Butler. Knoxville: University of Tennessee Press, 1993.

Hewitt, Clyde E. *Midnight and Morning: An Account of the Adventist Awakening and the Founding of the Advent Christian Denomination, 1831–1860*. Charlotte, N.C.: Venture Books, 1983.

Horowitz, Helen Lefkowitz. *Campus Life: Undergraduate Cultures from the End of the Eighteenth Century to the Present*. Chicago: Chicago University Press, 1987.

Knight, George R. *Millennial Fever and the End of the World: A Study of Millerite Adventism*. Boise, Idaho: Pacific Press Publishing Association, 1993.

Lucas, Christopher J. *American Higher Education: A History*. New York: St. Martin's Griffin, 1994.

Mendota Area Chamber of Commerce. *Tracks of Time: Mendota, Illinois, 1853–1978*. Mendota, Ill.: Wayside Press, 1978.

Mendota Centennial Committee. *Magnificent Whistle Stop: The 100-Year Story of Mendota, Ill*. Mendota, Ill.: Wayside Press, 1953.

Nichol, Francis D. *The Midnight Cry: A Defense of the Character and Conduct of William Miller and the Millerites, Who Mistakenly Believed that the Second Coming of Christ Would Take Place in the Year 1844*. Washington D.C.: Review and Herald Publishing Association, 1944.

Ringenberg, William C. *The Christian College: A History of Protestant Higher Education in America*. 2nd ed. Grand Rapids, Mich.: Baker Book House Co., 2006.

Rowe, David L. *God's Strange Work: William Miller and the End of the World*. Grand Rapids, Mich.: William B. Eerdmans Publishing Company, 2008.

Rowe, David L. "Millerites: A Shadow Portrait." In *The Disappointed: Millerism and Millenarianism in The Nineteenth Century*, edited by Ronald L. Numbers and Jonathan M. Butler. Knoxville: University of Tennessee Press, 1993.

Rowe, David L. *Thunder and Trumpets: Millerites and Dissenting Religion in Upstate New York, 1800–1850*. Chico, Calif.: Scholars Press, 1985.

Rudolph, Frederick. *The American College and University: A History*. 1962. Reprint, Athens, Ga.: University of Georgia Press, 1990.

Thelin, John R. *A History of American Higher Education*. Baltimore: Johns Hopkins University Press, 2004.

Wellcome, Isaac C. *History of the Second Advent* Message *and Mission, Doctrine and People*. Yarmouth, Maine: I. C. Wellcome, Publisher, 1874.

Woloch, Nancy. *Women and the American Experience*. 4th ed. Boston: McGraw Hill, 2006.

Master's Thesis and Doctoral Dissertations

Arthur, David Tallmadge. "Come Out of Babylon: A Study of Millerite Separatism and Denominationalism, 1840–1865." PhD diss., University of Rochester, 1970.

Palmer, Susan L. "Building Ethnic Communities in a Small City: Romanians and Mexicans in Aurora, Illinois, 1900–1940." PhD diss., Northern Illinois University, 1987.

Rowe, David L. "Northern Millerites and Virginia Millennialists, 1838–1847." Master's thesis, University of Virginia, 1972.

Rowe, David Leslie. "Thunder and Trumpets: The Millerite Movement and Apocalyptic Thought in Upstate New York, 1800–1845." PhD diss., University of Virginia, 1974.